WOMEN AND HEALTH
Cultural and Social Perspectives

MOTHERS & MOTHERHOOD

Readings in American History

EDITED BY
RIMA D. APPLE AND JANET GOLDEN

OHIO STATE UNIVERSITY PRESS
Columbus

Library of Congress Cataloging-in-Publication Data

Mothers and motherhood : readings in American history / edited by Rima
   D. Apple and Janet Golden.
      p.   cm. — (Women and health)
   Includes bibliographical references (p.) and index.
   ISBN 0-8142-0738-3 (cloth : alk. paper). — ISBN 0-8142-0739-1
(paper : alk. paper)
   1. Mothers—United States—History. 2. Motherhood—United States—
History. 3. Women—United States—History. I. Apple, Rima D.
(Rima Dombrow), 1944– . II. Golden, Janet Lynne, 1951– .
III. Series: Women & health (Columbus, Ohio)
HQ759.M885   1997
306.874′3′0973—dc21   97-15670
                                         CIP

Text and cover design by Donna Hartwick.
Type set in Adobe Garamond by Graphic Composition, Inc.
Printed by Edwards Brothers, Inc.

The paper in this publication meets the minimum requirements of American National Standard
for Information Sciences—Permanence of Paper for Printed Library Materials.
ANSI Z39.48–1992.

9 8 7 6 5 4 3 2 1

To our partners, children, and grandchild

CONTENTS

Acknowledgments

The shape of this book owes much to helpful conversations with our students as well as with our colleagues. Especially helpful were members of the Culture and Politics of Reproduction Seminar at the Center for the Critical Analysis of Contemporary Culture, Rutgers University-New Brunswick. Four students in particular assisted us in the compilation and production of this book; we are grateful for the library and computer skills of Jessica Brownell, Jessica Dixon, Judy Houck, and Sonya Sidky, University of Wisconsin-Madison in translating an idea into a finished book manuscript. Financial aid came through the University of Wisconsin Graduate School, the University of Wisconsin School of Human Ecology, and the Rutgers University Research Council. We appreciate their support of this project.

INTRODUCTION
Mothers, Motherhood, and Historians

RIMA D. APPLE AND JANET GOLDEN

Motherhood is a significant experience for the overwhelming majority of American women, while the work of mothering—in individual families and in communities—has shaped the lives of all Americans. Though mothers have always been present in American history, motherhood is not a static concept nor is it a homogeneous category.

Mothers: A *New Yorker* cartoon humorously presents a rack of Mother's Day cards bearing the labels biological, working, surrogate, adoptive, earth, single, in-law, unwed, and unfit.[1] A film history offers an analysis of how Hollywood portrays mothers as unwed, perfect, sacrificing, or destructive.[2] Even without a modifying adjective, "mother" conjures up a variety of roles: a female who bears offspring, who adopts a child or holds a maternal relationship toward another, or who creates, nurtures, and protects someone else. Clearly the word *mother* evokes a multiplicity of meanings in our culture, meanings that have evolved within a variety of scientific, legal, social, cultural, political, religious, and economic perspectives. Moreover, these meanings are constantly changing, shaped by structural elements and also through the individual and collective, conscious and unconscious work of mothers themselves.

Few textbooks or college courses have paid much attention to the phenomenon of mothering, the meaning of motherhood, or the lives of mothers. To study mothers we can examine books, films, paintings, photographs, and television shows, all of which are replete with images of mothers, and we can look for mothers in social, cultural, and psychological studies of families and of women. However, it is only recently that historians have begun to examine mothers and motherhood as distinct from and yet a part of family history and women's history. Through their work we have come to understand that the history of mothers and motherhood is also part of economic, political, and intellectual history, as well as the history of medicine, science, and technology.

The demand for historical studies of mothers and motherhood arises in part from the growing recognition of its significance in explaining our past, and in part from contemporary concerns. As politicians and policy makers confront issues facing mothers in the paid labor force; as they debate immigration, welfare, education policies, and health care policies; and as they make references to mothers and children to lure voters, they illustrate that motherhood has a political meaning. Historians, in turn, seek to understand the evolution and the impact of these ideas and policies, and to investigate the discussions of motherhood by mothers and by others.

Historians face many difficulties in studying how both real and rhetorical motherhood has changed over time. To begin with, they must understand and explain the differences between mothers separated by race, class, religion, region, and culture. Second, they must place the lives of mothers in political, intellectual, economic, and social context, all the while seeing how the context changes. Third, they must find sources. The availability of primary and secondary materials about the lives of urban, white, middle- and upper-class women has meant that a disproportionate amount of research has been done on some mothers while others remain relatively unstudied. Despite these obstacles, the study of motherhood is expanding, as scholars ask new questions and find new materials for answering them and thus for reshaping our understanding of American history.

Mothers in American History

Historians are beginning to examine the work and meaning of mothering in the seventeenth century for Native Americans, Euro-American immigrants, and African American slaves imported to the British colonies. Sources for these studies include diaries, letters, art, and artifacts, as well as more traditional sources. For example, a study of the legal system discloses statutes mandating that indentured servants who became pregnant have their term of servitude extended, one indication of the status of mothers in the period. Motherhood is treated quite differently in literary sources, such as the sermons preached on the duties of mothers. Then, too, there are church records and plantation records of births and burials, which enable us to see just how many years women spent pregnant, nursing, or rearing young children. In New England and the middle colonies, white women bore many children; in the southern colonies the birthrate was lower, largely because of greater maternal mortality among both African Americans and Euro-Americans and because many servants began childbearing only after completing their indenture and many female slaves were imported after they had completed some of their years of peak fertility. High death rates among white women in the southern colonies meant that many reared stepchildren when they married widowers, and that they reared their own children knowing it was possible that other women would replace them.

Racial, geographic, and demographic differences among mothers persisted in the eighteenth century, although three major trends began to reshape the experiences of mothers. First, slavery was transformed into a family-based system, meaning not that legal families were recognized but that the formation of families was encouraged, in large part to encourage childbearing and thus the growth of the slave population. Southern slave owners allowed pregnant and breast-feeding slaves to have more rest and time with their children; as a result, the slave system grew by natural increase rather than through importation (which ended in the early nineteenth century). Second, class distinctions grew sharper among free white women. This was manifested not only in the material conditions of their lives but in their expectations for their children. Pauper women who gave birth in the almshouse of a commercial seaport city had little hope of seeing their children survive or of finding the means for supporting them. Farm wives buried some children and trained those who lived to assist with the maintenance of the family, including the production of some goods for cash—a necessity in the expanding commercial economy. Wealthy mothers too saw some of their children die, but they could bring new resources to bear in an effort to preserve the health of their children. Some turned to imported advice manuals; others called for the services of physicians. A third transformation in motherhood occurred in the closing decades of the eighteenth century as political agitation and ultimately the American Revolution engulfed many mothers. Some sent sons off to battle; others experienced the hardships of raising and feeding children in wartime. For their efforts they received, not political power, but public honor as republican mothers who had reared and would continue to rear future generations of citizens.

The rhetorical links between political ideals and maternal practices in the wake of the American Revolution foreshadowed later efforts. Some nineteenth-century women used the discourse of motherhood to leverage new rights and to institute vast social changes. The fight to abolish slavery, obtain the vote, and establish moral reforms ranging from the control of prostitution to the outlawing of alcohol sales all involved communicating the significance of mothers and children to those in power. Ironically, while "home" and "mother" became unifying themes in some movements, the differences among mothers were growing sharper and more visible. In the West, the lives of Native American, Hispanic American, and Euro-American mothers diverged, even as the geographic distance between them narrowed. In the expanding cotton kingdom of the South, slave mothers and plantation mistresses lived in close geographic contact but with enormous differences between them. Greater even than the gaps caused by differences in their racial status, their material well-being, and the physical demands and social expectations placed upon them was the unbridgeable gap between freedom and slavery. When the Civil War brought this particular rift to an end, other vast differences remained. In the South as well as the North, race and racism continued to shape the experiences of mothers.

What else separated mothers? The conditions in which they worked, some on isolated farms, others in expanding cities; the technology that supported their work, from simple butter churns to rows of sewing machines; and the social distinctions marked through religion, nationality, language, and beliefs. Millions of immigrants poured into the rich farmland of the West and Midwest and into the urban centers of the North and Midwest during the nineteenth century, and the mothers among them struggled to reconcile the child-rearing practices and beliefs they brought from home with the conditions and ideologies they encountered in their new lives. What many mothers shared in the nineteenth century were high rates of fertility (and among some, an effort to restrain this fertility) and lives bounded by domestic responsibilities.

The transformations of America begun in the nineteenth century—the growth of cities and industries, and new modes of transportation and communication—accelerated in the twentieth century, punctuated by wartime expansions of the economy and postwar contractions. Growing numbers of mothers entered the paid labor force, growing numbers of mothers had access to technologies that made their lives easier—from indoor plumbing to washing machines—and growing numbers found a means of controlling their fertility. Yet, sharp distinctions among mothers remained. In many ways the communications revolution that began in the nineteenth century and advanced through the twentieth helped to obscure differences that race, class, and culture made in the lives of women. Just as wealthy mothers of the seventeenth and eighteenth centuries learned about ideal motherhood in books and sermons, so too did mothers of the nineteenth and later the twentieth century find representations of middle-class motherhood in a range of print media and eventually in radio and television. These images are accessible to us through cable television "nostalgia channels," but, as the *New Yorker* Mother's Day cartoon notes, we are increasingly aware of the many kinds of mothers, and of the vastly different lives they lead, as well as the ways in which motherhood is deployed as a rhetorical tool in political battles and in economic debates.

This book brings together some of the most exciting of recent scholarship on mothers and motherhood. We have included articles illustrating the shifting meaning of motherhood over time, the differences between mothers, and the kinds of evidence scholars use to study both the reality and the rhetoric of mothering. At the same time, we must acknowledge that there are gaps. We know far too little about Native American mothers, lesbian mothers, adoptive mothers, foster mothers, stepmothers, rural mothers, and mothers of many different ethnic and immigrant groups, to name just a few areas demanding further study.

In recognition of the work yet to be done in the history of motherhood, we have included a bibliography. It is not comprehensive but inclusive—developed to direct additional reading in the field and to serve as a starting point for others as they undertake their own research projects.

NOTES

1. D. Franden cartoon, *New Yorker,* May 15, 1995, p. 8.
2. Jeanine Basinger, *A Woman's View: How Hollywood Spoke to Women, 1930–1960* (New York: Knopf, 1993), pp. 392–444.

Part One

SOCIAL CONSTRUCTION OF MOTHERHOOD

"Social construction" refers to the process by which motherhood is culturally defined. Watching old movies or listening to old songs, for example, we can learn how motherhood was defined in earlier periods. Talking with mothers today, we can hear how they are affected by socially accepted styles of mothering. In much the same way, the articles in this section of the book examine historical materials instructing mothers about their behavior and data about their actual activities.

By saying that motherhood is socially constructed we are rejecting biological determinism—the idea that motherhood is a natural phenomenon. Instead we argue that idealized maternal roles and the relations of mothers to other social actors, to social structures, and to systems of belief are created and re-created by individuals and by society. Whether mothers reject prevailing social beliefs or embrace them fully, they are, through their daily practices, continually redefining the meaning of motherhood.

Collectively, the articles in this section raise five issues. First, they show that emotions can be socially constructed, as the accounts of motherlove and maternal grief demonstrate. Second, the articles suggest that ideal types of mothering, such as republican motherhood or scientific motherhood, develop in particular historical eras and are reflections of political, cultural, economic, and social forces. Third, the articles stress the difference between public depictions of maternal roles and the experiences of actual mothers. Fourth, the authors remind us that significant attention must be paid to the ways in which the social constructions of motherhood vary by race and class. Finally, the articles illuminate the variety of sources we must study in order to develop a clearer appreciation of the social construction of motherhood.

In order to learn about women's lives and roles as mothers in early modern England and America, Marylynn Salmon examines the cultural meanings attached to the act of breast-feeding. Salmon's article explores ministerial literature, medical texts, and women's own recipe books, carefully delineating what each source reveals about what she terms the "physical aspects of mothering."

In her study of Mary Palmer Tyler's letters, reminiscences, and popular child-care manual, Marilyn Blackwell suggests that new ideas about mothering emerged in the wake of the American Revolution. Termed "republican motherhood," this doctrine called for women to transmit to their children the religious, social, and emotional values that would enable them to thrive in the new nation. Blackwell shows how Tyler attempted to fulfill the tenets of republican motherhood as she reared her children.

Emotion is the central theme of Jan Lewis's discussion of "motherlove." While contemporaries considered maternal love to be natural and irrepressible, something that was imprinted on a child and ultimately shaped its character, Lewis shows that "motherlove" was socially constructed. It developed, she argues, as a fusion of nineteenth-century democratic and Christian thought.

Nineteenth-century descriptions of ideal mothers contained, as Janet Golden shows, hidden assumptions about class. In discussing the practice of wet-nursing, in which women were hired to breast-feed babies, she shows that wet nurses were portrayed in the medical literature as dangerous and ruled by instinct, while their well-to-do employers were idealized. In analyzing the actual encounters of wet nurses and employers, Golden finds the stereotypes did not always fit.

Turning to the late nineteenth and early twentieth centuries, Rima Apple discusses the creation of "scientific motherhood"—the idealogy that stressed women's need to follow expert advice in order to rear healthy children. Apple examines articles and advertisements in popular magazines, government pamphlets, popular films, and home economics education to show how women's traditional knowledge began to be devalued, while scientific authority grew. She shows us that by the twentieth century mothers ceased to be regarded as queens of the nursery and instead were taught to be servants of science.

Wendy Simonds investigates the construction of maternal grief—women mourning infant deaths, miscarriages, and stillbirths—as portrayed in the pages of *True Story* magazine from 1920 to 1985. Written for a working-class readership, the stories, Simonds finds, teach mothers to distrust themselves and to rely on other authorities and consumer goods. At the same time, these stories also help readers to understand that death is a part of life.

In the concluding article, Ruth Feldstein describes how Mamie Till Bradley, an African American mother, responded to the brutal murder of her fourteen-year-old son. Constructing herself, as Feldstein notes, as an attractive, patriotic, religious, and family-oriented woman, Bradley used her situation as a grieving mother to challenge the racial violence that took the life of her child. Her status was contested by segregationists and later challenged by political allies. Yet, so long as the Till murder remained in the news, this critical political event of the late twentieth century was seen in part through debates about motherhood.

1.

The Cultural Significance of Breast-Feeding and Infant Care in Early Modern England and America

MARYLYNN SALMON

In the late summer of 1752, the Reverend Ebenezer Parkman lay ill. His joints were stiff and painful; he frequently felt faint and feverish; and he had no appetite. As he confided to his diary on the 21st of August, "I am so wasted, that there appears to me Danger of consuming away."[1] Ebenezer Parkman had been suffering for weeks, the rheumatic pains that troubled him moving from limb to limb, his nights so tormented that his neighbors and adult children came in regularly to sit with him and watch. On August 22 Ebenezer grew worse. He wrote, "The Evening and night were most distressing with pain that ceased not, no not in any situation whatever, a Circumstance which I have not, I think, at any Time had till now."[2] The 24th was a night filled with "Fever, faintness and frequent waking."[3] Deacon Newton of the Westborough church came to pray with him.

On the 25th Ebenezer's wife, Hannah, sent her baby Samuel, age one year and three days, away to be weaned. That night she watched with her husband herself and stilled "a miscellany of Meat, Herbs, Roots, seeds, etc. by the Doctor's Direction." She sat up with her husband again the next night and from Ebenezer's diary we learn of the special care she was giving him. On the 26th he wrote, "My wife tends me o'nights and supply's me with Breast milk."[4] Little Samuel's loss was Ebenezer's gain. The father recovered from his illness to live another thirty years.

In England and America, breast milk was regarded as a beneficial medicine. Women provided milk for use in a wide variety of medicinal recipes and, in extreme cases like Ebenezer Parkman's, gave it as nourishment to adults as well as children. Reliance on breast milk as food for the weak and medicine for the sick is one of those striking historical facts that we sense, instantly, is significant for revealing

Reprinted from the *Journal of Social History* 28 (1994): 247–69, by permission of the publisher.

the secrets of the past. Such uses lead us to question whether breast milk and breast-feeding had meanings in the early modern period quite different from modern ones. In giving their milk to others, women were able to preserve not only the lives of their infants but also the health of their adult relatives, friends, and neighbors. What does this belief reveal about the cultural significance attached to women as breast-feeders? In this context, culture is defined as a shared system of meaning that determined attitudes and behavior.

Historians have uncovered little about the meaning of breast-feeding to most women and men. Our attention has focused more on the relatively few women who employed wet nurses than on the majority of mothers who breast-fed their own infants. Fortunately, readily available and varied sources contain a wealth of information on the meaning of breast-feeding. Writings long known to contain references to women's breast-feeding capacity—the ministerial literature with its rich maternal imagery—may be read for clues on attitudes toward breast milk, breast-feeding, and women's maternal roles. Medical texts also contain valuable information about infant feeding and general care. Perhaps most important, given the dearth of writings by women that have survived from the seventeenth and early eighteenth centuries, are women's own collections of medicinal recipes. They reveal mothers' day-to-day activities in feeding infants and caring for children's health, and concern that the work be done well. Although these manuscripts do not constitute the same kind of literature about infant and child care that women began to write at the end of the eighteenth century and that historians have found so useful for uncovering information about motherhood, they do demonstrate much about breast-feeding and the kind of child care that contemporaries believed was important.

All of these sources—the ministerial literature, the medical literature, and women's medicinal recipe books—reveal much about the nature of women's breast-feeding capacity and attitudes toward motherhood generally. Significantly, taken together it is the physical side of mothering that emerges as the focus of both women's and men's writings. The contemporary belief that women's efforts in breast-feeding and otherwise tending to the physical needs of their young children was work seems particularly important for understanding the cultural meaning of motherhood.

The material included here is a part of a larger attempt to study the work of motherhood and to address the question of how women and men regarded motherhood before the modern age. Breast-feeding is emphasized because we know so little about it despite the fact that infant care was a central part of women's day-to-day work as mothers. As we will see, throughout the period contemporaries regarded women's physical powers with respect and treated seriously women's responsibility for infant care. After the acceptance of the healthfulness of colostrum in the middle of the eighteenth century, we see a sudden cultural shift toward even greater regard for women's work as breast-feeders. Infant nurture was one aspect of the maternal role that consistently earned women praise, and very little criticism.

The focus of this paper is on breast milk and breast-feeding, but these are topics that can be understood only in the context of women's wider role as mothers. Therefore, questions about motherhood must be addressed alongside questions about breast-feeding. For example, our failure to understand the work women performed as mothers, including breast-feeding, has led us to conclude that motherhood was a secondary role for women, less culturally significant than women's work as economic providers.[5] In fact, our knowledge of motherhood before the end of the eighteenth century is so slight that we do not know how much time women spent on mothering or to what degree it played a part in determining either women's sense of self or the meaning of women's work.[6] Yet few historians would deny that motherhood, like other social roles, is constructed according to the cultural values of different eras, values that have changed over time and thus created a history of the meaning of motherhood. We need to understand much more fully the history of motherhood in all of its complexity.

Breast Milk as Medicine

The use of breast milk as food for weak adults probably was common in England and the colonies. "Neither is women's milk best only for young and tender infants, but also for men and women of riper years, fallen by age or by sickness into compositions," wrote the physician Thomas Muffet in 1584.[7] Its lightness and ease of digestion made it particularly useful in cases of loss of appetite or consumption. As Nicholas Culpeper explained in his *Directory for Midwives* (1660), "Milk digests soon, it being concocted by the Nurse; and thats the Reason, many in a Consumption (whose digestion is weak) are cured by sucking a Womans Breast."[8] Similarly, a late seventeenth-century recipe book claimed that "ye Consumption of ye Lungs . . . is best recover'd by Sucking Milk from a Womans Brest, as most familiar to our Livers & Blood, needing no Preparation (for it is only Blood discolored) but only Application to ye flesh."[9] Breast milk, the only fit food for a newborn infant, could also ease the distress of the weak and sick.

Medicinal use of breast milk in early modern Anglo-American society went beyond simple nourishment. In childbirth, a draught of another woman's milk was recommended as a way to speed delivery, and reliance on breast milk as a pain reliever, and as a prime ingredient in medicines for grievous ailments such as hysteria, faintness, and blindness, indicates that it had a special significance to early modern men and women.[10] Consider, for example, the recipes of Gulielma Penn, first wife of William Penn, which reveal reliance on breast milk as a pain reliever. In a section of the recipe book covering ear infections, she noted her success in easing the pain of one man's earache. "I dropt into it Womans milk warm with ye white of an Egg, & with this remedy ye pain ceased." Another man came to her in great pain from an infection, caused by a piece of garlic he had placed in his ear to cure a toothache. When he could not get the garlic out he called in a surgeon, but the man only pushed the garlic further into the ear canal so that "ye blood came out with great pain & heat of his Ear following." Before attempting to remove the garlic or treat the infection (which she did successfully through the application of two different elaborate remedies), Gulielma Penn dealt with the afflicted man's pain. "To ease him of his pain, I wished him to foment his Ear often with Womans-Milk & oyl of Roses warm, & drop it into his Ear."[11] Male professors at prestigious schools of medicine also might rely on breast milk as a pain reliever in the treatment of ear infections, if the example of Felix Platter is typical. He taught that "to asswage pain . . . take womans milke," mix it with other ingredients, and drop it into the affected ear.[12]

Reliance on breast milk to treat eye problems may have been extensive. Gulielma Penn used it in her recipe "for an eye yt is pricked, venomed swolne or such like."[13] Another seventeenth-century English healer, Elizabeth Dowinge, recommended "a lettle woman's milke" be mixed with various herbs, honey, frankincense, and urine to restore eyesight, "though near lost."[14] One recipe book from the end of the seventeenth century contained numerous cures for various eye ailments, many of them relying on breast milk. They ranged from treatments for sore or red eyes to cures for blindness, and marginal notations reflected the healer's belief in their efficacy. "Keep ye water in a Glass for this water is pretious of all waters for ye Eyes; And hath been often tryed." Beside another recipe, the compiler wrote, "This hath healed many blind People," and elsewhere "A Medicine that help'd One yt had a Thurst in ye White of his Eye."[15] At the beginning of the eighteenth century, breast milk was still being used in eye remedies. "An excellent Eye-Water," found in a collection of recipes published in 1716, directed: "Take of Juice of Sengreen and Red Fennel-Root, of each 2 Ounces; of Woman's Milk, a Spoonful; of White Rose-Water, a Quarter of a Pint; of fine Sugar-Candy, and White Vitriol powder'd, of each 2 Drams; being all mix'd, set them on the Fire, and as the Scum rises take it off, and keep it in a Glass for your Use, and with a Feather drop of it into your Eye, twice or thrice every Day."[16]

The use of breast milk as a treatment for eye ailments may have grown from mothers' custom of milking their breasts into infants' eyes. Breast milk was useful in clearing the discharges that collected in infants' eyes before the tear ducts began to work properly. Thus the French physician Jacques Guillemeau wrote in 1612, "The Nurse, besides a sufficient quantity for the nourishment of the child, must have some to milke into his eyes, if he should chance to have any imperfections there: as either heat, pimples, itching, that so it may be cooled."[17]

Other healers employed breast milk in salves and plasters. "Ffor swiming in ye head," an unidentified seventeenth-century Englishwoman thought that following purging and bleeding the ailing person should apply a salve of oil of roses, oil of cowslips, nutmeg, mace, rose water, wine, and "womans milk of a manchilde 2 spoonefulls [or] if ys be used for a man ye milke must be of a woman childe."[18] According to at least one seventeenth-century healer, insomnia could be cured by making a salve of opium and breast milk: "A Remedy—Rx Oyl of Violets Opium, Incorporate these together wth. Womans Milk, And with a fine Linen Cloth lay it to thv Temples. . . . Or—Rx Opium ye Bigness of a Pease, dissolve it in Cochy. of Womans Milk, make it Blood-warm, and Anoint ye Temples therewith, for want of Womans milk, take Rose-Water."[19] Cures for gout also sometimes included breast milk, as in the claim that "Ye yolks of Eggs, Womans milk, Linseed, & Saffron, altogether in a plaister, asswageth ye Diseases of ye Gout." Similarly, "For ye Gout—Rx Sevil Sope, [ca.] pennyworth of Camphire, a Sauser full of Woman's milk of a man child, then put ye Sope & Camphire into ye Milk, till it be thick, then put it into a clean box, or Vessel, & let it stand 24 hours, & then Anoint ye Patient therewith cold, & ever lay ye Medicine above ye Sore to draw it downwards. This was proved upon Sr Jon Wilton, & many more." Breast milk was also employed in a treatment "for heat in the Kidnies," in combination with houseleek, plantane, rose water, and wine vinegar.[20] As late as the second half of the eighteenth century, breast milk was still recommended as an ingredient in medicinal recipes. As an "outward medicine for [the phrensy]," *Aristotle's Masterpiece* (1766 edition) recommended, "Take juice of house-leek, mix it with woman's milk, apply it to the fore part of the head shaved."[21]

Respect for the medicinal properties of breast milk reflected faith in its power as a life-giving force. Contemporaries recognized that denial of breast milk in the first few months after birth led almost inevitably to sickness and death. In England and America, hand-feeding of animal milk through horns or boats therefore was practiced only in extreme cases of hardship. The majority of women breast-fed their infants as a matter of course.[22] Medical and religious writers urged hesitant mothers to nurse their children themselves, or if they could not, to hire wet nurses. In the early modern period, when a mother nursed her own infant, she was seen as providing it with the purest, lightest, and most easily digestible food available. Not only was breast milk so perfectly designed that newborns could not live without it, but older babies thrived so well on the breast that weaning generally was postponed for at least a year.

Early modern medical texts taught that breast milk was whitened blood, the same blood that had fed the fetus in the womb now diverted to the breasts, where it could continue to nourish the newborn baby.[23] "It were fit," wrote Guillemeau (1612), "that every mother should nurse her owne child: because her milke which is nothing else, but the bloud whitened (of which he was made, and wherewith hee had been nourished the time hee staide in his Mothers wombe) will bee alwaies more naturall, and familiar unto him, than that of a stanger."[24] A nursing mother represented selfless devotion to early modern men and women, for in feeding her child she gave, quite literally, of herself. Her milk was her own blood, her own life-sustaining fluid. As Hugh Smith explained women's breast-feeding capacity in 1777,

> Whether it be animal or vegetable diet, or a mixture of both, taken into the stomach; the quality of the food is so far altered by the digestive faculties, that a milky nutriment is produced from it; and as the aliment passes through the bowles, this milk is taken up by a great number of fine vessels, which, from their destined office, are called the milky vessels; and through them it is conveyed into the blood for our support: and, as before observed, Nature has so admirably contrived the animal fabric, that mothers are likewise enabled to support their young from this constant supply, which at the same time also affords to themselves their own proper nourishment.[25]

Early modern faith in breast milk as medicine for adults therefore may be seen not only as a reflection of the power of breast milk as a life-sustaining fluid but also as evidence of respect for this aspect of women's physical nature. Such an interpretation coincides well with Thomas Laqueur's recent discussions of what he calls the "one sex body," and the cultural values attached to specific bodily fluids. During the early modern period, the fluids of the human body were regarded as fungible, making one simply a different form of another. Some forms were more powerful than others. As Laqueur explains,

> In Aristotle's one-seed theory, *sperma* and *catemenia* refer to greater or lesser refinements of an ungendered blood. . . . The thicker, whiter, frothier quality of the male semen is a hint that it is more powerful, more likely to act as an efficient cause, than the thinner,

less pristinely white, and more watery female ejaculate or the still red, even less concocted, menstrua. Like reproductive organs, reproductive fluids turn out to be versions of each other; they are the biological articulation, in the language of a one-sex body, of the politics of two genders and ultimately of engendering.[26]

In this cultural setting, the white, frothy appearance of breast milk indicated its highly concocted, and therefore powerful, state. Like semen, it possessed life-giving force. While semen was necessary to create life, breast milk was necessary to sustain it. The proximity of the breasts to the heart explained the appearance of breast milk, for the heart was the "shop of heate," as the English anatomist Helkiah Crooke explained it.[27] Thus breast milk, like semen, arose from the heat that contemporaries associated with a higher physical state. Although women's bodies were, on the whole, colder than men's, in this one aspect of their physical nature they duplicated the superior abilities of men's bodies.

Positive attitudes toward breast milk are particularly striking when we contrast them with the negative connotations given to menstrual blood in early modern Anglo-American culture, for as fungibles they came from the same source. Menstrual blood, too, was created to nourish a new life, but when that life was not conceived it was sloughed off, extraneous, superfluous, foul and unclean. A menstruating woman was offensive; the blood that flowed from her body dangerous. Men were repelled by the sight and smell of menstrual blood, disdaining and derogating women for the unpleasantness associated with their bodies.[28] Attitudes such as these contributed to the persistence of a taboo on intercourse with a menstruating woman.

Historians and historical anthropologists have placed greater emphasis on the negative connotations of menstrual blood than on the positive connotations of breast milk.[29] Perhaps that imbalance should be corrected to recognize the symbolic as well as the practical value placed on lactating women's milk flow. White, sweet, and pure, breast milk also flowed from a woman's body. A woman whose breasts swelled and flowed with milk was the provider, nurturing and loving. Women and men praised breast-feeding women unequivocally. They were all that was good, not only redeemed in the eyes of God and cleansed of original sin—for even mothers who did not nurse earned such praise—but also particularly feminine in the positive sense of that word: concerned for the welfare of others, unselfish, giving. They took no chances with the health of their children, giving them the breast despite the strain nursing placed on their own bodies. The high cultural value placed on the physical side of motherhood in the early modern period is demonstrated by idealization of women as breast-feeders, the nurturers of new life.

Ministerial Representations of Breast-Feeding Mothers

The writings of seventeenth-century English and colonial religious leaders reveal respect for women's roles as the breast-feeders of infants and caregivers to young children. As Laurel Thatcher Ulrich has observed, ministerial representations of women's lives are useful for delineating cultural norms and expectations. In her own work on motherhood, Ulrich found that in ministerial pronouncements "the idealization of motherhood received its fullest expression."[30] Ministers' frequent reliance on breast-feeding as a symbol for divine love, and on weaning as a metaphor for spiritual loss and helplessness, is particularly striking for its idealization of maternal care.

Ministerial comparisons of eternal joy with infant contentedness at the breast reveal a deep respect for the power of breast-feeding mothers to soothe and comfort as well as nourish. Thomas Shepard described the gift of eternal life as being "laid in the bosom of Christ, when sucking the breasts of the grace of Christ, when you can go no further, though thou wert in heaven, for there is no other happiness there."[31] Eternal happiness was a gift from God, just as infantile bliss was a gift from mothers. "Grace goes directly to Christ, as a childe new borne goes to the mothers breast, and never leaves crying till it be laid there."[32] Similarly, final denial of the breast was a time of crisis, and used as a metaphor for the absence of grace. John Winthrop's famous description of his feelings before his conversion is telling in this regard. God "laid mee lower in myne owne eyes than at any time before, and shewed mee the emptines of all my guifts and parts, left mee neither power nor will, so as I became as a weaned child."[33]

According to David Leverenz, who has written the most detailed study of Puritan language and imagery, breasts ordinarily represented churches or ministers but could also stand for God's loving nurturance. "Ministers often called themselves breasts of God, and milk imagery was interchangeably dispensed among several theological roles: the minister, the Word, and God's promises."[34] Because breast-feeding represented God's gift of grace coming through his churches and ministers, good Christians should attend worship services on the sabbath prepared to "suck the breast while it is open," that is, attend to the minister's sermon.[35] Parishioners might also rely on breast-feeding imagery to describe the worth of their religious leaders. In commenting on the early death of Joseph Green, the peace-loving minister to distressed Salem Village in the years after the witchcraft hysteria, Joseph and Anna Gerrish said that he died with "his breast full of milk," that is, full of promise in bringing his parishioners to Christ.[36]

Ministers' recognition of the power of breast milk is seen in their comparisons of breast-feeding and hand-feeding. Just as the word of God conveyed by ministers in the sermon was more powerful than the word of God conveyed by the written word, including the Bible, so a breast-fed baby received nourishment and comfort far superior to that of the hand-fed baby. As phrased by Thomas Shepard, "Dish milk and slit milk may convey some nourishment, but breast milk hath spirit going with it; good books may be blessed, but there is not that spirit in them as in lively dispensations of the gospel by ministers themselves." His words speak to a widespread popular faith in mothers' milk as the only proper food for newborns, unmatched by animal substitutes or pap. "Give children milk in the dish, they cry still; they must have it from the mother, and there suck; so 2 Pet. i 2,3."[37]

Religious imagery focused on maternal feeding as a means of representing God's love. Nursing at the breasts of ministers during the hearing of the Word, or cuddling in God's bosom throughout eternity, was bliss. Although only one of several common images for feelings of joy and regeneration, breast-feeding clearly evoked a powerful sense of perfection in early modern religious sensibilities. Significantly, the ministerial literature demonstrates positive attitudes not only toward breast-feeding and breast milk but also toward motherhood generally. References to maternal love and care of children, and comparisons of God to good mothers, appeared frequently enough to indicate that they could evoke strong emotional responses in listeners. Seventeenth- and eighteenth-century English people in England and the American colonies believed in the importance of maternal love.

In fact, according to Leverenz, Puritan imagery exalted women only in their roles as pure mothers. If women attempted to excel in other areas, they earned derision rather than praise.[38] Similarly, Patricia Crawford has argued that "preachers taught their congregations that the ideal good woman was the good mother. The Bible was the basic authority in this, as in other areas of life. Concepts of motherhood were deeply embedded in the metaphorical discussion of Church and State. Thus, for example, the true Church was a mother, the false a whore."[39]

Although women's spiritual value as revealed in the sermon literature was limited to motherhood, we should not underestimate the significance of that role in the early modern period. Ministers' equation of God and good mothers, both full of care and concern for their offspring, both providing the necessities of life—even of eternal life—with selfless devotion, demonstrates the power of motherhood to evoke feelings of devotion and gratitude. The first two stanzas of "A thankful Acknowledgment of God's Providence" by John Cotton exemplifies the merging of everyday maternal care and heavenly solicitude:

In mothers womb thy fingers did me make, And from the womb thou didst me safely take: From breast thou hast me nurst my life throughout, That I may say never wanted ought.

In all my meals my table thou hast spread, In all my lodgings thou hast [made my] bed: Thou hast me clad with changes of array, And chang'd my house for better far away.[40]

Early modern religious writers accorded women honor for their performance of everyday chores, including even such lowly duties as changing diapers or washing sinks. In this vein, the equation of sin with filth, and of the power of God to cleanse with mothers' care of the body, is particularly important. Again, John Cotton provides a telling passage:

> Women, if they were not Mothers, would not take such homely offices up, as to cleanse their Children from their filth; why if God were not of the like affection to us, hee would not cleanse us from our filthiness, . . . if hee did not sweep the Sinck, and scum off the scum of our hearts, it would never bee done; . . . it is with us as it is with young Infants that would lye in their defilements, if their Mothers did not make them clean, and so would wee even wallow in the defilements of sin, if God did not cleanse us, therefore admire Gods love and mercy towards us.

Tender mothers, like God, would not let their children cry out unheard. Rather, they would take them up, clean and comfort them, and give them the breast. Good Christians were instructed to admire the tasks performed by women with dedication and love. Theirs was an appropriate model for true Christian humility.

Advice to Mothers in Medical Books

Like the ministerial literature, the printed medical literature is valuable for uncovering attitudes toward breast milk, breast-feeding, and women's work as mothers. Two points are particularly important. First, medical writers, like religious writers, praised breast-feeding mothers for their efforts and demonstrated respect for breast milk by advocating it as the only proper food for infants. Second, detailed medical advice to mothers about the proper feeding and care of infants and young children reveals widespread concern for the work of women as mothers, beginning in the sixteenth century. Medical writers recognized that infant care was a vital health is-sue and that without proper management, which they believed was often lacking, infants would sicken and die. They therefore published advice and instructions on all aspects of breast-feeding, weaning, and the care of both ill and healthy infants. Changing medical advice on feeding neonates colostrum is especially important for the period under consideration here, because it helps us understand the eigh-teenth-century shift toward more maternal breast-feeding among English elites.[41]

Medical writers praised breast-feeding mothers and criticized harshly women who declined their maternal duty. Their attitude demonstrates a strong respect for women's physical power to sustain life. In giving birth, women fulfilled only part of their duty as women. A second, equally burdensome duty was breast-feeding, for without it infants were immediately placed at great risk. Not only might they die if the wet nurse hid feeding problems, as many were rumored to do, but in addi-tion they absorbed any character failings of the wet nurse through the milk.[42] To mold a child properly, both physically and mentally, a mother had to devote the whole of her physical abilities to the task. Only those women who undertook the office of breast-feeder were true mothers.

After discussing the issue of who should feed the newborn, medical writers commonly turned to questions of how often infants should be fed, when supple-mentary feeding of pap and solid foods should begin, and when and how weaning should be undertaken. Advice on clothing, bathing, and airing of infants also ap-peared in the medical literature, again indicating concern that children be cared for properly and well. Specific instructions on topics such as diapering speak to com-mentators' belief that even the mundane details of child care deserved coverage. In *A Treatise of the Diseases of Infants, and Young Children* (English translation, 1612), for example, Jacques Guillemeau wrote on diapering,

> The time of shifting him is commonly about seven a clocke in the morning, then againe at noone, and at seven a clocke at night: and it would not be amisse, to change him againe about midnight; which is not commonly done. But because there is no certaine howre, ei-ther of the childs sucking, or sleeping; therefore divers, after he hath slept a good while, do every time shift him least he should foule and bepisse himself. And surely there be many children, that had need to be shifted, as soone as they have foul'd themselves which I would counsaile you to doe, and not to let them lie in their filth.[43]

It is important to note that Guillemeau addressed his comments to the women who would be caring for the children. While some writers wrote only for other physicians (Walter Harris, for example, published his treatise in Latin),[44] most directed their advice at women: midwives, professional baby nurses, wet nurses, and mothers. This is apparent not only from titles, prefatory remarks, and use of the vernacular but also from content.[45] A largely female readership can be assumed from the material covered in these books. In the early modern period few men concerned themselves with infant care. Those who did were physicians, caregivers to nobility and royalty, or pediatric specialists. They wrote their treatises to instruct the normal caregivers of infants and young children in the techniques they had found to be the most effective in managing elite patients. Thus as late as 1767, George Armstrong could write in the introductory section to his *On the Diseases Most Fatal to Infants,* "The care of infants, even with regard to medicine, has commonly been left to old women, nurses, and midwives, so that it has been long a common saying in this country, that the best doctor for a child, is an old woman."[46]

Accepting the fact that physicians wrote for women as well as other physicians, we can well wonder what use wet nurses and midwives had for male advice on diapering and mixing pap. Undoubtedly, these sections of the books were most useful to elite women who commonly employed wet nurses and therefore had little firsthand experience with infant care. It seems highly likely that the reason common details of infant care were covered in this literature was precisely because elite women lacked information about them. Mothers who wanted to assist in the care of their infants, or at least to understand whether or not their infants were receiving proper care, could now turn to these books for advice. In addition, elite women who did choose to breast-feed, as an increasing number did among seventeenth-century English Puritans, could rely on medical advice books in the absence of personal knowledge. This might have been particularly important because their mothers and other female relatives did not have the experience to guide them, as they had not breast-fed their own children. Reliance on the printed word undoubtedly supported mothers in making decisions about infant feeding and care, particularly when they disagreed with the practices of their baby nurses. Medical advice books therefore must have found a ready market among poorly trained but literate, elite mothers. The less well-to-do, that is, the vast majority of women who always had breast-fed and tended their own children, undoubtedly continued to rely on the guidance of relatives, neighbors, and local healers in an oral tradition.

The medical literature of the seventeenth and early eighteenth centuries maintained that infants should be fed on demand, initially in small amounts. "As to the time and hour it needs no limits, for it may be at any time, night or day, when he hath a mind; but let him have it rather little and often, than too much at a time, that his little Stomach may the better concoct and digest it without Vomiting."[47]

Most authors maintained that infants should be fed only on breast milk for at least two months, although they recognized that sometimes this was impossible. Physicians argued that mothers' tendency to begin supplementary feedings of pap and solid foods too early caused unnecessary distress in infancy. As one eminent practitioner observed, "It is very astonishing, that Mothers, who are so fond of their Children, as to be quite mad with Love of them, are not afraid to murder them with so improper a food."[48] He referred to mothers' habit of chewing meat to a soft consistency and then giving it to their infants.

Treatises frequently described the kinds of gruels and solid foods that children should be fed, and when they should be introduced. By gradually feeding a variety of solid foods to their children, mothers could ease their dependence on the breast. Gradual weaning was generally regarded as essential for a child's well-being.[49] Although final denial of the breast might be either sudden or extended over a period of weeks, the fact that virtually all children were fed supplementary foods beginning at only a few months old minimized the trauma of the final weaning. The recommended age for weaning varied according to a variety of circumstances, such as the health of the child and the season of the year. In the seventeenth century, physicians recommended that weaning take place during the second year, while in the eighteenth century many argued for the benefits of weaning at about eight to ten months.[50] Commentators sometimes noted mothers' tendency to breast-feed for unusually long periods of time. Nicholas Culpeper disapproved of mothers spoiling their children in this way. "The fondness of Mothers to Children doth them more mischief than the Devil himself can do them: one part (and not none of the least) of which appears in letting them suck too long."[51]

As these examples demonstrate, from the early seventeenth century Englishwomen received the advice of physicians on the proper care and feeding of infants. While it is always difficult to uncover evidence on maternal behavior, medical writers did open a window on women's attitudes in discussing what they saw as the common practices of the day, and then approving or disapproving of them. One area in which medical writers revealed women's behavior involves breast-feeding immediately following birth, when colostrum rather than milk is produced in the breasts. It appears that many women did not give their infants colostrum. In 1612, for example, Guillemeau observed that "Some women do make their keepers draw their breasts, and others draw them with glasses themselves," indicating they were not feeding their newborns.[52] Hugh Smith, writing in 1777, complained about women's custom of feeding newborns before the mother's milk came in, either with pap or another woman's milk. "The cries of an infant are generally occasioned by the uneasiness it suffers, either from its dress, or in consequence of thus cramming it. . . . Custom has rendered this ridiculous practice so universal, that the good women continually complain it is impossible for a child to remain without food till the milk comes."[53]

William Cadogan was the most explicit in describing common practice in the middle of the eighteenth century: "The child as soon as it is born, is taken from the mother, and not suffered to suck till the milk comes of itself, but is either fed with stronge and improper things, or put to suck some other woman, whose milk flowing in a full stream, overpowers the new-born infant, that has not yet learned to swallow."[54] But probably the most telling evidence is the belief that every woman would, as a matter of course, suffer from what was called a milk fever, and what we would identify as a breast infection. According to the anonymous author of "A System Concerning Fevers" (1677), a "milky fever" was common to "almost all childbed women . . . the third or fourth day after their delivery, upon the milk floeing into the breast."[55] Medicinal recipe books, both published and private, commonly included remedies for milk fevers, indicating that they were commonplace.

The taboo against colostrum, which has been found in a wide variety of cultural settings, stems from its color and consistency.[56] Colostrum looks and feels different from mature breast milk. It is yellow rather than white, sticky, and of a more watery consistency. The fear of colostrum was unfortunate, for modern research has demonstrated unmistakable benefits to neonates from drinking it. Colostrum purges the small intestines of meconium (a black, sticky substance present at birth), which contains bilirubin, a cause of jaundice if retained too long. It also contains twice the protein of mature breast milk and is high in vitamins A and E. Perhaps most important, colostrum holds concentrated amounts of antibodies that protect the neonate from gastrointestinal infections, and maternal antibodies that shield against various bacteria and viruses. As newborns do not begin to produce their own antibodies for about six weeks, maternal antibodies are a great help in-protecting infants from disease.

While early modern physicians echoed women's own fears of colostrum in arguing against maternal breast-feeding of neonates, they also influenced women by expanding on that fear, creating a more extensive taboo on the basis of the condition of the blood. Early modern physicians believed that any overexertion, excitement, or overheating was detrimental to the blood. Breast milk, as whitened blood, was poisoned because of the difficulties women experienced during childbirth. The discharge of the lochia, which can last anywhere from a week to a month and a half, indicated an instability in the woman's system that spelled impurity, and thus danger to a sucking infant. According to contemporary medical theory, only after the discharge ceased could infants safely be put to the breast. Therefore, although many mothers in western Europe must have denied their newborns the breast for two or three days following birth, when they produced only colostrum, women who came under the care of physicians probably waited longer than less privileged women to begin breast-feeding. Undoubtedly, this affected their ability to breast-feed at all, as early and frequent stimulation of the breasts is necessary to promote a good supply of milk. The result would have been a high rate of failure, especially for first-time mothers, and a consequent greater dependence on wet nurses. In contrast, less privileged women who could not afford the services of wet nurses in the days and weeks immediately following birth began their own breast-feeding sooner, and thus succeeded in establishing adequate supplies of milk.

Here we may have an explanation for commentators' assertions that it was primarily elite women who found their milk supplies insufficient to meet the needs of their infants.[57] In 1597, for example, the Puritan writer Henry Smith complained about the problems wealthy women experienced in establishing breast-feeding: "Whose breasts have this perpetual drought? Forsoothe it is like the goute, no beggars may have it, but citizens or Gentlewomen. In the ninth chapter of Hosea, drie breasts are named for a curse: what lamentable happe have Gentlewomen to light upon this curse more than other? Sure if their breasts be drie, as they say, they should fast and pray together that this curse may bee removed from them."[58] In 1773 the physician Charles White commented on the inability of some women to breast-feed, blaming fashionable corseting for the problem. After describing the tight and unpliable nature of women's stays, he wrote, "Hence it will appear evident why women of rank, and those in the middle stations of life meet with difficulty in giving suck to children . . . [and] why hard working, labouring women, who are obliged to go very loose about their breasts generally make good nurses, and that too with very little trouble."[59] And at the end of the eighteenth century William Moss, an opponent of maternal breast-feeding immediately following birth, still believed with regard to elite women that "a great many are not able to nurse at all, for want of suck."[60]

Although physicians may have contributed to elite women's breast-feeding problems in the seventeenth and early eighteenth centuries, it was, ultimately, physicians who demonstrated the benefits of colostrum to newborn infants. According to the historian Ian G. Wickes, the first recommendation to give neonates colostrum appeared in 1699, when the German physician Michael Ettmueller argued in favor of the purgative quality of the first milk.[61] The leading expert on English breast-feeding practices, Valerie Fildes, found that the physicians who wrote medical advice books began recommending colostrum as more nourishing than any other milk in 1719. She believes that it was mid-century before this viewpoint became generally accepted among physicians.[62]

In 1748, William Cadogan published a highly influential, popular treatise on maternal breast-feeding that criticized mothers' fears of colostrum. According to Cadogan, maternal nursing in the first hours and days after birth would prevent milk fevers, bring the mother's milk in sooner, and provide the newborn with a natural—and beneficial—purge. By following nature, rather than interfering with it, both mothers and babies would benefit. His views gained favor in England and America throughout the second half of the eighteenth century. By 1800 physicians rarely argued against giving infants colostrum. The result was a rather sudden cultural shift in attitudes toward maternal breast-feeding, and therefore in attitudes toward the relationship among mothers, fathers, and children. The new views on colostrum apparently contributed to the rise in maternal breast-feeding among elites that has been documented for the eighteenth century. Greater success due to earlier introduction of the breast must have meant that more women enjoyed suckling. Perhaps women who intended to breast-feed for only a short while, to give their infants the benefits of colostrum, found that they enjoyed the experience and decided to continue. The decision of elites to breast-feed meant that infants remained at home where close emotional ties could develop more easily. The resulting affectionate relationships contributed to greater emotional attachments among the members of elite families, as Lawrence Stone first posited in *The Family, Sex, and Marriage in England.*[63]

If we can accept the fact that many early modern women believed it was harmful to nurse their infants in the first days following a birth, then how did they feed them? François Mauriceau admitted that many women would not be able to follow his advice. "But often poor people cannot observe so many Precautions, and such Mothers are obliged to give their Children suck from the first day. . . . In this case, let their Breasts be a little drawn by some old persons, or some lusty sucking Child; or they may draw them themselves with a Glass."[64] Other medical writers assumed that a friend of the new mother would assist in feeding the child, which they saw as preferable to feeding the infant pap, or milk gruel. In 1724, John Maubray advised, "The Breast of some other clean and sound Woman may be given the Child, until the mother's Milk be purified for its proper Use."[65] Here we can see an important way in which women cared for one another in childbirth. For a short time, generally lasting for only a few days at the most, a friend or hired wet nurse might suckle the newborn. Thus in describing the birth of his first child, Samuel Sewell reported that "The first Woman the Child sucked was Bridget Davenport." Five days later Sewell wrote that they "First laboured to cause the child suck his mother, which he scarce did at all. In the afternoon my Wife set up, and he sucked the right Breast bravely, that had the best nipple." Two days later, "The Child sucked his Mothers left Brest well as she laid in the Bed, notwithstanding the shortness of the Nipple."[66] In theory, this kind of delay in initiating breast-feeding relieved the mother to recover from the rigors of birth and benefited the infant by giving it nourishment superior to what the mother could provide. These services were probably exchanged regularly, a part of the mutual support women gave and received during their childbearing years. William Moss, for example, could claim rather casually at the end of the eighteenth century that a newly delivered mother would have little trouble finding a friend to nurse her child. "Either in town or country," he wrote, "breast milk may be obtained from some relative, friend or other healthy woman . . . as the sex of all ranks feel much for each other in this situation."[67]

Women's Attitudes toward Breast-Feeding

As demonstrated by a number of authorities on the early modern family, many wealthy mothers in western Europe (and some in colonial America) hired wet nurses for their infants, turning over the biologically important and culturally significant role of breast-feeder to a paid employee.[68] Historians have pointed to parents' reliance on wet nurses as evidence of a lack of concern for their infants. Valerie Fildes argues convincingly that dependence on wet nurses did not indicate a lack of affection on the part of mothers. Instead, the weight of tradition virtually required elite women to use wet nurses, much as women today rely on bottle feeding. In addition, she found considerable evidence demonstrating that husbands objected to their wives' breast-feeding.[69] While among the English there was no longer a taboo on intercourse with a breast-feeding woman (upheld over centuries by the Catholic church), traditional fears about the ill effect of intercourse on the milk may have helped to justify husbands' objections to the demands breast-feeding placed on their wives' time and energy. And in addition, as we have just seen, attitudes toward colostrum must have affected the ability of elite women to breast-feed successfully, even when they attempted to do so against considerable social pressure.

Another factor in the decision not to breast-feed was concern about the physical difficulty of the breast-feeding routine. Commentators often mentioned women's fear for their health during breast-feeding as a primary reason for hiring a wet nurse.[70] At the end of the eighteenth century, for example, the physician William Moss explained why some women continued to rely on wet nurses. "They are mostly advised from [i.e., against] it, at first, by their older relatives or friends, either on the mistaken idea of their health, or on the score of fashion; very frequently by their husbands, who fancy they shall be incommoded and disturbed by it."[71] When elite women decided not to breast-feed, they were thinking of their own health as well as their convenience. Even women who could not afford to hire wet nurses sometimes limited the amount of time their infants spent on the breast, from a concern for their health.[72]

By acknowledging the dangers and difficulty of breast-feeding, we will better understand the respect granted to women who breast-fed successfully. The medical sources demonstrate that women's fears for their health were legitimate. Private collections of medicinal recipes and published medical tracts all include cures, sometimes numerous ones, for breast ailments. Taken in combination with the comments of diarists about problems with breast-feeding, we come to understand that the routine carried potentially serious risks for many, if not most, women.[73] In studying the Maine midwife Martha Ballard, whose early nineteenth-century experiences echoed those of earlier periods, Laurel Thatcher Ulrich found that "a considerable part of Martha's medical practice involved treating infants for 'sore mouths' and their mothers for 'painful breasts.'"[74] In addition to fatigue, and problems associated with the reduction or loss of their milk supply, breast-feeding mothers suffered from sore, cracked nipples and painful infections.

Medicinal recipe books, both published and unpublished, were filled with cures for plugged milk ducts, knots in the breast, and abscesses. Serious breast infections brought with them high fevers and general weakness in addition to the pain—often extreme—of a swollen, tender breast. Today such infections are treated with antibiotics and can be alleviated within twenty-four hours of starting medication. In the early modern period, women suffered for days or even weeks. In the most severe cases, the breast or nipple could be permanently damaged. Mauriceau presented the worst-case scenario in his medical treatise. "Very often Women that are Nurses, and especially the first time, are subject to have their Nipples, which are endued with an exquisite sence . . . chopped and excoriated; which is very painful to them, and insupportable. . . . And sometimes these Chops and Excoriations do so encrease by the Childs continual sucking, that in the end it takes the Nipple quite off from the Breasts, and the Woman is no longer capable of giving suck, and there remains sometimes an ulcer very hard to be cured."[75] The pain, and damage to the breast caused by infections, led some women who endured them to resist subsequent breast-feeding. As Moss observed, "A gathered breast in a former lying-in, is often given as a reason for preventing a future attempt at nursing; either for fear of a like accident, or lest there should not be suck enough from want of milk in that breast."[76]

Healers treated infections with a variety of salves and poultices, generally laid on warm as in "An oyntment for a swelling or soare or for a swelled breast," a recipe recorded by a seventeenth-century Englishwoman. Her ointment was made of fresh butter and herbs, and she recommended that "wn you use it heate it as hott as you can suffer it anoynte & bayth it in against ye fire."⁷⁷ Similar recipes were still being used in the eighteenth century. Elizabeth Smith's cure for "a Sore Breast before 'tis broken" was to "Boil white Bread and Milk to a Poultice, then put to it Oil of Lillies, and the Yolk of an Egg; set it over the Fire again to heat, and apply it as hot as can be endured: Dress it Morning and Night till 'tis broke, then dress it with the Poultice of Raisins."⁷⁸ It was the heat that worked in these remedies; hot compresses are still recommended as the most effective way to open a plugged duct. So, for example, when Sarah Cushing "was a good deal threatened with a sore in her left Breast," as her husband wrote to his brother-in-law in 1774, she relied on "ye application of Cow Dung" and found relief.⁷⁹ The cow dung probably was applied hot. Sarah was fortunate; she might have ended up with an abscess like her mother, Hannah Parkman.

Hannah suffered through a number of breast infections over her years of child rearing, but one illness was particularly serious. This infection worsened steadily over a period of two weeks, causing great distress for the entire family. Ebenezer described her condition as first "soreness," then "very bad." On the eighth day he wrote, "Miss Patty Dunlop here, and very Seasonably for my Wife's Breast is grown very bad, & Patty can tend ye Child better yn any one, as she also takes a singular please & Delight in it. Mrs. Hitty Rice came p.m. They both tarry over Night, & are very helpf. to my wife undr. her distress & pains." The next day Hannah was "weak and feverish," despite taking "physick," and all that week her condition remained critical. Finally the decision was made to call in professional help. Ebenezer wrote, "My Wifes breast so bad that I sent Thomas for Dr. Hemingway, who came. Dr. Rice here likewise. May God prepare for his holy will!" Three days later they decided to "open" the breast. Hannah bore the operation, "with a good spirit," but the pain must have been severe. Ebenezer probably observed the procedure, for he commented, "It was no more than a blood-letting as to ye Drs. part. . . . Its issue was corrupt Matter & Blood."⁸⁰

The hesitance of some mothers to breast-feed in the face of such dangers, and the inability of others to do so despite their attempts, made those women who did intensive nursing seem all the more nurturant, giving, and bountiful. Contemporaries recognized the excessive strain that breast-feeding placed on some women, particularly if they were weak, unhealthy, or malnourished. In diaries, letters, medical treatises, and sermons of the period, women and men praised breast-feeding mothers for their personal sacrifice, while babies who were dry-nursed, weaned early, or sent out to wet nurses were seen as the innocent victims of maternal weakness or parental selfishness. Respect for breast milk and breast-feeding mothers remained a cultural given throughout the seventeenth and eighteenth centuries, in part because people recognized just how difficult the work could be.

Laurel Thatcher Ulrich has pointed to the cultural importance of fertility for defining women's status.[81] By fertility, she means both fecundity and success at nurturing children until they reached adulthood and became parents themselves. Clearly, fertility was essential both to women's self-perceptions and to interpretations of their roles. As the New England minister Benjamin Colman observed in 1716, "A Mother with a Train of Children after her is One of the most admirable and lovely Sights in the Visible Creation of God."[82] Ministers and physicians valued highly women's ability to give birth, breast-feed, and care for their families in sickness, but even more important, women valued these qualities in themselves. In such a cultural setting, problems with breast-feeding and infertility caused severe stress. Women's collections of medicinal recipes invariably included remedies for increasing inadequate milk supplies as well as recipes for supplementary feedings of pap and panada, but mothers with breast-feeding problems often must have relied on the help of other women in feeding their infants. For infertile women, the inability to become pregnant or carry a fetus to term carried an even heavier social and psychological burden. Such women turned to prayer and active medical intervention in their attempts to become mothers. Both female healers and male physicians wrote at length about the causes and cures of barrenness, and ministers attempted to comfort barren women, but it was difficult to avoid the conclusion that barrenness was a sign of God's disfavor. In his printed sermon on motherhood, *Some of the Honours that Religion Does Unto the Fruitful Mothers in Israel,* Benjamin Colman observed "LET me add a Caution to the Barren: Not to be dejected for want of Children; as Rachel and Hannah were too much. For tho' it be such a favour to be the Mother of many, yet there are Greater favours than this to set our Hearts upon; and it may be you in your *Espousals* to Christ have much more to satisfie your Soul in; or at least thither let me direct you."[83] For women who could not fulfill their highest earthly duty, and receive the honor due them as good mothers, only the hope of an eternal reward could give solace.

Large areas of women's history remain obscure, hidden by our failure to understand basic assumptions about women's lives in the past. We have not grasped the importance of women's functions as mothers, and so we have assumed that other areas of women's lives were more culturally significant. Yet clearly fertility, and infertility, determined women's status and self-image alongside other factors more commonly considered by historians, such as wealth or reputation. That we have overlooked for so long the role of fertility in women's lives points more to its lack of importance in twentieth-century culture than to its lack of importance in the past.

As we have discovered from a variety of sources—sermons, medical books, collections of recipes, letters, and diaries—cultural assumptions about motherhood in the seventeenth and eighteenth centuries differed significantly from modern ones. Most important, contemporaries regarded motherhood as first and foremost a physical activity. Women were primarily responsible for the physical well-being of their infants and children, as in fact they were for all members of their households, and they demonstrated their emotional attachment to family members by giving them good physical care. When we consider healing in conjunction with women's work as the bearers and breast-feeders of infants, women's control over the body emerges as the focal point of motherhood before the modern age. After marriage, most seventeenth- and eighteenth-century women spent fully twenty to twenty-five years either pregnant or nursing. Many died in their old age with children still living at home. Their work as mothers filled their days: in the physical presence of the fetus kicking inside the womb, in the pull of the infant sucking at the breast, in the needs of the sick child lying in a cradle by the fireplace. Although matrons' work in kitchen and garden was never ending, children's needs probably came first. When the baby cried it had to be fed. The very physical realities of motherhood made it the center point of women's mature lives. In fulfilling their roles as both good housewives *and* good mothers, women lived up to a high cultural standard for female excellence.

NOTES

The author wishes to thank Norma Basch and Jan Lewis for their perceptive criticisms and comments on this paper. Earlier versions of the work were presented at the Eighth Berkshire Conference on the History of Women, Douglass College, 1990, and at a conference in honor of Lois Green Carr, "The Chesapeake and Beyond—A Celebration," held at the University of Maryland, College Park, in 1992.

1. Francis G. Wallett, ed., *The Diary of Ebenezer Parkman, 1703–1782. First Part: Three Volumes in One, 1719–1755,* with a foreword by Clifford K. Shipton (Worcester, Mass., 1974), p. 259.

2. Ibid., pp. 259–60.

3. Ibid., p. 260.

4. Ibid.

5. American historians, in particular, have devoted considerable energy to studying women's work as wives and economic providers and have produced little on the work of mothering. Chapter 1 of Jeanne Boydston's *Home and Work: Housework, Wages, and the Ideology of Labor in the Early Republic* (New York, 1990) is typical of the focus on economic production. For the colonial period, Boydston did not define childbirth, breast-feeding, or care of the sick as work and equated child care with such chores as tending fires and cleaning. Other studies of colonial and revolutionary era women that argue against motherhood as a valued social role

are Ruth Bloch, "American Feminine Ideas in Transition: The Rise of the Moral Mother, 1785–1815," *Feminist Studies* 4 (1978): 101–26; and Catherine Scholten, *Childbearing in American Society: 1650–1850* (New York, 1985). Bloch's work influenced Carl Degler, who made the same point in *At Odds: Women and the Family in America from the Revolution to the Present* (New York, 1980), p. 73. Laurel Thatcher Ulrich has produced the best work on colonial motherhood. She demonstrates the high regard New Englanders accorded women as mothers, particularly prolific ones. See *Good Wives: Image and Reality in the Lives of Women in Northern New England, 1650–1750* (New York, 1982), especially chap. 8. Ulrich's conclusion that women's work as mothers was extensive rather than intensive, owing to their many household obligations, is her most frequently cited point. Unfortunately, this somewhat undercuts her main argument about the respect accorded motherhood as a key female role. Nancy Schrom Dye and Daniel Blake Smith, for example, cite Ulrich as proof for an extensive mothering style in the colonial period and do not mention her arguments about the importance of good mothering for defining women's status in their communities and the wider culture. Their oversight allowed them to use Ulrich's study as proof for their own argument that only in the nineteenth century did mothers assume primary responsibility for the physical care of their children. See Dye and Smith, "Mother Love and Infant Death, 1750–1920," *Journal of American History* 73 (1986): 329–53. Similarly, Boydston ignored Ulrich's discussion of motherhood, focusing only on the discussions of household production in *Good Wives*. In *Liberty's Daughters: The Revolutionary Experience of American Women, 1750–1800* (Boston, 1980), chap. 3, Mary Beth Norton argues that mid-eighteenth-century women received their greatest satisfaction from their work as mothers. Julia Cherry Spruill, *Women's Life and Work in the Southern Colonies* (Chapel Hill, N.C., 1938; reprint, New York, 1972), chap. 3, includes useful information on motherhood. John Demos is one of the most frequently cited authorities on the prevalence of breast-feeding in colonial New England. See *A Little Commonwealth: Family Life in Plymouth Colony* (New York, 1970), p. 133.

6. English historians recently have produced a number of excellent studies on various aspects of motherhood in the seventeenth and eighteenth centuries. See Valerie Fildes, ed., *Women as Mothers in Pre-Industrial England: Essays in Memory of Dorothy McLaren* (New York, 1990); Fildes, *Breasts, Bottles, and Babies: A History of Infant Feeding* (Edinburgh, 1986); Linda A. Pollock, *Forgotten Children: Parent-Child Relations from 1500 to 1900* (Cambridge, 1983); Betty S. Travitsky, "The New Mother of the English Renaissance: Her Writings on Motherhood," in *The Lost Tradition: Mothers and Daughters in Literature,* ed. C. N. Davidson and E. M. Broner (New York, 1980).

7. Thomas Muffet, *Health's Improvement* (1584), quoted in Ian G. Wickes, "A History of Infant Feeding," *Archives of Disease in Childhood* 28 (1953): 157. Dorothy McLaren believed suckling of weak adults may have been a normal part of wet-nursing in pre-industrial England. See "Marital Fertility and Lactation 1570–1720," in *Women in English Society, 1500–1800,* ed. Mary Prior (New York, 1985), p. 29.

8. Nicholas Culpeper, *A Directory for Midwives: or, A Guide for Women, in their Conception, Bearing, and Suckling their Children* (London, 1660), p. 214.

9. Great Britain, Customs Establishment, 1688–1691, p. 69, Massachusetts Historical Society, Boston.

10. Gervase Markham wrote, "If a woman have a strong and hard labour, Take foure spoonefulls of another womans milke, and give it the woman to drinke in her labour, and she

shall bee delivered presently." *The English House-wife, Containing the inward and outward Vertues which ought to be in a complete Woman* (London, 1637), p. 39. See also *Aristotle's Complete Master-Piece, In Three Parts, Displaying the Secrets of Nature in the Generation of Man . . . To which is added A Treasure of Health, or the Family Physician* (London, 1766), p. 66.

11. Penn Family Papers, vol. 6, p. 103, Historical Society of Pennsylvania, Philadelphia.

12. Anonymous, *Enchiridum or an Abridgm[en]t of Platerous Golden Practise of Physick by T.W.* (London, ca. 1660), p. 180.

13. Penn Family Papers, vol. 6, p. 93.

14. Medicinae Liber, 10a/214, College of Physicians, Philadelphia.

15. Great Britain, Customs Establishment, 1688–1691, pp. 24–29.

16. Richard Lower, *Dr. Lower's and Several Other Eminent Physicians Receipts: Containing the Best and Safest Method for Curing Most Diseases in Human Bodies,* 4th ed. (London, 1716), p. 103.

17. Jacques Guillemeau, *Child-Birth or, The Happy Deliverie of Women* (London, 1612), p. 6.

18. Charles Brigham Account Book, Folder 3, Recipe #33, American Antiquarian Society, Worcester, Mass.

19. Great Britain, Customs Establishment, 1688–1691, p. 195.

20. Anonymous, *A Closet for Ladies and Gentlemen. Or, The Art of preserving, Conserving, and Candying. . . . Also divers soveraigne Medicines and Salves for Sundry Diseases* (London, 1635), D2.

21. *Aristotle's Master-Piece,* p. 139.

22. Fildes, *Breasts, Bottles, and Babies,* p. 98; Demos, *A Little Commonwealth,* p. 133. Even in continental Europe in the eighteenth century, when hand-feeding and animal feeding were more common, these methods were considered inferior to maternal breast-feeding or reliance on a wet nurse.

23. Patricia Crawford, "Attitudes to Menstruation in Seventeenth-Century England," *Past and Present* 91 (1981): 51–52; David Hunt, *Parents and Children in History: The Psychology of Family Life in Early Modern France* (New York, 1970), p. 115; Thomas Laqueur, *Making Sex: Body and Gender from the Greeks to Freud* (Cambridge, Mass., 1990), pp. 35–36, 104–5. Laqueur writes at length about ideas on the "fungibility of fluids." See especially pp. 103–8.

24. Guillemeau, *Child-Birth,* p. 1.

25. Hugh Smith, *Letters to Married Women,* 4th ed. (Dublin, 1777), p. 65.

26. Laqueur, *Making Sex,* pp. 38–39.

27. Ibid., p. 105.

28. Crawford, "Menstruation," pp. 57–65, 72–73.

29. *The Curse: A Cultural History of Menstruation,* ed. Janice Delaney, Mary Jane Lupton, and Emily Toth, rev. ed. (Chicago, 1988), is an excellent introduction to the anthropological literature on menstruation.

30. Ulrich, *Good Wives,* p. 153.

31. Quoted in David Leverenz, *The Language of Puritan Feeling: An Exploration in Literature, Psychology, and Social History* (New Brunswick, N.J., 1980), p. 130. This section of my paper is dependent on the work of Leverenz, who uncovered numerous examples of breast-feeding imagery in the writings of Puritans.

32. John Cotton, *The Way of Life* (London, 1641), p. 28, quoted in Leverenz, *Language of Puritan Feeling,* p. 131.

33. Quoted in Edmund S. Morgan, *Visible Saints: The History of a Puritan Idea* (Ithaca, N.Y., 1963), p. 72.

34. Leverenz, *Language of Puritan Feeling,* p. 143.

35. Thomas Shepard, *Parable of the Ten Virgins,* in *Works,* vol. 2, p. 40, quoted in Leverenz, *Language of Puritan Feeling,* p. 129.

36. Quoted in Ulrich, *Good Wives,* p. 264, n. 15.

37. Shepard, *Parable of the Ten Virgins,* 2:497, 131, quoted in Leverenz, *Language of Puritan Feeling,* pp. 143, 145.

38. Leverenz, *Language of Puritan Feeling,* p. 152.

39. Patricia Crawford, "The Construction and Experience of Maternity in Seventeenth-Century England," in *Women as Mothers in Pre-Industrial England,* p. 8. Crawford writes generally of English religious leaders, while Leverenz focuses on the Puritans. Yet he concludes, "Almost any point [on family relations] made by Puritan tracts can be found in non-Puritan writings" (*Language of Puritan Feeling,* p. 92).

40. Printed in John Norton, *Abel being Dead yet speaketh . . .* (London, 1658), p. 28, quoted in Leverenz, *Language of Puritan Feeling,* p. 124.

41. Medical books were static in much of their advice on infant care. This peculiarity reflects two issues. First, there were few advances in medical understanding of breast-feeding, breast ailments, or infantile diseases during the period studied. Second, medical writers frequently borrowed heavily from each other and their predecessors. Thus, advice first written in the early seventeenth century was still being repeated in texts at the end of the eighteenth century.

42. The fear that wet nurses might convey their character failings to their nurslings was expressed beginning in the sixteenth century, in Thomas Phayer's *Boke of Children* (ca. 1544). See Wickes, "History of Infant Feeding," pp. 157–58, 232, 239. Fildes, *Breasts, Bottles and Babies,* p. 112, comments on beliefs during the sixteenth and seventeenth centuries. On the eighteenth century, see Anonymous, *The Ladies Dispensatory, or Every Woman her own Physician,* 2d ed. (London, 1740), p. viii; and Bloch, "Feminine Ideals in Transition," pp. 110–11. In her survey of three centuries of medical writers on breast-feeding, Fildes found only one who advocated use of a wet nurse over maternal breast-feeding. See *Breasts, Bottles, and Babies,* p. 111 and table 3.3.

43. Guillemeau, *Child-birth,* p. 21.

44. Walter Harris, *A Treatise of the Acute Diseases of Infants. To Which are added, Medical Observations on Several Grievous Diseases. Written Originally in Latin by the late learned Walter Harris, M. D. Fellow of the College of Physicians at London, and Professor of Chirugery in the same College. Translated into English by John Martyn* (London, 1742). The Latin version was published in 1689.

45. Revealing titles, for example, include Nicholas Culpeper, *A Directory for Midwives: or, A Guide for Women, in their Conception, Bearing, and Suckling their Children* (London, 1660); and Anonymous, *The Nurses Guide, or the right method of bringing up children* (London, 1729).

46. George Armstrong, *Essay on the Diseases Most Fatal to Infants* (London, 1767), pp. 2–3.

47. François Mauriceau, *The Diseases of Women with Child, and in Child-bed,* trans. Hugh Chamberlin (London, 1672), p. 367.

48. Harris, *Treatise of Acute Diseases*, p. 19.

49. See, for example, Guillemeau, *Child-Birth*, p. 25; Abbot Quillet, *Callipaediae; or, An Art how to have Handsome Children: Written in Latin by the Abbot Quillet. To which is Added, Paedotrophiae, or, The Art of Nursing and Breeding up Children: Written in Latin by Monsieur St. Marthe, Physician to Henry III of France. Now done into English Verse.* (London, 1710), pp. 208–9. According to Wickes, the Latin poem appeared in 1655 ("History of Infant Feeding," p. 239).

50. Fildes provides a wealth of information on weaning practices in *Breasts, Bottles, and Babies*, pp. 351–97.

51. Culpeper, *Directory for Midwives*, p. 214.

52. Guillemeau, *Child-Birth*, p. 18.

53. Smith, *Letters to Married Women*, pp. 91–92.

54. William Cadogan, *An Essay Upon Nursing, and the Management of Children. From Their Birth to Three Years of Age*, 5th ed. (Philadelphia, 1773), p. 17. Cadogan's book was published in England in 1748.

55. Anonymous, "A System Concerning Fevers," unpub. ms., 1677, p. 153, Yale Medical Library, New Haven, Conn.

56. Wickes, "History of Infant Feeding," p. 151.

57. In *Breasts, Bottles, and Babies*, Fildes wrote that "religious authors complained that only the rich were afflicted with insufficient breastmilk," citing William Gouge, *Of Domesticall Duties. Eight Treatises.* (London, 1622); Henry [?] Newcome, *The Compleat Mother or, An Earnest Persuasive to All Mothers (Especially Those of Rank and Quality) to Nurse Their Own Children* (London, 1695); and William Perkins, *The Complete Works*, vols. 1 and 3 (Cambridge, 1612–18). In her investigation into breast-feeding difficulties, Pollock found that "the most common hardship was insufficient milk" (*Forgotten Children*, p. 214).

58. Henry Smith, *The Sermons of Maister Hertie Smith gathered into one volume* (London, 1597), quoted in Fildes, *Breasts, Bottles, and Babies*, p. 101.

59. Charles White, *A Treatise on the Management of Pregnant and Lying-In Women* (London, 1773), quoted in Fildes, *Breasts, Bottles, and Babies*, p. 102. Fildes believes women's tight corsets may have caused inverted nipples, which make breast-feeding more difficult.

60. William Moss, *An Essay on the Management, Nursing and Diseases of Children* (London, 1794), p. 439.

61. Wickes, "History of Infant Feeding," p. 332.

62. Fildes, *Breasts, Bottles, and Babies*, p. 86, fig. 2.2, "Chronology of Changes in Ideas about Colostrum."

63. Lawrence Stone, *The Family, Sex, and Marriage in England, 1500–1800* (London, 1977), pp. 431–32.

64. Mauriceau, *Diseases of Women*, p. 365.

65. John Maubray, *The Female Physician, Containing all the Diseases Incident to that Sex, in Virgins, Wives, and Widows* (London, 1724), p. 334.

66. Samuel Sewell, *The Diary of Samuel Sewell, 1674–1729*, in *Collections of the Massachusetts Historical Society*, 5th ser., vol. 5 (Boston, 1878), pp. 41–42 (April 1–9, 1677).

67. Moss, *Management, Nursing and Diseases of Children*, pp. 100–101.

68. See especially Fildes, *Breasts, Bottles, and Babies*, chap. 3; and George D. Sussman, *Selling Mothers' Milk: The Wet-Nursing Business in France, 1715–1914* (Chicago, 1982).

69. On the importance of tradition, see Fildes, *Breasts, Bottles, and Babies,* p. 102. Robert Schnucker also made this point in "The English Puritans and Pregnancy, Delivery and Breast-feeding," *History of Childhood Quarterly* 1 (1974): 631–58. Fildes's complete discussion appears on pp. 100–106. Pollock demonstrates that although women may have employed wet nurses, that fact alone did not necessarily indicate a lack of affection or concern for their infants. She cites many examples of parents visiting their children at the wet nurses' homes, and expressing concern for the quality of care their infants received (*Forgotten Children,* pp. 216–17).

70. Fildes, *Breasts, Bottles, and Babies,* p. 100.

71. Moss, *Management, Nursing and Diseases,* p. 462. See also Cadogan, *Essay Upon Nursing,* pp. 16, 24.

72. Cotton Mather, *Elizabeth in Her Holy Retirement. An Essay to Prepare a Pious Woman for Her Lying-In* (Boston, 1710), p. 35; Hunt, *Parents and Children in History,* pp. 119–20.

73. Pollock cites several useful examples of diarists' comments, in *Forgotten Children,* pp. 213–14. See also Fildes, *Breasts, Bottles, and Babies,* pp. 101, 109–11.

74. Laurel Thatcher Ulrich, *A Midwife's Tale: The Life of Martha Ballard, Based on Her Diary, 1785–1812* (New York, 1991), p. 196.

75. Mauriceau, *Diseases of Women with Child,* p. 349.

76. Moss, *Management, Nursing, and Diseases of Children,* p. 468.

77. Charles Brigham Account Book, Folder 5, Recipe #23.

78. Elizabeth Smith, *The Compleat Housewife: or Accomplish'd Gentlewoman's Companion,* 5th ed. (Williamsburg, Va., 1742), p. 204.

79. Correspondence, Box 3, Folder 3, Parkman Family Papers, American Antiquarian Society, Worcester, Mass. This is an excellent example of the open manner in which men discussed aspects of breast-feeding in the eighteenth century.

80. Ebenezer Parkman, Diary, July 17–August 2, 1758, Parkman Family Papers. Ross W. Beales, Jr., has written an enlightening article on colonial breast-feeding practices based on the Parkman diary. See his "Nursing and Weaning in an Eighteenth-Century New England Household," in Peter Benes, ed., *The Dublin Seminar for New England Folklife, Annual Proceedings* (Boston, 1985), pp. 48–63.

81. Ulrich, *Good Wives,* pp. 159–62.

82. Benjamin Colman, *The Honour and Happiness of the Vertuous Woman: More Especially Considered in the Two Relationships of Wife and Mother* (Boston, 1716), p. 5.

83. Benjamin Colman, *Some of the Honours that Religion Does Unto the Fruitful Mothers in Israel* (Boston, 1715), p. 9.

2.

The Republican Vision of Mary Palmer Tyler

MARILYN S. BLACKWELL

In 1811 Mary Palmer Tyler, a thirty-five-year-old matron living in Brattle-boro, Vermont, wrote a child-care manual that explained her understanding of a mother's role. "To say nothing of our duty, as *citizens*," she insisted, "while form-ing the future guardians of our beloved country, it is undoubtedly our duty, as *mothers,* to bring up our sons in such a manner as shall render them most useful and happy." Indeed, for Mary, "the future beauty, health, and happiness of the ris-ing generation, and, eventually, the welfare of the community at large" rested on the proper discharge of a mother's duties. After sixteen years of experience raising eight healthy children, Mary, the wife of the dramatist and judge Royall Tyler, felt competent to instruct other women on their responsibilities in the new republic.[1]

Mary Tyler's conception of female citizenship represents a classic statement of republican motherhood, written not by a political theorist but by a mother. This study examines her interpretation of that concept within the context of Tyler fam-ily life, showing the evolution of republican ideology within the consciousness of a New England woman. In addition, it explores her influence on her children to il-lustrate the psychological ramifications of this dominant mode of child rearing for sons and daughters of the next generation.

The historians Linda Kerber and Mary Beth Norton have used the concept of republican motherhood to describe the political significance assigned to maternal duties in postrevolutionary America. Focusing attention on their sons and encour-aging industry, frugality, temperance, and self-control, republican mothers would nurture virtuous citizens who served their communities; by educating their daugh-ters, mothers would ensure the virtue of future generations. The ideal had am-biguous results for women's social status. Recognition of mothers' importance

Reprinted by permission from the *Journal of the Early Republic* 12 (1992): 11–35. Copyright © 1992 Society for Historians of the Early American Republic.

provided a rationale for female education, yet at the same time women were ex-cluded from direct political participation. Using this ideal, other scholars have out-lined a more expansive role for women as custodians of virtue in American society. As civic virtue lost its importance in male political discourse during the 1780s and 1790s, women could conveniently preserve the concept outside public life by en-suring the private virtue of their husbands and children. This responsibility for the common good made mothers not only essential to a successful republic but also capable of reconciling the goals of classical republicanism and liberal individualism.[2]

The term "republican mother" has become commonplace in historiography on early nineteenth-century women, yet scholars have rarely explained how real women adapted this public ideal in private life. Emphasis on its political signifi-cance has overshadowed the way the ideology operated for mothers. Both Norton and Kerber suggest that, despite its ambiguity, the ideal helped women question fa-milial roles. Nonetheless, we have few case histories showing the interaction of re-publican ideology with the longer-term shift in family relations that began in the mid-eighteenth century. With the rise of the companionate, child-centered family, affectionate domestic relations and child rearing gained importance. Beyond their traditional roles as "helpmeets" to their husbands, wives and mothers gradually be-came responsible for the psychological well-being of their families. By the 1830s, as commercial development increasingly drew fathers' attention outside the house-hold, maternal affection, rather than patriarchal authority, dominated the middle-class home in the Northeast. Moreover, motherhood, now specifically linked to piety, had become a social role played out in churches and voluntary associations. While debate over the importance of this shift for women's status continues, their part in shaping female experience and gaining influence within families is gener-ally acknowledged.[3] Scant attention, however, has been given to the connection be-tween ideology and behavior. How did women translate republican virtue of the earlier period into the Christian virtue pious mothers championed in the 1830s and 1840s, and what were the results for their children?[4]

The story of Mary Tyler reveals these connections. A forerunner in articulat-ing a mother's role in child rearing, Mary formulated, reshaped, and then imple-mented her republican ideology to meet practical needs. It was not the political aspect of republican motherhood that gave it importance for Mary, but the ways in which it helped her expand her moral authority in the Tyler family. In her view, re-publican motherhood meant taking responsibility for her family's future. Given wide leeway to manage her household by an absent husband, Mary applied Enlightenment thought to the supervision of her children's physical, moral, and intellectual development. When economic difficulties threatened her family's survival, Mary turned to evangelical religion to ensure her children's virtue and her own financial security. The character she instilled in her children helped create her vision of a Christian republic while she preserved the family values that dominated her view of the world. Her efforts, similar to those of many women of her time, maintained classical republican ideals, ensuring that her children would serve the common good even as liberalism began to dominate American life.[5]

Mary Palmer Tyler (1775–1866) learned about civic duty from her family's political participation. Wealthy, Boston-area revolutionary activists, the Palmers believed in their obligation to serve the public welfare as intellectual and social leaders. Joseph Palmer, Mary's grandfather, had been a member of the Massachusetts Provincial Congress and Committee of Safety; both her father, Joseph Pearse Palmer, and grandfather had served in the Massachusetts militia. In fact, her father had risked his life disguised as an "Indian" during the Boston Tea Party. During the war, Elizabeth Hunt Palmer, Mary's mother, had made bandages, cooked for the troops during the occupation of Boston, and abstained from drinking tea. As the family recounted these events of her early childhood, Mary absorbed its patriotic history and sense of public duty.[6]

Equally important was her understanding of family obligation. The eldest Palmer daughter, Mary benefited from both the intellectual stimulation of an educated family and the practical experience that economic misfortune forced upon her. Her parents treated her with affection and respect while encouraging her to write and to read extensively. A graduate of Harvard, Joseph Palmer believed in education for women, encouraged his wife to read, and monitored his children's intellectual development. His family's donations to the war effort followed by postwar inflation, however, reduced the Palmers to near poverty; they could hardly consider formal education for their four sons, much less their five daughters. Instead, Mary helped manage and teach her younger brothers and sisters. When the family moved to a farm outside Boston, she learned to make butter and cheese and to spin, weave, and make clothes. By the time she married in 1794, Mary understood the importance of her contribution to the family welfare and had developed considerable self-confidence as well.[7]

While her marriage to Royall Tyler was based on affection, Mary and her husband had somewhat different expectations of their marriage roles, at least initially. Descended from a family of Boston merchants, Royall Tyler, a well-known playwright and lawyer and a close friend of Joseph Palmer, had established a legal practice in Guilford, Vermont, where he offered to take Mary. Like the Palmers, Royall sensed his civic obligations, but, disillusioned with Boston society, he sought both personal and political opportunities in a less developed community. Having extolled affectionate marriage and ridiculed marital unions based on property in his play *The Contrast* (1787), Royall had little difficulty proposing to penniless Mary Palmer. Yet, eighteen years her senior, Royall also felt a paternal protectiveness for his bride that hindered his sense of mutual obligation. Moreover, despite his profession of yeoman values, he expected Mary to exhibit the delicacy and manners of the genteel women of Boston. Remembering his foolishness, Mary later explained that Royall enjoyed dressing her in sprightly outfits and displaying her as proudly "as any little girl is of her doll." More practical than her husband, Mary looked forward to applying her domestic talents and to raising children in their new home.[8]

Mary's personal experience formed the basis of her child-rearing philosophy. Her parents, who had read John Locke's *Some Thoughts Concerning Education* (1693) as a guide, had raised her using rational methods. Assuming a child's natural goodness and malleability, Lockean theory stressed the importance of childhood health, learning through experience, and regular patterns of discipline to encourage self-control. As a young child, Mary had been allowed considerable freedom to explore the outdoors and to exercise her mind before her training in domestic arts. Still at her parents' home in Massachusetts during her first child's birth, Mary learned about infant care from her mother. Once removed from her family, however, she relied largely on her own experience as a guide in caring for her growing family.[9]

Royall's frequent absences from home gave Mary the opportunity to expand her child-rearing role as she implemented the enlightened methods of her own youth. Elected to the Vermont Supreme Court in 1801, Royall traveled twice annually up the Connecticut River and down the Champlain Valley on the court circuit, leaving his family for months at a time. Meanwhile, the Tylers moved from their village home in Guilford to a farm in neighboring Brattleboro. With a farm tenant to oversee and isolated from friends and neighbors, Mary's burdens increased. Hired help and Mary's younger sister, who temporarily lived with the Tylers, relieved her of some domestic work, but pregnancy, breast-feeding, and constant attention to her babies sapped much of her energy. Between 1794 and 1810 Mary had nine sons and two daughters.[10] Affectionate letters and Royall's intense but brief visits home kept their marriage vibrant. Meanwhile, with Royall away, Mary avoided their "little troubles," as she described it, over child management. Royall, for example, would not allow their young children at the table until they were old enough to behave properly. From Mary's point of view, "This would have been a real damage to their manners, had it not been for his long and frequent absences from home when we could do as we pleased." Royall sometimes believed in strict discipline, but on other occasions he indulged his children with affection and trinkets. Resenting his inconsistency, Mary preferred using regular patterns of reward and gentle persuasion.[11]

Daily infant care caused Mary to worry more about her children's health than their manners, and much of her child-rearing philosophy emerged from this focus.[12] When her babies were desperately ill, she called local doctors. But for routine problems, rather than defer to tradition in the model of her colonial ancestors, Mary turned to British health care manuals for guidance. William Buchan's *Domestic Medicine* (1769), a widely read manual in America, proved the most valuable, though Mary read at least four other manuals as well. Steeped in Enlightenment thought, Buchan applied Locke's teachings to health issues, insisting that improved health practices could prevent illness. Once contracted, diseases could be treated through early detection and the systematic use of herbal medicines. With this interventionist approach, Buchan insisted that parents were responsible for the future "health and usefulness" of children. Much of his infant health program, including cleanliness, exercise, loose clothing, and a mother's breast-feeding, was familiar to Mary Tyler from her own childhood.[13] Her reading reinforced these practices, gave her confidence in treating disease, and, most important, encouraged her to intervene in her children's behalf. Experimenting with her own herbal recipes, Mary felt increasingly competent to treat her children as well as any doctor. She discovered, for example, that blood root, which looked "very much like small red beets," could be sliced, toasted, bottled with spirits and water, and used as an emetic for "children who are subject to biles, and other purulent humours." With success in keeping her children healthy, Mary learned that attention to each child's physical condition and stage of development was the most important factor in child care.[14]

Eventually, Mary decided to assert her maternal expertise by writing her own infant care manual. While she believed the work might earn much needed cash, it also confirmed her role at home, fulfilled her sense of public service, and affirmed her status among the intellectual elite. Royall's contacts with book printers made publication easy. In 1811 Isaac Riley, his New York publisher, printed *The Maternal Physician*.[15] Maintaining conventional anonymity as an author, Mary protected herself from possible criticism from male professionals who might consider her book a deviation from traditional female deference. Few women writers had claimed the authority to give child-care advice.

The Maternal Physician was one of the earliest comprehensive child-care manuals by an American woman. Mary Tyler not only explained her treatment of childhood diseases and her approach to education and discipline but also used her experience to argue that women had greater authority in child care than men. It was this philosophy, embodying her concept of womanhood and her place in a republican society, that distinguished her approach to child rearing from Lockean educational theory and from that of colonial women, who rarely made such claims.

Her manual became part of the growing literature on the health and education of children addressed to literate women. Written largely by ministers, health reformers, and educators, a few of whom were women, that literature became abundant by the 1830s. Charging mothers with responsibility for the physical, moral, and intellectual development of children, it set new standards of domestic practice. Mary was unusual in her ability to articulate this concept in 1811 and in directly confronting doctors with her medical knowledge. At a time when some ministers were beginning to focus on pious motherhood, Mary modeled her child-rearing techniques after the enlightened methods popular among the literate elite.[16]

Emphasizing a mother's biological relationship to her children, her daily experience, and her emotional fulfillment through child nurture, Mary separated parental duties based on her understanding of gender differences. Repeating much of William Buchan's advice, she described infant problems of feeding and teething plus a long list of childhood diseases, including measles, smallpox, chicken pox, worms, dysentery, scald head (cradle cap), ringworm, whooping cough, earache, herpes, shingles, canker, chilblains, warts, and sties. Unlike Buchan and other male advisers, who insisted upon a mother's breast-feeding largely to improve children's health, Mary used the argument to ground a mother's nurturing role in her natural biological function. Only a mother, she stressed, who breast-fed her infant and bathed him or her daily could "detect in season any latent symptoms of disease" that might even "baffle the physician's skill."[17] Not only was a mother better positioned than a father, but she was also as competent as a doctor in most routine illnesses. By noting her own children's symptoms and explaining how her treatments helped them recover, Mary argued that a mother's relationship with children provided the proper experience to oversee child care. Her "lovely little girl," for example, contracted "morbid snuffles" at only one week old, exhibited "dreadful fits," and was finally cured with calomel and "my unremitted care and attentions." With deference to "the most approved medical authorities," Mary supported her claims by citing doctors' advice. But she also stated: "These gentlemen must pardon me if I think, after all, that a mother is her child's best physician, in all ordinary cases." Moreover, she asserted, a woman's naturally tender feelings made her especially suited to maternal responsibilities. Sprinkling her text with sentimental language and quotations from eighteenth-century poets, Mary sanctioned what she believed were natural mother-child attachments. As "sweet pledges of connubial love," children were the source of a woman's happiness.[18]

Because she connected her children's physical and mental well-being, Mary also claimed a mother's duty to oversee their intellectual and moral training. Whereas Puritan child-training advice had stressed Christian education to teach moral principles and to break a child's will, Mary's approach rested on learning through experience. Babies, she believed, should not only be exercised every day to stimulate physical growth but also constantly talked to for mental development. Once again, she cited examples from daily experience: "I said to my babe to day, George where is Rover? at the same time pointing to a favourite spaniel which lay upon the carpet: the dog advanced, and the child sprang forward delighted; and now when he is asked where is Rover? he immediately looks around to find him; thus he has acquired an idea productive of constant pleasure."[19]

Just as Mary believed children's intellects could be shaped, so she hoped to control their "passions and desires" with uniform discipline and affectionate persuasion. Eight or nine months, she insisted, was not too soon for infants to learn obedience and for mothers to gain "ascendancy" over children's minds to guarantee "a due degree of influence over them through life." Subduing her obstinate nine-month-old son, Mary had refused to indulge his desire for a large lump of sugar. Once he had succumbed, she rewarded him with affection and praise to ensure his continued good behavior. Yet, for Mary, children also claimed inherent rights to be treated fairly; mothers must be sensitive to their children's feelings and accept reasonable efforts at compromise. With a "just sense of right and wrong," children would only revolt at "arbitrary government."[20]

Mary Tyler's desire to shape her children's characters represented her adaptation of Locke's educational theory to republican goals, to her experience of family relationships, and to her understanding of a woman's role. Locke's independent, rational man had been educated by his father to serve society and achieve happiness by doing what he ought to do.[21] In Mary's formulation, children were similarly shaped but under a mother's affectionate guidance. A mother's influence was more important than a father's not because a woman was more moral, a position Mary would assume later, but because her natural relationship to children, her tender feelings, and her reason would act in a child's and the family's best interest. Mary understood children within the context of family life, not as autonomous individuals. Just as her primary goal was raising a successful family, so she believed her children should place the family's welfare before their own. Her duty to care for and teach her children and their duty to behave properly resembled the mutual obligations prevalent in colonial households. But Mary's system required internal controls developed in response to maternal affection and persuasion rather than patriarchal discipline.[22] As they practiced self-denial at home, her children would learn to serve the needs of the larger community rather than to follow their personal inclinations. Defining individual happiness as the result of virtue and usefulness, Mary believed her program would ensure her children's happiness and serve society as well. Meanwhile, republican motherhood allowed her to control an arena of family life and achieve self-fulfillment through her children.

Creating such an ordered world was more difficult than Mary envisioned. Her optimism about human behavior masked the consistency and self-control required to achieve her ideal. When her children were little, Mary could arbitrate compromises between her expectations and their behavior, but, often burdened with household cares, her patience ran thin. Edward, the pliant infant she had described in her manual, for example, won his mother over in repeated attempts to stay by her side after the birth of a new baby. Securing a peaceful household against his temper became more important than subduing his will.[23] Royall could also be frustratingly indulgent, as Mary explained in her manual: "I was here almost tempted to address a word or two of advice to fathers; but my own good man, who sits laughing on the sofa, whilst his favourite little Joseph is drawing his watch tied to a string round the carpet for a plaything, and who just now looked as if he thought me cruel for refusing the dear enchanting little innocent my inkstandish for a go-cart, might esteem it too presuming."[24]

While these difficulties weakened Mary's consistency, Tyler finances posed a greater threat to her ideal world. Privately, Mary had far less confidence in her ability to shape the future than she had expressed publicly. Fear of poverty, with its resulting loss of family status and respectability, and the Tylers' lack of funds for their sons' education soon dominated Mary's concerns. As a judge, Royall received a regular income, but he spent freely with little concern for his indebtedness. Meanwhile, the Brattleboro farm barely produced enough to feed the family; Mary often felt "meanly destitute of necessaries." Despite the self-confidence of her child-care manual, she worried about her sons' futures and their characters, expressing more faith in God than in her own powers. "May we be able to educate them well is my daily and hourly prayer," she confessed to Royall in 1806. A year later she exclaimed, "God of his infinite Mercy grant that they may never cease to be Men of Delicacy and Virtue! What pangs would it cost us to see them profligate and abandoned."[25]

Then in 1813 family disaster struck. Royall lost his judgeship, creditors called in his debts, and the Tyler's eldest son died of typhus. The triple blow threw Royall into depression while Mary sought to keep the family together. Eventually, after selling the farm to pay their debts, they moved to rented quarters in Brattleboro Village. Royall resumed his law practice, but his income barely covered their cash demands in the commercializing economy of the Connecticut River Valley. As his spirits and eventually his health deteriorated, Mary foresaw that she would have to rely on her sons for economic support as well as emotional fulfillment.[26]

Continuing to persuade with affection, Mary reinforced the psychological ties with her sons while she reminded them of their family obligations after they left home. With an upper-class heritage and expectations that their sons would have business or professional careers, the Tylers took advantage of family connections in Boston and New York to secure apprenticeships for them when they reached fourteen. In 1810 their second son, John Steele, became an apprentice to Mary's brother George Palmer, a merchant in Boston. At the Tylers' request, John began sending boxes of goods home regularly with treats for family members and cloth for new clothes. Meanwhile, Mary worried about his behavior in a city where the "artful and designing" might play upon his innocent nature. To ensure his virtuous behavior, she demanded that he "implicitly obey" his uncle's commands and "never to go to any places of amusement either public or private without asking" his leave. Playing on John's love for her, she threatened, "be assured my son that the tender love I bear you is the reward of your goodness and whenever you forfeit your right to it, altho it may break in the seperation you will tear yourself from my heart—and then farewell happiness this side of the grave—!"[27] Tied by these emotional bonds and a deep commitment to his parents' welfare, John continued to support the family through his business activities in Boston. In 1820 he even bought them a new home in Brattleboro, before marrying and setting up his own household.[28]

Beyond these affectionate ties, Mary fostered her children's spiritual development as a source of control. Like many parents, she had taught her children to read the Scriptures, but not until her husband's failure did Mary connect religion to motherhood. Remaining somewhat aloof from the Brattleboro community in company with a small group of lawyers and intellectuals, the Tylers had not joined the Congregational church, but they had attended meetings and befriended William Wells, its liberal minister. After a Calvinist minister replaced Wells in 1818, Mary eventually joined the new Episcopal Church in East Guilford, three miles away. Episcopalian doctrine matched her belief in a "Merciful God" and self-improvement, the liturgy and rituals appealed to her, and the East Guilford church gave her an opportunity to associate with former friends. Moreover, religious activity in Brattleboro had begun to increase. Mary joined the Female Friendly Society devoted to promoting "Christian knowledge," and other parents initiated Sunday schools for youths.[29] Meanwhile, Mary's burdens mounted as Royall developed a cancer in his left eye and their scant income from his law work decreased. Replacing her former reliance on her husband as a provider with faith in God and her own ability to instill pious habits in her children, Mary insisted that her family "persevere to the best of our abilities and opportunities trusting in Him to accept & bless us."[30]

Through her relationship with her third son, Edward, Mary developed her role as a moral mother. After a brief apprenticeship in business, Edward, influenced by the climate of revival in New England, decided to train for the ministry. With diligence, he secured loans to attend Andover Theological Seminary in 1819 and then

Yale, seat of Congregational revivalism. As Mary wrote to Edward encouraging his
"religious feelings, sentiments and progress," she reinforced her own spiritual
growth. Linking her love to his faith, she proclaimed: "I love you better, far better,
for the love you bear our blessed Lord & Savior. My heart clings to you with more
than maternal affection when I reflect upon your ardent Piety and examplary [*sic*]
conduct."[31] Believing that Edward's faith would guide him into virtuous and diligent behavior, Mary trusted in religion to secure her child's happiness and her own
peace of mind in an uncertain world. Religion provided a moral structure for controlling him that her rational child rearing had lacked. As she participated in Edward's religious awakening and listened to her local ministers preach the benefits
of ardent faith, Mary's own piety became increasingly emotional. "I want to have
my affections awakened," she wrote Edward, "and my conscience aroused to
watchfulness." Her newly evangelical faith was deeply interwoven with her role as
a mother and with her sense of a woman's natural emotionalism.[32]

By placing her child-rearing philosophy in a religious framework, Mary redefined her place in society as a moral agent. Her duty to raise her children as virtuous citizens for the republic had evolved by 1820 into a call to direct their spiritual
development as the chief means of achieving wisdom, self-control, and civic, as
well as religious, virtue. She now used religious rather than sentimental language
to describe family obligations. "Pray for us all continually my child," she urged Edward, "that we may be duely sensible of all his blessings and strive continually to
do our duty both to God and Man."[33] While the behavior she expected remained
the same, her moral suasion increased.

Mary's path from republican virtue to piety as a means of self-control mirrored
a similar change in much of northeastern society between 1790 and 1840, when
both men and women turned to evangelical religion and social reform to ensure a
virtuous republic. At the same time, moral influence within families was shifting
from fathers, as spiritual leaders, to mothers. Mary's experience typified this shift
in family dynamics. Her particular heritage and family circumstances, however, exaggerated a change that became widespread during the revivals of the 1820s and
1830s, as women and ministers led husbands and children to piety. The values Mary
preached—hard work and reliance on a benevolent God—resembled the doctrine
that Freewill ministers spread throughout the Northeast. Aligning herself with
them, Mary simply reinforced her child-rearing philosophy. At the same time she
reshaped her concept of womanhood; henceforth, female moral influence would
ensure her children's success and the family's future prosperity.[34]

That future depended on Mary's ability to elicit each child's contribution to
the household economy while compromising her individual expectations for her
children as little as possible. Still hoping to raise both "the hero and the sage," Mary

focused the Tyler resources on her sons' educations. Yet, allowing her sons to pursue their training, either as apprentices in business or at schools away from home, did not prevent her from insisting on their continued support of the Brattleboro household. John not only sent boxes of goods from Boston but also took in two of his younger brothers as apprentices when they reached fourteen; he helped the others with their educational expenses.[35] Mary solicited support from Edward by praising his "energetic virtue and true desire to do good" as she informed him of the dire circumstances at home. "I tell you how we are situated," she explained in 1825, "that you may not be surprised if you should be called upon for more than you expected." Ten months later Mary recorded in her journal: "Wrote Edward mentioning the cost for cutting wood." Though she hardly expected Edward to abandon his studies and come home, she needed any cash he could spare from his small salary as a tutor. After her youngest sons left home, she required physical labor as well. In 1834, for example, she wrote her son Thomas Pickman, entreating, "while you work in the garden I will work for you." Always insisting on their mutual obligations, Mary promised to make him new shirts.[36]

Even more than her sons, family goals circumscribed her daughters' behavior, forcing Mary to reconcile her expectations for them with her practical needs and with her concept of a woman's role. Believing that her daughters would remain in sheltered domestic worlds, she had less concern about their futures. But her hopes that they would be educated conflicted with her need for their companionship and their help in housekeeping and child care. Moreover, her sons' training was far more important to the family's welfare in a world that provided limited economic opportunities for women. Consequently, while the boys pursued their careers, the Tyler women supported them at home, an arrangement common to other middle-class households. The older Tyler daughter, Mary Whitwell, spent much of her adolescence cooking, cleaning, washing, ironing, and sewing. Mary tried to inspire her to teach her younger brothers, but lamented, "the poor girl has to work hard all day about house, and her evenings are all the time she has to rest and enjoy herself and sew for herself and the children. . . . I cannot have a heart to drive her to it."[37] Amelia, nine years younger, did her share of family sewing, but she was able to study with local tutors and later taught the younger boys at home. During the worst years of Royall's illness, when Mary sought income desperately, she sent Amelia to Salem, Massachusetts, to live with her sister and to teach young children. Earning $24 a term in 1825, Amelia sent a few dollars home when she could. Meanwhile, Mary suggested that her daughter try to make some shirts for her father. He would appreciate the gift, she implored, and had "not one decent for the last sad office."[38]

As poverty threatened her hopes for her children and the family's social status,

Mary adjusted to her situation by managing their labor and binding them to the common good of the family with intense emotional bonds. Her demands for obedience and support were little different from traditional family practices, but her affectionate child-rearing techniques forced her children's struggles inward to their own consciences. With individual attention, Mary had encouraged self-consciousness in her children, yet the controls she placed on them conflicted with the opportunities for self-development they sought away from home. Family obligations claimed her sons' financial contributions and good behavior; eventually they tied her daughters to the Tyler home. The Tyler children responded differently to Mary's methods, depending on their birth order, temperament, and sex.

Amelia Tyler, for example, encountered difficulties in fulfilling her duties as a daughter, pursuing her intellectual development, and assuming the role of wife and mother that Mary extolled. After Royall died in 1826, Mary helped Amelia set up a school in the Tyler home to teach the younger boys and to bring in income from neighboring children. In the mid-1830s Amelia temporarily abandoned her school to become a tutor in Baltimore and later in Boston. Considered "beautiful & highly accomplished," Amelia attracted numerous suitors, none of whom were ever successful. At the age of twenty-nine, her conflicts over marriage, her obligations to her mother, and her intellectual needs erupted over a suitor who failed to meet Mary's approval.[39] Amelia took to her bed with a "Rhumatic complaint" that lasted many months. Her "marriage trauma," or "neurasthenia" as the condition was later named, kept her from arduous domestic tasks while maintaining her position as a dependent daughter. Eventually, she returned to her school as the likelihood of marriage or an independent existence diminished. Though Mary exercised psychological control over all her children, she bound her daughters even more closely than her sons because she had shaped female identity around domestic duty. Ironically, her daughters would never fulfill Mary's ideal of motherhood, for neither ever married.[40]

The Tyler sons, on the other hand, eventually became independent, but they experienced considerable emotional upheaval along the way. Thomas Pickman, born in 1815, became the focus of Mary's concern after her youngest son died in 1832. Pickman, as he was known, needed to be educated and to find a livelihood. True to Tyler tradition, the older boys offered both advice and financial assistance, but Pickman was caught among Mary's demands that he be diligent and virtuous, the high standards his brothers had set, his hope of emulating his father's literary talent, and his own desires for sociability. Striving to follow his brothers' examples and to be diligent in his studies, Pickman prayed to "overcome the love of the world." But the pressures were too great. Seeking an outlet in social life, Pickman spent hours in male comradeship in Brattleboro Village and took young women on sleigh rides and hikes, all of which plunged him into despair for neglecting his studies. "I would become a Christian worthy of the name," he wrote in his journal, "but it seems almost impossible for me to acquire the necessary command of myself."[41]

During most of his young manhood, as he went in and out of the Tyler house in periods of apprenticeship and college training, Pickman struggled between self-assertion and submission to Mary's demands and family expectations. Other young men experienced similar conflicts in the 1830s as they left New England communities for new work or college opportunities among their peers. Concern over Pickman's behavior away from home led Mary to exert her moral influence more powerfully than ever. "You seem to have a true sense of my anxiety to see my children virtuous and respected," she encouraged in 1831. "I have the brightest hopes that you will make a useful & brilliant Man if Heaven spares your life." Pickman became convinced that his only hope rested "in living near to God"; if left to himself, he lamented, he would surely "make Shipwreck of every hope of usefulness or distinction." Delighting in his decision to pursue the ministry, Mary disclaimed her ability to direct him, for, she declared, "it is God and not Man you are now resolved to Serve."[42] When Pickman also chose a wife who met his mother's approval, Mary felt confident that his marriage, "based on true piety," would maintain a woman's moral influence throughout his life. As a minister with a pious wife, Pickman could fulfill family expectations for honor and respectability and serve his community as well.[43]

In this way Mary's influence remained with her children throughout their lives; they tempered their self-interest to meet her expectations as virtuous citizens. As adults, the Tylers translated their sense of family obligation into various forms of public service, either as civil or military officials, ministers, or teachers. Edward, who evidenced the greatest commitment to the public good, joined the social reformers advocating temperance and abolition.[44] For the Tylers, economic necessity had enhanced the principles of self-sacrifice stemming from Mary's republican ideology and her experience of family cooperation. Relying on traditional survival strategies, she had succeeded in teaching her children to renew their ancestors' commitment to communal goals. The self-control they learned guided their personal relationships to benefit both family and community. As revivalism and the literature of domesticity spread Christian nurture throughout the Northeast, other young men and women learned about moral virtue and social reform. At the same time, schools, churches, and voluntary associations reinforced their patriotism, ensuring that concern for the public good would restrain American individualism.[45]

The role of mothers like Mary Tyler in preserving these communal values provided one link in the creation of an orderly society. While her husband worked in public life upholding the rule of law, Mary sought personal security and community control by shaping individual character.[46] Once freed from her child-rearing responsibilities, she assumed a social role in Brattleboro. As vice president of the Maternal Association in the mid-1830s and president of the Martha Washington Society in the 1840s, Mary joined other benevolent women in teaching Christian nurture and temperance reform in the broader community.[47] By taking personal responsibility for the future of both her family and society, Mary felt part of the new republic. In 1863, when she finished a memoir for her family, she linked her identity as a mother to that of America in a telling conclusion: "Now I think I have written enough. I began with an account of my birth, and the great Revolution, the birth of the American Nation. And now I have lived to see her struggling for life with her own rebellious children."[48]

Just as she portrayed the Civil War as a struggle between parent and child, Mary personalized her role in American society. Republicanism held meaning for Mary because it promoted a sense of responsibility she could activate in facing the demands of her daily life. Whereas a few highly intellectual women became consciously politicized through the new role, women like Mary Tyler used the ideology of republicanism to enhance their self-confidence at home.[49] Through her combination of love and authority, she gained respect in the Tyler family and moral control over her children, control that colonial women had rarely sought. For many mothers, this was the crucial significance of republican ideology and the source of their sense of improved status, perhaps not fully realized until they transformed civic virtue into religious virtue. For it was through Christian nurture, remarkably like her republican beliefs, that Mary and numerous other middle-class women eventually reaped an influence they were denied in public life. Once established, this maternal responsibility became the basis of their future public activity.

To say that women gained moral authority through republican motherhood and its pious version is not to suggest that the ideal lacked an underside, even within family life. Not only did acceptance of the concept solidify women's exclusion from politics, but it also helped devalue their other household work. By focusing on the importance of the female nurturing role, the ideal denied women's contribution to the household economy and helped restrict their work outside the home.[50] Mary Tyler's situation reflects these contradictions. Though she achieved as much dignity as any woman of her day, economic dependence remained a lifelong frustration. Because Mary had little means of support other than her children and because her concept of womanhood was based on her relationship to them, she satisfied her economic needs and her desire for self-assertion largely through them. Ironically, by carving out an expanded role for herself and wielding her influence, she left her children, particularly her daughters, a mixed legacy, for the conflicting goals of republican society remained embedded within their consciences.

NOTES

For valuable suggestions and critical comment, the author wishes to thank Constance M. McGovern and the anonymous reviewers of the *Journal of the Early Republic*.

1. [Mary Palmer Tyler], *The Maternal Physician: A Treatise on the Nurture and Management of Infants, from the Birth Until Two Years Old. Being the Result of Sixteen Years' Experience in the Nursery. Illustrated By Extracts From the Most Approved Medical Authors. By An American Matron* (1811; reprint, New York, 1972), pp. 273, 278.

2. Linda Kerber, *Women of the Republic: Intellect and Ideology in Revolutionary America* (Chapel Hill, N.C., 1980), pp. 199–200, 227–31, 283–88; Kerber, "The Republican Mother: Women and the Enlightenment—An American Perspective," *American Quarterly* 28 (Summer 1976): 187–205; Kerber, "The Republican Ideology of the Revolutionary Generation," ibid., 37 (Fall 1985): 474–95; Mary Beth Norton, *Liberty's Daughters: The Revolutionary Experience of American Women, 1750–1800* (Boston, 1980), pp. 242–49; Norton, "The Evolution of White Women's Experience in Early America," *American Historical Review* 89 (June 1984): 616–19; Ruth Bloch, "The Gendered Meanings of Virtue in Revolutionary America," *Signs* 13 (Autumn 1987): 37–58. For the shift in republican ideology deemphasizing civic virtue, see Gordon Wood, *The Creation of the American Republic, 1776–1787* (Chapel Hill, N.C., 1969), pp. 50–73, 609–12. For wives' role as cultivators of virtue in their husbands, see Jan Lewis, "The Republican Wife: Virtue and Seduction in the Early Republic," *William and Mary Quarterly* 44 (Oct. 1987): 696–721. Following Kerber and others, I have used "republican ideology" as a cultural system. Though historians of the postrevolutionary period disagree over the relative importance of classical and liberal ideas and their material connections, they generally accept the language of republicanism as a common cultural understanding that men and women would take broad responsibility for the future of their society. See, for example, Lester Cohen, "Mercy Otis Warren: The Politics of Language and the Aesthetics of Self," *American Quarterly* 35 (Winter 1983): 482–84; and Gordon Wood, "The Significance of the Early Republic," *Journal of the Early Republic* 8 (Spring 1988): 1–20. For the recent debate over the varied meanings of republicanism, see Robert E. Shalhope, "Republicanism and Early American Historiography," *William and Mary Quarterly* 39 (Apr. 1982): 334–56; Joyce Appleby, "Republicanism and Ideology," *American Quarterly* 37 (Fall 1985): 461–73; Lance Banning, "Jeffersonian Ideology Revisited: Liberalism and Classical Ideas in the New Republic," *William and Mary Quarterly* 43 (Jan. 1986): 3–19; and Joyce Appleby, "Republicanism in Old and New Contexts," ibid., pp. 20–34.

3. For the companionate family, see Lawrence Stone, *The Family, Sex and Marriage in England, 1500–1800* (New York, 1977); Edward Shorter, *The Making of the Modern Family* (New York, 1975); Carl Degler, *At Odds: Women and the Family in America from the Revolution to the Present* (New York, 1980); Daniel Scott Smith, "Parental Power and Marriage Patterns: An Analysis of Historical Trends in Hingham, Massachusetts," *Journal of Marriage and the Family*

35 (Aug. 1973): 419–28; Daniel Blake Smith, *Inside the Great House: Planter Family Life in Eighteenth-Century Chesapeake Society* (Ithaca, N.Y., 1980); and Mary P. Ryan, *Cradle of the Middle Class: The Family in Oneida County, New York, 1790–1865* (Cambridge, 1981). For women's experience and the debate over their status, see especially Nancy F. Cott, *The Bonds of Womanhood: "Woman's Sphere" in New England, 1780–1835* (New Haven, 1977); Joan Jensen, *Loosening the Bonds: Mid-Atlantic Farm Women, 1750–1850* (New Haven, 1986); and Suzanne Lebsock, *The Free Women of Petersburg: Status and Culture in a Southern Town, 1784–1860* (New York, 1984).

4. For the connection between republican child-rearing advice, as opposed to actual behavior, and Protestant beliefs, see Ruth Bloch, "American Feminine Ideals in Transition: The Rise of the Moral Mother, 1785–1815," *Feminist Studies* 4 (June 1978): 101–26; and Jacqueline S. Reiner, "Rearing the Republican Child: Attitudes and Practices in Post-Revolutionary Philadelphia," *William and Mary Quarterly* 39 (Jan. 1982): 150–63.

5. This thesis in an expanded form can be found in Marilyn S. Blackwell, "Love and Duty: Mary Palmer Tyler and Republican Childrearing" (master's thesis, University of Vermont, 1990).

6. Mary Palmer Tyler, *Grandmother Tyler's Book: The Recollections of Mary Palmer Tyler (Mrs. Royall Tyler), 1775–1866*, ed. Helen Tyler Brown and Frederick Tupper (New York, 1925), pp. 20–46, 236; William S. Pattee, *A History of Old Braintree and Quincy With a Sketch of Randolph and Holbook* (Quincy, Mass., 1878), pp. 402, 487–90; [Edward R. Tyler], "Biographical Sketch of General Joseph Palmer," *The New Englander* 9 (Jan. 1845): 5–23; *Journals of Each Provincial Congress of Massachusetts in 1774 and 1775, and of the Committee of Safety* (Boston, 1838), pp. 7, 77, 273, 505, 530; Clifford K. Shipton, ed., *Sibley's Harvard Graduates: Biographical Sketches of Graduates of Harvard College in Cambridge, Massachusetts*, 17 vols. (Boston, 1881–1975), vol. 17, pp. 588–89. For an interpretation of the activities of the revolutionary generation of women as political, see Norton, *Liberty's Daughters*, pp. 155–77.

7. Tyler, *Grandmother Tyler's Book*, pp. 15–17, 51–176.

8. Ibid., pp. 73–82, 151–53, 177–85, 204–7, 219, 226–27 (quotation on 219). The best work on Royall Tyler is G. Thomas Tanselle, *Royall Tyler* (Cambridge, Mass., 1967). For marriage ideals as seen in *The Contrast*, see Lewis, "The Republican Wife," pp. 696–98. On the rise of affectionate marriage in the late eighteenth century, see Degler, *At Odds*, pp. 12–18, 32–42; Stone, *Family, Sex and Marriage*, chap. 8; and Smith, "Parental Power and Marriage Patterns."

9. Tyler, *Grandmother Tyler's Book*, pp. 48–85, 209–12; Peter Gay, ed., *John Locke on Education* (New York, 1964), pp. 21–26. For belief in Lockean child rearing among the educated elite in the late eighteenth century, see Peter Gregg Slater, *Children in the New England Mind: In Death and in Life* (Hamden, Conn., 1977), pp. 95–127, 142–46: Catherine M. Scholten, *Childbearing in American Society, 1650–1850* (New York, 1985), pp. 67–68; Jay Fliegelman, *Prodigals and Pilgrims: The American Revolution against Patriarchal Authority, 1750–1800* (New York, 1982), pp. 12–16; and Smith, *Inside the Great House*, chap. 1.

10. Tyler, *Grandmother Tyler's Book*, pp. 272–98, appendix A. Births of the Tyler children were as follows: Royall, Jr., December 1, 1794; John Steele, September 29, 1796; Mary Whitwell, June 23, 1798; Edward Royall, August 3, 1800; William Clark, August 28, 1802; Joseph Dennie, September 4, 1804; Amelia Sophia, January 29, 1807; George Palmer, December 10, 1809; Charles Royall, April 19, 1812; Thomas Pickman, November 20, 1815; Abiel Winship, November 9, 1818.

11. Tyler, *Grandmother Tyler's Book,* pp. 233–34; [Tyler], *Maternal Physician,* pp. 151–65.

12. For Mary's concern about her children's health, see Mary Palmer Tyler to Elizabeth Hunt Palmer, Jan. 30, 1800, and Mary Palmer Tyler to Royall Tyler, Jan. 1, 16, 1807, Royall Tyler Collection, Vermont Historical Society, Montpelier, gift of Helen Tyler Brown.

13. William Buchan, *Domestic Medicine or A Treatise on The Prevention and Cure of Diseases By Regimen and Simple Medicines. With an Appendix, Containing a Dispensatory for the Use of Private Practitioner* (Fairhaven, Vt., 1798), pp. 2–25. Mary mentions other British health care writers in *Maternal Physician,* pp. 25, 27, 33, 48, 208. In addition to Buchan, she probably read William Cadogan, *An Essay Upon Nursing, and the Management of Children, from their Birth to Three Years of Age* (London, 1750); Michael Underwood, *A Treatise on the Disorders of Childhood and Management of Infants from the Birth; Adapted to Domestic Use* (1797); Hugh Smith, *Letters to Married Women, on Nursing and the Management of Children* (Philadelphia, 1792); and *Edinburgh Dispensatory* (1699). For the influence of Enlightenment thought on British medical authors, see Reinier, "Rearing the Republican Child," pp. 151–53.

14. [Tyler], *Maternal Physician,* pp. 258–59.

15. Ibid., pp. 5–7; Ada Lou Carson, ed., "Thomas Pickman Tyler's 'Memoirs of Royall Tyler: An Annotated Edition'" (Ph.D. diss., University of Minnesota, 1985), pp. 277–78, 285; Tanselle, *Royall Tyler,* pp. 31–33, 236. Mary's authorship of *The Maternal Physician* has been generally known in Vermont and by scholars of Royall Tyler, but historians, who have used her manual extensively, have failed to identify its author. See, for example, Bloch, "American Feminine Ideals"; Scholten, *Childbearing in American Society;* and Reinier, "Rearing the Republican Child." Reiner errs in identifying the author as a Philadelphia woman. Charles E. Rosenberg reprinted the manual in 1972 without Mary Tyler's authorship. The only scholarly work specifically about Mary Tyler and her manual is Christina Gibbons, "Mary Tyler and *The Maternal Physician," Journal of Regional Cultures* 3 (Fall/-Winter 1983): 33–45. Gibbons suggests that Mary may have written the manual for financial gain.

16. An earlier existing health manual by an American woman is Mary Watkins, *Maternal Solicitude, Or, Lady's Manual* (New York, 1809). Though similar in philosophy to Mary's manual, Watkins's brief tract offers advice only about breast-feeding. For studies using the contemporary advice literature, see Bloch, "American Feminine Ideals"; Slater, *Children in the New England Mind;* Scholten, *Childbearing in American Society;* Sylvia D. Hoffert, *Private Matters: Attitudes toward Childbearing and Infant Nurture in Early Nineteenth-Century America* (Urbana, Ill., 1989); Anne L. Kuhn, *The Mother's Role in Childhood Education: New England Concepts, 1830–1860* (New Haven, Conn., 1947); and Bernard W. Wishy, *The Child and the Republic: The Dawn of Modern American Child Nurture* (Philadelphia, 1968).

17. [Tyler], *Maternal Physician,* p. 7; Buchan, *Domestic Medicine,* pp. 2, 23. British writers focused on breast-feeding to counter the widespread use of wet nurses, whom they feared harbored disease. A mother's breast-feeding was deemed more natural and therefore healthier. In Puritan New England, wet-nursing was rare, but it had gained popularity among wealthy urban women. See Bloch, "American Feminine Ideals," pp. 104, 110–11; Scholten, *Childbearing in American Society,* pp. 62, 71–73; and Hoffert, *Private Matters,* pp. 146–49.

18. [Tyler], *Maternal Physician,* pp. 62–64, 7. On the use of sentiment to describe maternal emotions, see Bloch, "American Feminine Ideals," pp. 116–17.

19. [Tyler], *Maternal Physician,* pp. 102–3.

20. Ibid., pp. 151, 159–63.

21. Fliegelman, *Prodigals and Pilgrims,* pp. 33–35. Fliegelman connects Lockean child rearing and parent-child relations to revolutionary ideology but does not differentiate a woman's role.

22. For colonial child-rearing practices, see John Demos, *A Little Commonwealth: Family Life in Plymouth Colony* (1970; 2d ed., London, 1971), pp. 131–44; Edmund Morgan, *The Puritan Family: Religion and Domestic Relations in Seventeenth-Century New England* (1956; rev. ed., New York 1966), pp. 65–108; and Philip Greven, *The Protestant Temperance: Patterns of Child-Rearing, Religious Experience, and the Self in Early America* (New York, 1977). For child-care ideology, see Scholten, *Childbearing in American Society,* pp. 50–66; Slater, *Children in the New England Mind;* and Melvin Yazawa, *From Colonies to Commonwealth: Family Ideology and the Beginnings of the American Republic* (Baltimore, 1985), pp. 10–58. For the child-centered, affectionate methods of the late eighteenth century, see Smith, *Inside the Great House,* chap. 1; and Degler, *At Odds,* pp. 66–94. For persistence of older methods and an example of the anxiety that could be aroused by the new methods in child rearing, see William G. McLoughlin, "Evangelical Child-Rearing in the Age of Jackson: Francis Wayland's View on When and How to Subdue the Willfulness of Children," *Journal of Social History* 9 (Fall 1975): 20–43.

23. Tyler, *Grandmother Tyler's Book,* p. 294.

24. [Tyler], *Maternal Physician,* p. 165; Gibbons, "Mary Tyler and *The Maternal Physician,*" p. 39. For the importance of differentiating between advice literature on child rearing and actual practices, see Jay E. Mechling, "Advice to Historians on Advice to Mothers," *Journal of Social History* 9 (Fall 1975): 44–63.

25. Mary Palmer Tyler to Royall Tyler, Jan. 28, 1806, Jan. 1, 1807, Tyler Collection. Royall received a yearly income of $900 as a supreme court judge and $1,000 after becoming chief justice in 1807. For his spending habits, see Royall Tyler to Mary Palmer Tyler, Feb. 2, 8, 1802, in Carson, ed., "'Memoirs of Royall Tyler,'" pp. 161–66; Royall Tyler to Mary Palmer Tyler, July 12, 1802, Tyler Collection.

26. Tyler, *Grandmother Tyler's Book,* pp. 320–26; Royall Tyler Daybook, June 1817–Dec. 1821, Tyler Collection. Mary wrote in Royall's book sporadically. He ceased writing in May 1820; she began regular notations in March 1821. For changes in the economy of the Connecticut River Valley, see Randolph A. Roth, *The Democratic Dilemma: Religion, Reform, and the Social Order in the Connecticut River Valley of Vermont, 1791–1850* (New York, 1987), pp. 16–22.

27. Mary Palmer Tyler to John S. Tyler, May 22, 1814, Elliot Papers, Mellen Chamberlain Autograph Collection, Boston Public Library. For John's contributions to the family economy, see Royall Tyler Daybook, June 1817–Dec. 1821, and Royall Tyler to John S. Tyler, May 15, 1812, Mar. 23, 1814, Tyler Collection.

28. Tyler, *Grandmother Tyler's Book,* pp. 325–26. John's finances were also precarious. When his business failed in 1822, he temporarily lost the Tyler home in Brattleboro and did not regained title until 1824. See Brattleboro Deeds, Vol. H, pp. 369–70, 534; Vol. I, p. 169, Vermont Department of Public Records, Montpelier.

29. On the religious education of the Tyler children, see Tyler, *Grandmother Tyler's Book,* p. 267; and Mary Palmer Tyler to Edward R. Tyler, July 4, 1819, Tyler Collection. For the Tylers' social life and Mary's growing interest in religion, see Royall Tyler Daybook, June 1817–Dec. 1821, and Mary Palmer Tyler to Sophia Palmer Pickman, Jan. 12, 1823, Tyler Collection. For re-

ligion in Brattleboro, see Mary R. Cabot, *Annals of Brattleboro, 1681–1895,* 2 vols. (Brattleboro, Vt., 1921–22), vol. 1, pp. 337–58; and Records of the Female Friendly Society, Centre Church, Brattleboro. Mary's early religious preferences are unclear. She had joined the Congregational meeting in Framingham, Massachusetts, before her marriage, and in her memoir claimed to have had a conversion experience just after the birth of her first child. See William Barry, *A History of Framingham, Massachusetts, Including The Plantation, From 1640 to the Present Time, With an Appendix . . .* (Boston 1847), p. 348; and Tyler, *Grandmother Tyler's Book,* pp. 212–15. Yet in her letter of 1823 to her sister Sophia Palmer Pickman, Mary explained an early preference for the Episcopal church and complained about the difficulty of attending Episcopal services until her youngest child was beyond infancy. Despite Mary's membership in Guilford's Episcopal church, she continued to attend the Congregational meetinghouse in Brattleboro.

30. Mary Palmer Tyler to Edward R. Tyler, Sept. 1, 1816, Tyler Collection. For Royall's declining health, see Royall Tyler Daybook, July 1817 –Dec. 1821, ibid.; Mary Palmer Tyler Journal, Dec. 1821–Aug. 1826, ibid.

31. Mary Palmer Tyler to Edward R. Tyler, Jan. 29, Dec. 19, 1819, ibid. For the "moral mother," see Bloch, "American Feminine Ideals in Transition."

32. Mary Palmer Tyler to Edward A. Tyler, Oct. 1, 1826, Tyler Collection; Royall Tyler Daybook, May 1821–Dec. 1821, ibid.; Mary Palmer Tyler Journal, Dec. 1821–Aug. 1826, ibid. For the emotional quality of female religious response during the period, see Barbara Welter, "The Feminization of American Religion: 1800–1860," in *Clio's Consciousness Raised: New Perspectives on the History of Women,* ed. Mary S. Hartman and Lois Banner (New York, 1974), pp. 138–42.

33. Mary Palmer Tyler to Edward R. Tyler, Dec. 19, 1819, Tyler Collection. For women's religious language as a symbolic medium, see Carroll Smith-Rosenberg, *Disorderly Conduct: Visions of Gender in Victorian America* (New York, 1985), pp. 45, 139–40.

34. Research on evangelicalism is abundant. For an overview and interpretation of the movement's importance as a value system in antebellum America, see Daniel Walker Howe, "The Evangelical Movement and Political Culture in the North during the Second Party System," *Journal of American History* 77 (Mar. 1991): 1216–39. For the Vermont movement, see Roth, *Democratic Dilemma;* and David M. Ludlum, *Social Ferment in Vermont, 1791–1850* (New York, 1939). On the connection between revivalism and mother-child relations, see Ryan, *Cradle of the Middle Class,* pp. 75–104. For collaboration between women and ministers, see Ann Douglas, *The Feminization of American Culture* (New York, 1977); and Welter, "Feminization of American Religion," pp. 139–41.

35. [Tyler], *Maternal Physician,* pp. 276–77. For the Tyler sons' mutual support, see Marilyn S. Blackwell, "Growing Up Male in the 1830s: Thomas Pickman Tyler (1815–1892) and the Tyler Family of Brattleboro," *Vermont History* 58 (Winter 1990): 9–11.

36. Mary Palmer Tyler to Edward R. Tyler, May 15, 1825, Tyler Collection; Mary Palmer Tyler Journal, Mar. 29, 1826, ibid.; Mary Palmer Tyler to Thomas Pickman Tyler, Mar. 9, 1834, ibid. The persistence of similar family values is evident among farm families in the nineteenth century. See James Henretta, "Families and Farms: *Mentalité* in Pre-Industrial America," *William and Mary Quarterly* 35 (Jan. 1978): 3–32.

37. Mary Palmer Tyler to Amelia S. Tyler, [1823], Tyler Collection; Mary Palmer Tyler Journal, Dec. 1821–43, ibid. For family demands on daughters, see Lee Chambers-Schiller, *Liberty, a Better Husband: Single Women in America: The Generations of 1740–1840* (New Haven,

1984), pp. 107–23. For a similar dynamic among other families, see Ryan, *Cradle of the Middle Class,* pp. 191–203; and Margo Horn, "'Sisters Worthy of Respect': Family Dynamics and Women's Roles in the Blackwell Family," *Journal of Family History* 8 (Winter 1983): 367–82.

38. Mary Palmer Tyler Journal, Apr. 1823–June 1826, Tyler Collection; Mary Palmer Tyler to Amelia S. Tyler, Jan. 1, 1826, ibid. Mary's sister Elizabeth Peabody was the mother of Elizabeth Palmer Peabody, founder of the kindergarten movement in America.

39. For the Tyler school, see Mary Palmer Tyler to Mary Whitwell Tyler, Oct. 3, 1826, Tyler Collection; Cabot, *Annals of Brattleboro,* 1:382–83. For Amelia's activities, see Mary Palmer Tyler Journal, May 1834–Nov. 1836, Tyler Collection; Joseph Tyler to Thomas Pickman Tyler, Mar. 26, 1835, recopied in Thomas Pickman Tyler Commonplace Book, ibid. Amelia's marriage proposal of 1836 created considerable family anxiety. It is mentioned in Thomas Pickman Tyler Journal, Sept. 14, 1836, but he erased her name. Mary Tyler's daily journal entries from Aug. 26 to Nov. 9, 1836, are intermittently crossed out. Pages covering the period Nov. 13 to 22 were removed. Helen Tyler Brown suggested that Amelia renounced her suitor for her mother's sake. See Tyler, *Grandmother Tyler's Book,* p. 347.

40. Mary Palmer Tyler Journal, Oct. 1836–Oct. 1838, Tyler Collection. For role conflict and women's health in the nineteenth century, see Smith-Rosenberg, *Disorderly Conduct,* pp. 197–216; and Chambers-Schiller, *Liberty, A Better Husband,* pp. 157–75. On "marriage trauma," see Cott, *Bonds of Womanhood,* pp. 80–83. The word *neurasthenia* was used to describe conditions similar to Amelia's after 1870. See F. G. Gosling, *Before Freud: Neurasthenia and the American Medical Community, 1870–1910* (Urbana, Ill., 1987), pp. 55–62, 97–100.

41. Thomas Pickman Tyler Journal, Nov. 1834–Jan. 1835, Tyler Collection (quotation at Nov. 29, 1834). See also Thomas Pickman Tyler Commonplace Book, ibid. For an analysis of Pickman's development, see Blackwell, "Growing Up Male."

42. Mary Palmer Tyler to Thomas Pickman Tyler, June 11, 1831, Mar. 27, 1832, Tyler Collection; Thomas Pickman Tyler Journal, Nov. 20, 1834, ibid. For male role conflicts, see E. Anthony Rotundo, "Manhood in America: The Northern Middle Class, 1770–1920" (Ph.D. diss., Brandeis University, 1982), pp. 134–248; and Charles E. Rosenberg, "Sexuality, Class and Role in Nineteenth Century America," in *No Other Gods: On Science and American Social Thought* (Baltimore, 1976). For problems of adolescents during the period, see Joseph F. Kett, *Rites of Passage: Adolescence in America, 1790 to the Present* (New York, 1977), pp. 17–35; and John Demos, *Past, Present, and Personal: The Family and the Life Course in Historical Perspective* (New York, 1986), pp. 99–102. For youths in Vermont, see Roth, *Democratic Dilemma,* pp. 117–41, 196–207.

43. Mary Palmer Tyler to Thomas Pickman Tyler, Mar. 29, 1841, Tyler Collection. Pickman married Mary Ann Clark of Brattleboro, Dec. 9, 1841. After his difficult adolescence, he chose to take a ministry in Canton, New York, away from family pressure. See Blackwell, "Growing Up Male."

44. John and William, businessmen in Boston, became civil and military officers as well; the ministers, Edward, George, and Pickman, oversaw the social and psychological well-being of their congregations. Joseph, also a trained minister, taught the deaf; Charles, a lawyer, held various civil offices in Vermont; Amelia taught Brattleboro's youth; and Mary Whitwell conducted Sunday school. See Tyler, *Grandmother Tyler's Book,* pp. 339–53; and Cabot, *Annals of Brattleboro,* 1:273–79, 540.

45. For family strategies, see Ryan, *Cradle of the Middle Class,* pp. 145–225. On the spread

of Christian nurture, see Douglas, *Feminization of American Culture;* and Kuhn, *Mother's Role in Childhood Education.* On the role of schools in teaching public virtue, see Yazawa, *From Colonies to Commonwealth,* pp. 143–88; and Jean Baker, "From Belief into Culture: Republicanism in the Antebellum North," *American Quarterly* 37 (Fall 1985): 532–50.

46. For women and the preservation of communal values, see Bloch, "Gendered Meanings of Virtue," pp. 54–58; and Ryan, *Cradle of the Middle Class,* pp. 184–85. Scholars of Royall Tyler have focused largely on his literary works with only minor attention to either his legal or political career. See, for example, Tanselle, *Royall Tyler;* Ada Lou Carson and Herbert L. Carson, *Royall Tyler* (Boston, 1979); Marius B. Peladeau, ed., *The Prose of Royall Tyler* (Montpelier, 1972); and Peladeau, ed., *The Verse of Royall Tyler* (Charlottesville, Va., 1968). For a recent study exploring his novels and social change during the postrevolutionary period, see Cathy N. Davidson, *Revolution and the Word: The Rise of the Novel in America* (New York, 1986), pp. 192–210.

47. Proceedings of the Brattleboro Maternal Association, 1834–36, Centre Congregational Church, Brattleboro, Vt.; Mary Palmer Tyler Journal, 1834–38, Tyler Collection; Mary Palmer Tyler to Thomas Pickman Tyler, May 8, 1836, Mar. 15, May 9, 1842, ibid. For women's public benevolence through voluntary activities, see, for example, Ryan, *Cradle of the Middle Class,* pp. 105–44; Cott, *Bonds of Womanhood,* pp. 149–58; Nancy A. Hewitt, *Women's Activism and Social Change, Rochester, New York, 1822–1872* (Ithaca, N.Y., 1984), pp. 44–50; and Barbara L. Epstein, *The Politics of Domesticity: Women, Evangelism, and Temperance in Nineteenth-Century America* (Middleton, Conn., 1981).

48. Tyler, *Grandmother Tyler's Book,* p. 326.

49. For a similar conclusion, see Hoffert, *Private Matters,* pp. 196–97. For examples of intellectual women, see Kerber, *Women of the Republic,* pp. 227–31; and Cohen, "Mercy Otis Warren."

50. See especially Jeanne Boydston, *Home and Work: Housework, Wages, and the Ideology of Labor in the Early Republic* (New York, 1990), pp. 42–48.

3.

MOTHER'S LOVE
The Construction of an Emotion in Nineteenth-Century America

JAN LEWIS

When the Reverend John Todd told the readers of *The Mother's Magazine* in 1839 that "God planted this *deep,* this *unquenchable* love for her offspring, in the mother's heart," he was expressing the conventional wisdom of his day. In mid-nineteenth-century America, a woman who opened any ladies' magazine or advice book would read that a mother's love was eternal, that "no circumstance, no earthly change can destroy the mother's love," that "to love children, is the dictate of [her] nature."[1] Nature and God both made women to be mothers and implanted in their hearts a love that was pure and holy. This was the premise upon which the doctrine of women's separate sphere rested. Just as the philosophy and form of democratic government proceeded from Jefferson's self-evident truths, so the nineteenth century's description of woman's nature and role derived from seemingly incontrovertible assumptions about the nature of a mother's love.

Historians, of course, may question that which earlier generations took for granted, asking how it was that certain propositions came to be accepted as self-evident truths. We know that in 1776 belief in the equality of man was more of a novelty than Jefferson's self-confident statements would lead us to suppose. Likewise, the irrepressible nature of a mother's love was, in the 1830s, an idea whose time had only recently come. The writers who proclaimed these truths were, as much as Jefferson, the architects of an ideology. They described a world as they wanted it to be, and they could not imagine an America, as they wanted it to become, without a mother's love.

To compare the antebellum exponents of maternal love to Jefferson is, perhaps, not so strained a conceit as it might at first appear, for the idealization of mother's

Reprinted from Andrew E. Barnes and Peter N. Stearns, eds., *Social History and Issues of Human Consciousness* (New York: New York University Press, 1989), by permission of the publisher.

love was brewed in the same cauldron as Revolutionary political thought. Historians have recently recognized that the histories of politics and the family in this era are entwined. The Revolutionary brew was seasoned by a variety of ingredients—republicanism, liberalism, evangelical Protestantism, sensationalist psychology—and just as each of these strands of thought would contribute to political thought, so too would they affect the conceptualization of family roles. The late eighteenth century's revolt against patriarchy dethroned both fathers and kings; and it said that citizens in a society, like members of a family, should be bound together by affection, rather than duty.[2]

This transformation in political and familial thought would make room for a new ideal of motherhood, one that would be flavored by all the ingredients in the Revolutionary brew. Indeed, as Ruth H. Bloch has shown, the first positive characterizations of motherhood date to this period.[3] Before the Revolution, early Americans, particularly in the Puritan colonies, were rather fearful of feminine emotion. They considered women more passionate and, hence, more dangerous than men. And even mother's love, because it was both indulgent and unqualified, was mistrusted. As Laurel Thatcher Ulrich has observed of northern New England, "Mothers represented the affectionate mode in an essentially authoritarian system of child-rearing." In a "patriarchal order . . . mother love or any other form of human love could never be an unqualified good."[4] The Revolution undermined patriarchy, and it made of affection a political virtue, the glue of civil society. In so doing, it allowed women, who were supposedly naturally affectionate, a political role.

This new appreciation for affection was the contribution of sensationalist psychology, which had also facilitated a new interest in the education of young children. Eighteenth-century faculty psychologists argued that the characters of children could be shaped, that human nature was to some degree malleable. Sensationalist psychology, in both its Lockean and Scottish Common Sense forms, had been popularized in eighteenth-century America, softening Calvinist notions of innate depravity.[5] By the end of the eighteenth century, many Americans were accustomed to believing that children were born with a set of faculties, some of which (reason and affection, for example) were to be developed, and others of which (self-interest and the passions) needed to be controlled. To be sure, different schools placed different premiums upon certain of the faculties, with some trusting more to reason and others with more confidence in affection, just as they disagreed about how dangerous self-interest might be. By the nineteenth century, such distinctions almost disappeared, as the popular writers who adapted faculty psychology for the American audience used Lockean, Common Sense, and Calvinist assumptions almost indiscriminately.[6] Nineteenth-century didactic writers adapted eighteenth-century sensationalist psychology in another way: they said that moral education should be performed especially—indeed, almost exclusively—by mothers. Locke, the Common Sense philosophers, and Calvinist ministers had all assumed that fathers—or, at the very least, parents—played the crucial role in the education of the young. Why, in the nineteenth century, was this responsibility shifted to women? Much of the answer lies in the growing belief that the work of moral education had to begin even earlier, for the child's character was formed in the early years, while it was still in the mother's care.

Moreover, once evangelical Protestant denominations were prepared to accept the validity of childhood conversion, as they increasingly were by the mid-nineteenth century,[7] mothers acquired an important new role. Evangelical views about youthful conversion built upon secular ones about the malleability of character, giving mothers a new responsibility. The work of redemption had to begin early, when a child was still in its mother's care, and, to the extent that evangelicals believed that the world had to be reclaimed individual by individual, the home became the main arena for conversions. As the Reverend John Abbott put it, *"Mothers have as powerful an influence over the welfare of future generations, as all other earthly causes combined."*[8] The redemption of the world depended upon "the power of divine truth . . . Christianity, as taught from a mother's lips. In a vast majority of cases the first six or seven years decide the character of the man . . . the mothers of our race must be the chief instruments of its redemption." Mothers, thus, had it in their power to achieve not only the salvation of their children but also that of the entire world. Mothers occupied the key "place in the grand scheme which shall renovate the world." Mrs. Elizabeth Hall expressed the millennial hopes of evangelical maternal advisers when she told American mothers, "the destiny of a redeemed world is put into your hands; and it is for you to say, whether your children shall be . . . prepared for a glorious immortality."[9]

Women were called by God to be mothers; their work was nothing less than His own. But it was a work that was to be performed first and foremost in the United States, giving the mothers' mission both a sacred and a secular cast. One author who advocated the conversion of the young insisted, "The designs which God seems to have respecting this Republic, are to be accomplished by the moral renovation of the young."[10] Religious writers believed that American society in the early nineteenth century was approaching a crisis; they looked to mothers for the solution. "By what means," asked *The Mother's Magazine* in 1833, "can the population of this great country, increasing as it is, with fearful rapidity, be so enlightened and reformed, that our boasted liberty shall not disintegrate into gross licentiousness?" Sarah Josepha Hale provided the answer: "If the future citizens of our republic are to be worthy of their rich inheritance, they must be made so principally through the virtue and intelligence of their mothers."[11] Secular and sacred advocates of the importance of maternal influence shared certain assumptions about the crisis "in a country where the people govern." Many would have agreed that "*Self-government* both for adults and children seems almost the only available resource left us in the present state of society in this country."[12] Self-government, of course, was a term with a resonance in both religious and political discourse; in a democratic society, which had rejected authoritarian forms of control, it became all the more necessary for individuals to learn to govern themselves, to control their sinful and antisocial impulses both.

Indeed, in the minds of the authors of maternal advice literature, sin and selfishness were usually considered one and the same. Although we may distinguish between the sacred and secular elements of the motherhood paradigm, they were often fused in the popular mind. The didactic writers who idealized motherhood envisioned an American empire that was also the Kingdom of God on earth,[13] precisely because their ideal for society drew jointly from evangelical Protestantism, late-Enlightenment political thought (both republican and liberal), and sensationalist psychology. These separate strands became part of the fabric of American culture; all were woven, for example, into an essay published in *The Mother's Magazine* in 1833: "It is the province of the mother, to cultivate the affections, to form and guard the moral habits of the child, for the first ten years of its life, and to all intents and purposes the character of the *man* or *woman is* substantially laid as early as that period of life." So argued the author of "Family Government Essential to National Prosperity." "While, therefore, the father is engaged in the bustling affairs of active life, the mother, with almost irresistible sway, is forming the characters of the future defenders of our faith, the administrators of our laws, and the guardians of our civil liberties and lives."[14] Here we see all the elements of the new paradigm: a liberal appreciation of civil liberties is grafted onto the older, republican insistence upon the importance of the character of the citizenry and the Scottish Common Sense philosophers' concern for the cultivation of the affections. And we see, also, the separation of the private sphere of the home from the "bustling"—and presumably corrupt—"affairs of the active life" in the public arena. As many historians have noted, the responsibility for training children fell to mothers almost by default, as more fathers began to work outside the home.[15] By the time this structural change had taken place, however, women were already assumed to be peculiarly suited to the task at hand.

The intellectual basis for the separation of woman's private sphere of the home from the public sphere of the world had been laid well before the United States turned into the industrial and urban nation early nineteenth-century critics feared it would become. Women, and consequently mothers, were assumed to be more moral than men because they were isolated from the world. As Nancy F. Cott has noted, Christian doctrine had always contrasted the virtues of heaven with the vices of the world; in the early nineteenth century, as women and men were increasingly segregated into separate spheres—and as the masculine, public sphere of the world became ever more suspect—women and their arena profited from the comparison, and the home took on the attributes Christians had once reserved for heaven.[16] The authors of maternal advice literature accepted this assumption when they likened home to Paradise and mothers' work to that of Christ. "Our first mother found a paradise," Catharine Sedgwick wrote, and "her daughters have each the more enviable privilege and distinction of creating one at pleasure."[17] The home was designed to redeem the world.

Although a mother's work was performed at home, in private, it had enormous public importance; it was, fundamentally, of a political and religious nature, for it aimed at preparing children for entry into a particular society.[18] And it was this logic—the needs of nineteenth-century American society, as informed by both political and religious thought—that would dictate the characteristics of the children who should be created and the qualities of the mothers who would create them.

So if the work of salvation were to be performed in woman's sphere, it necessarily meant that women were especially suited to the task. Much as the nineteenth century fragmented the world into a private, heavenly sphere and an amoral public domain, so it would divide the set of faculties that once had been thought to belong to men and women both. In the process, the rational faculties were assigned to men, and the emotional ones—which the rise of sentimentalism had endowed with a higher value—to women. This new formulation is evident in the new view of marriage that had become popular by the beginning of the nineteenth century. In this paradigm, man's reason was thought necessary to check woman's emotion, while feminine affection was required to socialize masculine rationality.[19] Thus, under the influence of faculty psychology, feminine qualities were deemed necessary to the social order, for it was women who fit men for society. In the early decades of the nineteenth century, this paradigm of republican marriage—like republican political thought itself—would collapse, but one of its fundamental assumptions, that feminine qualities served a social function, would endure, as the focus of feminine socializing was shifted from adult men to children.

By 1830, the feminine social role had been redefined: women were to prepare their children, and especially their sons, for membership in society. If this society, with its separate private and public spheres, was recognizably that of the nineteenth century, it still retained eighteenth-century moral philosophy's belief that social order could be maintained only by the affection that men bore for one another, the sympathies that they shared. "What," asked the *American Ladies' Magazine,* "are

the good works of women which she was created to perform? She was born to perpetuate the reign of all good and gentle affections in the world, and to diffuse
through all society a spirit of love, of forebearance, of happiness." Evangelicals
agreed that "it is the province of the mother, to cultivate the affections,"[20] and, like
more-secular writers, they believed that such qualities were necessary to society.

Like their colonial ancestors, nineteenth-century American family advisers
still thought of the family as a little commonwealth; as one magazine writer put it
in 1830, "A family is society in miniature; home is its location." But now, "woman
is its presiding spirit."[21] Put another way, the family represented society as these
writers wanted it to be. In the "world . . . we behold every principle of justice and
honor, and even the dictates of common honesty disregarded, and the delicacy of
our moral sense is wounded; we see the general good, sacrificed to the advancement
of personal interest." Only in the family could we "expect pure, disinterested attachment." Only "there sympathy, honor, virtue, are assembled; . . . there disinterested love, is ready to sacrifice everything at the altar of affection."[22] It was this love,
expressed in its perfect form by mothers, that was to remake and redeem the world.
"Can a more charming picture be drawn," asked *The Mother's Magazine* rhetorically, "than a family cemented together and governed by the control[l]ing influence
of love? Love—flowing from the hidden spring in a mother's heart . . . flowing
deeper and wider as it goes, till neighborhood, friends, and country are refreshed
by its living waters!"[23] Mother's love was the very basis of the social order, its blood
and sinew both.

At a sociological level, the doctrine of maternal influence said that the feminine principle of love was necessary in order to temper the selfishness evident in an
increasingly individualistic age. At a psychological level, it insisted that men, to
some extent, ought to be feminized; it was the responsibility of mothers to implant
in their sons, in particular, an affectionate heart. To be sure, many maternal advisers, such as Catharine Beecher,[24] believed women responsible for the intellectual
education of their children, but more often it was emphasized that "the mother
holds, as it were, the hearts of her children in her hand," and it was the heart that
she was intended to train. She was supposed to teach her children how to love; that
is, to teach them what she knew best. She was to make her children like herself. As
one adviser explained it, "The control of youthful appetite and passion, is . . . best
committed to those whose nature and situation best prepare them to enforce by example what they teach by precept. . . . The plastic hand of maternal affection
moulds the susceptible being after the likeness of its own loveliness."[25] Properly
trained, a mother's sons would meet adulthood with a woman's heart. Thus it was,
explained one writer, that "the talents of the female are the transmitted inheritance
of her sons."[26]

And by what process were children to be made like their mother? It was generally believed that "children learn more by example than by precept." Thus a mother was to be what she wanted her children to become. A mother was supposed "not . . . to teach virtue but to inspire it." This she would accomplish simply by being herself, experiencing her natural and irrepressible love for her children. The secret of "The Mother's Power" was "the principle of attachment [that] is as much a part of a mother's nature, as the heart and blood parts of the human frame."[27] A mother's love would inspire her children's love in return. The mother "teaches our hearts the first lesson of love . . . around [her] our affections twine as closely and surely, as the young vine clasps itself about the branch that supports it: our love for [her] becomes so thoroughly a part and portion of ourselves, that it bids defiance to time and decay." The children of such a mother would come to "revere her as the earthly type of perfect love . . . they cannot but desire to conform themselves to such models."[28] From their mothers' example, children would learn how to love. They would carry this affection with them always, not merely as the memory of maternal tenderness, but as the standard for human behavior in an unredeemed world.

The conventions of mother's love held that it was eternal; it was "untiring," "imperishable," "unquenchable," and "irrepressible."[29] Such judgments carried a double meaning: the mother's love was eternal not only because it outlived the mother herself as it was preserved in her children's memories. It was eternal in another sense as well, for it was reincarnated in her children, who carried it with them always, as a talisman and an almost corporeal part of themselves. *The Mother's Magazine* advised that "the mother must dwell in the heart of the child, and be, as it were, the soul of its every action—enter into all its joys—feel its every sorrow." This characterization of maternal love reflected Christian doctrines of eternal life. But if standard evangelical exhortations advised sinners to accept Christ into their hearts so that they might be born again, the paradigm of mother's love conveyed the message from Christ's point of view: you will live again. And so mothers were told that their children "will go forth with the impress of a mother's hand, deep, imperishable. Yes! you will live in your children."[30]

Different writers expressed the same idea in different ways, but always the message was the same: the child was the mother reborn. Mary Virginia Terhune instructed mothers to "ask your heart . . . if there is not a strange ful[l]ness of joy in watching the reproduction of your traits, physical, mental and moral in your child?"[31] Another writer regarded the influence of the mother on her child the same way: "Her expressions, her feelings, her passions become almost imperceptibly a part of his nature."[32] By this process of moral and emotional replication, the identities of mother and child were merged. If the mother's love was irresistible, it meant that the mother had "in her own hands" the "*perfect formation* of [her children's] *entire character*." She could not resist making "impressions" that would "stamp" her children "not only *indelibly*, but *eternally*." The mother's child became, as Lydia Sigourney put it, her "twin-soul." Although most advisers alerted mothers to the "great diversity in the natural dispositions of children," they never seriously considered that the child should become anything other than the mother writ large, in Dr. Joseph Hanaford's phrase, "a mental and moral daguerreotype of herself."[33] From the mother's perspective, then, the child was self, rather than other. That is why Lydia Sigourney, in another remarkable turn of phrase, could instruct her mother to regard her baby as "a fragment of yourself."[34]

We have come, then, to the kernel of the emotionology of motherhood.[35] A mother focused her love upon a susceptible infant mind. "Working like nature . . . she . . . sends forth from [her] heart, in pure and temperate flow, the life-giving current . . . her warm affections and irrepressible sympathies." The influence of eighteenth-century faculty psychology is clear; and, according to its doctrines, the infant would necessarily bear the imprint of his mother's love. He would mimic her affection, learning to love just as he was loved. Yet the object of this love was the mother herself; the very process of loving would obliterate the distinctions between—the separateness of—mother and child. The popular writer Fanny Fern understood the dynamic perfectly when she described the essence of motherhood: "Another outlet for thy womanly heart; a mirror, in which thy smiles and tears shall be reflected back; a fair page on which thou, God-commissioned, mayst write what thou wilt; a heart that will throb back to thine, love for love."[36] Like Narcissus, looking into the mirror, the loving mother adored her own reflection.

Here, in the doctrine of motherhood, we can see the creation of a powerful mythology. It offers the mother a sort of omnipotence. It denies, or offers the means for denying, the strangeness and separateness of her children, by making them part of the mother herself. In defining children as beings who are designed to embody and return their mother's love, it authorizes a profound form of self-love. And in suggesting that the mother's love will be replicated in the child, and the child's child, for generations to come, it promises immortality. No wonder that "maternity" could become, for women, "part of our religion."[37]

Yet if the nineteenth-century doctrine of motherhood was, in part, a religion that established rather grandiose notions about the power of a mother's love, it must be remembered that this effect was incidental. The doctrine was not designed to increase feminine power or even a sense of power, for it grew out of an ideology whose very objective was to vanquish power with love, to replace selfishness with affection and virtue. Thus, the doctrine of maternal influence was bound to take away with the same hand that which it gave. Mothers could be powerful only if they renounced power, loved only if they renounced self, immortal only if they were willing to die.

Consider Catharine Sedgwick's description of an ideal mother, her friend Anne, "one of those strong characters that must do for itself the hardest work." And how did she train her children? "By the atmosphere of affection and kindness with which she surrounded herself [rather] than by any direct bearing of authority upon them." The mother had to be what she wanted her children to become. Then, in the confines of the family circle, the "exercise of absolute power" might be "softened by perfect love."[38] Somewhat like Christ, a mother was to be active only in "the exercise of those virtues denominated *passive*." Indeed, mothers were barely to "exercise" at all. When observing her growing children, would not a mother naturally "say, with a smile, a sigh—perchance a tear—'I felt, or thought, or longed the same at her years.'"[39] "A mother could not act; she might feel, or think, or long; she should "surround herself" with an "atmosphere"; she could smile, sigh, and shed a tear.

The mother was, as the maternal advisers liked to say, "the first book read, and the last one laid aside, in every child's library. Every look, word, tone, gesture . . . makes an impression."[40] Because everything about her could leave an indelible mark, she had to make certain that everything about her was designed to create the right impressions. It was not only what she did but how she looked, sounded, and seemed that was important. Although advisers might tell mothers how to feed, clothe, and instruct their offspring, much of their attention was devoted to less active endeavors. An article entitled "How to Speak to Children" described, not the words and ideas to be conveyed, but how to achieve the right tone of voice.[41] In this sense, the real work of child rearing was to be focused upon the woman herself, as she tried to make herself a fit model for imitation.

Even her appearance had to be altered to make her a good mother. T. H. Gallaudet reminded the mother of "the influence of her *countenance, voice, and general air and manners*." Adapting eighteenth-century psychological assumptions for his own age, addressing the nineteenth century's anxieties about the discrepancies between appearance and reality, he argued that the face was the "*index and agent of the soul*." Character and countenance mirrored one another. Like a phrenologist, Gallaudet believed that the exterior of the person reflected her moral qualities. And like a Common Sense philosopher, he believed that the moral qualities of the parent might by "the sympathy of sentiment" be communicated to her offspring. Therefore, it was imperative that the mother learn "to improve in all the heaven like expressions of countenance," making herself look like Christ.[42]

If children were such impressionable creatures that they could absorb their mother's character from the expression upon her face, then she would have to be enormously careful not to disclose, even inadvertently, any thought or feeling she did not want her child to acquire. Mothers were warned not "to permit the anxieties of your mind to mantle your countenance with forbidding gravity or gloom." And because the countenance and the voice were reflections of the mother's character, it was likewise necessary for her to control her thoughts and feelings, lest they betray her and ruin her child. The mother "must always be dignified, calm, consistent with herself. . . . She must never be observed to betray a weakness, changeableness or vascillation [*sic*] of character. . . . the mother must be at all times, agreeable, entertaining and tender."[43] Mothers were urged to suppress all negative emotions and to cultivate a placid cheerfulness. Again and again mothers were told which feelings might be enjoyed and which were to be denied. Lydia Sigourney advised that "every irritable feeling should . . . be restrained." She asked her readers to forgive her "for repeatedly pressing on mothers, to wear the lineaments of cheerfulness." Similarly, Alphonse Perren told mothers that "an even temper is indispensable to the cheerfulness of home," while *The Mother's Magazine* insisted that "a good disposition," one that was kind, considerate, and unselfish, was "the most important requisite in domestic life."[44] All these advisers assumed that women could manipulate and control their emotions, that a mother was able "to cultivate all good dispositions and noble aspirations—to overcome and subdue all evil propensities."[45] Emotion could be overcome by will.

Although women were believed to be, in a general sense, more emotional than men, "possessing superior strength of heart,"[46] that did not mean they were to express whatever they felt. Feminine emotionality was fundamentally passive; women might register feeling, deeply and indiscriminately, but they were not to transmit everything they might feel. The nineteenth century expected women, no less than men, to exercise self-control. Indeed, for mothers to be able to teach their sons essential lessons in self-control, they must be able to control themselves. Hence, advisers told women to "bear in mind, that, in governing, we should begin with ourselves." A woman endowed with "warm feelings" and "quick apprehension" would have to exercise "self-control" so that she might display only a "calm good sense."[47] Emotion was not in itself an unqualified good. Rather, mothers were enjoined to govern and, indeed, to manipulate their feelings for the benefit of their children. Thus, in a chapter entitled "The Mother's Difficulties," John Abbott insisted, "We must bring our own feelings and our own actions under a rigid system of discipline, or it will be in vain for us to hope to curb the passions and restrain the conduct of those who are looking to us for instruction and example."[48] Put another way, the natural and spontaneous outpourings of a mother's heart might interfere with the mother's true mission. Her most strenuous efforts would have to be directed at herself.

Is there a contradiction here? After all, the maternal advisers certainly believed that the mother's love was natural and irrepressible, and they agreed that one of the attributes that qualified women for motherhood was their ability to sympathize with their children, to feel what they felt. Were women born to be mothers, or was it an office that was to be achieved? Were women suited as they were, or did they have to be changed? The maternal advisers did not confront this question directly, but taken as a body, their writings offer this answer. Individual women were to strive to realize their feminine potential by deliberately cultivating that within themselves which was supposed to be the most naturally and essentially feminine. The advisers thus betrayed their suspicion of female emotionality in the full range of its possible manifestations; they idealized feeling only to the extent that it was an expression of the generalized, socializing affections or sympathies that Common Sense philosophers had glorified. More particular, individualized emotion was quite another matter. It was the feelings that a woman had in *common* with other women that were prized, not intense or idiosyncratic emotions.

Emotion was construed instrumentally; it had certain purposes and was to be shaped to serve those ends. Only in this context does the advice given by *The Mother's Magazine* in 1833 make sense. P. told mothers to "*feel* for your child . . . for whatever your feelings are, he will know them; you cannot elude his eagle eye." So mothers must feel the right feelings, but they "must beware of disclosing [their] feelings, or at least, let there not be an apparent attempt to exhibit them, either to himself or to others. This would be most ruinous. Rather let him feel that there exists in your bosom a well spring of feeling and anxiety, which others know nothing of, and which even he cannot fathom." P. told mothers that they must craft a maternal persona, a woman who was quintessentially feeling and self-effacing. She must eradicate almost entirely all evidence of will and intention, perhaps modeling herself after P.'s own mother, who prayed early in the morning, before her family awoke, almost—but not quite—eluding the watchful eye of her child. She must create the illusion that she had subdued all feeling, any interest in self, and all desire to exercise power. She might reveal only the scintilla of the crafted self that escaped her extraordinary efforts as self-suppression.

The mother was an actor on the stage of eternal life and death. She must see herself as her children would see her; she must observe herself playing her assigned role. "Mother, watch yourself," wrote P. "Your child watches you; his eye watches every motion; his ear is bent to catch every sound from your lips." Again P. warned, "Mother, watch yourself; how can you expect your Saviour's blessing if you slight his most solemn and repeated injunction to watchfulness?" And a third time, most emphatically, "Mother! watch yourself; Should the inquiry be made about your children—Who slew all these? How could you bear to have all eyes turned on you, as their murderer?"[49]

The mother had it in her power to secure for her child eternal life, or to consign him to perdition. Because the stakes were so high, it was "a mother's imperious duty to make any and every sacrifice, to rescue her child." Maternal advisers insisted unequivocally that "a mother's duties ought to take precedence before everything else." Quite simply, a mother had "no right to seek her own pleasure more than that of her children, or her own improvement more than theirs."[50] Americans could exhort mothers to self-sacrifice because they considered unselfishness a cardinal virtue; indeed, it was just what mothers were supposed, by precept and example, to teach.[51] Moreover, self-sacrifice was thought to bring its own sort of pleasure. So reasoned Lydia Sigourney, who observed that "the disinterested, have the best materials for being happy. . . . May it not therefore be assumed," she asked, "that the subjugation of self, is happiness?"[52] The mother's mission was to live for her child; this would bring her happiness here, and her child happiness hereafter.

Curiously, the maternal advisers never predicted whether the mother herself might look forward to salvation; their interest was only in the future of the child. Indeed, mothers were reborn not in heaven, but in their children; they sacrificed themselves in a most profound sense. Here is the way Lydia Sigourney explained the "Privileges of the Mother": "No longer will you now live for self,—no longer be noteless and unrecorded, passing away without name or memorial among the people. It can no more be reproachfully said of you, that 'You lend all your graces to the grave, and keep no copy.'"[53] Life everlasting came to a woman only through her child. The subtext of the maternal advice literature was that women, like Christ, were the instruments of someone else's salvation.

And like Christ, they would have to die that their children might live. The maternal advice literature makes this point effectively, if indirectly. We may consider the exhortations to self-sacrifice and the suppression of feeling as a generalized expression of the belief that mothers must pay dearly for the happiness of their children. But it is in fiction, especially in short, instructive tales, that this message comes through most clearly.

Again and again, maternal advisers imagined the moment when mother and child separated. This was the test of maternal influence: had the child learned from his mother's example? John Abbott summarized the basic assumption: "When a son leaves home, and enters upon the busy world, many are the temptations which come crowding upon him. If he leaves not his mother with established principles of religion and self-control, he will most assuredly fall before these temptations."[54]

If all went as it was supposed to, the child would have internalized his mother's values, her voice, her countenance, and her prayers; they would serve as his conscience. Many men who wrote for women's magazines testified to the efficacy of maternal influence. S., for example, described his falling away from God after he left his mother's home and his later conversion, which he credited to his mother: "If my heart has ever been renewed—if my sins have been forgiven, I feel I owe it, through the mercy of God, to a *pious mother's prayers.* . . . The memory of those prayers, wherever I am, still, like a guardian angel, hovers over my heart to restrain me from evil, and cheer me onward in the way of live."[55] Just as the maternal advice literature postulated, S. carried his mother with him, in his heart; Christ's surrogate, she effected his salvation.

That is the way the paradigm worked, from the perspective of the child. Many confessions—or pseudoconfessions, for it is impossible to assess the veracity of these tales—told the same story.[56] Only occasionally were such tales recounted from the mother's point of view. If children, when grown, might expect to enjoy the fruits of their mothers' labors, the mothers themselves would have to trust to faith. *The American Ladies' Magazine* put it this way, beginning with the standard sentiment: "The Maternal influence in molding these wonderful minds, is a triumph of which our sex may well be proud. . . . there is a connexion between duties performed and blessings secured, which is always certain." Then follows the caution. "The faithful mother may not see this fulfillment during her life; but she can and will feel its benignant and cheering hope."[57] Mothers, then, should not expect fulfillment on this side of the grave. Implicit is the assumption that mothers will not see their labors rewarded; for that they will have to trust to God.

It is necessary to read these stories from the mother's perspective to understand fully the nature of the mother's mission and the purpose of maternal love as they were defined by nineteenth-century maternal advisers. One tale may serve to represent them all. Fanny Fern's "A Mother's Influence" focuses upon the moment when a young man takes his leave from the parental home. Young Will Low has decided to go to sea. His father, an old-fashioned patriarch, has made his life unbearable. The son, however, will miss his mother, who is, as he tells a friend, "the only humanized portion of my heart—the only soft spot in it. She came to my bedside last night, after she thought I was asleep, gently kissed my forehead, and then knelt by my bedside. . . . I shall never be an infidel while I can remember my mother." Mrs. Low has mastered the conventions; she reveals her emotion only when she thinks she is unobserved. She tries to suppress her feelings, but the next morning her "hand trembled as she passed her boy's cup" at his last meal at home. "She did not trust herself to speak—her heart was too full." Will, of course, observes the signs of his mother's emotion, her "swollen eyelids" and "his favorite little tea-cakes that she had busied herself in preparing for him." All that she could utter was the simple prayer "God keep my boy!" This was the ritual mother's prayer, an incantation to protect her son and secure his salvation.

And so Will Low went to sea, enacting a scenario that seems to have been the realization of a mother's greatest fears. In tale after tale, separated sons went to the city or, more often, to sea—the masculine communities that appear as the antitheses of the female-dominated home. And, as in all of these tales, the son gave in to temptation. Of course he felt guilt, but "when the angel whisper, 'God keep my boy,' palsied his daring hand," he would drink another cup "to drown again more recklessly 'that still small torturing voice.'" He was too ashamed even to write home. Finally satiated, Will returned home, on what proved to be the day of his mother's funeral. A neighbor explained that after Will left home "'she began to droop like a willow in a storm, and lose all heart, like. Doctor's stuff didn't do any good, as long as she had no news of the boy.'" Will's sins, then, have killed his mother.

Will's "conscience," however, "did its office. Long years of mad folly passed in swift review before him; and over that insensible form a vow was made, and registered in Heaven." Mrs. Low's death worked her son's conversion, and he, in turn, persuaded his father also to repent. The story ends with the two men entering church, as the older Low comments, "'Your mother should have lived to see this day, Will.'"[58] But of course, she could not have. So directly is Will Low's conversion linked to the death of his mother that we cannot miss seeing the causal connection. Finally and firmly transplanted into her son's heart, Mrs. Low has served her life's function: she now *may* die. And in order to secure her husband's and especially her son's rebirth, she now *must* die. The narrative and the logic both are established by the life of Christ. Mrs. Low's death, like that of Christ, was necessary for her son and her husband to be reborn. She made the greatest sacrifice that a mother—and a Christian—could make; she gave her life for her child. Ultimately, a mother's influence depended upon her willingness to give herself fully and to deny herself finally. And it was only after she had gone to this extreme that she realized her destiny. A correspondent to *The Mother's Magazine* explained the effect of a mother's death this way: "Blessed are they, in the earth, who possess the inestimable dowry of a pious mother's grave!—I had almost said, the example and counsel of a living mother could hardly equal in power, upon the filial heart, the silent but thrilling preaching of a departed one."[59] There was no "almost" about it. The mother atoned for her child's sins; she forgave him still; she died that he might achieve eternal life. The mother was Christ.

The paradigm of mother's love must be read as an elaborate parable that patterns the mother's nature and destiny after that of Christ. Not only the moral tales invented by Fanny Fern and the others, but the entire corpus of maternal advice literature in early to mid-nineteenth-century America was directed to achieving the conversion of the nation's children. Sometimes the message was secularized, and mothers were enjoined to prepare their children for entry into a democratic society. But even in those cases, the design bore an evangelical imprint: citizens of the republic were supposed to manifest the recognizably Christian traits of self-sacrifice, sinlessness, and benevolence toward their fellow man. So it is not surprising that if mothers were designated the instruments of conversion, a mother's life story, as it was imagined by the maternal advisers, would read like a parable. Endowed with "a love, next in patience to that of a Redeemer,"[60] her career would be like that of the great Converter; to redeem, she must die. The logic of the paradigm of maternal influence could have it no other way, so closely was it patterned after the narrative of Christ's life.

We see, then, theology and democracy engaged in a dialectic that would determine the shape of nineteenth-century American culture. The paradigmatic mother was this dialectic's creature, designed to serve its ends. Historians have usually linked the nineteenth century's idealization of motherhood to the early stages of industrialization and the removal of men's work from the home.[61] Yet if structural changes alone could explain the exaltation of self-sacrificing motherhood, that ideal surely would have been modified as the society and economy continued to change; in our current, postindustrial age, it might seem an anachronism. But because the ideal is part of our national civil religion, reflecting an American fusion of democratic and Christian thought, it persists. Even though most Americans no longer expect mothers to act as agents of conversion, they still think that maternal love can redeem.

Indeed, since the early nineteenth century, Americans have increasingly looked to love for salvation; they have attached to love a transcendent importance.[62] Yet love is an emotion, a feeling that can be experienced and expressed in a variety of ways. In commenting upon an earlier version of this article, John Demos suggested that those of us who study the history of emotions should consider making a commitment to a theoretical position regarding the study of emotion. He noted that he has found Silvan Tompkins's account of affective experience particularly useful. Tompkins has "identified eight 'primary affects,'" which are "inborn and intrinsic to the species": "(1) Interest/Excitement; (2) Distress/Anguish; (3) Fear/Terror; (4) Anger/Rage; (5) Disgust/Contempt; (6) Shame/Humiliation; (7) Surprise/Startle; (8) Enjoyment/Joy." Readers of Demos's *Entertaining Satan: Witchcraft and the Culture of Early New England* have an example of how effectively a historian can use Tompkins's work to illuminate a chapter in history.[63] But as Robert Levy noted in discussion, "love" nowhere appears on Tompkins's list; it would not seem to be a "primary affect."

Instead, "love" is a social construction, a term that, in different times and places, takes on different meanings. Historians, then, have a role in analyzing the changing cultural meanings of love, of helping us to understand—to use Raymond Carver's words—"what we talk about when we talk about love."[64] When Freud said that "a mother is only brought unlimited satisfaction by her relation to her son; this is altogether the most perfect, the most free from ambivalence of all human relationships,"[65] he was talking about love in a way not very different from the antebellum maternal advisers who also believed that a mother's love was pure, unconflicted, and fundamentally self-denying. Yet we must wonder about the effect of this advice literature upon the women who read it and, perhaps, took it to heart; family historians have barely begun to study the experience of mothers in the nineteenth century.[66] As in the paradigm, living, fully dimensional mothers slip from our view. Still, we may speculate whether certain pathologies that psychologists and psychoanalysts have attributed to women—their masochism, their narcissism, their calculated presentation of self—may be the unintended result of the peculiar definition Americans have attached to the term "mother's love."

In Robert Stone's novel *Children of Light,* the protagonist responds to his lover's plea for help: "'I would die for you,' he said. It was true, he thought, but not really helpful."[67] Nor, surely, is it very helpful for mothers to liken themselves to Christ or to see in their willingness to die for their children an appropriate test of their love.

NOTES

The author wishes to thank the National Endowment for the Humanities for a Fellowship for Independent Study and Research, the Newberry Library for a Short-Term Research Fellowship, and the Philadelphia Center for Early American Studies for a Senior Fellowship; and Barry Bienstock, John Demos, Peter Stearns, and the participants in the First Biennial Conference on Social History for their valuable suggestions.

1. Rev. John Todd, "Address to Mothers," *The Mother's Magazine,* Nov. 1839, p. 249 (hereafter referred to as *MM*); E. L., "The Mother's Affections," *American Ladies' Magazine,* July 1833, p. 320 (hereafter referred to as *ALM*); Lydia H. Sigourney, *Letters to Mothers* (Hartford, 1838), p. 47.

2. See Jay Fliegelman, *Prodigals and Pilgrims: The American Revolution against Patriarchal Authority, 1750–1850* (New York, 1982); Melvin Yazawa, *From Colonies to Commonwealth: Familial Ideology and the Beginning of the American Republic* (Baltimore, 1981); Ruth H. Bloch, "The

Gendered Meanings of Virtue in Revolutionary America," *Signs* 13 (1987): 37–58; Jan Lewis, "The Republican Wife: Virtue and Seduction in the Early Republic," *William and Mary Quarterly* 3d ser., 44 (1987): 689–721 (hereafter referred to as *WMQ*).

3. Ruth H. Bloch, "American Feminine Ideals in Transition: The Rise of the Moral Mother, 1785–1815," *Feminist Studies* 4 (1978): 101–26.

4. Laurel Thatcher Ulrich, *Good Wives: Image and Reality in the Lives of Women in Northern New England, 1650–1750* (New York, 1982), p. 154. See also Nancy F. Cott, "Passionlessness: An Interpretation of Victorian Sexual Ideology, 1790–1850," *Signs* 4 (1978): 219–36.

5. Useful discussions are provided by Fliegelman, *Prodigals and Pilgrims,* esp. pp. 9–29; Daniel W. Howe, "The Political Psychology of *The Federalist,*" *WMQ,* 3d ser., 44 (1987): 485–509; Garry Wills, *Inventing America: Jeffersons' Declaration of Independence* (Garden City, N.Y., 1978), esp. part 4. Consider also Perry Miller, "The Rhetoric of Sensation," in his *Errand into the Wilderness* (New York, 1956), pp. 166–83.

6. See, for example, Rev. John S. C. Abbott, *The Mother at Home, or, The Principles of Maternal Duty* (Boston, 1834), p. 66; "Hints for Maternal Education," *MM,* Aug. 1834, pp. 113–14; S. F. W. "Woman's Sphere," *ALM,* May 1835, p. 264; Sarah W. Gordon, "It Should Be Love," *The Mother's Assistant and Young Lady's Friend,* Mar. 1849, p. 53 (hereafter referred to as *TMA*); Rev. V. Clark, "The Ruined Son," *TMA,* Oct. 1845, p. 74; "The Beginning," *ALM,* Jan. 1829, p. 4; "On Early Domestic Education, *Mother's Monthly Journal,* 1837, p. 6 (hereafter referred to as *MMJ*); Mrs. C. Sedgwick, "A Plea for Children," *ALM,* Feb. 1835, p. 95; Virginia Cary, *Christian Parent's Assistant; or Tales for the Moral and Religious Instruction of Youth* (Richmond, 1829), p. x; G. W. H., "The Disadvantages of Childhood," *MM,* 1867, p. 7; "What Virtue Is," *MM,* Aug. 1834, p. 115; D. M. L., "Early Habits of Industry," *MM,* Feb. 1834, p. 17; "Let Reason Dictate," *MMJ,* Nov. 1837, pp. 170–71.

7. See "The Conversion of Children," *MM,* Nov. 1835, pp. 161–64, Dec. 1935, pp. 179–81; "Remarks on the Conversion of Children," *MM,* Feb. 1836, pp. 24–25; C. A. Goodrich, "Hints on the Conversion of Children," *MM,* May 1838, p. 97; *Religious Remembrancer,* 20 July 1816, p. 187.

8. Abbott, *Mother at Home,* p. 159.

9. "Be Wise to Do, as Well as Learn," *MMJ,* Apr. 1837, p. 56; "A Mother's Influence," *TMA,* Feb. 1849, p. 25. See also "Third Annual Report of the Louisville Baptist Maternal Association," *MMJ,* Feb. 1846, p. 50.

10. "The Conversion of Children," *MM,* Dec. 1835, pp. 179–81.

11. "Family Government Essential to National Prosperity," *MM,* Mar. 1833, p. 35; "The Beginning," *ALM,* Jan. 1829, p. 3.

12. "Letter from D. B. L. Wade to Sister Allen," *MMJ,* Jan. 1846, pp. 13–15.

13. H. Richard Niebuhr, *The Kingdom of God in America* (New York, 1937).

14. "Family Government," p. 36.

15. For evidence that would support this analysis, see S. F. W., "Woman's Sphere," p. 266.

16. See Nancy F. Cott, *The Bonds of Womanhood: "Woman's Sphere" in New England, 1780–1865* (New Haven, 1977).

17. Sedgwick, "A Plea for Children," p. 94. See similarly, S. F. W., "Woman's Sphere," p. 262.

18. See Mary P. Ryan, *Cradle of the Middle Class: The Family in Oneida County, New York,*

1790–1865 (New York, 1981), p. 15, for her analysis of the family's function as that of "social reproduction . . . whereby people, rather than goods, are created."

19. See Lewis, "Republican Wife."

20. Sedgwick, "A Plea for Children," p. 93; "Family Government," p. 36. See similarly, "The Beginning," p. 4.

21. "Woman," *ALM,* Oct. 1830, p. 441. See John Putnam Demos, *A Little Commonwealth: Family Life in Plymouth Colony* (New York, 1970).

22. L. E., "Home," *ALM,* May 1830, pp. 218, 217, 218.

23. "The Happy Family," *MM,* May 1839, p. 111.

24. See Kathryn Kish Sklar, *Catharine Beecher: A Study in American Domesticity* (New Haven, 1973).

25. S. F. W., "Woman's Sphere," p. 264; "The Peculiar Faculties Afforded Mothers for Training Up their Children for Good," *MM,* May 1837, p. 104.

26. "The Mother of Washington," *ALM,* Nov. 1831, p. 385.

27. "The Connection Between Piety and Usefulness in Mothers," *MMJ,* Jan. 1837, p. 12; "Maternal Influence," *MM,* Apr. 1841, p. 84; "The Mother's Power, *MM* 35 (1867): 221. Such language became conventional. See also Sigourney, *Letters to Mothers,* p. 16.

28. John A. Bolles, "The Influence of Women on Society," *ALM,* June 1831, p. 256; Maria J. McIntosh, *Woman in America: Her Work and Her Reward* (New York, 1850), p. 77.

29. Rev. E. H. Chapin, "A Mother's Love," *TMA,* July 1845, p. 9; Frederick, "Maternal Affection," *The Casket,* Apr. 1827, p. 134. Also, see note 1 above.

30. "Extracts from Reports of Maternal Associations," *MM,* Feb. 1841, p. 46; "Be Wise to Do," p. 56. See similarly Sedgwick, "Plea for Children," p. 97.

31. Marian Harland [Mary Virginia Hawes Terhune], "A Christmas Talk With Mothers," in *The Christmas Holly* (New York, 1866), p. 53.

32. "Extract," *MM,* Jan. 1830, p. 24; "Training," *MMJ,* Jan. 1846, p. 2; "Prospectus," *MM,* Jan. 1833, p. 3.

33. Sigourney, *Letters to Mothers,* p. 25; Abbott, *Mother at Home,* p. 40; "Friendly Suggestions to Mothers," *TMJ* 20 (1855): 189. See also T. S. Arthur, *Anna Lee; or, The Maiden, The Wife, and the Mother* (reprint, London, n.d.), p. 186.

34. Sigourney, *Letters to Mothers,* p. 31.

35. This very useful neologism has been coined by Peter N. Stearns and Carol Z. Stearns to denote "the collective emotional standards of a society." See "Emotionology: Clarifying the History of Emotions and Emotional Standards," *American Historical Review* 90 (1985): 813–36, quotation on p. 813.

36. McIntosh, *Woman in America,* p. 25; Fanny Fern [Sarah P. Parton], *Ruth Hall and Other Writings,* ed. Joyce W. Warren (New Brunswick, 1986), p. 24.

37. "Maternity," *The Casket,* Oct. 1828, p. 472.

38. "Look Before You Leap," *Columbian Lady's and Gentleman's Magazine,* Jan. 1846, p. 13; "Thoughts on the Education of Girls," *MMJ,* July 1837, p. 106.

39. "Woman," p. 445; Harland, "Christmas Talk," p. 53.

40. *MMJ,* Apr. 1846, p. 119. See similarly P., "Parental Consistency," *MM,* Feb. 1833, p. 22.

41. "How to Speak to Children," *TMA,* Jan. 1850, p. 12.

42. "The Mother's Face," *MM,* Jan. 1838, p. 16; ibid., Apr. 1838, p. 74; ibid., Jan. 1838, p. 17;

ibid., Apr. 1838, p. 74; ibid., Feb. 1838, p. 30: the ideal mother exhibited a "Christ like loveliness." See similarly "The Mother," *MM*, 1867, p. 57: "Heaven has imprinted on the mother's face something which claims kindred with the skies." For the nineteenth century's concern for sincerity, see especially Karen Halttunen, *Confidence Men and Painted Women: A Study of Middle-Class Culture in America, 1830–1870* (New Haven, 1982); Fliegelman, *Prodigals and Pilgrims,* pp. 240–42; Lewis Kern, *An Ordered Love: Sex Roles and Sexuality in Victorian Utopias—The Shakers, the Mormons, and the Oneida Community* (Chapel Hill, 1981), pp. 35–40.

43. "How Shall a Mother Secure the Confidence of Her Children," *MM*, June 1830, p. 105; "For Who Hath Despised the Day of Small Things," *MMJ*, July 1837, p. 101.

44. Sigourney, *Letters to Mothers,* pp. 28, 63; "Home and Its Influences, *MM*, Mar. 1853, p. 80; L. L. H., "The Most Important Requisite in Domestic Life," *MM*, Mar. 1854, p. 88. See similarly Rev. Ralph W. Allen, "Family Government," *TMA*, Dec. 1849, p. 126.

45. "Mental and Moral Qualities Transmissible from Parents to Children," *MM*, Feb. 1841, p. 41.

46. "Maternal Traits of Feeling," *ALM*, Aug. 1830, pp. 373–74. See Peter N. Stearns and Carol Z. Stearns, *Anger: The Struggle for Emotional Control in America's History* (Chicago, 1986), p. 49.

47. "Report of the Philadelphia Union Maternal Association," *MMJ*, June 1837, p. 93; "The Satin Pelisse," *ALM*, Dec. 1830, p. 540.

48. Abbott, *Mother at Home*, p. 66.

49. P., "Parental Consistency," pp. 23–24.

50. A Mother, "Thoughts on Mothers' Responsibility," *MMJ*, Mar. 1837, p. 41; Arthur, *Anna Lee*, p. 221; Sedgwick, "Plea for Children," pp. 96–97.

51. See, for example, "Extract from a Letter," *MM*, Apr. 1835, p. 63.

52. Sigourney, *Letters to Mothers*, p. 193; see also p. 56.

53. Ibid., p. 9.

54. Abbott, *Mother at Home*, p. 15.

55. "The Mother in Her Closet," *MM*, Oct. 1840, p. 226.

56. The following discussion is based upon C. D., "Maternal Influence," *MM*, July 1840, pp. 160–64; "I Had a Mother," *MM*, July 1838, pp. 157–58; P. R. W., "Maternal Influence," *MM*, Nov. 1840, pp. 254–55; Rev. William H. Thayer, "The Mother's Grave," *TMA*, Mar. 1849, pp. 83–84; "My Mother's Grave," *The Casket,* May 1829, p. 84; "My Mother's Death," *MM*, Mar. 1833, pp. 94–95; S. M. D., "The Deathless Influence of a Mother's Love," *MM*, 1867, pp. 75–77.

57. "Woman's Way to Eminence," *ALM*, Sept. 1834, p. 388.

58. Fanny Fern [Sarah P. Parton], "A Mother's Influence," in *Fern Leaves From Fanny's Port-Folio,* 2d ser. (Auburn and Buffalo, 1854), pp. 252–56.

59. H. M. S., "A Mother's Grave," *MM*, June 1837, p. 138.

60. Sigourney, *Letters to Mothers*, p. 55.

61. See, for example, Cott, *Bonds of Womanhood;* Ryan, *Cradle of the Middle Class;* Ann Douglas, *The Feminization of American Culture* (New York, 1977); Bloch, "American Feminine Ideals."

62. See, for example, Jan Lewis, *The Pursuit of Happiness: Family and Values in Jefferson's Virginia* (New York, 1983). Consider also this observation by Robert N. Bellah, Richard Madsen, William M. Sullivan, Ann Swidler, and Steven M. Tipton, in *Habits of the Heart: Individ-*

ualism and Commitment in American Life (Berkeley, 1985), p. 291: "Many Americans are concerned to find meaning in life not primarily through self-cultivation but through intense relations with others."

63. John Putnam Demos, *Entertaining Satan: Witchcraft and the Culture of Early New England* (New York, 1982), pp. 184, 461; for Demos's use of Tompkins, see pp. 184–94.

64. This is the title of Carver's collection of short stories *What We Talk about When We Talk about Love* (New York, 1981), which includes the story of the same title.

65. Sigmund Freud, *New Introductory Lectures on Psychoanalysis*, ed. and trans. James Strachey (New York, 1965), p. 118.

66. See, for example, Nancy Schrom Dye and Daniel Blake Smith, "Mother Love and Infant Death, 1750–1920," *Journal of American History* 73 (1986): 329–53; Ulrich, *Good Wives;* Lewis, *Pursuit of Happiness,* chaps. 3 and 5; Sylvia D. Hoffert, "'A Very Peculiar Sorrow': Attitudes toward Infant Death in the Urban Northeast, 1800–1860," *American Quarterly* 39 (1987): 601–16.

67. Robert Stone, *Children of Light* (New York, 1986), pp. 231–32.

4.

THE NEW MOTHERHOOD AND THE NEW VIEW OF WET NURSES, 1780–1865

JANET GOLDEN

In the late eighteenth and early nineteenth centuries families employed wet nurses for a variety of reasons: the death of a mother following childbirth, her illness, or her inability to produce milk. Nearly everyone believed that wet-nursing was the best substitute for mother's milk, so that even poor orphaned infants were placed with wet nurses paid from local government coffers. At the other end of the social spectrum, wealthy infants were often sent to wet nurses, not out of need, but because parents chose this method of infant feeding as a signal of their social rank. This growing dependency of the well-to-do on poor wet nurses had many ramifications.

A new view of wet nurses began to be articulated in the postrevolutionary era. As the physician William Potts Dewees described the women paid to suckle the offspring of others, "Perhaps nothing displays the selfishness of the nurse in such strong relief as the tyranny with which she attempts to govern the whole house— every body, and every thing."[1] Dewees, a professor of midwifery at the University of Pennsylvania, described the social relations between wet nurses and their employers invoking the language of the early republic. In his view, the wet nurse threatened to subvert the household commonwealth by substituting domestic tyranny for the natural hierarchy of the family. Furthermore, the wet nurse epitomized the threat to gender conventions posed by working-class women, for, according to Dewees, she sought not only to earn a living but also to gratify her "wayward pleasures." Fusing the language of politics with the politics of gender and class, Dewees offered a new interpretation of nursery relations.

This article examines the transformation of those nursery relations and wet-nursing in the period between the American Revolution and the Civil War. Using the histories of wet nurses and their employers, it assesses how both working-class motherhood and middle-class motherhood were reconfigured by structural changes and by resulting shifts in the culture that transformed child rearing into a special vocation for middle-class women. Historians have bestowed a variety of labels on the emerging ideals of nineteenth-century middle-class motherhood: the cult of domesticity, republican motherhood, moral motherhood, and imperial motherhood, to mention a few.[2] The most critical insight lies, not in naming, but in the explication of the growing cultural hegemony of the urban bourgeoisie and its remaking the role of mother.

For wet-nursing, the creation of this new form of motherhood had significant ramifications. To begin with, well-to-do families ceased sending their children out to board with wet nurses in the country and instead brought wet nurses into their homes. This allowed mothers to oversee the daily development of their infants. Second, as the site of wet-nursing changed, so too did the wet nurse labor force. Instead of employing rural married women, families hired poor urban immigrant women, many of whom had given birth out of wedlock.[3] Third, the growing cultural isolation of the working class meant that wet nurses began to be characterized as dangerous—because of their personal characteristics—and therefore viewed as threatening the sanctity of the home, because they strongly influenced the life of the family's most vulnerable member. Ultimately, this led to a reframing of wet-nursing from a form of domestic service to a subject of medical concern and a profession mediated by physicians.

Domestic service work remained the most common occupation for women in the nineteenth century, although both the composition of the household labor force and the nature of the work itself changed because of the emerging industrial economy and the increasing pace of urbanization. In 1820, 8 percent of the U.S. population lived in urban areas; by 1870 the figure was 25 percent.[4] Early in the nineteenth century the predominant model of service was one of "hired help," in which women and girls assisted rural families in producing for the marketplace; later, domestic work in private urban households became the standard form of service.[5] The corollary to this in terms of wet-nursing was a shift from informal, temporary arrangements to the practice of hiring wet nurses to live with a family for extended periods of time.

Accompanying changes in the structure of service was a shift in the population of servants. Native-born servants began to be replaced, first by Irish and later by Scandinavian and German immigrants.[6] The consequences for employers of wet nurses can be seen in an 1861 letter written by Elizabeth Cabot, a wealthy Boston matron. After her sister-in-law's wet nurse had "given out," Cabot canvassed immigrant enclaves to find a replacement: "I roused up and trotted over, and thought I would raise a wet nurse in the village and dressed forthwith and started in the carryall with Powell, invaded *four* Irish mansions, succeeded in raising a nurse and a woman to take her baby and sent her off with Powell into town to be examined by Sam and go to Lillie."[7] While earlier generations of mothers judged wet nurses on their own, Cabot apparently sought the advice of a physician—the unidentified Sam. Moreover, earlier generations hired neighbors or acquaintances, while Cabot crossed an abyss of social class by "invading" an Irish neighborhood to find a wet nurse.

As Cabot's recollection suggests, the geographic and social distance between the working poor and the middle and upper classes was expanding. The well-to-do gradually retreated from the urban core and clustered together in neighborhoods of increasing homogeneity. The poor had their own districts, which by the 1840s were labeled slums and seen as wells of poverty, social pathology, and disease.[8] That the offspring of the well-to-do sometimes drank, literally, from such wells could be deeply troubling.

The fear was not unjustified; cities were unhealthy, and the young were at greatest risk. Overall, life expectancy at birth declined in the half century before the Civil War, and one reason was the excess mortality in urban areas. The concentration of population, the contamination of food and water, and the poverty of the urban lower classes combined to shorten the length of life, in large measure by producing an excess of infant mortality.[9] Nineteenth-century statisticians demonstrated that it was the poor and particularly their children who suffered disproportionately from urban ills. Indeed, one consequence of the increased mortality was an expanding supply of wet nurses, as poor women whose infants had died offered their milk in the marketplace. Yet, for many decades the popular belief persisted that the rich were most vulnerable because of their high living. Wealth, the argument went, led to ill health, whereas the poor enjoyed the advantages of a vigorous life.[10] Even when this notion had largely faded, vestigial elements of it remained, most notably in the belief that some wealthy women found it difficult to suckle their children, although poor mothers could do so easily.

The number of antebellum families relying on wet nurses is beyond calculation. Two studies of childbearing and infant care suggest that maternal nursing predominated among the well-to-do, with wet-nursing a second choice and artificial feeding a distant third. Mothers in the urban North, Sylvia Hoffert suggests, found in breast-feeding a source of power, self-esteem, and autonomy. An analysis by Sally McMillen of seventy-three southern families yielded similar conclusions. Only fourteen relied either partially or exclusively on wet nurses.[11] The small samples in these studies, however, makes it difficult to generalize from the results. Assessing the demand for wet nurses in nineteenth-century America therefore remains a matter of inference.

Maternal mortality and morbidity were two critical factors. The 1850 census reported that 2 percent of the deaths of white women occurred in childbirth, although the rate varied considerably from a low of 1.2 percent in New Hampshire to a high of 5.4 percent in Florida.[12] In some instances, the babies probably perished along with their mothers; in others, the surviving infants needed to be fed, either by a wet nurse or, if necessary, by artificial means. Instances in which maternal morbidity led to a demand for wet nurses are harder to measure. In addition to the women who were physically, mentally, or physiologically incapable of feeding their infants, there were others who suffered from a sense that nursing was too enervating. Popular literature defined middle- and upper-class urban women as frail. Some women no doubt applied the diagnosis to themselves and found a ready-made excuse to avoid nursing.

One issue shaping the demand for wet nurses—sexual behavior—disappeared from popular discussion. Early medical and popular guidebooks asked men to practice self-restraint so that their wives could nurse their babies, as it was thought that sexual intercourse led to breast milk becoming "excited" and dangerous. Discussions of this issue ceased in the nineteenth century as a veil of modesty descended. If families were hiring wet nurses so that husbands and wives could engage in sexual intercourse, their decisions provoked little comment. A few medical authors did address the possibility that wet nurses might remain sexually active and therefore harm their milk. This became a reason for changing the venue of the work from the wet nurse's home to the house of her employer.

Of course, women did not need medical reasons to reject breast feeding, they could simply chose wet-nursing. A study of the small town of Rockdale, Pennsylvania, in the antebellum years uncovered a network of upper-class women who regularly employed wet nurses.[13] On the spectrum of wet nurse employers, the Rockdale elite stood at an extreme. They were wealthy, not middle-class; lived in a small town, not a city; and were accustomed to managing large staffs of servants, including wet nurses. Yet, their experiences reveal a number of important aspects about wet-nursing, including the effects of the social distance between wet nurses and their employers, and the problems of wet nurse management that were linked to the needs of the wet nurses' babies.

In 1857, Clementina Smith of Rockdale described the "baby show" she had recently witnessed at the home of her sister, Harriet, the mother of a newborn.[14] In rapid succession the household hired two wet nurses who, owing to unforeseen events, briefly brought their own infants to reside in the home. Although Smith ultimately regarded the situation with amusement, for a time it proved to be a taxing reminder that dependence on a wet nurse brought with it a unique set of problems.

When the first wet nurse, Mary, developed infections in her breasts she was quickly relieved of her duties, but she remained in the household to be looked after as she convalesced. The mutual obligations between upper-class mistresses and their servants compelled Smith to take care of Mary. Smith therefore spent "anxious days and nights" engaged in "the hardest nursing I ever did" helping Mary to recover.[15] Treatment of Mary's breasts included repeated lancings and the application of several breast pumps—common therapies that may have discouraged some women from even attempting to suckle their own infants lest they be subjected to similar treatments if they experienced any difficulties.

As Mary convalesced from her illness (and perhaps her treatment), her successor, a Welsh wet nurse, joined the household, bringing her baby with her. Employers, as a rule, did not allow women to keep their own babies with them, fearing that the wet nurse would favor her own baby over her assigned charge. Clearly, an exception had been made, and Mary knew it. She became jealous and demanded that she too be allowed to have her child with her, ostensibly to help draw her milk. At this juncture the brief "baby show" began. However, Mary's baby stayed only a short time and then returned to its nurse, while the child of the Welsh wet nurse was soon sent out to board. Soon thereafter Mary's infant fell ill, was brought back to her, and then died.[16]

Smith's patient care of Mary and consideration for her baby did not blind her to what she saw as the woman's defects of class, character, and religion. Mary, Smith believed, lacked the necessary stoicism when faced with pain, and the appropriate response when faced with tragedy. When Mary first became sick, Smith admitted that she supposed "no suffering is more intense."[17] Nonetheless, she expressed exasperation in terms that belied her sympathy and betrayed her true sentiments: "That class of people have little self control or patience in sickness." Mary's torment following the death of her infant also puzzled Smith, who wrote that "she rather disappoints not to have relief mixed up with a sort of maternal instinct of pain in not having been with the child."[18] Had a middle-class woman failed to grieve for her infant, she would have stood in violation of every stricture of moral motherhood. When a poor woman was seen anguishing over the loss of her baby she evoked a far different response.

Although the paternalism of an older system of servant-mistress relations still existed, clearly the fault lines of religion and class had ruptured in the nursery. Smith never identified Mary as the mother of a baby; she saw her only as a slightly hysterical and often disruptive member of the lower class. Following the burial of Mary's child, Smith complained of the "difficulties getting the truth about her" and remarked that the other servants, including her replacement, harbored "a protestant bitterness against her."[19] Religion not only isolated Mary from her fellow servants but also marked her as untrustworthy and in need of careful management.

For Smith and her sister, a lifetime of experience provided all the training necessary for coping with this brief episode. For mothers of smaller means and less practice, with no family members to guide them or with a diminished confidence in their own abilities to manage a nursery, help was available. Domestic manuals, home medical books, medical textbooks, and, eventually, family physicians, stood ready to advise in the selection of wet nurses and day-to-day management of wet nurses.

These books offered interpretations of the roles of women as well as descriptions of nursery relations. They are, therefore, a lens through which to view the transformation of early nineteenth-century motherhood. The literature refracted the theme of growing class estrangement by juxtaposing the nurturing middle-class mother against the threatening lower-class wet nurse. At the same time, the literature magnified what was seen as the emerging distinction between scientific knowledge and practical experience, suggesting a division that would not be fully manifested until the late nineteenth century. But as a lens the literature was sometimes cloudy. It obscured the most fundamental and obvious fact about nursery relations—that each encounter was unique. Finally, the popular and medical literature, written for a middle-class readership, was blind to the existence of both municipal wet-nursing and of informal wet-nursing arrangements working-class women made among themselves.

Popular literature exalted the home as the seedbed of spiritual wealth, needing only proper cultivation by wives, mothers, and daughters. Literate women could not escape the deluge of advice on home management and child rearing, some of it barely concealed in novels, much of it freely offered in household manuals. In urging women to follow the precepts of modern motherhood, writers assumed from religious authorities the task of defining the importance of women's roles in the nursery. On the surface, the advice echoed earlier recommendations. The writers lauded women who breast-fed, reprimanded those who chose not to, and detailed the exceptional circumstances that required a wet nurse. In *Two Lives; or, To Seem and To Be* (1846) the popular novelist Maria McIntosh described a dissolute American woman living in Paris who found it "quite impossible" to "fulfill the two characters of a lady of fashion and a nursing mother." Her choice of a dissolute lifestyle led, predictably, to an early and tragic death.[20] In contrast to the novelists, the authors of advice books sometimes referenced their own experiences and invoked themes of personal sacrifice. "Heaven has crowned my endeavors with success," wrote Mary Palmer Tyler, "why then may I not show my gratitude, by presenting to the matrons of my country the fruits of my experience."[21] Tyler's book explained how she successfully nursed and reared eight children, including one child whose suckling caused her such excruciating pain that her friends advised her to wean the baby. Her message was quite clear: she had suffered for her children; others should do the same.

Even as domestic writers brought the language of the pulpit into the parlor, they subtly moved maternal responsibility out of the realm of the sacred. In sandwiching advice about babies between hints for wash day and cooking instructions they suggested that not the Almighty but mothers were the chief architects of their infants' welfare. Catharine Beecher's enormously popular *Treatise on the Domestic Economy* (1841) exemplified the secularization of infant care. She placed her faith in a rational approach to the problems of household management in general and was strikingly unsentimental on the subject of nursery organization. Her book, which addressed subjects ranging from charity to the care of parlors, included a chapter on the care of infants that quoted liberally from the medical literature. Uniquely, Beecher refrained from reprimanding those mothers who did not suckle their infants and chose instead to hire a wet nurse.[22] Here, close observation may have substituted for personal experience. Beecher had no children. However, her younger sister and fellow author Harriet Beecher Stowe bore five children in the first seven years of her marriage and seven altogether.

For Stowe, in at least one instance, using a wet nurse proved to be a necessity. Stowe retained the wet nurse to suckle her son Charles Edward, born in 1850.[23] In a letter to another sister, Sarah, Stowe complained about problems with her breasts that had caused her incessant pain and described the "healthy young Irish woman" who was nursing her child.[24] The woman had her flaws; according to Stowe, she "didn't know how to do anything" and was "very slack and slovenly"—charges not infrequently lodged against the Irish servants who streamed into the United States in the middle of the nineteenth century.[25] Nevertheless, the baby apparently thrived on her milk, and Stowe kept the woman in her home for three months. As in earlier decades, the gap between private experiences and public expectations remained a broad one. Stowe settled for a less than ideal wet nurse, satisfied that her baby remained in good health. While domestic authorities and women employing wet nurses, such as Harriet Beecher Stowe, saw the nursery in the context of the larger household, medical writers viewed it as a space that needed to be regulated by physicians and governed by rules of hygiene. Nineteenth-century American physicians began producing health books for the home, intending to replace the imported volumes that previous generations had relied upon. The authors addressed infant care as a medical subject rather than a domestic duty. Comparing the successive editions on the topic of wet-nursing reveals both the growing attention paid to this subject and the enhanced focus on the needs of urban readers.

Early editions of American popular health guides were largely silent on the subject of wet-nursing. James Ewell, a Savannah physician whose early work *The*

Planter's and Mariner's Medical Companion (1807) was intended for residents of "warm climates," stated simply that if an infant could not receive milk from its mother, or from "a healthy woman who laid in about the same time," the best choice would be the milk of a goat.[26] John Gunn's treatise on domestic medicine, which appeared in 1830, remained altogether silent on the subject of wet nurses. Gunn, a Knoxville, Tennessee, physician, wrote for frontier residents who had little financial or geographic access to full-time hired help.[27] In later years, revised versions of both manuals appeared, aimed at an expanded and increasingly urban audience that was more familiar with wet nurses and more willing to embrace the emerging ideas of female debility and medical authority. An enlarged and revised edition of Ewell's work, published in 1856, informed readers, "It has been improperly imagined that all mothers ought to be nurses." Such a false belief, the book continued, could result in harm to both mother and child.[28] Gunn's extraordinarily successful book was similarly transmogrified. Eastern publishers significantly revised his book to appeal to an urban constituency, adding new material on infant feeding and a somber discussion of wet-nursing.[29]

In the 1840s and 1850s, a new theme emerged in the discussion of wet-nursing: the threat of the dangerous stranger. The subject inspired both the popular and the medical imagination, combining the growing alienation of the middle and upper classes from the urban poor with more specific fears about disease. The 1848 edition of the home medical guide written by the botanic practitioner Wooster Beach used the term "stranger" in reference to wet nurses who communicated "loathsome and fatal diseases" and gave milk "rendered unwholesome by age or other causes."[30] With great specificity, physicians such as Beach outlined the problems of infant feeding, linking them to the argument that the well-to-do were vulnerable to the afflictions of the lower classes and suggesting therefore that solutions lay in the careful application of medical as well as practical knowledge.

The fullest expression of the idea of medical management of infant feeding appeared in seven pediatrics books published between 1825 and 1850. As a collective achievement, they signaled a decreasing reliance on foreign authorities, the gradual maturing of the American medical community, and the growing intellectual ambitions of certain members of the medical profession.[31] Unlike the authors of popular medical books, the physicians who wrote pediatrics manuals addressed clinical subjects and employed technical language in a discourse aimed at fellow practitioners. However, the books also found a popular readership, as self-doctoring remained the rule in many homes and as popular writers began to refer their readers to the new medical literature.

It is tempting to portray the textbook authors as exemplars of modern science in contrast to the more populist physicians who wrote home health guides, but this accords too much to the former and suggests too wide a knowledge gap among the various practitioners. As the historian Charles Rosenberg has noted, all Americans, physicians and lay persons alike, shared a vernacular healing tradition, an understanding of the body in health and disease, and a knowledge of various remedies.[32] What distinguished analyses of infant feeding in medical textbooks from those found in popular guides was not their science but rather their belief in medical authority. The pediatrics books were beginning to assert that the nursery was a medical domain as much as it was a domestic space.

The new textbooks offered a more expansive and less moralistic assessment of employer's needs. Whereas popular writers championed mothers who overcame all varieties of pain and suffering to breast-feed their babies and popular medical guides similarly exalted maternal sacrifice, the textbook authors paid homage to ideal mothers but also enumerated the conditions that prevented women from nursing. The Cincinnati practitioner John Eberle explained that a mother with either insufficient or bad milk, a disease, or a painful condition could not nurse, and therefore a wet nurse had to be obtained.[33] Without explicitly sympathizing with women who considered breast-feeding immodest, wearisome, or déclassé, the long lists of exemptions implicitly sanctioned the women who chose to defy convention, enabling them to frame their decision as a medical necessity rather than a personal choice. The inventory of medical excuses had the effect of endorsing the use of wet nurses without contradicting the physicians' basic objections to hired substitutes.

A belief that middle- and upper-class women were weak vessels who could not fulfill their biological duties was a distinguishing characteristic of both the popular and the professional medical literature. Doctors had begun to suspect that some middle- and upper-class women lacked the physical stamina necessary to withstand the pain of childbirth and therefore required anesthesia. Similarly, they surmised that well-to-do women found breast-feeding more difficult than did lower-class women.[34] Caleb Ticknor argued that "women of the higher classes frequently possess such extremely sensitive and excitable temperaments as will render it imprudent for them to suckle their own children."[35] Under the circumstances, it was best to ask the doctor to find a wet nurse.

The pediatrics textbooks endorsed wholeheartedly the idea that families needed direct medical guidance in matters of child rearing, including the hiring of wet nurses. Ideally, the physician would hire the wet nurse. Failing that, the family would refer to a medical textbook to help them select a proper candidate. Wet nurses were to be treated not simply as servants but as individuals capable of transmitting either health or disease; they had to be judged by medical standards.

In selecting wet nurses, physicians scrutinized their health, their milk, and their children. They weeded out women with eruptions suggestive of venereal infection, with swollen necks that hinted at scrofula (tuberculosis of the lymph glands, usually those of the neck), or with a history of convulsions. Failure to examine potential wet nurses, doctors noted, could have tragic consequences. Dewees, in obvious reference to venereal infections, recounted two cases of babies acquiring "the most loathsome and horrible of all diseases" from their respective wet nurses. He also discussed an episode in Scandinavia involving a wet nurse who infected an entire family, including the father, mother, three children, a maid servant, and two clerks—a pattern of transmission that leaves much to the reader's imagination. Dewees's intention in recounting this near-epidemic episode was not to frighten employers away from wet nurses, although it may well have had that effect. Instead, he wanted to upbraid families who hired wet nurses without "previous inquiry into [their] character."[36]

The possibility of contracting a venereal disease from a wet was nurse was real, and frightening. In an 1845 letter to her mother, Laura Lenoir Norwood of Hillsboro, North Carolina, expressed her dread of employing a wet nurse. "I can't feel reconciled to the idea," she wrote, believing she would have "never had one if my children had not done so badly on feeding, and now I feel ten times more averse to it than ever." Norwood's reluctance stemmed from a previous "narrow escape" from a wet nurse infected with a venereal disease.[37] Infant feeding, her case illustrates, raised fundamental medical questions about the transmission of disease and the protection of health. With venereal disease perceived to spread upward from the lower classes, the hiring of wet nurses took on a heightened danger as the social class of workers fell.

Fulfilling the demand for thorough examinations of potential wet nurses proved difficult because investigations violated codes of morality and modesty. It was easy for the authors of textbooks to explain the need to scrutinize a woman's breasts and nipples. But how could an inspection take place in an era when medical professionals approached the female body with reluctance and when most physicians did not yet view women giving birth as part of their clinical training?[38] The recommendation that the doctor examine a woman's milk and pay attention to the quantity, appearance, and color seems equally unlikely to be followed, as does the suggestion that the doctor taste the milk to determine if it was sufficiently "sweet."[39] Such actions moved the doctor far beyond the bounds of proper professional decorum and gentlemanly behavior.

It was far simpler to rely on the traditional means of discovering a wet nurse's health: viewing her baby. Careful inspection of the infant helped to rule out the presence of a communicable disease, provided evidence that the woman gave milk capable of nourishing a child, and allowed prospective employers to see if the wet nurse's infant was close in age to the suckling. Many doctors believed that young infants could not consume "old milk," defined as having come from women who had nursed for six months or more. Constitutionally, physicians asserted, old milk did not suit the needs of a young baby; and physiologically, it became more likely that the wet nurse had resumed menstruating or become pregnant.[40] Both conditions, physicians believed, were detrimental to the milk's quantity and quality.

The age limit, however, proved difficult to enforce in light of the uncertain supply of wet nurses and the family's interest in finding a wet nurse who suited not only the baby but the needs of the entire household. In an 1858 article in the *American Medical Monthly,* William H. Cummings complained of a shortage of wet nurses, lamenting that in cities there were "not enough to supply the demand," and in the country they could "scarcely ever be obtained."[41] Perhaps the scarcity accounted for the singular case of a woman who employed the same wet nurse for three of her infants. At the mother's direction the wet nurse weaned one baby just in time to begin nursing the new arrival.[42] The arrangement, though highly unusual and counter to medical advice, allowed the family to solve several problems at once: it kept a trusted woman ready for service at a time when wet nurses were perceived as both scarce and dangerous.

The new maternal ideology that anointed mothers as the molders of the health and character of their children ironically served to vest greater power in wet nurses. Writing in *Godey's Lady's Book,* the educator Almira Phelps conceded that even if the mind could not be transfused from one soul to another, the "moral character of the future man may be influenced by the treatment he receives at the breast and in the cradle."[43] Such potential power could not be granted lightly. A mother needed to be absolved of responsibility for feeding her baby, not simply permitted to abdicate her role. This required the doctors to determine, first, whether a woman could breast-feed, and, second, if she could not, who would be hired to take her place. As the ideology of middle-class maternity grew more fixed, the rules governing the nursery became more rigid.

A key change involved the placement of the infant. Under the new regimen babies no longer went to wet nurses in the country but lived at home under the watchful gaze of their mothers. Even though urban living was recognized as less healthy than country life, only one of the textbook authors endorsed outplacement. The Philadelphia physician D. Francis Condie believed, "A country residence for a nurse has one important advantage," explaining "it indemnifies, in some degree, the infant for its removal from the maternal breast, particularly when the mother inhabits the confined and illy ventilated streets of a crowded city."[44] His colleagues and many families disagreed.[45] The need to oversee the work of the wet nurse far outweighed the benefits of country air. Physicians placed aside their scientific understanding of the deleterious effects of urban living, echoing the opinions of domestic advisers that no woman who expected to exert a strong moral influence over her children could send an infant away to be reared in the home of a stranger.

The effects of the new geographic imperatives proved significant. First, urban wet nurses came from a different social class than their rural counterparts. As a result, the wet-nursing vignettes in the medical and popular literature became stylized presentations of urban class antagonisms. Second, and more critically, the new arrangement meant separating the wet nurse from her own child. The literature thus began to depict wet nurses who missed their babies and took desperate measures to visit them. A frequent scenario involved a woman who clandestinely visited her child after putting her suckling into a deep sleep. Dewees reported a case in which a wet nurse applied laudanum—tincture of opium—to her breasts to quiet the baby and make time for an afternoon visit.[46] Lydia Maria Child, a domestic expert, offered a fuller explanation of the laudanum problem: "If the nurse have her own child with her, she is naturally tempted to give it a greater proportion of nourishment; if the child be removed, there is the painful consideration of deriving benefit from the privations and sacrifices of another; however conscientious she may be, it is more difficult to perform her duties patiently and well for mere money, than it is from instinct, or feeling; hence the great dangers of injuring a babe by putting it to sleep with laudanum."[47] The motherly desires of the wet nurse demanded fear, not reverence. If they tried to ensure the future for their own babies, by suckling them first or making a brief visit, they posed a threat to their employers' infants.

In Child's account there were two possibilities: allowing a wet nurse to keep her child—something most employers frowned upon—or making her cast the infant aside. A third possibility was, of course, hiring a woman whose infant had died. The physician John Eberle favored this plan, thinking that a mother who had "no child of her own to take care of" was safer than one who would somehow find a way to express her feelings for her own baby.[48] The scheme had a serious drawback, however; without an infant to inspect, many doctors and employers had no way of determining whether a potential wet nurse was healthy and whether she produced good milk.

Even as they stood accused of maternal feelings, wet nurses also faced charges that they acted from greed alone. Eberle warned that women who lacked sufficient milk might resort to clandestine feedings in order to retain their situations and, more important, their income. The life of a nursling, he alleged, was "often sacrificed to the secret practices of a mercenary and unprincipled nurse."[49] Mrs. C. A.

Hopkinson, author of *Hints for the Nursery* (1863), provided a graphic account of a wet nurse whose milk failed after eight or nine months, causing the infant to starve. A physician misdiagnosed the problem and recommended sending the complaining baby to the seashore with his wet nurse. Only a chance encounter with a nursing mother, during which the baby "screamed and stretched out his arms to the woman," allowed the family to discern the truth.[50] The saga presented the evil counterpart to the wet nurse who missed her own baby—the wet nurse who sacrificed her suckling in order to fatten her purse. Wet nurses, the literature suggested, acted as both instinctive mothers and instinctive entrepreneurs. Indeed, it was instinct that was thought to separate middle-class from lower-class mothers. The former reared their children by following moral precepts, by rationally determining how to nurture them, and by consciously instilling in them proper bourgeois values. Lower-class women in general and wet nurses in particular also had strong feelings for their children, but their feelings were steeped in instinct, not enlightened motherhood. And, Condie alleged, emotions such as "grief, envy, hatred, fear, and jealousy" could alter a wet nurse's milk and ultimately destroy the child and the family.[51]

The characterization of wet nurses in the prescriptive literature as instinctive mothers and instinctive entrepreneurs was more accurate than the authors might have realized. Records from the Orphan Society of Philadelphia reveal both the pragmatism and the sentimentality of women who wet-nursed the offspring of other working women. More critically, the records show that although the vicissitudes of working-class life forced women to earn what they could, the emotional dimensions of the job sometimes overcame material considerations.

While the offspring of the well-to-do were suckled in their homes, wet nurses were forced to place their own babies with other women. In addition, working-class women took in the children of mothers who had died. Employed in an informal system of care, home-based wet nurses were of little interest to doctors or domestic writers. The women did, however, concern municipal authorities, for when they failed to be paid for their work, they handed their charges over to the town. In 1830, for instance, the wet nurse Grace McDernish sent the infant in her care to the Philadelphia Orphan Asylum after the child's father died and the payments stopped.[52] Jane Courtney, another Philadelphia wet nurse, also attempted to turn her suckling over to the authorities when its father died, but she was persuaded to keep the girl after the Guardians of the Poor of Philadelphia promised her fifty cents a week.[53]

When sentiment collided with self-interest, the latter typically won, but there were exceptions. Some wet nurses kept babies long after the payments for their maintenance ceased to arrive. Philadelphian Matilda Thorne, hired to wet nurse a girl whose mother went to New York to work as a wet nurse, received only two payments, despite repeated efforts to collect what she was owed. Rather than send the infant to the city's care and earn a stipend suckling another baby (or perhaps being paid to continue her work), she simply continued to rear the girl on her own for several years before depositing her at the Orphan Society.[54] Thorne was not alone in her generosity. After Hugh Devine's mother died, he was kept "on charity" by his nurse, Lydia Vannater, until he turned five.[55] Had Thorne or Vannater turned the babies over to authorities and perhaps taken in another child from the Guardians of the Poor, they could have earned fifty cents a week. It was not a large sum—the amount equaled the stipend given to the indigent and was less than the seventy-five cents to one dollar per week usually paid to servants—but it was, at least, something.[56] Keeping the infants abandoned to their care meant a loss of income for the women and the additional costs of rearing the child. Few physicians or domestic experts knew or cared that poor women sometimes voluntarily mothered abandoned babies.

The relationships between Vannater and Thorne and the infants they suckled began in the marketplace but concluded in the private household. In a sense, both women were acting like middle-class mothers—making the tender rearing of a child a vocation. Yet, their actions were grounded in emotion; after all, they overlooked their own rational, economic interests. Although Vannater and Thorne were not instinctive entrepreneurs, a charge often lodged against wet nurses, they were instinctive mothers—a fact that set them apart from the middle-class ideal, which cherished mother-love as an intellectual as well as an emotional entity.

The social dichotomies of motherhood presented in the medical and popular literature reflected a larger reality of deepening social class divisions and functioned as propaganda for the emerging ideal of middle-class motherhood. Still, the descriptions hardly qualify as an accurate analysis of the relationships that arose between wet nurses and employers. The aim of the literature was not to chronicle the possibilities or exceptions, but to share and shape the modern understanding of home, family, and health. Thus, the literature presented an abstract, schematic view of wet nurses and wet-nursing. Personal accounts bring additional factors into view, including the way in which the perception of wet nurses intersected with the popular understanding of motherhood, medical authority, and household service.

As motherhood began to be reconfigured after the American Revolution, the perception of wet nurses and the work of wet-nursing changed. The authors of popular household advice books and medical treatises portrayed wet nurses as morally deficient women who traded their duties to their children for money and who stealthily infiltrated the nurseries of the middle class. Middle-class mothers, by contrast, were described by these authors as morally superior, capable of rearing children because they were guided by rational precepts rather than by instinct alone.

The private writings of these women reveal that relations with wet nurses were more complex than the prescriptive literature suggested. The work and meaning of wet-nursing was mediated by expectations about servants, by the growing belief that mothers could determine the health and well-being of their babies, by the shift in the site of wet-nursing from the wet nurse's home to that of her employer, and by the resulting change in the population of wet nurses. Together these structural and cultural shifts remade the work of mothering in the nineteenth century for both poor and well-to-do women.

NOTES

1. William Potts Dewees, *A Treatise on the Physical and Medical Treatment of Children,* 2d ed. (Philadelphia: Carey & Lea, 1826), pp. 59–60.

2. Ruth H. Bloch, "American Feminine Ideals in Transition: The Rise of the Moral Mother, 1785–1815," *Feminist Studies* 4 (1978): 101–26; Linda K. Kerber, *Women of the Republic: Intellect and Ideology in Revolutionary America* (Chapel Hill: University of North Carolina Press for the Institute of Early American History and Culture, 1980); Jan Lewis, "Mother's Love: The Construction of an Emotion in Nineteenth-Century America," in Andrew E. Barnes and Peter N. Stearns, eds., *Social History and Issues in Human Consciousness: Some Interdisciplinary Connections* (New York: New York University Press, 1989), pp. 209–29; Mary P. Ryan, *The Empire of the Mother: American Writing about Domesticity, 1830–1860* (New York: Institute for Research in History and Haworth Press, 1982); and Barbara Welter, "The Cult of True Womanhood: 1820–1860," *American Quarterly* 18 (1966): 161–74.

3. Race was not a critical factor in nursery relations. In the North, families typically hired white, working-class wet nurses. Southern families made use of both free white and African American slave wet nurses, and in some cases white plantation mistresses suckled the offspring of slave women who died in childbirth. See Janet Golden, *A Social History of Wet Nursing in America: From Breast to Bottle* (New York: Cambridge University Press, 1996).

4. Bayrd Still, *Urban America: A History with Documents* (Boston: Little, Brown, 1974), p. 76.

5. Faye E. Dudden, *Serving Women: Household Service in Nineteenth-Century America* (Middletown, Conn.: Wesleyan University Press, 1983), pp. 1–103.

6. David M. Katzman, *Seven Days a Week: Women and Domestic Service in Industrializing America* (Urbana: University of Illinois Press, 1981).

7. Elizabeth (Dwight) Cabot to Ellen Twistleton, April 8, 1861. In Elizabeth (Dwight) Cabot, *Letters* (Boston: privately printed, 1905; New Haven: Research Publications, microform), pp. 220–21.

8. Blumin, *Emergence of the Middle Class;* David Ward, *Poverty, Ethnicity, and the American City, 1840–1925: Changing Conceptions of the Slum and the Ghetto* (Cambridge: Cambridge University Press, 1989), pp. 13–45. Residential segregation of the poor was, of course, the obverse of the on-going residential segregation of the rich. See Edward Pessen, *Riches, Class, and Power before the Civil War* (Lexington: D. C. Heath, 1973), pp. 169–204; and William H. Pease and Jane H. Pease, *The Web of Progress: Private Values and Public Styles in Boston and Charleston, 1828–1843* (New York: Oxford University Press, 1985), pp. 1–11.

9. R. W. Fogel, "Nutrition and the Decline in Mortality since 1700: Some Additional Preliminary Findings," National Bureau of Economic Research, Working Paper no. 1802, cited in Samuel H. Preston and Michael R. Haines, *Fatal Years: Child Mortality in Late Nineteenth-Century America* (Princeton: Princeton University Press, 1991), p. 51.

10. Richard A. Meckel, *"Save the Babies": American Public Health Reform and the Prevention of Infant Mortality, 1850–1929* (Baltimore: Johns Hopkins University Press, 1990), pp. 20–21.

11. Sylvia D. Hoffert, *Private Matters: American Attitudes toward Childbearing and Infant Nurture in the Urban North, 1800–1860* (Urbana: University of Illinois Press, 1989), p. 148 n. 34, and pp. 163–64; Sally McMillen, "Mothers' Sacred Duty: Breast-feeding Patterns among Middle- and Upper-Class Women in the Antebellum South," *Journal of Southern History* 51 (1985): 333–56.

12. Sally G. McMillen, *Motherhood in the Old South: Pregnancy, Childbirth, and Infant Rearing* (Baton Rouge: Louisiana State University Press, 1990), appendix 1, table 3.

13. Anthony F. C. Wallace, *Rockdale: The Growth of an American Village in the Early Industrial Revolution* (New York: Knopf, 1978), pp. 22–32.

14. Clementina Smith to Sophie du Pont, January 22, 1857, W9–26035, Hagley Museum and Library, Wilmington, Delaware (hereafter HML).

15. Ibid.

16. Clementina Smith to Sophie du Pont, January 17, 1857, W9–26033; January 22, 1857, W9–26035; February 7, 1857, W9–26037, HML.

17. Ibid., January 17, 1857, W9–26033, HML.

18. Ibid., February 7, 1857, W9–26037, HML.

19. Ibid.

20. Maria J. McIntosh, *Two Lives; or, To Seem and To Be* (New York: D. Appleton, 1846; microfilm, American Fiction Series, Woodbridge, Conn: Research Publications, 1970–78), p. 293.

21. [Mary Palmer Tyler], *The Maternal Physician: A Treatise on the Nurture and Management of Infants, from the Birth Until Age Two Years Old* (New York: Isaac Riley, 1811), p. 6.

22. Catharine Beecher, *A Treatise on Domestic Economy* (1841; reprint, New York: Schocken Books, 1977), pp. 207–24. See also Kathryn Kish Sklar, *Catharine Beecher: A Study in American Domesticity* (New York: Norton, 1976), pp. 151–67.

23. It is possible that some of her other children were wet-nursed. A letter from Catharine Beecher mentions that one of Harriet's twin daughters had been "put out for the winter." Catharine Beecher to Mary Beecher Perkins, 1838, cited in Kathryn Kish Sklar, introduction to Beecher, *Treatise on Domestic Economy*, pp. viii and xvii n. 5.

24. Harriet Beecher Stowe to Sarah Beecher, December 17, 1850, Harriet Beecher Stowe papers, Folder 9A, Schlesinger Library, Radcliffe College, Cambridge, Massachusetts.

25. Hasia R. Diner, *Erin's Daughters in America: Irish Immigrant Women in the Nineteenth Century* (Baltimore: Johns Hopkins University Press, 1983).

26. James Ewell, *The Planter's and Mariner's Medical Companion . . .* (Philadelphia: Bioran, 1807), p. 266.

27. John Gunn, *Gunn's Domestic Medicine, or Poor Man's Friend, In the Hours of Affliction, Pain and Sickness* (Knoxville: the author, 1830).

28. James Ewell, *The Medical Companion, or, Family Physician . . . ,* 11th ed. enl. (Philadelphia: Keen & Lee, 1856), p. 488.

29. Criticisms of rich mothers and poor mothers alike can be found in John C. Gunn, *New Family Physician: or Home Book of Health . . . ,* 200th ed. rev. and enl. (Cincinnati: Wilstach, Baldwin, 1880), p. 590.

30. Wooster Beach, *The American Practice Condensed or, the Family Physician . . . ,* 14th ed. (New York: James McAlister, 1848), p. 631.

31. The textbooks are cited in Thomas E. Cone, Jr., *History of American Pediatrics* (Boston: Little, Brown, 1979), pp. 78–83. They are George Logan, *Practical Observations on Diseases of Children . . .* (Charleston: A. E. Miller, 1825); William Potts Dewees, *A Treatise on the Physical and Medical Treatment of Children* (Philadelphia: H. C. Carey & I. Lea, 1825); John Eberle, *A Treatise on the Diseases and Physical Education of Children . . .* (Cincinnati: Corey & Fairbank, 1833); James Stewart, *A Practical Treatise on the Diseases of Children* (New York: Wiley & Putnam, 1841); D. Francis Condie, *A Practical Treatise on the Diseases of Children* (Philadelphia: Lea & Blanchard, 1844); John Forsyth Meigs, *A Practical Treatise on the Diseases of Children* (Philadelphia: Lindsay & Blakiston, 1848); and Charles Delucena Meigs, *Observations on Certain of the Diseases of Young Children* (Philadelphia: Lea & Blanchard, 1850).

32. Charles E. Rosenberg, "John Gunn: Everyman's Physician," in Rosenberg, ed., *Explaining Epidemics and Other Studies in the History of Medicine* (Cambridge: Cambridge University Press, 1992), pp. 62–70.

33. Eberle, *Treatise on the Diseases and Physical Education of Children,* p. 33.

34. On upper-class women lacking stamina for birth, see Hoffert, *Private Matters,* pp. 67–68; and Judith Walzer Leavitt, *Brought to Bed: Childbearing in America, 1750 to 1950* (New York: Oxford University Press, 1986), p. 126.

35. Caleb B. Ticknor, *A Guide for Mothers and Nurses in the Management of Young Children . . .* (New York: Taylor & Dodd, 1839), p. 92.

36. Dewees, *Treatise on the Physical and Medical Treatment of Children,* p. 60.

37. Letter from Laura Lenoir Norwood to her mother, cited in Erna Olafson Hellerstein, Leslie Parker Hume, and Karen M. Offen, eds., *Victorian Women: A Documentary Account of Women's Lives in Nineteenth-Century England, France, and the United States* (Stanford: Stanford University Press, 1981), p. 218.

38. On the viewing of women giving birth, see Virginia G. Drachman, "The Loomis Trial: Social Mores and Obstetrics in the Mid-Nineteenth Century," in Susan Reverby and David Rosner, eds., *Health Care in America: Essays in Social History* (Philadelphia: Temple University Press, 1979), pp. 67–83; and Leavitt, *Brought to Bed,* pp. 40–50.

39. Ticknor, *Guide for Mothers and Nurses,* p. 102; Stewart, *Practical Treatise on the Diseases of Children,* pp. 189–90.

40. The English physician Burns, whose work was reprinted in several American editions,

suggested that families refrain from hiring wet nurses who have nursed for some months "as the milk is apt to go away in some time, or become bad." John Burns, *The Principles of Midwifery; Including the Diseases of Women and Children,* rev. and enl. (Philadelphia: Hopkins & Earle, Fry & Kammer, 1810), p. 381. See also M. K. Hard, *Women's Medical Guide; Being a Complete Review of the Peculiarities of the Female Constitution . . .* (Mt. Vernon, Ohio: Cochran, 1848), p. 217; and Meigs, *Practical Treatise on the Diseases of Children,* p. 219.

41. William H. Cummings, "On a Substitute for Human Milk," *American Medical Monthly* 9 (1858): 196.

42. Stephen Tracey, *The Mother and Her Offspring* (New York: Harper, 1853) p. 204. The author admitted that this situation was "rare."

43. Almira H. Phelps, "Remarks on the Education of Girls," *Godey's Lady's Book* 18 (1839): 253, quoted in Anne L. Kuhn, *The Mother's Role in Childhood Education: New England Concepts, 1830–1860* (New Haven: Yale University Press, 1947), p. 57.

44. Condie, *Practical Treatise on the Diseases of Children,* p. 37.

45. Discussions of outplacement can be found in Edward H. Parker, *The Handbook for Mothers; A Guide in the Care of Young Children,* 2d ed. rev. (New York: Hurd & Houghton, 1867), p. 59; and Tracey, *The Mother and Her Offspring,* p. 208.

46. Dewees, *Treatise on the Physical and Medical Treatment of Children,* pp. 57–59.

47. Lydia Maria Child, *The Family Nurse; or Companion of the Frugal Housewife* (Boston: Charles J. Hendee, 1837), p. 39.

48. Eberle, *Treatise on the Diseases and Physical Education of Children,* p. 33.

49. Ibid.

50. Hopkinson was equally critical of a mother whose milk failed but was reluctant to hire a wet nurse. Mrs. C. A. Hopkinson, *Hints for the Nursery or, The Young Mother's Guide* (Boston: Little, Brown, 1843), pp. 29–30, 33–34.

51. Condie, *Practical Treatise on the Diseases of Children,* p. 35.

52. Orphan Society of Philadelphia, Admittance Book, 1815–1833, p. 626, Historical Society of Pennsylvania, Philadelphia, Pennsylvania (hereafter HSP).

53. Ibid., p. 261.

54. Orphan Society of Philadelphia, Folder "Admitting and Binding Indentures, 1815–," document signed by Matilda Thorne, March 1825, HSP.

55. Orphan Society of Philadelphia, Admittance Book, 1815–1833, p. 597, HSP.

56. Philadelphia's poor laws were revised in 1828 to limit outdoor relief. It is unclear whether this influenced the practice of taking in babies. Priscilla Ferguson Clement, *Welfare and the Poor in the Nineteenth-Century City: Philadelphia, 1800–1854* (Rutherford, N.J.: Fairleigh Dickinson University Press, 1985), pp. 70, 79. On wages, see Matthew Carey, "Essays on the Public Charities of Philadelphia . . . ," in *Miscellaneous Essays* (Philadelphia: Carey & Hart, 1830), pp. 193–94.

5.

CONSTRUCTING MOTHERS
Scientific Motherhood in the Nineteenth and Twentieth Centuries

RIMA D. APPLE

In the past century and a half, the growing impact of science and medicine in women's daily lives has dramatically transformed mothering practices as the emergence of the ideology of scientific motherhood has emphasized women's increasing reliance on medical and scientific expertise. A compelling illustration of this change is the movement from breast-feeding to physician-directed bottle feeding in the United States between 1890 and 1950; but this change in infant feeding routines is merely one example of the significant shift in women's mothering roles. This essay represents a preliminary analysis of the complex and dynamic relationships that led to mothers' dependence on scientific and medical expertise and experts and focuses in particular on the United States experience.[1] It investigates the various ways, including formal and informal educational structures, cultural icons and mass media, that women learned about mothering and about the shifting idealizations of motherhood.

Scientific motherhood is the insistence that women require expert scientific and medical advice to raise their children healthfully. As the ideology emerged in the nineteenth-century United States, a myriad of interested parties—including educators, social commentators, physicians, health reformers, and mothers themselves—promoted the idea that mothers needed to learn about science and medicine. Women were advised to seek out the most up-to-date and "scientific" information they could find. Doctors were popular sources, but so too were childcare manuals (produced by physicians, scientists, nurses, manufacturers, and lay writers), advice columns, and letters to the editor in women's magazines and general interest journals; and the new field of domestic science or home economics offered classes at all levels of a girl's education.

Reprinted from *Social History of Medicine* 8 (1995): 161–78, by permission of Oxford University Press.

As scientific advice for successful child rearing gained in prominence, the source of this expertise slowly changed. In its early manifestations, scientific motherhood encouraged mothers to find and evaluate information for themselves, to be actively involved in decision making about the health of their families. By the twentieth century, the scientific motherhood ideology had been refined. Increasingly women were told not just that they needed to learn from scientific and medical expertise but that they needed to follow the directions of experts. This aspect of the ideology presented women with a tension-laden contradiction: it made them responsible for the health and welfare of their families, but it denied them control over child rearing. In other words, women were both responsible for their families and incapable of that responsibility. Two advertisements clearly illustrate this transition.

A 1885 Mellin's Food advertisement (figure 1) from the child-care journal *Babyhood* is headed "Advice to Mothers" and the body of the copy cautions readers: "The swelling tide of infantile disease and mortality, resulting from injudicious feeding, the ignorant attempts to supply a substitute for human milk, can only be checked by enlightened parental care." The advertisement goes on to say most reassuringly: "Men of the highest scientific attainments of modern times, both physiologists and chemists, have devoted themselves to careful investigation and experiment in devising a suitable substitute for human milk." The result, of course, was Mellin's Food, a food "worthy the confidence of mothers."

In contrast, another advertisement published in *Parents' Magazine* more than 50 years later (figure 2) has a young father objecting: "But your mother says he's much too young for vegetables!" And the modern mother replies, "Well dear, you'd better argue that with Doctor Evans. He says babies do better if they have vegetables early in life."

These two advertisements share several characteristics. Both are selling food products for infants; both seek to convince mothers to buy the product; both imply that use of the product will ensure good health for the baby; both suggest that science provides the best guide for raising children. Yet, despite these similarities, the two advertisements are quite dissimilar in form and tone. While both, to some extent, play on the emotions of the reader, the emotional content of the 1885 advertisement is more muted. It attempts to sell with gentle persuasion, informing the consumer of a problem, "the swelling tide of infantile disease and mortality," and explaining in rather technical terms that "a compound suitable for the infant's diet must be alkaline in reaction; must be rich in heat-producers, with a proper admixture of albuminoids of a readily digestible nature, together with the necessary salts and moisture." It then claims that Mellin's Food is the solution to that problem. It is a wordy advertisement, fairly typical of the day.

Fig. 1. Mellin's advertisement, *Babyhood* (1885)

The 1938 advertisement attracts the reader with an eye-catching visual of a smiling baby and smiling parents. It graphically demonstrates the result of using Libby's Homogenized Baby Food. The copy in the lower half of the advertisement is informative, "special homogenization—which breaks food cells into tiny particles," but the information imparted in the text is less important than the emotional appeal. Of greater significance is the dialogue in the visual which cites a physician and urges readers to "Ask your doctor." Healthful child rearing would not result from mother's, or grandmother's, experience, this advertisement suggests; nor

Fig. 2. Libby's advertisement, *Parents' Magazine* (1938)

would women study science for themselves. Rather, mothers interested in the health of their families would proudly follow the directions of their doctors.

The differences between these two advertisements reflect technological advances and philosophical developments in magazine advertising, it is true, and, most strikingly, changes in the idealization of motherhood. These advertisements document how the commonly accepted views of motherhood changed and how scientific motherhood was used to promote specific merchandise.

Throughout the nineteenth and into the twentieth century, certain core elements in the idealization of motherhood remained fairly constant. Central was the correspondence between motherhood and womanhood: it was through motherhood that women were to find their identity and life fulfillment. As one writer neatly expressed it in 1886: "For motherhood is the crown and glory of a woman's life. It comes sometimes as a thorny crown, but it is worth all it costs. The blessing of motherhood, which is like nothing else on earth, is placed in compensation over against all the pain and care which so often seem to be woman's peculiar burden. And it compensates."[2] Though new options took some women outside the domestic sphere into the worlds of paid labor and the women's club movement, the overwhelming majority of women became wives and mothers and popular imagery persisted in equating praiseworthy womanhood and the maternal role.[3] "Women's labors and success in the various fields and affairs of life, are calling daily for more and more attention," noted one woman physician in her 1901 manual for women. But, she cautioned, "while we admire her in her new role, with her efforts toward success in society, literature, science, politics and the arts, we must not lose sight of her most divine and sublime mission in life—womanhood and motherhood."[4]

Yet, even with the persistence of this image, over the decades the size of the average American family shrank and women spent less years in child rearing. In 1880, the total fertility rate for white women was 4.24 children. The number decreased over the decades: by 1900 it was 3.56, and by 1930 the rate was 2.45, dropping to 2.19 in 1940.[5]

In addition to declining family size, technological innovations and other social and cultural factors altered women's lives. Devices such as carpet sweepers, vacuum cleaners, refrigerators, and washing machines slowly became available to growing numbers of households. Cookbooks became more "scientific," more exacting, speaking of a tablespoon of an ingredient, not a walnut-sized piece. The emerging commercial food industry further modified American women's cooking tasks, as the variety of canned foods first available in the mid-nineteenth century expanded greatly by the second decade of this century. Furthermore, modern and expanding networks of communication and transportation, including such developments as rural free delivery, mail-order merchandising, mass-circulation magazines, the telephone and railroads, facilitated the movement of goods and services and transformed the domestic experiences of women.[6]

Regarded in a negative light, these changes could appear to devalue the importance of women's work in the home and could encourage women to seek an identity outside the domestic sphere. Concurrently, though, the ideology of scientific motherhood served to elevate the nurture of children to the status of a profession.

The expectation that science should shape domestic work dates from at least as early as the 1840s with the publication of Catharine Beecher's *Treatise on Domestic Economy*. Beecher gathered together in one volume the whole spectrum of domestic tasks, including household maintenance, child rearing, gardening, cooking, cleaning, and nursing, providing scientific rationale for her advice. She did not present herself as an expert in matters such as physiology and health but instead acknowledged the scientific sources she used and implied that any woman could learn from them. For Beecher and her followers, just as men studied and trained for their professions, so must women educate themselves for their life's work, mothering. Women needed to "equip themselves for motherhood as thoughtfully, conscientiously, and zealously as any other scientist prepares himself for an exacting career," opined one early home economist in 1895.[7]

Moreover, as the prestige of science grew in American society, the application of scientific discoveries in the domestic sphere could enhance the status of women's domestic labor.[8] As one mother wrote in an 1899 issue of the popular women's magazine *Ladies' Home Journal,* "Ideal motherhood, you see, is the work not of instinct, but of enlightened knowledge conscientiously acquired and carefully digested. If maternity is an instinct, motherhood is a profession." Women, she insisted, needed to "cultivate a new way of looking at their children";[9] they needed to adopt a male, "scientific" perspective. Scientific motherhood exalted science and devalued instinct and traditional knowledge. A 1915 anonymous poem from *Forecast: A Magazine of Home Efficiency* playfully captures this message:

A Modern Lullaby

Rock-a-bye, baby, up on the bough
You get your milk from a certified cow.
Before your eugenic young parents were wed
They had decided how you should be fed.
Hush-a-bye, baby, on the tree-top,
If grandmother trots you, you tell her to stop;
Shun the trot-horses that your grandmother rides—
It will work harm to your little sides.
Mamma's scientific—she knows all the laws—
She kisses her darling through carbolized gauze.
Rock-a-bye, baby, don't wriggle and squirm:
Nothing is near you that looks like a germ.[10]

Though lighter in tone than other calls for educated motherhood, this poem is representative of the period.

Into the twentieth century, scientific motherhood more and more accentuated the positive necessity of mothercraft education. Giving birth made a woman a mother in the physical, biological sense only; a good mother had to learn about mothering from authoritative sources. The growing belief that science should inform mothering practices could and did lead to the claim that women should receive professional training for motherhood. Declared one mother of six writing in 1919, "It now seems to me that it is about as rational for a woman to learn by experience with her own children to be a good mother, as it would be for a doctor to get his education merely by practicing on his patients. Motherhood offers no less opportunities for success than do the professions of law or medicine."[11] Some commentators carried the analogy further, claiming that untrained mothers were dangerous to their children's health. Acknowledging the importance of "maternal instinct," which she described as "love, patience, and unselfishness," one mother writing in *Good Housekeeping* in 1911 claimed that "maternal instinct left alone succeeds in killing a large proportion of the babies born into this world."[12] Soon, ill health, excessive crying, or any negative characteristic of an infant could be, and was, blamed on maternal ignorance. Counseled the editor of *Parents' Magazine* in 1935, "Doctors, teachers, nutritionists and research workers are daily proving that not mother love alone but mother love in combination with the best that science has to offer in all fields of child care is needed."[13]

Not surprisingly, child-care journals and general women's magazines were among the leading proponents of scientific motherhood from the late nineteenth century onward. As the magazine *Babyhood* stated in 1893, "There is a science in bringing up children and this magazine is the voice of that science."[14] Other journals articulated the ideology of scientific motherhood through articles and advice columns such as "Mother's Corner," edited by a trained nurse for the *Ladies' Home Journal,* and the "Health and Happiness Club," edited by a physician for *Good Housekeeping,* another popular women's magazine.[15] In 1910 in a more targeted move, Dr. Emelyn Coolidge established the "Young Mother's Register" in the *Ladies' Home Journal.* Within one year over five hundred mothers registered; they sent monthly reports to Coolidge and questions that the doctor promised to answer personally. By 1912, Coolidge proudly announced, "The young mother is fast becoming educated, being no longer satisfied to follow the advice of well-meaning but inexperienced neighbors, but preferring to turn to a higher authority for help in solving nursery problems."[16] In this case, and increasingly, that higher authority was the science or medical expert.

In the twentieth century, another source for "scientific motherhood" was government pamphlets, most especially the federal government's pamphlet *Infant Care.* This most popular of all government publications was produced by the Children's Bureau. As a result of reformers' extensive efforts, the federal government had established the bureau in 1912. Originally designed as a fact-finding agency to report on the welfare of children, the reformers who staffed the agency sought to maximize their influence through educational initiatives; among the most important were their publications.[17] *Infant Care* was first published in 1914. By 1940 over 12 million copies had been distributed and by the 1970s over 59 million. People could and did write in for the pamphlet, but it was also frequently sent unsolicited by congressional representatives to their constituents with newborns. The history of the production of *Infant Care* is a good example of the shifting definition of scientific motherhood in this century and the shifting focus of authority in motherhood education.

The first edition of *Infant Care* was written by Mrs. Max West. A widowed mother of five and a graduate of the University of Minnesota, West had turned to writing to support her family. She fused her knowledge of the work of leading physicians with her own practical experience, a combination that reflected the Children's Bureau's belief that children's health encompassed more than medicine.[18] Following the initial distribution of the pamphlet, the medical profession pressured Julia Lathrop, chief of the Children's Bureau, to involve medical practitioners more directly in the production of bureau publications dealing with the techniques of child care. They insisted that she appoint a Medical Advisory Committee to review all such publications. The committee included representatives of the American Pediatric Society, the Pediatric Section of the American Medical Association, and the American Child Hygiene Association. In a letter date 9 October 1919, the committee claimed that *Infant Care* was "merely a compilation" and as such should not have an author's name attached. West, bowing to the pressure exerted on Lathrop by the committee, accepted the decision to delete her name. By 1921, she appears only in the letter of transmittal, not on the title page. Shortly thereafter she disappears from the publication; by the late 1920s, all the compilers of *Infant Care* were physicians.[19] In the 1931 edition of *Infant Care,* readers learned that "the care of a baby is a great responsibility, but it can be carried successfully if the parents regularly seek the advice of a physician trained in the care of infants. . . . The doctor should be the mother's guide, and this bulletin is intended to help her carry out his orders intelligently."[20] No longer were mothers envisioned as actively involved in making decisions about their child-rearing practices; they were now to follow the orders of the physician.

Books, mainly child-care manuals and home medical manuals, also advocated the ideology of scientific motherhood. Dr. L. Emmett Holt's book, though certainly not the first, was one of the most popular. First issued in 1894, Holt's *Care and Feeding of Children* went through 75 printings, 12 revisions, and several translations by the 1920s. It was taken up by his son and, at least as late as 1957, was in print under the auspices of *Good Housekeeping*. Many other physicians published baby care books with varying success. And the tradition continues today, with *Dr. Spock's Baby and Child Care* in its fifth edition.[21] Also, physician-authored manuals face stiff competition from child-care books produced by psychologists and lay writers.

In addition to publications, women learned about scientific motherhood and received training in other, more immediate settings. Slowly in the early years of the twentieth century and then rapidly in the 1920s and 1930s, school systems all over the country instituted home economics or domestic science classes. Often these courses were mandatory for girls. Educators rationalized that "it is expected that every woman will have at some time in her life the care of babies and young children. It is not reasonable to expect that she should know how to care for them wisely without definite instruction and training in the skill and art of mother craft."[22] Domestic science instruction was preparation for a girl's lifework.

Middle-class home economists promoted their subject as beneficial for the future of individual girls and for society in general. They viewed with alarm what they and many other contemporaries saw as the breakdown of American family life. All around they saw a society disrupted by increased urbanization, industrialization, and immigration. They believed they identified the remedy. Ellen Richards, founder of the Lake Placid Conferences, the first professional organization of home economists in the United States, confidently promoted home economics as "nothing less than an effort to save our social fabric from what seems inevitable disintegration."[23] This social reform outlook continued to influence the calls for home economics education. Declared one writer in the *Journal of Home Economics* in 1919, "Much of what is unwise in the rearing of children is due to the indifference, the inertia, and the lack of insight that arise from unpreparedness for the responsibility. Each generation of graduates from the eighth grade and high school courses in home economics should increase the number of homes in which babies and children will have better chances for survival and health."[24]

Contemporary curriculum reform movements also reflected this belief in the efficacy of education to alleviate social problems.[25] In its 1910 report on the place of industries in public education, the National Education Association clearly articulated the role leading educators saw for girls in American society. They explained that courses for girls should "enable them, thru the right sort of home-making training, to enter homes of their own, able to assume the most sacred duties with an intelligent preparation, and to perpetuate the type of home that will bring about the highest standard of health and morals."[26]

Alternatively, mothercraft education was promoted through Little Mothers' classes, usually offered by city public health departments. These courses were first established in 1910 by Dr. S. Josephine Baker in New York City. Her interest in educating girls in mothercraft was spurred by the realization that many young children in the slums of New York were left for long periods of time in the care of only slightly older sisters. Baker had two goals in developing Little Mothers' Clubs. First, she wanted the girls to receive practical instruction in child care, which she believed would improve the health of their younger charges. Second, she intended that these young girls would, in turn, instruct their mothers and neighbors in scientific motherhood, making the girls, in Baker's words, "our most efficient missionaries." By 1912, some 20,000 girls attended weekly meetings of the city's Little Mothers' Leagues.[27] Other states followed suit. For example, Wisconsin offered a series of ten one-hour lessons on infant hygiene for school-age girls, starting in the 1920s. If the student successfully completed the course, passed an oral or written examination, and demonstrated her expertise in bathing an infant and mixing a bottle formula, she received a diploma naming her a "Wisconsin's Little Mother."[28] The photographic records of the Rockefeller Archives document the extensive networks of homemakers' clubs established by the General Education Board in the years 1902 to 1964.[29] Courses provided women and girls in elementary and secondary schools with training in child-care practices informed by contemporary scientific knowledge.

Manufacturers too, as seen in figures 1 and 2 above, recognized the power of the image of scientific motherhood and produced advertisements that stressed the importance of scientific advice. More and more through the first half of the twentieth century, the use of scientific and medical "experts," usually men, dispensing scientific advice, sold a variety of consumer products. While flattering the readers' perceptiveness ("Your own intelligence tells you"), one 1928 advertisement (figure 3) establishes the critical role of physicians in selecting an appropriate toilet tissue by describing the "three requirements doctors say toilet tissue must have." Furthermore, the advertisement insists, because of the medical endorsements, there is no doubt that "housewives should insist on [these requirements] in buying toilet tissue." Clearly, this and many other advertisements of the time seem to be saying that in order to purchase the appropriate bathroom tissue and any number of other products, women need direction from medical experts. Another example is the 1938 advertisement for a set of course material (figure 4). The publisher uses a combination of negative appeal (the disadvantages of not having purchased the advertised product) with the promise of a hopeful future (namely, the success of scientifically directed child care). Modern, up-to-date mothers, this advertisement seems to say, will replace traditional advice networks with scientific advice. The statement that "instead of blindly following instinct alone or laboriously duplicating the tedious methods of previous generations, you turn to specialists and

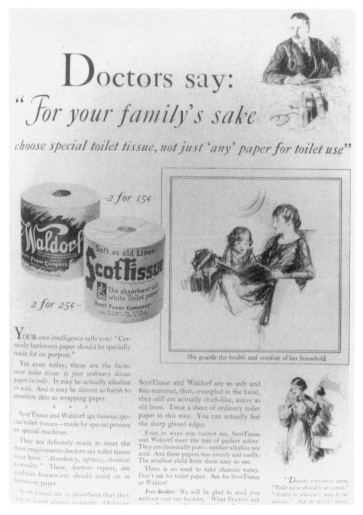

Fig. 3. Scott advertisement, *Good Housekeeping* (1928)

authority" implies that without them mothering would be a dismal failure. "Specialists and authority" replace "instinct" and the knowledge of "previous generations." The appeal to science is strengthened by the grandmother extolling the virtues and benefits of modern motherhood. The copy underscores her advice: "Add science to love and be a 'perfect mother.'"

The extent to which scientific motherhood permeated U.S. culture raises several crucial questions. In the face of all these manuals and pamphlets and classes and advertisements, how did women react to the ideology of scientific motherhood? How did they participate in its development and spread? How did they in-

Fig. 4. "Extension course on the care and feeing of young children" advertisement, *Parents' Magazine* (1938)

fluence its shape and scope? Though these queries demand further study, some preliminary answers are clear at this time.

Evidently women came to accept the essence of the ideology: that successful and healthful child rearing should be informed by scientific expertise. It is also evident that women actively sought out expert advice. Women acted on the basic tenets of scientific motherhood, namely, that while women maintained the primary responsibility for infant and child care, they were dependent on experts, scientific and medical, to tell them and to teach them how best to raise their children.

Ultimately, they believed that the most successful child rearing was done under scientifically informed medical supervision. This is not to say that all women everywhere and at all times slavishly followed the dictates of scientific and medical experts in raising their children. They could and did temper their faith in scientific expertise with greater or lesser doses of common sense and self-confidence in their own abilities. Indications that women accepted scientific motherhood and the balancing act are, on the whole, indirect and impressionistic.

Popular culture presents some hints about this balancing act. In the 1939 comedy film *Bachelor Mother,* Ginger Rogers is self-confident in her care of an infant; yet, as David Niven helpfully reads to her from a child-care manual written by a doctor with "twenty years' experience," she begins to doubt her ability. When Niven reads that Rogers should rub some warm food into the child's navel, she is torn between her methods, which have satisfied the child, and this "expert advice." She starts to lay the child down and undress him as if to follow the doctor's instructions. Then rethinking the situation, she takes the book from Niven and discovers that in his reading several pages had stuck together, and the instructions he read had concerned a treatment for colic. This scene captures very clearly the confusion that many women felt; they appreciated scientifically based advice but were perplexed when the "expert" opinion contradicted their own proven abilities and common sense. Though an example from Hollywood, this film is one indication of the widespread recognition of the basic tenets of scientific motherhood in the United States.[30]

The multitude of child-care books based on the ideology is another sign of its acceptance. These publications were extremely popular, running through many editions each. For example, Spock's book first appeared in May 1946. Within three years, paperback annual sales reached one million copies. Despite stiff competition from a multitude of other child-care manuals, by 1985 Spock's had sold over 30 million copies in 38 languages.[31] While historians may debate to what extent Spock's publication signified a major shift in the philosophy of child-care advice, in one very significant aspect at least he represents continuity with his predecessors. In the opening of his book, he counsels readers, "You know more than you think you do. . . . Bringing up your child won't be a complicated job, if you take it easy, trust your own instincts, and follow the directions that your doctor gives you."[32] Some analysts of the 1940s and 1950s consider that the popularity of books such as Spock's is to some extent class-related; however, additional research is needed in this area. It is clear that the audience for much of this child-care literature was the literate middle-class; yet, Holt's book was initially conceived as a catechism for working-class nursemaids employed by upper-class mothers in New York City and was quickly revised for the use of the *employers,* rather than the *employees.*

The many letters received over the years by the Children's Bureau in praise of its pamphlet *Infant Care* also demonstrate the complex interaction of class and scientific motherhood. This correspondence came from rural and urban mothers and cut across class and, to some extent, racial and ethnic groups.[33] Women's acclaim for the bureau's publications reached beyond the internal bureau files. One mother, writing in *Cosmopolitan* in 1940, declared, "My constant companion was that Bible of the 1940 young mother, the infant Care pamphlet printed by the United States Government. The title was just too prosaic for the singing hearts of the mothers, so someone rechristened it The Good Book, and by that name it is generally known."[34] Other letters and articles in women's magazines and child-care journals talk about raising their children "by the book" and counseled other readers to use child-care manuals. In late nineteenth-century women's magazines, readers frequently advised each other through letters columns. This sisterly support continued into the twentieth century, but the content of the advice slowly shifted. In the earlier period, women were more likely to use their own experiences to instruct others. Gradually, letters relied less on women's practical experience and began to reflect more what women were reading and the advice they received from physicians. Consequently, by the second quarter of this century, mothers wrote about "what my doctor told me to do" and directed others to medical practitioners.[35]

While letter writers and authors of articles in women's magazines were primarily middle-class, the students in public school home economics classes spanned a wider range. Since home economics educators, as well as public health officials who established Little Mother's Clubs, were very pointed about the role of their courses in the uplifting and "Americanizing" of working-class and immigrant girls, the role of these educational efforts in the spread and popularity of scientific motherhood requires a complex, nuanced study of the education of girls in the period.[36]

In the first four decades of this century, there were a few surveys that attempted to ascertain actual child-rearing practices among various class and ethnic groups. These investigations report that women read advice printed in sources such as Holt and *Infant Care* and that they followed what they read. The Lynds' classic study of American culture, *Middletown*, disclosed the importance of published sources, classes, and health practitioners to mothers raising children in Muncie, Indiana, though the specific forms popular with mothers varied among classes.[37] My own interviews with women document their growing appreciation and reliance on scientific and medical expertise. Mothers who attended child-care classes at the university saved their books and notes and later read them again while raising their children. One of my informants fondly remembered a University of Wisconsin course popularly called "The Bride's Course," which included instruction in prenatal and postnatal care. Years later she continued to refer to her class notes in raising her children.

The reasons for mothers' increasing adherence to scientific motherhood from the late nineteenth century to our own time require analysis beyond the scope of this essay. However, preliminary research suggests several factors that begin to explain why women turned more and more frequently to medical expertise and experts. Throughout the period, the prestige of science and medicine grew in American culture.[38] Moreover, declining family size along with a fear of continuing high infant mortality and morbidity rates made each child that much more precious; one sought out the best, most up-to-date information for the sake of one's children. Then, too, economic considerations encouraged the spread of scientific motherhood in both the commercial and professional worlds. Manufacturers found that promoting "science" helped to sell products; since scientific motherhood remained a popular theme for advertisers, they must have believed it was a successful tool for advancing a variety of products.[39] Doctors found that pediatrics provided a lucrative portal to an expanding practice, as the specialty of pediatrics grew and as more general practitioners incorporated pediatrics into their practices.[40]

A most critical and as yet not fully examined component in the growing acceptance of scientific motherhood is gender. True, the experts were most frequently depicted as male, usually physicians; science, medicine, and professionalism in general were described in male terms. Yet, scientific motherhood is more than an expression of male physicians intervening in the lives of female patients. Whether viewed as passive or as active recipients of medical knowledge, mothers were actively involved in caring for their children in their homes, negotiating between the instructions of medical practitioners and the exigencies and beliefs of their own lives. Moreover, though medicine and medical science were gendered male, the insistence on the importance of medical expertise and experts came from a multitude of sources, including, very significantly, the emerging field of home economics. It is important to remember here that home economics was the only science gendered female—that is, a niche within which women could pursue science.[41] Therefore, gender must be analyzed not only in terms of a male medical system. An important question that is beginning to receive much more historical attention addresses the relationship between home economics and the ideology of scientific motherhood in patriarchal American culture.

The development of scientific motherhood was not limited to the United States. It appeared in various forms in many parts of the globe, including Europe, other parts of North America, and the Antipodes. For example, Mein Smith's close study of one town in Australia attempts to document some mothering practices in a similar time of transition.[42] Her evidence implies that though there is no simplistic link between prescription and practice, changes in mothers' routines and beliefs over time do reflect changes in prescribed routines and beliefs, many of which are similar to the elements in the U.S. form of scientific motherhood. The concern for motherhood education is also apparent in Klaus's study of France and the United States.[43] She elucidates structural, political, and cultural differences that affect the development and implementation of maternal and child health public policy, in many regards the political expression of scientific motherhood. Such work points to the importance of expanding beyond national borders. Scientific motherhood was a broad-based, socially sanctioned ideology prescribing women's relationship to medical expertise and experts. Subsequent research will undoubtedly disclose how local political, social, and cultural factors of different countries, counties, cities, and even neighborhoods shaped the ideology in unique ways and provided women with distinctive avenues to accommodate and resist the direction of medical experts.[44]

Under the tenets of scientific motherhood, woman's place remained in the home, where mothers were accorded full responsibility for all things domestic, including, most significantly, the care and raising of children. At the same time, and with increasing intensity, scientific motherhood denigrated women's skills and knowledge by insisting that mothers needed the assistance of medical and scientific authorities in order to carry out their maternal duties successfully. The development of scientific motherhood did not represent a sharp break with past practices, but rather a gradual realignment of power relationships within the domestic setting. The nineteenth century promoted the image of woman as "queen of the nursery," responsible for and in control of her domain. Through the late nineteenth and early twentieth centuries, increasing numbers of advisers insisted on the importance of scientific expertise to the successful accomplishment of her tasks. By the second third of this century, the form of the expertise had shifted from counsel to direction. The image of the scientific mother changed from the queen of the nursery to the servant of science. By the twentieth century, scientific motherhood endowed the image of women with positive and negative attributes: responsibility implies independence of action and strength—that mothers are important in child care; yet the need for assistance suggests dependence and weakness—that women lack intelligence.

Scientific motherhood was not and is not a disembodied, reified theoretical construct. It was and is defined by science, culture, and society. It reinforced and

reinforces, it reproduced and reproduces patriarchal sex roles: women in the domestic sphere, men outside; women instructed by scientific and medical authorities—males. Scientific motherhood was and is disseminated through cultural
forms. The study of the development and spread of scientific motherhood can help
us to understand the interrelationships between science, medicine, and social roles.

NOTES

I wish to thank Diane Worzala, Anne Crowther, and an anonymous reviewer for their helpful
comments on earlier versions of this paper.

1. This study is part of a comprehensive, on-going investigation of "scientific motherhood," *"Science + Love": A History of Scientific Motherhood, 1850–1990.*

2. L. W. Palmer, "The Coming Guest," *Babyhood* 2 (1886): 313.

3. In the United States, only a small minority of married women entered the paid labor
force. In 1890, approximately 4 percent of all married women were employed outside the home.
By 1900 this figure had grown to only 5 percent and by 1940 had reached barely 15 percent. S.
H. Van Horn, *Women, Work and Fertility, 1890–1986* (New York, 1988). According to statistics
analyzed by Weiner, approximately 770,000 married women were in the labor force in 1910. L.
Y. Weiner, *From Working Girl to Working Mother: The Female Labor Force in the United States,
1820–1980* (Chapel Hill, 1985). In contrast, many women, especially middle-class women, both
white and African American, joined the expanding club movements. Organizations ranged
from literary and self-help groups to those involved in social reform. In the 1890s they combined
to form a national umbrella organization, the General Federation of Women's Clubs, which by
1910 claimed a membership of over one million. For more on women's organizations, see A. F.
Scott, *Natural Allies: Women's Associations in American History* (Urbana, 1993); T. Skocpol, *Protecting Soldiers and Mothers: The Political Origins of Social Policy in the United States* (Cambridge,
Mass., 1992), esp. pp. 328–33.

4. M. R. Melendy, *Perfect Womanhood for Maidens—Wives—Mothers* ([Chicago?],
1901).

5. It rose again in 1950 to 3.0. For more on fertility rates, see D. S. Smith, "Family Limitation, Sexual Control, and Domestic Feminism in Victorian America," in M. S. Hartman and
L. Banner, eds., *Clio's Consciousness Raised: New Perspectives on the History of Women* (New York,
1974), pp. 119–36; Van Horn, *Women, Work, and Fertility, 1900–1986.*

6. For more on the impact of these changes on women's lives, see E. Arnold, ed., *Voices of
American Homemakers* (Bloomington, Ind., 1985); E. T. May, *Homeward Bound: American
Families in the Cold War Era* (New York, 1988), esp. pp. 162–82; R. S. Cowan, *More Work for
Mother: The Ironies of Household Technology from the Open Hearth to the Microwave* (New York,
1983); L. Shapiro, *Perfection Salad: Women and Cooking at the Turn of the Century* (New York,
1986).

7. E. B. Dietrick, "A Scientifically Trained Baby," *New England Kitchen Magazine [Home
Science]* 2 (1895): 179–80.

8. B. Berch, "Scientific Management in the Home: The Empress's New Clothes," *Journal of American Culture* 3 (1980): 440–45; Shapiro, *Perfection Salad;* B. Ehrenreich and D. English, *For Her Own Good: 150 Years of the Experts' Advice to Women* (New York, 1979); K. K. Sklar, *Catharine Beecher: A Study in American Domesticity* (New York, 1973), esp. pp. 151–67; B. J. Harris, *Beyond Her Sphere: Women and the Professions in American History* (Westport, Conn., 1978), esp. pp. 32–72; L. M. Newman, *Men's Ideas/Women's Realities: Popular Science, 1870–1915* (New York, 1985), pp. xxiv–xxvi, 156–91.

9. H. W. Moody, "The True Meaning of Motherhood," *Ladies' Home Journal* 16, no. 6 (1899): 12; J. Stewart, "Is the Mother Ready for the Baby? Training Versus 'Instinct' and 'Experience,'" *Ladies' Home Journal* 30, no. 2 (1913): 76.

10. *Forecast: A Magazine of Home Efficiency* 9 (1915): 391.

11. C. V. Gulick, introduction to M. L. Read, *The Motherhood Manual* (Boston, 1919), p. ix.

12. "A Trained Mother," "Maternal Instinct Run Riot," *Good Housekeeping* 52 (1911): 245–47.

13. C. S. Littledale, "Thanks to the Quintuplets," *Parents' Magazine* 10, no. 10 (Oct. 1935): 11.

14. *Babyhood* 9, no. 103 (1893): xii. By 1928 an article in *Parents' Magazine* pointed to thousands of research scientists, doctors, dietitians, and nurses who were trying to determine how to give children the best possible start in life. Yet, their endeavors would mean nothing "unless the mother picks up the work there and carries it wisely." A. Pierce, "What to Feed the Baby and Why," *Parents' Magazine* 3, no. 5 (1928): 16–17, 60, 61.

15. The nurse was Elizabeth Robinson Scovil; the physician, Josephine Hemenway Kenyon. For more on their columns and the booklets they provided mothers, see R. D. Apple, *Mothers and Medicine: A Social History of Infant Feeding, 1890–1950* (Madison, 1987), esp. chaps. 6 and 7.

16. E. L. Coolidge, "The Young Mother's Guide," *Ladies' Home Journal* 28, no. 1 (1911): 37; Coolidge, "The Young Mother's Guide," *Ladies Home Journal* 29, no. 1 (1912): 65; S. H. Steinberg, *Reformer in the Marketplace: Edward W. Bok and the "Ladies Home Journal"* (Baton Rouge, 1979), p. 36. Similar articles and correspondence columns appear in other journals, such as *Babyhood, Mother's Friend, Home Science,* and *Farmer's Wife.*

17. For more on the Children's Bureau and its relationship with mothers across the country, see M. Ladd-Taylor, *Raising a Baby the Government Way: Mothers' Letters to the Children's Bureau, 1915–1932* (New Brunswick, N.J., 1986).

18. Ibid., pp. 33–34.

19. N. Weiss, "Mother, the Invention of Necessity: Dr. Spock's *Baby and Child Care,*" *American Quarterly* 29 (1977): 519–46.

20. U.S. Children's Bureau, *Infant Care,* Bureau Pub. No. 8, 1931.

21. B. Spock, *The Common Sense Book of Baby and Child Care* (New York, 1945, 1946); B. Spock and M. B. Rothenberg, *Dr. Spock's Baby and Child Care* (New York, 1985).

22. C. A. Harper, in the introduction to G. S. Hasbroucke, *Handbook for Teachers of Infant Hygiene Classes* (Madison, 1927), p. 8. For more on home economics, see R. D. Apple, "Liberal Arts or Vocational Training: Home Economics Education for Girls," in S. Stage and V. B.

Vincenti, eds., *Rethinking Women and Home Economics in the Twentieth Century* (Ithaca, forth-coming); and Apple, "The Science of Homemaking: A History of Middle School Home Eco-nomics to 1970," in F. M. Smith and C. O. Hausafus, eds., *The Education of Early Adolescents: Home Economics in the Middle School,* 14th Yearbook of the American Home Economics Asso-ciation (Peoria, 1994).

23. E. Richards, 1909, quoted in J. Rury, "Vocationalism for Home and Work: Women's Education in the United States, 1880–1930," in B. E. McClellan and W. Reese, eds., *The Social History of American Education* (Urbana, 1988), p. 237.

24. A. L. Binzel, "For the Homemaker: Making Children Worth While," *Journal of Home Economics* 11 (1919): 28. See also E. S. Eppright and E. S. Ferguson, *A Century of Home Econom-ics at Iowa State University: A Proud Past, a Lively Present, a Future Promise* (Ames, 1971), pp. 86–87.

25. B. Brenzel, C. Roberts-Gersch, and J. Wittner, "Becoming Social: School Girls and Their Culture between the Two World Wars," *Journal of Early Adolescence* 5 (1985): 480. This de-veloped against a background of a changing school population. In 1900, only 59 percent of all children between 5 and 17 attended schools; by 1928, this proportion had grown to 80 percent. Several interrelated factors induced the sharp increase in school attendance. Before the turn of the century, secondary education was primarily college oriented. In the twentieth century, the occupational structure of the U.S. economy created increasing numbers of jobs that demanded high school education, if not graduation, and evolving elementary and high schools curricula were slowly, though unevenly, incorporating vocational education. The high school was no longer an elite institution for the college-bound; it was a popular institution with a pragmatic outlook: to prepare women and men for their roles in society. Rury, "Vocationalism," p. 252.

26. National Education Association, "Report of the Committee on the Place of Industries in Public Education to the National Council of Education," July 1910 (Chicago), p. 110. See also C. C. Greer, "When, How Much, and to Whom Should Home Economics Be Taught?" *Jour-nal of Home Economics* 11 (1919): 235–41.

27. S. J. Baker, *Fighting for Life* (New York, 1939), pp. 126–37.

28. Hasbroucke, *Handbook for Teachers,* p. 10; E. S. Whitcomb, *Typical Child Care and Parenthood Education in Home Economics Departments* (Washington, D.C.: U.S. Bureau of Ed-ucation, 1927), pp. 8–9.

29. *Rockefeller Archive Center Newsletter,* Fall 1993, p. 11.

30. *Bachelor Mother* proved to be a very popular film. Remade in 1956 as *Bundle of Joy,* star-ring Debbie Reynolds and Eddie Fisher, most of the dialogue remained, but a few songs were added for Fisher. Other films also insisted that mothers needed education. See, for example, *Rock-A-Bye Baby,* a 1958 film starring Jerry Lewis. Faced with needing to prove that he is a "real mother," Lewis is able to attend the University Child Care Clinic of Chicago, an institution ded-icated to educating mothers. He is the only male student.

See also R. D. Apple, ed., "Special Section on History of Science in Film," *Isis* 84 (1993): 750–74, esp. R. D. Apple and M. W. Apple, "Screening Science," pp. 750–54; E. A. Kaplan, *Motherhood and Representation: The Mother in Popular Culture and Melodrama* (London, 1992).

31. For more on Spock's success, see G. Collins, "Heir Apparent to Dr. Spock," *New York Times,* 1 March 1985.

32. B. Spock, *The Common Sense Book of Baby and Child Care* (New York, 1945, 1946), p. 3. This advice can be found in all subsequent editions as well.

33. For an indication of the range of correspondents in the Children's Bureau files, see Ladd-Taylor, *Raising a Baby the Government Way.*

34. J.B., "My $100 Baby," *Cosmopolitan* 108, no. 6 (1940): 54.

35. For more on these writings, see Apple, *Mothers and Medicine,* esp. pp. 135–66.

36. Apple, "Liberal Arts or Vocational Training"; and Apple, "The Science of Homemaking."

37. R. S. Lynd and H. M. Lynd, *Middletown: A Study in Contemporary American Culture* (New York, 1929), pp. 149–52; *The Young Child in the Home: A Survey of Three Thousand American Families,* section 3: *Education and Training,* White House Conference on Child Health and Protection, Committee on the Infant and Preschool Child, J. E. Anderson, chairman (New York, 1936), pp. 73–80.

38. J. C. Burnham, "American Medicine's Golden Age: What Happened to It?" in J. W. Leavitt and R. L. Numbers, eds., *Sickness and Health in America,* 2d ed. (Madison, 1985), pp. 248–58; H. Hart, "Changing Social Attitudes and Interests," *Recent Social Trends in the United States: Report of the President's Research Committee on Social Trends* (New York, 1933), pp. 382–97.

39. Roland Marchard, *Advertising the American Dream* (Berkeley, 1985).

40. R. Stevens, *American Medicine and the Public Interest* (New Haven, 1971); S. A. Halpern, *Pediatrics: The Social Dynamics of Professionalism, 1880–1980* (Berkeley, 1988).

41. R. D. Apple, "Science Gendered: Nutrition in the United States, 1840–1940," in H. Kammminga and A. Cunningham, eds., *The Science and Culture of Nutrition,* Wellcome Institute Series in the History of Medicine (Amsterdam, forthcoming).

42. P. Mein Smith, "Mothers, Babies, and the Mothers and Babies Movement: Australia through Depression and War," *Social History of Medicine* 6 (1993): 51–83. See also K. M. Reiger, *The Disenchantment of the Home: Modernizing the Australian Family, 1880–1940* (Melbourne, 1985); and R. A. Meckel, *Save the Babies: American Public Health Reform and the Prevention of Infant Mortality, 1850–1920* (Baltimore, 1990).

43. A. Klaus, *Every Child a Lion: The Origins of Maternal and Infant Health Policy in the United States and France, 1890–1920* (Ithaca, 1993). Examples of other works that provide data for developing a comparative analysis include K. Melby, "The Housewife Ideology in Norway between the Two World Wars," *Scandinavian Journal of History* 14 (1989): 181–93; C. Dyhouse, "Working-Class Mothers and Infant Mortality in England, 1895–1914," *Journal of Social History* 12 (1978): 248–67; J. Lewis, *The Politics of Motherhood: Child and Maternal Welfare in England, 1900–1939* (London, 1980); D. Dwork, *War Is Good for Babies and Other Young Children: A History of the Infant and Child Welfare Movement in England, 1898–1918* (London, 1986); R. M. McKinlay, "Where Would We Be without Them? Motherhood and Self-Definition in New Zealand" (Ph.D. thesis, Victoria University, Wellington, 1983); M. Tennant, "Natural Directors: The New Zealand Movement for Sexual Differentiation in Education during the Early Twentieth Century," in B. Brookes, C. Macdonald, and M. Tennant, eds., *Women in History: Essays on European Women in New Zealand* (Wellington, 1986), pp. 87–100; E. Olssen, "Truby King and the Plunket Society: An Analysis of a Prescriptive Ideology," *New Zealand Journal of History*

15 (1981): 3–23; Mein Smith, "Mothers, Babies, and the Mothers and Babies Movement"; Reiger, *The Disenchantment of the Home;* K. Arnup, *Education for Motherhood: Advice for Mothers in Twentieth-Century Canada* (Toronto, 1994); C. R. Comacchio, *Nations Are Built of Babies: Saving Ontario's Mothers and Children, 1990–1940* (Montreal, 1993).

44. R. D. Apple, "The Medicalization of Infant Feeding in the United States and New Zealand: Two Countries, One Experience," *Journal of Human Lactation* 10 (1994): 31–37.

6.

CONFESSIONS OF LOSS
Maternal Grief in True Story, *1920–1985*

WENDY SIMONDS

There has been a recent surge in professional interest in women's experiences of miscarriage, stillbirth, and infant death. Fueled by the medical profession's technological quest for the "perfect"—well-planned, disease- and defect-free, irreplaceable—baby, this interest primarily concerns the losses of white middle- and upper-middle-class, well-educated parents. The popular psychological literature has addressed the grief of middle- and upper-class women, but not that of working-class women. The new literature unanimously deplores the lack of sensitivity toward these experiences in parents' lives (especially those of mothers) on the part of the medical profession and society in general (Borg and Lasker 1981; Friedman and Gradstein 1982; Pizer and Palinski 1980; Schiff 1977).

Women's popular literature has served as a forum for the grief of mothers since the early nineteenth century, when women's magazines began their climb to success. During the 1800s, these magazines published a plethora of poetry about women's reactions to infant death. From its inception in 1919, *True Story,* the first American confessional magazine, has addressed this topic. *True Story* serves as a transitional link between nineteenth-century religious and poetic writing on infant death and twentieth-century professional and popular psychological writings on maternal grief. Unlike most other past and current successful women's magazines, *True Story* is marketed expressly for working-class women and offers them the advice and solace the psychological literature provides middle- and upper-class women. The presence of such material in *True Story* (during a time when more mainstream women's periodicals remained virtually mute on this subject) testifies to the timelessness of the theme of maternal grief.

Reprinted from *Gender and Society* 2 (2): 149–71, copyright © 1988 by *Gender and Society.* Reprinted by permission of Sage Publications, Inc.

The Story of *True Story*

Bernarr Macfadden began publishing *True Story* in 1919. The cover of the first issue featured a photograph of a man and a woman looking into each other's eyes,
captioned "And Their Love Turned to Hatred!" and "swarms of people put their
double dimes down on the newsstands to find out why" (Macfadden and Gauvreau
1953, p. 222). According to her biography of her ex-husband, the original idea for
True Story came from Mary Macfadden. In prophetic reverie, she describes her
"thirty-million-dollar idea" that would change the course of magazine fiction in
America: "Let's get out a magazine to be called *True Story*, written by its own readers in the first person. This has never been done before. I believe it will have a wide
readership. It might lead to all sorts of other publications in the same vein" (Macfadden and Gauvreau 1953, pp. 218–19).

After a year, *True Story* had gained a circulation of one million (Oursler 1929,
p. 226). Currently, it has a readership of 5,958,000. Its publication was soon followed by *True Romance*, and eventually the Macfadden Women's Group included
True Story, True Romance, True Confession, True Experience, and *True Love. True
Story* has always been the biggest seller of the group. It has long endeavored to separate itself from less reputable publications. Originally, it hired a board of clergymen to serve as "moral censors" of the magazine (Macfadden and Gauvreau
1953, p. 234), and early writers were made to sign affidavits swearing their stories
were true.

The narrators of *True Story* are almost always women, but in my sample, there
are two informative pieces written by men ("Babies Need Not Die" and "A Baby in
Your Arms . . . or MISCARRIAGE?") and another credited to "*True Story's* Child
Care Clinic" ("If SIDS Strikes Your Baby").

The problems that arise in the stories are inseparable from women's involve-
ments with men. *True Story* writers tend to employ a standard Gothic theme—
women are constantly the victims of situations in which they feel trapped or
helpless. Unlike Gothic heroines, whose behavior is usually above reproach under
uncontrollable and miserable circumstances, *True Story* heroines often lose control
of themselves and commit evil (often sexual) deeds for which they must later atone.
True Story adventures are stripped of the usual elegant Gothic trimmings. Instead
of the young orphaned governess terrorized in a venerable, sea-surrounded castle
by a lustful widowed employer, the *True Story* heroine might be married to a
plumber who continually gets drunk and beats her. Out of loneliness, she might
begin an affair with the manager of her supermarket, become pregnant, and miscarry, all without (and in fear of) her husband's knowledge. Both Gothic heroines
and *True Story* narrators eventually manage to extricate themselves, or to be extri-

cated from, the terrifying circumstances that made the stories worth telling in the first place.

True Story characters are nearly always white. Macfadden was the first magazine publisher to use live models, instead of conventional illustrations, to pose for the photographs that accompany the stories. Photographs accompanying the stories are of white models unless it is explicitly stated that blacks or people of other minority groups are the subjects of a story, which occurred only once in my sample ("I Gave Birth to a Black Baby").

Narrators often write that they are motivated by altruism and compassion, especially in circumstances involving death, loss, and grief. They send in stories because they have learned something from their experience and hope, among other things, to save other women some time and difficulty in their own lives. Resignation is often offered as an answer to women's problems—a grin-and-bear-it attitude that assumes a better time will come. *True Story* writers teach their readers that self-blame can be best mitigated by self-sacrificing service.

Like the evangelical poetry that predates it, which was often meant as a token of sympathy from one woman to another, *True Story* narratives about infant or fetal loss are intended as affirming didactic tools by their writers. In "Just in Time," the author begins, "It seems that almost every one has had some experience in his life . . . that is worth telling. By doing so, he might, perhaps, warn another. That is what I hope to do in writing of a most trying experience" (Feb. 1925, p. 65). Authors' interjections recur fairly frequently, recalling nineteenth-century novelists' countless "Dear Reader!" exclamations:

> To those who have loved and lost babies of their own, an explanation of my grief will be unnecessary; to others of you, the scratching of this pen for the next hundred years could not possibly express the blackness of the depths into which I was plunged. ("No Children Wanted," Dec. 1932, p. 8)

> When my heart hurts and I don't think I can go on, I like to read a poem from a book my sister gave me after Jenny's death. It helps me and maybe it can help someone else who has lost a loved one. ("A Doll for Jenny," Mar. 1985, p. 98)

True Story narrators are no different from many writers of the consolation literature of the 1970s and 1980s who find the impetus to write to help other women in their own experiences of child loss or miscarriage. In *Coping with a Miscarriage*, Christine O'Brien Palinski writes: "My experiences over the past two and a half years have been painful and difficult. A portion of that difficulty came from the lack of support available for women who miscarry. . . . I searched for things to read in the popular literature, in medical books, in women's magazines, but met with nothing but frustration. . . . I know what a comfort it would have been *the first time* to sit and read the information that took me two years to accumulate" (Pizer and Palinski 1980, pp. 19–20).

True Story narrators' efforts to help readers do not go unrewarded. Letters about specific stories or addressed to their writers demonstrate that a community of readers exists. For instance, in September 1982, "Ginny" writes of a traumatic miscarriage in "Why Couldn't He Have Lived? How I Found the Courage to Accept My Loss." She describes the insensitivity of everyone but one friend whose conversations helped Ginny face the reality of her child's death. In December, a woman who calls herself P. F. writes, "Ginny, don't ever give up praying and hoping for another child. The Lord took your son for reasons of his own." P. F. explains that she has had nine miscarriages and two living children: "I thank the Lord every day for giving them both to me" (p. 2). P. F. affirms Ginny's right to grieve by telling of her own similar but prolonged experience of miscarriage and urges Ginny to seek comfort where P. F. feels she has been satisfied. In most letters printed in *True Story,* readers express gratitude for stories that touched them by recalling their own experiences and problems and that made them feel less alone.

In a recent promotional description of *True Story* titled "About the Magazine," marketers assert that it "is edited specifically to working class women. . . . largely from the homes of hourly paid workers in manufacturing, mining, transportation, etc." *True Story* promoters present its readers as uninterested in "white-collar" middle-class magazines that "are written almost entirely for, and about, a kind of society that is largely alien" to them. They claim to offer advertisers a unique brand of women readers who, despite their access to less money, "have more discretionary spending power than their white-collar sisters."

Its promoters have always treated the successful reader-writer chemistry of *True Story* as a miraculous and mysterious relationship with which they would never interfere. In a pre–1958 booklet titled *The Women That Taxes Made; An Editor's Intimate Picture of a Large But Little Understood Market,* the editor-in-chief of *True Story* explained: "Remember, these women never were, and never will be, the avid readers of textbooks nor the patients of psychiatrists. . . . They cannot and do not often read the conventional women's magazines. They read very little that is not written in their conversational language. . . . Their interests are almost entirely in people. . . . The abstract is seldom discussed" (cited in Gerbner 1958, p. 31). Today, *True Story's* advertising copy retains the same tone: "Lacking the self-assurance and often the education of her middle-class counterpart, the working-class woman brings to her problems and conflicts an emotional rather than a logical approach. . . . She responds to the emotional appeal of the magazine by becoming involved in the problems, conflicts and activities of other women whom she feels are much like herself. . . . She is reassured and thus encouraged to find a solution to her own problems" ("About the Magazine").

The average *True Story* reader the magazine's publicists portray for potential advertisers is a conglomerate of stereotypical feminine traits: she is not rational but emotional, which implies that because of her vulnerability she will be drawn to buy products she doesn't need. She is insecure and needs affection and affirmation from others, especially men. These ultrafeminine characteristics are linked specifically to the reader's class by marketers. Included in *True Story*'s promotional packet is a two-page blurb called "Blue-Collar Women and Brand Name Products," which cites a number of sources concurring that "blue-collar women" depend emotionally on brand-name products for "status recognition" from others, especially husbands. It is implied that as a consumer of *True Story* and its sponsoring products, the average reader will receive some of the guidance she greatly needs.

According to a 1986 Mediamark Research Inc. audience profile, *True Story* has a total audience of 5,958,000, of which 85.8 percent are women. The median age of readers is 35.2 years. Slightly more than half (51.4 percent) of women and 71.4 percent of men readers are employed outside the home. Seventy-eight percent of women and 10 percent of men readers define themselves as homemakers. Women readers, like women narrators, are far more likely than their male counterparts to live in poverty. The individual yearly earned income median for women is $9,388; for men, $26,042. More than a third of women readers are heads of households. Less than 3 percent of women, as opposed to 38.4 percent of men, earn more than $25,000 a year. At the other extreme, 24.4 percent of women and 6.6 percent of men readers earn less than $10,000 yearly. More than half (56.3 percent) of readers are married, 17.5 percent are single, and 26.3 percent are divorced, widowed, or separated. Nearly half (46.3 percent) are parents. As for race, 79.5 percent of *True Story* readers are white, 17.5 percent are black, and 2.7 percent are of other minorities.

True Story continually presents women as self-abnegating nurturers, wives, homemakers, and child rearers (Honey 1984, p. 311). Themes and exposition style have changed little since the magazine's beginning. During the 1960s, stories began to provide more explicit sexual detail, but the moral order remained unchallenged. For instance, a woman might describe her repeated visits to a motel for wild passionate lovemaking, but in the end, she discloses that her wild passionate lover has been her husband all along. Current events appear to have very little impact on *True Story*. Wars and social movements are rarely mentioned. Since the mid-1970s, the tone of the magazine has become slightly more religious and conservative. When religion plays a prominent role in a story, the heroine is usually Christian (the stories I collected include one mixed marriage between a Jew and a Catholic, and one Jewish couple.) Antiabortion sentiments surfaced in the 1950s and continue to the present. Narrators are often poor, and many of the stories are complicated by their authors' daily efforts to survive. Often, children are the only part of these women's lives that give them any pleasure; so this special relationship serves as a likely target of threat and danger.

The stories collected for this study are less likely than the more common *True Story* narratives about romance to furnish unqualified happy endings, because maternal loss is experienced as a grave and long-lasting tragedy. These stories vary in plot more than love stories that do not involve children, and the struggle between men and women is often not the main focus of the stories. Authors do offer some sort of resolution or closure, which often consists of a heroine's resignation to the reality of her loss.

Maternal Grief in Women's Magazines

Between 1840 and 1870, the two most popular nineteenth-century women's magazines, *Godey's* and *Peterson's,* published a great deal of material about mothers' reactions to infant death. The number of such articles gradually decreased as the century progressed. Toward the end of the 1800s, poetry—the primary source for maternal consolation material in these magazines—gradually lost its place as a prominent feature.

Fashion features and short stories about romance and adventure moved to the fore. Heroines were introduced when they were young and unmarried, and their stories usually ended on or soon after their wedding days. Motherhood, especially "failed" motherhood, had become an inappropriate topic for magazines that focused on elegant, sophisticated courtships and what to wear during them. Along with motherhood, the dominant Christian morality that had been enthusiastically propounded in the poetry of the mid-1800s slowly receded. The moral tone of magazine stories became secularized, and subjects that had been religiously charged, such as infant death, were dropped by mainstream periodicals.[1]

Methodology

I found a total of 71 items in *True Story* from 1920 to 1937, and from 1950 to 1985, including 21 letters to the editor, which dealt on some level with maternal grief concerning infant death, miscarriage, stillbirth, abortion, or loss due to kidnap-

TABLE 1
Type of Articles in *True Story*

				Type of Loss			
Years	*Death*	*Stillbirth*	*Miscarriage*	*Regretted or Unwanted Adoption*	*Regretted or Unwanted Abortion*	*Feature by "Authority"*	*Totals*
1920–29	4	0	0	3	0	0	7
1930–39	4*	0	0	1	0	1*	6*
1940–49	0	0	0	0	0	0	0
1950–59	4	0	4	0	1	0	9
1960–69	7	0	3*	0	1	1*	12*
1970–79	15*	1	2	3*	4	1*	16*
1980–85	6	1	7*	0	1*	0	15*
Totals	40	2	16	7	7	3	77

Note: Totals do not add to 71 because items marked with an asterisk include stories or letters that fell into more than one category.

ping or adoption.[2] (See table 1.) Forty of the collected articles have titles that strongly indicate that maternal grief or infant or fetal loss will figure prominently in the story: for example, "He Called Me Baby Killer" or "Tears for My Little Boy." Others, such as "Afraid to Give My Husband a Child" or "God Sent Me a Miracle," are less obviously titled. I found no stories between 1937 and 1950 dealing with infant death. It is likely that the absence of stories about infant loss is due at least in part to preoccupation with World War II in stories during this time.

The Stories

True Story mothers' descriptions of their infants often echo the idealized language of nineteenth-century poetry. In the earliest article in my sample, "In Every Woman's Heart" (Oct. 1923), the narrator's husband physically abuses her and their infant daughter. Frantic, with nowhere to go for help, the author decides she must get her daughter out of danger. In true *True Story* spirit, she pursues a rather extreme route. She takes out an ad in the *Morning News:*

> "A BABY FOR SALE—Girl baby, six months old, with blue eyes and gold hair." . . . Next morning, I dressed the baby in her fine white dress and tied on her lacy cap. She reached out with her soft little hand and laid it against my lips the way she always did when I dressed her. . . . My throat ached with the tears I did not shed. (p. 33)

The author's descriptions of her child are identical to those of the nineteenth-century idealized infant who died in poem after poem. These children are blue-eyed and irresistibly sweet, like "Little Emily" in Abby Allin's 1851 poem:

> I see thee in my dreams, baby,.
> In visions of the night;
> Thy blue eye full of blessedness,
> Is glancing on my sight:
> Again upon my heart, baby
>
> Thy little hand is pressed;
> Again thy little nestling head
> Is pillowed on my breast. (*Godey's* 43 [July 1851]: 56)

The "white dress" and "lacy cap" worn by the *True Story* teller's child proclaim her vulnerability and purity, like the clothing in which nineteenth-century infants were buried.

After selling her baby, the narrator begins to feel the gravity of her deed:

> Thirty dollars—thirty pieces of silver. I wondered where I had heard that before. Then my mother's voice, tender and broken, sounded in my ears—like the echoes of my own heart. "Then Judas who had betrayed him, when he saw that he was condemned, repented himself and brought himself and brought again the thirty pieces of silver. . . . " (p. 35)

Like Christ, the lost child is a symbol of goodness and a possible means to the redemption of others. The narrator's guilt and grief at her betrayal of the child seem unbearable, yet deserved, to her:

> My arms longed for the softness of her, the touch of her fingers across my face; I felt I couldn't stand it. Then I thought of Charlie [her husband] with that sudden cruel light in his blue eyes, of the way he had held her curling fingers across the red-hot stove. I'd have to stand it. If I loved her enough I could stand it. (p. 127)

Though she compares herself to Judas, the narrator realizes on some level that she has done something positive for her child, which does not acquit her of guilt feelings, however. She spends the rest of her story (told in three installments) looking for her baby.

Many of the writers view their children's deaths as punishment for some grave error they have committed, often neglect of some kind. In "And I Didn't Want Children," Lorry gives her second child up for adoption while her husband is away and tells him she had a miscarriage. Lorry acts against her doctor's advice:

> Mother love is in the heart of every woman. Yours may be dormant now but as surely as there is a God above, some day it will come back to life. I know. Other women have given away their babies. Most have come back, begging, pleading, groveling at our feet, praying to have their babies given back, which we cannot do. They are pitiful sights. (Feb. 1937, p. 86)

Lorry's attempts to buck patriarchy (by going behind her husband's back and not listening to her doctor) do not go unpunished. The doctor's words are a self-fulfilling prophecy. Eventually Lorry becomes obsessed with the lost child and confesses her secret to her husband. They search in vain for the child. Their other child, a daughter, dies at the age of two. At this point, Lorry is a "pitiful sight," as the doctor predicted. Guilty, lonely, and miserable, Lorry finds her only hope for relief in the fulfillment of her womanly duties. The only way to make up for stepping out of bounds is to keep herself firmly within the walls she refused to recognize earlier.

No matter what, she can never forget the tragedy that resulted from her rash act; so instead she builds a shrine to it. Though she and her husband have more children, she keeps a room in their new house for her "abandoned child" and buys presents for both of her lost children on their birthdays. At the end of her narrative, Lorry writes that she is on the path toward mental peace: "By devotion to my husband, my children, my family and my friends . . . God is allowing me to atone" (p. 89).

Lorry's story serves as just one example of how many (but not all) *True Story* women accept blame for the death of their children. The notions that the self ought to be treated as suspect and that one's actions should be measured for their offensiveness to a patriarchal God complement traditional prescriptive ideas of how a woman should behave.

Even if a woman accedes completely to her designated role as loving wife and mother, she must still watch her step. In "No Children Wanted," Dorothy interprets her child's death as a possible punishment for overindulgence. She writes, "We are taught not to worship anything on this earth. Perhaps that is why God took her from me" (Dec. 1932, p. 97). In the nineteenth-century poetry about infant loss, women commonly asserted a biblical morality like Dorothy's; they knew that they were not supposed to think of the love between a mother and a child as an all-consuming passion. That feeling should be reserved for one's relationship with God; on earth, it was considered selfish to overlove another. In this vein, when an infant was "taken back" by God, mothers consoled each other with the idea that God could take better care of their babies than even they could. God was looked on as the ultimate mother, and mothers' grief was lessened by their faith that their children were in better hands. "A Mother's Story," by Aidyll, published by *Godey's* in 1874, outlines the emotions that are echoed in *True Story* nearly 60 years later:

> Oh, selfish mother-love! to dare.
> To grudge God's angels though aware
> That he in mercy calls them home—
> Their little feet to never roam
> In paths of sorrow or of sin,
> But safe, in his loving arms within! (Aug. 1874, p. 143)

In "Just in Time," when Madge's "little baby was taken suddenly," she vows to "never care for another thing" and to live "right," so that she will meet him again in heaven (Feb. 1925, p. 65). Sustained by the religious conviction brought on by her baby's death, Madge does not act on the lustful attraction she feels toward her cousin Jim. "I resolved to keep myself pure and good so I would go to him [her son] when God was ready to take me" (p. 66). Madge does not accomplish her end without a struggle, but by associating her grief over her lost child with her behavioral goals, she is able to tread the straight and narrow path in which she believes: "It always seemed that when I thought of things I shouldn't the baby would creep into my thoughts, as though to remind me of the promise I had made to him" (p. 42). By remaining faithful to her husband, Madge tailors her behavior to her traditional notion of what is right and believes her goodness will pay off. What separates Madge from the mourning writers of the nineteenth century is her recognition of herself as a woman with sinful sexual desires.

Sometimes narrators do not accept full blame for the tragedies afflicting them. At times, they realize that they ought not bear the emotional burden of guilt along with their grief over miscarriage or death. In "Ours to Love But Not to Keep," the narrator gains this knowledge only after two of her children die.

> Suddenly I knew He [God] was not taking Susan away to punish me
> for any sin of mine but because she, like little Matt, was one of his
> special angels, only loaned to us. He was taking her, but sending us
> another precious baby in answer to our prayers. (Sept. 1963, p. 101)

Many *True Story* writers, like the authors of the current prescriptive literature, recognize the fact that having another child helps remedy the grief but does not replace the child who died or the fetus lost in miscarriage. The conviction that a baby is irreplaceable counters the sentiments commonly heard by grieving mothers, presented as unfortunate and clearly refutable examples by a recent *Compassionate Friends Newsletter:*

> "At least you didn't bring it home."
> "Luckily you never really knew the baby."
> "You're young, you can have another."
> Do these statements sound familiar? . . . Those who have lost newborns or who have experienced stillbirth have found it common for many people not to recognize the loss as being quite as tragic as the loss of an older child. ("When a Baby Dies," 1980, p. 1)

In "Tears for My Little Boy" (Nov. 1950), even though it has been a year since her son's death, to Barbara "it was still as if we'd lost him only yesterday." Her husband, Art, like most *True Story* husbands, has had little problem adjusting to the death and patiently endures Barbara's constant expressions of grief. Barbara, like many other *True Story* writers, feels religious doubts as a result of her son's death:

> What was the good of going to church when I no longer believed in God? If there was a God, why had He taken Bobbie from us? Why had He reached out and struck down a happy, healthy, loving little boy who'd been all the world to his parents? (p. 36)

Barbara begins to baby-sit for a neighbor's child on weekends. She becomes very involved with the child, much to her husband's chagrin. "Don't you see what you're doing—building your life around him? You know it can't go on, Barbara. . . . He isn't ours, and there's no way he can be" (p. 130). Art says she should stop baby-sitting for Johnny. Barbara realizes he is right but cannot bring herself to stop seeing the child. Art's view is never acted upon because Nora, Johnny's mother, is dying. She asks Barbara to adopt him when she dies. Johnny does not replace Bobbie, but having him to mother takes the bitterness out of Barbara's grief.

> The ghosts of Bobbie that are still with me are happy ones. . . . Because I can't help but feel, now, that Somewhere, a gently, gallant, and selfless mother is with my boy, loving and caring for him as I love and care for hers. I've got back my faith in life, and my faith in God. (p. 131)

New children can help parents to replace their love in the world by satisfying their need to nurture, but they can never fit into the specific void left by the child who died. By loving Johnny, Barbara is able to transform her grief from a destructive into a constructive force.

An attempt to mold one child into another proves dangerous in "No One Believes Me, But I Know My Baby's Come Back from the Dead." The narrator becomes convinced that her son Kenny is a reincarnation of her son Kevin, who died before Kenny was born. It takes Kenny's near death to show her she was deluding herself and denying Kenny his individuality. Her experience restores her faith in God, which was shaken at Kevin's death. "Somewhere a part of Kevin lives because God lives," she concludes.

Though most of the stories I collected (38 of 71) dealt with infant death, 13 dealt specifically with miscarriage. Narratives centered on miscarriage experiences do not differ markedly in substance, plot, or degree of expressed grief from stories dealing specifically with infant death. *True Story* authors who experience miscarriage grieve the loss of what to them was a wanted baby, just as mothers of dead infants do. The earliest miscarriage story in this sample, "Greedy Mother," appeared in October 1954. After three miscarriages, Dot writes, "misery closed in on me" (p. 8). Her husband, Dan, appears to have an easy time dealing with the situation and urges her to forget about having children: "'You've got to snap out of this funk. I love you, and the life we have together is all we need. Children aren't everything, Dot.' How easily he could dispose of my dreams!" It seems clear to Dot that being a mother is obviously more powerful than being a father. She can't follow Dan's advice, and their relationship begins to fall apart. Angry at Dan, and feeling like a "half-woman" (p. 8), Dot seeks the advice of a doctor. Despite Dan's objections, she undergoes an operation to suspend her uterus, which would at least decrease her chance of miscarrying.

The operation works. Dot gives birth to a son and becomes obsessively jealous of Dan's attentions to him. "What right had Dan to be wild about him? He was my baby. If I'd taken Dan's advice, there'd never have been a baby for us at all" (p. 18). Dot's selfishness and overprotection of the baby alienates everyone around her. In the end, she comes to recognize her error in misconstruing Dan's concern for her into indifference. She sees that Dan cares about their son and realizes she should be thankful for such a wonderful husband. The experience of miscarriage helps transform Dot and Dan's marriage into a more mutual and satisfactory partnership.

True Story writers who have experienced stillbirth go through the same grief process as writers who have experienced miscarriage or infant death. Writers are aware that the grief they suffer is unique because no one else in their families can relate to it or understand that it never goes away. In "The Empty Crib," Barbie writes on the fourth anniversary of the stillbirth of her son Timmy: "there *is* a birthday no one remembers—no one but me" (Dec. 1955, p. 48). Barbie writes in detail of her (fairly good) experience in the hospital and of the eventual birth of two more children, and concludes her narrative on a positive note:

> Some people say we never get our reward here on earth—but I have. What more could a woman want than a wonderful husband and children? People ask, "How do you have so much patience with your children?" Well, maybe it's because I know what it is to lose one child; I know how precious every moment of a child's life can be. (p. 107)

When abortion is the subject of a narrative, it is depicted as an immoral, traumatic experience that will cause a woman to feel guilt and remorse. In most cases, the narrator has been coerced (or almost coerced) into having an abortion against her better judgment. In "If You Have This Child, I'll Leave You," Ben threatens exactly that. Both Cathy and Ben have regrets afterward, but Cathy's affect her self-image as a woman. "Through my tears . . . I looked at my husband—this handsome man who had said he'd leave me if I had his baby. And all at once everything inside me went dead" (Feb. 1965, p. 125). Despite the fact that she was coerced into an abortion she did not want, Cathy must ultimately shoulder the blame. Cathy realizes she has wronged Ben as well as her unborn "baby":

> Our baby could have been born if I had fought for it! Yes, I was the one who should have fought for our baby—with my love for it, I should have fought for it! God plants that love in a mother when she first knows she is with child. . . . [Ben] had needed me to be strong, and I hadn't been strong enough. He had needed me to get him past the place of fearing to the place of loving and caring and protecting. And I failed him. (p. 127)

The strength Cathy lacked is not contradictory to traditional womanly characteristics but is akin to a maternal instinct (which Cathy sinfully denied in herself). Antiabortion stories are grounded in ultraconservative attitudes regarding women's self-sacrificial role in the family. Husbands are not to be defied but should be brought around to proper behavior by womanly persuasion.

There are several stories about women who attempt in a semiconscious way to induce miscarriage rather than seek full-fledged medical abortions. In such cases, the women come to learn that they were denying their true feelings about their pregnancies. In "He Called Me Baby Killer," Ann does strenuous exercise, even though her doctor has cautioned her against it, because she feels resentment toward the "baby." She miscarries. During the painful labor experience, Ann prays: "Let me live, dear God, and I'll never sin the rest of my life." Afterward, she immediately regrets what she has done:

> I lay with closed eyes, but the full enormity of what I'd done was a leaden weight on my soul. I'd murdered my baby. Adultery hadn't been enough—now I was a murderess as well. And if God had let me die, He would have been justified. (Jan. 1957, p. 96)

Her husband Johnny does indeed call her "baby killer," as his behavior toward her gradually worsens. However, no punishment—even rape—is less than what Ann feel she deserves. When Ann becomes pregnant after the rape, Johnny becomes repentant, and they reconcile. This time, her doctor advises her to abort for the sake of her own life, but by now Ann really doesn't care whether she lives or not, because she feels so worthless and sinful. She does live long enough to write the story, and to exclaim in closing:

> I know that [Johnny] has forgiven me for more than he realizes, but I'm not apt to forget what I still carry on my soul. My only prayer is that I may live the rest of my life in such a way that God, keeping His records, will some day decide, "This woman's debt is paid." (p. 99)

True Story writers who tamper with or allow others to tamper with their pregnancies end up feeling extremely guilty. Narrators writing about abortion accept procreation as women's lot, believe that it is a sacred area, and feel that ultimately women should be thankful for the opportunity to have children. The author of "Is the Child I Killed Still Alive?" (Apr. 1971) writes that her psychiatrist and her minister have urged her to write for *True Story* as an exercise to help her "concentrate on rebuilding my life instead of losing myself in memories" (p. 54) of her abortion at a clinic that she later discovered had been selling live fetuses for experimentation. The purpose of these stories is to frighten women away from abortion by making it seem not only immoral but repulsive and grisly. Unlike stories about infant death, miscarriage, and stillbirth, the responsibility for an abortion cannot be reconciled at all with the traditional, "pro-life" sensibility of the women who confess to them.

Self-Blame and Penance

Whatever the circumstances of her relationship with her child, a mother is likely to experience self-doubt in response to the child's death. This response commonly surfaces in the prescriptive twentieth-century literature, in which guilt is recognized as a normal part of the grieving process and parents are reassured that they will pass through this phase of mourning: "Psychiatrists now recognize a pattern in [parents'] reactions and talk about the stages of grieving through which the bereaved person must almost inevitably pass before regaining peace of mind. These stages are shock, denial, sadness, despair, guilt, anger, and eventual resolution and reorganization" (Borg and Lasker 1981, pp. 17–18).

True Story women often vow to amend any misbehavior that they perceive as possible causes of their children's deaths and do not necessarily absolve themselves from blame. Thus *True Story* confessions do not afford working-class women an overwhelmingly supportive consolation literature, nor the peace of penance and absolution, but some of each, with lingering regrets. Women's powerlessness is recognized but not amended, perhaps because narrators are unable to see a way out. Self-blame and helplessness are reinforced most strongly in articles written for *True Story* by doctors and psychologists.

Lawrence Galton's "Babies Need Not Die," September 1950, is the earliest example of professional advice on the subject of infant death. Galton asserts that mothers' ignorance and neglect are the causes for most infant deaths. He cautions against malnutrition and emotionality in pregnant women and advises: "The sensible thing to do is to pick a good doctor and leave the whole business up to him" (p. 17). In May 1966, Lester David extends a similar argument to the problem of miscarriage. David asserts that two to three out of every ten pregnancies end in miscarriage and that the primary cause is the pathological emotional state of pregnant women. Like Galton, he recommends medical solutions (such as Depo-Provera) to cure the problems of pregnant women. He urges women to rely wholly on their doctor's advice: "Your doctor . . . can ferret out all the possible things that might cause miscarriage and correct them" (p. 78). This prescriptive writing indicts pregnant women's emotionality as one of the main causes of miscarriage and advocates medicine—or what the authors consider to be objective and technically demonstrable—as the cure. Thus authoritative men writers offer rationality and science as the remedy for the excessive emotion and passion they believe women display. For a pregnant woman to achieve success, she must deny the more dangerous aspects of her femininity and cultivate the passive side of it. David urges: "Try to cultivate a placid disposition" (p. 78).

These articles, like much of the popular scientific material of the twentieth century, champion the delegation of authority and control to the medical profession and denigrate or ignore lay wisdom. In the process, the fears and self-doubts of pregnant women and young mothers are no doubt exacerbated. Advertisements in *True Story* and other women's magazines have reiterated these themes over the course of this century. A Johnson's Baby Powder ad from August 1921 states: "A noted baby specialist . . . has informed us that the infantile death rate is literally three times as great in summer as in winter. 'Tell mothers,' says this physician, 'to be very careful all during summer.' . . . It is impossible to list all this splendid man's ideas for safe-guarding baby during the trying hot-weather months. Using a special baby powder was one of the foremost" (*Woman's Home Companion,* p. 68). In a later ad, Johnson's begins even more boldly: "*Three times more babies fall ill in Summer than at any other time. Will your baby come safely through?*" (*Woman's Home Companion,* July 1922, p. 87). Frigidaire calls itself "First aid to mothers in safe-guarding baby's health" (*Woman's Home Companion,* May 1929, p. 5). An ad for Eagle Brand baby food in December 1932 proclaims, "MOTHER THOUGHT HER BABY WOULD DIE!" and rejoins in smaller letters, "Then she found a wonderful baby food" (*True Story,* p. 94). A February 1937 ad for Squibb dental cream features a photograph of an infant captioned "Life is Real . . . Life is Earnest." Below, it cautions: "Unchecked, [dental infection] can become one of the worst enemies of health—retarding physical and mental development—contributing to serious illness of vital organs—standing in the way of success—even shortening life" (*True Story,* p. 75). Ads, like *True Story* narratives, link mothers' consumer negligence with the possibility of sickness, even death, of their children. A Drano ad in *McCall's* magazine warns "2 inches from where you washed your baby's cup . . . your sink is a *hotbed* of live Sewer Germs. Sink-scrubbing won't touch them—the *danger* remains—*until* you use Drano" (Apr. 1944, p. 67). The moral responsibility of women for the spiritual development of their children in the nineteenth century developed a secular twist in the twentieth. Working-class mothers' guilt was reinforced by profit-seeking advertisers, as infant care was presented as a grave and complicated endeavor for which mothers bore the sole responsibility (Ehrenreich and English 1978).

As children have come to be seen as precious commodities (Zelizer 1985), mothers have been depicted as negligent caretakers by the media, and *True Story* has been no exception. The bizarre tactics of advertisers and strange turns in *True Story* narratives reinforce the powerlessness and desperation of working-class mothers. Yet *True Story* also gives voice to women's feelings of powerlessness and desperation and allows readers the possibility, not furnished by mainstream periodicals, of reading about the conditions of their lives. Every weird or horrible event that takes place in *True Story* narratives may be an opportunity for readers to slip deeper into their empathy with the writer, to imagine themselves more and more the "I" in the seemingly no-win situation, which they know will turn into a story with a resolved, if not happy, ending. The experience can be both frightening and reassuring, since the narrator must progress from peril and chaos to safety and

restoration in order to deal with her grief. Every bizarre and horrible
also to help the readers put their own troubles in perspective.

Confessional Literature and Catharsis

Like much of women's literature, *True Story* and other confession magazines have
been labeled insignificant, sentimental, and formulaic and have largely been ignored by scholars, despite their popularity. (For biting critical commentary on
women's popular literature in general, see Douglas 1977; Fiedler 1960; Pattee 1966.)

Gerbner (1958) argued that confessionals locate the source of misfortune
within the individual confessor and ignore larger societal issues such as class. "The
flame of rebellion is first kindled, then controlled in scope and divorced from its
broader social context, and then doused in jet streams of remorse, sacrifice and
compromise" (p. 40). Kosinski vehemently labeled confessionals a damaging influ-
uence on readers: "They reveal a significant popular need for yet another soporific:
a literature that can defuse the imagination, dismiss emotion, and ultimately leave
the reader disarmed, unable to face his very self or to cope with the unknown—his
own existence" (1972, p. 204).

In "He Admits . . . But She Confesses," Stewart (1980, p. 111) described confession magazines as providers of "illusory relief to isolation" for their working-class
readers. Stewart asserted that confessionals portray women as masochistic, emotional creatures struggling to obtain the primary goal of a marriageable man. She
saw confessionals as a reinforcement of women's subordinate position in a society
dominated by men. Honey's analysis of 48 stories selected from four Macfadden
magazines of November 1981 led her to conclude that confessionals deliver mixed
messages to women; she writes, "While affording some relief from the pain of victimization and powerlessness, the formula ultimately fails to serve the interests of
its readers" (1984, p. 316). Honey concurred with earlier critics in stating that ultimately any radical urges a narrator—and hence a reader—might feel are defused
by the moralistic end of each formulaic story, when traditional values are expounded and womanly submission of some sort prevails (p. 131).

The activity of reading confession magazines, like that of reading romances,
has been deemed ultimately fruitless and unsatisfying escapism (Douglas 1980;
Modleski 1980). Radway (1984), however, credits readers of women's popular literature with active participation and shows that romance reading can have a positive
effect in their lives. Drawing on reader-response criticism, Radway analyzed a
group of romance-novel readers' own descriptions of their reading experiences and
preferences. She concluded that reading romance literature involves staging a mild

rebellion in real life, by creating time for idealistic and quasi-feminist fantasies: "In effect, the vision called into being at the end of the process of romance reading projects for the reader a utopian state where men are neither cruel nor indifferent, neither preoccupied with the external world nor wary of an intense emotional attachment to a woman. This fantasy also suggests that the safety and protection of traditional marriage will not compromise a woman's autonomy or self-confidence" (p. 215).

Like contemporary romances, *True Story* reinforces traditional values and presents a world in which men and women's relations are ultimately successful, once they have suffered through a violent transition process. The end result is heterosexual marriage based on idealized, woman-constructed utopian fantasies, despite the patriarchal structure within which they take place.

At its worst, *True Story* can be seen as doing all it has been accused of by its critics. In order to escape the grief that results from miscarriage (spontaneous or planned) or infant death, most *True Story* women come to see themselves as guilty for the creation of their own tragedies. To atone, they become self-denying, even masochistic, and take pleasure only from their service to others and their feelings that they are living as God has deemed they should. Mothers are taught to distrust themselves and to rely on paternalistic authorities and consumer goods. Oppressive class and gender positions are reinforced. These women are entrapped and alone.

At its best, however, *True Story* presents women who have discovered a less rigid alternative than constant misery, women who learn to accept death as part of life, or as part of a religious conception of reality. In many cases, narrators use their grief in what they consider to be productive directions—they enjoy other relationships more fully and reach out to validate other women's experiences by their very acts of writing.

NOTES

This article is part of larger project I am working on with Barbara Katz Rothman; I would like to thank her for her valuable help at every stage of research and writing, and for making the project possible. Judith Lorber, Randy Malamud, Janice Radway, and Gaye Tuchman offered helpful suggestions and comments on earlier drafts. I would also like to thank Helen Vincent, Florence J. Moriarty, and Nitaya Permsap for their assistance at *True Story,* and Lisa Schwartz for the Mediamark Research Inc. statistics. This research was funded by PSC—CUNY Grant 666–246. An earlier version of this article was awarded the Candace Rogers Award of the Eastern Sociological Society and was presented at the ESS Annual Meeting in May 1987.

1. Other popular women's magazines of the late nineteenth and early and mid-twentieth

century yielded little on maternal grief, and virtually no firsthand descriptions of mothers' losses. I examined *McCall's* from 1940 to 1975; *Reader's Digest* from its inception in 1922 to 1975; The *Woman's Home Companion* from 1900 to its last issue in 1975; *Woman's Day* from its inception in 1938 to 1975; *Lippincott's* from 1875 to its last issue in 1915; and *Cosmopolitan* from its inception in 1886 to 1975. *True Story,* however, printed narratives dealing with infant loss beginning in 1923.

2. Because *True Story* is not available in the New York Public Library system, I went directly to the publishing company, which was reluctant to allow me to use its collection for scholarly work. Permission was granted by the vice president and editorial director, who allowed me to peruse *True Story* for four days.

REFERENCES

Borg, Susan, and Judith Lasker. 1981. *When Pregnancy Fails: Families Coping with Miscarriage, Stillbirth and Infant Death.* Boston: Beacon.

Douglas, Ann. 1977. *The Feminization of American Culture.* New York: Knopf.

———. 1980. "Soft-Porn Culture." *New Republic,* Aug. 30, pp. 25–29.

Ehrenreich, Barbara, and Deirdre English. 1978. *For Her Own Good: 150 Years of the Experts' Advice to Women.* Garden City, N.Y.: Anchor.

Fiedler, Leslie. 1960. *Love and Death in the American Novel.* New York: Criterion Books.

Friedman, Rochelle, and Bonnie Gradstein. 1982. *Surviving Pregnancy Loss.* Boston: Little, Brown.

Gerbner, George. 1958. "The Social Role of the Confession Magazine." *Social Problems* 6:29–40.

Honey, Maureen. 1984. "The Confession Formula and Fantasies of Empowerment." *Women's Studies* 10:302–20.

Kosinski, Jerzy. 1972. "Packaged Passion." *American Scholar* 42:193–204.

Macfadden, Mary, and Emile Gauvreau. 1953. *Dumbbells and Carrot Strips: The Story of Bernarr Macfadden.* New York: Holt.

Modleski, Tania. 1980. "The Disappearing Act: A Study of Harlequin Romances." *Signs: Journal of Women in Culture and Society* 5:438–48.

Oursler, Fulton. 1929. *The True Story of Bernarr Macfadden.* New York: Lewis Copeland.

Pattee, Fred Lewis. 1966. *The Feminine Fifties.* Port Washington, N.Y.: Kennikat.

Pizer, Hank, and Christine O. Palinski. 1980. *Coping with a Miscarriage.* New York: New American Library.

Radway, Janice A. 1984. *Reading the Romance: Women, Patriarchy and Popular Literature.* Chapel Hill: University of North Carolina Press.

Schiff, Harriet S. 1977. *The Bereaved Parent.* New York: Crown.

Snitow, Ann Barr. 1983. "Mass Market Romance: Pornography for Women Is Different." Pp. 245–63 in *Powers of Desire: The Politics of Sexuality,* ed. Ann Barr Snitow et al. New York: Monthly Review.

Stewart, Penni. 1980. "He Admits . . . But She Confesses." *Women's Studies International Quarterly* 3:105–14.

"When a Baby Dies." 1980. In *Compassionate Friends Newsletter,* vol. 3, no. 4, edited by Cindy
    Bouman et al. Oak Brook, Ill.: The Compassionate Friends, Inc.
White, Cynthia Leslie. 1970. *Women's Magazines, 1693–1968.* London: Michael Joseph.
Zelizer, Viviana A. 1985. *Pricing the Priceless Child: The Changing Social Value of Children.* New
    York: Basic Books.

7.

"I Wanted the Whole World to See"
Race, Gender, and Constructions of Motherhood in the Death of Emmett Till

RUTH FELDSTEIN

The murder of the fourteen-year-old African American Emmett Till in the summer of 1955 was a grisly one. Late Saturday night on August 28, Roy Bryant, twenty-four years old, and his half-brother J. W. Milam, thirty-six, kidnapped Emmett Till, a native of Chicago, at gunpoint from his relatives' cabin in Money, Mississippi. Several days after the abduction, a white teenager found Till's body in the nearby Tallahatchie River. He had been brutally beaten, one eye was gouged out, and he was shot in the skull. In the hope of weighting the mutilated body in the water, Till's murderers had tied a 100-pound cotton gin fan to his neck with barbed wire.[1] Till allegedly had whistled at Carolyn Bryant, Roy Bryant's wife, and mother of two young sons. The two white men felt compelled to avenge what they perceived as a racial and sexual transgression.

The brutal murder transfixed the country. Thousands attended Till's funeral in Chicago and saw his mangled body. Bryant and Milam were arrested, indicted, and tried for murder. During the five-day trial in September, three television networks flew footage from Mississippi to New York daily for the nightly news.[2] "Will Mississippi Whitewash the Emmett Till Slaying?" asked *Jet* magazine in a photo essay depicting Till in life and death.[3] On Friday, September 23, the all-white, all-male jury deliberated for only sixty-seven minutes before returning a verdict of not guilty. Less than two months later, a grand jury chose not to indict Milam and Bryant on charges of kidnapping. They were free men. The acquittal fueled the horror and collective anger that the murder had evoked. In the weeks before and after the trial, dozens of protest rallies with thousands in attendance were held

---

around the country. Till's relatives and others involved in the trial told of their experiences, raised funds for the NAACP, and urged voter registration. "Not since Pearl Harbor has the country been so outraged as by the . . . [Till] lynching . . . and the unconscionable verdict," commented one magazine.[4]

Till's murder occurred in 1955, a year of growing defensiveness and violence on the part of many white southerners. It marked the first year in the life of White Citizens' Councils, "respectable" and middle-class white supremacist organizations born in response to the Supreme Court's 1954 decision in *Brown v. Board of Education of Topeka*.[5] In Mississippi alone, two other black males were shot to death between May and August 1955; both had registered to vote. Yet 1955 was also a year of cautious optimism in some black communities and activism for civil rights workers. The African American newspaper the *Chicago Defender*, for example, celebrated its fiftieth anniversary with an 80-page edition that "epitomizes the position of the American Negro today in relation to his native country. All of the elements that have gone into his development and progress in the United States are embodied in this issue . . . a hefty, tangible symbol of our democracy."[6] The year would end with the onset of the Montgomery bus boycott, a campaign that would break segregated public transportation in the Deep South city and bring an obscure black minister, Martin Luther King, Jr., to national attention.

Of course, the year of Till's murder was marked by many other, seemingly unrelated, events and attitudes. These included a sexually conservative message emphasizing that a "good" woman was concerned primarily with her home and family and, perhaps most important, was a nurturing mother. In a commencement address at Smith College in May 1955, liberal Democrat Adlai Stevenson urged each graduate to become a mother and inspire "in her home a vision of the meaning of life and freedom . . . help her husband find values that will give purpose to his specialized daily chores."[7] Television moms projected images of fulfilled and fulfilling white motherhood onto recently acquired screens across the country, and these representations of motherhood frequently prevailed despite increases in women's labor force participation and alternative gender roles offered in popular culture. And although these were prescriptions for white women, African American periodicals, too, often celebrated motherhood and domestic security.[8] "Goodby Mammy, Hello Mom," declared *Ebony*, heralding the alleged postwar retreat of black women to the home and giving thanks that "Junior" has "been getting his bread and butter sandwiches regularly after school and [now] finding that rip in his blue jeans mended when he goes out to play." Indeed, columnist Roi Ottley praised black mothers for disciplining their children successfully—more readily and effectively than did "modern" white mothers. "Perhaps the Negro mother's attitude is old-fashioned," he wrote, "but in the final analysis it is more practical and indeed involves a sense of personal responsibility."[9]

Mamie Till Bradley,[10] a thirty-three-year-old African American woman, worker, and mother living in Chicago, was a part of these overlapping and seemingly conflicting currents on race relations and gender roles. When Bryant and Milam murdered her son, these currents forcefully collided and their interdependence crystallized. As this essay makes clear, a discourse on motherhood was not incidental to the widely publicized murder of Emmett Till—an episode frequently cited as critical to the "birth" of the civil rights movement.[11] Instead, constructions of gender were at the center of a case hailed solely as a landmark in the history of the civil rights movement. An analysis of the southern-born but Chicago-bred Mamie Bradley demonstrates that motherhood itself was a battleground on which the meaning of Till's death was fought. Both racists and antiracists, conservatives and liberals invoked, constructed, and relied on meanings of motherhood to formulate their views both on race relations and on American citizenship.[12]

Scholars analyzing this murder have emphasized the racial, regional, and class conflicts that Till's death brought to the fore. Initially, the majority of white southerners condemned the murder and praised the speedy indictment of two men now labeled "white trash" or "peckerwoods" by many southern whites who, regardless of Bryant and Milam's financial positions, used class distinctions to distance themselves from such blatant and violent racism.[13] In the days after their arrest, local lawyers intentionally demanded payment they knew Bryant and Milam could not afford, and the men had no counsel.[14] But as white southerners concluded that the South itself was under attack and on trial, and as blacks around the country mobilized politically to protest the murder, a racially specific alliance developed to defend Milam and Bryant—and to protect power relations in the region. Within a week of the murder, all five of Sumner's attorneys agreed to collaborate in Bryant and Milam's defense; a "defense fund" raised $10,000 for the two. The impact of the case, then, scholars have argued, stemmed in part from the way in which one region of the country felt itself set against another.[15] Because Bryant and Milam murdered Till for alleged "advances" toward Carolyn Bryant, gender has not been wholly overlooked in discussions of the murder. But analyses situate gender onto a white woman exclusively, so Carolyn Bryant becomes "the woman" relevant to these events. Similarly, race is situated onto black men exclusively, so either Till or Moses Wright, Till's uncle and a prominent witness at the trial, are "the blacks" relevant to these events. As a result, the relationships among gender, race, and class and the ways in which together these fluid categories interact and structure power relations have not been considered. The power of Carolyn Bryant's gender as racially specific and class informed, for example, is obscured. Further, a central figure in understanding how the meaning of Till's death was constructed has been largely effaced: Mamie Till Bradley.[16]

Mamie Bradley—as an African American woman and an African American mother—was central to the politicization of her son's murder. She chose to open her son's casket to the world and thus helped make his death an international civil rights issue. Bradley actively involved herself in the events that followed the murder—the funeral, the trial, and the political mobilization the murder spurred—and in the process defined her own subjectivity as a black woman. She claimed the public role of grieving mother and thus reformulated conceptions of both white and African American motherhood.[17] Her actions enable a consideration of the political—even radical—potential of motherhood in the 1950s and a reconsideration of a women's history paradigm that renders mothers in the 1950s apolitical.[18] Bradley explicitly politicized motherhood on a number of levels—challenging black women's exclusion from the racially specific discourse of white motherhood and challenging women's exclusion from the gendered discourse of politics.[19] She thus exposed the ways in which citizenship relied on false distinctions between public and private and unquestioned assumptions about race and gender.[20]

As the story of Mamie Till Bradley suggests, an intervention into the dominant discourse on motherhood could have multiple meanings and consequences. In claiming her role as a grieving mother she helped inject motherhood more forcefully into the political landscape, but she could not control the terms of the debate or the ways in which she herself was a symbol. Till opponents consistently invoked assumptions about natural motherhood that privileged Carolyn Bryant and excluded Mamie Till Bradley in order to preserve citizenship as it was defined in the South. But more progressive claims to citizenship that included African Americans were also gendered, dependent on traditional divisions between a public and rational masculinity and a private and emotional femininity. As part of its political battle for black citizenship, the NAACP, too, would ultimately seek to contain Bradley and define the meaning of motherhood on these more "progressive" terms. Representations of Bradley underscored the fact that meanings of motherhood sat on the cusp between public and private—clearly relegated to the private sphere, yet infused with political meaning. The meaning of Till's death was structured around these tensions between public and private, between exposure and concealment. And precisely because Mamie Till Bradley existed and acted as she did—as mother, woman, and African American, in the public and private spheres—she became an object to be positioned, defined, and contained by those across the political spectrum.

"A Mother's World Came to an End": The Meanings of Respectable Motherhood

The meanings of Till's death pointed to the contested meanings of motherhood and respectability. Who and what was a "natural" or a "good" mother? What sources of authority did this role confer, and who was excluded from this category? Who was and was not respectable? Could either the African American and northern Mamie Till Bradley or the white, southern, less financially stable Roy and Carolyn Bryant be cast as respectable?

Powerful as these categories were, their meanings were not fixed in 1955. Motherhood did not automatically confer on Mamie Bradley or Carolyn Bryant authority or sympathy. Indeed, despite the fact (or perhaps because of it) that motherhood was considered the ultimate form of womanhood, "experts" in psychology, sexology, sociology, and other "sex role" or "race relation" disciplines understood motherhood as the linchpin to a range of social and political problems—from communism and homosexuality to juvenile delinquency and poverty. In many instances, middle-class white mothers in particular were vilified in this period.[21] Nevertheless, white motherhood afforded potential power and demanded at least rhetorical loyalty. Since well before World War II, motherhood, for white women, had been explicitly prescribed and at least conditionally valorized.[22] In the same week that thousands waited in lines to view Till's body, reviewers praised Herman Wouk's novel *Marjorie Morningstar*—the tale of aspiring actress turned mother and homemaker. She "fulfilled her destiny," sang one voice in the chorus of praise, and was a model for women everywhere—"their lives at last disposed into the state which becomes them."[23] Even as mom bashing became something of a national pastime, then, critiques of "bad" white mothers were based on a basic belief in their potential power and importance as civilizers of men. Or, in the words of the anthropologist Ashley Montagu, author of *The Natural Superiority of Women*: "It is the function of women to teach men how to be human . . . the true genius of women."[24]

The historian Elaine Tyler May has analyzed the emphasis on "early marriage, sexual containment and traditional gender roles" in the context of the Cold War: "Domestic containment," she explains, was a way men and women could "bolster themselves against potential threats"—including atomic war and communism within America.[25] When the quest for civil rights is considered part of the 1950s, the political implications of domestic containment widens. For whites, and especially for financially insecure southern whites like Roy and Carolyn Bryant, adherence to traditional gender roles and the belief in motherhood's power were ways of

containing "threats" to the racial caste system on which they depended for their socioeconomic security. Although both white families were notches above the share-
croppers and tenant farmers of both races who populated the rural South, the
Bryants in particular lacked economic security.[26] Whiteness established the code in
which "protecting" white womanhood enabled violence against African Americans. Relying on idealized images of white womanhood to strengthen white racial
dominance was surely not new in 1955;[27] doing so, however, meant something different when it drew on a prevailing emphasis on motherhood to contest a bur-
geoning racial liberalism.

Although for Bryant and Milam definitions of masculine power and respectable womanhood were informed by both race and class, over the course of the
trial their class status was curiously elided. Indeed, for racially conservative white
southerners defending the two men, Milam and Bryant became symbols of all that
was good about the middle-class white family—veritable commercials for *Father
Knows Best:* clean-cut, seemingly pillars in their communities; quintessential family men; veterans of the Korean war; and "heroes."

Consequently, Carolyn Bryant had access to the image of motherhood as the
ultimate state of womanhood despite her family's financial insecurities. The "feminine mystique" might envision women in middle-class suburbia and in fact rely
on an economic expansion that depended on working women's labor outside the
home; nevertheless, symbolically this ideology of womanhood accommodated *all*
white women. *Mama,* for example, a popular television program on CBS, celebrated a working-class Norwegian immigrant family, especially the hard-working
but domestic "mama" of the title. A 1956 *Look* magazine on American women
lauded "this wondrous creature" who "married younger than ever, bears more babies and looks and acts far more feminine than the emancipated girl of the 1920s
or even 1930s. *Steelworker's wife and Junior Leaguer alike* do their own housework."[28] Carolyn Bryant, twenty-one years old in 1955, was married and had two
young sons; she worked in her home as well as in the small country store she and
her husband struggled to maintain. She too, then, was a "wondrous creature."

African American motherhood was far more fraught with potential pitfalls and
damaging effects, according to "race relations" authorities in sociology and psychology in this period. In part because of discriminatory hiring practices toward
black men, a third of all black wives worked for wages in 1950, compared to a quarter of all married women in the population.[29] Nevertheless, as black women struggled to support and care for their families, twentieth-century race relations
scholarship rendered them the cause of "Negro pathology" and as "not only damaged but also as *damaging* to black masculinity" and the black community generally.[30] According to an emerging consensus of liberal researchers led by E. Franklin

Frazier in the 1940s, unmarried or otherwise overly dominating black mothers (the "matriarchy") transmitted "loose sexual behavior" and caused "moral degeneracy" in their children.[31]

By the 1950s, in part the result of the ascendancy of Frazier's theories, matriarchy and black pathology had become so interwoven, particularly for progressive intellectuals fighting discrimination, that "black departures from patriarchal gender relations and white-defined sexual norms became equated with the Negro's cultural inferiority and therefore inequality."[32] According to this analysis of race relations, to fight both racism and "Negro pathology" black men and women had to adhere to "traditional" (white-defined) gender roles. In this contradictory context Bradley's "credentials" as a mother, as a working single mother especially, were highly contested issues. Those who condemned the murder required confirmation that Bradley was a good mother and an appropriately feminine woman.

Thus, for Till defenders, constructing Mamie Bradley as a respectable mother was a means through which African Americans could assert their right to the American credo of equal rights for all.[33] The message was that if Till came from a family that loved him, that cried for him—a "good" family—then his murder, and racial discrimination generally, violated these American values. Indeed, the degree to which Till had been successfully mothered would corroborate his innocence and his "Americanism." His identity as an innocent victim depended on his position as a son in a stable family.

Mamie Till Bradley worked as a voucher examiner in Chicago's Air Force Procurement Office and earned $3,900 annually, well above the median income of black families in this period. Bradley could afford the $11.10 ticket for her son to take the segregated train for a vacation in Mississippi.[34] That the urban-bred Till was killed while vacationing in the country—a wholesome teenage experience gone awry—was not lost on observers, particularly sympathetic whites. "The boy's mother could not send him to the mountains, not to the seashore," editorialized *Commonweal.* "His uncle is poor and his home is a cabin, but to the boy from Chicago's streets, a vacation in Mississippi sounded fine." Race had intruded into the vacation, continued this editorial, and "tragically, a mother's world came to an end and thousands of Negroes stood in line to see what a vacation in Mississippi had done to one of their sons."[35] In 1955, a vacation was a desirable and potent symbol, signifying respectability, a healthy family life, and a strenuous work ethic that entitled one to leisure. Situating the teenager on vacation was a way of assigning a respectable and moral middle-class ethos to Till and his mother; indeed, garnering sympathy from progressive white audiences depended in part on erasing her race and foregrounding this middle-class lifestyle as a sign of respectability.

Within Chicago's black community, however, visiting southern kin had a long history and neither salary nor class position necessarily reflected a person's status or respectability. "What's a Middle Classer?" asked a *Chicago Defender* editorial unrelated to Till's murder. The answer, in a complex interweaving of class and race, indicted the African American "so-called middle class" for "adding to the racial separation" and indicted the poor who "strive to be middle class with a two car garage, a bath room and a powder room." Middle classers are "eagle-eyed against 'rosion' and 'intrusion,' they are America's most vigilant snobs."[36] For black women in particular, money or class position did not confer respectability. The Association of Mannequins' tenth annual "Ten Best-Dressed Women" awards, for example, honored "those women of the Race who have achieved an appearance that is fashionable and *appropriate.* . . . such women help to hold high the standard of good grooming . . . they deserve the accolade of best dressed, *regardless of financial status.*"[37] One columnist bemoaned the black working woman who "flaunts her independence and makes it clear that she can take care of herself. She resents and resists any inclinations to lean upon a man and to seek his help. She hardly ever cries."[38] A woman's competitive salary, then, was dangerous, even if it might enable a seemingly respectable middle-class lifestyle, because it endangered the equally important respectable femininity. These ideas would culminate in *The Black Bourgeoisie,* E. Franklin Frazier's scathing critique of an effeminate and frivolous black middle class. Women play a salient role in this analysis, appearing as selfish social climbers, dominating emasculators, and sexually frustrated self-haters—all qualities that Mamie Till Bradley would have to avoid in order to "earn" the politically necessary designation of respectable mother.[39]

As the coverage of Till's funeral, trial, and protest rallies indicates, Bradley's "status" as a good mother and a respectable, feminine woman was as precarious as it was essential to a condemnation of the murder. Reestablishing the innocence and respectability of both Emmett Till and his mother was of particular importance to antiracists because of accusations that Till had violated racial and sexual boundaries. Bradley needed to confirm her role as a respectable mother in order for her son to be cast as an "innocent victim," but she needed to do so along multiple valences: to emerge as protective of Emmett, yet not emasculating; fashionable and well-groomed, yet not ostentatious and luxury laden; hardworking, yet not ambitious; and "universal" enough to attract the sympathy of whites without distancing herself from the black community.

"Mother Breaks Down": Constructing Mamie Till Bradley

Mamie Bradley learned on Wednesday, September 1, that her son's corpse had been discovered in the Tallahatchie River. Till's body then became the physical sign of what Mississippi wanted to forget and Bradley wanted remembered. The sheriff of Tallahatchie County and soon-to-be vocal defender of Bryant and Milam, Harold Strider, ordered that Till be buried in Mississippi—immediately. But Bradley insisted that her son's body be returned for burial in Chicago. "We [relatives] called the governor [William Stratton, Illinois governor], we called the sheriff. . . . We called everybody we thought would be able to stop the burial," she later explained. To the sympathetic white and black press in the North chronicling Till's murder, it was "the grieving mother of a Chicago boy" who "barely averted" this "hasty burial."[40]

When the casket arrived in Chicago, Bradley insisted that it be opened so that she could know for sure that it carried her son. And at that point, when she saw Till's beaten and bullet-ridden body, she decided he would have an open-casket funeral to "let the people see what they have done to my boy!"[41] Till's body lay first at Rayner Funeral Home and then at Roberts Temple of the Church of God in Christ until the burial on Tuesday, September 6. Thousands stood in long lines winding around the block outside the church to view the disfigured corpse dressed in a suit and the three enlarged photographs of Emmett Till in life. A public-address system broadcast the Saturday memorial service to crowds outside the church. Bradley postponed the burial for a day so that the many who wanted to could pay their respects.[42] Estimates regarding attendance vary, ranging from ten thousand to six hundred thousand, but there was little dispute that "the memorial service for young Till" had mobilized Chicago's "Negro community as it has not been over any similar act in recent history."[43]

Emmett Till's funeral blurred the boundaries between public and private; as a result of the open casket, his body and the individual pain he endured became the locus for a collective political mobilization of African Americans demanding citizenship for all blacks.[44] At the same time, this collective mobilization occurred on gender-specific terms. As thousands passed the bier, for example, one observer noted that "stern men gritted their teeth and turned tear-filled faces away from the ghastly sight, while women screamed and fainted."[45] Indeed, images of femininity were consistently central to the meaning of Till's death and funeral. And because the meanings of motherhood and respectability were so negotiable, crucial "American" categories—motherhood, femininity, citizenship. and respectability—were involved and contested during the funeral, during the trial, and during the protest rallies before and after the trial.

The symbolic construction of Mamie Till Bradley during the funeral provided the basis on which Till's murder was challenged and at once afforded Bradley a degree of power even as it contained her. Sympathetic accounts of the funeral and protest rallies offered images of her that reconciled the various positive meanings of motherhood and respectability. She was represented not just as a mother but as "*Mrs.* Mamie Till Bradley," "a cautious, God-fearing, law-abiding mother."[46] In photographs, she was frequently flanked by ministers or pictured in familial do-mestic settings: "the elm-shaped stretch of St. Lawrence Avenue where Bobo [Em-mett's nickname] lived. It is a family neighborhood where many own the buildings where they live."[47] Descriptions of Till as "polite and mild-mannered . . . with a near-perfect attendance at Sunday School" enhanced the image of Bradley as a good mother. A neighbor shared an anecdote about when the dutiful son "was go-ing to surprise his mother with a cake." One photograph even pictured Mamie Bradley holding a dog; according to the caption, "Mike [the dog] keeps nightly vigil in the boy's room, not knowing that his young master will never play with him any more."[48]

Mamie Bradley's patriotism was another component in her construction. *Newsweek* reported her "concern that the murder would be used by the Commu-nists for anti-American propaganda."[49] (According to one account, Bradley "found it necessary to play sick . . . as a means of ducking 'Red' rallies"—a curious example of women's notoriety for dissemblance harnessed to patriotism.)[50] Patriotism was invoked most explicitly in ubiquitous accounts that the "bereaved mother" was the widow of a war hero. "Private Louis Till must have turned in his grave last week" began one account of the murder. Bradley had suffered "a double tragedy . . . for the boy's father had died abroad as a soldier in World War II." Indeed, Louis Till's allegedly heroic death was the cornerstone to a dramatic editorial in *Life,* saturated with religious imagery comparing Till to Jesus. Southerners who condoned the murder "are in far worse danger than Emmett Till ever was. He had only his life to lose, and many others have done that, including his soldier father who was killed in France fighting for the American proposition that all men are equal."[51] The con-demnation of the murder in *Life* and elsewhere thus relied on Louis Till's heroism and patriotism.

But being religious, familial, and patriotic was not sufficient in the construc-tion of Mamie Bradley as an appropriate symbol of exemplary motherhood and womanhood. References to Bradley as "the attractive Chicago woman" abound and serve multiple functions.[52] To some degree, the equation between "successful" womanhood and physical appeal suggests that certain types of sexism knew no racial boundaries. "At What Age Is a Woman Most Beautiful?" queried *Jet* (shortly after an issue with pages of bathing suit–clad "1955 Calendar Girls").[53] But stories and advertisements that seemed simply to highlight black women's physical appeal "counter[ed] the image of black women as domestic drudges."[54] A repeated em-phasis on Bradley's stylish appearance and physical appeal thus contested a racially specific standard of womanhood and beauty that had historically excluded black women. Photographs and physical descriptions of both Emmett Till and Mamie Bradley were integral to coverage of the case. Their bodies became icons and, in evoking horror and pleasure respectively, were agents in the politicization of the murder.

Simultaneously, images of Bradley as "well-dressed" or attractive reassured readers that she was "feminine," had not usurped any "male" prerogatives, and was ladylike—all without being overtly sexual.[55] Descriptions of her appearance and body, and references to her as "Till's Mom," tend to appear at precisely those moments when she was most public—during public speeches or her testimony at the trial, for example—and thus "prove" that while she might make her private grief a public and political issue, she was not questioning that feminine private role as her primary source of identity. In New York, "Mamie Bradley hardly had time to powder her nose from the time she stepped off a plane until after the rally."[56] Bradley had brought a long-denied racial violence and motherhood into the public and political sphere. These transgressions needed to be contained, even by her "supporters."

Bradley's emotionalism and her consequent dependence on men or male-dominated institutions were the crucial components in assuaging doubts regarding her respectability and motherhood. From the outset, her weakness, even hysteria, and her need to defer to men confirmed her femininity and her religiosity and were vehicles for asserting Bradley's "authenticity" as an American woman and mother. "Mother Breaks Down," announced the *Chicago Tribune*. "Mother's Tears Greet Son Who Died a Martyr," proclaimed the *Chicago Defender*. She was a woman "limp with grief"; an accompanying photograph showed her in a wheelchair, "sobbing" and "near collapse."[57] Bradley's physical weakness was politically valuable—an important resource in the mobilizations the trial generated—even as the emphasis on her body's limits suggested that, somehow, she was not a part of the active political community around her seeking power.

Contemporary depictions and subsequent analyses of the funeral are more readily understandable in this context. For although numerous accounts acknowledge that Mamie Bradley insisted on the open-casket funeral, representations of her as hysterical obscured her role in this political process.[58] Emotion, long coded as a feminine quality, precluded consideration of her as a political player, even as foregrounding emotionalism afforded Bradley some moral and maternal authority. Evidence indicates, however, that this emotionally infused decision was neither haphazard nor apolitical. "Lord, you gave your only son to remedy a condition, but who knows, but what the death of my only son might bring an end to lynching!"

she said when she first saw the body at Illinois Central Station. In the days before the burial Bradley explained that "she wanted people 'to realize the threat to Negroes in the Deep South and to what extent the fiendish mobs would go to display their hate.'"[59] Opening the casket, then, represented a challenge to false though enduring dichotomies between political, public (and masculine) subject and emotional, private (and feminine) nonsubject.

Segregationists and others drew on these same values—religion, family, patriotism, and femininity—to paint a very different picture of Mamie Bradley. The funeral was not a religious event but a fund-raising spectacle that attracted "curiosity seekers" because "against the advice of the undertakers" Bradley had insisted that the casket be opened—"macabre exhibitionism," according to a "moderate" southern newspaper. In these accounts, "Mamie Bradley of Chicago" was not a religious woman, but (at best) a pawn of NAACP "rabble rousers"; the funeral was not a religious ritual with political meaning but cheap "exploitation."[60] According to the journalist William Bradford Huie, at the funeral "cash was collected at the bier in wastebaskets: Mamie Bradley received five thousand dollars the first week. . . . The explosion was a godsend to the NAACP. . . . It was a godsend to the Negro press."[61] Suggesting that the NAACP exploited Till's death also cast suspicion on Bradley's status as a mourning mother experiencing "authentic" grief in her church.

Milam and Bryant defenders also drew on a discourse of patriotism. Accusations ranged from the NAACP being "Red-inspired" to suggestions that a communist-NAACP plot had staged the murder to make the South—and the United States—look bad abroad. After Milam and Bryant had been acquitted, southern reporters learned that the army had hanged Louis Till in Italy for alleged murder and rape; Mississippi Senators James O. Eastland and John Stennis had obtained and released the information from the War Department. Although the details remained unclear, this news was the "most explosive of the developments" in the Till case, according to the *New York Times*. "Till's Dad Raped 2 Women, Murdered a Third in Italy," shouted an oversized headline on the front page of one Mississippi paper.[62] To many, clearly, "like father like son"; given racist stereotypes of black men, if Louis Till had been hanged for rape, then his son must certainly have been guilty. Not only was Emmett's innocence imperiled, but so too were his family's claims to Americanism and Bradley's claims to respectable motherhood.

Images of Carolyn Bryant as a victim and as the wife of a hero provided the necessary antithesis to the rendering of Mamie Bradley as greedy, unfeeling, and unwomanly. One reporter, for example, located Mamie Till Bradley at Emmett's heavily publicized funeral, where "a collection was *still* being taken up at his casket," in the same story that located Carolyn Bryant "in seclusion" (with her two sons of course). Carolyn, according to her mother-in-law, "went all to pieces after the incident. She has been unable to sleep and has to take sedatives."[63]

Indeed, opposing images of Mamie Till Bradley or Carolyn Bryant as *the* good or *the* bad woman were central to both indictments and defenses of the murder. The meaning of Till's death evolved out of these binary views of "good" versus "bad" women, which in turn suggested who was victim and who was perpetrator. In the *Chicago Defender,* for example, Mamie Bradley, the "grief-stricken mother" and innocent victim, was set against a photograph of Carolyn Bryant with the caption "The Cause of It All."[64] Similarly, according to at least one southern white woman, Till had died because his mother "permit[ted] her boy to visit here. . . . *She* should have had better sense than to let such a child come here."[65] Rendering either woman the "cause" of Till's murder deflected attention away from Roy Bryant and J. W. Milam and exemplified how women became sites for social anxieties regardless of whether or not they had access to power.[66]

The discourse in which Mamie Bradley appeared as greedy and unmaternal, on the one hand, and hysterical and unrefined, on the other, and morally weak in any case, spun together racial and gender stereotypes that coded emotionalism as an inherently feminine and "negro" quality. This race/gender analogue conceptualizing African Americans as a weak and "feminine" race dated back to antebellum antislavery campaigns, and these links between African Americans and femininity pervade both racist and antiracist constructions of Mamie Bradley.[67] Huie, for example, sought "the truth" about the murder but also disapproved of the "emotional explosion" of the open-casket funeral, where "the corpse was displayed 'as is' to thousands of cursing, shrieking, fainting Negroes."[68] He and others scorned the primitive qualities—coded as feminine *and* black—they saw in the funeral.

Significantly, however, the antiracist construction of Bradley coded emotionalism as an inherently and exclusively feminine quality and thus rested on sexist stereotypes that undermined black women's strength and political agency. Only ostensible dependence and weakness enabled Bradley to transgress certain boundaries. It was permissible for her to go to Mississippi for the trial or to attend protest rallies, since she had the support of her "advisers," was "accompanied by her father," and had deferred to the NAACP to prevent communist-front organizations from "trying to line her up for big meetings." She might recount events at the trial at a New York rally in a "calm intelligent voice," but she would be speaking from her "heart" and as "the victim's mother" exclusively. And she might even plan a civil suit against the Bryants and raise funds for the NAACP, but that was commended because she had abdicated control "and is placing her crusade in the hands of the

NAACP."[69] These contradictory configurations of race and sex, and the degree to which emotionalism was a sign for race or for gender would be even more pronounced during the trial of Roy Bryant and J. W. Milam—a trial in which far more was being judged than the actions of two men.

"Who Else Could Identify That Child?": Black Motherhood on Trial

The murder trial of Roy Bryant and J. W. Milam began on September 19, 1955, in Sumner, Mississippi. Above a Coca-Cola billboard, a sign welcomed some seventy reporters to a town with a population of 527: "*Sumner, A Good Place to Raise a Boy.*"[70] Here, for five brutally hot days, competing notions of womanhood, motherhood, and respectability—what it actually meant to raise a son successfully—occupied center stage and helped determine the outcome of the trial. Few had expected a conviction of two white men for the murder of a black teenager. Criteria for the defense and acquittal of the two men, however, revolved around a racially specific gender discourse that excluded Mamie Till Bradley. The defense refused to acknowledge that a black woman could be a worthy mother, and the prosecution countered by asserting a universal version of motherhood that crossed racial boundaries. Nevertheless, this assertion of universal motherhood, radical as it could be, further circumscribed Bradley and was, in any event, compromised by other constructions of her as a racialized mother, used by the prosecution as well as the defense. Meanings of motherhood, then, were central in the outcome of what has been hailed exclusively as a "race relations" battle.

The state presented its case first. Special prosecutor Robert Smith III and District Attorney Gerald Chatham offered six witnesses who confirmed the fact that Milam and Bryant had kidnapped Till and, with Bradley's testimony, confirmed the identity of the body found in the river three days later. Two "surprise witnesses" filled in some of the intervening time, testifying that they had seen Till with Milam and Bryant in a truck and had heard them beating the youth in a barn.[71] Moses Wright, a sixty-four-year-old preacher and sharecropper, "Uncle Mose" to defense attorneys and simply "Mose" to the prosecution, stood up in the witness chair and with his "Dar he" and an outstretched arm identified J. W. Milam and Bryant as Till's abductors.[72]

Four key witnesses for the defense raised questions regarding the identity of Till's body on the one hand and reminded the all-male, all-white jury of his alleged advances toward Carolyn Bryant on the other.[73] These strategies simultaneously cast doubts on the death and implied that in any case, it had been deserved. Sheriff Strider asserted that the body had been in the water for "at least ten days, if not fifteen," so it could not be Till's. "Experts"—physicians and morticians L. B. Otken and H. D. Malone—agreed and elaborated; the former testified that no one could identify this body because even the race of the body was a mystery.[74]

The position that motherhood and its power knew no lines of race—and challenges to this perspective—began during coverage of the funeral and continued in representations of Mamie Bradley during the trial. It "was her duty as a mother" to be in Mississippi, according to forty out of fifty blacks polled in the Washington, D.C., area; but, as her (male) "spokesperson" conveyed to the press and to District Attorney Gerald Chatham, she would not travel to Mississippi without official protection. As one headline proclaimed, "Mother Arrives with Her Pastor." Her agreement to testify reinforced the image that Bradley was a mourning mother, committed to her dead son's memory. Speaking through a spokesperson, appearing most frequently with two male relatives "who stood like bodyguards," and demanding protection for herself further reinforced the image that she was a respectable woman, who adhered to "traditional" gender roles.[75]

This position was in fact highly untraditional. Mamie Bradley effectively drew attention to a long history of black women's physical vulnerability at the hands of white men. By insisting on physical protection, she challenged assumptions about black women's promiscuity; moreover, she bridged the chasm between women that had enabled the dichotomy between "chaste white woman" and "promiscuous black woman" to persist.[76] As well, in accommodating the two positions of mourning—emotional mother and public, respectable woman—in suggesting that emotional expressiveness and public decisiveness could coexist, Mamie Till Bradley bridged the chasm between the public man and the private woman.

White supremacists repeatedly challenged this view of womanhood that crossed racial boundaries. Many southern newspapers suggested that Bradley's wariness about coming to Mississippi stemmed not from her physical vulnerability but from her indifference toward her son. According to the *Memphis Commercial Appeal*, District Attorney Chatham had to remind Bradley, repeatedly, of her duties as a mother: "It is important to the state's case that you appear," said one telegram. "Your failure to make yourself available as a witness for the state is not understandable."[77] Indeed, Till opponents would permit no rivals to their racially specific version of womanhood. According to one southern paper, Mamie Bradley, "the fashionably dressed Negro woman . . . caused a sensation [among the press] when she walked into the courtroom flanked by her father and advisers" and consequently "swept an expression of almost painful dislike across the faces of local spectators."[78]

The juxtaposition of Mamie Till Bradley to Carolyn Bryant escalated throughout the trial. Contrasting images of the two were central to competing views of

who—and what—was on trial. Captions below adjacent head shots of "Mrs. Carolyn Bryant" and "Mrs. Mamie Bradley" in the *Pittsburgh Courier,* for example,
were "doesn't like whistles" and "would avenge her son." While "Mrs. Bradley" was
"plump and dimpled," the "coldly attractive" Carolyn Bryant appeared in "a family portrait which can be described in one word: unhappy."[79]

Similarly, those hoping to preserve the racial status quo relied on images of
Carolyn Bryant to convey the message that the white nuclear family itself was on
trial and must be preserved at all costs. Cooperative if embarrassed Carolyn Bryant
"wore a black dress with a white collar and red sash" on the stand and "demurely
told a court" that "a Negro man" (the teenage Till) had grabbed her. One defense
attorney positioned himself as Till to re-create the alleged scene between them.
Judge Swango ruled that most of her testimony was inadmissible to the jury;
"Woman's Story Barred," explained one headline. Nevertheless, she was still regarded as the "key witness" for the defense, and jury members (who had heard these
accusations previously) were reminded of the threats to "the pretty brunette" when
they were briefly removed from the courtroom.[80] Carolyn Bryant's name rarely appears anywhere without the adjectives "attractive," "comely," or even more typically, as "Roy Bryant's wife, an attractive twenty-one-year-old mother." *Newsweek*
successfully condensed the multiple attributes of respectable white motherhood
into one sentence: "It was Bryant's wife, Carolyn, an attractive, dark-haired mother
of two, whom Emmett was accused of insulting."[81]

Carolyn Bryant was thus central in the campaign to underscore her husband's
innocence and to cast him, too, as a respectable and upstanding southern citizen.
"Wives Serious, Children Romp as Trial Begins," declared one headline, in a story
with detailed attention to Milam and Bryant playing peek-a-boo with their "four
handsome sons" as attorneys selected the jury. While guards frisked African Americans at the door of the jammed courtroom and had them sit at a segregated,
crowded bridge table, Milam and Bryant came to the courtroom with "their wives
and children" in a new "green 1955 Chevrolet" and sat "quietly and without hand-
cuffs." The two men received daily shaves at the Sumner barber shop and lunched
with the wealthy Sheriff Strider "at an air conditioned cafe."[82] In many respects the
trial deflected attention away from class differences in Mississippi and provided
Bryant and Milam and their families access to middle-class standards and values—
temporarily.[83] That segregationists managed to shape the trial into a tale about the
white nuclear family tragically imperiled by Emmett Till and his family is evident
in coverage of the acquittal: the not-guilty verdict marked a "happy ending" and
was "a signal for Roy Bryant and his half brother J. W. Milam to kiss their wives."
The sheer repetition of these accounts—of the two lighting cigars, of the women,

both "the mother of two small sons," smiling radiantly—served to celebrate the reconstituted white families.[84]

Mamie Bradley's testimony was the crucial space in which motherhood's meaning as universal or racially specific was negotiated. Because the defense challenged the identity of the body, her identification based on her authority as "the boy's mother" was pivotal; she was the "expert."[85] Bradley testified on Thursday, September 22, that she knew that the body was that of her son because she had "recognized Emmett's hair line, his hair, the general shape of his nose and his teeth. Especially his teeth, because I used to tell him daily to take care of his teeth." The jury could not discount Bradley's identification, according to Robert Smith in his closing statement, because "the last thing in God's creation a mother wants is to believe that her son is dead." Prosecutor Gerald Chatham concurred. "Who else could identify that child?" he asked dramatically. "Who else could say, 'That's my boy'?"[86] Black women "too," this argument went, loved and cared for their offspring and recognized their bodies almost viscerally.

But on closer inspection, "the grief-stricken mother's" authority was in fact predicated on racially specific behavior; further, assertions of universal womanhood were highly problematic and based on gendered distinctions between public and private.[87] Once again, Mamie Bradley's efforts to define herself as a subject were open to manipulation on all sides. First, as had been the case throughout the funeral and the rallies, Bradley had to "prove" that she had been a good mother to Till and had raised him "correctly." Concern about juvenile delinquency was widespread in 1955 and ineffective parenting was perceived as causing this new social ailment. "Discipline is a must, starting in infancy," stressed one advice column.[88] Mamie Bradley thus testified that she had warned Till "to be very careful" in Mississippi, cautioning him to "say 'yes sir' and 'no, ma am'" and "to humble himself to the extent of getting down on his knees" to whites if necessary.[89] This portion of her testimony—widely quoted in the white press North and South—indicates that Bradley had to prove herself a credible mother not in "universal" but in racialized and racist terms. Assigning guilt to Bryant and Milam required proof that Mamie Till Bradley had raised her son to "know his place"—specifically to know his race—and that being polite and respectful was itself constructed by race.[90]

Second, Bradley's expressiveness during her testimony was highly contested, intersecting as it did with assumptions about respectability and motherhood, race, and gender. According to the *New York Times,* "young Till's mother . . . stoutly maintained that the dead body sent to her was that of her son. . . . Mrs. Bradley was a composed and well-spoken witness," who, when shown photographs of her son's body, "removed her glasses and wiped at her eyes."[91] In choosing to maintain her composure throughout these public proceedings, Bradley resisted gender and racial stereotypes that rendered women and African Americans emotional and lacking control.

Nevertheless, many Till defenders who condemned Milam and Bryant did not mention self-control; instead, Bradley was represented as a highly emotional "tragic figure" who "wept on the witness stand as she identified a police picture of the body of her son. . . . She ran her hand quickly across her eyes as tears trickled down her cheeks."[92] More "objective" accounts, too, foregrounded her inability to control her emotions as "proof" of her maternal authority. "The boy's mother, Mrs. Mamie Bradley, a $3,600 civil-service employee, weepingly told the jury that she was certain the body was that of her son," wrote *Newsweek*.[93] Images of the "naturally" emotionally distressed mother were resources in the condemnation of the verdict; those fighting racism *needed* Mamie Till Bradley to express her private emotions to corroborate her femininity and her maternalism. To Till defenders, private emotion was a sign for gender, "evidence" of her womanliness, which surpassed that of Carolyn Bryant, and of respectable gender difference among African Americans generally.[94]

The jury of white southern men "chose to believe" that the body was not Till's as a way to acquit Milam and Bryant and preserve power relations in Mississippi. "What could a black mother say that would be of any value?" asked *L'aurore,* a French daily.[95] They thus rejected Bradley's identification of the body and rejected a definition of "natural" motherhood that included black women, privileging instead the rational, "scientific" testimony of the "experts." The jury's dismissal of her testimony derived from what they perceived as her lack of authentic expression of maternal grief. "If she had tried a little harder," said jury foreman J. A. Shaw, "she might have got out a tear."[96] In this interview with Shaw, in fact, Bradley emerges as a manipulative, defeminized woman who did not cry "naturally" and had thus forfeited her moral and maternal authority to identify her son's body.[97] This depiction was consistent with racist representations of the funeral and the protest rallies: Bradley was not a "natural" mother because she did not express or experience true grief; she was, instead, a public performer of sorts, capitalizing on her son's death. This version of Mamie Bradley as morally undeveloped and unwomanly drew on race- and gender-specific constructions of morality and motherhood.

In sum, during the trial, Bradley's potential power as a respectable African American mother was simultaneously subversive and reactionary. Her authority as a mother relied on racist assumptions that required Till to be "humble" and on an essentialist discourse that required mothers to be emotionally overwrought. And the all-male, all-white jury rejected even these conditional sources of power.

"Where else," asked the liberal critic I. F. Stone, "would a mother be treated with such elementary lack of respect and compassion?"[98] Racially specific constructions of both motherhood and respectability prevailed in Sumner, most powerfully evoked in photographs of the reconstituted Bryant and Milam families. But, significantly, Mamie Bradley chose not to be in the courtroom when the jury returned the verdict. "I was expecting an acquittal," she said, "and I didn't want to be there when it happened."[99] Her absence indicated her ongoing rejection of the values through which the verdict had been offered and her refusal to be contained—even in the walls of the courtroom. Even as Mamie Bradley absented herself, she further exposed the inequities of the southern judicial system; or in the words of one front-page editorial, the unpunished murder of blacks now lay "Naked Before the World!"[100]

"What Is True Story about Mrs. Bradley?": The Tide Turns

Protest rallies continued for six to eight weeks after the acquittal of Bryant and Milam, with their focus shifting from the case itself to the ongoing battle for African American citizenship and civil rights. It was time to "stop being emotional and start being smart," according to the NAACP executive secretary, Roy Wilkins. "Worry about those who are alive," said NAACP lawyer Thurgood Marshall at a New York protest rally, and he repeatedly urged the crowd to register to vote.[101] The NAACP placed a nearly full-page advertisement in the *New York Times* on October 3 entitled "Help End Racial Tyranny in Mississippi." The ad detailed a "slaughter of personal rights" that included "Three Unpunished Murders—Open Defiance of Supreme Court School Decree" and "Over 900,000 Mississippi Negroes without an Effective Voice in Their Government" and concluded that Till's murder "climaxed a series of blows to American ideals that has horrified the country." Within a month, the ad generated $5,500 in donations and multiple requests for similar fund-raising appeals from newspapers across the country.[102] But the sympathetic construction of Mamie Bradley as the perfect mother—respectable, all-American, feminine, and deferential—did not persist alongside this bid for equal rights.

On November 8, the NAACP publicly severed its relationship with Mamie Bradley. The rupture—or divorce, as the marriage metaphors suggest—occurred as rumors regarding the propriety of Till-related fund-raising drives percolated, immediately after a grand jury refused to indict Milam and Bryant on kidnapping charges and on the eve of Bradley's NAACP-sponsored West Coast speaking tour.

Executive Secretary Roy Wilkins publicly condemned Bradley's request for remuneration, declaring that the "NAACP does not handle such matters on a commercial basis." Shortly thereafter, NAACP attorney William Henry Huff resigned as her legal representative. Reporters wondered, "Will Mamie, NAACP Kiss, Make Up?" but the organization quickly made the separation official when they arranged for Moses Wright to replace Bradley on the West Coast speaking tour.[103]

The conflict triggered a transformation in constructions of Mamie Till Bradley within the African American press that drew with remarkable consistency on entrenched images of motherhood and respectability. NAACP officials implied and others concurred that if Till's mother had asked for a $5,000 fee for public speaking engagements, she was neither a respectable woman nor a good mother, and in fact was little better than racist representations had suggested all along. Whereas those who defended Mamie Till Bradley did so by emphasizing her gullibility, vulnerability, and poor judgment—qualities implicit in earlier positive depictions of her.[104] No one changed the terms of this debate by suggesting that as a public figure working exclusively for the NAACP—she had been on an unpaid leave of absence from her job since Till's murder—Bradley might be entitled to a professional salary or might even be ambitious. Both sides in this conflict, then, reinscribed motherhood as a private, pure, and apolitical role—the very assumptions that Mamie Bradley had troubled.

As a result, the antiracist dichotomy that pits the good, respectable, and maternal Mamie Till Bradley against the bad, immoral, and cold Carolyn Bryant was reconfigured. Polarized views of good versus bad woman endured but were now contained in opposing views of one woman—Mamie Bradley. Or in the words of one headline, "What Is True Story about Mrs. Bradley?"[105]

The backdrop to this "rift over money" was the ongoing negotiation of the ideas of respectability and motherhood as each informed civil rights activism. From the moment that Mamie Bradley helped make her son's death a public issue, there were those who expressed concern about the money being raised. Fears of exploitation were allayed with guarantees that funds were for the collective cause rather than for personal gain. Immediately after the funeral, for example, the *Chicago Daily Tribune* reported that "the mother" authorized the NAACP to use donations made in her behalf for legal expenses the Till case incurred. Local NAACP branches asked churches to assume fund-raising responsibilities to ensure an air of virtue to these campaigns; the organization designated October 2 "NAACP Church Day."[106] By mid-October, however, hostility toward "the sycophants, moochers, jackals and charlatans who are always ready to ply their trade of capitalizing on human outrage" and who were "as busy as a pack of vultures on a freshly killed carcass in the Till case" would not be quelled—and were fueled by anger about the acquittal. "It is the opinion of myself and perhaps that of thousands of other Negroes throughout the country," wrote an Ohio woman, "that if the NAACP had worked as hard presenting evidence in the Till case as they did collecting money, more would have been done to convict the suspects. . . . The NAACP [should] make publicly known the amount of money they collected and the amount to which they have participated in gathering evidence in the Till case."[107] Proliferating rumors were evident in their denial: William Henry Huff, for example, issued a formal statement that he was not "clearing a lot of money in the unfortunate Till case"; in another instance, an editorial assured readers that Bradley "is taking her job very seriously of speaking out against the lynching of her son . . . in spite of reports to the contrary, she is not making any profits from her appearances."[108]

During the period after the trial, representations of Bradley continued to underscore her emotionalism and dependence on men and her relative unimportance to the larger political forces around her: "HEAR THE MISSISSIPPI STORY!! FROM THE LIPS AND HEARTS OF EMMETT TILL'S MOTHER and Mrs. Ruby Hurley," said one advertisement; the name "MRS. MAMIE BRADLEY" appears in parentheses, in small type and below "EMMETT TILL'S MOTHER."[109] According to a "verbal agreement" made in mid-October, the NAACP *exclusively* would coordinate Bradley's public appearances during her unpaid leave of absence from her job; the "mother of the slain boy" was to be at their disposal.[110]

Nevertheless, while her deference was highlighted and her authority emanated from these seemingly traditional sources, Bradley was increasingly a public figure with something to say. In late October, she went to Washington, D.C., in an (unsuccessful) effort to urge federal intervention into the case and to speak before the Senate Subcommittee on Constitutional Rights.[111] This extension of her public role was met by many with surprise, if not derision. "The demand for Mrs. Bradley at these mass meetings is astounding," wrote one black male columnist. Following her Washington, D.C., trip, a *Chicago Defender* editorial referred to "*Mamie,* who is really learning fast the ways of public officials."[112] The tension between two positions—grieving mother and public figure—was evident when Mamie Bradley asserted at a rally in New York that perhaps her sacrifice had not been in vain, if "a little nobody like me and a little nobody like my boy can arouse the nation."[113] It was this tension which could not be sustained indefinitely.

Doubts about Mamie Bradley's role, allegations about the propriety of Till fund-raising, and frustrations regarding NAACP campaigns for African American citizenship were resolved conjointly through the "break-up" between the NAACP and Bradley. She became a scapegoat of sorts, a receptacle for anger at the trial's outcome and overlapping anxieties about gender relations and the future of civil rights activism. Many reacted to reports that Bradley had requested a speaking fee by characterizing her as a "mercenary hard-hearted gold digger, seeking to capitalize on the lynching of her child," or as a "greedy" woman who "had changed from a simple grief-stricken mother to an arrogant celebrity full of her own importance."[114] "Don't Need to Worry About Ma'—She's Loaded!" was the title of a sardonic letter in the *New York Amsterdam News,* which described the less-than-positive transformation of one mother after Till's death: "Ordinarily, Ma is the quiet sort and legs it off to church every Sunday. . . . But ever since those two peckerwoods up and killed Mamie Bradley's boy, she's been riled up to the point of blaspheming." This fictional Ma had even "broke loose from her religion and . . . sent the rent money off to the NAACP Legal Fund."[115] With Bradley's credentials as a respectable mother jeopardized, the African American press referred to her simply as "Mamie" with far greater regularity.

But even more significantly, the defense of Bradley depended on her basic inability to conduct herself as a public, political, or professional player—an image that echoed representations of Carolyn Bryant by white supremacists. Reinterpreters of the "misunderstanding" argued that Bradley was "the victim of bad advice" or that the "plain, ordinary woman . . . has been misrepresented by those she trusted." Clearly, she was "ill-prepared for public life" and had been "catapulted from a humdrum existence . . . into a living martyrdom."[116] Defenders also drew attention to Bradley's emotional and physical frailty: her "nervous condition prevented her handling the business end"; she was "worn to a frazzle," according to Anne B. Crockett, "special representative" to Bradley; and she had yet "to pay her own hospital bill when she suffered a nervous breakdown" (she was hospitalized for "nervous fatigue" in early October).[117] Indeed, Bradley's reaction to the public rebuke *proved* that she was "a sensitive woman": "Her almost complete withdrawal" into "semi-seclusion" followed the canceled speaking tour; the "announcement hit her hard and she hasn't recovered yet."[118]

NAACP leaders had behaved with an "obnoxious display of insensitivity [and] lack of loyalty" toward this "ordinary woman baffled and bewildered," according to Bradley's defenders.[119] A critique of the organization in the *Chicago Defender* titled "Indiscreet Rebuke," carefully reinforced progressive assumptions that more healthful race relations required healthful gender relations, as defined by a middle-class white norm. Although Bradley's "requests for money were seemingly greedy and conscienceless," the male-dominated organization "wield[ed] power in behalf of others" and, as such, had the responsibility to "accept certain disabilities and even tenuous loyalties" and to renounce emotional displays and "public demonstrations of petty irritations." By suggesting that the NAACP had erred in departing from traditional gender roles with its unmanly "public demonstration" of displeasure (Wilkins had "snarled," according to *Jet*), these critiques of the organization effectively bolstered the gendered and racialized split between public and private that Mamie Bradley had challenged.[120]

Finally, several of Bradley's defenders argued that she neither requested, demanded, nor perhaps deserved $5,000, and that Franklin Williams, the West Coast regional director of the NAACP, made the offer after learning of her mounting expenses.[121] She was thus positioned once again as a passive and nonconfrontational figure being done to rather than actively doing, and as a woman who "wants to make it clear that she is not engaged in a fight with the NAACP" and "was anxious to straighten out the mess."[122] The need for Bradley's defenders to circumscribe her actions and feelings was most evident in the coverage of a press conference she held in New York. Headlines such as "NAACP Criticized," "Mamie Bradley Says NAACP Used Son," and "Mother of Till Bitter!" suggested some anger toward the organization. But in the texts, only her father, John Carthan, is "vehement in his condemnation" and legitimizes any request for remuneration. It is he who suggests that Roy Wilkins "was attempting to punish his daughter," that the organization "is using Emmett Till and his mother," or that "as long as my daughter can be useful to them, everything's all right, but the minute she asks for something, it's a different story." With the anger and the demands displaced onto a male authority figure, Bradley emerges as hurt but remarkably conciliatory, "nonetheless hopeful" and "still interested in seeing justice done."[123]

At this press conference, Mamie Till Bradley released a letter she had written to Roy Wilkins after her dismissal from the NAACP. It reveals the contradictory ways in which she defied any one subject position and simultaneously relied on and transgressed gendered and racialized conceptualizations of motherhood, respectability, and citizenship:

> The objective of the NAACP is of much greater concern to me than my pocketbook. I set out to trade the blood of my child for the betterment of my race; and I do not now wish to deviate from such course. I feel very bad that the opportunity to talk for the association would be taken from me. I know th[a]t you have tried very hard and sincerely to see to my day-to-day financial needs. It is unfair and untrue for anyone to say otherwise. If the NAACP is willing to continue to do what it has to defray my travel and living expenses that should suffice. Please let me go forward for the NAACP. It is a duty. I would not want it said that I did anything to shirk it.[124]

Once again Bradley asserted, with some emotion, that the public cause was as important as her personal needs; that her private and maternal grief and her public and political service could and did reinforce each other and did not contradict NAACP claims for black citizenship. Implicit is a critique of political strategies "for the betterment of the race" that segregated these positions. Yet, in this letter, any rebuke is at most implicit. Mamie Bradley, too, ultimately relied on her authority as a respectable woman and good mother to make her bid for credibility. Indeed, she emerged here as emotional, dutiful, respectful, and conciliatory to NAACP authorities. Ultimately, there may have been no other place from which she might hope to be heard or speak with any degree of authority. For racists, antiracists, and for Mamie Bradley herself, then, the "good mother" was a category potentially beyond criticism and, as such, was a visible if not potent position from which to shape politics.

Conclusion

Mamie Till Bradley's departure from the NAACP lecture and fund-raising circuit was permanent. She returned to school and became a public school teacher. Out of Till's death, she later explained, came a "burning . . . to push education to the limit,"[125] but her actions following her son's murder reverberated beyond 1955. An analysis of constructions of her point to the interdependence of assumptions about sexual and racial difference and the interdependence of racial liberalism and sexual conservatism that seem at first to be at odds.

On the one hand, Bradley as symbol and person—the respectable woman, with an authority devolving from motherhood—posed a significant challenge to American power relations: to the racial caste system most prevalent in the South that valorized Carolyn Bryant, to dominant theories of sexual difference that often marginalized and depoliticized women, and to dominant theories of racial difference that held defeminized and emasculating black women responsible for racial inferiority. In laying claim to the overlapping values of the roles of "good mother" and respectable, moral woman, Bradley resisted definitions of womanhood that either excluded black women by virtue of their race or rendered black mothers as dominating and pathological. She politicized and publicized motherhood and racial violence with composure and emotion, dignity and grief.

That women could reach across lines of race, class, and even region to identify with Bradley confirms the subversive potential of explicitly politicizing motherhood in terms that challenged the split between public, masculine citizenship and private, emotional motherhood. "Womanhood without regard to color must be aroused," wrote one New Yorker. Another, a Canadian white woman, wrote to

Milam and Bryant, condemning their violation of the "joys of parenthood that are so dear to us all. Young or old, black or white." And writing to Governor Hugh White of Mississippi "as a white woman, a Texan, an American and the mother of a son," E. H. Johnson asked, "Since when did the testimony of strangers take priority over a mother's identification of a body—a mother who bore and raised the son? Do you think if someone took my boy and beat him to a pulp and threw him in the river, that I couldn't recognize him? . . . Think of his mother. Think of the Negro race. Think of the blot on Mississippi." She concluded by assuring White that she was not a "crackpot" but an "outraged American woman . . . taking action to see that the same justice is given for the death of a Negro boy as I would want for my own son. Do you have a son? How would you feel? Can we do less?"[126] For some, universal definitions of womanhood enabled a condemnation of Bryant and Milam and of American race relations generally.

Further, the political mobilization of blacks that the funeral and rallies helped generate was neither local nor short term. "It was the best advertised lynching that I had ever heard," recalled Amzie Moore, an NAACP Mississippi activist in 1955.[127] With a prescient accuracy, one reporter suggested that Bradley's desire to "'let the people see'" could "easily become the opening gun in a war on Dixie which can reverberate around the world."[128] "Congratulations to your paper for putting the picture of the murdered Till boy on the front page," wrote one reader, "so the whole world can see what goes on in Mississippi."[129] And the world did see. As the famous and ordinary construct their own memories of that period, the case often figures as a pivotal moment. The teenage Cassius Clay (later Muhammad Ali) "couldn't get Emmett out of my mind."[130] Writing on the twenty-fifth anniversary of the *Brown* decision, the sociologist Joyce Ladner recalled that "more than any other single atrocity, the *Jet* magazine photograph of Emmett Till's grotesque body left an indelible impression on many young Southern blacks who, like my sister and I, became the vanguard of the Southern student movement."[131] Bradley's decision to "let the whole world see" was instrumental in the impact the case had on the American body politic.

On the other hand, the symbolic construction of Bradley as a perfect and "natural mother" was fraught with contradictions. Frequent references to Bradley as "the mother" effaced her as a decision-making person even as it empowered her, as was evident during Till's funeral. A cross-racial definition of womanhood and motherhood relied on essentialist assumptions that women were emotional and that their identities were based on the biology of reproduction, as was evident during the trial. And the political impact she had as a speaker and fund-raiser was predicated on her deference to the male-dominated NAACP, as was most evident during Mamie Bradley's conflict with the organization. The discourse on mother-hood was consistently subject to conservative responses and symbolic manipula-tion—by both racial conservatives and racial liberals—and the radical potential of her position was thus undercut.

The reactionary responses to Mamie Till Bradley, despite the very different sources from which they sprang, illuminated how ostensibly universal notions of citizenship relied on race and gender. White southerners' efforts to contain her claims to motherhood enabled them to fight *against* racial integration; they claimed racially exclusive rights to respectable, rational, and masculine citizenship by propping up a discourse of white motherhood. At the same time, the NAACP's efforts to contain her claims to motherhood enabled them to fight *for* racial inte-gration; they claimed racially inclusive rights to respectable, rational, and mascu-line citizenship by adhering to traditional gender roles that constrained Mamie Bradley. In either case, notions of citizenship relied on meanings assigned to motherhood.

The ways in which ideas about motherhood and respectability infused and constructed the meaning of this event were not unique. In underscoring the radi-cal potential and political meaning of women's "traditional" roles, Mamie Till Bradley offers an important lens through which to consider continuities in women's activism. This radical potential of traditional roles was realized, for ex-ample, by women in the civil rights movement in particular—the women who cooked for and fed civil rights activists, the "mamas" of many southern black com-munities who formed the "backbone" of the movement.[132] And in exposing how and why both racists and antiracists relied on a discourse of motherhood to con-tain Mamie Bradley, this incident offers an important lens through which to un-derstand how many seemingly "universal" political categories are in fact gendered and racialized. Indeed, constructions of femininity would play a central though problematic role in civil rights and New Left activism. When Mamie Till Bradley opened her son's casket "to let the people see," she exposed more than her dead son's body. She had the courage and the determination to translate her personal pain and her family's tragedy into political terms. In negotiating her private role as a mother into the public and political sphere, she helped change the terms on which her son's death was understood and debated. Emmett Till was not just another statistic in the tragic history of American lynching.

NOTES

I thank Mari Jo Buhle, Jacqueline Jones, Elaine Tyler May, Joanne Meyerowitz, and Jack Thomas for comments and questions on earlier versions of this essay. I particularly appreciate suggestions and support from Lucy Barber, Krista Comer, Dorothee Cox, Linda Grasso, Andrea Levine, Melani McAlister, Uta Poiger, Miriam Reuman, Jessica Shubow, and Lyde Sizer. Jane Gerhard read countless drafts; her insights and patience were invaluable.

1. Juan Williams, *Eyes on the Prize: America's Civil Rights Years, 1954–1965* (New York: Viking Penguin, 1987), p. 43; Henry Hampton and Steve Fayer, *Voices of Freedom: An Oral History of the Civil Rights Movement from the 1950s through the 1980s* (New York: Bantam Books, 1990), pp. 1–16. Shortly after the trial, the journalist William Bradford Huie paid Milam and Bryant $3,600 to tell "the real story," and they confessed to the murder. Huie's accounts were quite popular and, despite their many ambiguities, are frequently assumed to be the definitive texts on the murder. See William Bradford Huie, *Wolf Whistle* (New York: Signet, 1959); Huie, "The Shocking Story of Approved Killing in Mississippi," *Look,* January 24, 1956, pp. 46–49, and in *Reader's Digest,* April 1956, pp. 57–62; Huie, "What's Happened to the Emmett Till Killers?" *Look,* January 22, 1957, pp. 63–68. Others who have tried to determine just what transpired include Hugh Stephen Whitaker, "A Case Study in Southern Justice: The Emmett Till Case" (master's thesis, Florida State University, 1963); and Stephen Whitfield, *A Death in the Delta: The Story of Emmett Till* (New York: Free Press, 1988). Yet details regarding these events— the most controversial being whether or not Till actually whistled at Carolyn Bryant and who accompanied Bryant and Milam when they took Till—have never been clarified and are not my central concern. In particular, debates about Till's behavior often imply that what he did or did not do should determine his fate and our responses to it.

2. Whitfield, *A Death in the Delta,* p. 34.

3. "Will Mississippi Whitewash the Emmett Till Slaying?" *Jet,* September 22, 1955, p. 8.

4. Meeting of the NAACP Board of Directors, October 10, 1955, NAACP Papers, supp. to pt. 1, 1951–55, reel 1, Widener Library, Harvard University; Report of the Secretary for the Month of September 1955, NAACP Papers, supp. to pt. 1, 1951–55, reel 2; "Till Protest Meeting," *The Crisis,* November 1955, p. 546.

5. Southern whites formed the first White Citizens' Council in July 1954 in Indianola, Mississippi—barely two months after the landmark Supreme Court decision. By that November, there were 25,000 members in councils across the south. The Ku Klux Klan was also newly invigorated in this period. See Whitaker, "A Case Study in Southern Justice," p. 71.

6. *Chicago Defender,* August 13, 1955, p. 1; Harvard Sitkoff, *The Struggle for Black Equality, 1954–1980* (New York: Hill and Wang, 1981), p. 23; Hampton and Fayer, *Voices of Freedom,* p. 2.

7. Adlai Stevenson, quoted in Betty Friedan, *The Feminine Mystique* (New York: Dell, 1963), pp. 53–54; and Sara Evans, *Born for Liberty: A History of Women in America* (New York: Free Press, 1989), p. 255. Historians have successfully revised the myth of the 1950s as a decade of monolithic conformity and passivity; women's historians in particular have shown that not all women in this period were ensnared in what Friedan would later label the "feminine mystique." See, for example, Sara Evans, *Personal Politics: The Roots of Women's Liberation in the Civil Rights Movement and the New Left* (New York: Knopf, 1979); Susan Lynn, "Gender and Post World War II Progressive Politics: A Bridge to Social Activism in the 1960s U.S.A.," *Gender and History* 4 (Summer 1992): 215–39; Joanne Meyerowitz, "Beyond the Feminine Mystique: A Reassessment of Postwar Mass Culture, 1946–1958," *Journal of American History* 79 (March 1993):

1455–82; Joan Nestle, *A Restricted Country* (New York: Firebrand Books, 1987); Susan Ware, "American Women in the 1950s: Nonpartisan Politics and Women's Politicization," in *Women, Politics and Change,* ed. Louise Tilly and Patricia Gurin (New York: Russell Sage Foundation, 1990), pp. 281–99. Other scholarship that suggests continuities between the 1950s and the civil rights movement, the sexual revolution, or the 1960s counterculture includes Robert Korstad and Nelson Lichtenstein, "Opportunities Found and Lost: Labor, Radicals and the Early Civil Rights Movement," *Journal of American History* 75 (December 1988): 786–811; W. T. Lhamon, *Deliberate Speed: The Origins of a Cultural Style in the American 1950s* (Washington, D.C.: Smithsonian Institution Press, 1990); Uta Poiger, "Rock 'n' Roll, Female Sexuality and the Battle over German Identities in the Cold War," paper presented at a Brown University History Department Workshop, May 1992. All this scholarship is important in delineating the diversity of experiences in the 1950s; I am seeking to understand aspects of this diversity in relation to each other. In other words, I am exploring how and why sexually conservative prescriptive literature emphasizing motherhood and domesticity ran parallel to and informed other values and experiences in 1950s America.

8. For the preoccupation with security among white women, see Elaine Tyler May, *Homeward Bound: American Families in the Cold War Era* (New York: Basic Books, 1985), esp. pp. 28–36. This emphasis on domesticity and security did not preclude constructions of femininity that emphasized glamour. For a discussion of these "utterly incompatible scenarios" for white women, see Wini Breines, *Young, White, and Miserable: Growing Up Female in the Fifties* (Boston: Beacon Press, 1992), p. 37. For a discussion of conflicting images and roles for black women, see Paula Giddings, *When and Where I Enter: The Impact of Black Women on Race and Sex in America* (New York: Morrow, 1984), pp. 238–58; Jacqueline Jones, *Labor of Love, Labor of Sorrow: Black Women, Work and the Family from Slavery to the Present* (New York: Basic Books, 1985), pp. 268–74; and Jeanne Noble, *The Negro Women's College Education* (New York: Bureau of Publications, Teachers College, Columbia University Press, 1956).

9. "Goodby Mammy, Hello Mom," *Ebony,* March 1947, p. 36, quoted in Jones, *Labor of Love, Labor of Sorrow,* p. 271; *Chicago Defender,* October 15, 1955, p. 3. Clearly, this celebration of black motherhood is complicated, and I do not intend to suggest a parallel or equal "feminine mystique" for black women. As both these quotations suggest, an emphasis on black women as good mothers countered white-defined racial stereotypes. Nevertheless, this maternalist ethos, even if marshaled in part to resist racism, ultimately constrained women.

10. Mamie Till Bradley remarried and divorced after the death of Till's father, Louis Till. She used the name Mamie Bradley in 1955. I do the same throughout this article, unless I am specifically referring to her in the present, when I use the name she now uses, Mamie Till Bradley Mobley.

11. For peers' views that Till's death was a catalyst to the civil rights movement, see Ruby Hurley and Amzie Moore interviews in Howell Raines, *My Soul Is Rested: The Story of the Civil Rights Movement in the Deep South* (1977; New York: Viking Penguin, 1983), pp. 131–37, 233–37; Myrlie Evers and Charles Diggs interviews in Williams, *Eyes on the Prize,* pp. 46–47, 49. For scholarly interpretations that link Till's death to the civil rights movement, see, among others, Sitkoff, *The Struggle for Black Equality,* p. 49; William Simpson, "Reflections on a Murder: The Emmett Till Case," in *Southern Miscellany: Essays in History in Honor of Glover Moore,* ed. Frank Allen Dennis (Jackson: University Press of Mississippi, 1981), pp. 177–200; Whitfield, *A Death*

in the Delta, p. 107. Indeed, Henry Hampton's critically acclaimed documentary on the civil right's movement, *Eyes on the Prize,* begins with a segment on the Till murder. These accounts underscore the psychological impact of Till's murder and, for the most part, do not pinpoint a direct cause-effect relationship.

12. This is a discursive analysis in two ways. For one, I am looking rather literally at how Till's funeral, the protest rallies, and the trial were talked and written about. (Because the transcript of the trial has either been lost or was never saved, there is no other point of entry into the "material reality" of the trial. See Simpson, "Reflections on a Murder," p. 187.) I also assume that the discourse about the case constitutes, rather than reflects, the "material reality" and that meanings of these events were constructed through and by discourse. With this in mind, discourse means more than simply "language" and instead refers to a system that produces material reality. Thus, throughout this analysis I do not delineate the boundaries between texts (most frequently, newspaper and periodical accounts) and social relations and events themselves; nor do I seek to pinpoint individual agency. For more on this theoretical framework, see Michel Foucault, *The History of Sexuality,* vol. 1, *An Introduction* (1976; New York: Random House, 1978); Joan Scott, *Gender and the Politics of History* (New York: Columbia University Press, 1988); Carolyn Dean, "Discourse," in *Encyclopedia of Social History,* ed. Peter Stearns (New York: Garland Press, 1994).

13. Harold Strider's reference to the men as "peckerwoods" quoted in Whitaker, "A Case Study in Southern Justice," p. 127.

14. Simpson, "Reflections on a Murder," p. 181; Whitaker, "A Case Study in Southern Justice," pp. 119–21.

15. In particular, many southerners reacted angrily to accounts labeling the murder a "lynching." See *Chicago Daily Tribune,* September 18, 1955, p. 1. For this line of analysis, see Simpson, "Reflections on a Murder"; Whitaker, "A Case Study in Southern Justice"; and Whitfield, *A Death in the Delta.*

16. In what is perhaps the most notorious reading of gender and race in the Till case, Susan Brownmiller argues that Till's alleged whistle (which she assumes to be fact) proved what "Emmett Till and J. W. Milam shared"—a domination of women "just short of physical assault." See *Against Our Will: Men, Women and Rape* (New York: Simon & Schuster, 1975), pp. 245–48. Angela Davis successfully changes the terms of this debate in her cogent analysis of white antirape feminists' reliance on racism. See *Women, Race and Class* (New York: Random House, 1981), pp. 172–201. For the historical effacement of black women's sexuality in particular, see Darlene Clark Hine, "Rape and the Inner Lives of Black Women in the Middle West: Preliminary Thoughts on the Culture of Dissemblance," *Signs* 14 (Summer 1989): 912–20. For the contemporary effacement of race in feminist theory and for formulations of black feminist thought, see, among others, Elsa Barkley Brown, "'What Has Happened Here': The Politics of Difference in Women's History and Feminist Politics," *Feminist Studies* 18 (Summer 1992): 295–312; Patricia Hill Collins, *Black Feminist Thought: Knowledge, Consciousness, and the Politics of Empowerment* (Boston: Unwin Hyman, 1990); Evelyn Brooks Higginbotham, "African-American Women's History and the Metalanguage of Race," *Signs* 17 (Summer 1992): 251–74; bell hooks, *Yearning: Race, Gender, and Cultural Politics* (Boston: South End Press, 1990). In *Reconstructing Womanhood: The Emergence of the Afro-American Woman Novelist* (New York: Oxford University Press, 1987), Hazel Carby provides a particularly helpful model for interrogating

race in all women. See also Vron Ware, *Beyond the Pale: White Women, Racism and History* (London: Verso, 1992).

17. For excellent analyses of how black women could alter and assign meaning to gender ideologies, see Carby, *Reconstructing Womanhood,* chap. 1; Jones, *Labor of Love, Labor of Sorrow.*

18. See n. 7 above. For analyses of the political meanings and uses of "traditional" sex-role ideology for white women, see May, *Homeward Bound;* and Amy Swerdlow, "Ladies' Day at the Capitol: Women Strike for Peace versus HUAC" (1982), in *Unequal Sisters: A Multi-Cultural Reader in U.S. Women's History,* ed. Ellen DuBois and Vicki Ruiz (New York: Routledge, 1990), pp. 400–17.

19. I emphasized "explicitly" here because it is clear, even from Adlai Stevenson's speech, for example, that motherhood was always infused with political meaning. What is new here is the reformulation of motherhood's political meaning.

20. Citizenship here refers not just to suffrage (a right that most southern African Americans were denied in 1955) but, in the words of Nancy Fraser, to "capacities for consent and speech, the ability to participate on a par with others in a [public] dialogue . . . capacities that are in myriad of ways deemed at odds" with femininity and blackness. See Nancy Fraser, *Unruly Practices: Power, Discourse and Gender in Contemporary Social Theory* (Minneapolis: University of Minnesota Press, 1989), quotation on p. 126. See also Jean Bethke Elshtain, *Public Man, Private Woman* (Princeton: Princeton University Press, 1981). For historically specific analyses of gendered citizenship, see Lynn Hunt, *The Family Romance of the French Revolution* (Berkeley: University of California Press, 1992). My thanks to Jane Gerhard for helping me clarify these ideas in this context.

21. See, for example, Philip Wylie, *Generation of Vipers* (1942; New York: Holt, Rinehart and Winston, 1955). Wylie coined the term *momism* in this best-selling diatribe against the bad white mother, revised and republished in 1955. Other texts in "sex role" literature through which "momism" developed include Helene Deutsch, *The Psychology of Women,* vol. 2 (New York: Grune and Stratton, 1945); Ferdinand Lundberg and Marynia F. Farmham, *Modern Woman: The Lost Sex* (New York: Harper & Brothers, 1947); and Edward A. Strecker, *Their Mothers' Sons: The Psychiatrist Examines an American Problem* (Philadelphia: J. B. Lippincott, 1946, 1951).

22. May, *Homeward Bound,* pp. 140–50; Susan M. Hartmann, *The Home Front and Beyond: American Women in the 1940s* (Boston: Twayne, 1982). See also Ruth Milkman, *Gender at Work: The Dynamics of Job Segregation by Sex during World War II* (Urbana: University of Illinois Press, 1987), esp. chap. 7; Rickie Solinger, *Wake Up Little Susie: Single Pregnancy and Race before Roe v. Wade* (New York: Routledge, 1992); Julie Weiss, "Womanhood and Psychoanalysis: A Study of Mutual Construction in Popular Culture" (Ph.D. diss., Brown University, 1990).

23. *Chicago Tribune Magazine of Books,* September 4, 1955, p. 1.

24. Ashley Montagu, "The Natural Superiority of Women," *Ladies Home Journal,* July 1952, p. 37.

25. May, *Homeward Bound,* pp. 91, 102. Nor was the domestic containment that May analyzes a racially specific phenomenon. See *Chicago Defender,* September 1955, p. 9.

26. The Bryants owned a small country store, and J. W. Milam rented mechanical cotton pickers. The store could not support the family of four, and Roy Bryant engaged in a variety of other jobs to make ends meet. At the time of the alleged incident between Emmett Till and Car-

olyn Bryant, Roy Bryant was working in Texas. See Whitfield, *A Death in the Delta,* pp. 16–23: U.S. Department of Commerce, *Statistical Abstract of the United States 1955* (Washington, D.C.: Government Printing Office, 1956), p. 553; Huie, *Wolf Whistle,* pp. 17–19. Huie also details their financial woes after the trial. For a discussion of how whiteness functioned as a compensatory wage of sorts for white workers in the nineteenth century, see David R. Roediger, *The Wages of Whiteness: Race and the Making of the American Working Class* (London: Verso, 1991).

27. See, for example, Gail Bederman, "'Civilization,' the Decline of Middle-Class Manliness, and Ida B. Wells's Anti-Lynching Campaign (1892–1894)," *Radical History Review* 52 (1992): 5–30; Jacquelyn Dowd Hall, *Revolt against Chivalry: Jesse Daniel Ames and the Women's Campaign against Lynching* (New York: Columbia University Press, 1979).

28. George Lipsitz, *Time Passages: Collective Memory and American Popular Culture* (Minneapolis: University of Minnesota Press, 1990), p. 77; *Look,* October 16, 1956, p. 35, and quoted in Sara Evans, *Born for Liberty,* p. 249, emphasis added.

29. Jones, *Labor of Love, Labor of Sorrow,* p. 269.

30. Patricia Morton, *Disfigured Images: The Historical Assault on Afro-American Women* (New York: Praeger, 1991), p. 88, emphasis in original. Frazier first developed what would become the "matriarchy thesis" in *The Negro Family in the United States* (1939; Chicago: University of Chicago Press, 1947). Other progressive "race relations" texts that elaborated on matriarchy as damaging include John Dollard, *Caste and Color in a Southern Town* (New York: Harper & Brothers, 1937); St. Clair Drake and Horace R. Cayton, *Black Metropolis: A Study of Negro Life in a Northern City* (1945; New York: Harper & Row, 1962); Abram Kardiner and Lionel Ovesey, *The Mark of Oppression: Explorations in the Personality of the American Negro* (1945; New York: Meridian Books, 1962). Despite similarities in discussions of black and white women and despite the similarities between "momism" and "matriarchy," debates about women remained segregated: within dominant white culture, black women were not part of the large literature on "sex roles" but remained the object of concern only within the parameters of "race relations."

31. Morton, *Disfigured Images,* pp. 74–84; Frazier, *The Negro Family,* p. 299. See also Regina G. Kunzel, "White Neurosis, Black Pathology: Constructing Out-of-Wedlock Pregnancy in the Wartime and Postwar United States," in *Not June Cleaver: Women and Gender in Postwar America, 1945–1960,* ed. Joanne Meyerowitz (Philadelphia: Temple University Press, 1994).

32. Morton, *Disfigured Images,* p. 76.

33. For an example of how and why respectability could be central to black women's political activism, see Jo Ann Gibson Robinson, *The Montgomery Bus Boycott and the Women Who Started It: The Memoir of Jo Ann Gibson Robinson* (Knoxville: University of Tennessee Press, 1987). See, too, Brown, "'What Has Happened Here,'" esp. pp. 304–6.

34. Whitfield, *A Death in the Delta,* p. 15; Williams, *Eyes on the Prize,* p. 41. Although black women's yearly pay was still less than half of white women's (itself less than two-thirds of white men's), the percentage of black women working as domestics declined from 60 percent in 1940 to 42 percent in 1950, and the percentage of black men and women in white-collar work doubled between 1940 and the mid-1950s. See Jones, *Labor of Love, Labor of Sorrow,* p. 261; Sitkoff, *The Struggle for Black Equality,* p. 18; Giddings, *When and Where I Enter,* p. 241.

35. *Commonweal,* September 23, 1955, pp. 603–4. Sympathetic whites tended not to see the ways in which the lives of whites and blacks were structured by race; rather, race became a relevant issue only when Till was murdered.

36. *Chicago Defender,* October 22, 1955, p. 2.

37. Ibid., November 5, 1955, p. 14, emphasis added.

38. *Pittsburgh Courier,* August 20, 1955, p. 9.

39. E. Franklin Frazier, *Black Bourgeoisie* (1957; New York: Free Press, 1966).

40. Hampton and Fayer, *Voices of Freedom,* p. 5; *Chicago Daily Tribune,* September 2, 1955, p. 1.

41. Hampton and Fayer, *Voices of Freedom,* p. 5; *Pittsburgh Courier,* September 10, 1955, p. 1. The exact words Bradley used at this point vary slightly from one account to the next, but the message is remarkably consistent in every report. The quotation "I wanted the whole world to see what I have seen" appears in Hampton and Fayer, *Voices of Freedom,* p. 6.

42. *Chicago Defender,* September 17, 1955, p. 4; ibid., September 10, 1955, p. 1; *Chicago Daily Tribune,* September 4, 1955, p. 2.

43. Quotation on impact of the service from "Chicago Boy," *The Nation,* September 17, 1955, p. 235. For estimates of 10,000, see "Mississippi: The Accused," *Newsweek,* September 19, 1955, p. 38; and *New York Times,* September 4, 1955, sec. VI, p. 9; for other figures, see *Chicago Daily Tribune,* September 4, 1955, p. 2 (40,000); *Chicago Defender,* September 10, 1955, p. 1; and *New York Amsterdam News,* September 10, 1955, p. 1 (50,000); *Pittsburgh Courier,* September 10, 1955, p. 1 (100,000); "Nation Horrified by Murder of Kidnapped Chicago Youth," *Jet,* September 15, 1955, pp. 6–9 (600,000). Discrepancies could stem from daily versus cumulative estimates.

44. Jessica Shubow has helped me to see that black control of the body was in marked contrast to a long history of white-controlled displays of lynched African Americans in which published photographs of lynchings were designed to intimidate and disempower black communities. The near unanimous outrage outside the South and the unprecedented media coverage of these events (the latter due in part to the advent of television) also distinguished the Till case from the heavily publicized, though always controversial, trial of the "Scottsboro boys."

45. *Chicago Defender,* September 17, 1955, p. 9.

46. Ibid., emphasis added.

47. Ibid.; *Afro-American,* September 17, 1955, p. 1; *Chicago Defender,* October 1, 1955, p. 4; *Chicago Defender,* September 10, 1955, p. 5; *Afro-American,* September 10, 1955, p. 1.

48. "Mississippi: The Place, the Acquittal," *Newsweek* October 3, 1955, p. 24; *Chicago Defender,* September 10, 1955, p. 1; *Pittsburgh Courier,* September 17, 1955, p. 1; *Chicago Defender,* October 1, 1955, p. 4; *New York Amsterdam News,* September 24, 1955, p. 1. Whether or not the teenage Till was a boy or a man and what black masculinity and sexuality should mean were also implicit in these and other images of both Till and Bradley. For example, Huie emphasized Till's size and tried to uncover his sexual history, while some critics of the murder specifically defended Till's "right"—as an American male—to whistle. According to the liberal *Commonweal,* for example, "coming from a 14-year-old white boy this [whistle] would have been dismissed as rudeness . . . and many would have laughed at the indication that the boy was on his way to becoming a man." See "Death in Mississippi," *Commonweal,* September 23, 1955, p. 603. Others constructed images of Till as young, innocent, and anything but masculine. In a fiery speech to an

interracial crowd of twenty thousand, for example, Congressman Adam Clayton Powell declared that murdering Emmett Till was akin to "the lynching of the Statue of Liberty." See *New York Amsterdam News,* October 15, 1955, p. 1.

49. "Mississippi: The Accused," p. 38. Many in the liberal press feared that the negative publicity surrounding the murder and acquittal would be used by communists. According to the *New Republic,* for example, when Milam and Bryant were acquitted, "communists around the world got a new weapon against the United States." See "Notes," *New Republic,* October 3, 1955, p. 2. Others saw different international implications to the murder; a French reporter linked Till's death to "the eternal problem of colonialism . . . that numerous Americans are so quick to denounce in others." See "L'Affaire Till in the French Press," *The Crisis,* December 1955, pp. 596–602.

50. *Pittsburgh Courier,* October 29, 1955, p. 9.

51. *Chicago Defender,* September 17, 1955, p. 9; *New York Amsterdam News,* October 1, 1955, p. 7; "In Memoriam, Emmett Till," *Life,* October 10, 1955, p. 48. Bradley's status as a "widow" deflected attention away from her second marriage and divorce. According to several sources, however, Bradley and Louis Till had divorced before he entered the army. See Whitaker, *A Death in the Delta,* p. 15.

52. *New York Amsterdam News,* October 1, 1955, p. 7.

53. "At What Age Is a Woman Most Beautiful?" *Jet,* March 3, 1955, pp. 26–29 (the answer—"Experts Say All Women Beautiful at Least Twice in Life"); "*Jet's* Calendar Girls for 1955," *Jet,* January 6, 1955, pp. 28–42.

54. Jones, *Labor of Love, Labor of Sorrow,* p. 272. In her analysis of *Ebony,* Jones also points out that an emphasis on attractive women accompanied an emphasis on prominent women—in politics, in the entertainment industry, and in other traditionally male-dominated professions. See n. 8 above.

55. Black women are conspicuously absent in defenses of Till that do address sexuality. An editorial decrying the "mongrelization obsession" of southern whites, for example, argued that the "great majority of Negroes . . . do not aspire to wed the 'pure' womanhood of Dixie." See *Pittsburgh Courier,* October 1, 1955, p. 6. This absence countered long-standing stereotypes that rendered black women promiscuous and was part of a tradition in which, in the words of Elsa Barkley Brown, "black women, especially middle class women, have learned to present a public image that never reveals their sexuality." Brown, "'What Has Happened Here,'" p. 306.

56. *Chicago Defender,* October 1, 1955, p. 2; ibid., p. 4; ibid., October 8, 1955, p. 2. This editorial discussed "petty jealousy" between the NAACP and the AFL/Brotherhood of Sleeping Car Porters regarding Bradley's attendance at an AFL-sponsored rally (which the NAACP suspected of "pinkish tendencies"), but in this account Mamie Bradley had no role in the dispute.

57. *Chicago Tribune,* October 7, 1955, p. 5; *Chicago Defender,* September 10, 1955, p. 1; ibid., September 17, 1955, p. 4. In some accounts, Bradley's dependence extended to her relationship with her son. See *Afro-American,* September 10, 1955, p. 1.

58. The *Eyes on the Prize* documentary is an exception in that it draws attention to Bradley's role. Nevertheless, according to an accompanying text, "in vengeance" Bradley "declared" that the world would see her son's corpse. This language and other descriptions of her as overly emotional effectively depoliticize her actions. See Williams, *Eyes on the Prize,* pp. 43–44. See also "30 Years Ago: How Emmett Till's Lynching Launched the Civil Rights Drive," *Jet,* June

17, 1985, pp. 12–18. These more recent analyses duplicate accounts at the time. For example, her declaration, "Darling, you have not died in vain, your life has been sacrificed for something," is followed by "Mrs. Bradley hysterically shouted." See *Chicago Defender,* September 10, 1955, p. 2.

59. *Chicago Defender,* September 10, 1955, p. 1; *Pittsburgh Courier,* September 10, 1955, p. 3.

60. *Memphis Commercial Appeal,* September 4, 1955, sec. 2, p. 4; ibid., pp. 1, 2; ibid., September 7, 1955, p. 6; *Greenville Delta-Democrat Times,* quoted in Whitfield, *A Death in the Delta,* p. 29.

61. Huie, *Wolf Whistle,* p. 26.

62. Whitaker, *A Death in the Delta,* pp. 117–19; *Chicago Defender,* October 29, 1955, p. 2; *New York Times,* October 30, 1955, p. 87; *Jackson Daily News,* October 15, 1955. The guilt or innocence of Louis Till and the details surrounding his court-martial and hanging remain in dispute, particularly in light of the fact that in Europe during World War II, eighty-seven of the ninety-five soldiers hanged for rape and murder of civilians were African American. At least one of Till's peers in the segregated unit suggested that he had been "railroaded" by MPs enforcing "nonfraternization bans." At the time, Bradley asserted that the federal government had never told her how or why her husband had died; she has since noted that "Louis was never allowed to testify . . . the case was built on the testimony of what someone else said." See "GI Buddies Say Till's Dad Was 'Railroaded' in Italy," *Jet,* November 3, 1955, pp. 4–5; *New York Amsterdam News,* October 1, 1955, p. 7; "Time Heals Few Wounds for Emmett Till's Mother," *Jet,* April 9, 1984, p. 55.

63. *Memphis Commercial Appeal,* September 6, 1955, pp. 1, 8. *Memphis Commercial Appeal,* September 4, 1955, sec. 2, p. 4, emphasis added.

64. *Chicago Defender,* September 17, 1955, p. 1. One black woman wrote that she would like to see a photograph of Carolyn Bryant, "the woman who started this 'shot heard around the world'— . . . this delicate example of female virtue, this outraged accuser of children and babies." See *Afro-American,* September 24, 1955, p. 4.

65. Mary Cain, quoted in Ira Harkey, *The Smell of Burning Crosses: An Autobiography of a Mississippi Newspaperman* (Jacksonville, Ill.: Harris-Wolfe, 1967), p. 106, emphasis added.

66. See Lynn Hunt, "The Many Bodies of Marie Antoinette: Political Pornography and the Problem of the Feminine in the French Revolution," in *Eroticism and the Body Politic* (Baltimore: Johns Hopkins University Press, 1991), pp. 108–30; Solinger, *Wake Up Little Susie.* My thanks to Carolyn Dean for helping me to understand this dynamic.

67. Morton, *Disfigured Images,* pp. 70–72. It is worth noting that links between African Americans and femininity were used toward progressive and reactionary ends at different points in American history. See Deborah Gray White, *Ar'n't I a Woman? Female Slaves in the Plantation South* (New York: Norton, 1985), esp. pp. 13–61.

68. Huie, *Wolf Whistle,* p. 26. In contrast to accounts in the African American press, which seem intent on underscoring gender difference, he does not distinguish between male and female mourners.

69. *Chicago Defender,* September 17, 1955, p. 2; *New York Amsterdam News,* October 1, 1955, p. 12; ibid., p. 8; *Pittsburgh Courier,* October 29, 1955, p. 9; ibid., October 22, 1955, p. 1. It is important to note that there were black women assuming increasingly prominent and political roles in this period, including civil rights activists Ruby Hurley, Daisy Bates, and Ella Baker; entertainment figures Lena Horne and Mahalia Jackson; and professional educators or public ser-

vants Mary McLeod Bethune and Edith Sampson. While sexism and racism informed these women's lives as well, they were not subject to the same symbolic construction as was Mamie Till Bradley.

70. *Chicago Defender,* September 24, 1955; Whitfield, *A Death in the Delta,* p. 33.

71. Ruby Hurley and Medgar Evers, NAACP staff workers in Mississippi, located Amanda Bradley and Willie Reed, the two "surprise witnesses," and encouraged them to testify. Report of the Secretary for the Month of September 1955, NAACP Papers, supp. to pt. 1, 1951–55, reel 2; David Shostak, "Crosby Smith: Forgotten Witness to a Mississippi Nightmare," *Negro History Bulletin* 37 (December 1974): 320–25.

72. *New York Times,* September 22, 1955, p. 64; Hampton and Fayer, *Voices of Freedom,* p. 11; Whitfield, *A Death in the Delta,* p. 39.

73. Although 63 percent of the population in Tallahatchie County was African American, no blacks were eligible for jury service, dependent as it was on voter registration. In fact, jury duty in Tallahatchie County was so severely restricted through age, gender, literacy, and residency requirements that, ultimately, only 5 percent of the county population was eligible. See Whitfield, *A Death in the Delta,* p. 35.

74. There were six other "character witnesses" for the defense. Sheriff Strider raised questions about the identity of the body shortly after Till's funeral, in direct contradiction to statements he had made earlier. Casting doubts on the identity of the body was an important part of the shift in southern whites' opinions generally, and in the condemnation of the NAACP in particular. See "Mississippi: The Place, the Acquittal," p. 25; Simpson, "Reflections on a Murder," p. 192.

75. *Afro-American,* September 24, 1955, p. 14; ibid., p. 1; *Memphis Commercial Appeal,* September 22, 1955, p. 8.

76. After the trial, Mamie Bradley reported that she had not been molested in Sumner but that men had pretended to shoot at her, yelling "'Bang! Bang!' while others laughed." See *Memphis Commercial Appeal,* September 25, 1955, p. 1. Certainly, the physical dangers she faced were multiple. For more extensive analyses of polarized constructions of women, see, among others, Morton, *Disfigured Images,* esp. pp. 1–27: White, *Ar'n't I a Woman?,* esp. pp. 27–61.

77. *Memphis Commercial Appeal,* September 8, 1955, p. 1; ibid., September 20, 1955, p. 15. The texts of these telegrams suggest an adversarial attitude toward Mamie Bradley on the part of the district attorney and underscore just how difficult those days in Sumner were. Clearly, even the men prosecuting the case were not allies of Till's family. For more information on the legal team, see *Memphis Commercial Appeal,* September 18, 1955, sec. V, p. 10; Simpson, "Reflections on a Murder," pp. 185–87; Whitfield, *A Death in the Delta,* pp. 31, 41, 56; Whitaker, "A Case Study in Southern Justice," p. 131.

78. *Memphis Commercial Appeal,* September 21, 1955, p. 8.

79. *Pittsburgh Courier,* September 21, 1955, p. 1; ibid., p. 4; *Chicago Defender,* October 1, 1955, p. 4.

80. *Memphis Commercial Appeal,* September 21, 1955, p. 8; *New York Times,* September 23, 1955, p. 15; *Memphis Commercial Appeal,* September 22, 1955, p. 1; ibid., September 23, 1955, p. 2; Whitfield, *A Death in the Delta,* pp. 40–42. According to Judge Swango, the alleged incident between Bryant and Till had occurred "too long before the abduction" and hence was inadmissible.

81. *Memphis Commercial Appeal,* September 8, 1955, p. 1; *New York Times,* September 23, 1955, p. 15; "Mississippi: The Place, the Acquittal," p. 24.

82. *Memphis Commercial Appeal,* September 20, 1955, p. 1; *Chicago Defender,* September 24, 1955, p. 5; *Memphis Commercial Appeal,* September 7, 1955, p. 1; ibid., September 22, 1955, p. 33; Whitfield, *A Death in the Delta,* p. 37. Congressman Charles C. Diggs (D-Mich.) was among those at this segregated table and was frequently referred to as "the nigger congressman."

83. After the trial (and after their paid confession to Huie), Milam and Bryant lost the support of the Mississippi establishment. Their economic difficulties increased when Mississippi blacks refused to buy at the Bryant store and local banks refused to give either man loans; both ultimately left Mississippi. See Hampton and Fayer, *Voices of Freedom,* p. 14; Raines, *My Soul Is Rested,* p. 392; Huie, *Wolf Whistle.* For analyses of race and gender in relation to class tensions, see Dolores Janiewski, *Sisterhood Denied: Race, Gender, and Class in a New South Town* (Philadelphia: Temple University Press, 1985); Jones, *Labor of Love, Labor of Sorrow;* Jacqueline Jones, "The Political Implications of Black and White Women's Work in the South, 1890–1965," in *Women, Politics, and Change,* ed. Louise Tilly and Patricia Gurin (New York: Russell Sage Foundation, 1990), pp. 108–29. In "The Leo Frank Case Reconsidered: Gender and Sexual Politics in the Making of Reactionary Populism," *Journal of American History* 78 (December 1991): 917–48, Nancy MacLean offers a particularly helpful analysis of how gender informed class conflicts, anti-Semitism, and racism during this notorious murder trial in 1913.

84. *Memphis Commercial Appeal,* September 24, 1955, p. 17; *Chicago Daily Tribune,* September 24, 1955, p. 1. See also *Memphis Commercial Appeal,* September 24, 1955, p. 1; ibid., p. 3; ibid., p. 4; *New York Times,* September 24, 1955, p. 1. Antiracists challenged this image of the happy family. A liberal Parisian weekly, *Aux écoutes,* labeled Carolyn Bryant a "cruel shrew"; in *Le canard enchaîné* she was "a crossroads Marilyn Monroe." Others, nationally and internationally, drew attention to the irony of "Roy . . looking like the model family man," to the "'phony' sad faces of the wives," and to Milam and Bryant "playing with their children, seemingly callous of the charges against them, while their wives 'mugged' for the cameras." See "L'Affaire Till in the French Press," pp. 596–601; *Pittsburgh Courier,* October 1, 1955, p. 1; *New York Amsterdam News,* October 15, 1955, p. 1. Roi Ottley both clung to and inverted notions of respectability in a biting column that characterized the trial as endorsing "vicious, lawless and barbarous" behavior and the southern whites as primitives. See *Chicago Defender,* October 8, 1955, p. 8.

85. Although the state called one funeral director who testified that he thought the body was Till's, prosecutors made no effort to confirm the identity of the body scientifically. See Simpson, "Reflections on a Murder," p. 189. In fact, as rumors about the identity of the body continued to circulate after the trial, Bradley expressed her willingness "to have my boy's body exhumed from the vault for a thorough examination if that would dispel these wild rumors." See *New York Times,* September 30, 1955, p. 18.

86. *New York Times,* September 24, 1955, p. 1.

87. *Chicago Defender,* October 1, 1955, p. 4.

88. *Chicago Daily Tribune,* September 1, 1955, p. 4; *Chicago Defender,* October 15, 1955, p. 3.

89. "Trial by Jury," *Time,* October 3, 1955, p. 18; *Memphis Commercial Appeal,* September 22, 1955, p. 1; I. F. Stone, "The Murder of Emmett Till," in *The Haunted Fifties* (New York: Random House, 1963), p. 107.

90. Many African Americans consequently objected to this emphasis on Till's willingness

to humble himself. See, for example, NAACP Correspondence, Mississippi Pressures, 1955, NAACP Papers, Library of Congress, Washington, D.C.; *Chicago Defender,* September 17, 1955, p. 9.

91. *New York Times,* September 23, 1955, p. 15; ibid., September 24, 1955, p. 1. Speaking at a Cleveland, Ohio, NAACP chapter meeting on her way to Sumner, Bradley "appeared quiet and composed, (and) urged the groups to write congressmen . . . and called on the audience to promote membership in the NAACP," according to the *Chicago Daily Tribune,* September 19, 1955, p. 2.

92. *Pittsburgh Courier,* October 1, 1955, p. 1; *Chicago Defender,* October 1, 1955, p. 1.

93. "Mississippi: The Place, the Acquittal," p. 25. (In one sentence *Newsweek* corroborated her respectability from a variety of perspectives—rendering Bradley a good mother, a hard worker, an emotional woman, and an ex-wife.) Gendered and racialized representations of Bradley did not always break down along regional lines. According to the *Memphis Commercial Appeal,* September 22, 1955, p. 35, Bradley "wept silently" when shown the photograph of the body.

94. *Chicago Defender,* September 17, 1955, p. 2.

95. *Pittsburgh Courier,* October 1, 1955, p. 8; *L'aurore,* quoted in "L'Affaire Till in the French Press," p. 600.

96. *New York Times,* September 24, 1955, p. 1; *Chicago Daily Tribune,* October 24, 1955, p. 1. The defense also tried to "prove" a relationship between Bradley and a public organization (particularly the NAACP), one that would discredit the "grieving mother" and make her motherhood itself suspect. This need for a woman to act exclusively as a "private" person has echoes in the Anita Hill–Clarence Thomas hearings; hostile senators repeatedly asked Hill if she was "acting alone." Any public or official affiliation would clearly have undercut her claims as a private woman who had experienced sexual harassment. For more on the Hill-Thomas hearings, see Brown, "'What Has Happened Here,'" pp. 302–7; Toni Morrison, ed., *Race-ing Justice, En-Gendering Power: Essays on Anita Hill, Clarence Thomas and the Constructions of Social Reality* (New York: Pantheon, 1992); Geneva Smitherman, ed., *African American Women Speak Out on Anita Hill–Clarence Thomas* (Detroit: Wayne State University Press, 1995).

97. This "damned if you do, damned if you don't" framework, which renders Mamie Bradley's words irrelevant because of both her composure *and* her irrationality, was replayed by the all-white, all-male "jury" of senators in the Hill-Thomas hearing. Anita Hill presented as a very rational, composed subject and not as the stereotypically "hysterical woman." Arlen Specter used this composure and dignity against her when he argued that if she were in fact telling the truth, she would have either quit her job, kept notes after incidents of harassment, or reported her boss. Her rational behavior and demeanor were thus suspect; using those standards of rationality, he accused her of perjury and dismissed her charges. At the same time, Orin Hatch struggled to represent Anita Hill as the classically irrational, hysterical, and delusional woman by quoting *The Exorcist* and other sources. Using those standards, he too dismissed her charges.

98. Stone, "The Murder of Emmett Till," p. 108.

99. *New York Times,* September 24, 1955, pp. 1, 38.

100. *Pittsburgh Courier,* October 1, 1955, p. 1. Mamie Till Bradley Mobley appeared on the Oprah Winfrey show in October 1992; at that time, she again emphasized that she had not wanted to be present when the verdict was offered.

101. *New York Amsterdam News,* October 1, 1955, p. 8; ibid., October 8, 1955, p. 21.

102. Board of Directors Meeting, October 10, 1955, NAACP Papers, supp. to pt. 1, 1951–55, reel 1; *New York Times,* October 3, 1955, p. 19. According to the Report of the Secretary to the Board of Directors for the month of October 1955, as a result of the *New York Times* advertisement, letters and contributions "came from persons in all walks of life, a New England judge . . . business men . . . fraternities. A score of letters came from white Southerners." See NAACP Papers, supp. to pt. 1, 1951–55, reel 2.

103. *Pittsburgh Courier,* November 19, 1955, p. 2; *New York Amsterdam News,* November 19, 1955, p. 2; Board of Directors meeting, November 14, 1955, NAACP Papers, supp. to pt. 1, 1951–55, reel 1. Wright apparently agreed to NAACP terms for the tour: the organization would pay for travel expenses plus $100 per appearance, "which amount will be increased if the receipts for the meeting warrant it." Details of this conflict are unclear and again not my central concern. More significant to me is how the meaning of these events was constructed and how gender implicitly and explicitly informed the NAACP's political agenda. Further, I am less concerned with Bradley's intentions than with perceptions of them and the meaning derived from this "rift" with the NAACP.

104. *Chicago Defender,* November 19, 1955, p. 2; Board of Directors meeting, November 14, 1955, NAACP Papers, supp. to pt. 1, 1951–55, reel 1.

105. *Chicago Defender,* November 26, 1955, p. 1.

106. *New York Amsterdam News,* November 19, 1955, pp. 1, 2; Report of the Secretary for the Month of September 1955, NAACP Papers, supp. to pt. 1, 1951–55, reel 2.

107. *Pittsburgh Courier,* November 26, 1955, p. 12.

108. *Chicago Defender,* October 15, 1955, p. 2; *Pittsburgh Courier,* October 29, 1955, p. 1; *Chicago Defender,* October 22, 1955, p. 2.

109. *New York Amsterdam News,* October 1, 1955, p. 9.

110. *Pittsburgh Courier,* December 24, 1955, p. 3; *Chicago Defender,* October 22, 1955, p. 2. For her leave being unpaid, see *Chicago Defender,* November 19, 1955, p. 2. According to statements by Wilkins in the NAACP papers, the organization also agreed to pay the travel expenses of her father.

111. *New York Times,* October 25, 1955, p. 27; *Chicago Defender,* October 29, 1955, p. 1. Bradley had also sent a telegram to President Eisenhower, then recovering from a heart attack; the president, who once told Chief Justice Earl Warren that white supremacists "were not bad people," did not respond. See Whitfield, *A Death in the Delta,* pp. 72–74. Two rallies in Washington were held to coincide with her visit and "12,000 turned out to see her . . . the crowds were so great that Mrs. Mamie Bradley of Chicago, mother of the dead little Till boy, was almost prevented from entering the auditorium to address the throngs that awaited her." See *New York Amsterdam News,* October 29, 1955, p. 3.

112. *Pittsburgh Courier,* October 29, 1955, p. 9; *Chicago Defender,* October 29, 1955, p. 2, emphasis added. This editorial appears to be the first time Bradley is referred to simply as "Mamie" in the African American press; indeed, reporters and other observers had paid close attention to the titles—and lack thereof—whites had shown to black principals in the case.

113. *Pittsburgh Courier,* October 1, 1955, p. 1.

114. *Chicago Defender,* November 26, 1955, p. 1.

115. *New York Amsterdam News,* November 26, 1955, p. 8; "How the Till Case Changed 5 Lives," *Jet,* November 24, 1955, p. 10.

116. *Pittsburgh Courier,* November 19, 1955, p. 2; *Chicago Defender,* November 26, 1955, p. 1, 2; "How the Till Case Changed 5 Lives," p. 10. Chicago reporters seemed particularly intent on salvaging Mamie Bradley's reputation; perhaps, to them, the city in general was potentially implicated in any scandal.

117. *Chicago Defender,* November 19, 1955, p. 2; *New York Amsterdam News,* November 19, 1955, p. 2; *Chicago Defender,* October 8, 1955, p. 1.

118. *Chicago Defender,* November 26, 1955, p. 1.

119. Ibid., November 19, 1955, p. 2.

120. Ibid.; "How the Till Case Changed 5 Lives," p. 13.

121. *Chicago Defender,* November 19, 1955, pp. 1, 2; *New York Amsterdam News,* November 19, 1955, pp. 1, 2. The argument that the $5,000 fee was not her idea was made alongside descriptions of her financial problems (with quotations such as "It is a strain to get food for my table"). Bradley, quoted in *New York Amsterdam News,* November 19, 1955, pp. 1, 2. See also "How the Till Case Changed 5 Lives," pp. 10–13.

122. *Chicago Defender,* November 19, 1955, p. 2; *Pittsburgh Courier,* December 24, 1955, p. 3.

123. *Pittsburgh Courier,* December 24, 1955, pp. 3, 6; *Chicago Defender,* December 24, 1955, p. 1. Efforts to "rehabilitate" Bradley are also evident in the two-installment "Mamie Bradley's Untold Story, Told by Mamie Bradley, as Told to Ethel Payne," *Chicago Defender,* April 21, 1956, p. 8, and April 28, 1956, p. 10. In these autobiographical pieces, Bradley alludes to the controversy when she writes, "People wonder why I am so calm, and some even think I am cold," but then turns to a detailed description of her childhood, writing at length about her own mother's work ethic and religious commitment.

124. Quoted in *Pittsburgh Courier,* December 24, 1955, p. 3.

125. Studs Terkel, *Race: How Blacks and Whites Think and Feel about the American Obsession* (New York: Norton, 1992), p. 22; of her time with the NAACP in 1955, Mobley said only, "I was one of the best fundraisers they ever had." See also "30 Years Ago: How Emmett Till's Lynching Launched the Civil Rights Drive," *Jet,* June 17, 1985, pp. 12–18.

126. *Afro-American,* September 24, 1955, p. 4; "Inside You and Me," *The Crisis,* December 1955, pp. 592–95.

127. Moore, in Raines, *My Soul Is Rested,* pp. 234–35.

128. *Pittsburgh Courier,* September 10, 1955, p. 1.

129. *New York Amsterdam News,* October 18, 1955, p. 8; *Afro-American,* September 24, 1955, p. 4.

130. Clay quoted in Whitfield, *A Death in the Delta,* p. 94; *New York Times,* May 17, 1979, p. A23. For other memories of Till's death, see interviews in Hampton and Fayer, *Voices of Freedom;* Raines, *My Soul Is Rested;* and Williams, *Eyes on the Prize.* Endesha Ida Mae Holland, "Memories of the Mississippi Delta," *Michigan Quarterly Review* 26 (Winter 1987): 246–58; Anne Moody, *Coming of Age in Mississippi* (New York: Dell, 1968), pp. 125–29; Cloyte Murdock Larsson, "Land of the Till Murder Revisited," *Ebony,* March 1986, pp. 53–58; Shelby Steele, "On Being Black and Middle Class," *Commentary,* January 1988, pp. 42–47. For fiction that draws

on Till's murder, see, among others, Alice Walker, "Advancing Luna—and Ida R. Wells," in *You Can't Keep a Good Woman Down* (San Diego: Harcourt Brace Jovanovich, 1981); and Bebe Moore Campbell, *Your Blues Ain't Like Mine* (New York: Putnam's, 1992).

131. *New York Times,* May 17, 1979, p. A23.

132. Jones, *Labor of Love, Labor of Sorrow,* pp. 279–80; Jones, "The Political Implications of Black and White Women's Work," pp. 108–29. I am grateful to Jacqueline Jones for helping me think more carefully about women's "traditional" roles.

Part Two

MOTHERHOOD AND REPRODUCTION

The subject of reproduction encompasses efforts to prevent, terminate, and achieve pregnancy as well as the completion of a pregnancy through birth. While reproduction is, at its core, a biological function, the articles we have selected examine reproduction as a social phenomenon. They ask how reproduction is thought of and experienced by individual women, by communities, and by society. In posing these questions, the authors inquire about how social beliefs about fertility, birthing practices, and the desire to control reproduction give meaning to the lives of mothers and define the culture in which they live.

The articles in this section suggest some of the continuities and changes in the lives of mothers over the past centuries. One continuity is the cultural expectation that women will become mothers; a second and related issue is the concern that women have about surviving pregnancy and childbirth and seeing that their offspring survive and are healthy. A third continuity is the quest for control. Whether women sought to attain or avoid pregnancy, and whether they gave birth at home with a midwife or in the hospital with a physician, they sought to manage their reproductive lives as best they could. Yet, as the transition from home to hospital births suggests, there were significant changes in mothering and reproduction over the course of American history. One important shift was the growth of medical authority over fertility, pregnancy, and childbirth. Another was the overall decline in fertility. Tracing these phenomena requires an examination of demographic data about birthrates within populations, and it necessitates the examination of individual accounts often hidden in diaries and reminiscences. While demographic data can, for example, tell us that overall rates of childbirth declined over a particular era, the private writings of women will tell us how some individuals attempted to limit the size of their families.

Laurel Thatcher Ulrich's discussion of midwife and physician practices in rural, postrevolutionary New England illuminates the roles played by each kind of practitioner. Her examination of the diary of midwife Martha Ballard reveals how a midwife managed birth. Moreover, it documents the effectiveness of Ballard's methods by demonstrating the low rates of maternal and infant mortality among her patients.

Turning to the South, Jan Lewis and Kenneth Lockridge show how Virginia gentry women began to control their fertility in the early nineteenth century. Using diaries and letters, they disclose how women used prolonged breast-feeding and sexual abstinence to control the size of their families, and they discuss how husbands' interests in family limitation were critical to the drop in fertility rates.

In tracing the history of infertility, Margaret Marsh considers both the enduring cultural expectation that women become mothers and the shifting meaning of childlessness. In the seventeenth, eighteenth, and most of the nineteenth century infertility was explained as the will of God. In the late nineteenth and twentieth centuries medical explanations of infertility became more dominant.

Judith Walzer Leavitt provides a case study of women's search for control in her analysis of the movement for "twilight sleep," a form of anesthesia used in childbirth in the early decades of the twentieth century. In their campaign for painless childbirth, women helped move birth out of the home and into the hospital, where it could be overseen by physicians.

Studying the perspective of African American women in the areas of abortion and birth control, Loretta Ross finds a continuing quest for reproductive freedom. She discusses slave women in the early nineteenth century using abortion as a form of resistance, recounts the methods women used later in the nineteenth century to control their fertility, and shows how the late twentieth-century demand for access to birth control also required women to fight against the eugenics movement and sterilization programs.

In the final article, Joan Mathews and Kathleen Zadak describe the development of the alternative birth movement in the United States, beginning with the prepared childbirth movement of the 1940s. The authors explain how the convergence of consumer and feminist movements created a demand for an alternative to medicalized hospital births that emphasized technological intervention. They show that while technology remains a key part of hospital births, there is a growing interest in responding to women's demands by providing family-centered, personalized care.

8.

"The Living Mother of a Living Child"
Midwifery and Mortality in Post-Revolutionary New England

LAUREL THATCHER ULRICH

Forty-one years ago, Richard Harrison Shryock could summarize the history of early American midwifery in a few sentences. "The history of obstetrics and of pediatrics," he wrote, "affords other illustrations of the way in which inadequate medical science affected the public health. Maternity cases were left, in English-speaking lands, almost entirely to midwives.... And since midwives lacked any scientific training, obstetrics proceeded on the level of folk practice, and with consequences which may be easily imagined."[1] The consequences could be imagined because few persons in 1948 doubted the superiority of medical science over folk practice.

The advent of "natural" childbirth, culminating in recent years in the revival of lay midwifery, has changed historical judgments as well as obstetrics. In revisionist histories of childbirth, the pleasant story of scientific progress has been replaced by a darker tale of medical competitiveness and misplaced confidence in an imperfect science. Medical science did not on the whole increase women's chances of surviving childbirth until well into the twentieth century, the new histories argue, and may actually have increased the dangers. As Richard W. Wertz and Dorothy C. Wertz explain, puerperal fever, the dreaded infection that killed so many women in the nineteenth century, "is probably the classic example of iatrogenic disease—that is, disease caused by medical treatment itself."[2]

Although historians trace to the eighteenth century the gradual supplanting of midwives by physicians, most detailed studies have concentrated on the nineteenth century or later. The few discussions of childbirth in early America have dealt with

Reprinted from *William and Mary Quarterly,* 3d ser., 46 (1989): 27–48, by permission of the Institute of Early American History and Culture.

urban centers and with the work of prominent physicians such as William Shippen of Philadelphia.[3] Almost nothing is known about rural obstetrics or about the activities and attitudes of midwives. This essay begins to fill that gap. Its central document is the manuscript diary of a Maine midwife, Martha Moore Ballard, who lived at Augusta (then part of Hallowell) from 1778 to 1812. It also uses English obstetrical literature, scattered physicians' and midwives' records from Maine and New Hampshire, and the papers of Dr. Jeremiah Barker of Gorham, Maine.

Martha Ballard performed her first delivery in 1778, though her diary does not begin until six years later. Between 1785 and 1812 she recorded 814 deliveries. The expansiveness of her record is unusual not only among midwives (few of whom left any written evidence of their practice) but among country physicians as well. Yet the diary has received little scholarly attention. Historians who have used it have relied on an abridged version published in Charles Elventon Nash's *History of Augusta*. For most, the details of Ballard's practice have seemed less important than her symbolic image as a "traditional" midwife. One work portrays her as an untrained, intensely religious, and poorly paid practitioner, who nevertheless shared some of the attitudes of contemporary physicians. Another associates her with nineteenth-century controversies between midwives and physicians, emphasizing her helplessness when accused by a local physician of "meddling by giving her opinion of a disease."[4]

Serious study of the entire diary shatters such stereotypes. Although physicians were delivering babies in Hallowell as early as 1785, Martha Ballard was clearly the most important practitioner in her town. Because her record documents traditional midwifery at a moment of strength, it allows us to shift the focus of inquiry from the eventual triumphs of medical science to the immediate relations of doctors and midwives in an era of transition. What is most apparent on close examination is the *success* of Ballard's practice, measured on its own terms or against contemporary medical literature. Although elements of the new obstetrics had begun to filter into the region, the old rituals of childbirth remained powerful. In her record, it is the physicians—particularly the young physicians—who appear insecure and uncomfortable.

The diary also extends and deepens recent discussions concerning eighteenth-century modes of delivery. A number of historians have argued that English innovations, such as William Smellie's improved forceps, encouraged an interventionist obstetrics that eventually displaced the gentler practices of midwives. Edward Shorter has countered that eighteenth-century English midwives were themselves "wildly interventionist" and that physicians, not midwives, introduced the notion of "natural" childbirth. This new obstetrics, he argues, was in part a response to general cultural trends—a medical reflection of Enlightenment respect for nature—and also a consequence of the work of pioneering physicians like Charles White, whose textbook published in London in 1773 was the first example of a fully noninterventionist obstetrics.[5]

By shifting the balance of attention from obstetrical prescriptions to obstetrical results, Ballard's diary provides a new vantage point for assessing this controversy. Although it reveals little about the particulars of Ballard's methods (we do not know, for example, whether she applied hog's grease to the perineum or manually dilated the cervix), it offers compelling evidence of her skill. Maternal and fetal mortality rates extracted from the diary compare favorably with those for physicians in both England and America, countering the horror stories of eighteenth-century literature as well as the casual assumptions of twentieth-century historians. The consequences of Ballard's practice need not be imagined.

In most respects Martha Ballard's is a typical eighteenth-century rural diary—a laconic record of weather, sermon texts, family activities, and visits to and from neighbors. Obstetrical and general medical entries are interwoven with this larger accounting of ordinary life, although she gave birth records a special significance by summarizing them in the margins, numbering each year's births from January to December. Each delivery entry gives the father's name, the child's sex, the time of birth, the condition of mother and infant, and the fee collected. Many also include the time of the midwife's arrival and departure, the names of the attendants who assisted her, and the arrival of the "afternurse," who cared for the woman during lying-in (the week or two following delivery). Succeeding entries record follow-up visits or hearsay reports about the mother and child.

The account of Tabitha Sewall's delivery on November 12–13, 1790, is typical:

> I was Calld by Colonel Sewall to see his Lady who was in Labour. Shee was not so ill as to Call in other assistance this day. I slept with her till about 1 hour morn when shee calld her Neighbours to her assistance. Mrs Sewal was ill till 3 hour pm when shee was thro divine asistance made the Living Mother of a Living Son her 3d Child. Mrs Brooks, Belcher, Colman, Pollard & Voce assisted us . . . Colonel Sewall gave me 6/8 as a reward. Conducted me over the river.

The only unusual thing about this account is the reference to "divine asistance," suggesting that Mrs. Sewall or her midwife encountered some difficulty along the

way. Everything else about the description is routine. The father or a near neighbor summoned the midwife. The woman remained "ill" for several hours. Just before the birth she called her female neighbors. The child was delivered—safely. The
father paid the midwife and escorted her home. In the eight deliveries Martha Ballard performed for Tabitha Sewall, the description of one differs very little from another. Mrs. Sewall "was safe delivered at 7 hour morn of a fine Daughter and is
Cleverly," Ballard wrote, or "Mrs Suall Delivard at 1 this morn of a son & is
Cleaverly."[6]

Ballard performed her first delivery at the age of forty-three shortly after moving to the District of Maine from Oxford, Massachusetts. Although she had no
doubt assisted in many births in Oxford (she was herself the mother of nine children), she seems not to have practiced alone until she came to Hallowell. Demographics may explain her entry into the profession. In Oxford she had been
surrounded by older women; her maternal grandmother was still alive in 1777. In
Hallowell she was one of the older women in a young and rapidly growing town.
The diary opens in January 1785, the year she turned fifty. It ends with her death in
May 1812, just ten days after she performed her last delivery at the age of seventy-
seven.

The diary tells us nothing of how she acquired her skills, though genealogical
data suggest that her family had something of a medical bent. Two of her sisters
married doctors; a maternal uncle was a physician. Certainly, her family demonstrated an unusual commitment to education. Her uncle Abijah Moore was Oxford's first college graduate. Her younger brother, Jonathan, was the second.[7] She
probably learned midwifery in the same way her husband, Ephraim, learned
milling or surveying—by practice, by observation, and by working alongside
someone who knew more than she.

Ballard's assurance as a midwife is the best evidence we have of her training. In
almost 1,000 births she did not lose a single mother at delivery, and only five
women died in the lying-in period. Infant deaths were also rare. The diary lists
fourteen stillbirths in 814 deliveries and five infant deaths within an hour or two of
birth. When Mrs. Claton and her infant both died in the autumn of 1787, a week
after delivery, Ballard noted the singularity of the event: "I asisted to Lay her out,
her infant Laid in her arms, the first such instance I ever saw & the first woman that
died in Child bed which I delivered."[8] The sight was as unusual as it was affecting.
Under Martha Ballard's care, a woman could expect to become "the living mother
of a living child."[9]

By twentieth-century standards, of course, both maternal and infant mortality were high. The diary records one maternal death for every 200 births. Today the
rate for the United States is one per 10,000. But as Judith Walzer Leavitt has

demonstrated, such dramatic gains in obstetrical safety have come in the past fifty years; as late as 1930 there was one maternal death for every 150 births in the United States. A recent study of early twentieth-century births in a Portsmouth, New Hampshire, hospital gives stillbirth rates five times as high as Ballard's. The turning point for fetal as well as maternal deaths was the 1940s.[10]

The appropriate question is how Martha Ballard's record compared with those of her contemporaries, particularly with New England physicians who began the regular practice of obstetrics in the eighteenth and early nineteenth centuries. Direct comparisons are difficult, in part because physicians' records tend to be organized much differently from hers. Most are simply a record of fees collected. Some doctors kept notes on unusual cases; a few compiled mortality tables for their towns. Account books, obstetrical case notes, and mortality tables seldom overlap, however, so that we know the numbers of deliveries performed by one physician but not the results, the management of extraordinary cases by another but not the overall caseload, and the incidence of stillbirths for a given town but not the numbers of maternal deaths or the names of practitioners. Comparison with midwives' registers is easier, since midwives typically listed all births, live as well as stillbirths, chronologically from the beginning to the end of their careers. Few such lists survive, however, and none that I have found offers the kind of narrative detail available in the Ballard diary.

Despite the difficulties, it is nevertheless possible to construct some comparisons. Table 1 gives stillbirth ratios derived from Ballard's diary, two physicians' records, two midwives' registers, and several published mortality tables. At first glance it is the success of Ballard's practice that stands out. Whether her record is compared to that of Hall Jackson, a prominent eighteenth-century physician, or to Lydia Baldwin's, a contemporary Vermont midwife, it is eminent.[11] Yet none of the mortality ratios are as high as impressionistic accounts would lead us to believe, nor are there clear differences between midwives and physicians.

Most obstetrical treatises published in the first three-quarters of the eighteenth century emphasized the terrors of obstructed birth. Even authors who mistrusted "man-midwifery" and the use of forceps acknowledged the problems. Sarah Stone, an English midwife writing in 1737, described a breech delivery in which it took her an hour and a half to turn and extract the fetus. When she reached for the child, it "suck'd my fingers in the Womb, which concern'd me, fearing it impossible for the poor Infant to be born alive." Writing two decades later, Dr. Edmund Chapman, an English physician, included more gruesome tales. Among cautionary examples he cited one ignorant doctor who, not knowing "the Method of *Turning* a Child, made frequent use of the *Hook* and the *Knife,* and several other shocking and barbarous instruments, even while the Child was *Living.*" Dr. William Smellie,

TABLE I
Comparative Stillbirth Rates

	Total Births	Total Stillbirths	Stillbirths per 100 Live Births
Martha Ballard Augusta, Maine 1785–1812	814	14	1.8
Hall Jackson Portsmouth, N.H. 1775–94	511	12	2.4
Lydia Baldwin Bradford, Vt. 1768–1819	926	26	2.9
James Farrington Rochester, N.H. 1824–59	1,233	36	3.0
Jennet Boardman Hartford, Conn. 1815–49	1,113	36	3.3
Portsmouth, N.H. 1809–10	541	14	2.7
Marblehead, Mass. 1808	222	7	3.3
Exeter, N.H. 1809	53	1	1.9
United States* 1942			2.0

*Fetal death ratio, defined as fetal deaths of 28 weeks' or more gestation per 1,000 live births.

Sources: Martha Moore Ballard Diary, 2 vols., Maine State Library, Augusta, Maine; J. Worth Estes, *Hall Jackson and the Purple Foxglove: Medical Practice and Research in Revolutionary America, 1760–1820* (Hanover, N.H., 1979), p. 120; A Copy of Records from an Original Memorandum Kept by Mrs. Lydia (Peters) Baldwin, typescript, Baker Library, Dartmouth College, Hanover, N.H.; James Farrington Medical Record Books, 1824–1859, Special Collections, Dimond Library, University of New Hampshire, Durham; "Midwife Records, 1815–1849, Kept by Mrs. Jennet Boardman of Hartford," Connecticut Historical Society, *Bulletin* 33 (1968): 64–69; Lyman Spalding, *Bill of Mortality for Portsmouth,* broadside (Portsmouth, N.H., 1809, 1810); John Drury, *Bill of Mortality for Marblehead, 1808,* broadside (Marblehead, Mass., 1809); Joseph Tilton, M.D., *Bill of Mortality for Exeter, New Hampshire,* broadside ([Exeter, N.H., 1809]); Helen M. Wallace, "Factors Associated with Perinatal Mortality and Morbidity," in Helen M. Wallace, Edwin M. Gold, Edward F. Lis, eds., *Maternal and Child Health Practices: Problems, Resources, and Methods of Delivery* (Springfield, Ill., 1973), p. 507.

the London physician whose improved forceps supposedly solved such problems as these, included vivid case studies in his published works, evenhandedly distributing the blame for mismanaged deliveries among superstitious midwives and poorly trained physicians. In comparison, Ballard's delivery descriptions are remarkably bland: "the foet[u]s was in an unnatural posetion but I Brot it into a proper direction and shee was safe delivered." Usually she said even less: "removed obstructions" or "used means."[12]

Just as striking, given the tenor of the prescriptive literature, is her independence of Hallowell's physicians. Although the English authors agreed that midwives were capable of handling routine deliveries, authorities differed on the question of their ability to negotiate emergencies. Most publishing physicians argued that the sign of a good midwife was her willingness to call for help when needed. As Brudenell Exton put it, "the more knowledge they have, the readier they are to send for timely Assistance in Cases of Danger." Sarah Stone, the English midwife, disagreed, as did Nicholas Culpeper, a seventeenth-century herbalist and astrologer whose books were still being reprinted in New England in the early nineteenth century. Culpeper told the "Grave Matrons" who followed his advice that "the Lord will build you Houses as he did the Midwives of the *Hebrews,* when *Pharaoh* kept their Bodies in as great bondage as *Physitians* of our times do your Understandings." Both authors believed that experienced midwives were better equipped to handle difficult deliveries than officious but poorly prepared physicians.[13]

Ballard's philosophy was closer to Culpeper's than to Exton's. Although she had cordial relations with Hallowell's physicians, several of whom occasionally officiated at routine births, she seldom needed their help. A handful of her patients called *both* a doctor and a midwife at the onset of labor, but even in those cases she usually handled the delivery. Only twice in her entire career did she summon a doctor in an emergency, once in 1785 and again in 1792. She was not herself responsible for the first emergency. Arriving late, she found the patient "greatly ingered by some mishap," though the midwife or neighbor who had delivered the child did "not allow that shee was sencible of it." Calling the doctor may have been Ballard's way of resolving a disagreement over the severity of the injury.[14]

In the other case she described her feelings in vivid language, though characteristically she offered little obstetrical detail:

> My patients illness Came on at 8 hour morning. Her women were Calld, her Case was Lingering till 7 p.m. I removd difuculties & waited for Natures opperations till then, when shee was more severly

atackt with obstructions which alarmed me much. I desird Doct
Hubard might be sent for which request was Complid with, but by
Divine assistance I performed the oppration, which was blisst with
the preservation of the lives off mother and infant. The life of the latter I dispard off for some time.

In the margin of the day's entry she added, "The most perelous sien I Ever past thro
in the Course of my practice. Blessed be God for his goodness."[15] Whether Dr.
Hubbard's emergency skills included the forceps delivery of a living child or only
the dismemberment of a dead one, we do not know. Fortunately, in this case as in
all the others, Ballard and her patient got along without him.

In difficult deliveries, she typically gave God the credit for her success. The
phrases are formulaic: "Her illness was very sever a short space but Blessed be God
it terminated in Safety and the infant is numbered among the living," or "She had
a Laborious illness but Blessed be God it terminated in safety. May shee and I ascribe the prais to the Great Parent of the universe."[16] One should not assume from
such language, however, that Ballard lacked confidence in her own ability or that
she relied on faith to the exclusion of skill. She knew that God worked through her
hands.

Her confidence may actually have increased with the arrival of Dr. Benjamin
Page in Hallowell in 1791. Page is remembered in local history as an extraordinarily successful physician. When he died in 1844, after more than fifty years of practice, the *Boston Medical and Surgical Journal* published an eleven-page biography
proclaiming his skills as a general practitioner, surgeon, and gentleman. According
to the anonymous author, Page was also "unequalled in the success of his obstetric
practice. . . . [H]e attended upwards of *three thousand females in their confinement,
without the loss of a single life from the first year of his practice!* This is almost miraculous, and may challenge the professional records of Europe or America for anything to compare with it."[17]

This is not the picture of Page preserved in Ballard's diary. Her first encounter
with the young doctor was at the delivery of his near neighbor, Mrs. Benjamin
Poor, the wife of a printer newly arrived in the town. Perhaps the woman intended
medical delivery; perhaps she was simply worried that her midwife would not arrive in time. "I Extracted the child," Ballard wrote. "He Chose to close the Loin."
The language is opaque here, suggesting either a friendly division of duties or an
officious takeover by the doctor. The second encounter was more troublesome.
Ballard had been sitting up all night with twenty-year-old Hannah Sewall, who had
recently arrived in Hallowell from the town of York. "They were intimidated," she

wrote, "& Calld Dr. Page who gave my patient 20 drops of Laudanum which put her into such a stupor her pains (which were regular & promising) in a manner stopt till near night when she pukt & they returned & shee delivered at 7 hour Evening of a son her first Born."[18] Hannah Sewall's intimidation, so called, may have had something to do with the fact that she had grown up in an elite family in a coastal town and was already familiar with medical delivery. As for Ballard, she was openly annoyed. Thereafter she was unmerciful in reporting Page's mistakes.

"Sally Cocks went to see Mrs. Kimball," she wrote. "Shee was delivered of a dead daughter on the morning of the 9th instant, the operation performed by Ben Page. The infants limbs were much dislocated as I am informed." She even questioned the doctor's judgment on nonobstetrical matters. Called to treat an infant's rupture, she recommended the application of brandy. "They inform me that Dr. Page says it must be opined [opened], which I should think improper from present appearance," she added. In June 1798, while she was engaged in another delivery, the doctor again delivered a stillborn child. Her report of the event was blunt: "Dr Page was operator. Poor unfortunate man in the practice."[19]

Page was unfortunate, but in eighteenth-century terms he was also ill prepared, as his administration of laudanum at Hannah Sewall's delivery suggests. The prescriptive literature recommended the use of opiates for *false* pains but not for genuine labor; Page was apparently having difficulty telling one from the other. Experience was the issue here as in so many other aspects of midwifery. Ballard had sat through enough lingering labors to know promising pains from false ones. Her reference to the doctor's dislocation of an infant's limbs also suggests lack of familiarity with the difficult manual operation required in breech births. The English midwife Sarah Stone had warned against doctors like him, "boyish Pretenders," who having attended a few dissections and read a few books professed to understand the manipulative arts so important to midwifery. Even Henry Bracken, an author who insisted that midwives should call in a doctor in difficult births, cautioned, "I would never advise any one to employ a *young* physician."[20]

After 1800, Page's misadventures disappear from the diary. Presumably, he eventually learned the obstetrical art in the way Ballard did—by experience.

Extracting the child was only part of the problem. Toward the end of the eighteenth century, English writers began to give as much attention to the dangers of the lying-in period, particularly the problem of childbed fever, as to delivery itself. Puerperal fever may in fact have been rare in England in the early years of the eighteenth century; obstetrical treatises published before 1760 rarely comment on its treatment.[21] Thomas Denman's *Essays on the Puerperal Fever* appeared in London in 1768. Four years later, Charles White appended a detailed account of puerperal mortality in British hospitals to his *Treatise on the Management of Pregnant and Lying-In Women.*[22]

Puerperal fever is a wound infection caused by bacterial invasion of the uterine cavity. The infectiousness of the disorder was first suggested in the 1840s by Dr. Oliver Wendell Holmes in the United States and Dr. Ignaz Semmelweis in Austria, though the bacteriology of the disease was not settled until the 1880s, when Louis Pasteur demonstrated the presence of what is now known as streptococcus in patients suffering from the affliction. The symptoms—elevated temperature, headache, malaise, and pelvic pain—usually do not appear until several days after delivery. With certain strains of bacteria there is a profuse and foul-smelling discharge.[23]

At least one of Martha Ballard's patients probably died of puerperal infection. Mrs. Craig was "safe Deliverd of a very fine Daughter" on March 31, 1790, but after five days finding her "not so well as I could wish," Ballard administered a "Clister [enema] of milk, water, & salt" and applied an "ointment & a Bath of Tansy, mugwort, Cammomile & Hysop which gave Mrs. Cragg great relief." A week later the woman was still "Exceeding ill." Someone (perhaps a physician) prescribed rhubarb and Peruvian bark but without effect. A day or two later Dr. Cony "plainly told the famely Mrs. Cragg must die." She expired that night. Ballard helped dress her body for burial. "The Corps were Coffined & sett in the west room," she wrote. "Purge & smell very ofensive." Meanwhile, neighbors came by turns to "give the infant suck."[24]

Although Ballard attempted no diagnosis in this case, the symptoms fit the clinical description of puerperal fever. Perhaps one or two others among the five maternal deaths in her practice can also be attributed to infection. One woman was "safe delivered," fell ill a few days later, and died two weeks after delivery. Another died four days after giving birth at a time when scarlet fever, a form of streptococcus infection, was present in the town. In the two remaining maternal deaths, however, other symptoms were apparent. One woman was suffering from measles.[25] The other was in convulsions when delivered of a stillborn daughter and was still experiencing "fitts" four days later when she died. She was no doubt a victim of eclampsia, the most severe stage of an acute toxemia of pregnancy, a condition that is still considered one of the gravest complications of childbirth today.[26]

The Ballard diary suggests that puerperal infection was present in late eighteenth-century Maine, but the random appearance of the disease shows why it was seldom identified and discussed. In contrast, contemporary English physicians were encountering a truly alarming phenomenon. Charles White reported mortality rates for several London and Dublin hospitals that at midcentury were losing

TABLE 2
Comparative Maternal Mortality Rates

	Total Births	*Maternal Deaths*	*Deaths per 1,000 Births*
London A			
1767–72	653	18	27.5
1770	63	14	222.2
London B			
1749–70	9,108	196	21.5
1770	890	35	39.3
London C			
1747–"present"	4,758	93	19.5
1771	282	10	35.4
London D	790	6	7.5
Dublin A			
1745–54	3,206	29	9.0
Dublin B			
1757–75	10,726	152	14.1
1768	633	17	26.8
1770	616	5	8.1
Martha Ballard			
1777–1812	998	5	5.0
1785–1812	814	5	6.1
United States			
1930			6.7
1935			5.8
1940			3.8
1945			2.1

Sources: Charles White, *A Treatise on The Management of Pregnant and Lying-In Women* (London, 1772; Worcester, Mass., 1793); Ballard Diary; Wallace, Gold, and Lis, eds., *Maternal and Child Health Practices,* p. 285.

one out of every thirty or forty patients to puerperal fever. In 1770, in one London hospital, one of every four women died, most from infection. (See table 2.) White was astonished that two hospitals that had been established at the same time, were an equal distance from the center of London, were directed by eminent physicians, and treated the same number of patients should have markedly different death rates. In true Enlightenment fashion he concluded that one hospital smothered patients with an artificial regimen, while the more successful one not only was less crowded and closer to fields and fresh air but obliged patients to do more for themselves.

White believed that bad habits led to childbed fevers. "Violence used either by instruments or by the hand, in the extraction of the child or the placenta," might bring on an inflammation of the womb, a condition made worse by the custom of pampering women in childbed. A woman should not be delivered in a hot room, or have her child or placenta dragged from her, or lie in a horizontal position in a warm bed drinking warm liquids for a week after delivery. Physicians and midwives were both to blame for practices that all too frequently led to maternal death. He suspected that lower-class women, who could not afford pampering, did better in childbirth than their more affluent neighbors, and he cited christening and death ratios from London and Manchester parish records to prove his point.[27]

Had White known about Martha Ballard, he would have had a ready explanation for her success: she practiced among frontier women who lived close to nature. In fact, Ballard was probably guilty of one of the practices White deplored—using hot drinks laced with alcohol. Still, there is plenty of evidence in the diary of the kind of vigor he admired. Ballard's patients were not all as sturdy as Mrs. Walker, who was "sprigh about house till 11 [and] was safe delivrd at 12," or as courageous (or foolhardy) as Mrs. Herriman, who "wrode in a sleigh 13 miles after her illness was on her"; but few Hallowell women could afford to lie in bed.[28] Ballard's own daughter, Dolly Lambert, was "so well as to be helpt up and sett at table for breakfast" twenty-four hours after giving birth to her fourth child. Ballard generally left her patients in the care of an afternurse a few hours after delivery, but when she stayed overnight she helped to get the woman out of bed in the morning. "Got my patient up, Changd her Lining and came home," she wrote (in this case, twelve hours after delivery), and "help[ed] Mrs Williams up & maid her Bed and returned home" (twenty-four hours after birth).[29]

Modern epidemiology confirms Charles White's belief that environment affected mortality, though, of course, the theoretical explanations differ from his.[30] Because Ballard was a part-time practitioner who delivered women at home and shared their postpartum care with nurses and family members, she had little opportunity to spread puerperal infection from one patient to another. The opposite conditions existed in the London hospitals, where as White himself suspected, the use of instruments in delivery probably increased the lacerations and tears that encouraged septicemia. Higher incidence of venereal disease in London may also have been a factor.[31]

That childbearing was safer in rural Maine than in London hospitals hardly seems surprising. The more interesting question for our purposes is how the literature emanating from those hospitals affected obstetrical practice in country places. Here the writings of Dr. Jeremiah Barker of Gorham, Maine, are particularly revealing. In February 1785 Barker initiated a discussion in the *Falmouth (Maine) Gazette* over the causes of an unusual "mortality among child-bed women, which has prevailed of late." Dr. Nathaniel Coffin, whose practice was in Falmouth (now Portland), submitted an angry response that was published in the next issue of the paper. Yes, several women had died in childbed in and about the town, but since the cause was unknown there was nothing that could have been done to save them. He denied that there was an epidemic, and he accused Barker of awakening "all those fears and apprehensions, which are but too often cherished by the sex." The debate continued through four issues of the newspaper, Barker insisting that an excess of bile characterized all the cases of puerperal fever he had studied, Coffin retorting that Barker had misread the symptoms.[32]

Barker included additional detail on the puerperal fever controversy in "History of Diseases in the District of Maine," a manuscript that he wrote after his retirement from active practice in 1818. Taken together, the newspaper stories and the "History" tell us a great deal about how medical reforms, initiated in London, were received in America. In his letters to the *Falmouth Gazette* Barker appears as a bold empiric asserting the power of direct experimentation against the dated theories of academic physicians. In his manuscript he reveals that the source of his ideas was a work by Thomas Denman, presumably his 1768 essays on puerperal infection.[33]

According to Barker's history, the puerperal fever outbreak began at the same time as an equally troubling rash of wound infections. In the spring of 1784, he recalled, "some unusual appearances took place in wounds & bruises, even trivial ones, which baffled the skill of the Surgeon, and issued in the death of the patient. . . . Local inflammations chiefly from injuries were more frequent and untractable during the year than I ever knew them to be before or since. The subjects of these complaints were chiefly males and apparently of good constitutions."[34] At the same time, several women in Gorham, Falmouth, and adjoining towns contracted puerperal fever. Although Barker made no connection between the two phenomena, it is difficult for a twentieth-century reader to avoid doing so.

Since Barker gave no statistics on the number of men who died from infected wounds or of women who suffered from childbed fever, and since birth and death records for the region are incomplete, it is impossible to know how serious the problem really was. Barker simply tells us that few women who suffered childbed fever survived, and that he attended autopsies in three different towns. Yet his description confirms the rarity of the disorder in the region. "The ill success which attended my practice," he wrote, "induced me to write to several aged & experienced physicians in different portions of Massachusetts, for advice, as puerperal fever had never appeared among us excepting in a few sporadic cases, which yielded to common means." His correspondents had never seen such an epidemic themselves, but they referred him to the works of Denman and other unnamed British authors. It was from Denman's book, apparently, that Barker got his notions about bile and the use of "the bark" (quinine) as a remedy. He also wrote to Dr. Ammi

Ruhamah Cutter of Portsmouth, New Hampshire, who had reportedly experienced high mortality from childbed fever. Cutter suggested applying "fermenting cataplasms to the abdomen composed of flower & yeast."[35]

Barker credited none of these sources in his 1785 newspaper letters, however, nor did he elaborate on the problems in his own practice. Alluding to an unusual childbed mortality, "especially in the town of Falmouth" (where Nathaniel Coffin practiced), he offered his remedies as a disinterested effort to "secure the happiness of mankind." Although he claimed to have "taken the opinion of the Massachusetts Medical Society," he gave no names.[36] Whom was he addressing? Surely not his fellow doctors. If that had been his intent, he would have limited himself to the private correspondence he had already begun. Instead he reached beyond the medical fraternity to the literate public of his region. The very form of his argument suggests that some part of his intended audience was female.

When Barker asserted that his patients could testify to the effectiveness of his methods, Coffin countered, "I am sorry the Dr. is obliged to have recourse to the female sex for a vindication of them." He suggested that the young doctor read "Astruc, Brooks, and others" to correct his faulty diagnosis. Barker retorted that the proposed authors were not only "Obsolete" but "esteemed of less consequence, in many respects, than the opinion of some of the female sex, founded on experience, in this more enlightened age."[37] The reliance on experience was, of course, a staple of Enlightenment medicine. Whereas earlier physicians had relied on theoretical learning, English reformers like William Smellie had emphasized the necessity for practical training in the manual arts of midwifery. Ironically, the obstetrical Enlightenment encouraged physicians to assume women's work in the very act of celebrating its importance. As Thomas Denman expressed it, "A natural labour was the last thing well understood in the practice of midwifery, because scientific men, not being formerly employed in the management of common labours, had no opportunity of making observations upon them."[38]

Barker's regard for female experience was conditional. He praised enlightened women who sought his care but mistrusted traditional midwives and nurses. His case notes from 1774 describe his efforts to deliver a woman with an imperforate vagina after the ministrations of her "friends" had failed. "I found that nothing could be done but to dilate the Perineum for the egress of the Child," he wrote, "and 'tho the operation is simple, yet fearing the sensure of the Vulgar (if any misfortune should befall the patient, afterwards) advised to send for Dr. Savage as an assistant." As it happened, the dead fetus was delivered before the second physician arrived.[39] Barker's concern about the censure of "the Vulgar" suggests the difficulties many physicians had in establishing credibility in the region, not only in obstetrical but in general medical cases. One young man entering practice in

Waterville, Maine, in the 1790s even signed contracts with prospective patients, promising not to charge them if his remedies failed.[40]

Like Benjamin Page of Hallowell, Barker had begun his medical career after a brief apprenticeship with a Massachusetts physician. In 1774 he was twenty-two and in his second year of practice. The newspaper debate suggests that, ten years later, he had grown tired of his practice in Gorham and adjoining towns and perhaps hoped to attract the attention of prosperous families in the port of Falmouth.[41] Jeremiah Barker knew that women, whether vulgar or enlightened, were guardians of a doctor's reputation.

For his part, Coffin was furious at Barker for questioning the skills of other physicians. He was also dismayed that the younger doctor should invoke the authority of the Massachusetts Medical Society, even though he was not a member. When Coffin wrote to the society in 1803 recommending a number of new members from Maine, he explicitly excluded Barker, partly on the basis of the 1785 affair, which still rankled. (The society ignored his advice and elected Barker anyway.)[42] Thus a young physician moving into obstetrical practice in the 1780s and 1790s had two obstacles to overcome—folk reliance on traditional midwifery and the mistrust of older, more conservative physicians.

For our purposes, however, the more important issue is the way in which the puerperal fever incident of 1784–85 began to shape Barker's practice. All of the cases of childbed fever described in his history came from that outbreak, yet he used them to support a long, detailed discussion of the cure and prevention of the disorder. Even by his own account, puerperal fever cannot have been a serious problem in the region. Most of the physicians to whom he wrote had seen only scattered cases; all of them referred him to British authors for an understanding of the subject. Coffin even doubted that the deaths could be attributed to a single disease, and he questioned whether he or any other physician could have done anything to prevent them. In Barker's own practice the trouble also faded away. There were additional cases during the winter of 1784–85, he wrote, yet the disease showed "decreasing malignancy and mortality. Since which it has not appeared among us, excepting in a few sporadic cases, which seldom proved fatal."[43] Yet by 1818 his interpretation of the 1784–85 cases had expanded to encompass citations from medical literature published as late as 1817.[44] Barker measured his entire career against that single early disaster. Since it was never repeated, he assumed that his preventative practices were successful.

Barker combined the noninterventionist prescriptions of the late eighteenth century—better ventilation, lighter food, avoidance of alcohol—with more heroic measures. "The means of prevention may be reduced to two," he argued. First, the physician should treat the patient during labor as though she were already a victim of the disease, drawing blood, administering emetics and cathartics, debarring her "entirely from spirits," and keeping her "on a low diet, without any animal food, in a well ventilated apartment without any curtains, on a mattress or straw bed." The second method involved "facilitating or rather hastening, by artificial means, the termination of labour."[45] Presumably, this meant using forceps and possibly ergot, a powerful and dangerous drug that, when given orally, stimulates uterine contractions.[46] In this, Barker departed from the advice of his 1784 mentor, Thomas Denman, who, like Charles White, believed that forceps should be used rarely and that hastening labor led to postpartum complications.[47]

What we have, then, is a clear example of the way in which medical literature in combination with local experience came to define a practice. Barker's need to differentiate himself from other practitioners, as well as his desire to apply the latest in scientific knowledge to the management of his practice, made it impossible for him to see the 1784–85 outbreak as an anomaly. Thereafter, he was convinced that it was his own intervention that had prevented a similar disaster from occurring. In contrast, Martha Ballard's nonscientific, even providential interpretation of events enabled her to treat each case on its own terms. For every patient, she did what she knew how to do and let God determine the outcome. This is not to say that she was incapable of experimentation or that she never wondered why one infant died and another lived. It is simply to argue that her craft was oriented toward practical results rather than theoretical explanation. The death of Mrs. Claton or Mrs. Craig did not destroy her confidence in the soundness of her methods. Hers was not an approach that encouraged innovation, but neither did it promote ill-considered intervention.

Adrian Wilson has estimated that, in nature, 96 percent of births occur spontaneously. Approximately 4 percent involve serious obstruction of some kind and cannot be delivered without intervention. An additional 1 percent, though spontaneous, result in complications—minor ones such as fainting, vomiting, and tearing of the perineum, or major events like hemorrhaging or convulsions.[48] Martha Ballard's records fit Wilson's typology well. Approximately 95 percent of her entries simply say "delivered" or "safe delivered." In the remaining 5 percent, some sort of complication is indicated, by explicit reference to obstructions, an oblique comment on the severity of the labor, or simply an acknowledgment that the delivery was accomplished through the mercy of God. Her records thus attest to the relative safety of childbearing as well as to her skill in managing difficult labors. Her ministrations no doubt improved the conditions of birth, but, perhaps even more important, she did little to augment the dangers.

In this regard it is interesting to compare her records with those of James Farrington of Rochester, New Hampshire, a nineteenth-century physician whose caseload was similar to hers and whose records, unlike those of his eighteenth-century predecessors, are extraordinarily complete. Dr. Farrington began the study of medicine in 1814, two years after Ballard's death. His manuscript records include a systematic register of 1,233 deliveries performed between 1824 and 1859. At first glance, his stillbirth and mortality ratios confirm the conclusions of revisionist histories—that childbirth became more dangerous in the nineteenth century. Farrington's stillbirth ratios are higher than any of the eighteenth-century practitioners and closer to those of the nineteenth-century midwife Jennet Boardman. (See table 1.) Even more striking is the number of maternal deaths at delivery. That he was occasionally called to complete someone else's mismanaged delivery is certain, though those few cases that include extended descriptions suggest that, regardless of practitioner, nineteenth-century obstetrical practice added new dangers to the old problems of obstructed birth. Curiously, there is no indication of puerperal fever in Farrington's records. One might have expected at least a few cases of infection over such a long career. Since his tightly organized accounts, with one exception, list deliveries *only*, it is possible that such cases, usually arising a week or so after delivery, appeared in another set of more general medical records.[49]

Farrington recorded five maternal deaths. One woman, he wrote, was "enfeebled by intemperance." Another had a severe cold and "spoke but few words after delivery, but sunk away without a groan." The most dramatic case had been abandoned by another physician. Farrington described it as "preternatural labor requiring in the end the dissection of the infant," adding details that might have come from English obstetrical literature a hundred years before: "the external parts of generation much lacerated and mangled by *hooks, pincers, and knives*." The woman survived Farrington's extraction of the dismembered fetus but died five days later. A fourth woman died of bleeding after an unidentified attendant failed to extract the placenta. The fifth woman suffered a ruptured uterus: "in a few minutes the whole child could be felt expelled from the Uterus within the abdominal cavity." The woman lived about an hour.[50]

The numbers are small, however, and, without more detail on postpartum infection, inconclusive. The most striking contrast between Farrington's and Ballard's records is not in mortality rates themselves but in their characterizations of delivery. The process of labor was biologically the same, yet their descriptions differ markedly. Whereas Ballard thought in terms of the general outcome ("left mother and child cleverly"), Farrington focused on theoretical categories. Labors were "natural," "tedious," "premature," "preternatural," "complicated," or, after 1838, "instrumental," regardless of whether the mother and child survived.[51] Twenty percent of the deliveries in his records are listed as something other than "natural."[52]

Here the telltale category may be his 102 cases of "tedious" labor, defined in the medical literature as lasting longer than twenty-four hours. In one case, which terminated safely at twenty-six hours, Farrington reported taking blood from the woman's arm, then giving an opiate. Four hours before the birth he gave her "Ergot in Infusion" and was pleased when he was able to deliver the child "without Instruments though for several hours no alteration was made by the force of the Pains."[53] Reading such an account, one finds it difficult not to think of Ben Page's administration of laudanum at the delivery of Hannah Sewall. Ironically, the remedy that so dismayed Martha Ballard was by now a standard part of the physician's arsenal. The three remedies—laudanum, ergot, and forceps—went together, accomplishing, as the physicians and perhaps many of their patients thought, an artificial hastening of labor.[54]

Judith Walzer Leavitt has argued that women chose medical intervention. Sally Drinker Downing, for example, sought out the services of the Philadelphia physician William Shippen, who administered opium during her 1795, 1797, and 1799 deliveries. Leavitt concludes that "the prospect of a difficult birth, which all women fearfully anticipated, and the knowledge that physicians' remedies could provide relief and successful outcomes led women to seek out practitioners whose obstetric armamentarium included drugs and instruments."[55] Leavitt may be right about Downing, yet Martha Ballard's diary adds a new dimension to the question of choice. At ten o'clock on the evening of October 21, 1794, she was summoned to the house of Chandler Robbins, a Harvard graduate and new resident of Hallowell. "Doctor Parker was calld," she wrote, "but shee did not wish to see him when he Came & he returnd home. Shee was safe delivered of a son her first Born at 10 hour 30 minutes Evening"—that is, twenty-four and one-half hours after summoning the midwife. Ballard's reward for officiating at this "tedious labor" was eighteen shillings and the satisfaction of knowing that God and the parents were pleased.

This brief survey of Martha Ballard's diary and related documents supports the reformist point that birth is a natural process rather than a life-threatening event. It suggests that rural midwives were capable of managing difficult as well as routine births, that the need for medical intervention was by no means obvious, and that puerperal infection, though present, was still only a random problem in the last years of the eighteenth century. For midwives like Martha Ballard or Lydia Baldwin, experience defined competence, yet in the years following the Revolution a number of brash young men with more confidence than experience took up the practice of delivering babies. Not content with the more restrained role of older doctors, they consulted British literature and sought advice from other physicians to solve their problems and validate their skills. That they gravitated toward works that emphasized the necessity of intervention is hardly surprising. In a competitive environment no bright young physician could embrace Charles White's advice that the less done in childbirth the better. Employing forceps, letting blood, administering opiates and ergot, they set themselves apart from the manual skills and the providential faith of the midwives.

During the earlier years of Martha Ballard's midwifery in Hallowell, however, the success of such physicians was by no means assured. In 1800, when age, ill health, and a move to a more distant part of the town forced her to cut back her practice, she was the single most important practitioner in her town, and she knew it.

NOTES

Versions of this article were presented at meetings of the Benjamin Waterhouse Medical Society, Boston University; the Maine Society for the History of Medicine; the American Antiquarian Society Seminar in Political and Social History; and the comparative history seminar at the University of New Hampshire. I am grateful to those groups and to Worth Estes, Judith Walzer Leavitt, Janet Polasky, and Cornelia Dayton for helpful comments. Some parts of this essay appeared in my *A Midwife's Tale: The Life of Martha Ballard, Based on Her Diary, 1785–1812* (New York, 1990).

1. Richard Harrison Shryock, *The Development of Modern Medicine: An Interpretation of the Social and Scientific Factors Involved*, rev. ed. (London, 1948), pp. 77–78.

2. Judith Walzer Leavitt, *Brought to Bed: Childbearing in America, 1750 to 1950* (New York, 1986), pp. 56–57; and Leavitt, "'Science' Enters the Birthing Room: Obstetrics in America since the Eighteenth Century," *Journal of American History* 70 (1983): 281–304; Richard W. Wertz and Dorothy C. Wertz, *Lying-In: A History of Childbirth in America* (New York, 1977), pp. xi, x, 128.

3. Catherine M. Scholten, "'On the Importance of the Obstetrick Art': Changing Customs of Childbirth in America, 1760 to 1825," *William and Mary Quarterly*, 3d ser., 34 (1977): 429–31; and Scholten, *Childbearing in American Society, 1650–1850* (New York, 1985), chap. 2; Wertz and Wertz, *Lying-In*, chap. 2; Leavitt, *Brought to Bed*, pp. 36–44, 263–65.

4. Charles Elventon Nash, *The History of Augusta: First Settlements and Early Days as a Town, Including the Diary of Mrs. Martha Moore Ballard (1785–1812)* (Augusta, Me., 1904); Wertz and Wertz, *Lying-In*, pp. 9–10; quotation from Scholten, *Childbearing*, p. 45; Leavitt, *Brought to Bed*, p. 37.

5. Wertz and Wertz, *Lying-In*, pp. 34–43; Scholten, *Childbearing*, pp. 34–36; Leavitt, *Brought to Bed*, pp. 38–40; Shorter, "The Management of Normal Deliveries and the Generation of William Hunter," in W. F. Bynum and Roy Porter, eds., *William Hunter and the Eighteenth-Century Medical World* (Cambridge, 1985), pp. 371–83.

6. Martha Moore Ballard Diary, 2 vols., Maine State Library, Augusta, Me., Apr. 2, 1788, Dec. 31, 1786. According to the *Oxford English Dictionary*, "cleverly" means "well" or "in health"

in some dialects. This is obviously the meaning Ballard intended. Henry Sewall, Tabitha's husband, also kept a diary. He mentioned Martha Ballard's presence on only four of the eight occasions, never recorded paying a fee, and only twice mentioned the presence of other birth attendants. Henry Sewall Diary, Massachusetts Historical Society, Boston, Mass.

7. The medical tradition continued into the nineteenth century. Ballard's diary was inherited and preserved by her great-granddaughter, Dr. Mary Hobart, who practiced obstetrics at New England Hospital in Boston. Clara Barton, the Civil War nurse and founder of the American Red Cross, was Ballard's grandniece.

8. Ballard Diary, Aug. 16, 20, 1787. Since the first fatality occurred during the diary period, I have included the 177 pre-diary births in arriving at the total of 991 births.

9. The phrase was conventional, and it persisted into the nineteenth century. Leavitt, for example, quotes a woman who gave thanks for having become "the living mother of a living and perfect child" (*Brought to Bed*, p. 34). Ballard's version of the statement was usually gender specific, as in "the living mother of a living son" or "the living mother of a fine Daughter" (Ballard Diary, Dec. 30, 1789).

10. Leavitt, *Brought to Bed*, pp. 23–26; Helen M. Wallace, Edwin M. Gold, and Edward F. Lis, eds., *Maternal and Child Health Practices: Problems, Resources, and Methods of Delivery* (Springfield, Ill., 1973), p. 185; J. Worth Estes and David M. Goodman, *The Changing Humors of Portsmouth: The Medical Biography of an American Town, 1623–1983* (Boston, 1986), p. 298. In 2.3 percent of Ballard's deliveries the child was stillborn or died in the first 24 hours of life. For Portsmouth Hospital the figures were 11.4 percent (1915–17), 4.8 percent (1925–41), 1.2 percent (1954–57), and 0.8 percent (1971–83). Because methods of compiling statistics vary markedly over time, these numbers must be considered approximations. Stillbirth ratios, for example, might be affected by abortions, spontaneous or induced. On the development of obstetrical record keeping in general, see James H. Cassedy, *American Medicine and Statistical Thinking, 1800–1860* (Cambridge, Mass., 1984), pp. 80–83.

11. The lack of detail in the other sources makes it difficult to know whether the data are precisely comparable. Ballard's diary distinguishes between stillbirths and deaths within a few minutes or hours of birth. If other records melded those two categories, her record would look better by comparison. Still, adding the five very early deaths in her practice to stillbirths results in a ratio of only 2.3, almost identical with Jackson's and slightly lower than Baldwin's. Jennet Boardman's register includes three categories: "born dead," "died," and "died at age — or on —." I list all those infants described as "dead" or "born dead" as stillborn, but exclude the "died" entries, some of which deaths may have occurred immediately after birth.

12. Stone, *A Complete Practice of Midwifery* . . . (London, 1737), pp. 76–77; Chapman, *A Treatise on the Improvement of Midwifery, Chiefly with Regard to the Operation* . . . , 3d ed. (London, 1759), p. xiv; Smellie, *A Collection of Cases and Observations in Midwifery*, 3d ed., vol. 3 (London, 1764), for example, pp. 1–69, 416–27; Ballard Diary, Aug. 29, 1797, July 19, 1794, Feb. 18, 1799.

13. Nich[olas] Culpeper, *A Directory for Midwives; or, A Guide for Women, in Their Conception, Bearing, and Suckling Their Children* . . . (London, 1651), "Epistle Dedicatory"; Stone, *Complete Practice*, p. ix; Henry Bracken, *The Midwife's Companion; or, A Treatise of Midwifery, Wherein the Whole Art Is Explained* . . . (London, 1737), p. 146; *Chapman, Improvement of Mid-*

wifery, pp. vii–xiii; Brudenell Exton, *A New and General System of Midwifery . . .* (London, 1751), p. 11. The library of the College of Physicians and Surgeons, Philadelphia, has an autographed and annotated copy of Exton owned by Dr. John McKechnie, who emigrated from Scotland to Maine in 1755 and apparently practiced medicine until his death in 1782. Martha Ballard may have known him; three of his married daughters were among her patients (James W. North, *The History of Augusta* [Augusta, Maine, 1870], pp. 913–14).

14. Ballard Diary, Nov. 11, 1785.

15. Ibid., May 19, 1792.

16. Ibid., June 30, 1807, Mar. 31, 1800.

17. "Memoir of Benjamin Page, M.D.," *Boston Medical and Surgical Journal* 33 (1845): 9, 173.

18. Ballard Diary, Nov. 17, 1793, Oct. 9–10, 1794. For additional detail on relations between midwives and physicians in Hallowell, see Laurel Thatcher Ulrich, "Martha Moore Ballard and the Medical Challenge to Midwifery," in James Learnon and Charles Clark, eds., *From Revolution to Statehood: Maine in the Early Republic, 1783–1820* (Hanover, N.H., 1988), pp. 165–83.

19. Ballard Diary, July 8, Aug. 14, 1796, June 14, 1798.

20. Thomas Denman, *An Introduction to the Practice of Midwifery,* 2 vols. (London, 1794, 1795; New York, 1802), 1:179; Stone, *Complete Practice,* pp. 76–77, xiv; Bracken, *Midwife's Companion,* p. 194.

21. Exton, for example, gives no more attention to childbed fever than to afterpains (*System of Midwifery,* p. 150). In addition to the English works cited above, I have read the Worcester 1794 edition of Alexander Hamilton, *Outlines of the Theory and Practice of Midwifery,* first published in Edinburgh in 1784. It also ignores the problem.

22. White, *A Treatise on the Management of Pregnant and Lying-In Women . . .* (London, 1772).

23. Erna Ziegel and Carolyn Conant Van Blarcom, *Obstetric Nursing,* 6th ed. (New York, 1972), pp. 522–26; Wertz and Wertz, *Lying-In,* pp. 119–28; Leavitt, *Brought to Bed,* pp. 154–55.

24. Ballard Diary, Mar. 31, Apr. 4, 5, 10, 11, 12, 13, 15, 16, 1790.

25. Ibid., Oct. 18, 21, 24–29, 1802.

26. Ibid., Feb. 26, 27, Mar 1, 2, 4, 1789; Ziegel and Van Blarcom, *Obstetric Nursing,* pp. 208–13.

27. White, *A Treatise on the Management of Pregnant and Lying-In Women* (Worcester 1793 ed.), pp. 17–31, 219, 236–40. White's estimates for London and Manchester work out to maternal mortality rates of 13/1,000 and 6/1,000 respectively. For a modern effort to compute maternal mortality ratios from parish christening and death records, see B. M. Willmott Dobbie, "An Attempt to Estimate the True Rate of Maternal Mortality, Sixteenth to Eighteenth Centuries," *Medical History* 26 (1982): 79–90. Dobbie believes that maternal mortality in England may have been as high as 29/1,000, as compared with earlier estimates of 10–15/1,000.

28. Ballard Diary, Mar. 11, 1790, Jan. 19, 1800.

29. Ibid., Apr. 17, 1801, May 31, 1799, Nov. 28, 1787; see also ibid., June 30, 1794, June 3, 1795, Aug. 10–11, 1799.

30. Some nineteenth-century Americans debating the causes of childbed fever used the

same environmental argument, anticipating the conclusions but not the logic of twentieth-century historians (Charles E. Rosenberg, *The Care of Strangers: The Rise of America's Hospital System* [New York, 1987], pp. 124–26, 376 nn. 10, 11).

31. Dorothy I. Lansing, W. Robert Penman, and Dorland J. Davis, "Puerperal Fever and the Group B Beta Hemolytic Streptococcus," *Bulletin of the History of Medicine* 57 (1983): 70–80. On the complexities of the puerperal fever debate in the nineteenth and early twentieth centuries, see Leavitt, *Brought to Bed,* chap. 6.

32. *Falmouth Gazette and Weekly Advertiser,* Feb. 12, 26, Mar. 5, 12, 1785.

33. Jeremiah Barker, "History of Diseases in the History of Maine," chap. 3, Barker Papers, Maine Historical Society, Portland.

34. Ibid.

35. Ibid.

36. *Falmouth Gazette,* Feb. 12, 1785.

37. Ibid., Feb. 26, Mar. 5, 12, 1785. Coffin was perhaps referring to Richard Brookes, *The General Dispensatory . . .* (London, 1753), or *The General Practice of Physic . . .* (London, 1754); and to Jean Astruc, *A Treatise of the Diseases of Women . . . ,* 2 vols. (London, 1762), or *Elements of Midwifery, containing the Most Modern and Successful Method of Practice in Every Kind of Labor . . .* (London, 1766). Astruc's works were translated from the French.

38. Smellie, *Collection,* 3:533–43; Denman, *Introduction,* 1:171.

39. Jeremiah Barker, Medical Cases, 1771–1796, Barker Papers.

40. Loose paper dated Apr. 29, 1802, Moses Appleton Papers, Waterville Historical Society, Waterville, Me. On the larger question of lay resistance, see William G. Rothstein, *American Physicians in the Nineteenth Century: From Sects to Science* (Baltimore, 1972), pp. 128–38; and Joseph F. Kett, *The Formation of the American Medical Profession: The Role of Institutions, 1780–1860* (New Haven, Conn., 1968), pp. 101–7.

41. Barker was born in Scituate, Mass., began his practice in Gorham, Me., in 1772, removed to Barnstable on Cape Cod after a year, returned to Gorham in 1779, and finally went to the Stroudwater section of Falmouth in 1796 (James Alfred Spalding, *Jeremiah Barker, M.D., Gorham and Falmouth, Maine, 1752–1835,* reprinted from *Bulletin of the American Academy of Medicine* 10 ([1909]: 1–2). Barker had an indirect link to British medicine. In mid-career his mentor, Dr. Bela Lincoln of Hingham, Mass., had spent a year studying in London hospitals and acquiring an M.D. from King's College, Aberdeen. Spalding, *Barker,* pp. 1–2; Clifford K. Shipton, *Sibley's Harvard Graduates: Biographical Sketches of Those Who Attended Harvard College,* vol. 13 (Boston, 1965), p. 456.

42. Nathaniel Coffin to Massachusetts Medical Society, May 8, 1803, and Jeremiah Barker to Joseph Whipple, July 12, 1803, Countway Medical Library, Boston. In the long run, Barker may have been more forgiving than Coffin. His manuscript history describes Coffin as a physician "who commanded an extensive practice in physic, surgery and obstetrics, with good success" ("History," chap. 2).

43. Barker, "History," chap. 2.

44. Ibid. The citations on puerperal fever are, as he gave them, "Dr. Terriere, 1789; Dr. Biskell, *Medical Papers,* v. 2, 1798; *London Medical Repository,* May 1815; *New England Journal,* v. 4, 5; Dr. Channing, *New England Journal,* vol. 6, 1817; *Medical Repository,* vol. II."

45. Barker, "History," chap. 2.

46. Leavitt, *Brought to Bed*, pp. 144–45.

47. On some things Denman had changed his own mind by 1794. Although he continued to oppose intervention in labor, he did accept bloodletting as a cure for puerperal fever, something he had dismissed in his earlier treatise, as had Barker in his *Falmouth Gazette* letters. Denman, *Introduction*, 1:184–190, 2:253–254; *Falmouth Gazette*, Feb. 26, 1785.

48. Adrian Wilson, "William Hunter and the Varieties of Man-Midwifery," in Bynum and Porter, eds., *William Hunter*, pp. 344–45.

49. Franklin McDuffie, *History of the Town of Rochester, New Hampshire, from 1722 to 1890*, ed. Silvanus Hayward (Manchester, N.H., 1892), 1:345–46; James Farrington Medical Record Books, 1824–1859, Special Collections, Dimond Library, University of New Hampshire, Durham. Farrington added an entry about the woman dying five days after delivery in different colored ink at the end of his delivery record. On the general pattern of listing childbed deaths under other causes, see Wertz and Wertz, *Lying-In,* pp. 125–26.

50. Farrington Medical Record Books, Case #451, Sept. 9, 1835; #118, Feb. 24, 1825; #442, May 28, 1835; #292, Jan. 30, 1831.

51. Farrington used forceps before 1838; he just did not have a separate category to cover instrumental labors.

52. Joan M. Jensen's analysis of 109 deliveries by an early nineteenth-century Chester, Pa., physician shows no maternal deaths at delivery, 7 percent stillbirths, and 30 percent difficult labors (*Loosening the Bonds: Mid-Atlantic Farm Women, 1750–1850* [New Haven, Conn., 1986], pp. 30–33). The low caseload of this physician, roughly 14 deliveries a year, suggests the presence of other practitioners, probably including midwives.

53. Denman, *Introduction*, 1:171; Farrington Medical Record Books, Case #539, Aug. 8, 1839.

54. Leavitt, *Brought to Bed*, pp. 43–44.

55. Ibid., p. 40.

9.

"Sally Has Been Sick"

Pregnancy and Family Limitation among Virginia Gentry Women, 1780–1830

JAN LEWIS AND KENNETH A. LOCKRIDGE

The great legend that has grown up around them says, among many things, that antebellum Southerners were fatalists, their women no less than their men. Statistics seem to bear this out; the lesson read from census and impressionistic evidence both is that before the Civil War Southern gentry women continued to accept the eight to ten children God gave them.[1] Their "traditional" behavior is often contrasted to that of their Yankee sisters, who by 1860 had already entered the transition to limited fertility within marriage and were bearing, at that time, perhaps five children apiece. The consensus among Southern historians and historical demographers has been that Southern gentry women found neither a need nor a way to broach with their husbands so delicate and bold a subject as reduced fertility, even while Yankee couples were, presumably, beginning to carry on a rational and effective dialogue in which a kind of "domestic feminism" gave women an equal role with their husbands.[2]

It is perhaps unfair to fault American historians for not having tested further this comparison, for any demographer will affirm that very little indeed is known about the discussions between husbands and wives anywhere about reproduction on the eve of the great transition to lower marital fertility that struck the Western world in the nineteenth century, and little enough is known about actual reproductive behavior. Given this vacuum in our knowledge, it was easy to go on seeing, in cursory glances at the American evidence, fatalistic and repressed Southern wives lagging far behind their Northern sisters in their quest for reproductive autonomy. Indeed, our own data in the aggregate initially seemed to confirm this picture. Our statistics, which are based on a sample of 298 Virginia gentry women

Reprinted from the *Journal of Social History* 22 (1988): 5–20, by permission of the publisher.

born between 1710 and 1849, indicate that, thus aggregated, married gentry women born in Virginia between 1760 and 1799, and bearing children between 1780 and 1840, bore nearly as many children as their sisters bore between 1710 and 1759—just over eight apiece.[3]

Yet a preliminary look at the letters and diaries written by hundreds of Virginia gentry women between 1760 and 1830 reveals that after 1790 or 1800 some of them, at least, were becoming ever more articulate and insistent in their complaints about the burdens of repeated pregnancies and childbirths.[4] Their dialogue with their husbands, dwelling as it did on their pain and suffering alone, was perhaps not wholly the language of feminine autonomy, let alone rational economic discourse, but it may eventually have been effective. For a closer analysis of the childbearing experience of our sample of 298 Virginia gentry women born 1710–1849 and bearing children in the years 1760 to 1870 indicates that the faint beginnings of the fertility transition were in evidence as early as the 1820s, and that a definite trend to lower marital fertility had commenced by the 1840s and 1850s, well before the Civil War.

In the letters of Virginia gentry women written between 1760 and 1790 or 1800, childbirth was already regarded as a difficult time for a woman. This can hardly be surprising, as the connection between childbirth and female suffering goes back at least as far as Genesis. The risks and painful realities of human reproduction made such an association inevitable. But what is striking is the relative brevity, directness, and stoicism with which eighteenth-century Virginia women discussed childbirth—when they discussed it at all. Even as late as the 1790s (and indeed in some instances later still), the entire business, including its fears, was discussed in routinized language, as in this letter from Martha (Jefferson) Carr to Lucy Terrell of 9 August 1794: "[Patsy Randolph will have a child soon.] How happy should I be could I repeat my attentions to you on the same occasion but I have not a dou[b]t of your being blest with some good female friend that will act the Mother [and] sooth you with her compassion when the painful hour arrives and soften [you] by her tenderness. The necessary time of retirement may God of his mercy grant you a favorable time." In this letter, the woman's need of companionship can be met by any "female friend" who will fill a standard role by "acting the Mother" in "the painful hour," that is, in "the necessary time of retirement." This is still largely the standardized language of the stoical eighteenth century, in which such conventionalized formulas at once expressed and yet controlled the fear and other emotions that, by the very use of such language, were assumed to be simply the *inevitable* concomitants of childbirth. Childbirth was, in short, frightening, but, like all other occasions of emotion, in the eyes of the eighteenth century it was nothing to make a great fuss about. Men similarly subsumed childbirth's recognized problems under routine formulas. To William Byrd, it was simply "breeding," as in "my wife is breeding again." To David Meade, his daughter's impending delivery of a child was called "being taken to the Chamber for a season." "She will not," he continued, "be without your anxious wishes for her speedy recovery from so critical a state."[5] Again here, the recognized dangers were being subsumed under formulas that both expressed and contained human fears.

Yet by the turn of the eighteenth century, some Virginia gentry women (and, eventually, men) were beginning to discuss childbirth much more frequently and to make it ever more clear that they faced childbirth with hesitation, and even fear and trembling. Theirs became the standard mode of future discussions. It was not that they did not love their children. But, if anything, the increasing value that the nineteenth century attached to the individual tended to make a mother more satisfied with a smaller family upon whom she could lavish, proportionately, more affection. Thus, Eleanor Lewis, anticipating the birth of her second child in 1801, could tell a friend, "You say my Dear Mrs. Pinckney, that you shall be pleased to hear I have another little darling to divide my affection with my precious Frances—in August or September [three or four months hence] I expect to inform you of such an event if no accident intervenes—I often think what I shall do with more, when one engrosses me so much—".[6] Similarly, Ellen Coolidge, also anticipating the birth of a second child, told her sister that "my present poppet is such a source of hope and comfort to me that I do not allow myself to repine at the thought of another, although I should certainly have preferred to defer the arrival of the little sister another year."[7] Thus, women with only one child, and one they loved dearly, might express reservations about the impending arrival of a second.

Similar reservations were expressed by women who were, to all indications, happily married; so the anxiety women expressed about childbirth cannot be read as a covert protest against marriage itself or against the physical intimacy that was an accepted, indeed welcomed, part of marriage. One of the euphemisms for pregnancy was being "in the way that ladies love to be who love their lords."[8] Because this phrase was one used among women rather than with men or in mixed company, it should not be read literally, as an acknowledgement of male mastery, so much as female appreciation of the sexual dimension of marriage: it is women who love their husbands who will find themselves pregnant. That also is the meaning of the confession to her sister of a woman pregnant for the first time. "Oh my dear Jane how can I ever get through[.] I feel as the time approaches that I would rather die than bear so much pain. What a fool a girl is ever to get married, if I should be so fortunate as to have a daughter my first lesson to her shall be to despise everything that wears breeches."[9] Sidney Carr held herself, not her husband, responsible for her predicament. Ironically, then, those forces that worked in the early nineteenth century to make marriage more intimate and to increase the acceptance of romantic love as the only legitimate basis for marriage would ensure that the sex that was attracted to the one that wore breeches would find itself pregnant time and again.[10]

That was the catch. The very women who expressed love of their children and their husbands also feared childbirth, so much so that a married woman, gossiping with a female friend about an unmarried woman who had become pregnant, could not comprehend the maiden's lapse: "How ca[n you] account for a young woman's so far losing all . . . fear of what even *we* dread so much. . . ."[11] Not shame, or the economic insecurity, but the pain and danger were what impressed, and these were discussed in the blunt language of fear and dread. What woman would undertake such risks without the benefits of marriage? The prospect of pain and the very real possibility of dying in childbirth combined to make women's descriptions of the experience strikingly negative. It was richly, variously, and sometimes appallingly termed "this dreadful event," a "trial," "an affliction," "one of the evils of this life."[12] The stoicism of the eighteenth century was being strained to, and beyond, its limits by this amplifying terminology.

Women approached the moment of childbirth with grave trepidation. According to one letter writer, a relative was "in miserable spirits at her approaching confinement, which is to take place next month."[13] Another, even more despondent, was "in a very gloomy state of Mind . . . she expects the birth of her child will put a period to her existence as her constitution is far too exhausted to bear the distresst state to which she is exposed in childbirth."[14] During the eighteenth century, female mortality rates in the Chesapeake consistently exceeded those of men, with perhaps 30 percent of women dying before their 45th birthdays; historians have attributed women's lower life expectancy to the hazards of childbirth.[15] By the beginning of the nineteenth century, women themselves ever more frequently made this association between childbirth and maternal death. Further, their language of dread was by now seldom rendered in brief formulas alone but was amplified into such varying chronicles of individual misery and fear.

Women who well knew the hazards of childbirth made it clear that they dreaded facing the trial, which might, to use a conventional term—but one seldom used in this context previously—"put a period to their existence." They wanted with them, not just any female, but their loved ones, especially their mothers, women who they knew for a fact had successfully passed through the same danger. Sally Lacy, for example, implored, "What would I not give if you my dear Mother could be with me or rather if I could be with you—."[16] Similarly, Mary Anderson explained to her brother, "Believe me Duncan the company of a much loved

Mother to comfort & sooth in affliction & pain is a blessing indeed."[17] Any woman who could "act the Mother" would no longer do. Again, these were not women who were alienated from their husbands; Sally Lacy's was in her words "the best nurse I ever saw," while Mary Anderson described hers as a "kind friend and affectionate husband." Even women who believed themselves to be living out the nineteenth century's ideal of the affectionate marriage wanted their mothers with them when they gave birth.

Perhaps women looked to their mothers because they sensed that, as much as they loved their husbands, men could not fully empathize with their increasingly articulated fears. Indeed, until perhaps 1820, the letters written by husbands and fathers still reveal much less anxiety about the dangers of childbirth than did women's. Few Virginia men after the dawn of the nineteenth century were as patriarchal in their views as David Meade had been in 1799, when he proclaimed to a kinswoman that his "newly married Daughter promises to support the credit of our race by duly answering the most important purpose of her creation—already she discovers strong indications of that disposition."[18] Meade's circumlocutions are revealing; in his mind, pregnancy was woman's natural state. Rather, more characteristic of the attitudes of early nineteenth-century men is the postscript Sally Lacy's husband appended to the rather anxious letter she wrote her brother: "Sally intends to give me another little boy, as much finer and smarter than little Ned, as her health and spirits (which are as good as possible) are better now, than previous to Ned's entrance into life."[19] His focus was upon the prospect of another child—indeed, another boy—as much as upon his wife's very real fears. Much more than women, men tended to regard the pains and dangers of childbirth as necessary and inevitable; and more than women, they hoped for sons. Thus, Randolph Harrison announced to his good friend John Hartwell Cocke that "last night at 11 o'clock, my wife presented me with a little Nancy Cocke, instead of a John Hartwell as I expected. I say expected, because after so many daughters I thought I had a right [to] calculate on a son. . . . Poor Dear Soul, she has suffered more than on any former occasion. She was taken slightly on the night of the 16th, lingered for two days, and for several hours before the birth suffered the most excruciating torture that can be imagined." But in the long run, Harrison's desire for sons overrode his sympathy for his wife's ordeals; ten years later he reported to Cocke that "after two days of pain, generally slow and lingering but lately extremely violent, my wife at 11 last night was made the happy mother of the 8th daughter, and 10th child. She is now Thank God (who has always dealt with me more bountifully than I deserve), as well as I could reasonably expect."[20] Tellingly, Harrison deemed himself, not the mother of his ten children, the beneficiary of God's mercy.

At least until about 1820, women appear to have been considerably more anxious about childbirth than were their husbands. Thus, any woman who wanted to limit her fertility would have to devise or discover her own means. That, at least, is what women seemed to believe. Ann Barraud, for example, repeated to her married daughter a kinswoman's observation "about Women's being with child, unless they chose it."[21] (The daughter, incidentally, would die six years later, in 1816, shortly after giving birth to her sixth child in 14 years of marriage.) Such a comment suggests that women believed that they, and they alone, could exercise *some* control over their own fertility. Such also is the conclusion to be drawn from the letter of another mother to her daughter. Peggy Nicholas wrote that "I was not surprised, nor would I have been grieved to hear that you were again in the family way; but I must acknowledge to hear that your confinement was to take place next Month, dashed me not a litle. I had hoped that you had got into a confirmed habit of an intervall of two years, that there was no doubt of your continuance in this, and that [there] might be some reasonable guide in calculating your number. But now that you have got into your old habits, there is no saying where will be the end."[22]

Between 1815 and 1839, Peggy Nicholas's daughter Jane Randolph bore 13 children, at an average interval of 23 months, an experience that virtually duplicated her mother's 12 children, also at a rate of one every 23 months.[23] Both women had several more than the average of 8.32 for their age cohort. Though neither woman suggested what an ideal number of children might have been, the mother clearly believed, to put it in demographers' terms, that *some* control of fertility might be achieved by effective spacing and that the ideal birth interval was no less than 24 months. Such maternal advice is significant for several reasons. First, it suggests that Virginia women in this period may have tried to limit the frequency of births, if not family size. Second, it suggests that without some conscious effort, a birth interval shorter than two years would be the usual result. And third, this goal—and, presumably, the means by which it could be accomplished—were part of a women's tradition, passed on from mother to daughter. Peggy Nicholas had learned of her daughter's pregnancy from her son-in-law, but she addressed her complaint not to him but to her daughter.[24]

In fact, our evidence suggests that Virginia gentry wives had long been successful in maintaining the modest goal of an average two-year interval espoused by Peggy Nicholas and practiced by her and her daughter. Thus the median birth interval for women in our sample born between 1710 and 1759 was 23 months, while that for women born between 1760 and 1799 increased slightly to between 23 and 24 months.[25] What means were at a woman's disposal to assure that she could give birth, on the average, at two-year intervals? The most likely was breast-feeding. Not only does lactation seem to retard ovulation, but there is some evidence that

Virginia women realized that prolonged breast-feeding might extend the interval between pregnancies.[26] The two-year interval that we have found for gentry women born between 1710 and 1799 and that was Peggy Nicholas's ideal is certainly consistent with the practice of breast-feeding. We would expect women who were not breast-feeding, who were instead using wet nurses, to give birth every 18 to 24 months and, as a consequence, to bear a greater number of children than their breast-feeding sisters. For example, Frances Tasker Carter, who used a wet nurse for many of the 16 children to whom she gave birth between 1757 and 1784,[27] delivered a child about every 17 months (median; average: 18.5 mo.). Our figures, which indicate, as we have noted, a longer median birth interval and a lower fertility rate among Virginia gentry women, provide additional confirmation for the assertions of Daniel Blake Smith and Sally McMillen that the vast majority of Southern women breast-fed their own infants.[28]

So it is likely that our women born between 1760 and 1799, like their predecessors, relied upon breast-feeding as a strategy to space their children and possibly as an effort, albeit one with feeble effect, to limit their fertility. This method was perhaps not totally ineffective, but it still meant that a married woman born between 1760 and 1799 and who survived her childbearing years could expect to give birth to an average of 8.3 children, as had her predecessors in the earlier generation.[29] That figure, which is characteristic of the high fertility of colonial American women,[30] represents the limits of female-controlled, breast-feeding-based fertility limitation—and very feeble limits they were. A woman without the cooperation of her husband could accomplish no more.[31]

To put it another way, further limitation of fertility on the part of early nineteenth-century women would require the participation of husbands. How might men who regarded frequent pregnancies with more equanimity than their wives be persuaded to extend spacing further or in another way unquestionably to limit family size? One might think that economic considerations would be important, that men who could not afford to support in independence large families would be inclined to control fertility. By this logic, the group born 1760–99 and bearing children from roughly 1780 to 1840 should have borne fewer children than our earlier (born 1710–59) cohort, for the post-Revolutionary decades in Virginia were characterized by serious economic woes; soil exhaustion, falling tobacco prices, a series of depressions, and land pressures combined to undermine the economic security of the gentry. Yet it was in the letters of women only that the connection between economic pressures and a large family was confronted;[32] men, in contrast, never seemed to consider family limitation as a strategy for coping with hard times, and in fact, family size for the cohort of women born 1760–99 fell almost insignificantly (from an average of 8.37 to 8.33).

Rather, the only instances in which men accepted some form of family limitation were when the wife's life clearly would have been endangered by pregnancy. Thus one Virginian explained to a kinswoman, "It is not probable that I shall ever have a numerous family, if any. My wife has been accidentally unfortunate last winter in a miscarriage, which has rendered her health very delicate." Similarly, James Parker noted that his son's "poor Wife has lost another Little One. It lived only two days, so Dr. Currie writes me. & he thinks that absence from her husband and another climate are the only chances she has of ever doing better."[33] In such cases, the husband would, presumably, avoid intercourse with his wife or would separate from her in order to spare her health. To be sure, not every husband with a delicate wife was willing to forgo sexual relations with her; Thomas Jefferson is a case in point. It is worth noting, however, that the doctor's remedy of a woman's "absence from her husband" strongly suggests that the practice of coitus interruptus, often regarded by historical demographers as the most common pre-twentieth-century method of family limitation,[34] was not used by Virginians; instead, abstinence is recommended, a remedy so difficult that it was thought to require the separation of husband and wife.

That, apparently, was the conclusion reached by Ellen Coolidge and her husband, Joseph, who announced the birth of his sixth child to his mother-in-law this way: "Only think of it—four sons, the oldest of whom is but two years and eight months! I can hardly realize it, and as for Ellen what a melancholy idea of suffering does it give to be told that—with six children she has barely been married six years—; take out the weary months of pregnancy, and nursing, and how little is left to restore her strength of mind a[nd] body—! . . . If we could but feel that we had come to the end of the chapter, I should soon be reconciled, and so would she, to our present number,—which the loss of one would so painfully diminish, (and can we hope to go through life and never lose a child?)."[35] A year later, in 1832, Coolidge, who was a merchant, departed for Canton, China. He was not permanently reunited with his family until his wife had passed out of her childbearing years.[36] If loving couples had to resort to separation, it is unlikely that they had at their disposal less drastic means of birth control. Abstinence, though surely effective, was no easy solution. And it was accepted only by husbands who had grave fears for their wives' health and well-being.

These examples suggest that men may have proved more susceptible to a feminine reason for birth control, fear of maternal death in childbirth, than to the more "masculine" one of economic necessity, which simply does not appear in their correspondence. In order for such a rationale to become a spur to widespread family limitation, however, it would be necessary for men as a class to perceive pregnancy as dangerous in the way that their wives already had come to do. In other words, most men would have to consider all women, and not merely particular husbands their exceptional and obviously ill wives, as delicate. Pregnancy would have to become an acknowledged pathology in which childbirth was dangerous to all women. (And, presumably, means less drastic than abstinence would have to be adopted.)

Perhaps Virginia women somehow knew that this was the only appeal that would persuade their husbands to engage in a mutual program of family limitation. Whether or not this was the case, slowly after the turn of the century, Virginia men as well as women began to describe pregnancy as an illness, using a language of pathology that had been uncommon in earlier descriptions. In 1728, for example, William Byrd II exploited his wife's impending confinement to display his wit: "I wonder any Mother shoud be affraid of dying in child-bed; considering tis dying in obedience to the first command, and consequently in the best cause in the world.... I fancy if there were any such thing as seeing into Female hearts we shoud find this is the reason the whole Sex wants to be married, that by being with child they may have a chance to dye Martyrs."[37] Pregnancy was no cause for concern.

By the early nineteenth century, however, women and men both were beginning to describe pregnancy and childbirth as something unnatural, a disruption of a woman's health. Of course it is not unusual that miscarriage should have left one man's wife "a good deal indisposed & much debilitated," nor that childbirth left another's "as well as I could reasonably expect."[38] What is exceptional is the use of the language of pathology to describe pregnancy itself. Thus one man alluded to his wife's impending confinement by saying that she was "indisposed." Another Virginian, searching for the right words to inform his daughter of a kinswoman's pregnancy, said merely, "Laura looks very badly...." The adjectives of ill health— "indisposed," "unwell," "sick"—became euphemisms for pregnancy. Sally Lacy, for example, described herself as "restless" and "generally ... unwell at night."[39] By a process of cultural synecdoche, pregnancy's discomforts became the part that stood for the whole. As one woman put it, using terms whose meaning was quite clear, "Sally S—— has been sick almost since she went down, she is in the way to increase her family." Such an illness, of course, lasted nine months. Another woman, using a similar terminology, was "delighted to hear of her [sister's] improved health, I pray it may continue; and that she may indeed have had her quantum of children."[40]

The gradual redefinition of pregnancy as disease, in evidence by the beginning of the nineteenth century, did not immediately result in family limitation. Instead, it was a prelude to the very different demographic experience of women born between 1800 and 1839. Although we see a slight lengthening of the median birth interval for women born at the end of the eighteenth century and a small (4 percent) drop in fertility among women born in the 1790s, it is only for the women born af-ter the turn of the century that we see an unmistakable decline in family size.[41] For these women, born between 1800 and 1839, there was a slight further increase in median birth interval (to just over 24 months), but the most important factor lead-ing to limited family size was the sharp drop in fertility of women in their thirties, which resulted in an average completed-family size of 5.81 for women born between 1800 and 1839, compared to 8.37 for the 1710–59 cohort and 8.33 for the 1760–99 cohort.[42]

Our preliminary calculations suggest to us that men agreed to limit family size only when their wives had entered their thirties and had given them a healthy male heir or two. Although our figures for women born between 1800 and 1839 show some drop in fertility for women aged 20–24, the fertility rate is consistent with effective spacing, that is, a child born every two and a half years or so, while the rate for women aged 25–29 remains rather consistent for all Virginia gentry women born between 1710 and 1839. On the other hand, the sharp decline in the fertility rate of women in the 1800–1839 cohort aged 35–39 and 40–44 (along with data for later cohorts) suggests strongly that after 1830 many married women stopped, or tried to stop, bearing children after they reached age 35 and had delivered what they considered their "quantum" of children.

We do not know what means these families used. It is unlikely that many Vir-ginia men joined Joseph Coolidge in Canton. Perhaps after a certain number of births Virginia's husbands and wives resorted to shorter periods of separation or agreed to abstinence when they were together. Our sources are mute on this sub-ject. What they do tell us is that an inchoate desire for family limitation was voiced first among women, and that the description of pregnancy as pathological by both women and men preceded the clear and irreversible drop in fertility.

Most historians of the South and historical demographers, as we have noted, have assumed that antebellum Southern couples did not attempt to limit family size and that, in contrast to the North, no demographic transition took place in the pre–Civil War South.[43] Our statistics, preliminary though they are, may indicate otherwise. Our Virginia gentry women born in the first five decades of the nine-teenth century seem to have borne progressively fewer children, especially after age 35, than their mothers, even if their fertility did not drop as early and as sharply as that of their Northern sisters. Their success in limiting family size might in some sense be considered a Southern instance of the domestic feminism that Daniel Scott Smith has found among Northern women, for now it seems possible that here in Virginia as well, control of fertility depended upon a woman's persuading her husband to accede to her desire for a smaller family.[44]

Still, this victory for Virginia's elite women was not necessarily proof of—as

Smith puts it—"women's increasing autonomy within the family."[45] Family limitation may have had its costs. It could be purchased only by sacrificing the physical intimacy that the nineteenth century's cult of romantic love had awakened. And it may have required women to depict themselves as weak, frail, and too delicate to endure the rigors of repeated pregnancies. Indeed, women themselves, and not, as some have suggested, their physicians,[46] may have played the leading role in medicalizing pregnancy and describing it as a pathology. In this way, ironically, women themselves may have encouraged the belief that they were frail, that the essence of their femininity posed a grave and, finally, unnatural threat to their health. Such a view perhaps gave them leverage over their husbands, in a sort of "domestic feminism," but it was possibly as "the weaker vessel" and not as autonomous equals that Virginia gentry women finally prevailed on their husbands to liberate them from the pain of childbirth.

As a sort of coda, we might add that this Virginia evidence, aside from being seen as strictly preliminary, should not be rendered too pessimistically. The great attitudinal changes of the early nineteenth-century evangelical religion, romanticism, and emerging medical "science"—had all helped free these women to express more eloquently than before what was certainly an ancient concern, indeed an ancient slavery, for women. From all the evidence, once they expressed this concern, Virginia gentry women *did* prevail on their husbands, at whatever cost to their own self-image, to help liberate them. By the time of the cohort born in 1800, Virginia gentry women were having seven rather than nine children. By the time of the cohort born in 1840, that number was probably closer to five, and by the turn of the twentieth century, four. Further, since our research in the correspondence of this class of women does not in fact extend to cover many of the letters of the cohorts born after 1800 and bearing children chiefly after 1830—that is, those who finally succeeded in limiting their families—it is entirely possible that a more optimistic construction could be placed upon the evident adoption of family limitation practices among these later generations of women. These women and their husbands, born after 1800 and growing up in the 1800s and 1810s and 1820s, heard on their parents' lips the ample language of suffering and pathology used to describe pregnancy and childbirth. And they saw their parents fail, by and large, to limit their families substantially. This experience may have led both the women and the men of these younger generations, born after 1800, quietly to agree not to endure such extensive suffering and "sickness" as a part of their own marriages. Recent Swedish research indicates that such a sober, *mutual* resolution "not to have ten children like our mothers," reached by young women and men alike, lay behind the advent of family limitation in far northern Sweden in the 1930s and 1940s.[47] So the desperate, almost demeaning frustrations of the Virginia mothers bearing children in the period of 1800–1830, who did not generally succeed very well in having fewer children, may have become a quieter, more mutual resolution in their daughters—and in their sons—born after 1800, who did succeed in having fewer children thereafter. Thus in these younger and more successful generations, the net product could have been something closer to Daniel Scott Smith's "domestic feminism"— namely, a quiet, mutual, and effective decision to change reproductive behavior.

Which model is characteristic of the advent of fertility limitation elsewhere in America—the desperate appeal to weakness characteristic of Virginia gentry women at least up to 1830; a quieter, more mutual decision not to prolong such suffering, as was possibly found in later generations in Virginia and probably in northern Sweden a century later; or the classic "domestic feminism" posited by Daniel Scott Smith—is anyone's guess.[48] W. Seccombe, of the Ontario Institute for Studies on Education, has recently completed a study of working-class women in Britain circa 1910–30 remarkably similar to this one in its sources and conclusions. His study implicitly suggests that within each social class in its respective historical place and time, all three of these models, perhaps in the order specified, across several generations, could have entered into a fertility transition that was generally led by women's concerns.[49] These questions and possibilities aside, the only certainty is that all our theories of the advent of family limitation in Western society, some relating it more closely to structural change and others to attitudinal revolutions,[50] must take greater cognizance of the varied conversations women carried on with one another and with their husbands. These conversations and the views they embodied were the final lens through which both structural change and attitudinal modernization were focused into radically changed behavior.[51]

NOTES

We are indebted to Sarah Bearss of the Virginia Historical Society, for her assistance in obtaining genealogies, and Norma Basch, Colleen Isaac, Rhys Isaac, Martin Pernick, Daniel Scott Smith, and Maris Vinovskis for their advice.

1. Richard H. Steckel, *The Economics of U.S. Slave and Southern White Fertility* (New York, 1985), esp. p. 176; Catherine Clinton, *The Plantation Mistress: Woman's World in the Old South* (New York, 1982), pp. 152–53; Bertram Wyatt-Brown, *Southern Honor: Ethics and Behavior in the Old South* (New York, 1982), p. 205.

2. Daniel Scott Smith, "Family Limitation, Sexual Control, and Domestic Feminism in Victorian America," *Feminist Studies* 1 (1973): 40–57.

3. We have drawn our demographic sample from unpublished genealogies of Virginia gentry women available at the Virginia Historical Society, from published genealogies of the same group, also from the collection of the society, and from the *William and Mary Quarterly,*

1st ser., and the *Virginia Magazine of History and Biography.* "Gentry" is defined throughout as slave-owning families with possessions and pretentions indicating, and in many cases with actual self-identification confirming, membership in the planter elite of Virginia. It should be noted that this was often a rather upper-middle-class elite, however, hence the term "gentry," which many at the time preferred. We have not used genealogies that appear to be "tainted," that is, ones that appear to have excluded children who died young or did not themselves produce issue, as well as those that in other ways seem incomplete or unreliable. (As a result, our figures for completed family size may be shaded toward the high side, and our age-specific fertility rates, particularly for women over age 25, may likewise be slightly high. That is, in trying to make certain that we excluded from our sample all genealogies in which the compiler chose to follow only those individuals who achieved adulthood or those lines that produced issue, we may have eliminated a very few women who simply bore relatively few children. But most cases of data tainted in this way are clearly tainted and thus must be excluded from the sample.) We have divided our demographic sample into three cohorts: women born 1719–54 (*n* = 44), born 1760–99 (*n* = 121), born 1800–1839 (*n* = 97); we also have data on 36 women born in the 1840s. We should also note that we have, whenever possible, included in this sample the actual fertility histories of those women from whose correspondence we have quoted. It is this demographic sample that provides the evidence cited here in the text.

> Live births per married woman surviving to age 45:
> Women born 1710–59   8.37 (*n* = 24)
> Women born 1760–99   8.33 (*n* = 38)

4. The women whose correspondence is to be used in developing this argument come from the primary sample used in this article. That "sample" is nothing more or less than the letters of hundreds of Virginia gentry women in the years 1760–1830, totaling more than half and as much as two-thirds of all such letters surviving in Virginia archives. In general, while the majority of such letters surveyed are not articulate about the issues of childbirth, pregnancy, etc., considered here, they are nonetheless, in their tone and often actual language, not inconsistent with, and often implicitly or explicitly support, the more articulate minority of women who wrote in some detail on these issues and who are quoted here. This articulate minority within Virginia gentry women's culture circa 1760–1830—perhaps 100 women in all—might therefore be seen as the voice of their feminine culture on fertility issues, the voice of a given sex, class, culture, and milieu. The actual fertility histories of these more articulate women have been traced wherever possible (in a majority of cases) and have been included in and in all known cases are consistent with the fertility histories of the women of their generation in the appropriate and larger demographic subsample of women of the same class (i.e., women born 1710–59, 1760–99, etc., cited in n. 3 above) analyzed to check for actual fertility behavior among the various generations of Virginia gentry women of this era. In this pilot study, then, *correspondence* sampled is, therefore and perforce, not strictly identical with the *demographic behavior* sampled in women of the same class and generations. For some women we have only correspondence, for others only demographic behavior, as is inevitable from the nature of the surviving sources. But all of the most vital examples from the correspondence where demographic information is available in fact show demographic behavior consistent with that of the larger demographic samples invoked.

5. Martha Carr to Lucy Terrell, August 9, 1794, Terrell-Carr Papers, Alderman Library, University of Virginia; William Byrd, in *The Correspondence of the Three William Birds of Westover, Virginia* (Charlottesville, Va., 1977), 1:391; David Meade to Ann Randolph [1799?], Bolling Papers, Perkins Library, Duke University.

6. Eleanor P. Lewis to Mrs. Pinckney, May 9, 1801, Custis Family Papers, Library of Congress.

7. Ellen Wayles Coolidge to Virginia Trist, March 20, 1827, Ellen W. Coolidge Papers, Alderman Library, University of Virginia.

8. Sarah Nicholas to Jane H. Randolph, January 1, 1830, Edgehill-Randolph Papers, Alderman Library, University of Virginia; see also Martha J. Randolph to Ellen W. Coolidge, November 16, 1825, Coolidge Papers.

9. Sidney Carr to Jane Randolph, December 31 [1825–30], Edgehill-Randolph Papers.

10. Jan Lewis, *The Pursuit of Happiness: Family and Values in Jefferson's Virginia* (New York, 1983), chap. 5; Ellen W. Rothman, *Hands and Hearts: A History of Courtship in America* (New York, 1984), chap. 1.

11. F. H. Allison to Margaret Coalter, July 15, 1797, Brown, Coalter, and Tucker Papers, Earl Gregg Swem Library, College of William and Mary.

12. Betsy Carrington to Ann Fisher, November 22, 1799, Carrington-Ambler Papers, Alderman Library; Virginia Trist to Ellen W. Coolidge, March 23, 1827, Coolidge Papers; Peggy Nicholas to Jane H. Randolph, May 25, 1827, Edgehill-Randolph Papers. See also Peggy Nicholas to Jane H. Randolph, April 28 [1828], Edgehill-Randolph Papers; and William Shepard to Ebenezer Pettigrew, August 5, 1818, Pettigrew Papers, Southern Historical Collection, University of North Carolina.

13. W[ilson] J. Cary to Virginia Cary, July 21, 1821, Carr-Cary Papers, Alderman Library.

14. Ann Barraud to Ann Cocke, May 18 [1812], Cocke Deposit, Alderman Library.

15. Allan Kulikoff, *Tobacco and Slaves: The Development of Southern Cultures in the Chesapeake, 1680–1800* (Chapel Hill, N.C., 1986), p. 63. Approximately 30 percent of the women in our sample born 1710–99 died before age 45; only about 10 percent of women in that cohort were preceded in death by their husbands (men who were, typically, several years older than their wives). The higher female mortality rate may well be related to childbirth and, in particular, the debilitating effects of malaria; Darrett B. Rutman and Anita H. Rutman have hypothesized that Chesapeake women of childbearing age were weakened by malaria. ("Of Agues and Fevers: Malaria in the Early Chesapeake," *William and Mary Quarterly*, 3d ser., 33 [1976]: 51–52). For women's fear of childbirth, see also Judith Walzer Leavitt and Whitney Walton, "'Down to Death's Door': Women's Perceptions of Childbirth in America," in *Childbirth: The Beginning of Motherhood, Proceedings of the Second Motherhood Symposium, April 1981* (Madison, 1982), reprinted in Judith Walzer Leavitt, ed., *Women and Health in America* (Madison, 1984), pp. 155–65; and Judith Walzer Leavitt, *Brought to Bed: Childbearing in America, 1750–1950* (New York, 1986), pp. 20–35.

16. Sally Lacy to [Margaret Graham], July 21, 1817, Graham Family Papers, Perkins Library, Duke University.

17. Mary Anderson to Duncan Cameron, August 17, 1798, Cameron Papers, Southern Historical Collection.

18. David Meade to Ann Randolph [1799?], Bolling Papers, Perkins Library; see similarly David Meade to Ann Randolph, May 6, 1798.

19. Sally Lacy to William A. Graham, February 7, 1819, Graham Family Papers.

20. Randolph Harrison to John Hartwell Cocke, February 19, 1819, and February 1829, Cocke Deposit.

21. Ann Barraud to Ann Cocke, August 13 [1810], Cocke Deposit. See also Milton Rugoff, *The Beechers: An American Family in the Nineteenth Century* (New York, 1981), p. 237, quoting Catharine Beecher's letter to her sister Mary about their sister Harriet, who "says she shall not have any more *children, she knows for certain* for one while. Though how she found this out I cannot say, but she seems quite confident about it."

22. Peggy Nicholas to Jane H. Randolph, April 28 [1828?], Edgehill- Randolph Papers. See similarly Peggy Nicholas to Jane H. Randolph, February 18, 1829.

23. Both married younger than the average of their cohort. (Average age at first marriage for women born 1710–59, 20.9; born 1760–99, 20.3; 1800–1839, 21.46.) Peggy Nicholas married at 19, and her daughter Jane at 17.

24. See n. 22 above.

25. Smith has found a typical birth interval of 24–30 months. Daniel Blake Smith, *Inside the Great House: Planter Life in Eighteenth-Century Chesapeake Society* (Ithaca, 1980), p. 27.

26. Catherine M. Scholten, *Childbearing in American Society: 1650–1850* (New York, 1985), p. 14; Smith, *Inside the Great House,* pp. 36–37. Smith believes that most women breast-fed about eighteen months.

27. Smith, *Inside the Great House,* p. 51.

28. Ibid., pp. 36–37; Sally McMillen, "Mothers' Sacred Duty: Breast-Feeding Patterns among Middle- and Upper-Class Women in the Antebellum South," *Journal of Southern History* 51 (1985): 333–56.

29. See n. 3 above.

30. For example, John Demos found an average of 9.3 births to third-generation Plymouth families. *A Little Commonwealth: Family Life in Plymouth Colony* (New York, 1970), p. 192.

31. There is some evidence that Virginia women of this period may have been aware of some methods of abortion and could even imagine infanticide, but both were considered the remedies of desperate women, certainly not appropriate for married women. See F. H. A[llison] to Margaret Coalter, July 15, 1797, Brown, Coalter, and Tucker Papers; and Francis Biddle, "Scandal at Bizarre," *American Heritage* 12 (August 1961): 10–82, esp. p. 79, for knowledge of abortifacients. We have found no evidence, however, that those artificial means of birth control, such as syringes, that Joan Jensen has found available in Philadelphia by the 1790s could be obtained in Virginia. See her *Loosening the Bonds: Mid-Atlantic Farm Women, 1750–1850* (New Haven, 1986), p. 29.

32. Cary Ann Smith to Jane H. Randolph, June 16, 1819, Edgehill-Randolph Papers; Peggy Nicholas to Jane H. Randolph, September 19, 1829, Edgehill- Randolph Papers; Virginia Trist to Ellen W. Coolidge, March 23, 1827, Coolidge Papers. For problems in the Virginia economy, see Lewis, *Pursuit of Happiness,* chap. 4.

33. Gideon Fitz to Elizabeth Fitz, September 22, 1808, George Carr Manuscripts, Alder-

man Library; James Parker to Charles Steuart, April 21, 1791, Steuart Papers, Colonial Williamsburg Foundation, Research Archives.

34. In ten years of marriage to Thomas Jefferson, Martha Wayles Skelton (a widow with an infant son at the time of her marriage to Jefferson in 1772) bore six children (of whom only two survived infancy). Throughout her marriage, Martha Jefferson suffered from poor health; she never recovered from the birth of her last child. See Dumas Malone, *Jefferson the Virginian* (Boston, 1948), pp. 214, 241, 245–46, 393–96, 434. Those who have argued that coitus interruptus was the most common method of birth control include Carroll Smith Rosenberg and Charles Rosenberg ("The Female Animal: Medical and Biological Views of Woman and Her Role in Nineteenth-Century America," *Journal of American History* 60 [1973]: 332–56).

35. Joseph W. Coolidge to Martha J. Randolph, August [28 and 30], [1831], Coolidge Papers. Note that Coolidge first mentions his four sons and only later that his wife is the mother of six children in all; his calculation that at least one of these children will fail to survive to adulthood suggests strongly that his desire for a male heir has entered into his reckoning. Fathers seemed to consider limiting family size only after they were assured of a male heir. See similarly Cary Ann Smith to Jane H. Randolph, June 16, 1819, Edgehill-Randolph Papers.

36. Walter Muir Whitehall, "Eleanora Wayles Randolph and Joseph Coolidge, Jr.," in George Green Shackelford, ed., *Collected Papers to Commemorate Fifty Years of the Monticello Association of the Descendants of Thomas Jefferson* (Princeton, 1965), pp. 89–99.

37. William Byrd II to Cousen Taylor, July 28, 1728, Letter Book 1, pp. 23–24, Colonial Williamsburg (original at Virginia Historical Society).

38. Larkin Smith to Littleton Tazewell, October 16, 1804, Tazewell Papers, Colonial Williamsburg (original at Virginia State Library); Randolph Harrison to John Hartwell Cocke, February 1829, Cocke Deposit; see also Mary Anderson to Duncan Cameron, August 17, 1798, Cameron Papers.

39. Jean Cameron (quoting her brother Duncan) to Rebecca Cameron, January 6, 1804, Cameron Papers; W. H. Cabell to Louisa Carrington, May 21, 1829, Cabell-Carrington Papers, Alderman Library; Sally Lacy to Margaret Graham, July 21, 1817, Graham Papers; see also Sarah Preston to Mrs. Susanna McDowell, February 27, 1826, The Papers of the Carrington and McDowell Families of Virginia, Library of Congress. Abigail Adams used similar terminology in describing pregnancy, once referring to it as "*her old sickness.*" See Paul C. Nagel, *The Adams Women: Abigail and Louisa Adams, Their Sisters and Daughters* (New York, 1987), p. 97.

40. S[ally] Faulcon to Ann Cocke, May 14, 1810, Cocke Deposit; Agnes Cabell to Louisa Cabell, February 16, 1819, Cabell-Carrington Papers. Randolph Trumbach notes that an influential midwifery manual, published in French in 1672 and available in England in the eighteenth century, described pregnancy as an illness, albeit a necessary and unavoidable one (*The Rise of the Egalitarian Family: Aristocratic Kinship and Domestic Relations in Eighteenth-Century England* [New York, 1978], p. 176). We have no evidence that this work or its assumptions were shared by early Virginians.

41. See above for birth intervals. We have subdivided our post–1759 cohorts and obtained the following completed-family sizes (*n* = no. of women with completed families):

Born	No. of Children	n
1760s	8.43	10
1770s	9.26	3
1780s	8.41	12
1790s	7.98	13
1800s	6.54	16
1810s	6.31	16
1820s	5.39	22
1830s	5.47	31
1840s	5.17	24

Because the numbers in each cohort are small, these calculations are rough. They do show a rather steady decline in family size beginning in 1790, but with the clearest drop for women born after 1800. We have also broken the cohort down because those born at the end of it (after 1830) would have been of childbearing age during and after the Civil War. One would assume that the difficulties of that period would have encouraged family limitation, yet clearly the trend toward a smaller family size was well under way before that time, as was the sharp drop in fertility for women 35 and older (see below).

42. Although the average age of marriage for women increased by 1.2 years for the cohort born 1830–39, that increase is not sufficient to account for so sharp a drop in fertility. (For age at first marriage, see n. 23 above.) Our calculations of age-specific marital fertility rates are preliminary. They suggest a drop in fertility for women born after 1800 of 22 percent for women aged 30–34, and just over 50 percent for women aged 35–39 and 40–45. We hope to refine these data and then apply to them Coale and Trussell's "m" to obtain a more precise measure of the possible presence of family limitation, but in general, this sort of decline in fertility over age 35 is one indication of such limitation. So is the irreversibility of the trend to smaller family size, also found in this data.

43. See n. 1 above.

44. Smith, "Family Limitation."

45. Ibid.

46. See, in particular, G. J. Barker-Benfield, *The Horrors of the Half-Known Life: Male Attitudes toward Women and Sexuality in Nineteenth-Century America* (New York, 1976), pt. 2. Barker-Benfield argues that nineteenth-century physicians were hostile to their female patients; hence, he believes, the medicalization of pregnancy and childbirth represented "the male drive to take control of women" (p. 61). Analyses of the medicalization of pregnancy and childbirth that are more sympathetic to physicians and recognize the desire of at least some of them to alleviate feminine suffering are provided by Scholten, *Childbirth,* chap. 2; and Regina Markell Morantz-Sanchez, *Sympathy and Science: Women Physicians in American Medicine* (New York, 1985), pp. 26, 222–31. Both note, as well, that the medicalization of childbirth was associated with the professionalization of medicine. In her study of childbearing among the British aristocracy, Judith Schneid Lewis has found that women were the first to question the inevitability of maternal suffering, and that hence they, and not their physicians, were the first to insist upon medical intervention in childbirth (*In the Family Way: Childbearing in the British Aristocracy,*

1760–1860 [New Brunswick, N.J., 1986]). See also Martin Pernick's fascinating discussion of the use of anesthesia for childbirth in the nineteenth century; because women were thought to be especially sensitive to pain, they were among those who were most often afforded anesthesia. Thus the availability of relief from pain, including that associated with childbirth, depended upon the cultural assumption of feminine frailty (*A Calculus of Suffering: Pain, Professionalism, and Anesthesia in Nineteenth-Century America* [New York, 1985], especially pp. 149–54).

47. Unpublished interview-based research by Sune Ackerman, Department of History, University of Umeå, Umeå, Sweden.

48. Although the demographic transition in the North may have preceded that of the South, the experience of women in the two regions may otherwise have been similar. Nagel's *The Adams Women* provides evidence from the correspondence of this family of Massachusetts women of a pattern strikingly similar to the one we have observed in Virginia. By the end of the eighteenth century, the Adams women were worrying, in their letters to each other, about the burdens and dangers of repeated pregnancies. They cautioned and commiserated, without providing any specific advice about techniques for family limitation. (Nagel hypothesizes that the preferred method was absence from their husbands.) Not until well into the nineteenth century did the men in the family voice the sorts of concerns the women had been expressing for several decades. See, for example, pp. 80, 96–97, and 267–71. It was apparently only at or after this point that effective fertility limitation within marriage began in this context as well, suggesting a generational effect rather like that hypothesized for Virginia in the preceding paragraph of the text.

49. W. Seccombe, "Starting to Stop: Working Class Fertility Decline in Britain." Draft, Ontario Institute for Studies in Education, 1987. See also J. Caldwell, "Demographic Change in Rural South India," *Population and Development Review* 8 (1982): 689.

50. See *The Fertility Transition in Sweden,* K. Lockridge, Demographic Database, Umeå University, S–901 87 (Umeå, Sweden, 1983).

51. See, as another recent approximation of this goal, John Knodel's "Fertility Transition in Thailand: A Qualitative Analysis," *Population and Development Review* 10 (June 1984): 297–328.

10.

MOTHERHOOD DENIED
Women and Infertility in Historical Perspective

MARGARET MARSH

Throughout American history there has always been a cultural expectation that nearly all women will want to become mothers. Those who choose childlessness, or express no maternal feelings, often find themselves accused of unwomanliness. Those who marry are generally *expected* to reproduce. What some psychologists have called "the motherhood mandate" has been invoked to stigmatize not only those who choose not to have children but also those who are involuntarily childless. Furthermore, opponents of women's involvement in the world beyond the confines of home and family have traditionally used the motherhood mandate to castigate career women as well as to valorize women's fertility. This essay provides a historical exploration of the ways in which women in infertile marriages have coped with these cultural expectations and their own desires for motherhood. Its focus is both on social attitudes toward involuntarily childless women and on the ways in which women dealt with their infertile marriages. In the seventeenth and eighteenth centuries, colonial Americans generally viewed the inability to procreate as the will of God, or (sometimes) the work of the Devil. But by the end of the nineteenth century infertility had become a medical condition, one often brought on, many believed, by unconventional or inappropriate behavior on the part of women. Such "medicalization" engendered the transformation from an emphasis on coping with involuntary childlessness through social means, such as the rearing of others' children, to dependence on medical intervention.

Corresponding with the rise of medical treatment for infertility was an equally significant transformation in the cultural perception of family life. Beginning in the early nineteenth century among the rising middle classes, and continuing ever since, the family has become more privatized. Instead of the bustling household of the colonial era, filled with sundry kin and unrelated individuals, the family ideal became that of a married couple and their "own" children, bound (at least in theory) by ties of love rather than economics, and increasingly dependent on these relationships. As the new attitudes toward family evolved, women in infertile unions found their situations compounded by new difficulties.

Coping with Childlessness in Colonial America

The typical colonial woman brought six or more children into the world, and her life centered around repeated cycles of pregnancy and childbearing. High fertility and high infant mortality continued to the end of the eighteenth century. As late as 1800 the average white woman bore seven living children, which usually meant that she had more than seven pregnancies, since many ended in miscarriage or still-birth.[1] In a society in which the large family was the rule, couples without biological children were clearly atypical, although exactly how uncommon they were remains unclear. There are no definitive statistics on the number of childless marriages in the seventeenth or eighteenth centuries. Neither the genealogical studies of the late nineteenth and early twentieth centuries, which asserted an extraordinarily low rate of infertility—2 percent—nor most of the more recent community studies, which rarely mention its existence, are very helpful. Some data do exist, however, from which recent historians have estimated that about 8 percent of the marriages in colonial New England were childless. The figure may have been larger for other colonies, where higher rates of mortality and morbidity prevailed. The Dutch families in New Amsterdam at the time of the English conquest were, perhaps because of particularly stressful circumstances, especially unfruitful; nearly 23 percent of marriages apparently were childless.[2]

Although childless couples were never so rare in colonial America as to be considered curiosities, neither did they conform to the colonial familial ideal. Especially in Puritan New England, it was commonly thought that childlessness signified either the Lord's disfavor or His desire to test the faith of the couple. In both cases, at least according to religious teaching, the best comfort would come from prayer and reflection.[3] Men were never considered to be incapable of procreation unless they were impotent; only women could be "barren." Even those who were barren, however, were not invariably destined to remain childless, nor were they necessarily excluded from the family-centered rituals of the community. Those women who never bore children could nevertheless participate in the communal rituals—from the birth of a neighbor's child to the "sitting up" visits that attended the entrance of a child into the world. And wife and husband together had a number of means of bringing children into their families.

Because the household, and not so much the conjugal unit, defined the colonial family, it does not appear to have been terribly difficult for couples to accept children who came their way by various means other than conceiving them themselves. Somewhat akin to modern adoption (although no adoption laws existed in the colonies), such practices were nevertheless sufficiently different to require some explanation. First, as far as it is possible to tell, most couples took in the children of family members. Second, a childless couple might "adopt" the child of a living family member in order to provide themselves with an heir without the biological parent having to relinquish the child completely. The concept of a couple having an absolute "right" to a child they brought up would emerge much later, in the nineteenth century, as a part of a more general transformation taking place in ideas about the family.[4]

Women without children of their own, in fact, may even have been expected to rear the children of deceased siblings or cousins. From Puritan New England through the Chesapeake and southward, maternal deaths left many half-orphans. When a wife died leaving young children, a father who did not remarry quickly was likely to send the youngsters to relatives to be reared. If half-orphanhood was the rule, in some parts of the colonies full orphanhood was also common. In one Chesapeake county, for example, almost 20 percent of the children were orphaned before the age of thirteen and more than 30 percent by the age of eighteen.[5]

Childless couples welcomed orphaned nieces, nephews, and cousins into their homes and hearts. In Massachusetts, when Thomas and Bethiah Lothrop adopted a cousin's orphaned daughter in the 1670s, Bethiah recalled that Thomas expressed thankfulness "for the providence of God in disposing of the child from one place to another till it must be brought into his house that he might be a father to it." Elsewhere in the colony the very rich but childless Lydia and Thomas Hancock brought their nephew John, the future signer of the Declaration of Independence, into their house when the boy was eight. They had been married for thirteen years without having children. John's widowed mother, living with her children in the household of her late husband's father, kept her two daughters with her but sent John to Boston, where he became the virtual son of Lydia and Thomas, and their heir.[6]

These intimate dramas of orphanhood and adoption were played out against the backdrop of a distinctive kind of familial and communal life. As the historian Helena Wall reminds us, colonists from New England through the Middle Atlantic states and into the South "conceived of the family almost entirely within the context of community." Families and households in the seventeenth and eighteenth centuries were often quite elastic, and most of them included the sons and daughters of kin as well as unrelated youngsters "put out" (in the parlance of the day), often when very young, to learn a trade, husbandry, or housewifery, or simply because the parents had too many younger mouths to feed.[7] A widespread practice, "putting out" was not limited to families in crisis but was a way for families to relieve themselves of the care of too many offspring. "Putting out" could also provide a means for the childless to enjoy some of the benefits of having children, ideally including both ties of affection and the more tangible attributes of extra hands on the farm or in the kitchen.[8]

Throughout the seventeenth and eighteenth centuries, adoptive practices, guardianship, and being on the receiving end of the putting out system served the community by creating households and providing for children, and they served childless couples by enabling them enjoy some of the benefits of parenthood. Such solutions were possible in a society in which the boundaries between family and community were highly permeable. Biological parenthood, of course, was preferable, but it was not the only way to create a family. Although some childless women in New England found themselves under suspicion as witches, for the most part childlessness was viewed as something beyond a woman's control. She might pray, consult a midwife who might provide various botanical remedies for specific conditions such as leucorrhea (a range of vaginal discharges) or amenorrhea (failure to menstruate), but for the most part she would not have viewed her situation either as a medical condition or as an irrevocable obstacle to rearing children.[9]

Privatizing Motherhood

In the postrevolutionary era, Americans began to cut ever deeper lines of separation between the community and the family. Bearing one's own biological children took on new significance. In the seventeenth and early eighteenth century, the principal value of children lay in the benefits they could bring to the family and the community. But beginning in the late eighteenth century, historians have noted, changes occurred both in patterns of family formations and in cultural attitudes toward the family. Historians disagree about what caused the changes. Some have viewed the transformation as a manifestation of revolutionary democracy. For others it appears to constitute evidence of the development of an individualism derived at least in part from eighteenth-century evangelistic religion. Finally, it has been argued that the turn from communalism and hierarchy toward privacy and greater if not absolute equality, which marked the end of the dominance of the household family form and its replacement by the conjugal unit, had its origins in the rise of capitalism.[10]

However historians choose to explain them, the changes in the family—both in real and in ideal terms—had profound implications for the ways in which women dealt with infertility. In a communal society composed of households it might matter somewhat less, to the society if not to the individual, how children came into those households. But in a society where the fundamental unit was the married couple and their offspring, having one's "own" children became increasingly important.

As cultural attitudes toward the relationship between the family and the larger society shifted so too did perceptions of infertility. Elusive but unmistakable signs of such a change emerged in the closing decades of the eighteenth century and became clearly manifest in the early years of the nineteenth, as the first signs of defining infertility as a medical condition appeared. Over the course of the nineteenth century women faced with an involuntarily childless marriage would come to rely more and more heavily on medical expertise, and to accept the definition of infertility as a disease. This process, however, would take several generations. Reliance on prayer did not die in the eighteenth century; neither did the belief in roots and herbs. Moreover, although elite physicians may have aspired to become authorities on infertility as early as the turn of the nineteenth century, the initial impact of medical interest in infertility in the late eighteenth and early nineteenth centuries was not so much to encourage women to seek out a physician to treat her as it was to give her the tools to treat herself. A great deal of medical advice—on infertility as well as other matters—came not in the shape of a physician but in the form of one or another of the guides to domestic medicine.[11]

In the early nineteenth century, as earlier, it was assumed that only impotent men were unable to procreate; hence women were considered responsible for a couple's childlessness. Irregular or painful menstruation, everyone agreed, constituted the most likely cause of a woman's inability to conceive. Women with such menstrual irregularities (generally called "obstructions") were advised to improve their overall state of health. Exercise, a diet "chiefly of milk and vegetables," cold baths, and the use of "astringent medicines" (tonics) were all recommended. Although not every domestic medical guide included a chapter on infertility, nearly all dealt with menstruation. Women attempting to conceive would not have had difficulty in finding suggestions for treatment.[12]

Although recommendations for self-treatment dominated advice on the treatment of infertility in the guides to domestic medicine, a number of physician-writers also discussed more "heroic" or invasive therapies, such as venesection (bloodletting) for amenorrhea. The aim of both kinds of therapies was the same. As one of the many "handbooks" for medical students advised, practitioners should attempt to promote menstrual regularity, to remove local disease, and to restore "vigour" to the uterus. This therapeutic continuum—from mild to ever more interventionist treatment—laid out in the early nineteenth century, has survived for nearly two centuries.[13]

The heightened interest in promoting the medical treatment of infertility reflected new anxieties about both the capacity and the will of American women to reproduce, anxieties fueled by the decline in the birthrate. By 1850 the national birthrate had slipped from 7.04 births (in 1800) to 5.42. As the historian James H. Cassedy has argued, "People worried increasingly about the effects produced on 'delicate' female nervous systems by their increased exposure to the physical stresses of modern living—the cacophony of city noise, the bustle of travel, the excitements produced by newspaper reading, [and] the tensions produced by their husbands' ventures and risks in business."[14]

Eventually, many feared, the nation would be forced to rely on immigrants to populate its vast reaches. Some medical advice givers indicted contraceptive practices for damaging women's reproductive systems. Most medical advice writers in fact castigated American women from the 1830s to the 1850s for using various means to limit the size of their families, including abortion. Any form of contraception, as well as abortion, these doctors claimed, almost always resulted in permanent sterility. The few skeptics among them, who remained unconvinced that contraception and abortion were as widespread as most of their colleagues believed, nevertheless warned women that succumbing to the pleasures and luxuries of modern life could cause them to forfeit their chances of motherhood. At stake was not only their marital happiness but also the nation's future.[15]

Such dire forebodings notwithstanding, there is little evidence that wives were abandoning motherhood entirely. Bearing and rearing children remained, as Judith Walzer Leavitt has noted, "a vital component in the social definition of womanhood." It represented, in fact, women's "most valued work." In colonial America, that "work" had added to the family's and the community's economic well-being; by the middle decades of the nineteenth century, however, an unprecedented public and private glorification of motherhood suggested that bearing and rearing children constituted a woman's principal reason for existing. In middle-class America by midcentury the mother-child bond had become—at least in theory—the most important family tie, taking precedence even over the husband-wife relationship. As the historian Sylvia Hoffert has argued, the "ideology of motherhood assured [women] that having children could fulfill both private and public needs. Bearing children, it promised, was certain to guarantee personal happiness because it renewed the bonds of intimacy that served as the basis of a stable marriage."[16]

This was a significant new interpretation of the place of motherhood in the

culture and one that was likely to raise anxieties. The majority of colonial "good-
wives," women who worked in cooperation with their spouses to sustain the household and communal economy, had been mothers, of course, and in some ways
motherhood was their most important function; but it was not the only thing that
defined them as women.[17] By the middle of the nineteenth century, however, it had
become a middle-class article of faith that healthy family life required a woman to
direct her emotional and physical energies into creating the proper home life. Domestic reformers such as Catharine Beecher made it clear that women were an-
swerable for the nation's moral vision, and the only place to instill that vision was
in the home. As the domestic writer Mrs. L. H. G. Abell reminded her readers, the
influence of mothers was indeed "far reaching." A mother, she insisted, had a task
much more important than whatever accomplishments men may enjoy in the
larger world, for "she must sow the seed, and watch with ceaseless anxiety its
growth, plant the tender and delicate germs of principle, and train the young ten-
drils of the feelings and affections. She is set to guard, to instruct, to mould the
moral nature." In addition to what we might call this public function of motherhood, however, there was also a woman's responsibility to make her husband
happy; and marital happiness was, according to the advice givers, "a condition
made possible only by the presence of a child, whose birth was guaranteed to enhance the affection that husband and wife felt for each other."[18]

Of course, it is always difficult to know how powerfully the injunctions of the
advice givers affected the women who read them, but several studies of mid-
nineteenth-century family and community history have offered portraits of
middle-class family life that conform quite remarkably to the prescriptive literature. It is not that women were real-life counterparts of fictional heroines or that
people's behavior conformed exactly to the directions given in advice books; rather,
it is that they believed in the cultural values embodied in the literary material,
whether or not their own lives seemed to confirm those values.[19]

Such veneration of motherhood united both reformers who wanted to enlarge
women's educational opportunities and others who adhered to more conventional
notions. Naturally, these two groups tended to view the decline in the birthrate differently. According to some of the reformers, those women and their husbands who
chose to limit their family size were not rejecting parenthood. Far from it; if women
were to "mould the moral nature" of their offspring they needed the time and the
health to do so. A woman who spent her entire life pregnant or nursing, some reasoned, would have used up so much strength in childbearing as to have little left
for child rearing. Although this may have been cold comfort for those who
were convinced that the decline in the birthrate boded ill for American society, the
two groups were more in agreement than disagreement over the significance of

motherhood, if not the number of children each couple should have. It was one thing to be single: Catharine Beecher, the most famous domestic reformer of her generation, and a single woman herself, claimed that the unmarried could employ their maternal instincts as teachers, nurses, and physicians. But wives were expected, by nearly everyone, to be mothers. In such a world, childlessness often became more than a disappointment. It could be a tragedy.

Although it is very difficult to move beyond generalized evidence to locate the voices of those women who experienced infertility during the era in which the ideal of republican motherhood became transformed into the ideology of domesticity, a few women of this period have left a record of their emotional reaction to childlessness and the ways in which they attempted to deal with it. Three of them who did were the novelist and antislavery reformer Lydia Maria Child (1802–80), who came of age before the full flowering of the cult of motherhood; and the women's rights reformer Amelia Bloomer (1818–94) and the Civil War diarist Mary Chesnut (1823–86), both of whom became women in the midst of it and felt its full weight. Their experiences of infertility offer some insight into both the range of individual responses and the kinds of pressures—internal and external—that childless women faced as the century wore on.

As a solitary young girl growing up in the New England countryside, Lydia Maria Francis had looked forward not to marriage and motherhood but to a literary career. By her early twenties she already enjoyed a taste of modest fame (at least among the Boston literati) as the author of *Hobomok,* a tale of interracial love set in colonial Massachusetts. Her season of celebrity in the salons of Boston was followed by a long and productive career, first as a novelist, juvenile writer, and advice giver, later as a well-known antislavery journalist.[20]

In 1828 Maria married David Lee Child, a dreamy, impractical intellectual and stubborn idealist. As his wife would soon discover, David Child was wholly unsuited to the role of family breadwinner. Objectively, perhaps, she should have considered it just as well that no children appeared in this marriage fraught with such economic uncertainty. But in fact both she and David wished very much for children. Still, although her childlessness disappointed her, there is no evidence that she sought medical advice. Nor did she and David adopt, although apparently they considered doing so at one point.[21]

Lydia Maria Child had a rich and full career, and she also had all of the cares and anxieties of being the family breadwinner. Nevertheless, the thought of her and David's childlessness seemed never far from consciousness. In the first year or two of her marriage she appeared relieved that there was no extra mouth to feed. Complaining to her sister-in-law Lydia B. Child about their financial woes, she suggested that thank goodness, at least she was not yet pregnant, that for the moment, there was "no prospect of anybody but ourselves to take care of."[22] But after another year had passed and still no sign of pregnancy appeared, she wrote her mother-in-law, "I do wish I would be a mother, and that even more for my husband's sake than for my own. But God's will be done. I am certain that Divine Providence orders all things for our good." Her acceptance of the will of Providence never entirely assuaged her disappointment. In a letter congratulating her friends the Lorings on the news of Mrs. Loring's pregnancy, Child once again came face-to-face with her own childlessness: "I never felt so forcibly as within the last year, that to a childless wife, 'life is almost untenanted.[']" If in the early years of her marriage she seemed to think that fatherhood would have made David less irresponsible, she cherished no such illusions later on, tellingly remarking to her friend Sarah Shaw in 1859 that "my good David serves me for husband and 'baby and all.'" But she never ceased to regret her childlessness, expressing her regret throughout her life.[23]

Like Lydia Maria Child, Amelia Jenks Bloomer was a writer and editor, most remembered for the costume that still bears her name. Married at the age of twenty-two to the editor Dexter Bloomer, she became a women's rights advocate and temperance reformer. Encouraged by a husband who admired her journalistic abilities, Amelia Bloomer, having written for several local and regional newspapers, became editor and publisher of the reformist *Lily* at its founding in 1848. She continued at this post until 1854, when she sold the paper in preparation for moving with her husband to what was then the frontier outpost of Council Bluffs, Iowa.[24]

While Lydia Maria Child was either rarely ill or downplayed whatever health problems she may have had, Amelia Bloomer was often in what the nineteenth century referred to as "delicate health." Indeed, for the first year of her marriage she was repeatedly ill, suffering from "intermittent fever." (Intermittent fever was a general-purpose term that referred not just to malaria but also to a variety of ailments distinguished by fevers that came and went.) Whether any of her numerous trips to medicinal springs or various health resorts were related to her childlessness, neither she nor her husband disclosed. For whatever reason, for the first twenty years or so of her married life, Bloomer spent time at various health resorts; in her husband's recollections, she was often unwell.[25]

Amelia and Dexter Bloomer adopted two children—first a little boy and then his younger sister—shortly after moving to Council Bluffs. Her husband recalled after Amelia's death that they had always had nieces or nephews staying with them from the early years of their marriage. But she, at least (he is reticent about his own feelings), wanted children of her own. When the Bloomers adopted their first child, she was thirty-seven and he thirty-nine. For the next several years Amelia concentrated most of her attention on her family and her home.[26] Upon selling the

Lily she wrote that "home and husband being dearer to us than all beside," her publishing career had become of "secondary importance." And although she remained involved in reform causes between 1855 and 1870, most of her activities were on the local level. Her adopted children would have been adolescents before she once again took on any major responsibilities.[27]

Lydia Maria Child left behind professions of regret for her childlessness, but she accepted it as the will of Providence. Amelia Bloomer chose adoption as the only way to have children "of her own." Mary Boykin Chesnut did neither, but she seems to have suffered far more over her childlessness. Born into a distinguished South Carolina family—her father served as governor and later as a United States senator—Mary Boykin married James Chesnut when she was just seventeen. Her husband began a career in politics, and she herself made friends with the wives of rising Southerners, including Varina Davis, the wife of Jefferson Davis. Unlike Lydia Maria Child or Amelia Jenks Bloomer, Mary Chesnut was not a public figure during her lifetime. The public came to know of her only after her death, as a result of her posthumously published Civil War diaries. During her own life, she was simply a childless wife in a prominent family.[28] In Mary Chesnut's world, large families were not just encouraged but expected. When she and James married, they planned for numerous children. Her failure to have any, according to her biographer, brought on her "despondency." Friends apparently tried to keep up her spirits by urging her to continue to hope for a pregnancy, keeping her informed of their friends who had conceived after long years of marriage.[29]

Constant remarks on her childlessness from her mother-in-law only worsened her feelings. She complained of the senior Mrs. Chesnut's "bragging *to me* with exquisite taste—me a childless wretch"—of her numerous grandchildren. Even her father-in-law, "who rarely wound[ed]" her, could be insensitive, once remarking to his wife in Mary's presence, "You must feel that you have not been useless in your day and generation. You have now twenty-seven great grandchildren." Mary was distraught. "God help me," she wrote, "no good have I done—to myself or any one else. . . ."[30]

Of these three women, Mary Chesnut seems to have found childlessness most painful, although her greater emotional expressiveness may have been as much a matter of personality or the times as of greater depth of feeling. Mary Chesnut managed to conceive at least once and possibly more often, but she was unable to carry a pregnancy to term. Like Amelia Bloomer, she often traveled to spas and health resorts—albeit more fashionable ones than Bloomer frequented—and she spent time in Philadelphia with her uncle, a prominent physician. Her sudden 1845 trip to Europe with James may have been as much in pursuit of pregnancy as diversion. Alone of the three women she may have actively sought medical help, however unavailing. For her, childlessness was a tragedy, the pain of which she tried to alleviate by "borrowing" the children of relatives for long extended visits. She may also have eased her pain through drugs. Having suffered from what her physicians diagnosed as a heart condition since her childhood, she continued to experience periodic bouts of ill-health that were severe enough to cause alarm in her family. Some of her doctors prescribed opium, which it seems she took for her emotional as well as her physical pain.[31]

The experience of these three women may be seen as emblematic of the ways in which nineteenth-century women came to cope with involuntary childlessness. Lydia Maria Child accepted the will of the Lord with sadness but with resignation. Perhaps, having come of age nearly twenty years before the other two women, she was the least touched by the cultural belief of the era that bearing children was the most glorious thing to which a woman could aspire. Amelia and Dexter Bloomer chose to adopt, which may seem like a very eighteenth-century solution to childlessness, but in fact adoption was beginning to mean something different in the nineteenth century. The Bloomers' adopted children were not the orphans of other family members nor were they brought into an expansive household community. Rather, the Bloomers adopted in order to have their "own" children, to complete their conjugal family. And Bloomer in fact suspended her career as a national reformer until the children were nearly grown, although she did not retire entirely into private life. Mary Chesnut seems to have sought medical help, having both the financial resources to travel to the urban centers where such help was increasingly becoming available, and the desire, fueled by her own wishes and pressure from her husband's family, to bear her own children.

Medicalizing Maternal Desires

Mary Chesnut might have been seeking medical help just about the time that American elite physicians began to turn their attention in earnest to the problem of infertility, influenced both by the growing national anxiety about the fertility of American women and by new medical ideas. Beginning in the 1850s, and continuing ever since, women in infertile unions increasingly sought help from physicians to help them conceive. Dramatic changes occurred in the two decades between 1850 and 1870. A woman seeking medical help to become pregnant in almost any American city in 1850 most likely came away with advice to get more exercise and change her diet. If she complained in addition of menstrual discomfort or leucorrhea, she might also receive a vaginal douche or a tonic. Almost any physician who was conversant with current theory and who had on hand some "nitrate of silver for ulcerations, . . . a cylindrical speculum, . . . astringent injection[s]," and perhaps a "Physics globe pessary" (used for uterine prolapse, or "falling of the womb") felt prepared to treat almost any known condition of the female reproductive system. But by 1870, should a childless woman happen upon a practitioner who kept up with new medical developments, especially one associated with an urban voluntary hospital, she would probably find herself diagnosed with a defective cervix, for which the recommended treatment was surgery. In neither year would a physician have been likely to ask to see her husband. Data documenting the existence of male sterility began to appear in the 1860s; nevertheless, physicians to a man (the gender-specific term is intentional) continued to believe that it was an extremely rare condition.[32]

In the course of these two decades, ideas about the proper treatment of the "diseases of women," as they were still called during the years just before the emergence of gynecology, changed dramatically. Technological developments, in the form of new instruments and surgical techniques, burst on the medical scene. These instruments and techniques provided new opportunities for seeing—and for reconfiguring—the interior of women's bodies. Controversial at first, the use of instrumentation and surgery on women's sexual organs became commonplace by the end of the nineteenth century among physicians eager to establish themselves as experts in the emerging medical field of gynecology. Dramatic innovations in the treatment of infertility demonstrated the profound nature of the changes occurring in both the theory and practice of physicians who treated women with reproductive disorders. Women themselves, apparently in increasing numbers, actively sought instrumental and surgical treatment, demonstrating the existence of demand for these methods and encouraging more physicians to provide them.

After the Civil War, the reproductive behavior of American women came under even greater scrutiny than it had in the 1840s and 1850s. As the marriage rate among highly educated women dropped and the birthrate in general among the white Protestant middle-classes continued its sharp fall, discussions and arguments over the significance of these changes became an important part of the nation's public discourse. Women seemed to be rebelling against conventional ideas of their appropriate roles. Although in the final analysis most women did not turn their backs on matrimony and maternity, choosing instead to make room in their lives for outside interests in addition to their domestic responsibilities, a noticeable minority explicitly chose to seek higher education and productive careers rather than marriage and family life. Debates raged within individual families, in popular and serious periodicals, and among public figures over the best methods of either encouraging—or stifling—the changes that were taking place.

Among those attempting to take a leading role in defining the terms of the discussion were physicians interested in the diseases of women, who considered themselves well placed to provide explanations and solutions to what many viewed as a
growing problem. These physicians—many of them now calling themselves gynecologists—set themselves the task of monitoring and regulating women's reproductive behavior. They formed a vanguard of experts on the process of human
reproduction. Because the fertility of American women was a major social concern
in the late nineteenth century, the problem of infertility, while it by no means dominated the field of gynecology, held an important place in its early development.
Although they were only a minority of physicians who treated women in this period—most Americans received their care from generalists, many of whom may
have trained decades earlier in proprietary medical schools or as apprentices—gynecologists established the intellectual infrastructure that made new research into
fertility and infertility possible. Disseminating their findings in new journals and
societies, they also trained the next generation of physicians who would apply that
new knowledge.

Historians are familiar with the attempt of physicians to influence women's behavior during the post–Civil War era; as Regina Morantz-Sanchez has noted,
"Doctors found themselves the spokespersons for the affirmation of traditional
verities."[33] The problem of infertility provided numerous opportunities for the
assertion of conventional values, as physicians articulated an explanation of its
etiology that centered on women's inappropriate behavior. Such confident pronouncements about the root causes of infertility were designed to advance the
claims of gynecologists to authority in both reproductive and behavioral matters.

There is no denying that the demographic and social changes of the late nineteenth century were dramatic. Family size continued to drop, reaching an average
of 3.56 children by 1900; the marriage rate was also declining to the lowest level ever
attained in American history, with about 10 percent of women never marrying.
Moreover, the fertility rate was lowest among urban native-born whites and highest among immigrants and African Americans. The closing years of the nineteenth
century brought this country its greatest "extremes of differential fertility," as one
demographic historian has expressed it.[34]

Notwithstanding these changes, the overwhelming majority of women still
expected to marry and bear children. Until well after the turn of the century, even
among women's rights advocates there lurked the idea that motherhood and a full-
scale career were incompatible. Only the most radical of feminists before the turn
of the twentieth century were publicly willing to assert otherwise.[35] In spite of such
seemingly conventional behavior, however, women's roles—and the roles of men

as well—were undergoing significant changes, especially within the middle classes. The women whose vision of their own roles had expanded to include social service and club membership increasingly urged their husbands to share more intimately in their domestic lives. In the middle of the nineteenth century, as a number of historians have documented, the most important bond in the family was between mother and child. In Mary Ryan's words, it held "the central place in the constellation of family affection."[36] By the end of the century, women advice givers were urging men to educate themselves for fatherhood. Within a decade, their male counterparts would be urging men to seek greater emotional closeness to their wives and to spend time with their children as companions. Indeed, as women were making incursions into the public realm, their husbands began to take a greater interest in the domestic one.[37]

The transformation of the intimate familial relations among husbands and wives is one of the most significant factors for understanding the emotional dimensions of infertility in the late nineteenth century. It is true that, among the middle-classes, children had ceased to be an economic necessity. Americans, however, still reserved their highest approval for mothers, who were celebrated in essays, fiction, and verse for their wisdom and devotion. Women who were not mothers, unless they were single and exhibited devoted self-sacrifice in some other capacity, were viewed with suspicion. The culture labeled married women who chose not to have children as selfish and cold. According to the popular writer Jennie June, only a wife whose "heart and brain" were "deformed and misshapen" would make the choice to have a marriage without children.[38] Among the immigrant poor, where children *were* needed to contribute to the household income (although too many children too quickly were an economic burden), to be unable to conceive was considered a failure of one's womanhood. One woman physician who treated poor immigrant women for sterility in Philadelphia remarked on the "ignominy" faced by women "among the lower classes when they do not bear children."[39]

For most women children had long been the focus of family life, and it now appeared that for men as well parenthood was taking on new meaning. Children were not less important simply because there were fewer of them. Couples did clearly use contraception to limit the size of their families, but few desired to opt out of parenthood altogether. To the contrary, historians of the middle-class family have found that stronger affectional ties between parents and children accompanied the decline in family size.[40]

As powerful a record as nineteenth-century mothers and fathers have left to posterity concerning their feelings about their children, those who wished for offspring in vain have left little to enable historians to understand how they coped with their involuntary childlessness. The extraordinary reticence of those late nineteenth-century Americans who vainly wished for children cannot be accounted for simply by reference to Victorian sensibilities. The freely shared confidences between sisters and mothers and daughters about their hopes and fears in pregnancy, or between brothers about their wives' confinements, which historian Judith Walzer Leavitt has so poignantly delineated, had no parallel among the infertile. But toward the close of the century a few women did leave behind some evidence of the ways in which involuntary childlessness affected them.[41] Like Lydia Maria Child and Amelia Bloomer two generations before them, they were well-known figures. All three—Kate Douglas Wiggin, Margaret Deland, and Ella Wheeler Wilcox—were writers.

Wiggin was the popular author of *Rebecca of Sunnybrook Farm* and one of the early leaders of the kindergarten movement in the United States. Nora Smith, her sister and biographer, claimed that Wiggin continued her commitment to the kindergarten movement, even after she became famous, because it enabled her to assuage her sadness over her inability to bear her own children. It is unclear whether Wiggin ever sought infertility treatment, although Smith referred delicately to "a serious surgical operation" (a widely used euphemism for gynecological operations) that Wiggin underwent, which might have either accounted for her childlessness or have been in pursuit of pregnancy.[42] The novelist Margaret Deland also was veiled in her expressions of regret for her childlessness. As her biographer has noted, Deland was not given to talking about her personal problems, even to close friends in her personal correspondence, informing them "briefly" that she had undergone surgery. Among the childless late nineteenth-century writers, only Ella Wheeler Wilcox openly wrote about her anguish, and with her the situation was somewhat different; she had borne one child, who lived less than a day.[43]

For the reactions of ordinary women of the middle and working classes, one must consult sources that reflect their views more indirectly—records of private and clinical practices to which women turned in increasing numbers in the late nineteenth century to find solutions to their involuntary childlessness. Although the numbers of women who sought infertility treatment in this period cannot be counted with any accuracy, articles in the gynecological journals suggested that private practices in large cities, as well as clinics serving low-income women, were experiencing an increase in demand. The gynecologist H. Marion Sims claimed in 1888, "Probably the gynecologist of today is consulted more often in regard to the sterile condition of woman than for any [other] disease."[44]

Women who consulted a physician for infertility in this era were setting out on an uncertain course. In our own day visits to the gynecologist are far more commonplace, but a century ago people rarely saw doctors for anything less than a serious condition. Those women who took themselves to clinic or consulting room in search of solutions to their childlessness, therefore, clearly assumed that they were suffering from a treatable medical condition and believed that such a condition was serious enough for medical intervention. Physicians increasingly had the upper hand in this interaction because they asserted their mastery over the mysteries of science and technology. This did not mean, however, that women were willing to accede to everything the physician said. Indeed, some women, who appeared to be quite well informed about their medical options, were not reluctant to say what therapies they would or would not tolerate. Gynecologists might have denominated themselves "priests" of women's health, but women do not appear to have been willing to play the role of a passive icon. Nevertheless, a doctor had something a woman did not, access to diagnostic and therapeutic tools to provide her with a reason for her childlessness and perhaps an alleviation of it. As a result, the interaction between physician and patient was fraught with ambiguity.[45]

That women often insisted on having their own way is clear from the numerous complaints of practitioners, who expressed considerable annoyance at their patients' refusal to take their advice. Some women rejected surgery. One gynecologist grumbled about the "large number of cases" in which his patients refused "to submit to the use of the knife."[46] But others demanded operations so insistently that conscientious physicians had difficulty dissuading them. Practitioners regularly noted the presence of women who made the rounds of their consulting rooms, demanding surgery from a new doctor when the former one refused. One physician told his colleagues of a patient who "so begged and so urged me to perform any operation which would be likely to make her fruitful" that in spite of his belief that the surgery was uncalled for he came close to agreeing.[47]

In addition, practitioners were contending more often with husbands. By the 1890s, as elite gynecologists argued for the necessity to analyze seminal fluid, the recalcitrant husband who refused semen testing became a staple of doctors' anecdotes. One outraged husband knocked his wife to the floor in the doctor's office and loudly proclaimed that the physician himself was "insane" to suggest he might be sterile. Such behavior on the part of husbands led many physicians simply to give up on the idea of demanding semen specimens. In fact, outside of the practices of eminent gynecologists semen analysis did not become a routine part of arriving at a diagnosis of infertility until the 1950s; and even today many physicians remain very sensitive to male anxieties about the relationship of their sperm count to their sexual capacities.[48]

Although men had become a more common presence in physicians' consulting rooms, it remained true that *wives* were almost always the focus of medical intervention. Infertility treatment was most often a female experience, even if sometimes mediated by a husband's involvement. It was also an experience that cut across ethnic, racial, and class lines. Although the scene of their interactions with physicians differed—paying patients waited their turn in physicians' consulting rooms and the poor lined up at hospital outpatient clinics—the recommended course of treatment was generally the same. The difficulty, of course, was that poor women rarely had the leisure to devote to an extensive period of treatment, which might involve days of bed rest or a series of operations.

Some practitioners, it is evident, had little sympathy for their clinic patients, valuing them principally as case material for experimental treatments to be presented at meetings or published in journal articles. Annoyance and irritation appeared to constitute the whole of their attitude toward these women, who, these unsympathetic doctors complained, rarely bothered to complete their treatment. As one New York gynecologist snapped, his clinic patients "underrate[d] the value of medical services which cost them no money."[49] However, it is important not to rush to the conclusion that poor or working-class women were invariably shortchanged. At the Woman's Hospital in New York, the gynecological pioneer Thomas Addis Emmet treated women of all social classes with care and dignity until he retired at the close of the century. Others followed suit. In Baltimore, Thomas Ashby recalled with sympathy one of his patients, an African American domestic worker, who underwent two surgeries in the 1890s for pelvic adhesions that Ashby believed were causing her infertility. Although she was able to conceive, he recalled, because her life was a round of unending hard labor, she was unable to carry a pregnancy to term.[50]

Although no definitive breakdown by class, race, or ethnicity exists for the women who sought treatment for infertility, the physicians who discussed its treatment in the medical journals described the cases of people from all walks of life. The evidence is scattered, but social class seems neither to have distinguished women's willingness to seek treatment nor determined the kind of treatment they received. Geographic factors may have been much more influential. African American women in the South appear to have had virtually no access to infertility treatment; neither did poor whites in rural America. In the North, African American women do appear in physicians' records, although to a lesser extent than women from low-income immigrant families. In general, however, up-to-date infertility treatment was much more readily available in large urban areas in the North than anywhere else for women across lines of social class and ethnicity.[51]

If women were seeking treatment in greater numbers, as the anecdotal evidence suggests they were, one might wonder whether they did so out of any sense that treatments were becoming more successful. This is a difficult question to answer. Very few gynecologists in the 1870s gave success rates for their treatments, although they all had success stories. The New York gynecologist Joseph Kammerer's statistical study, in which he reported 25 pregnancies out of a group of 176 women, was unusual. In spite of the fact that the profession as a whole was moving toward a statistical model in reporting operative results in other kinds of surgery, the treatment of infertility was different. It often took a long time, and follow-up was difficult. Not until around World War I would physicians make any sustained attempts at determining the efficacy of their infertility treatments. That said, it is probably also true that physicians continued to use the anecdotal model of reportage because they did not have very many successes.[52]

Most women treated for infertility in the late nineteenth century, therefore, left their doctor's care without a pregnancy. Indeed, even Kammerer's figures, drawn from his private practice because he had so little success with his clinic patients, represented a cure rate of less than 15 percent. Some of these women were able to create a family through adoption; and although an analysis of adoption is beyond the scope of this essay, it served by the late nineteenth century as well as in the twentieth as the other "cure" for infertility.

In spite of the low success rates of medical treatment, women's faith in it continued to grow. Even those women who never consulted a physician about their involuntary childlessness were not necessarily rejecting medication. The success of Lydia Pinkham's tonic, which for a while was advertised as having "a baby in every bottle," attests to the strength of popular faith (or hope) in self-medication. Pinkham's tonic, the formula of which was based on the botanic medicines of the previous generation, contained some of the same roots and leaves that practitioners of botanical medicine would have given women who had come to them with an infertility problem in the 1840s and 1850s. Lydia Pinkham's Tonic and others such as Dr. Pierce's Golden Medical Discovery in some ways simply replaced the tonics that doctors of an earlier era would have concocted themselves.[53]

By the turn of the twentieth century, medical treatment for infertility began to take on its modern trappings. It had become an important part of gynecology, and gynecology itself had become a recognized specialty. Whereas in 1875 medical schools had limited their gynecological instruction to a few lectures, now there were entire courses devoted to the subject. And the increase in the journal literature, with its detailed descriptions on how to recognize gonorrhea (a significant factor in infertility) in a patient, and its explanations of exactly how to perform a surgical procedure, allowed practitioners removed from their medical school days to read about new developments. Although elite medical practitioners were only a small part of the medical profession, they taught the courses on gynecology and genitourinary surgery, and most medical students in the last twenty years of the nineteenth century had exposure to the new ideas. This is not to say that every involuntarily childless woman who went to a local physician in city or country was told to bring in her husband for a semen examination (indeed, the constant exhortation in the journals by the very few eminent practitioners who did so that their colleagues emulate them suggests the reverse), or that discredited or outmoded procedures were no longer performed. And for every successful treatment there were numerous failures.

As the new century opened, treatment for infertility had become a routine service offered by gynecological specialists as well as by some general practitioners who had been trained both in regular and in homeopathic institutions. Physicians expressed confidence that their increasing operative skills would enable more women to conceive, and that these skills would be in great demand. This confidence helped to form the attitudes toward infertility that would permeate the twentieth century's response to involuntary childlessness.

From the Past to the Present

Before the turn of the twentieth century, nearly all of the elements that would shape the ways in which twentieth-century Americans would think of infertile women were in place, although they have neither remained static nor gone unchallenged in the intervening century. Nevertheless, the parallels are striking. All three of the ideas at the core of the late nineteenth century's attitude toward infertility—that women often bring on their own infertility by their behavior, that infertility is principally a woman's problem rather than a man's, and that medical treatment can alleviate infertility—are also central to the views of the late twentieth century.

The idea that women are at fault for their infertility problems, although it had ceased to dominate the medical profession's assessment of the problem for much of the twentieth century, returned with renewed emphasis in the 1980s. It is probably no accident that this idea seems most compelling to a society during eras in which substantial numbers of women are rebelling against conventional roles—the period of the women's rights movement in the late nineteenth century and the feminist movement of the late twentieth.[54]

Beginning in the 1980s and continuing into the 1990s there has been an antifeminist backlash that has encouraged high achieving women to abandon the "fast track" for the "mommy track." Although contemporary demographic studies show that poor and working-class women have higher rates of infertility than do their highly educated counterparts, the belief remains powerful that middle-class women, who are castigated for bringing infertility upon themselves by delaying childbearing in order to pursue a career, are most likely to experience infertility. Even one writer highly sympathetic to the plight of infertile women nevertheless states flatly, "Infertility was the unexpected fallout of the women's revolution."[55]

Perhaps because women find themselves "blamed" for infertility in contemporary America, they also continue to take the primary responsibility for finding a solution to the problem, just as they did in the late nineteenth century. By the 1930s, at the latest, physicians knew that men were infertile as often as women; nevertheless, men resisted taking responsibility for a couple's infertility in a number of ways. They refused to have their semen analyzed, refused to believe the results, resisted treatment when treatment was available, and refused to carry the emotional burden. The evidence suggests that little has changed.[56]

Most recent studies agree that the experience of infertility affects women more deeply than it does men. The "motherhood mandate" remains a strong force in most women's lives. As Margarete Sandelowski has argued, women perceive their infertility "as a social impediment preventing them from gaining admission into what one woman called 'the special club of motherhood.' Although women now have greater opportunities than ever before to pursue life goals other than motherhood, . . . biological maternity remains a critical factor in a woman's sense of herself as a normal woman." As a result, for women, in the words of the sociologist Arthur Griel, "infertility present[s] itself as intolerable, identity threatening." His field study of infertile couples demonstrated that in contrast to their wives "the majority of husbands viewed the experience [of infertility] as disappointing but not devastating." As one husband said, "My personal infertility has . . . never eaten away at me." The psychotherapist Aline Zoldbrod also found that "women [infertility] patients are obsessed to an extraordinary extent with getting pregnant . . . , much more than are their partners." Even when the husband rather than the wife is afflicted with the medical condition causing the couple's inability to conceive, the wife apparently takes responsibility for the problem. Among Griel's couples, wives took the lead in seeking treatment and making decisions about what therapies to accept. In another study, a husband diagnosed as the sole cause for a couple's infertility said that he had "not felt the involved party."[57]

Finally, the belief in the efficacy of medical treatment has not abated since the end of the nineteenth century. The range of medical services has multiplied dramatically, and many couples resort to high technology services—in vitro fertilization seems almost commonplace compared to egg and embryo donation, or techniques to inject a single sperm into an egg. More than a million couples a year undergo infertility treatment, either of the more conventional sort or that involving the new techniques of assisted reproduction.[58] Women undergo the vast majority of the procedures. And although success rates are higher than they were a century ago—today, about half of all couples undergoing treatment eventually bring a baby home—still a large proportion of couples, like those at the end of the nineteenth century, either seek adoption or resign themselves to remaining childless.

For all of the vast social, cultural, and demographic changes over the past three hundred years, the inability to conceive a child remains a source of pain and anguish for many women. To argue, as do the members of the Feminist International Network of Resistance to Reproductive and Genetic Engineering (FINNRAGE), that this desire to conceive is imposed upon women by a patriarchal society that values women only for their ability to reproduce, vastly oversimplifies the issue.[59] Without denying that there are coercive aspects to the motherhood mandate, it remains true that many women as well as men desire children because they want to be parents—to pass on their love, family traditions, and heritage to another generation. To suggest that women who seek medical treatment because of an intense desire to bear children are doing so merely out of some cultural imperative that restricts women's choices is to do these women an injustice.

NOTES

Prepared specifically for this volume, this essay is in large measure adapted from *The Empty Cradle: Infertility in America from Colonial Times to the Present,* by Margaret Marsh and Wanda Ronner (Baltimore: Johns Hopkins University Press, 1996).

1. For one example, see Mary Vial Holyoke's diary, available in printed form, along with diaries of other Holyoke family members, in George Francis Dow, ed., *The Holyoke Diaries* (Salem, Mass.: Essex Institute, 1911), entries for May 14 through May 23, 1770; April 13, 1763; February 12, 1765; March 4, 1765; September 14, 1766; and April 28, 1782. Judith Walzer Leavitt, *Brought to Bed: Childbearing in America, 1750–1950* (New York: Oxford University Press, 1986), p. 14.

2. Steven Mintz and Susan Kellogg, *Domestic Revolutions: A Social History of American Family Life* (New York: Free Press, 1988), p. 12, is the source for the 8 percent figure; Joyce Goodfriend, *Before the Melting Pot: Society and Culture in Colonial New York City, 1664–1730* (Princeton: Princeton University Press, 1991), p. 30.

3. See, for example, Benjamin Wadsworth, *The Well-Ordered Family; or Relative Duties* (1712), available in *The Colonial Family: Collected Essays* (New York: Arno Reprints, 1972), pp. 25–26.

4. See William M. Fowler, Jr., *The Baron of Beacon Hill: A Biography of John Hancock* (Boston: Houghton Mifflin, 1980), pp. 10–11; Helen L. Witmer et al., *Independent Adoptions* (New York: Russell Sage Foundation, 1963), pp. 19–30.

5. Helena M. Wall, *Fierce Communion: Family and Community in Early America* (Cambridge, Mass.: Harvard University Press, 1990), pp. 86–87, 90–91, and 204 n. 1. See also Gordon S. Wood, *The Radicalism of the American Revolution* (New York: Knopf, 1992), p. 46.

6. Wall, *Fierce Communion,* p. 99. The name was variously spelled as Lathrop and Lothrop; Goodfriend, *Before the Melting Pot,* p. 44; Wood, *Radicalism,* p. 47; Fowler, *Baron of Beacon Hill,* pp. 10–11, 18.

7. Laurel Thatcher Ulrich, *A Midwife's Tale: The Life of Martha Ballard, Based on Her Diary* (New York: Vintage Books, 1991). Also, Wall, *Fierce Communion,* pp. 8, 86; Mintz and Kellogg, *Domestic Revolutions,* p. 44.

8. Wall, *Fierce Communion,* pp. 8, 86.

9. Margaret Marsh and Wanda Ronner, *The Empty Cradle: Infertility in America from Colonial Times to the Present* (Baltimore: Johns Hopkins University Press, 1996), esp. pp. 13–17. Another work on childlessness is Elaine Tyler May, *Barren in the Promised Land: Childless Americans and the Pursuit of Happiness* (New York: Basic Books, 1995).

10. Wood, *Radicalism,* pp. 146–49; Mary Ryan, *Cradle of the Middle Class* (New York: Cambridge University Press, 1981); see also Edward Shorter, *The Making of the Modern Family* (New York: Basic Books, 1975); Randolph Trumbach, *The Rise of the Egalitarian Family* (New York: Academic Press, 1976).

11. See, for example, William Buchan, *Domestic Medicine* (New York: Richard Scott, 1812). Paul Starr, *The Social Transformation of American Medicine* (New York: Basic Books, 1982), pp. 32–33. See John B. Blake, "From Buchan to Fishbein: The Literature of Domestic Medicine," in Guenter Risse et al., *Medicine without Doctors: Home Health Care in American History* (New York: Science History Publications, 1977), pp. 11–30, on pp. 15–17.

12. Joseph Brevitt, *Female Medical Repository and Treatise on the Primary Diseases of Infants* (Baltimore: Hunter and Robinson, 1810), pp. 72–75; Horatio Gates Jameson, *American Domestic Medicine* (Baltimore: by the author, 1818). See also *American Lady's Medical Pocketbook and Nursery Advisor* (Pittsburgh: James Kawson and Brother, 1833).

13. James Hamilton, *Outlines of Midwifery for the Use of Students* (London: Bell and Bradfute, 1826), p. 162.

14. James H. Cassedy, *Medicine and American Growth, 1800–1860* (Madison: University of Wisconsin Press, 1986), pp. 173, 175.

15. See ibid., pp. 174–75; James Mohr, *Abortion in America: The Origins and Evolution of National Policy* (Oxford: Oxford University Press, 1978). See, for example, William A. Alcott, *The Physiology of Marriage* (New York: Selden, Lamport, & Blakeman, 1856), p. 121.

16. Leavitt, *Brought to Bed,* p. 3: Sylvia Hoffert, *Private Matters: American Attitudes toward Childbearing and Infant Nurture in the Urban North, 1800–1860* (Urbana: University of Illinois Press, 1989), p. 2.

17. Nancy Cott, *The Bonds of Womanhood* (New Haven: Yale University Press, 1977), p. 200; Kathryn Kish Sklar, *Catharine Beecher: A Study in Domesticity* (New Haven: Yale University Press, 1973).

18. (Mrs.) L. H. G. Abell, *Woman in her Various Relations* (New York, 1851), p. 209. For a

fuller discussion of this issue, see Margaret Marsh, *Suburban Lives* (New Brunswick: Rutgers University Press, 1990), pp. 22–25; Hoffert, *Private Matters,* p. 2.

19. Catharine Beecher and Harriet Beecher Stowe, *The American Woman's Home* (New York: J. B. Ford and Company, 1869), p. 216; Mary Ryan, *Cradle of the Middle Class* (New York: Cambridge University Press, 1981), pp. 230–42 (quotation on p. 232).

20. There are several biographies of Lydia Maria Child, including Milton Meltzer, *Tongue of Flame: The Life of Lydia Maria Child* (New York: Crowell, 1965); Bernice Grieves Lamberton, "A Biography of Lydia Maria Child" (master's thesis, University of Maryland, 1952); Helene Gilbert Baer, *The Heart Is Like Heaven* (Philadelphia: University of Pennsylvania Press, 1964); and Deborah Clifford, *Crusader for Freedom: A Life of Lydia Maria Child* (Boston: Beacon Press, 1992).

21. Marsh, *Suburban Lives,* pp. 33–35; Baer, *The Heart Is Like Heaven,* p. 59; Meltzer, *Tongue of Flame,* p. 76; and Clifford, *Crusader for Freedom,* esp. p. 84.

22. Lydia Maria Child to Lydia (Bigelow) Child, June 23, 1831, p. 2, Letter 48, Microfilm Collection, Library of Congress.

23. Lydia Maria Child to Louisa (Gilman) Loring and Ellis Gray Loring, April 30, 1839, p. 2, Letter 179, ibid. She expressed her disappointment yet again to the Lorings in a later letter: Lydia Maria Child to Ellis Gray Loring and Louisa (Gilman) Loring, May 14, 1849, Letter 751, ibid. Lydia Maria (Francis) Child, *Letters of Lydia Maria Child* (1883; New York: Arno Reprints, 1969), p. 140.

24. After Amelia Bloomer died, her husband, Dexter Bloomer, published a memorial to her, which included a biography and a selection of her writings and letters. Dexter Bloomer, *Life and Writings of Amelia Bloomer* (1895; reprint, New York: Schocken Books, 1975).

25. Marilyn Thornton Williams, *Washing "The Great Unwashed": Public Baths in Urban America, 1840–1920* (Columbus: Ohio State University Press, 1991), p. 11; Bloomer, *Life and Writings,* pp. 17–18, 128–29.

26. Bloomer, *Life and Writings,* pp. 299–300.

27. Ibid., pp. 189, 241–42.

28. Mary Boykin Chesnut, *A Diary from Dixie* (Boston: Houghton Mifflin, 1949). In 1984 C. Vann Woodward and Elisabeth Muhlenfeld, Chesnut's biographer, edited and published the original diaries, as *The Private Mary Chesnut: The Unpublished Civil War Diaries* (New York: Oxford University Press, 1984).

29. Elisabeth Muhlenfeld, *Mary Boykin Chesnut: A Biography* (Baton Rouge: Louisiana State University Press, 1981), pp. 62–63, 235 n. 34; Chesnut, *Diary from Dixie,* p. xvii.

30. Chesnut, *Diary from Dixie,* p. 22; Muhlenfeld, *Mary Boykin Chesnut,* pp. 64, 127.

31. Woodward and Muhlenfeld, preface to *The Private Mary Chesnut,* p. xx.

32. See, for example, Thomas Addis Emmet, *Reminiscences of the Founders of the Woman's Hospital Association* (New York: American Gynecological Association, 1899), p. 2 (reprinted, with additional information, from the *American Gynecological and Obstetrical Journal* [April 1899]); on male sterility, James Whitehead, *On the Causes and Treatment of Abortion and Sterility* (Philadelphia: Lea and Blanchard, 1848), p. 346.

33. Regina Markell Morantz-Sanchez, *From Sympathy to Science: Women Physicians in American Medicine* (New York: Oxford University Press, 1985), pp. 203–8 (quotation on p. 207).

34. Judith Walzer Leavitt, *Brought to Bed: Childbearing in America, 1750–1950* (New York: Oxford University Press, 1986), p. 19; Susan Householder Van Horn, *Women, Work, and Fertility* (New York: New York University Press, 1988), pp. 17–18; Marsh, *Suburban Lives,* p. 51; Peter Filene, *Him/Her/Self: Sex Roles in Modern America,* 2d ed. (Baltimore: Johns Hopkins University Press, 1986), p. 41.

35. Filene, *Him/Her/Self,* p. 26; Nancy Cott, *The Grounding of Modern Feminism* (New Haven: Yale University Press, 1987), pp. 179–80. Also, Julia Ward Howe, "The Joys of Motherhood," *The Delineator* 71, no. 5 (May 1908): 806, 879. Radicals did challenge the family, and often with vehemence, but they were a minority. See Margaret S. Marsh, *Anarchist Women, 1870–1920* (Philadelphia: Temple University Press, 1981); Charlotte Perkins Gilman, *The Home: Its Work and Influence* (New York: McClure, Phillips, 1903); Dolores Hayden, *The Grand Domestic Revolution* (Cambridge, Mass.: MIT Press, 1981), pp. 188–92.

36. Mary Ryan, *Cradle of the Middle-Class* (New York: Cambridge University Press, 1981), p. 232.

37. Harriet Beecher Stowe, *My Wife and I; or, Harry Henderson's History* (New York, 1870), p. 478; Margaret Marsh, "Suburban Men and Masculine Domesticity, 1870–1915," *American Quarterly* 40 (Summer 1988): 165–86; "From Separation to Togetherness: The Social Construction of Domestic Space in American Suburbs, 1840–1915," *Journal of American History* 76 (September 1989): 506–27; and Marsh, *Suburban Lives,* esp. pp. 35–40, 74–83.

38. Jennie June [Jane Cunningham Croly] considered herself a suffragist and reformer, but her attitudes about voluntarily childless women reflected the dominant view of the culture. *Jenny Juneiana* (Boston: Lee and Shepard, 1869), p. 63.

39. Sheila Rothman, *Woman's Proper Place* (New York: Basic Books, 1978), pp. 97–134; "Report from the Women's Hospital," *Transactions of the Alumni Association of the Woman's Medical College of Pennsylvania,* 16th Annual Report, May 7 and 8, 1891, pp. 92–93. See also case records for the "Hospital and Dispensary of the Alumnae of the Women's Medical College of Pennsylvania," Book I, Dr. Griscom, 1895–96, esp. pp. 5, 21, 73, 146, Archives of the Medical College of Pennsylvania.

40. See Shorter, *Making of the Modern Family;* Lawrence Stone, *The Family, Sex, and Marriage in England* (London: Weidenfeld & Nicolson, 1977); Trumbach, *Rise of the Egalitarian Family;* J. A. Banks, *Victorian Values: Secularism and the Size of Families* (London: Routledge & Kegan Paul, 1981); Anne C. Rose, *Victorian Americans and the Civil War* (New York: Cambridge University Press, 1992), chap. 4; Marsh, *Suburban Lives,* pp. 39–40.

41. I say this with some confidence because I made an intensive search among the memoirs and papers of dozens of nineteenth-century women who appeared to be infertile. Friedrich, *Clover,* p. 215; Leavitt, *Brought to Bed,* chap. 2; Diana Reep, *Margaret Deland* (Boston: Twayne Publishers, 1985), preface.

42. Kate Douglas Wiggin, *My Garden of Memory* (Boston: Houghton Mifflin, 1923); Nora Archibald Smith, *Kate Douglas Wiggin as Her Sister Knew Her* (Boston: Houghton Mifflin, 1925), pp. 313–14.

43. Reep, *Margaret Deland,* p. 3; Ella Wheeler Wilcox, *The Worlds and I* (New York: G. H. Doran, 1918), pp. 69, 118–24, 134–35.

44. H. Marion Sims, "Sterility, and the Value of the Microscope in Its Diagnosis and

Treatment," *Transactions of the American Gynecological Society* 13 (1888): 291–300. H. Marion was the son of J. Marion Sims. For demand for infertility treatment among working-class women, see Max Huhner, *Sterility in the Male and Female* (New York: Rebmen, 1913), p. 60.

45. See Starr, *Social Transformation of American Medicine*, pp. 136–37; and Blake, "From Buchan to Fishbein."

46. Paul Munde, "Report on the Progress of Gynecology," *American Journal of Obstetrics* 4 (1876): 159.

47. See, for example, William Goodell, "A Case of Sterility," *American Journal of Obstetrics* 10 (1877): 121; Thomas Ashby, "Laparotomy for Intra-Pelvic Pain," *Transactions of the American Gynecological Society* 15 (1890): 325.

48. Goodell, "Case of Sterility," pp. 121–22; Emil Noeggerath, "Latent Gonorrhea, Especially in Regard to Its Influence on Sterility in Women," *Transactions of the American Gynecological Society* 1 (1876): 300.

49. See "Review of Literature Pertaining to Diseases of Women," a condensation of Joseph Kammerer, "Pathological Conditions," *American Journal of Obstetrics* 2 (1870): 549.

50. Thomas Ashby, "The Influence of Minor Forms of Ovarian and Tubal Disease in the Causation of Sterility," *Transactions of the American Gynecological Society* 19 (1894): 260–71.

51. See Goodell, "Case of Sterility," pp. 121–22; Noeggerath, "Latent Gonorrhea," p. 300.

52. Kammerer, "Pathological Conditions," pp. 546–49; T. Gaillard Thomas is quoted in William B. Atkinson, *The Therapeutics of Gynecology and Obstetrics* (Philadelphia: D. G. Brinton, 1881), p. 213.

53. On Lydia Pinkham, see Sarah Stage, *Female Complaints: Lydia Pinkham and the Business of Woman's Medicine* (New York: Norton, 1979); James Harvey Young, "Patent Medicines and the Self-Help Syndrome," in Risse et al., *Medicine without Doctors*, esp. pp. 102–3.

54. Margarete Sandelowski has argued for a continuum in medical attitudes that blame women for infertility, in "Failures of Volition: Female Agency and Infertility in Historical Perspective," *Signs* 13 (Spring 1990): 475–99. Ronner and I have argued otherwise. See Marsh and Ronner, *Empty Cradle*, esp. pp. 246–49.

55. Susan Lang, *Women without Children: The Reasons, the Rewards, the Regrets* (New York: Pharos Books, 1991), p. 43. See also Arthur L. Griel, *Not Yet Pregnant: Infertile Couples in Contemporary America* (New Brunswick: Rutgers University Press, 1991), p. 33.

56. There is an enormous literature on the experience of infertility. One of the best of the memoirs is Susan T. Viguers, *With Child: One Couple's Journey to Their Adopted Children* (New York: Harcourt, 1986). For representative examples of scholarly studies, see Aline P. Zoldbrod, *Men, Women, and Infertility: Intervention and Treatment Strategies* (New York: Lexington Books, 1993); Griel, *Not Yet Pregnant;* Margarete Sandelowski, *With Child in Mind* (Philadelphia: University of Pennsylvania Press, 1993). Several British studies confirm the American experience. See, for example, James Monach, *Childlessness, No Choice: The Experience of Involuntary Childlessness* (New York: Routledge, 1993).

57. Nancy Felipe Russo, "Overview: Sex Roles, Fertility, and the Motherhood Mandate," *Psychology of Women Quarterly* 4 (Fall 1979): 7–9; Sandelowski, *With Child in Mind*, p. 75; Zoldbrod, *Men, Women, and Infertility*, pp. 12, 111 (she suggests that, at least in part, this may be be-

cause men are expected to be less expressive, but in fact most of her evidence supports the fact that they are truly less affected); Griel, *Not Yet Pregnant,* pp. 56–57, 77; Monach, *Childlessness, No Choice,* p. 117.

58. Marsh and Ronner, *Empty Cradle,* pp. 206–9, 221–22, 248–49, 252–55.

59. Ibid., pp. 251–52.

11.

BIRTHING AND ANESTHESIA
The Debate over Twilight Sleep

JUDITH WALZER LEAVITT

"At midnight I was awakened by a very sharp pain," wrote Mrs. Cecil Stewart, describing the birth of her child in 1914. "The head nurse . . . gave me an injection of scopolamine-morphin. . . . I woke up the next morning about half-past seven . . . the door opened, and the head nurse brought in my baby. . . . I was so happy."[1] Mrs. Stewart had delivered her baby under the influence of scopolamine, a narcotic and amnesiac, that together with morphine produced a state popularly known as "twilight sleep." She did not remember anything of the experience when she woke up after giving birth. This 1914 ideal contrasts with today's feminist stress on being awake, aware, and in control during the birthing experience. In 1914 and 1915, thousands of American women testified to the marvels of having babies without the trauma of childbirth. As one of them gratefully put it, "The night of my confinement will always be a night dropped out of my life."[2]

From the perspective of today's ideology of woman-controlled births, it may appear that women who want anesthesia sought to cede control of their births to their doctors. I will argue, however, that the twilight sleep movement led by women in 1914 and 1915 was not a relinquishing of control. Rather, it was an attempt to gain control over the birthing process. Feminist women wanted the parturient, not the doctor or attendant, to choose the kind of delivery she would have. This essay examines the apparent contradiction in the women's demand to control their births by going to sleep.

The Process

The attendants, location, and drugs or instruments used in American women's birthing experiences varied in the early decades of the twentieth century. America's

Reprinted from *Signs: Journal of Women in Culture and Society* 6 (1980): 147–64. Copyright © 1980 by the University of Chicago Press; reprinted by permission of the publisher.

poorer and immigrant women delivered their babies predominantly at home, attended by midwives who seldom administered drugs and who called physicians only in difficult cases. A small number of poor women gave birth in charity or public hospitals where physicians attended them. Most upper- and middle-class women, who had more choice, elected to be attended by a physician, usually a general practitioner but increasingly a specially trained obstetrician, rather than a midwife. At the turn of the twentieth century, these births, too, typically took place in the woman's home; however, by the second decade of the century, specialists, aided partly by the twilight sleep movement, were moving childbirth from the home to the hospital.[3]

Physicians used drugs and techniques of physical intervention in many cases, although the extent cannot be quantified accurately. In addition to forceps, physicians relied on opium, chloroform, chloral, cocaine, quinine, nitrous oxide, ergot, and ether to relieve pain, expedite labor, prevent injury in precipitous labors, control hemorrhage, and prevent sepsis.[4] In one study of 972 consecutive births in Wisconsin, physicians used chloroform during the second stage of labor in half of their cases and forceps in 12 percent.[5] The reports indicate that drugs and instruments may have made labors shorter but not necessarily more enjoyable. Because most drugs could not be used safely throughout the labor and delivery, either because they affected muscle function or because they were dangerous for the baby, women still experienced pain. The use of forceps frequently added to discomfort and caused perineal tears, complicating postdelivery recovery. Maternal mortality remained high in the early decades of the twentieth century, and childbirth, whether attended by physicians or midwives, continued to be risky.[6]

Most women described their physician-attended childbirths as unpleasant at best. Observers of the declining birthrates among America's "better" classes worried that the "fear of childbirth has poisoned the happiness of many women"[7] and caused them to want fewer children. One woman told her doctor that her childbirth had been "hell. . . . It bursts your brain, and tears out your heart, and crashes your nerves to bits. It's just like hell, and I won't stand it again. Never."[8] In scopolamine deliveries, the women went to sleep, delivered their babies, and woke up feeling vigorous. The drug altered their consciousness so that they did not remember painful labors, and their bodies did not feel exhausted by their efforts.[9] Both the women who demanded scopolamine and the doctors who agreed to use it perceived it as far superior to other anesthesia because it did not inhibit muscle function and could be administered throughout the birthing process. It was the newest and finest technique available—"the greatest boon the Twentieth Century could give to women," in the words of Dr. Bertha Van Hoosen, one of its foremost medical advocates.[10]

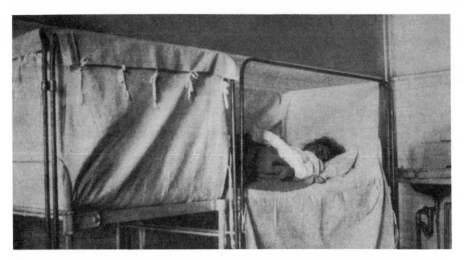

Fig. 1. Patient in crib-bed ready for examination. Source: Bertha Van Hoosen, *Scopolamine-Morphine Anaesthesia* (Chicago: House of Manz, 1915), p. 48.

However, women's bodies experienced their labors, even if their minds did not remember them. Thus observers witnessed women screaming in pain during contractions, thrashing about, and giving all outward signs of "acute suffering." Residents of Riverside Drive in New York City testified that women in Dr. William H. W. Knipe's twilight sleep hospital sent forth "objectionable" noises in the middle of night.[11]

A successful twilight sleep delivery, as practiced by Dr. Van Hoosen at the Mary Thompson Hospital in Chicago, required elaborate facilities and careful supervision. Attending physicians and nurses gave the first injection of scopolamine as soon as a woman appeared to be in active labor and continued the injections at carefully determined intervals throughout her labor and delivery. They periodically administered two tests to determine the effectiveness of the anesthesia: the "calling test," which the parturient passed if the doctor could not arouse her even by addressing her in a loud voice, and the "incoordination test," which she passed if her movements were uncoordinated. Once the laboring woman was under the effects of scopolamine, the doctors put her into a specially designed crib-bed to contain her sometimes violent movements (see fig. 1). Van Hoosen described the need for the bed screens: "As the pains increase in frequency and strength, the patient tosses or throws herself about, but without injury to herself, and may be left without fear that she will roll onto the floor or be found wandering aimlessly in the corridors. In rare cases, where the patient is very excitable and insists on getting out

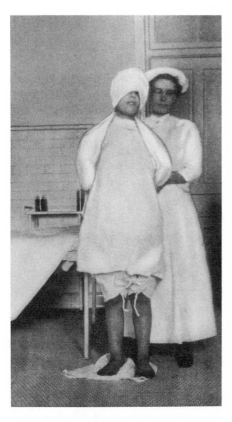

Fig. 2. Gown with continuous sleeve
behind neck. Source: Bertha Van Hoosen,
Scopolamine-Morphine Anaesthesia
(Chicago: House of Manz, 1915), p. 88.

of bed. . . . I prefer to fasten a canvas cover over the tops of the screens, thereby
shutting out light, noise and possibility of leaving the bed."[12] When delivery began, attendants took down the canvas crib and positioned the patient in stirrups,
familiar in modern obstetrical services. Van Hoosen advised the use of a continuous sleeve to ensure that patients did not interfere with the sterile field (see fig. 2).
The canvas crib and the continuous sleeve were Van Hoosen's response to a common need in twilight sleep deliveries: a secure, darkened, quiet, contained
environment.

The Events

Twilight sleep became a controversial issue in American obstetrics in June 1914,
when *McClure's Magazine* published an article by two laywomen describing this
newly popular German method of painless childbirth.[13] In the article, Marguerite

Tracy and Constance Leupp, both visitors at the Freiburg women's clinic, criticized high-forceps deliveries (which they called the common American technique) as dangerous and conducive to infection. They contrasted these imperfect births to the safety and comfort of twilight sleep. The new method was so wonderful that women, having once experienced it, would "walk all the way [to Germany] from California" to have their subsequent births under twilight sleep. The physicians at the Freiburg clinic thought the method was best suited for the upper-class "modern woman . . . [who] responds to the stimulus of severe pain . . . with nervous exhaustion and paralysis of the will to carry labor to conclusion." They were less certain about its usefulness for women who "earn their living by manual labor" and could tolerate more pain.[14]

The women who took up the cause of twilight sleep concluded that it was not in general use in this country because doctors were consciously withholding this panacea. Physicians have "held back" on developing painless childbirth, accused Mary Boyd and Marguerite Tracy, two of the most active proponents, because it "takes too much time." "Women alone," they asserted, "can bring Freiburg methods into American obstetrical practice."[15] Others echoed the call to arms: the journalist Hanna Rion urged her readers to "take up the battle for painless childbirth. . . . Fight not only for yourselves, but fight for your . . . sex."[16] Newspapers and popular magazines joined the chorus, advocating a widespread use of scopolamine in childbirth.[17]

The lay public's anger at the medical profession's apparent refusal to adopt a technique beneficial to women erupted into a national movement. The National Twilight Sleep Association, formed by upper-middle-class clubwomen,[18] was best epitomized by its leaders. They included such women as Mrs. Jesse F. Attwater, editor of *Femina* in Boston; Dr. Eliza Taylor Ransom, active women's rights advocate and physician in Boston; Mrs. Julian Heath, of the National Housewife's League; the author Rheta Childe Dorr, of the Committee on the Industrial Conditions of Women and Children; Mary Ware Dennett, of the National Suffrage Association (and later the National Birth Control League); and Dr. Bertha Van Hoosen, outspoken women's leader in medical circles in Chicago.[19] Many of these leaders saw the horrors of childbirth as an experience that united all women: "Childbirth has for every woman through all time been potentially her great emergency."[20] Dr. Ransom thought that the use of twilight sleep would "create a more perfect motherhood" and urged others to work "for the betterment of womenkind."[21] Because they saw it as an issue for their sex, not just their class, and because many of the twilight sleep leaders were active feminists, they spoke in the idiom of the woman movement.[22]

The association sponsored rallies in major cities to acquaint women with the issue of painless childbirth and to pressure the medical profession into adopting the new method. In order to broaden their appeal, the association staged meetings "between the marked-down suits and the table linen" of department stores, where "the ordinary woman" as well as the activist clubwoman could be found.[23] At these rallies, women who had traveled to Freiburg testified to the wonders of twilight sleep. "I experienced absolutely no pain," claimed Mrs. Francis X. Carmody of Brooklyn, displaying her healthy baby at Gimbels. "An hour after my child was born I ate a hearty breakfast. . . . The third day I went for an automobile ride. . . . The Twilight Sleep is wonderful." Mrs. Carmody ended with the familiar rallying cry: "If you women want it you will have to fight for it, for the mass of doctors are opposed to it."[24]

Department-store rallies and extensive press coverage brought the movement to the attention of a broad segment of American women. Movement leaders rejoiced over episodes such as the one in which a "tenement house mother . . . collected a crowd" on a street corner where she joyfully told of her twilight sleep experience.[25] Many working-class women were attracted to twilight sleep not only because it made childbirth "pleasanter" but because they saw its use as "an important cause of decreased mortality and increased health and vitality among the mothers of children."[26] Some feared, however, that twilight sleep would remain a "superadded luxury of the wealthy mother" because it involved so much physician time and hospital expense.[27] Although different motivations propelled the physician-advocates who believed twilight sleep was safe, the middle- and upper-class women who wanted the newest thing medicine had to offer, and the working-class women who wanted simple relief from childbed suffering, they were all united by their common desire to make childbirth safer and easier for women.

Van Hoosen emerged as the most avid advocate of twilight sleep in the Midwest. She received her M.D. from the University of Michigan Medical School and worked at the New England Hospital for Women and Children in Boston before setting up practice in Chicago in 1892. Her enthusiasm for the method came from two sources: her commitment to the best in obstetrical care and her equally strong commitment to women's rights. Through her use of scopolamine in surgery and obstetrics, she became convinced that twilight sleep offered women a "return of more physiological births" at the same time that it increased the efficiency of physicians, giving them "complete control of everything."[28] She guided many other physicians to the twilight sleep method.[29] In terms of safety and comfort, she could not imagine a better method of birthing.

Increasingly, doctors began to deliver twilight sleep babies. Some traveled to Germany to learn the Freiburg technique and subsequently offered it to both private and charity patients.[30] A few physicians even became enthusiastic about the possibilities of twilight sleep. "If the male had to endure this suffering," said Dr. James Harrar of New York, "I think he would resort very precipitously to something that might relieve the . . . pain."[31] Dr. W. Francis B. Wakefield of California went even further, declaring "I would just as soon consider performing a surgical operation without an anesthetic as conducting a labor without scopolamin amnesia. Skillfully administered the best interest of both the mother and the child are advanced by its use."[32] Another physician listed its advantages: painless labor, reduction of subsequent "nerve exhaustion that comes after a prolonged hard labor," better milk secretion, fewer cervical and perineal lacerations, fewer forceps deliveries, less strain on the heart, and a "better race for future generations" since upper-class women would be more likely to have babies if they could have them painlessly.[33] There was also, it was claimed, an "advantage to the child: To give it a better chance for life at the time of delivery; a better chance to have breast-feeding; a better chance to have a strong, normal mother."[34]

Despite the energy and enthusiasm of the twilight sleep advocates, many American doctors resisted the technique. They lashed out against the "pseudo-scientific rubbish" and the "quackish hocus-pocus" published in *McClure's*[35] and simply refused to be "stampeded by these misguided ladies."[36] These physicians did not believe that nonmedical people should determine therapeutic methods; it was a "question of medical ethics."[37] Other physicians refused to use scopolamine because they feared its dangers either to the mother or to the child. The *Journal of the American Medical Association* concluded that "this method has been thoroughly investigated, tried, and found wanting, because of the danger connected with it."[38]

Because the evidence about safety was mixed, many doctors were frustrated in their attempts to find out whether scopolamine was harmful or safe for use in obstetrics. Earlier experience with the unstable form of the drug led some to refuse to try scopolamine again, although at least one pharmaceutical company had solved the problem of drug stability by 1914. "The bad and indifferent results which were at first obtained by the use of these drugs we now know to have been due entirely to overdosage and the use of impure and unstable preparations," concluded one physician in a report on his successful results with 1,000 twilight sleep mothers in 1915.[39] Dr. Van Hoosen had successfully performed surgery on 2,000 patients with the help of scopolamine by 1908[40] and began using the drug routinely in deliveries in 1914. She concluded after 100 consecutive cases that scopolamine, properly administered, "solves the problems of child-bearing" and is safe for mother and child.[41] But the medical literature continued to express concern about the possible ill effects of a breathing irregularity in babies whose mothers had been given scopolamine and morphine late in labor.[42] Doctors trying to understand the evaluation of twilight sleep must have been confused. In one journal they read that the procedure was "too dangerous to be pursued," while another journal assured them that scopolamine, when properly used during labor, "has no danger for either mother or child."[43] Increasingly, by 1915, medical journals published studies that at least cautiously favored twilight sleep (the January 1915 issue of *American Medicine* published nine such articles),[44] although they frequently ran editorials warning of the drug's potential dangers and stressing the need for caution. Practicing physicians faced a dilemma when pregnant women demanded painless childbirth with scopolamine.[45]

While physicians debated the desirability of using scopolamine in 1914 and 1915, the public, surer of its position, demanded that twilight sleep be routinely available to women who wanted it. Hospitals in the major cities responded to these demands and to physicians' growing interest in the method by allowing deliveries of babies the Freiburg way.[46] In order to gain additional clinical experience, and possibly in response to some women's requests, some doctors used twilight sleep in hospital charity wards. But the technique was most successful in the specialty wards where upper- and middle-class patients increasingly gave birth and hospital attendants and facilities were available. By May 1915 *McClure's Magazine's* national survey reported that the use of twilight sleep, although still battling for acceptance, "gains steadily" around the country.[47]

Because of the need for expertise and extra care in the administration of scopolamine, the twilight sleep movement easily fed into widespread efforts in the second decade of the twentieth century to upgrade obstetrical practice and eliminate midwives.[48] Both the women who demanded the technique and the doctors who adopted it applauded the new specialty of obstetrics. Mary Boyd desired to put an end to home deliveries when she advocated twilight sleep for charity patients: "Just as the village barber no longer performs operations, the untrained midwife of the neighborhood will pass out of existence under the effective competition of free painless wards."[49] Not only did scopolamine advocates try to displace midwives, but they also regarded general practitioners as unqualified to deliver twilight sleep babies. "The twentieth century woman will no more think of having an ordinary practitioner attend her in childbed at her own home," said two supporters, "she will go to a [twilight sleep] hospital as a matter of course."[50] Specialists agreed that "the method is not adapted for the general practitioner, but should be practiced only by those who devote themselves to obstetrics."[51] Eliza Taylor Ransom went so far as to recommend the passage of a federal law forbidding "anyone administering scopolamine without a course of instruction and a special license."[52]

Some obstetricians used this issue to discredit their general practitioner colleagues and the midwives who still delivered large numbers of America's babies. Another factor that might have pushed obstetricians to support twilight sleep was that births under scopolamine could be managed more completely by the physician. As one succinctly put it, anesthesia gave "absolute control over your patient at all stages of the game. You are 'boss.'"[53] Physicians' time at the bedside could even be used for other pursuits. "I catch up on my reading and writing," testified one practitioner, "I am never harassed by relatives who want me to tell them things."[54]

The Issue of Control

How do we explain the seeming contradictions in this episode in medical history? Why did women demand to undergo a process which many physicians deemed risky and in which parturients lost self-control? Why did some physicians resist a process that would have given women an easier birthing experience and would have reinforced physicians' control over childbirth in a hospital environment?

Several factors contributed to the open tensions about the use of twilight sleep. One was safety. Many physicians rejected scopolamine because they did not have access to facilities like those at Mary Thompson Hospital or because they believed the drug too risky under any circumstances. Because of the variability among physicians' use of scopolamine and the contradictory evidence in the professional journals, we know that safety was a guiding motivation of many physicians. However, this is not enough to explain physician reluctance, since so many doctors administered other drugs during labor despite questionable safety reports.[55] Differing perceptions about pain during childbirth also contributed to the intensity of feeling about twilight sleep in 1914 and 1915. Although many physicians believed that women's "extremely delicate nervous sensibilities" needed relief, others were reluctant to interfere with the natural processes of childbirth. One anti–twilight sleep physician argued, "when we reflect that we are dealing with a perfectly healthy individual, and an organ engaged in a purely physiological function . . . I fail to see the necessity of instituting such a measure in a normal labor and attempt[ing] to bridge the parturient women over this physiological process in a semi-conscious condition."[56] Women perceived, too, that some physicians used anesthesia only for "suffering when it becomes a serious impediment to the birth process."[57] However, women who had suffered greatly, or whose friends had suffered greatly, actively sought relief from their "physiological" births: they thought pain in itself was a hindrance to a successful childbirth experience and "demanded" that their physicians provide them with more positive, less painful, experiences in the future.[58]

Both sides in the twilight sleep debate grappled with a third important question: whether the women or the attendants should determine and control the birthing process.⁵⁹ The women who demanded that doctors put them to sleep were partially blind to the safety issue because the issue of control (over pain, bodily function, decision making) was so important to them. Control became important when doctors refused to allow women "to receive the same benefits from this great discovery that their sisters abroad are getting."⁶⁰ Twilight sleep advocates demanded their right to decide how they would have their children. Tracy and Boyd articulated this issue: "Women took their doctor's word before. They are now beginning to believe . . . that the use of painlessness should be at *their* discretion."⁶¹ Although women were out of control during twilight sleep births—unconscious and needing crib-beds or constant attention to restrain their wild movements— this loss of control was less important to them than their determination to control the decision about what kind of labor and delivery they would have. Hanna Rion, whose influential book and articles had garnered support for the method, wrote:

> In the old-fashioned days when women were merely the blindfolded guardians of the power of child-bearing, they had no choice but to trust themselves without question in the hands of the all-wise physician, but that day is past and will return no more. Women have torn away the bandages of false modesty; they are no longer ashamed of their bodies; they want to know all the wondrous workings of nature, and they demand that they be taught how best to safeguard themselves as wives and mothers. When it comes to the supreme function of childbearing every woman should certainly have the choice of saying how she will have her child.⁶²

Twilight sleep women wanted to control their own births by choosing to go to sleep. They were not succumbing to physicians or technology but were, they thought, demanding the right to control their own birthing experiences.

This feminist emphasis on control over decision making appears in the writings and lectures of the twilight sleep movement; its followers sought simple relief from pain.⁶³ Many leaders were active suffragists whose commitment to twilight sleep was rooted in their belief in women's rights.⁶⁴ Although these activists agreed with most physicians that birth should increasingly be the domain of the obstetricians and that women should not suffer unnecessarily, they disagreed vehemently about who should decide what the birthing woman's experience would be. They clearly and adamantly wanted women to have the right to decide their own method of birthing.⁶⁵

In the face of advancing obstetrical technology, many physicians wanted to retain their traditional professional right and duty to decide therapy on the basis of their judgment about the medical indications. They refused to be "dragooned" into "indiscriminate adoption" of a procedure that they themselves did not choose.[66] Even the doctors who supported twilight sleep believed that, in the final analysis, the method of childbirth was "a question for the attending man and not the patient to decide."[67] It was principally this question of power over decision making that separated the movement's proponents from its opponents.

The Decline

In the very successes of the twilight sleep movement lay the seeds of its demise. Pressured by the clubwomen's associations and their own pregnant patients, doctors who had not been trained in the Freiburg method delivered babies with scopolamine. There was an enormous variation in the use of the drug, its timing through labor, the conditions in which the woman labored, and the watchfulness of attendants. As its advocates had feared, problems emerged when scopolamine was not properly monitored in a hospital setting. Following reports of adverse effects on the newborn, the drug fell into ill repute, and some hospitals that had been among the first to use it stopped administering it routinely.[68]

Those physicians who continued to advocate twilight sleep believed that accidents were due to misuse of the Freiburg method and not to the drug itself. Commenting on its discontinuation at Michael Reese Hospital in Chicago, Dr. Bertha Van Hoosen noted that "it is . . . probable that this adverse report demonstrates nothing more than the inexperience of the people using this anesthetic."[69] Dr. Ralph Beach agreed that "there is no doubt that all of the bad results which have been reported due to this method, are due to an improper technic, or the administration of unstable preparations."[70] Simultaneously, in 1915, some hospitals expanded their obstetric services to offer twilight sleep, and others began cutting back its use. Either because they judged the drug dangerous or because they did not use it correctly, some hospitals found the method too troublesome to administer on a routine basis to all patients. Most reached a compromise and continued to use scopolamine during labor's first stage (when it was deemed safe), thus preempting their patients' protests without compromising their medical beliefs. A second inhibitory factor appeared in August 1915 when Mrs. Francis X. Carmody, one of the country's leading exponents of twilight sleep, died during childbirth at Long Island College Hospital in New York. Although doctors and her husband insisted that her death was unrelated to scopolamine, it nonetheless harmed the movement.[71] Mrs. Carmody's neighbor started a new movement to oppose twilight sleep, and women became more alert to the question of safety than they had been.[72] Doctors and some former twilight sleep advocates, emphasizing the issues of safety and difficulty of administration, began exploring other methods of achieving painless childbirth.[73]

The obstetric literature after 1915 indicates that twilight sleep did not die in that year. The women's movement may have failed to make scopolamine routinely available to all laboring women, but it succeeded in making the concept of painless childbirth more acceptable and in adding scopolamine to the obstetric pharmacopoeia. In fact, obstetricians continued to use scopolamine into the 1960s during the first stage of hospital births.[74] The use of anesthesia (including scopolamine) in childbirth grew in the years after 1915, since women, aware of the possibility of painlessness, continued to want "shorter and less painful parturition" and since physicians felt they could disregard these desires "only at great risk to [their] own practice."[75]

The attempt by a group of women, including some feminists, to control their birthing experiences backfired. The medical profession retained the choice of birth procedures and perhaps gained additional control as a result of this episode. Partial acceptance by the profession quieted the lay revolt, and women lost the power they had sought. Ironically, by encouraging women to go to sleep during their deliveries, the twilight sleep movement helped to distance women from their bodies. Put to sleep with a variety of drugs, most parturient women from the 1920s to the 1960s did not experience one of their bodies' most powerful actions and thus lost touch with their own physical potential.[76] The twilight sleep movement helped change the definition of birthing from a natural home event, as it was in the nineteenth century, to an illness requiring hospitalization and physician attendance. Parturient feminists today, seeking to experience childbirth fully, paradoxically must fight a tradition of drugged, hospital-controlled births, itself the partial result of a struggle to increase women's control over their bodies.

NOTES

I am grateful to William J. Orr, Jr., and Susan Duke for their assistance in the preparation of this study. I would also like to thank Mari Jo Buhle, Norman Fost, Susan Friedman, Lewis Leavitt, Elaine Marks, Regina Morantz, and Ronald Numbers for their comments on earlier drafts of this paper.

1. Testimony quoted in Marguerite Tracy and Mary Boyd, *Painless Childbirth* (New York: Frederick A. Stokes Co., 1915), pp. 188–89. For a thorough account of the twilight sleep controversy in America, see Lawrence C. Miller, "Pain, Parturition, and the Profession: The Twilight Sleep in America," in *Health Care in America: Essays in Social History*, ed. Susan Reverby and David Rosner (Philadelphia: Temple University Press, 1979), pp. 19–44.

2. Tracy and Boyd, *Painless Childbirth,* p. 198.

3. For more information on childbirth practices in this period, see Judy Barrett Litoff, *American Midwives: 1860 to the Present* (Westport, Conn.: Greenwood Press, 1978).

4. J. F. Ford, "Use of Drugs in Labor," *Wisconsin Medical Journal* 3 (1904–5): 257–65.

5. Ibid.

6. See, e.g., Dorothy Reed Mendenhall, "Prenatal and Natal Conditions in Wisconsin," *Wisconsin Medical Journal* 15 (1917): 353–69, who reported, "The death rate from maternity is gradually increasing in Wisconsin, as it is throughout the United States" (p. 364). Dr. Mendenhall also noted that death rates for physician-attended births were higher than for midwife-attended births in Wisconsin (p. 353). I would like to thank Dale Treleven for calling this article to my attention.

7. Mary Boyd, "The Story of Dammerschlaf: An American Woman's Personal Experience and Study at Freiburg," *Survey* 33 (1915): 129.

8. Quoted in Russell Kelso Carter, *The Sleeping Car "Twilight," or Motherhood without Pain* (Boston: Chapple Publishing Co., 1915), pp. 10–11.

9. Scopolamine is an alkaloid found in the leaves and seeds of solanaceous plants. It is a sedative and a mild analgesic as well as an amnesiac, causing forgetfulness of pain rather than blocking the pain sensation. For obstetrical twilight sleep, scopolamine was administered with morphine—the most active alkaloid of opium—in the first dose and alone for subsequent doses.

10. Bertha Van Hoosen, *Scopolamine-Morphine Anaesthesia* (Chicago: House of Manz, 1915), p. 101.

11. *New York Times,* June 9, 1917, p. 13.

12. Van Hoosen, *Scopolamine-Morphine Anaesthesia,* p. 12.

13. Marguerite Tracy and Constance Leupp, "Painless Childbirth," *McClure's Magazine* 43 (1914): 37–51.

14. Ibid., p. 43. For the same sentiment among American physicians, see, e.g., John O. Polak, "A Study of Scopolamin and Morphine Amnesia as Employed at Long Island Hospital," *American Journal of Obstetrics* 71 (1915): 722; and Henry Smith Williams, *Painless Childbirth* (New York: Goodhue Co., 1914), pp. 90–91. The classic descriptions of the ideal scopolamine delivery are Bernhard Kronig, "Painless Delivery in Dammerschlaf" (1908); Carl J. Gauss, "Births in Artificial Dammerschlaf" (1906); and Gauss, "Further Experiments in Dammerschlaf" (1911), all translated and reprinted in Tracy and Boyd, *Painless Childbirth,* pp. 205–308.

15. Mary Boyd and Marguerite Tracy, "More about Painless Childbirth," *McClure's Magazine* 43 (1914): 57–58.

16. Hanna Rion, *Painless Childbirth in Twilight Sleep* (London: T. Werner Laurie Ltd., 1915), p. 239; see also her "The Painless Childbirth," *Ladies Home Journal* 31 (1914): 9–10.

17. See, e.g., "Is the Twilight Sleep Safe—for Me?" *Woman's Home Companion* 42 (1915): 10, 43; William Armstrong, "The 'Twilight Sleep' of Freiburg: A Visit to the Much Talked of Women's Clinic," *Woman's Home Companion* 41 (1914): 4, 69; *New York Times,* September 17, 1914, p. 8; November 28, 1914, p. 2.

18. On women's clubs and clubwomen, see Mary P. Ryan, *Womanhood in America: From Colonial Times to the Present* (New York: New Viewpoints, 1975), pp. 227–32; Edith Hoshino Altbach, *Women in America* (Lexington, Mass.: D.C. Heath & Co., 1914), pp. 114–21; William

L. O'Neill, *Everyone Was Brave: A History of Feminism in America* (Chicago: Quadrangle Books, 1969), pp. 107–68; Sheila M. Rothman, *Woman's Proper Place: A History of Ideas and Practices, 1870 to the Present* (New York: Basic Books, 1978), pp. 63–93.

19. Carter, *The Sleeping Car "Twilight,"* pp. 174–75.

20. Tracy and Boyd, *Painless Childbirth,* p. 145.

21. Eliza Taylor Ransom, "Twilight Sleep," *Massachusetts Club Women* 1 (1917): 5. I am grateful to Regina Markell Morantz for this reference.

22. The connections between clubwomen and suffrage or other women's issues are explored in Altbach, *Women in America,* pp. 114–15; O'Neill, *Everyone Was Brave,* pp. 49–76, 146–68; Ryan, *Womanhood in America,* pp. 230–49; and Eleanor Flexner, *Century of Struggle: The Woman's Rights Movement in the United States* (New York: Atheneum Publishers, 1970), pp. 172–92. The term *woman movement,* in the nineteenth and early twentieth centuries, described the movement to better women's condition, including, but not limited to, the drive for suffrage.

23. Tracy and Boyd, *Painless Childbirth,* p. 145.

24. Quoted in *New York Times,* November 18, 1914, p. 18.

25. Tracy and Boyd, *Painless Childbirth,* p. 145.

26. Clara C. Stillman, "Painless Childbirth," *New York Call,* July 12, 1914, p. 15.

27. Sam Schmalhauser, "The Twilight Sleep for Women," *International Socialist Review* 15 (1914): 234–35. I am grateful to Mari Jo Buhle for this and the previous reference.

28. Bertha Van Hoosen, *Petticoat Surgeon* (Chicago: Pellegrini & Cudahy, 1947), pp. 282–83.

29. See, e.g., Bertha Van Hoosen, "A Fixed Dosage in Scopolamine-Morphine Anaesthesia," *Woman's Medical Journal* 26 (1916): 57–58; and Van Hoosen, "Twilight Sleep in the Home," ibid., p. 132.

30. For early American trials, see William H. Wellington Knipe, "'Twilight Sleep' from the Hospital Viewpoint," *Modern Hospital* 2 (1914): 250–51; A. M. Hilkowich, "Further Observations on Scopolamine-Narcophin Anesthesia during Labor with Report of Two Hundred (200) Cases," *American Medicine* 20 (1914): 786–94; William H. Wellington Knipe, "The Freiburg Method of Dammerschlaf or Twilight Sleep," *American Journal of Obstetrics* 70 (1914): 364–71; and James A. Harrar and Ross McPherson, "Scopolamine-Narcophin Seminarcosis in Labor," *Transactions of the American Association of Obstetricians and Gynecologists* 27 (1914): 372–89.

31. Quoted during discussion of Rongy, Harrar, and McPherson papers, *Transactions of the American Association of Obstetricians and Gynecologists* 27 (1914): 389.

32. W. Francis B. Wakefield, "Scopolamine Amnesia in Labor," *American Journal of Obstetrics* 71 (1915): 428. For more of this kind of enthusiasm, see also Elizabeth R. Miner, "Letter and Report of Nineteen Cases in Which 'Twilight' Was Used," *Woman's Medical Journal* 26 (1916): 131.

33. Ralph M. Beach, "Twilight Sleep," *American Medicine* 21 (1915): 40–41.

34. Bertha Van Hoosen, *Scopolamine-Morphine Anaesthesia,* p. 101. Some physicians reported success using twilight sleep at home, but most thought the method best suited to hospital deliveries.

35. Quotation from the *Journal of the American Medical Association* in "Another 'Twilight

Sleep,'" *Literary Digest* 50 (1915): 187; W. Gillespie, "Analgesics and Anesthetics in Labor, Their Indications and Contra-Indications," *Ohio Medical Journal* 11 (1915): 611.

36. "Twilight Sleep Again," *American Medicine* 21 (1915): 149.

37. "'Twilight Sleep' in the Light of Day," *Scientific American* 79, suppl. 2041 (1915): 112. See also *New York Times*, October 20, 1914, p. 12; November 28, 1914, p. 12; February 5, 1915, p. 10; February 11, 1915, p. 8.

38. *Journal of the American Medical Association*, June 6, 1914, quoted in "'Twilight Sleep' and Medical Publicity," *Literary Digest* 49 (1914): 60.

39. Ralph M. Beach, "Twilight Sleep: Report of One Thousand Cases," *American Journal of Obstetrics* 71 (1915): 728.

40. Frederick A. Stratton, "Scopolamine Anesthesia," *Wisconsin Medical Journal* 8 (1908–9): 27.

41. Van Hoosen, *Scopolamine-Morphine Anaesthesia*, p. 101.

42. This condition, called "oligopnea," usually resolved after a few hours, but it was frightening to observe, especially for attendants who had no experience with it (Gauss, "Further Experiments in Dammerschlaf," p. 302).

43. See discussion of the Polak paper (n. 14 above) in *American Journal of Obstetrics* 7 (1915): 798; and Hilkowich, "Further Observations," p. 793.

44. *American Medicine* 21 (1915): 24–70.

45. See, e.g., the discussion following Knipe's paper (n. 30 above) in *American Journal of Obstetrics* 70 (1914): 1025. For articles with positive conclusions, see John Osburn Polock, "A Study of Twilight Sleep," *New York Medical Journal* 101 (1915): 293; Robert T. Gillmore, "Scopolamine and Morphine in Obstetrics and Surgery," *New York Medical Journal* 102 (1915): 298; Knipe, "'Twilight Sleep' from the Hospital Viewpoint," p. 250; W. Francis B. Wakefield, "Scopolamin-Amnesia in Labor," *American Journal of Obstetrics* 71 (1915): 428; Samuel J. Druskin and Nathan Ratnoff, "Twilight Sleep in Obstetrics—with a Report of 200 Cases," *New York State Journal of Medicine* 15 (1915): 152; Charles B. Reed, "A Contribution to the Study of 'Twilight Sleep,'" *Surgery, Gynecology and Obstetrics* 22 (1916): 656. For a negative conclusion, see Joseph Louis Baer, "Scopolamin-Morphin Treatment in Labor," *Journal of the American Medical Association* 64 (1915): 1723–28. The actual dangers of the drug varied according to dosage and timing, and it is impossible for the historian to assess the events accurately without individual case records. Any drug can be dangerous if misused, and the variability in scopolamine suggests that some disasters occurred with it.

46. E.g., see *New York Times*, August 22, 1914, p. 9, and September 10, 1914; and the American hospitals mentioned in Tracy and Boyd, *Painless Childbirth*.

47. Anna Steele Richardson's survey was reported in the *New York Times*, May 10, 1915, p. 24.

48. Litoff, *American Midwives*, pp. 69–70.

49. Mary Boyd, "The Story of Dammerschlaf," *Survey* 33 (1914): 129. See the same statement in Tracy and Boyd, *Painless Childbirth*, p. 69.

50. Constance Leupp and Burton J. Hendrick, "Twilight Sleep in America," *McClure's Magazine* 44 (1915): 172–73. The argument about expertise appeared repeatedly; see, e.g., William H. W. Knipe, "The Truth about Twilight Sleep," *Delineator* 85 (1914): 4. Twilight sleep women were aware that theirs was an expensive demand. They expected the cost of physician-

attended childbirth to jump from twenty-five to eighty-five dollars (Tracy and Boyd, *Painless Childbirth,* p. 180).

51. Druskin and Ratnoff, p. 1520.

52. *New York Times,* April 30, 1915, p. 8.

53. Quoted from the *New Orleans Medical and Surgical Journal* in Miller, "Pain, Parturition, and the Profession," p. 74.

54. Van Hoosen, *Petticoat Surgeon,* p. 282.

55. Fifty percent of 100 general practitioners surveyed in rural districts and small towns in Wisconsin indicated that they used ergot during labor, although its use was blamed for "a very large per cent of necessary operations for repair injuries to the floor and pelvic organs of the female patient" (Ford, "Use of Drugs in Labor," p. 257).

56. Dr. Francis Reder, during a discussion of Rongy, Harrar, and McPherson papers, *Transactions of the American Association of Obstetricians and Gynecologists* 27 (1914): 386.

57. Tracy and Boyd, *Painless Childbirth,* p. 149.

58. For physicians' perceptions of "demanding" women, see, e.g., the discussion following the Rongy and Harrar papers, *Transactions of the American Association of Obstetricians and Gynecologists* 27 (1914): 382–83.

59. Other contributing factors cannot be developed here. Growing professionalization and specialization within medicine produced tensions among groups of doctors that surfaced during this debate. The method's German "origins" invalidated it with many Americans during the war years. My emphasis here on the issue of control is not meant to minimize these and other factors. However, because others, especially Lawrence Miller ("Pain, Parturition, and the Profession"), have explored the general outlines, I have focused on the previously unanalyzed question of decision-making power. Its importance, I think, is indicated by the intensity in the women's arguments on this issue.

60. Letter from "Ex-Medicus" in *New York Times,* November 28, 1914, p. 12.

61. Tracy and Boyd, *Painless Childbirth,* p. 147 (emphasis in original).

62. Rion, *Painless Childbirth in Twilight Sleep,* p. 47.

63. Tracy and Boyd claimed "four to five million" twilight sleep followers, obviously an exaggeration (*Painless Childbirth,* p. 144).

64. See, e.g., *New York Times,* November 28, 1914, p. 12.

65. See esp. Tracy and Boyd, *Painless Childbirth;* Rion, *Painless Childbirth in Twilight Sleep;* Ransom, "Twilight Sleep"; and Van Hoosen, *Scopolamine-Morphine Anaesthesia.*

66. *New York Times,* September 26, 1914, p. 10.

67. Dr. Arthur J. Booker, in his remarks defending Van Hoosen's use of scopolamine, quoted in Van Hoosen, *Scopolamine-Morphine Anaesthesia,* p. 12.

68. *New York Times,* April 24, 1915, p. 10; April 30, 1915, p. 8; May 29, 1915, p. 20; August 25, 1915, p. 10; August 16, 1916, p. 7.

69. Van Hoosen, "A Fixed Dosage," p. 57.

70. Beach, "Twilight Sleep," p. 43.

71. *New York Times,* August 24, 1915, p. 7.

72. Ibid., August 31, 1915, p. 5.

73. See, e.g., Frank W. Lynch, "Nitrous Oxide Gas Analgesia in Obstetrics," *Journal of the American Medical Association* 64 (1915): 813.

74. See, e.g., Henry Schwarz, "Painless Childbirth and the Safe Conduct of Labor," *American Journal of Obstetrics and Diseases of Women and Children* 79 (1919): 46–63; and W. C. Danforth and C. Henry Davis, "Obstetric Analgesia and Anesthesia," *Journal of the American Medical Association* 81 (1923): 1090–96.

75. See the assessment of anesthesia used in childbirth in New York Academy of Medicine Committee on Public Health Relations, *Maternal Mortality in New York City: A Study of All Puerperal Deaths, 1930–1932* (New York: Commonwealth Fund, 1933), p. 113; see also Joyce Antler and Daniel M. Fox, "Movement toward a Safe Maternity: Physician Accountability in New York City, 1915–1940," *Bulletin of the History of Medicine* 50 (1976): 569–95.

76. The legacy for the parent-infant bond and for subsequent child development is explored in M. H. Klaus and J. H. Kennell, *Maternal Infant Bonding: The Impact of Early Separation or Loss on Family Development* (St. Louis: C. V. Mosby, 1976). For a feminist perspective on women's missing their deliveries, see Adrienne Rich, *Of Woman Born: Motherhood as Experience and Institution* (New York: W. W. Norton, 1976).

12.

African American Women and Abortion, 1800–1970

LORETTA J. ROSS

> Homage I pay
> to the mothers who
> became mothers
> before their time.
> & the mothers
> that became mothers
> when there were no mothers
> to be found.
> —KIMBERLY COLLINS

Introduction

My quest to understand the activism of African American women seeking abortions and birth control stems from experiences shared with millions of women who want real choices as to when, and under what conditions, we will have children. Here is my definition of what it means to be "pro-life" *and* "pro-choice"—the right to have, or not to have, children and the right to raise them free from racism, sexism, and poverty.

Many people mistakenly view the African American women's struggle for abortion rights and reproductive freedom as a relatively recent phenomenon, rather than placing it in the context of our historical struggle against racism, sexism, and poverty. Whether these assumptions come from population experts or the African American community, they fail to credit us with the power to make responsible decisions for ourselves. To ask whether African American women favor

Reprinted from *Theorizing Black Feminism: The Visionary Pragmatism of Black Women* (1993), by permission of the publisher, Routledge: London and New York.

or oppose abortion is the wrong question. We obtain 24 percent of the abortions in the United States, more than 500,000 annually (Henshaw et al., 1991: 75–81). The question is not *if* we support abortion but *how*, and when, and why.

African American women have a long history in the struggle for reproductive freedom, but racist and sexist assumptions about us, our sexuality, and our fertility have disguised our contributions to the birth control and abortion movements in the United States. Distilling facts from the myths is difficult because so many accounts of African American history are written from perspectives that fail even to acknowledge our presence in the reproductive freedom movement.

Similarly, if a decline in African American birth rates occurs, the population experts usually ascribe it to poverty, coercive family planning, or other external factors, ignoring the possibility that we Black women were in any way responsible for the change.

The absence of discussion about abortion rights activism by African American women in most feminist literature is also disappointing, reflecting a commonly held view that African American women either are too politically naive or have an underdeveloped consciousness on issues of gender equality and abortion rights.

While volumes could be written on this topic, this chapter merely aspires to be one step in the process of recording our "herstory." It remains for others to cover comprehensively various aspects of abortion, such as its medical technology, and the judicial and legislative battles that determined the legality of abortion and contraception.

Instead, I have chosen to focus on the activism; the *agency* of African American women in the struggle both to obtain abortions and to participate in the national debate. I have also chosen to tell my own story in this chapter because, in the tradition of Paula Giddings and others, I believe it is the deliberate combination of the personal and the objective that creates the authority, authenticity, and uniqueness of the African American female experience.

Recording our history of activism is important because the voices heard in support of abortion are usually white. Even with the best intentions, white women cannot speak for us. They cannot see the world through our history or represent the authority of our lives. And, while volumes could also be written about the racism and elitism historically besetting the feminist movement, white women are not the focus of this paper.

African American women have been reluctant to analyze our history regarding abortion and to speak out collectively and publicly in support of abortion. To do so once seemed to further arguments of Black genocide, a charge that was not necessarily paranoid in view of past attacks on African Americans. To speak out also risked replicating the narrow focus of the white abortion rights movement, by engaging in "privileged bias," of isolating abortion from other forms of control imposed on African American women, through racism and poverty (Joseph and Lewis, 1981: 50).

If we are to connect ourselves to our foremothers who preceded us, we must transcend the tensions between these two extremes. To paraphrase bell hooks, our struggle is not so much to move from silence into speech as to change the nature and direction of our speech, to make a speech that is heard (hooks, 1989: 6).

I chose to write on abortion because reproductive health activism has been a part of my life for more than 20 years. I have been privileged to be a part of both the Black liberation and the women's movements and to meet many other African American women who share a commitment to improving the quality of life for African American women by ending racism and poverty, and by advancing gender equality.

Abortion rights and reproductive freedom are not intellectual abstractions for me but have determined many aspects of my life. By the time I was in my twenties, I had experienced many of the reproductive crises consistent with being Black, poor, and female in America. At age 15 I became a teen mother because of sexual activity coupled with sexual ignorance, not an unusual combination even today. I realized for the first time the lack of options available to pregnant teens in the 1960s. Because abortion was illegal and traveling anywhere else was not possible, I had my son in a very difficult pregnancy, after staying in a home for unwed mothers.

As a college student two years later, I became pregnant again, owing to contraceptive failure. I had an abortion, which fortunately was legal in Washington, D.C., at the time.

It is providential that I kept my child rather than giving him up for adoption, because I was permanently sterilized by the Dalkon Shield IUD at age 23. I sued A. H. Robins, the maker of the shield, and became one of the first Black women to prevail against this multinational corporation. The company was eventually bankrupted by thousands of other women who were also sterilized. Thus my reproductive career lasted a brief eight years and included a full-term pregnancy, an abortion, and sterilization.

Although winning against A. H. Robins was a moral victory, it did not mitigate the burning anger I felt because my IUD was inserted years after its dangers had already been substantially documented. Why was a defective contraceptive recommended to me? Why did I nearly die from acute pelvic inflammatory disease, which several doctors failed to link to the defective IUD, preferring to believe in bizarre theories of rare venereal diseases among Black women? Doctors' diagnoses of African American women were distorted by theories of diseases brought back by soldiers returning from Vietnam. My pelvic infection from the IUD was treated as a mysterious venereal disease. I wondered who really controlled my body. It certainly didn't seem to be me.

In the process I learned that simply surviving against the odds was personally liberating. But I also learned that for African American women to survive, we all need liberation from devices and doctors and politicians who control our bodies.

Abortion, in and of itself, does not automatically create freedom. But it does allow women to exert some control over our biology, freeing us from the inevitability of unwanted pregnancies, and is therefore indispensable to bodily and political self-determination.

There is much yet to be written about our activism. But it was not persuasive analysis, arguments, or ideology that influenced African American women to support abortion. We did so because we *needed* to. Necessity was the midwife to our politics.

Abortion in the 1800s

Before the Civil War, almost 20 percent of the total U.S. population consisted of African American slaves. By 1900, African Americans were 12 percent of the total population, as the forced breeding of slavery came to an end (Littlewood, 1977: 18). However, even before the Civil War, African American women sought to control their fertility.

Controlling women's reproduction was important to maintain the race, class, and gender inequality of the slave economy. Plantation owners tried to keep knowledge of birth control and abortion away from both slaves and white women to maintain the caste system of white supremacy used to justify slavery (P. H. Collins, 1991: 50). Black women's fertility increased the owners' labor force and property value, and "slave masters wanted adolescent girls to have children, and . . . they practiced a passive, though insidious kind of breeding" (D. G. White, 1985: 98). Techniques included giving pregnant women lighter workloads and more rations and bonuses to increase Black women's willingness to have children. Punitive measures were also used: infertile women were treated "like barren sows and . . . passed from one unsuspecting buyer to the next" (D. G. White, 1985: 101).

African Americans used birth control and abortion as a form of resistance to slavery. Abortion and infanticide were acts of desperation, motivated not by a desire to avoid the biological birth process or the burdens of parenting but, instead, by a commitment to resist the oppressive conditions of slavery. When Black women resorted to abortion, the stories they told were not so much about the desire to be free of pregnancy as about the miserable social conditions that dissuaded them from bringing new lives into the world (A. Davis, 1990: 17).

Abortion as a means of controlling fertility has been a part of African culture since the time when Egypt was the cradle of civilization. Abortion-inducing herbs and methods have been discovered in ancient societies in Africa, China, and the Middle East (Petchesky, 1990: 28; S. E. Davis, 1988: 17). African queen and pharaoh Hatshepsut, who reigned in Egypt from 1486 to 1468 B.C., invented a method of birth control (Simmons, 1990: 121). Most of these skills were lost during slavery, except the knowledge retained by midwives, which spanned across time. This folk knowledge blurred the distinction between birth control and abortion.

Historians declare that it is almost impossible to determine whether slave women practiced birth control and abortion. However, careful readings of slave journals and narratives reveal that some southern whites were certain that slave women knew how to avoid pregnancy as well as how to deliberately abort their pregnancies. When Daph, a woman on the Ferry Hill plantation in Virginia, miscarried twins in 1838, the overseer reported that she had taken an abortifacient to bring about the miscarriage (D. G. White, 1985: 84).

Suspicions about slave abortions ran high enough to spur public comment. In an 1856 essay, Dr. E. M. Pendleton claimed that planters regularly complained of whole families of women who failed to have children. Pendleton believed that "blacks are possessed of a secret by which they destroy the foetus at an early age of gestation" (D. G. White, 1985: 85). A Tennessee physician, Dr. John H. Morgan, said that he was certain that slave women were aborting either by "medicine, violent exercise, or by external and internal manipulations" (Sterling, 1984: 40).

Toward the end of the nineteenth century, "alum water" was one of many birth control measures used in southern rural communities served by midwives. Women in urban areas used petroleum jelly and quinine. Widely available and purchased very cheaply in stores, it was placed over the mouth of the uterus. Some remedies served both purposes. For example, boiling rusty nails created a douche used either as an abortifacient or as a contraceptive. Some women used quinine tablets or turpentine (orally or as a douche) and laxatives. Such concoctions were reputed to bring about severe cramps and contractions which approximated giving birth. Plant compounds like pennyroyal and papaya seeds were also used (Sterling, 1984: 40).

Despite this knowledge, folk methods of birth control and abortion were usually regarded as a sin by those influenced by Christianity. For example, the secret techniques for abortion kept by a midwife named Mollie became too much for her to bear when she converted to Christianity. She begged for forgiveness for having assisted hundreds of women in obtaining birth control and abortions (D. G. White, 1985: 126).

Nevertheless, African American women informally discussed abortion and birth control and passed along the knowledge (Ward, 1986: 13–14). In 1894, *The Women's Era,* an African American women's newsletter, wrote that "not all women are intended for mothers. Some of us have not the temperament for family life" (Giddings, 1984: 108). By the 1900s, Black women were making gains in controlling their fertility. "Their grandmothers married at twelve and fifteen," W. E. B. Du Bois, one of the founders of the National Association for the Advancement of Colored People (NAACP), observed in the *Souls of Black Folk.* In 1910, he found 27 percent of African American women still single past the age of 15. They were also having fewer children. Half of all married, educated African American women had no children at the turn of the century. Even more revealing, one-fourth of all Black women—the majority of them rural and uneducated—had no children at all (Giddings, 1984: 137).

Birth Control and Abortion, 1915–1950

One perception of the birth control movement is that it was thrust upon reluctant African Americans by a population control establishment anxious to control Black fertility. While the population establishment may have had an agenda, African Americans had their own view of the matter. Probably the best documented source of information about the use of birth control by African Americans was written by Jessie M. Rodrique, who asserts that "Black women were interested in controlling their fertility and the low birth rates reflect in part a conscious use of birth control. . . . Blacks were active and effective participants in the establishment of local clinics and in the birth control debate" (Rodrique, 1990: 333). It is both wrong, and racist, to assume that African American women had no interest in controlling the spacing of their children and were the passive victims of medical, commercial, and state policies of reproductive control.

Black fertility declined toward the end of the nineteenth century, indicative of the growing social awareness among African Americans that birth spacing was integral to economics, health, race relations, and racial progress. In fact, between 1915 and 1920, Black infant mortality actually dropped from 181 per 1,000 births to 102 for states registering 2,000 or more Black births (Giddings, 1984: 149).

African American women saw themselves not as breeders or matriarchs but as builders and nurturers of a race, a nation. Sojourner Truth's statement "I feel as if the power of a nation is within me!" affirmed the role of African American women as "seminal forces of the endurance and creativity needed by future generations of Blacks not merely to survive, but to thrive, produce, and progress" (Burgher, 1979: 117).

W. E. B. Du Bois wrote in 1919 that "the future [African American] woman . . . must have the right of motherhood at her own discretion" (Rodrique, 1990: 336). Joining him was the historian J. A. Rogers, who wrote, "I give the Negro woman credit if she endeavors to be something other than a mere breeding machine. Having children is by no means the sole reason for being" (ibid.).

The Colored Women's Club Movement, the organized voice of African American women during the late nineteenth and early twentieth centuries, directly addressed issues of Black women's sexuality. This movement sought to "confront and redefine morality and assess its relationship to 'true womanhood'" (Giddings, 1984: 85). Stereotypes about Black women's sexuality and alleged immorality prompted many African American women to "make the virtues as well as the wants of the colored women known to the American people . . . to put a new social value on themselves" (Lerner, 1972: 576).

The Club Movement also denounced the rampant sterilization of Black women and supported the establishment of family planning clinics in Black communities. In 1918, the Women's Political Association of Harlem announced a scheduled lecture on birth control. The National Urban League requested of the Birth Control Federation of America (the forerunner to Planned Parenthood) that a clinic be opened in the Columbus Hill section of the Bronx. Several ministers held discussions about birth control at their churches, and Adam Clayton Powell, an influential Congressional leader, spoke at public meetings in support of family planning (Rodrique, 1990: 338).

African American organizations, including the NAACP and the National Urban League, and leading Black newspapers like the *Pittsburgh Courier* and the *San Francisco Spokesman* promoted family planning. The African American newspapers of the period reported the mortality rates of women who had septic abortions and also championed the causes of Black doctors who were arrested for performing illegal abortions (Rodrique, 1990: 335).

The *Baltimore Afro-American* wrote that pencils, nails, and hat pins were instruments commonly used for self-induced abortions and that abortions among Black women were deliberate, not the result of poor health or sexually transmitted diseases. This was clearly a "means of getting rid of unwanted children" (Rodrique, 1990: 335). Many women died as well, a fact not lost on African American women.

Eugenics and Genocide

> It is up to science to meet the demands of humanity . . . that life shall
> be given . . . "frankly, gaily," or—not at all. Which shall it be? (Stella
> Browne, 1922, quoted in Petchesky, 1990: 92)

Although motherhood was a highly prized social status in Africa, fears of depopulation were not a tremendous concern before American slavery. Africa's population decreased because of the slave trade, exploitative colonial labor policies, and the introduction of new diseases from Europe. In the eighteenth century, 20 percent of the world's population lived in Africa; by the year 2000, the figure is expected to be less than 13 percent.

In the United States, as racism, lynchings, and poverty took their heavy toll, fears of depopulation produced among African Americans toward the end of the nineteenth century a pronatalist trend that had not previously existed. This trend also built successfully on traditional Black values that conferred adult status on women who became biological mothers, the first significant step toward womanhood (P. H. Collins, 1991: 134). This shift in the critical thinking of African Americans on population and motherhood presaged an inevitable conflict between the right of women to exercise bodily self-determination and the need of the African American community for political and economic self-determination. In both schools of thought, wombs were to be the weapon against racism and oppression.

The opposition to fertility control for African American women in the 1920s came primarily from the Catholic Church for religious and political reasons, from white conservatives who feared the availability of birth control for white women, and from Black nationalist leaders like Marcus Garvey who believed that the continuation of the Black race demanded increasing, rather than decreasing, the African population as a defense against racial oppression.

When the movement for birth control began, proponents like Margaret Sanger advocated giving women control over their fertility as a means of social mobility. This argument persuaded middle-class women, both Black and white, to support birth control. However, the early feminism of the movement, which prioritized women's control over their own bodies, collapsed under the weight of support offered by the growing number of people who were concerned about the rising population of African Americans, other people of color, and immigrants. Birth control advocacy quickly became a tool of racists, who argued in favor of eugenics, or other population control policies based on fears of African Americans and others thought to be "undesirable" by the politically powerful. The elite sought to improve their control of society through the control of breeding (Corea, 1985: 138).

The eugenics movement, begun in the late 1800s and based on pseudoscientific theories of race and heredity, evolved into a movement of biological determinism. To promote the reproduction of self-defined "racially superior" people, its proponents argued for both "positive" methods, such as tax incentives and education for the desirable, and "negative" methods, such as sterilization, involuntary confinement, and immigration restrictions for the undesirable (Petchesky, 1990: 86). It was assumed that Black and immigrant women had a "moral obligation to restrict the size of their families." While birth control was demanded as a right for privileged women, it became a duty for the poor (A. Davis, 1990: 20).

A leading eugenicist proposed sterilization, based on IQ tests, of at least ten million Americans because they were mentally or physically disabled, criminal, or simply "feeble-minded" (Hartmann, 1987: 96). By 1932, the Eugenics Society could boast that at least 27 states had passed compulsory sterilization laws and that thousands of "unfit" persons had already been surgically prevented from reproducing (A. Davis, 1983: 214). Many birth control advocates believed it was important to "prevent the American people from being replaced by alien or negro stock, whether it be by immigration or by overly high birth rates among others in this country" (Hartmann, 1987: 97).

The eugenicists' view that social intervention should be used to manipulate biological reproduction echoed other white supremacist views of the day. The Ku Klux Klan had an estimated five million members at this time, including representatives in Congress (Blee, 1991: 20). It should not be difficult to understand why birth control (and abortion) came to be regarded as genocidal by some African Americans. This view was exacerbated by the high incidence of involuntary sterilization of African American women.

It was not helpful that Margaret Sanger, like others who followed her, opportunistically built alliances with the oftentimes racist population control establishment, thereby advancing her cause at the expense of people of color. Sanger's campaign succeeded and benefited middle-class women because it concentrated on legal rights, medical acceptance, and public policy. The result was the enactment of policies that were racist enough to be supported by the population control establishment and weak enough that control over the technology and techniques of birth control would remain in the hands of the professional medical community. The eugenics movement was broader and encompassed far more historical trends than just the feminist movement. It was international in scope, and its roots were firmly established in the colonialism of the era. Feminism played its part, both wittingly and unwittingly, in the advancement of the eugenics movement in particular and white racism in general (Petchesky, 1990: 93).

The Birth Control Federation designed a "Negro Project" in 1939 to hire several African American ministers to travel through the South to enlist the support
of African American doctors for birth control (Gordon, 1990: 328). The project did
not necessarily want strong involvement of other portions of the African American
community, especially women, and argued that "the mass of Negroes, particularly
in the South, still breed carelessly and disastrously, with the result that the increase
among Negroes, even more than among Whites, is from that portion of the population least intelligent and fit, and least able to rear children properly" (ibid.).

Not all advocates of birth control and abortion were as insensitive as the eugenicists. The *Courier*, a Black newspaper whose editorial policy favored family
planning, said in 1936 that African Americans should oppose sterilization programs
being advanced by eugenicists because the burden would "fall upon colored people
and it behooves us to watch the law and stop the spread of [eugenic sterilization]"
(Rodrique, 1990: 338). A clear sense of dual or "paired" values also emerged among
African American women: to want individual control over their bodies while simultaneously resisting government and private depopulation policies that blurred
the distinction between incentives and coercion (Petchesky, 1990: 130). African
American women supported birth control, but at the same time they offered a
strong critique of the eugenicists.

Ironically, because of the unavailability of family planning services, sterilization through hysterectomies was frequently chosen by African American women
desperate to control their fertility. Often women pleaded for the operation because
of the absence of organized, alternative birth control services. As had been proven
earlier, women adapted themselves to whatever limited choices were available to
help them control their lives.

The Underground Movement, 1950–1970

The majority of abortions provided to African American women in the 1950s and
early 1960s were provided by doctors and midwives operating illegally. For example, Dr. Edgar Keemer, a Black physician in Detroit, practiced outside the law
for more than thirty years until his arrest in 1956. Women also traveled to Mexico
to have abortions (Simmons, 1990: 121).

Middle-class women could sometimes persuade doctors to arrange for a dis-
creet abortion or to provide a referral. Poor women either had the unplanned children or went to "the lady down the street" or the "woman downstairs"—either
midwives or partially trained medical personnel. Abortions from these illegal

providers were usually very expensive, and many white women came to Black neighborhoods to obtain abortions this way (Ward, 1986: 15; Baehr, 1990: 13). Fees for abortions were between $50 and $75, which was expensive considering that a pregnant woman might earn $10 a day (Ward, 1986: 15).

Long after the majority of "granny" midwives in other ethnic groups had been replaced by medically based hospital practices, there were still hundreds of Black lay midwives practicing in the Deep South, with midwifery lineages extending as far back as slavery. They provided most of the abortion and contraceptive services for Black southern women (E. C. White, 1990: 98). If complications developed, women visited physicians who operated in the poor sections of the city. Only as a last resort did they go to hospitals, fearing the legal consequences of having obtained an illegal abortion. Thus, the rate of septic abortions reported to hospitals was very low.

Dr. Dorothy Brown, the first Black female general surgeon in the United States, graduated from Meharry Medical College in 1948 and, while in the Tennessee State Legislature, became in the 1950s the first state legislator in the United States to introduce a bill to legalize abortion (E. C. White, 1990: 47). In an interview at the 1983 founding conference of the National Black Women's Health Project, Dr. Brown asserted, "We should dispense quickly the notion that abortion is genocide, because genocide in this country dates back to 1619" (Butler, 1988: 38).

The pseudoscience of eugenics had been largely discredited after the Second World War, when worldwide condemnation followed the Nazi extermination, not only of six million Jews, but of countless Germans with African, Indian, or Asian blood, as well as gypsies, gay men and lesbians, the disabled, and the mentally ill. In the mid-1950s, population "time bomb" theories from demographers gave rise to a newer, more legitimate and "scientific" approach to eugenics. The proponents of time bomb theories sanctimoniously argued that they were simply saving the poor from themselves.

Brochures published by groups like the Draper Fund and the Population Council showed "hordes of black and brown faces spilling over a tiny earth" (Petchesky, 1990: 118). The fund dated from 1958, when President Eisenhower appointed General William Draper, a New York investment banker and a key figure in the postwar reconstruction of Europe, to study foreign aid. The committee eventually developed an ideological link between population growth in the Third World and the United States' ability to govern world affairs. Draper told the Senate Foreign Relations Committee in 1959 that "the population problem . . . is the greatest bar to our whole economic aid program and to the progress of the world" (Hartmann, 1987: 103). By the early 1960s, the U.S. government began supporting population control policies overseas, and linked foreign aid with depopulation policies.

The domestic side of this worldview coincided with the growth of the civil rights movement, perhaps in response to the militancy of the movement and its potential for sweeping social change. The "political instability" of the African American population convinced many members of the white elite and middle class that Black population growth should be curbed. White Americans feared, out of proportion to reality, that a growing welfare class of African Americans concentrated in the inner cities would not only cause rampant crime but exacerbate the national debt and eventually produce a political threat from majority Black voting blocs in urban areas (Littlewood, 1977: 8).

The new "politics of population" that emerged in the mid–1960s gave rise to family planning programs in the South that were directed at predominantly Black urban areas. Family planning was designed to reduce the number of Black births to control the ever expanding Black population. This occurred at the same time as African American leaders were expressing interest in "taking over" the big cities and "holding them as enclaves against increasing repression" (Littlewood, 1977: 910). The U.S. Congress took note and pressured the newly created Office of Economic Opportunity to wage its war on poverty by emphasizing family planning programs for African Americans the year after passage of the 1965 Voting Rights Act. It is interesting to note that George Bush, a Texas Congressional representative at the time, supported family planning, even though his father once lost a Senate election in Connecticut after the columnist Drew Pearson, on the weekend before the ballots were cast, "revealed" the candidate's "involvement" with Planned Parenthood (Littlewood, 1977: 51). This support was affirmed by Richard Nixon when he took office in 1969.

Medicaid was established in the 1960s to cover medical costs for the poor. Family planning was included only after a series of fights with Catholics and conservatives at the state level. Publicly supported birth control developed in the 1960s, aided by the mass availability of the pill and the IUD. In 1967, Congress passed the Child Health Act, which specified that at least 6 percent of all maternal-child health grants to public health agencies had to be spent on family planning. This law stated that federal funds could be used to pay for services to any woman who had in the past needed, or might in the future need, welfare. It allowed family planners to offer a wide range of maternal and child care services to poor women. Joan Smith, current head of Louisiana's statewide family planning program, said at the time, "What caught my fancy was the idea of offering services to indigent women the same as private doctors were giving. Nobody treated poor women with dignity. We said we'd do it and we did" (Ward, 1986: 42).

Some medical experts opposed family planning for African Americans, convinced that African American women "wanted to be pregnant and have all those children and that even if they did not want repeated pregnancies, they could not possibly understand the principles of birth control because they were not bright enough and lacked behavioral control" (Ward, 1986: 17).

Although abortion was still illegal, some public health agencies operated an "underground railroad" of referrals for women to have illegal abortions (Ward, 1986: 58). It is estimated that from 200,000 to one million illegal abortions occurred annually in the late 1960s (S. E. Davis, 1988: 12). A major strength was the informal networks of African American women who spread the news about the availability of services and became activists in support of birth control and better health care and for abortion rights. Underground abortions were facilitated by church- and community-based referral services and cooperative doctors' networks that emerged in cities and states in the 1960s (Petchesky, 1990: 113).

Because of the blatant racism of the population control establishment that promoted family planning, Black nationalist campaigns against family planning reemerged. Several birth control clinics were invaded by Black Muslims associated with the Nation of Islam, who published cartoons in *Muhammad Speaks* that depicted bottles of birth control pills marked with a skull and crossbones or graves of unborn Black infants. The Pittsburgh branch of the NAACP declared that the local family planning clinic was an instrument of genocide. William "Bouie" Haden, leader of the militant United Movement for Progress, went one step further and threatened to firebomb the Pittsburgh clinic (Littlewood, 1977: 69).

Whitney Young, leader of the Urban League, also reversed his organization's support for family planning in 1962. Marvin Davies, head of the Florida NAACP, said, "Our women need to produce more babies, not less . . . and until we comprise 30 to 35 percent of the population, we won't really be able to affect the power structure in this country" (Littlewood, 1977: 75). This was a major ideological shift away from the early days of the NAACP and the Urban League; both organizations had formerly supported women's rights as a means of racial progress. The NAACP of the 1920s would have been horrified to find itself in the 1960s sounding more like Marcus Garvey and less like Du Bois.

The Black Power conference held in Newark in 1967, organized by Amiri Baraka, passed an anti–birth control resolution. Two years later, the May 1969 issue of the *Liberator* warned, "For us to speak in favor of birth control for Afro-Americans would be comparable to speaking in favor of genocide" (Giddings, 1984: 318).

The Black Panther Party was the only nationalist group to support free abortions and contraceptives on demand (Ward, 1986: 92), although not without considerable controversy within its ranks. "Half of the women in the party used birth control and we supported it because of our free health care program. We understood the conditions of the Black community," remembers Nkenge Toure, a former member, who also recalls that there were no formal political education discussions around the issue, but there was support from many party women.[1] Kathleen Cleaver, the wife of Eldridge Cleaver, wrote that "in order for women to obtain liberation, the struggles [Black liberation and women's rights] are going to have be united" (Giddings, 1984: 311).

This view of women's liberation within the Black Panther Party often collided with male opposition to abortion and birth control. Some male members tried to shut down family planning clinics in New Orleans and Pittsburgh (Littlewood, 1977: 97). As Angela Davis concluded, the late 1960s and early 1970s were "a period in which one of the unfortunate hallmarks of some nationalist groups was their determination to push women into the background. The brothers opposing us leaned heavily on the male supremacist trends which were winding their way through the movement" (Giddings, 1984: 317).

White conservatives saw family planning as an assault on traditional values of motherhood, while some Black radicals saw it as a race- and class-directed eugenics program; thus the assault on birth control and abortion came from both the left and the right. That such disparate forces aligned themselves against African American women proved that both white bigots and Black leaders could find common cause in the assertion of male authority over women's decisions regarding reproduction. Both tendencies sought to reverse a trend that saw women becoming more autonomous and presenting greater social and economic threats.

In contrast, African American women exerted a dynamic and aggressive influence on the family planning movement. They constituted the largest single bloc of support for family planning and were so visible that politicians in some states began to see them as a potential political force (Ward, 1986: 59). They were assisted in their efforts by coalitions of Presbyterian, Episcopal, Unitarian, Baptist, Lutheran, and Jewish congregations, representatives of which signed a "freedom-of-conscience" statement supporting the women in Pittsburgh and other cities.

African American women noticed that "most of the commotion about the clinics . . . seemed to be coming from men—men who do not have to bear children" (Littlewood, 1977: 72). Even when Black men successfully shut down clinics, as in Cleveland and Pittsburgh, women organized to reopen them because they "did not appreciate being thought of as random reproduction machines that could be put to political use" (ibid., 79), reported William Austin, who reviewed the dispute for a study by the Urban League. African American women fully understood that there were no Planned Parenthood clinics in poor white neighborhoods, but they still perceived the free services to be in their own best interests (ibid.). Quoting from Du Bois, they declared, "We're not interested in the quantity of our race. We're interested in the quality of it" (Ward, 1986: 93).

In Pittsburgh, about 70 women members of the National Welfare Rights Organization rebuffed attempts by African American men to close family planning clinics. In particular, they rejected the leadership of William "Bouie" Haden who, it was discovered, was on the payroll of the Catholic Church. "Who appointed him our leader anyhow?" inquired Georgiana Henderson. "He is only one person—and a man at that. He can't speak for the women of Homewood. . . . Why should I let one loudmouth tell me about having children?" (Littlewood, 1977: 72). Other African American women around the country declared they would not tolerate male expressions of territorial rights over women's bodies.

Shirley Chisholm, a Black congresswoman from Brooklyn, dismissed the genocide argument when asked to discuss her views on abortion and birth control: "To label family planning and legal abortion programs 'genocide' is male rhetoric, for male ears. It falls flat to female listeners and to thoughtful male ones. Women know, and so do many men, that two or three children who are wanted, prepared for, reared amid love and stability, and educated to the limit of their ability will mean more for the future of the black and brown races from which they come than any number of neglected, hungry, ill-housed and ill-clothed youngsters" (Chisolm, 1970: 114–15).

African American women were also profoundly committed to the clinics because they knew teen pregnancy and death from septic abortions were the leading causes of death for Black women. Before the legalization of abortion, 80 percent of deaths caused by illegal abortions involved Black and Puerto Rican women (A. Davis, 1983: 204). In Georgia between 1965 and 1967, the Black maternal death rate due to illegal abortion was 14 times that of white women (Tervalon, 1988: 136). Based on these grim statistics, programs to curb adolescent pregnancy and obtain contraceptives gained support in the African American community. Emphasis was also placed on establishing programs for education, like Head Start, and homes for unwed mothers. Women were not blind to the incongruity of the government plan to make contraceptives free and extremely accessible to African American communities that lacked basic health care. They used infant and maternal mortality figures to overcome resistance to family planning. "I showed them the maternal mortality statistics for the previous five years," said one birth control advocate. "Fifty-four women lost their lives during childbirth in the District of Columbia, two of them white. So if [the family planners] were really interested in something genocidal, I'd tell all the black women to go out and get pregnant, and they'll die at the rate of 25-to-1" (Littlewood, 1977: 77).

Black women succeeded in keeping family planning clinics open, and they understood the essential difference between population control and birth control in their "paired values." They organized to remove Haden as a delegate from the Homewood-Brushton Citizens Renewal Council in a demonstration of political strength that frightened both Black and white men. They also learned a valuable lesson about sexist backlash that equated Black male domination with African American progress.

A distinct Black feminist consciousness emerged to counter the reactionary views promulgated by African American men. In 1969, Frances Beal, then New York coordinator of the Black Women's Liberation Committee of the Student Nonviolent Coordinating Committee (SNCC), wrote, "Black women have the right and the responsibility to determine when it is in *the interest of the struggle to have children or not to have them and this right must not be relinquished to anyone* . . . to determine when it is in *her own best interests* to have children" (Beal, 1970: 349; emphasis in original).

This sentiment was echoed by Toni Cade (Bambara) in 1970 when she wrote, "I've been made aware of the national call to Sisters to abandon birth control . . . to picket family planning centers and abortion-referral groups and to raise revolutionaries. What plans do you have for the care of me and the child?" (Petchesky, 1990: 137). Black feminists argued that birth control and abortion were, in themselves, revolutionary—and that African American liberation in any sense could not be won without women controlling their lives. The birth control pill, in and of itself, could not liberate the African American woman, but it "gives her the time to fight for liberation in those other areas" (Petchesky, 1990: 172).

By the late 1960s, family planning became "synonymous with the civil rights of poor women to medical care" (Ward, 1986: xiii). It was regarded as a key to the prevention of disease and death, and as a public health measure to address many of society's problems. However, African American women warily watched state legislative proposals to sterilize poor women who had too many "illegitimate" children, which fueled the genocide debate. None of the proposals succeeded, largely because of the militance of women like Fannie Lou Hamer, who said that "six out of every ten Negro women were . . . sterilized for no reason at all. Often the women were not told that they had been sterilized until they were released from the hospital" (Littlewood, 1977: 80). A national fertility study conducted by Princeton University found that 20 percent of all married African American women had been sterilized by 1970 (A. Davis, 1990: 23).

To African American women, it seemed absurd to coerce them to limit their family size through involuntary sterilization when they were willing to do so voluntarily if safe methods were accessible. This combined support for birth control and abortion and opposition to sterilization, a view unique to African American women at the time, did much to inform both the feminist and the civil rights movements in later decades. African American women rejected the single-issue focus of the women's movement on abortion, which excluded other issues of reproductive freedom. They also opposed the myopic focus on race of the male-dominated civil rights movement, which ignored concerns of gender equality.

Conclusion

> Historical patterns suggest that just as Black women are vital to
> Black movements, Black movements are vital to the progress of
> feminist movements. Feminism always had the greatest currency
> in times of Black militancy or immediately thereafter. (Giddings,
> 1984: 340)

African American women have always been concerned about our fertility, despite the myths and assumptions of others. When birth control and abortion were available, African American women used them. When they were not, women resorted to dangerous methods limited only by their imaginations and physiology.

It is critical that the civil rights and the feminist movements acknowledge this history. We understand that we are needed in both movements, but we refuse to be pawns in a population numbers game or tokens to colorize a white movement. As we deepen our understanding of our history, we will reconceptualize how our activism is recorded, because male-dominated or Eurocentric views of the political process produce definitions of power, activism, and resistance that fail to capture the meaning of these concepts in the lives of African American women (Collins, 1991: 140).

The fast-paced growth and militancy of the African American women's movement will probably produce, again, its own form of backlash from some African American men, a reaction that I call "blacklash." As Paula Giddings has predicted, "We are entering, once more, an era of Black assertiveness, one which will trigger historical tensions over the relationship of race and sex" (Giddings, 1984: 349). These tensions, however, will not keep us from taking control over our lives. As the Black Women's Liberation Group of Mount Vernon, New York wrote in 1970, "Birth control [including abortion] is the freedom to *fight* genocide of black women and children" (Black Women's Liberation Group, 1970: 360–61).

Winning reproductive freedom will reward African American women with true choices in our lives. We may learn, along the journey, to trust in the words of Audre Lorde:

> For Black women, learning to consciously extend ourselves to each other and to call upon each other's strengths is a life-saving strategy. In the best of circumstances surrounding our lives, it requires an enormous amount of mutual, consistent support for us to be emotionally able to look straight into the face of the powers aligned against us and still do our work with joy. It takes determination and practice. (Lorde, 1988: 123)

NOTE

1. Telephone interview by the author with Nkenge Toure, former member of the Black Panther Party, March 8, 1992, Washington, D.C.

REFERENCES

Baehr, Ninia. 1990. *Abortion without Apology: A Radical History for the 1990s.* Boston: South End Press.

Beal, Frances M. 1970. "Double Jeopardy: To Be Black and Female." In Morgan, pp. 340–53.

Black Women's Liberation Group, Mount Vernon, New York. 1970. "Statement on Birth Control." In Morgan, pp. 360–61.

Blee, Kathleen. 1991. *Women of the Klan: Racism and Gender in the 1920s.* Berkeley: University of California Press.

Burgher, Mary. 1979. "Images of Self and Race in the Autobiographies of Black Women." In Roseann P. Bell, Bettye J. Parker, and Beverly Guy-Sheftall, eds., *Sturdy Black Bridges: Visions of Black Women in Literature,* pp. 107–22. New York: Anchor Books.

Butler, Edith. 1988. "The First National Conference on Black Women's Heath Issues." In Worcester and Whatley, pp. 37–42.

Chisolm, Shirley. 1970. *Unbought and Unbossed.* Special limited ed. New York: Hodge Taylor Associates.

Collins, Kimberly A. 1991. *Slightly Off Center.* Atlanta: Say It Loud Press.

Collins, Patricia Hill. 1991. *Black Feminist Thought: Knowledge, Consciousness, and the Politics of Empowerment.* London: Routledge.

Corea, Gena. 1985. *The Hidden Malpractice: How American Medicine Mistreats Women.* New York: Harper & Row.

Davis, Angela. 1983. *Women, Race and Class.* New York: Vintage Books.

———. 1990. "Racism, Birth Control and Reproductive Rights." In Marlene Gerber Fried, ed., *From Abortion to Reproductive Freedom: Transforming a Movement,* pp. 15–26. Boston: South End Press.

Davis, Susan E., ed. 1988. *Women under Attack: Victories, Backlash and the Fight for Reproductive Freedom.* Committee for Abortion Rights and against Sterilization Abuse. Boston: South End Press.

Giddings, Paula. 1984. *When and Where I Enter . . . : The Impact of Black Women on Race and Sex in America.* New York: William Morrow.

Gordon, Linda. 1990. *Woman's Body, Woman's Right: Birth Control in America.* Rev. ed. New York: Penguin.

Hartmann, Betsy. 1987. *Reproductive Rights and Wrongs: The Global Politics of Population Control and Contraceptive Choice.* New York: Harper & Row.

Henshaw, Stanley K., Lisa M. Koonin, and Jack C. Smith. 1991. "Characteristics of U.S. Women Having Abortions, 1987." *Family Planning Perspectives* 23, no. 2 (March/April): 75–81.

hooks, bell. 1989. *Talking Back: Thinking Feminist, Thinking Black.* Boston: South End Press.

Joseph, Gloria I., and Jill Lewis. 1981. *Common Differences: Conflicts in Black and White Feminist Perspectives.* Boston: South End Press.

Lerner, Gerda. 1972. *Black Women in White America.* New York: Vintage Books.

Littlewood, Thomas B. 1977. *The Politics of Population Control.* Notre Dame: University of Notre Dame Press.

Lorde, Audre. 1988. *A Burst of Light.* Ithaca, N.Y.: Firebrand Books.

Morgan, Robin, ed. 1970. *Sisterhood Is Powerful: An Anthology of Writings from the Women's Liberation Movement.* New York: Random House.

Petchesky, Rosalind Pollack. 1990. *Abortion and Woman's Choice: The State, Sexuality and Reproductive Freedom.* Rev. ed. Boston: Northeastern University Press.

Rodrique, Jessie M. 1990. "The Black Community and the Birth-Control Movement." In Ellen Carol DuBois and Vicki L. Ruiz, eds., *Unequal Sisters: A Multicultural Reader in U.S. Women's History,* pp. 333–42. London: Routledge.

Simmons, Judy D. 1990. "Abortion: A Matter of Choice." In Evelyn C. White, pp. 120–27.

Sterling, Dorothy, ed. 1984. *We Are Your Sisters: Black Women in the Nineteenth Century.* New York: W. W. Norton.

Tervalon, Melanie. 1988. "Black Women's Reproductive Rights." In Worcester and Whately, pp. 136–37.

Ward, Martha C. 1986. *Poor Women, Powerful Men: America's Great Experiment in Family Planning.* Boulder: Westview Press.

White, Deborah Gray. 1985. *Ar'n't I a Woman? Female Slaves in the Plantation South.* New York: W. W. Norton.

White, Evelyn C., ed. 1990. *The Black Women's Health Book: Speaking for Ourselves.* Seattle: Seal Press.

Worcester, Nancy, and Mariamne H. Whatley, eds. 1988. *Women's Health: Readings on Social, Economic, and Political Issues.* Dubuque: Kendall/Hunt.

13.

The Alternative Birth Movement in the United States
History and Current Status

JOAN J. MATHEWS AND KATHLEEN ZADAK

The alternative birth movement is a reaction by women against a predominately male medical establishment that has controlled obstetrical care in the United States. Most vocal in this reaction are women of childbearing age and nurse midwives. The movement developed from a realization that medical interests had appropriated a natural process and turned it into a depersonalized medical procedure in which women had no voice.

From the turn of the century through the 1960s the birthing process was almost completely removed from the domain of women. By the early 1970s the medicalization of childbirth, with its emphasis on technological intervention and depersonalizing procedures, had created a crisis in American birthing. In reaction, an increase in home births among educated, middle-class Americans began to take place. The response of the obstetrical community to the home birth trend was to appease public demand for a more personalized, family-centered, patient-controlled birthing experience; however, the medical establishment still maintained medical control over most decisions. The changes instituted took the form of a more homelike setting for labor and delivery, the diminution of unnecessary procedures, and a decrease in the use of technological interventions for women who chose "alternative" birthing methods. However, in keeping with medicine's desire to maintain control over its practice, these new alternatives to traditional medical obstetrical management are restricted almost exclusively to highly motivated, well-prepared women who anticipate a completely normal pregnancy and delivery. Thus, alternative birth methods symbolically meet the demands of parents-to-be while they maintain the control and prerogatives of the obstetrical com-

Reprinted from *Women and Health* 17 (1991): 39–58. Copyright © 1991 by The Haworth Press, Inc., Binghamton, N.Y.; reprinted by permission of the publisher.

munity. This paper (1) traces the historical antecedents and social factors leading to the alternative birthing movement, (2) describes the types of alternative birthing methods and the freedom and controls each exerts upon the parturient woman, and (3) describes the ways in which the obstetrical community has maintained and rationalized dominance over the birthing process in the United States.

Historical Perspective

Throughout most of the world the birthing process is managed primarily by women, and family participation takes a central place in the birthing experience (Mead and Newton 1967; Kay 1982; McCormack 1982; Jordan 1983). Similarly, birthing practice in the United States was managed predominately by women until the present century. Although "lying-in" hospitals had been built in the nineteenth century, these were established mainly for indigent women (Speert 1980). The preferred location for giving childbirth remained the private home.

Shortly after the turn of the century several factors combined to lead to the displacement of the home and the emergence of the hospital as the place for giving birth. These factors included the proliferation of hospitals and the development of modern nursing to provide continuous observation and care, the evolution of structured medical education with the consequent need for large numbers of women to be in one place for medical student experience, and the emergence of specialization within medicine, including the development of the specialty of obstetrics.

About 1915 the use of scopolamine during labor was introduced. This agent induced amnesia to erase the memory of pain and produce "twilight sleep" labor. The use of this procedure required careful supervision, which hospitals and nurses could provide. Ironically, while women were demanding access to scopolamine, physicians were highly divided about its desirability (Leavitt 1980). However, services followed demand, and hospitals responded by facilitating its use in the delivery of babies.

At the turn of the century more than 95 percent of babies were born at home (Wertz and Wertz 1977). However, it became fashionable among upper-class women to give birth in a hospital with a male physician in attendance. By 1940 more than half of births were taking place in hospitals. Following World War II a rapid rise in hospital births occurred, so that by 1945 78.9 percent of births took place in these institutions. This was followed by a gradual increase to 99 percent by 1969, a rate that has remained constant (National Center for Health Statistics 1988).

Although the hospital birth rate climbed through the first half of the twenti-eth century, many deliveries continued to be managed at home, especially among rural and low-income urban women. Increasingly, educated nurse-midwives re-placed lay midwives in the management of maternity care and birthing. This change in attendants was facilitated by the development of social service agencies that arose to meet the needs of underserved women. Early agencies for the care of indigent pregnant women and the training of professional midwives were New York's Maternity Center Association (established 1915), Frontier Nursing Service in rural Kentucky (1925), and Chicago Maternity Center (1932).

Following the transformation of maternity care for middle-class women to a physician-dominated specialty, professional nurse-midwives were allowed to prac-tice only among medically indigent women. In the 1950s nurse-midwives at-tempted to gain access to hospitals, since this was where the majority of women were giving birth. However, their entry was confined to public hospitals, which largely served the poor (Burst 1985). In the 1960s nurse-midwives became more in-fluential because of their participation in maternal-infant programs sponsored by the federal government under the Johnson administration. Although these pro-grams were designed to meet the needs of urban and rural underserved women, nurse-midwifery came to be valued for safe obstetrical outcome, cost reduction, and patient satisfaction by educated consumers in the private sector. Thus, nurse-midwifery was in a position to nurture and provide services for the alternative birthing movement that emerged in the 1970s and 1980s.

Impetus for Change

Consumer dissatisfaction with the medical management of birthing began as early as the 1940s. Having appropriated birthing from lay midwives and the home, the male-dominated medical community turned the process into a completely mech-anistic procedure. The laboring woman was subjected to procedures that were often more ritualistic than scientific (Haire 1976; Jordan 1983). The delivering woman was physically restrained, heavily draped, and veiled under general anes-thesia. The mother was separated from her spouse during delivery and from her in-fant shortly after delivery. As Arney and Neill note, the woman's psychology and subjective experience never entered into the physician's awareness or decision mak-ing (1982).

The first efforts to humanize maternity care emerged in the 1940s as the "pre-pared" or "natural" childbirth movement began to take form. The concept of psy-choprophylaxis to gain control over fear and pain associated with labor was imported from England (Dick-Read 1944) and France (Lamaze 1958). Around this time obstetrical practice underwent a transition as the fetus was recognized as the second patient. Concern developed for its environment and for the effects of pain-relieving medications on fetal outcome. This resulted in a move away from general anesthesia and toward the increased use of local anesthesia (Arney and Neill 1982).

The nursing profession also had an impact on changing the obstetrical environment. Nurses, studying the effects of natural childbirth on a woman's experience, began to teach breathing and relaxation techniques in prenatal care classes (Burst 1983). About this time a nurse-midwife implemented the concept of rooming-in (Burst 1983), an arrangement that allowed the mother and her infant to be cared for in the same room. Rooming-in was intended to facilitate mother-father-infant bonding. However, because of resistance by both nurses and mothers, rooming-in often meant little more than the infant being brought to the mother for several hours a day.

In spite of these efforts to refocus the birth experience onto the woman, her partner, and the infant, most women continued to give birth in hospitals. Through the 1970s and 1980s this practice was enhanced by the ability of physicians to manage pregnancy in "high risk" women such as those with diabetes and heart disease and by the advent of powerful technologies used to save pre-term infants.

The natural childbirth movement gained momentum when it converged with the feminist and consumer movements of the late 1960s and 1970s. At issue in all three movements was control and decision making in what had become a paternalistic environment. A predominant theme of the feminist movement was the idea of women regaining control over their bodies in relation to reproductive functions and the obstetrical experience. Increasing numbers of women would no longer submit passively to medical paternalism. Instead, they wanted the birthing experience to proceed on their own terms, and to some extent in their own territory.

The consumer movement in health care found expression in the questioning of physicians, the seeking of second medical opinions, comparison shopping for medical services, and self-help programs. The latter included self-diagnosis of pregnancy, husband-coached labor, and home birthing. The consumer movement placed particular emphasis on public education and informed choice. During the 1970s no fewer than ten national organizations were formed by consumers and professionals who were allied in their beliefs concerning the management of childbirth (Koek and Martin 1988). Organizations such as the International Childbirth Education Association and the American Society for Psychoprophylaxis in Obstetrics arose to challenge the necessity of "routine" obstetrical practice, to question the effectiveness and possible iatrogenic effects of technological intervention, and to press for family-centered maternity care. Feminist and consumer texts of the era informed women about their consumer rights and provided information regarding birthing alternatives (Boston Women's Health Book Collective 1971; Ashford 1983).

Conventional Birthing

The traditional design of obstetrical units in the United States is based on the surgical transfer system and specialized provider functions. In this system the woman is placed in one room for the duration of labor, transferred to a surgically equipped suite for delivery, and subsequently separated from her infant when she is moved to a recovery area and the baby is moved to a newborn nursery. Separate nursing staffs render services in each of these areas, and a pediatrician oversees the neonate upon its transfer to the nursery. In addition to its impersonal elements and fragmented care, this system is cost inefficient, since it requires separate nursing staffs as well as duplication of equipment and supplies.

Until the alternative birthing movement had a liberating influence on conventional obstetrics, procedures such as shaving the perineum, giving enemas, confining the laboring woman to bed, withholding maternal nutrition, and placing the woman in lithotomy position for delivery were routine. The application of obstetrical technologies became standard practice. Analgesia, local anesthesia, induction and augmentation of labor, and electronic fetal monitoring are now common. Surgical delivery of the infant by means of cesarean section is increasingly performed (Young and Mahan 1980). These technologies have potential physical and psychosocial hazards. For instance, pharmacological stimulation of labor may increase fetal heart rate, and chemical methods of pain relief for the mother may produce respiratory depression in the newborn (Bowers 1970). The use of analgesics and the immediate separation of mother and infant may interfere with the development of early parent-infant attachment, which is believed to be essential to stimulate appropriate parenting behavior (Klaus and Kinnel 1976).

Alternative Methods of Birthing

Until the mid-1970s the only alternative women had to conventional obstetrical care was home birth. Initially, home birth gained popularity in the California counterculture of the 1960s. Nationally, the home birth movement gained momentum as a result of criticism of the American method of childbirth. One of the most vocal critics was Suzanne Arms (1975), who advocated home birth as the only way in which women could retain control over their birth experience.

The safety of home birth, however, has been a greatly debated issue. Health professionals argue that home birth should not be encouraged. In 1977 the executive director of the American College of Obstetricians and Gynecologists even declared that home birth constituted "child abuse" and "maternal trauma" (ACOG official 1977). However, evidence from countries where home birth is widely practiced demonstrates that this method can be safe. Japan, Denmark, Sweden, and the Netherlands report infant mortality rates well below that of the United States (Foster 1981; Jordan 1983). In the United States home birth outcome statistics also support the safety of this method of delivery. The Frontier Nursing Service in Appalachia performed home births for 23 years without a single maternal death, and the Chicago Maternity Center performed over 12,000 home births from 1950 to 1960 without a maternal death (Jensen and Bobak 1985). The national maternal mortality incidence during this period was 8.3 per 10,000 births (National Center for Health Statistics 1984). In spite of these promising statistics, health care professionals armed themselves to turn the tide against home births and to ensure that birthing remained a medically conducted process. This effort took the form of alternative birth settings.

An alternative birth setting is any medically supervised, nonconventional birth setting. Such a setting may be located within a hospital or it may be a free-standing birth center (FSBC) separate from a hospital. The structure within a hospital combines labor, delivery, and recovery (LDR) and sometimes postpartum (LDRP) within a single room. Free-standing birth centers are structurally and administratively separate from a hospital (Burst 1983). However, they have arrangements for expeditious transfer of the laboring woman to a hospital should complications arise. The earliest freestanding centers were established by not-for-profit agencies and many were administered and staffed by nurse-midwives. Soon for-profit health care corporations began developing FSBCs (Johnson 1983).

The first in-hospital birth room was developed at Manchester Memorial Hospital in 1969 (Sumner and Philips 1981). This was a rudimentary setup that consisted of little more than a conventional hospital room with curtains on the window. The first freestanding center was opened in 1975 by the Maternity Center Association, New York (Lubic 1981). The concept of alternative birth centers grew rapidly. In 1975 there were only three FSBCs, but by 1987 the number had increased to 160 (Rooks et al. 1989). In 1979, 158 hospital-based alternative birthing centers were identifiable (Jensen and Bobak 1985). By 1987, 80 percent of the nation's 3,700 hospital maternity care units had some form of single room maternity care (Perry 1989).

Whether hospital-based or freestanding, alternative birth settings have similar ideological and structural approaches. Ideologically, most adherents of alternative birthing view birth as a normal process rather than an illness. They encourage participation by the mother in decision making, and they seek participation by "significant others," including the father and siblings; they avoid unnecessary invasive procedures, and they provide continuity of care throughout the experience.

A pregnant woman and her "significant other" birth attendants must be highly committed to an alternative birth experience. This usually requires consistent prenatal care, attendance at prepared childbirth classes, and preadmission orientation to the unit. In some settings candidacy also requires a commitment to unmedicated labor and delivery. The use of technological intervention varies from center to center. Analgesia, local anesthesia, episiotomy, forceps delivery, electronic fetal monitoring, and oxytocin may or may not be employed (NACC 1985).

When a woman decides to use an alternative birth approach, she and the primary health care professional negotiate a plan of care. This establishes whether medications will be used, which support persons will be in attendance, and whether the mother plans to breast-feed. However, decisions concerning technological intervention or transfer to conventional care remain within the judgment of the attending midwife or physician.

Although some early centers were founded on the philosophy that alternative-style birthing could be managed regardless of the woman's physical condition, current eligibility criteria usually eliminate all women who are expected to have a complicated pregnancy or delivery. In some centers the list of conditions that qualify as potential complications is extremely comprehensive. Therefore, women who are marginally in danger may be barred from selecting an alternative birthing option. For instance, a woman who has had several normal deliveries may be excluded because a history of pregnancies is defined as a potentially hazardous condition. In addition, policies allow for any woman who is admitted to an alternative birth center to be transferred to conventional obstetrical care for a variety of potential complications. At least two factors have led to the current conservative approach. One is the potential threat by obstetricians to use legal or coercive means to close alternative birth centers. Such threats, although based on fear of competition, are usually voiced as concerns about maternal and infant safety. This has led freestanding centers to transfer women to a back-up hospital at the first sign of potential difficulty. Another is the increase in litigation over undesired obstetrical outcomes. This has encouraged the use of technological monitoring and intervention for any fetus considered to be even minimally "at risk."

Structurally, alternative birth settings provide a single room for labor, delivery, and recovery; minimal intrusion by health professionals; and a homelike environment with such amenities as carpeting, artwork, refrigerators, and television. As consumers have increased their demands, hospitals have added whirlpool tubs, champagne dinners, hair stylists, and even fireplaces. The self-contained birthing and recovery room permits the mother, infant, and other significant persons to remain together.

In summary, alternative birth settings represent a model of family-centered, personalized obstetrical care in which the mother may exercise control over nonmedical decisions. Even then, agency policies may prescribe who can attend the mother, how many persons at a time may be in attendance, how long the baby remains with the mother after birth, and so on.

Medical Response and Rationale

In 1978 the Interprofessional Task Force on Health Care of Women and Children issued the *Joint Position Statement on the Development of Family-Centered Maternity/Newborn Care in Hospitals* (ACOG 1978). The task force was composed of representatives from the American College of Obstetricians and Gynecologists, the American Academy of Pediatrics, the Nurses Association of the American College of Obstetricians and Gynecologists, the American College of Nurse Midwives, and the American Nurses Association. The task force was convened to provide an official response to consumer demands for changes in traditional obstetrical practice. The task force's document espoused a philosophy of family-centered care and identified ways in which a satisfying birth experience could be achieved. In-hospital birth rooms were described as one alternative.

Following this recognition by organized professional groups that some changes were needed in maternity care, the American College of Nurse Midwives published guidelines for the establishment of home birth services, hospital birth rooms, and freestanding birth centers (ACNW 1979). The American Public Health Association also endorsed the establishment of demonstration projects in freestanding centers (Eakins 1984). As the concept of out-of-hospital alternative birth centers grew, the association published guidelines for their licensing and regulation (American Public Health Association 1983). Ironically, at this same time the American College of Obstetricians and Gynecologists was joined by the American Academy of Pediatrics in the issuance of a joint statement that opposed freestanding alternative birth centers and endorsed only the hospital as a safe environment for labor, delivery, and the postpartum period (ACOG 1983). This position was reiterated in 1988 (ACOG 1988). The American College of Obstetricians and Gynecologists also released a policy statement disapproving of home birth (ACOG 1982).

Why did organized medicine recognize the need for radical change in obstetrical care, yet reject all but in-hospital methods of birthing? The safety of mother and infant is the issue upon which the medical profession based its objections to out-of-hospital birth. Additional issues, however, are that physicians fear economic competition and resist loss of control over obstetrical practice.

The view promoted by many physicians is that out-of-hospital childbirth is unsafe because of a lack of immediately available technology and operating room facilities. Analysis of alternative center birth data by physicians often concludes that the transfer of some women to a conventional obstetrical setting is adequate evidence that the hospital is superior to a freestanding center (Averitt 1980; DeJong 1981). Many obstetricians cite the long-term decline in maternal and infant mortality as proof that traditional in-hospital obstetrical care is safer than other forms of birthing. This argument does not consider the effects of improved prenatal care, better nutrition, and fewer pregnancies on improved mortality rates. Likewise, physicians fail to appreciate the excellent outcomes of out-of-hospital centers and of home birth services both in the United States and abroad. For instance, Lieberman and Ryan (1989) question the significance of a study of outcomes among 12,000 freestanding birth center patients (Rooks et al. 1989) because "a large number of centers did not participate in the survey."

On the other hand, alternative childbirth advocates cite the decreased risk of infection, absence of iatrogenic injuries due to technological interventions, and lower maternal and infant mortality rates as evidence that the natural process of birthing is safer than the high technology medical model. Proponents of alternative methods of birthing also conclude that transfers (16 percent) (Rooks et al. 1989) reflect a conservative adherence to transfer guidelines imposed by operational policies of freestanding centers.

The real issues in the debate over the location for childbirth are loss of control and the competition created by freestanding centers that can offer maternity services at costs substantially lower than fees typically charged by hospitals and obstetricians.

In-hospital obstetrical services were slow to respond to consumer demand through the actual establishment of homelike birthing rooms. Hospital finances, physician convenience and training, and nursing staff resistance contributed to the hospital situation.

In many hospitals, obstetrical services are provided primarily as a community service, while the hospital depends on more expensive services for revenue production. In the 1970s some hospital administrators resisted expending money for physical plant conversions for a service that does not, overall, produce significant revenues. This has changed in the 1980s as the marketing of hospital services has become essential for hospital survival (Alpern 1987). Further, studies show that women make most of their families' health care purchasing decisions. Hospital administrators believe that a satisfied maternity customer is likely to return to the same hospital for other services (Petty 1989). The use of expensive technologies for normal patients also distributes capital expenditures for equipment that must be obtained for high-risk patients. This also served to discourage the development of alternative birth services.

Physicians frequently resist even minor changes in practice. The inconveniences of having to stoop to deal with a delivery bed, subdued lighting, and significant others "getting in the way" have been used by obstetricians to resist new practices. Physicians who have been trained to view pregnancy as an illness and delivery as a form of surgery have also resisted the changes necessitated by a new approach. Moreover, the rise of obstetrical litigation makes physicians reluctant to abandon the technology that they view as essential for detecting and intervening in fetal distress. Some nursing staffs also have opposed alternative birthing because change requires them to alter routines and to relinquish their power to other women. In many cases where in-hospital birth rooms were developed in response to out-of-hospital competition, physicians and nurses have merely utilized these facilities without changing either their attitudes or their practices (Klein and Westreich 1983).

While hospitals resisted change, other agents arose to fill the need for a different type of maternity service. These were the freestanding birth centers. Several factors combined to allow freestanding centers to charge a moderate fee that created competition for hospitals and obstetricians. A significant cost-saving factor is the reduction of overhead costs. These include stand-by technology, laboratory services, delivery suites, and redundant nursing staff. Second, insurance carriers initially did not cover out-of-hospital maternity services, so that clients of freestanding centers had to pay the costs themselves. This situation induced freestanding centers to obtain voluntary physician and hospital back-up services in order to hold fees down. Third, freestanding centers often were staffed by nurse-midwives, who themselves command low fees as compared to obstetricians.

Freestanding birth centers provide professional care and delivery services for fees 50 percent below the fees for delivery by a physician in a hospital (HIAA 1989). Within a short time the major insurance carriers became avid proponents of out-of-hospital birth centers because of the low cost of these services.

Economic competition is not the only source of physician objection to freestanding centers. The conflict between obstetricians and midwives over the control of maternity services has a lengthy history (Ehrenreich 1973). Throughout much of this century physicians confined nurse-midwifery practice to the rural and urban poor. Obstetricians excluded nurse-midwives from serving middle-class patients by refusing to provide back-up physician services and by influencing hospitals to deny admitting privileges to nurse-midwives. This prevented nurse-midwives from being able to make referrals for middle-class women who developed complications. The poor traditionally have no such options. In recent years, however, the momentum of the alternative birth movement has permitted nurse-midwives access to a portion of the middle-class maternity services market. Nevertheless, the total number of births attended by midwives outside the hospital is a minuscule 0.4 percent (National Center for Health Statistics 1988).

Conclusions

During the 1970s conventional obstetrics focused on advancements in technology. Women who formerly could not safely bring a fetus to term often could be successfully managed to sustain pregnancy at least until the fetus achieved probable viability. Powerful technologies and neonatal intensive care units were developed to save and nurture low birth weight, underdeveloped infants. Even in normal pregnancies, new technologies made it possible to monitor the development of the fetus, and to induce delivery when there was indication of fetal "distress" or maternal dystocia (difficult labor).

Concurrent with the reliance on technology outlined above, there was a growing trend in society for a more naturalistic, family-centered birth process in which the couple and their experience, not medical personnel and their protocols, were the center of attention. These developments essentially are mutually exclusive.

One consumer-driven response to this conflict was to remove childbirth from the province of the hospital. At first the only available alternative was home birth. Health care professionals, believing that home birth was inherently unsafe, developed other family-centered, homelike birth alternatives. Alternative birth settings developed either as in-hospital birth rooms or freestanding birth centers. These alternatives expanded rapidly during the late 1970s and early 1980s.

Currently, the design, philosophy, and policies of both types of alternative birth settings are similar. Both offer a homelike, low technology atmosphere and family-centered care. Both employ a medically conservative approach that eliminates all women who are expected to have a complicated pregnancy or delivery. In addition, women who are admitted to an alternative setting may be transferred to conventional obstetric care if a medical problem develops.

Some writers (DeVries 1980; Eakins 1984) suggest that alternative birthing co-opts women by allowing them to make only those decisions which are nonmedical while health care professionals remain in control of the birthing process. There is another possible explanation. The alternative birth movement is largely a phenomenon of well-educated, self-determining women. For many women in this group, childbearing is a planned occurrence that will happen only once or twice in a lifetime. For many women, and their partners, a perfect pregnancy outcome is imperative. This expectation is reflected by the sharp increase in maternity-related malpractice suits in recent years. Therefore, many well-educated, middle-class women demand ultrasonography during pregnancy, accede to electronic fetal monitoring for early recognition of fetal distress, want analgesia during labor, and readily accept cesarean section. In other words, many middle-class women trust technology yet desire the family-centered, homelike environment provided by alternative birth services. This position is supported by published data. Even though 85–90 percent of women will have a normal labor and delivery (Moore 1983: 466), only 1 percent of births occur outside the hospital (National Center for Health Statistics 1988). A 1981 study conducted by the American College of Obstetricians and Gynecologists involving 102 hospitals with alternative birth rooms reported only a 16 percent utilization of alternative birth services (ACOG 1981).

It is unlikely that technology will be abandoned in an effort to personalize childbirth. DeVries (1980) notes that to do so would deny years of accumulated medical knowledge and research. More likely, the future will see hospitals developing more alternative birthing rooms, although currently most hospitals have converted only one or two rooms to LDRs. This will occur in order for hospitals to keep their vast share of maternity care. In addition, freestanding centers will continue to develop. Some industry consultants predict that more FSBCs will be owned and operated by physicians, although physicians themselves will not necessarily provide the care ("Maternity Services Shift" 1985). It is likely that technology will seep into these facilities. The rationale will be cost-effectiveness and safety.

Hospitals currently are finding ways to facilitate personalized, family-centered care for high-risk women. This approach reflects a response to consumer demands more than it does changes in physician acceptance of nonconventional birthing. As hospitals have become increasingly market-oriented, they have committed millions of dollars for the development of LDRs. This trend has spawned the development of new industries in conversion consultation and the manufacture of furniture-like birthing beds, bassinets, and headboards that conceal stand-by monitoring and emergency equipment, radiant heat ceiling pads to warm mother and baby, ceiling retractable obstetrical lamps, and other items designed to naturalize birthing. Clearly, the alternative birth movement has initiated a major transformation in the birthing process in the United States.

REFERENCES

American College of Nurse Midwives (ACNM). 1979. *Guidelines for Establishing a Home Birth Service. Guidelines for Establishing a Hospital Birth Room. Guidelines for Establishing an Alternative Birth Center.* Washington, D.C.: American College of Nurse Midwives.

American College of Obstetricians and Gynecologists (ACOG). 1978. *Interprofessional Task Force on Health Care of Women and Children, Joint Position Statement on the Development of Family Centered Maternity/Newborn Care in Hospitals.* Chicago: American College of Obstetricians and Gynecologists.

———. 1981. *Alternative Birthing Centers: A Survey and Bibliography.* Washington, D.C.: American College of Obstetricians and Gynecologists.

———. 1982. *ACOG Statement of Policy: Alternative Birth Centers.* Washington, D.C.: American College of Obstetricians and Gynecologists.

———. 1983. *Guidelines for Perinatal Care.* Elk Grove Village, Ill.: American Academy of Pediatrics; Washington, D.C.: American College of Obstetricians and Gynecologists.

———. 1988. *Guidelines for Perinatal Care.* 2d ed. Elk Grove Village, Ill.: American Academy of Pediatrics.

ACOG official. 1977. "Home Delivery 'Maternal Trauma, Child Abuse.'" *OB-GYN News,* October 1, 1977, 1.

Alpern, B. B. 1987. *Reaching Women: The Way to Go in Marketing Health Care Services.* Chicago: Pluribus Press.

American Public Health Association. 1983. "Guidelines for Licensing and Regulating Birth Centers." *American Journal of Public Health* 73:331–34.

Arms, S. 1975. *Immaculate Deception: A New Look at Women and Childbirth in America.* Boston: Houghton Mifflin.

Arney, W. R., and J. Neill. 1982. "The Location of Pain in Childbirth: Natural Childbirth and the Transformation of Obstetrics." *Sociology of Health and Illness* 4 (1): 1–24.

Ashford, J. I., ed. 1983. *The Whole Birth Catalog: A Sourcebook for Choices in Childbirth.* Trumansburg, N.Y.: Crossing Press.

Averitt, S. S. 1980. "Adapting the Birthing Center Concept to a Traditional Hospital Setting." *JOGN Nursing* 9 (March/April): 103–6.

Boston Women's Health Book Collective. 1976. *Our Bodies, Our Selves.* New York: Simon and Schuster.

Bowes, W. A. 1970. "Obstetrical Medication and Infant Outcome: A Review of the Literature." In *The Effects of Obstetrical Medication on Fetus and Infant,* 3–23. Monographs of the Society for Research in Child Development, vol. 35, no. 4. Chicago: University of Chicago Press for the Society for Research in Child Development.

Burst, H. V. 1983. "The Influence of Consumers on the Birthing Movement." *Topics in Clinical Nursing* 8 (3): 42–54.

———. 1985. "Alternative Birth Settings and Providers." In J. C. McClaskey and H. K. Grace, eds., *Current Issues in Nursing.* Boston: Blackwell Scientific Publications.

DeJong, R. N., K. S. Kirkwood, and K. Camacho. 1981. "An Out-of-Hospital Birth Center Using University Referral." *Obstetrics and Gynecology* 58 (6): 703–7.

DeVries, R. G. 1980. "The Alternative Birth Center: Option or Cooptation?" *Women and Health* 5 (3): 47–61.

Dick-Read, G. 1944. *Childbirth without Fear.* New York: Harper and Brothers.

Eakins, P. S. 1984. "The Rise of the Free-Standing Birth Center: Principles and Practice." *Women and Health* 9 (4): 49–64.

Ehrenreich, B. 1973. *Witches, Midwives and Nurses: A History of Women Healers.* Westbury, N.Y.: Feminist Press.

Foster, F. H. 1981. "Trends in Perinatal Mortality." *World Health Statistics Quarterly* 34 (3): 138–46.

Haire, D. B. 1976. *The Cultural Warping of Childbirth.* Minneapolis: International Childbirth Education Association.

Health Insurance Association of America (HIAA). 1989. *The Cost of Maternity Care and Childbirth in the United States.* New York: HIAA.

Jensen, M. D., and I. M. Bobak. 1985. *Maternity and Gynecological Care.* St. Louis: Mosby.

Johnson, D. E. 1983. "40% of Births in Hospitals Could be Borne by Birthing Centers." *Modern Healthcare* 13:124.

Jordan, B. 1983. *Birth in Four Cultures: A Cross-Cultural Investigation of Childbirth in Yucatan, Holland, Sweden and the United States.* Montreal: Eden Press.

Kay, M. A. 1982. *Anthropology of Human Birth.* Philadelphia: F. A. Davis.

Klaus, M. H., and J. H. Kinnell. 1976. *Maternal-Infant Bonding: The Impact of Early Separation or Loss on Family Development.* St. Louis: Mosby.

Klein, M., and R. Westreich. 1983. "Birth Room Transfer and Procedure Rates: What Do They Tell about the Setting?" *Birth* 10 (2): 93–97.

Koek, K. E., and S. B. Martin, eds. 1988. *Encyclopedia of Associations.* Vol. 1, *National Organizations of the United States.* Detroit: Gale Research.

Lamaze, F. 1958. *Painless Childbirth: Psychoprophylactic Method.* Chicago: Henry Regnery.

Leavitt, J. W. 1980. "Birthing and Anesthesia: The Debate over Twilight Sleep." *Signs: Journal of Women in Culture and Society* 6 (1): 147–64.

Lieberman, E., and K. J. Ryan. 1989. "Birth-Day Choices." *New England Journal of Medicine* 321 (26): 1824–25.

Lubic, R. W. 1981. "Alternative Maternity Care: Resistance and Change." In S. Romalis, ed., *Childbirth: Alternatives to Medical Control,* 217–49. Austin: University of Texas Press.

MacCormak, C. P. 1982. *Ethnography of Fertility and Birth.* London: Academic Press.

"Maternity Services Shift in Response to Consumer Demand." 1985. *Hospitals* 59 (8): 82, 84, 88.

Mead, M., and N. Newton. 1967. "Cultural Patterning of Perinatal Behavior." In S. A. Richardson and A. F. Guttmacher, eds., *Childbearing: Its Social and Psychological Aspects.* Baltimore: Williams and Wilkins.

Moore, M. 1983. *Realities in Childbearing.* 2d ed. Philadelphia: W. B. Saunders.

National Association of Childbearing Centers (NACC). 1985. *Birth Center Update: 1983 NACC Survey.* Perkiomenville, Pa.: National Association of Childbearing Centers.

National Center for Health Statistics. 1984. "Advance Report of Final Mortality Statistics." *Monthly Vital Statistics Report,* vol. 35, no. 6, supp. 2. DHHS Pub No. (PHS) 86–1120. Hyattsville, Md.: Public Health Service.

————. 1988. *Vital Statistics of the United States 1986.* Vol. 1, *Natality.* DHHS Pub No. (PHS) 88–1123, Public Health Service. Washington, D.C.: Government Printing Office.

Perry, L. 1989. "Nurturing Single Room Maternity Care." *Modern Healthcare* 19 (19): 18–26.

Rooks, J. P., N. L. Weatherby, E. K. Ernst, S. Stapleton, D. Rosen, and A. Rosenfeld. 1989. "Outcomes of Care in Birth Centers: The National Birth Center Study." *New England Journal of Medicine* 321 (26): 1804–11.

Speert, H. 1980. *Obstetrics and Gynecology in America: A History.* Baltimore: Waverly Press.

Sumner, P. E., and C. R. Phillips. 1981. *Birthing Rooms: Concept and Reality.* St. Louis: Mosby.

Wertz, W., and D. C. Wertz. 1977. *Lying-in: A History of Childbirth in America.* New York: Free Press.

Young, D., and C. Mahon. 1980. *Unnecessary Caesareans: Ways to Avoid Them.* Minneapolis: International Childbirth Education Association.

Part Three

SOCIAL AND CULTURAL SETTINGS

It is easy to understand that societies influence the ways in which women go about the work of mothering and the value placed on that work. At the same time, it is difficult to grasp the sheer diversity of social and cultural settings that have emerged over the course of American history, and how these settings have changed over time. The articles in this section offer only a few examples of the different cultural and social settings of motherhood. Some of these settings are defined by race, class, or ethnicity; others are culturally defined, by membership in particular movements or organizations.

Together these articles demonstrate the many ways in which cultures transmit beliefs about mothering—for example, through language, as with the "sweet good mothers" described in the Irish-American press, or simply through the practices of daily life. They also show how mothers are often charged with transmitting to their children a sense of their religious, racial, and ethnic identity. Cultures are neither static nor fully resistant to external forces; these articles disclose how new ideas are assimilated, while older practices can continue as well, albeit in ways that change over generations.

In investigating the experiences of slave mothers, Stephanie Shaw studies how they sought to fulfill the needs of their children while coping with the harsh conditions of life and the knowledge that they could be separated from their children by sale. She argues that, rather than accept the subsistence level of support offered by the slave owners, mothers sought to provide additional sustenance for their children. Slave mothers also tried to transmit to their offspring the values that would enable them to survive as individuals and share in the culture of the slave community, while at the same time preparing them for life beyond enslavement.

The role of the community in shaping expectations about mothering is further explored in Timothy Meagher's study of Irish American women in the late nineteenth and early twentieth centuries. In contrasting the roles prescribed for single women and mothers, he shows how motherhood was both physically restricting for Irish American women and highly prestigious, earning them enormous respect.

Sidney Stahl Weinberg conducted oral histories of immigrant Jewish women who came to the United States from Eastern Europe after 1925. She shows how Jewish mothers transmitted traditional knowledge about household skills, family values, and gender roles. In addition, these mothers facilitated their daughters' assimilation by supporting their ambitions and allowing them to take on roles and responsibilities that would have been denied to women living in Eastern Europe.

Susan Matoba Adler also relies on oral histories in her investigation of how child-rearing practices among midwestern Japanese American mothers changed over the course of the late twentieth century. Adler contrasts Japanese and Euro-American traditions of child rearing and shows how succeeding generations of mothers tried to blend aspects of each. Her work demonstrates that motherlove has had a very different meaning in each culture.

Lynn Weiner's case study of the La Leche League, an organization founded to promote breast-feeding, illustrates that an intellectual community can be the foundation of a particular style of mothering. La Leche League supporters challenged the prevailing cultural authority of scientific motherhood and argued for an alternative view of motherhood that emphasized its "natural" and biological aspects. The values promoted by the La Leche League both complemented and conflicted with ideas about women's roles espoused by late twentieth-century feminists.

The term *feminist* encompasses many different kinds of women, as M. Rivka Polatnick demonstrates. She compares two women's liberation groups of the 1960s, one composed of black women of the working class or on welfare and the other largely comprising white, middle-class women. The former group included many mothers and argued for a very positive view of motherhood. The latter group had few mothers and feared that motherhood required women to become isolated, dependent on men, and less engaged in community life.

14.

MOTHERING UNDER SLAVERY IN THE ANTEBELLUM SOUTH

STEPHANIE J. SHAW

Mothering under slavery was truly contested terrain. The process of mothering in the antebellum South serves as one of many useful case studies for examining social constructions of mothering from a variety of viewpoints. Questions related to single parenting, women's working outside the home, surrogacy, and reproductive rights have historical antecedents in the political economy of slavery. While aspects of this essay reflect consideration of many of these questions, the focus is on the mothering of enslaved children by women who sought to define the process for themselves while living in a system where others claimed control of the process outright.

Because the successful operation of a political economy of slavery depended on the effective management of both productive labor (physical labor related to the production of ordinary goods and services) and reproductive labor (all the tasks related to the generation of and maintenance of human life), it was not possible for any aspect of slave life, including mothering, to develop entirely under the control of and based on the desires of those who were enslaved. But perhaps more significantly, because mothering, as the philosopher Sara Ruddick suggests, involves the protection and preservation of life, the fostering of emotional and intellectual development, and the preparation of a child for his or her expected social roles, slave owners and enslaved women participated in the processes of mothering in ways that often, ironically, reinforced each others' interests.[1]

While slaveholders and the women they enslaved often necessarily acted in these ways, the historian Lawrence W. Levine provides a poignant example suggesting that their views were sometimes in opposition. He writes of a New Orleans freedman who remarked: "I was once whipped ... because I said to my misses, 'my mother sent me.' We were not allowed to call our mammies 'mother.' It made it

Reprinted from *Mothering: Ideology, Experience, and Agency*, by Evelyn Nakano Glenn (1994), by permission of the publisher, Routledge: New York and London.

come too near the way of the white folks."[2] The freedman's interpretation was that slaveholders would go to violent extremes to protect what they perceived as white culture. Perhaps also embedded in his remark is a suggestion about the extent to which the alleged ownership of human chattel brought with it a construction of mothering that, from the slaveholders' point of view, defied both biological matters of fact and contemporary social traditions. Neither the slaveholders nor the women they claimed to own, however, had complete control over the process.

The history of antebellum slavery is fraught with paradoxes. In the first instance, slaveholders had routinely to demonstrate their power or control over those who were enslaved; yet absolute rigidity would only reveal the slaveholders' tenuous grip. Slaveholders had to provide some food, clothing, and shelter to those they claimed to own, because a semblance of dependency was critical to maintaining the system. But they could not provide too much because they also wanted to turn as handsome a profit as possible. And, at a time when slavery had been abolished in the rest of the Western world, slaveholders had to argue that the system was a benevolent one with one purpose—the protection and support of a class of people not competent to provide for themselves. Yet all the while, slaveholders had to count on those very slaves they claimed paternalistically to protect to use wit and skills to provide the many services and necessities they demanded for themselves. These contradictions, and the ways in which both slaveholders and the women they enslaved supported them, are especially apparent in the processes by which all those involved sustained the lives of children born into the system.

Anna Bishop, born a slave in 1849 in Alabama, remembered during her old age that "all de women on Lady Liza's place had to go to de fiel' ev'y day an' dem what had suckerlin' babies could com in 'bout nine o'clock in the mawnin' an' when de bell ring at twelve an' suckerlin' 'em."[3] The women were not relieved of their productive responsibilities simply because they had children, but because of the productive consequence of their reproductive labor, adjustments had to be made. Enhancing the survival of those newborns would eventually add to the labor force, because those children would be in the field, too, before the age of ten, pulling up weeds, carrying buckets of water back and forth to the field hands, or otherwise employed in some productive capacity, and thus contributing to the system.[4] Consequently, allowing the women to leave the fields to nurse not only enhanced the survival of the children but also relieved the owners of the obligation to provide extra food for the infants and to place more women in the nursery (losing their labor elsewhere) in order to feed the babies. Nursing mothers fulfilled the job requirement and in so doing gained some relief from the demands on them for physical labor. Some women, no doubt, also saw these feedings not as another work assign-

women fulfilled both their own interest in mothering and the owner's interest in their productive and reproductive responsibilities.[5]

Though many former slaves remembered their owners as compassionate people who showed special concern for women, infants, the elderly, and families, most available documentation is of a nature that makes it difficult to draw out slave owners' compassion and separate it from their business interests.[6] In an especially clear example, Virginian Robert Snead expressed concerns to his wife, Octavia, about the health of one slave child: "You should be more than cautious, and especially with the children and Effia; Effia is often complaining with her throat and it may go hard with her. I should dislike for you to lose her as she is handy about sewing and our family is getting so large it would be a great loss on[?] her."[7] Most examples, however, are more ambiguous. Slave owners, for example, regularly supplemented the diet of pregnant and nursing women by giving them extra food. In some instances, doing so was an act of generosity, but such acts also helped to protect the economic investments in human chattel while allowing enslaved women to provide better for the nourishment of their children.[8]

Enslaved women, however, did not always depend on slaveholders to provide the means for sustaining the children's lives. While seemingly acting within the various restrictions of their owners' mandates, some women made legendary efforts to preserve the lives of their children, to nurture them, and to encourage their development. Linda Brent explained their successes in terms of "determined will" and "mother love." When she was about to be separated from her children for the first time, upon determining that no one could or would help her, she concluded: "I had a woman's pride, and a mother's love for my children; and I resolved that out of the darkness of this hour a brighter dawn should rise for them. My master had power and law on his side, I had a determined will. There is might in each."[9] Brent's and other slave women's testimonies contradict slave owners' regular portrayal of the system as a benevolent one in which slaveholders provided for those unable to provide for themselves.

Enslaved women regularly demonstrated their ability to provide a higher standard of life for their children than their owners were willing to provide. Rose, whose family name is not known, was separated from her mother when she was a child in Virginia, but partly because she was not a great distance from her mother and because they both remained in the same white family, her mother regularly sent money and fruit with the white family members, who visited back and forth.[10] Many slaves maintained small gardens in order to supplement their own and their children's diets. And while hunting and fishing are regularly characterized as a part of male slave efforts to support their families, Addie Vinson, born in the 1840s, remembered his mother performing these duties. She fished for her family at night after working all day at her other required tasks. "Many's de time," he recalled, "i'se seed my mammy come back from Barbers Crick wid a string of fish draggin' from her shoulders down to de ground." Moreover, his mother did not take the four days after Christmas as holidays, as did most of the adults in the slave community; instead, she used the four days to weave and wash for white people who lived in the area, and with the meager pay was able to provide materially for her children beyond what their owner provided.[11]

The ability of slaves to earn money, buy fruit, plant a garden, or catch a fish made some difference in the lives of their children. But if those opportunities were not present, and often that was indeed the case, all was not lost, at least not for ingenious and daring slaves. Especially willful, courageous, clever, and perhaps lucky ones succeeded at "taking" some of what they needed to sustain themselves and their families. Georgia house servant Charlotte Raines accomplished the feat by wearing a flour sack tied around her waist under her skirts, into which she dropped so much food on a day-to-day basis that it bumped her knees when she walked. Alice Marshall, a Virginia woman who was nearly grown when the Civil War ended, also remembered her mother appropriating food for the children.

> I tell you, honey, mistiss Sally had a plenty, but we ain' fared de bes' by no means. She ain' never give us 'nough to eat; so my mother had to git food de bes' way she could. I 'member one way special. When de preacher come to mistiss' for Sunday morning breakfast, de white folks all git together an' have prayers. Den' tis my mother tek basket, go in de smoke house, git all de meat she want. When de preacher der, mistiss ain' bother 'bout nothing. Minds you, we ain' 'lowed to ever put our foot inside de meat house. Ole mistress kept de floor covered wid sawdus' an' dat smoothed off even. An' she better not find nary track in dat sawdus'. Anyhow my mother gwan in der, but she ain' never fergit to rub out her tracks. We got meat an' my mother ain' got caught neither.[12]

From the point of view of slave owners, clothing for young children was as unnecessary a luxury as meat. They were, after all, nonproductive beings and would not begin to pay for their upkeep (through work) until they were about ten years old. Slave owners at first allocated children two shirts a year—a lightweight one for the warm seasons and a heavier one for the winter. Boys and girls wore this pullover sliplike shirt and received no other clothing from their owners until they were nearly teenagers. Delia Garlic, who was separated during her childhood from her mother, never even owned an undershirt until just before the birth of her first child.

She possessed but a "shimmy an' a slip for a dress . . . made out of de cheapes' cloth that could be bought." Frederick Douglass and other male slaves recalled receiving their first pairs of pants as historic events. And sometimes even the cold weather of winter had little effect on this practice unless other slaves undertook the task of providing additional clothing for the children.[13]

Former Alabama slave Sara Murphy, born in the early 1850s, noted that the mothers of enslaved children where she lived regularly wove long underwear from cotton for the children. Linda Brent's grandmother provided her with most of her clothing during her childhood and adolescence, giving her an alternative to the linsey-woolsey dress that she received every winter as her clothing ration, which, incidentally, marked her as a slave. Brent's grandmother also bought her a new pair of shoes one winter, but Mrs. Flint, her young mistress's mother, took them because they squeaked, and it disturbed her. Slaveholders rarely allocated shoes to slave children before they were capable of performing productive labor. But even when the children were fortunate enough to have leather shoes, they were usually very crude items, and special care had to be taken of them if they were to protect the children's feet, which often went without socks. Horace Muse, who was nearly thirty-two years old at the end of the Civil War, remembered that "no matter what tasks mother got to do, fo' she go to bed she clean dem shoes an' grease em' wid tallow grease. Git stiff as a board in cold weather, an' lessen you grease 'em dey burn your feet an' freeze 'em too."[14]

Where enslaved women and men provided necessary food and clothing for their children, slave owners did not have to worry about deficiencies. This regular demonstration of resourcefulness proved the fallacy of slave owners' claims that the institution served a necessary and benevolent purpose. In the owners' views, those whom they enslaved were not capable of caring for themselves. But women's interest in their children, and their ability to raise them to some extent by their own standards, regularly gave the lie to the slaveholders' claims. These women's efforts, however, also simultaneously supported the owners' interest and made it possible for owners to continue to neglect the needs of these women and children whom they claimed to own.

Those who mothered slave children on a day-to-day basis recognized that nutritional and material neglect endangered the health of their children, who might or might not have the sense to come in out of the cold if they were playing outdoors. And when they did come in, this did not necessarily guarantee warmth and comfort, because allocated housing was often shabby at best. Beyond recreation, too, slave children had work responsibilities that required them to be out-of-doors sometimes, and little could be done to change that. Fannie Berry's owner once sent her five miles during a storm to get liquor for him. As Berry ran in the rain, trying to make it home, she finally stopped to take off her shirt and put it over her head. Had she had on anything else, her action might have served the purpose for which she intended it, but instead she quite possibly only made herself even more vulnerable to the weather by this act. Her mother, however, recognizing all the dangers facing her child traveling alone, in the storm, half-dressed, came to meet her and brought another wrap to keep her warm and dry. After Berry got home, "Sallie an' June, ol' gals," rubbed her down with warm grease until she felt warm. Her owner's wife gave her a stiff drink of whiskey. And then she went to bed.[15]

While slave owners' interest in maintaining their property led them to provide most of the basic necessities, those committed to mothering slave children invariably provided more. For Linda Brent, it meant a dress made of something other than so-called negro cloth. Or it meant being handed food for breakfast or dinner as she passed her grandmother's gate on her way to complete errands for her owner.[16] For Sally Murphy, Everett Ingram, and many others who endured slavery as children, it meant withstanding the doses of turpentine, castor oil, or teas made from Jerusalem oak and other ingredients their elders prepared for them in an effort to protect their health. And few children grew up without wearing bags of asafetida around their necks, which mothers believed prevented illness.[17]

There is much evidence to suggest enslaved women's interest in mothering their children, but often women's efforts were brutally conditioned by the structure of the larger political economy, and by the slaveholders who worked to sustain it. For example, scholars have presented substantial evidence to prove the persistence of the nuclear slave family, traditionally defined, but tradition had little to do with how those families survived intact. At a time when femininity was defined by motherhood and mothering in the larger society, slave owners frequently did not allow slave women to mother their children. The women's productive labor was often viewed as much more valuable to their owners than the reproductive labor involved in rearing a child who, as yet, had no value. As a consequence, new patterns of child care emerged, with a variety of people mothering slave children. The historian Deborah Gray White has demonstrated the importance of an existing network among enslaved women that helped to facilitate adequate child care.[18] When slave owners chose the ones to perform these tasks, they usually called upon people whose own productive capacities had significantly diminished but who could still perform the (presumably) less physically demanding tasks of mothering.

All children where Phoebe Faucette lived were cared for by "some old man or some old woman." Georgia Baker, born in the 1840s in Georgia, was cared for by her grandfather, about whom she said "all he done was to sit by the fire all day with a switch in his hand and tend the children whilst their mammies was at work." Allen Sims, who was probably not yet ten years old at the end of the Civil War, recalled that "Aunt Mandy, what was too old to work, looked atter all de little nigger chilluns, whilst dey mammy's working." An elderly male slave named Payne had to move every time his daughter was relocated in order to care for her children. And though this arrangement might have served this family's interest well, the slave owners' feminization of this man's work role was mostly a matter of expediency. The daughter would take care of herself, the master's work, and her father. And he would take care of her children while she was engaged in other work. The slave owner did not have to care for anyone. Callie Williams's mother kept slave children in a small cabin with homemade cradles while the other women worked in the fields. The mothers returned from the fields to feed their nursing infants twice a day. And while both the nurse and the mother shared some time with the children, both were limited in what they could do, for in this case the mothers had to return to the fields, and the nurse usually had other tasks to perform as well.[19]

The assignment of extra tasks seems to have been common in the case of women nurses. Williams's mother had to spin two to four cards of cotton while she watched the children. The Tennessee planter Benjamin Bedford's nurse tended the children in addition to her main duties as a laundress and cook. Bedford advised his overseer that "the negro woman who cooks and washes when not engaged in that business [is] to churn, work butter, work in the garden, make up negro clothing or attend to little negroes or such needful employment about the yard that is necessary and proper because it does not consume all her time to cook and wash." Many of those who cared for slave children had other major work responsibilities, because slave owners rarely considered child care an activity requiring all of the nurse's time.[20]

Particularly in cases where those assigned to care for children had many other responsibilities, there was a great chance the children would not receive close attention; they might even unavoidably be neglected. While Mandy McCullough Cosby's recollection about slavery, "de way de chillun rol roun' in the big nurses room," could indicate that the children enjoyed a carefree and uninhibiting environment, for example, it could also suggest the lack of attention they received. McCullough, born in the 1830s, witnessed these events as an adult, and her memory of what might have been haphazard child care was not all that different from the memory of slightly younger George Womble, who characterized mealtime in the nursery. The horrible scene involved children eating with animals from a trough, a popular method of feeding when there were a lot of children. The children gathered around the trough were not allowed to hit the animals, and they ate with their hands up to the sides of their heads so that the dogs and pigs could not lick them in the face as they ate. While this form of feeding might not have been typical for most slave children, it probably inspired many mothers to devise alternatives to the child care arranged by their owners. They knew that the nursery was not necessarily the best place for their small children.[21]

One alternative involved requiring older children to care for the younger ones. Sylvia Witherspoon's mother left Sylvia in charge of her siblings when she (the mother) had to report to the fields. "She would tie the smalles' baby on my back so's I could play wid out no inconvenience," Witherspoon recalled. Joseph Holmes's mother had eight children, and she made each one of them responsible for another. Holmes remarked: "We was raised in pairs. I had a sister who come along wid me, an' iffen I jumped in the river she done it too. An' iffen I go th'ough a briar patch, her[e] she come along too." Mary Smith's mother left her in charge of her younger siblings. Smith, who reported being only seven years old at the time of surrender, was but a child herself. In order to help her with her large responsibilities, she noted that her mother would "pin a piece of fat back [meat] on my dres' before she went to de fiel' and when de baby cry I tek him up and let 'em suck 'em."[22]

We can never know precisely why these child-care responsibilities often went to other children. No doubt, in some instances, these children and their mothers were owned by people who did not have a nursery where older men and women took care of those too young to work or take care of themselves. It is likely that in some instances these individual women and their children were the only slaves on the site. But perhaps some mothers had the ability to choose not to leave their children in nurseries where they were available. And considering that a well-instructed child could provide some personal attention to the child being cared for, while a nurse, assigned by the owner to care for numerous children and also to attend to other work details, could not, such a decision was not necessarily irresponsible. And, moreover, if mothers were not able or allowed to care for their children, those siblings could also help to reinforce family bonds in a system where slaveholders often ignored them.

In any case, under some circumstances, either none of these alternatives were available or they simply were not acceptable, and slave women took their children to the fields with them, though doing so represented no small amount of danger. During the early nineteenth century, women on Saint Simons Island carried their infants with them to the field in baskets they carried on their heads. According to Julia Rush, a former slave, Oliver Bell's mother was a plow hand, but she took him to the field with her every morning and sat him under a post oak tree, where he usually remained until she called or went for him. "Dat tree was my nurse," Bell recalled. Sara Colquitt, who was born in the 1830s, took her two children with her to the field as well; she tied the youngest to a tree limb (perhaps making a swing, in effect) to keep him or her away from bugs on the ground. And Roxy Pitts, born in

1855, whose mother succeeded in escaping from her owner, was taken to the field along with her younger sister by her father, who "kep' a bottle of sweeten water in he shirt to keep [it] warm to gib de baby when it cry."[23] To a large degree, it was simply not possible for those who were enslaved to determine totally for themselves the method by which or the extent to which their children would be cared for. But as some of the above examples suggest, the extent to which these children were nurtured (or the extent to which they could be) depended not only on their owners' whims and resources but on the women's need, willingness, and ability to improvise.

It is possible, however, to overestimate the ability of enslaved women to work the system to their own advantage. The work requirements that slaveholders and overseers imposed on them and their children often made it impossible for mothers to carry out or even to improvise this personal maternal work. Women of childbearing age were in their prime as productive laborers, and neither the biological fact of motherhood nor the traditional gendered construction of mothering applied to them, as far as slaveholders were concerned. Maternal work under this system was not simply a social responsibility left to the interests and abilities of mothers; it was a work assignment that utilized the labor of men, women who were not the biological mothers, and children. Children were fortunate when these workers saw their responsibilities as more than a work assignment and sought to fulfill the broader responsibilities of mothering. But the fact is that the recollections of some freed men and women growing up in the system suggest that not all slave children experienced the benefits of mothering.

Enslaved adults often worked from sunup to sundown at one task, and after that, they attended to weaving, spinning, shucking corn, mending tools, and other indoor work assignments. And as Cordellia Thomas said, "Come day, go day, no matter what happen, growin' chillun had to be in bed at deir reg'lar time."[24] Former Georgia slave Will Sheets noted that the most he ever saw of his mother was when she came to the cabin at night, and "den, us chilluns was too sleepy to talk. Soon as us et, us drapped down on a pallet and went fast asleep." More to the point, and indicating both adult and childhood work responsibilities, Tom Singleton remembered that the adults "were too busy to talk in de daytime, and at night us wuz so wiped out from hard work [us] just went to sleep early and never talked." Mandy McCullough, reared in Alabama, recalled that children who did not yet have work responsibilities played all day, ate their supper at the trough in the yard, and "some of dem jes' fall ovah on de groun' asleep, and is picked up, and put on dey pallet in de big chillen's room." During the work week at least, these children were, by necessity, mothered by others or not at all.[25]

Perhaps the most difficult aspect of slavery for mothers came with the breakup of families because of being sold or hired out. Under these circumstances, sometimes the best that they could do was to ask and hope that someone else would care for their children. Mingo White, probably born in the 1840s, moved to Alabama with his family when he was four or five years old. He was "jes' a li'l thang; tooked away from my mammy an' pappy jes' when I needed 'em mos'. The only caren' that I had ever knowed anything 'bout was give to me by a frien' of my pappy. His name was John [W]hite. My pappy tol' him to take care of me for him. John was a fiddler 'n many a night I woke up to find myse'f 'sleep 'twix his legs whilst he was playin' for a dance for de white folks." Laura Clark, only a few years younger than White, was one in a group of children sold from their North Carolina home to an Alabaman. The new owner either bought or hired elder slaves Julie Powell and Henry to care for them during the trip by wagon to the Deep South. "Wa'n't none of dem ten chillin no kin to me," Clark recalled, "and he never brout my mammy so I had to leave her behine. I recollect mammy said to ond [aunt] Julie, 'take keer my baby chile . . . and iffen I never sees her no mo' raise her for God." Clark's referral to Julie as aunt should be read not simply as the traditional respect that slaves showed for elders by giving them kinship titles but also as an indication that there developed a bond between them based on a caring, familial relationship.[26]

In spite of the extensive efforts of all those who mothered slave children, the overall conditions of slavery were often not conducive to preserving the lives of slave children. While infant mortality rates generally declined over the decades, some mothers experienced death rates among their children that were as high just before the demise of slavery as they were at the end of the eighteenth century. Slaveholders sought solutions to protect their investments, which were not only a source of their wealth, of course, but a source of their political power and social status as well. One London businessman who owned slaves in the United States wrote to his correspondent, probably a relative who was acting as his overseer:

> I am grieved to hear of the mortality among the negro children, and am very much afraid there is not proper care taken of them. You tell me there were ten born last year, and but one of them is living, and that [one] but three days old. . . . [I]s there no method to be fallen on to prevent it; suppose something by way of [illegible] was given to such of them as raise their children and to wenches that took care of them in the lying in aft[?] the children were brought you [illegible] to make them more careful and attentive.

More than fifty years later, Nicholas Edmunds recorded the following vital statistics for his slave woman Harriet: She gave birth to Washington on August 28, 1851, and he died on November 14, 1851. Dolly was born on March 4, 1853, and died on August 31, 1853. Luke, born on March 20, 1854, died on September 17, 1854. Sally, born on April 5, 1857, died six months later. A son, not named, was born on August 25, 1860, and died four days later. And Albert was born on November 1, 1861, and died nine months later (on August 10, 1862). Four of Harriet's children were listed with no death dates (b. 1850, 1855, 1858, and 1859) and therefore quite possibly lived to be set free. Still, five of her ten children did not see the first anniversary of their births, and one made it only to his first birth anniversary.[27]

Notwithstanding all the possible "natural" factors contributing to high infant mortality rates in the eighteenth century and isolated problems in the nineteenth, the letter from the British slaveholder cited above suggests other considerations. He proposes that enslaved women could be induced to take better care of the infants and raises a question about the extent to which adults deliberately contributed to the deaths of their children. Undoubtedly, many women made choices not to preserve the lives of slave children. And in these instances the evidence of contested terrain is vivid.

A Fairfax County, Virginia, court convicted Ally, the slave of George Miller, for "exposing [her child] as causing its death" in 1835. A Buckingham County Court convicted Polley of murdering her child in 1818. Kesiah allegedly killed her infant daughter on April 13, 1834. The courts sentenced all of the women to hang.[28] Between the 1840s and the 1860s, William Massie, the prominent Virginia planter and diarist, regularly noted his suspicions regarding the deaths of slave children on his plantation. In one instance he noted that Gabriel, the sixteen-month-old child of Lizzie, "was murdered right out by his mother's neglect and barbarous cruelty." At another point he wrote that Rhoda's fourteen-month-old son "was neglected . . . by its mother and died like a dog." And about Lucy's children, Romulus and Remus, born in 1844, Massie wrote that Remus died of neglect, and "Romulus died by waste caused by the natural neglect of his infamous mother."[29]

The accounts of alleged infanticide cases may, of course, be suspect in the light of more recent medical discoveries that indicate the importance of their contexts. Poor nutrition, low birth weights, poor pre- and postnatal care, and even genetic disposition quite possibly caused some or all of these infants to fall victim to Sudden Infant Death Syndrome (SIDS).[30] When the Mississippi farmer T. S. Jones wrote to a relative in Tennessee in 1852 about his slave woman Milly, who had recently "overlaid" her child, he noted that this incident made "three out of four children [that] she has killed in that way in eight years. This last one was a fine, likely, healthy child about seven months old." Milly could have, in her exhaustion, unknowingly "overlaid" her children. She might even have deliberately killed them.

The only thing certain is that children who succumb to SIDS are likely to have siblings who suffer the same fate. And, consequently, Milly might simply have been destined to suffer the loss of her children.[31]

Still, there are many irrefutable examples of infanticide. Amey, slave of John Grisham from King and Queen County, Virginia, killed her two infant children, Isbell and Harrison, on April 13, 1799. She cut their throats with an ax. Sixteen years later, Jenny (Powhatan County, Virginia) killed her three children. And Hannah, a Granville County, North Carolina, slave, killed her child Soloman. One witness at her trial testified that after Hannah cut her child's throat, she attempted to slit her own and, upon failing, asked Bob, another slave, to "put her away."[32]

On occasion, slave women threatened infanticide in an attempt to affect an owner's behavior. One often cited example involves a woman who successfully prevented her owner from selling her away from her child as punishment for some offense. Upon hearing that she could not take her child with her, the woman raised the infant into the air by its feet, threatening to smash its head into the ground rather than to leave it behind. She fully understood her master's value system and his proprietary interest in her child, and she used that understanding to ensure the maintenance of her values and to take the child with her. Though the latter example is an important one to the contrary, one must also acknowledge the possibility that some of these women suffered from postpartum depression and acted as a result of some psychological trauma beyond their control.[33]

Certainly there remain many questions about the extent to which slave mothers killed their children. Undoubtedly some did, and many did not. Where they did, infanticide sometimes represented a powerful example of women's opposition to this form of sexual and economic exploitation. But these examples could also reflect that the women possessed such a reverence for humanity and a level of self-determination that they simply decided to prevent a child, whose life they felt responsible for, from growing up in a system in which their owners demonstrated little respect for either.[34] Vincent Harding provides a chilling example of this, in which a husband and wife "shut up in a slave baracoon and doomed to the southern market . . . did by mutual agreement send the souls of their children to Heaven rather than have them descend to the hell of slavery." Both parents killed themselves after killing their children.[35]

Several scholars have noted the records of Southern physicians who remarked on the high rate of abortion among slave women. (No doubt some spontaneous abortions or miscarriages were included here.) One physician said planters believed "that the Blacks are possessed of a secret by which they destroy the fetus at an early stage of gestation." Another noted with some surprise that "whole families of women . . . fail to have any children." One planter claimed to have discovered that "the slaves had concocted a medicine with which they were able to terminate their unwanted pregnancies." And another said he had "an older female slave [who] had discovered a remedy for pregnancies and had been instrumental in all . . . the abortions on his place."[36]

Women's decisions to have abortions might represent a political act of defiance if they determined that they would not give birth to children in a system that allowed no consistent recognition of them as those children's mothers. That is, after some analyses of their situations, they could have decided not to have children because those children would belong to slave owners, not to themselves. The famous successful runaway Ellen Craft, at least, at first refused to marry because "marriage meant children—children who would belong to Robert Collins" rather than to her and her husband. But Ellen Craft's ability to decide, while enslaved, not to marry and not to conceive might represent an unusual case. Rather, what is most evident is that many women did not have a choice. Many were "married up" against their will. And whether "married" or not, many were raped.[37] Still, even when slave women had abortions, refused to conceive, or committed infanticide in order to protect children from a lifetime of slavery, they often did so in the interest of mothering. And even when they made such decisions without considering the child's future, they made mothering decisions—decisions not to mother.

Probably, most slave women allowed children they conceived to be born, to live, and to grow up in the slave system. And just as these adults often provided children with more food and clothing than their owners allowed, they also attempted to nurture the youngsters and to minimize their encounters with the most brutal aspects of the system. In a rare slave letter, which exemplifies one woman's attempt to prepare a future for her grandchildren and great-grandchild, Nancy Venture Woods presented a most convincing case to her owner.

> Dear Master   I will now inform you about my little family   six grandchildren and one great grand child and I am now a great grandmother Virgin is the eldest   Nancy the next who has now become a mother William Brutus Venten Jane & George is the names of the children that I have taken care of—Virgin desires to be put to a trade and I think it would be the best for him   a tailor or shoe maker would suit him best in consequence of a hurt he has had in his ancle which he still feels at times   I had rather keep the rest if agreeable to you to assist me in supporting the small ones but I feel willing that you should do by them as you please as for my own part I am a good

deal afflicted with the rhe[u]matic pains and I hope Daer M[as]ter if
I should be the longest liver you will remember your old servant for
I wish to end my days in this place   if I was to be carried from her[e]
now it seems that I could not be satisfied   I also wish to keep the
children as long as I live except such as you think best to put to a
trade

you will please write to mr. guion concerning the putting of Vir-
gin to a trade and he will see to the business.[38]

Woods's finely crafted letter carefully combined a good amount of expectation,
deference, and humility in a clever attempt to remain in the city of Raleigh, North
Carolina, rather than to return to the plantation in New Bern, to keep these children with her, to place the eldest of them at a particular kind of work—skilled
work—and to place any others, which she might not keep with her, in a trade. She
probably began her letter by informing her owner of the expansion of her family to
affect the way in which he would receive her requests. That is, her letter first made
the point that her owner's property had increased because of her. And in every instance where she acknowledged his authority in the matter, she also reminded him
of why her desires should prevail. Though Woods's letter is a rare document, her
intention to create a particular kind of future for the children was probably not uncommon among enslaved women; it carries the hallmark of mothering. But examples of women's attempts to prepare a specific kind of future for their children are
difficult to come by. It is much easier to show how parents and others attempted to
prepare children for the actual future that awaited them, which in most cases involved living within the slaveholders' reach and almost always included the possibility of being separated from the family unit.[39]

Parents began very early to discipline children in ways that would be important for their survival as they matured, and as their contact with owners and overseers increased. The process began during childhood and in the "nursery," where
lessons could be taught clearly but gently. Aunt Mandy, who took care of Allen
Sims and numerous other children while their mothers worked in the fields and
elsewhere, would "pop" him and the others with a brush when they did not obey
her. But Sims added, "she fuss more dan she whipt." It was important for the children not only to respect the authority of their Black elders but also to learn to respect authority figures in general if they were to survive under the supervision of
slaveholders and overseers. Reflecting the importance of such lessons, one woman
recalled being beaten during her childhood by her owner for not calling a nine-
month-old white child "miss." Theodore Fontaine Stewart's mother, a cook, beat
her children if she caught them stealing anything from the kitchen where she

worked. In doing so, she was instilling in them a moral code that prohibited random theft and was discouraging them from participating in acts that would bring severe punishment if they were caught by whites. Simultaneously, she was protecting her job, which probably allowed her to provide for her children—with leftover food and cast-off clothing—in a manner better than she could have if she had been forced to go to the field to work because of problems her children had created.[40]

Martha Showvley's mother made concerted efforts to teach her children not to meddle in the affairs of others. The importance of such a lesson is illustrated by the death of a Richmond County, Georgia, slave woman whose owner beat her to death after hearing a child's innocent conversation. The woman had given birth to twins one day and on the next day was ordered to scrub the floors of her owner's home. After she fainted while working, her mistress had a slave take her to her cabin and another one finish the scrubbing. The mistress's husband was satisfied that the work was done when he returned, but a slave child innocently told him what had happened in his absence. The owner mercilessly beat the woman because, he said, she was lazy and deceitful, and she died the same day while still tied to the whipping post. Teaching children to hear and not repeat, to see and not disclose, was critical to controlling the conditions of their survival, and to survival itself, because many of things that happened in the slave quarters would not have been acceptable to the owners.[41]

Probably most important, in terms of their preparation for future roles, slave children were taught to work and to work well. From birth, the futures of these children were geared toward work, and it was the job of their parents and other adults to see that they were able to fulfill that responsibility. But as much as it was the job of adult slaves to socialize children to their roles as workers, the adults' commitments to mothering also motivated them to psychologically prepare the children for this work. The adults provided with their strict disciplinary measures some protection for the children because, as the historian Eugene Genovese observes, "parents knew that soon enough the indulgence [of slave owners] would give way to the whip. Better they instill elementary habits and discipline in their children early and according to their own measure."[42]

Jennie Kendricks's mother probably took her oldest daughters with her to the spring to wash at night, not simply to have their help and their company, but to teach them how to wash and to convey to them that, being girls, that is what they would eventually have to do, even after working all day at something else. Ferebe Rogers said she virtually "come up twix the plow handles" because her mother took her to the fields and began to teach her how to plow when she was quite young. Will Sheets learned from an older slave woman named Mandy to drive cattle to and from the pasture. And Mary Smith's mother provided Smith, when she was only seven years old, with her first lessons in chopping cotton. Many children learned to spin thread from their mothers who were weavers. And Charlie Dink, when he was seven or eight years old, walked the rows in the field with his mother "totin' cawn for her to drap." By this process, he not only began to learn to work but also relieved his mother of concerns about his care while she worked.[43]

Because the work roles slave children faced very early came under the direct supervision of sometimes sadistic owners and overseers, teaching children to work hard and well was, quite possibly, the best way in which their parents could protect them—short of running away with them. By the time many of these children were five years old, they were assigned to fanning flies away from slave owners or their visitors.[44] At a very young age many children began to carry food to the fields and water to both the house and the fields from nearby wells and springs.[45] Between the ages of five and ten, they set and waited on tables in the big house, threaded needles, spun thread, picked up cow chips, swept yards, and performed a variety of other work details.[46] Doing these tasks diligently and effectively could save them from severe punishment.

Mollie Mitchell, born around 1845, went to work hoeing in the field at the age of seven, but she got whipped often because she could not "keep in the row." Tom Singleton, born in 1838, had occasional childhood whims that caused him to neglect his work role; he received his only beating as a child because he got involved in a marble game after his mistress had sent him to get thread. Easter Jones, a dishwasher in her owner's house, had to remove the dishes from scalding water, but she knew, even as a youngster, that "if I drap it dey whip me. Dey whip you so hard your back bleed." One ex-slave woman claimed to have had bones broken as a child on more than one occasion by her mistress, who beat her with a fire iron for not waking up quickly enough to see to the crying white infant to whom she was supposed to attend. And Delia Garlic's mistress ran a hot iron down Delia's arm and hand after she accidently hurt the white child to whom she attended.[47]

Those who mothered slave children had good reason, then, to work hard at preparing the children for their eventual work assignments. These children would too soon be caught between the labor requirements inherent in the system and their own natural inclinations and abilities as children. Thus it is not surprising that Emmaline Kilpatrick vividly remembered Black children growing up faster than white children did. Jasper Battle noted that slave children grew so fast that most of those assigned to nursing "warn't no older dan de white chillun dey tuk keer of." He also claimed that slave children "12 or 14 years old [in] dem days was big as a white child 17 or 18 years old." Battle was around 21 years old upon emancipation and therefore spoke not only from personal experience but also from years of observation.[48] Clearly, Battle was equating responsibility with age and size, because slave owners subjected the children they owned to an accelerated passage from childhood to adulthood. Very early in the children's lives, owners began to characterize them as "grown" or "most grown," thereby justifying putting them to work at a young age. The children's parents and others who mothered them could do little to alter this reality. And so they reared their children in a way that would better prepare them for it.

The exigencies of day-to-day life, in fact, necessarily resulted in a type of mothering that often reinforced the oppressive system of which it was a part. As women provided food, clothing, and shelter for children beyond that provided by slave owners, they helped to fortify the system. And as they taught those children to work in fields, in kitchens, at sewing and spinning machines, they prepared the children for a future of work and possibly a future as slaves. When they devised alternative child-care arrangements that allowed them to keep up their work in the fields, the big houses, or on some property other than that of their owners, the slaveholders' proprietary interest in these children was further protected at no additional expense to themselves.

But mothering under slavery was not always a matter of women's indirect and unavoidable support of the system. When women engaged, directly and indirectly, in abortions and infanticide, they picked away at one of the bases of the system's life itself—reproduction. And even as they performed mothering tasks that reinforced the system of slavery, they also chipped away at institutional assumptions about dependency (cultural, material, and political) and thereby helped to prepare their children for freedom.

They did this in part by transmitting a set of values and traditions to the children that reinforced a kind of self-sufficiency, community culture, and group identity that could help to sustain them within and beyond their enslavement. When mothers left their older children in charge of younger ones, they not only answered their child-care problems but also provided the children with important lessons in assuming responsibility for one another. When women taught children to address other Black people not related to them by blood as "aunt," "uncle," and "granny," they taught children that "family" had a basis not only in kinship but in community as well.[49] When members of the slave community devised the means or took advantage of opportunities to supplement their allotted rations of food, clothing, or shelter, they demonstrated their ability to care for themselves despite persistent portrayals of them as perpetual dependents. And ultimately, while the teaching of children to work effectively prepared those children for work as slaves, it also prepared them for freedom. More profoundly than slaveholders could have predicted, the efforts of enslaved women who mothered children in the antebellum South simultaneously served the interests of both slaveholders and slaves.

NOTES

Comments provided by John B. Boles, John C. Burnham, Evelyn Nakano Glenn, and Pat Washington were especially helpful in this revision of the original conference paper. This paper, concerning primarily North Carolina, Virginia, Texas, Georgia, and Alabama, is part of a larger study in progress on slave women. The larger study has been supported by an Ohio State University Seed Grant, a North Caroliniana Society Archie K. Davis Fellowship, a Mellon teaching fellowship at Rice University, a grant from the Virginia Historical Society, and a fellowship at the Virginia Foundation for the Humanities and Public Policy.

1. See Sara Ruddick, *Maternal Thinking toward a Politics of Peace* (Boston: Beacon Press, 1989).

2. Lawrence W. Levine, *Black Culture and Black Consciousness: Afro-American Folk Thought from Slavery to Freedom* (Oxford: Oxford University Press, 1977), p. 139.

3. George P. Rawick, ed., *The American Slave: A Composite Autobiography,* 19 vols. (Westport, Conn.: Greenwood Publishing Co., 1972), vol. 6, p. 36. References from these volumes will hereafter be cited as: Rawick, Alabama, 6:36.

4. See Rawick, Alabama, 6:181, in which Adeline (last name unknown) recalled: "I was jes' a li'l gal den. I was jes' big 'nuff to tote water to de fiel' to de folks wukking and to min' de gaps in the fence to keep de cattle out when dey was gatherin' de crops." Ella Grandberry couldn't remember having time to play as a child. She said "ever since I kin 'member I had a water bucket on my arm totin' water to de han's. Iffen I wan't doin' dat, I was choppin' cotton." Bishop, at the age of six or seven, was at work helping to tend to the women workers' babies and going back and forth to the field to call those who were needed for feedings. Hanna Johnson became a nurse at the age of ten, and Caroline Hunter began polishing silver and setting the tables of the big house at the age of five. Before Hunter was ten, she was put in the field to work all day. See Rawick, Alabama, 6:157; Georgia, part 3, 13:47, 58; Georgia, part 4, 13:183; Charles L. Perdue, Jr., Thomas E. Barden, and Robert K. Phillips, eds., *Weevils in the Wheat: Interviews with Virginia Ex-Slaves* (Bloomington: Indiana University Press, 1980), pp. 158–59.

5. This, of course, is not to say that all women wanted to nurture their children. In fact, later discussions will show that some did not. But for those who did want to, nursing the children provided one of the few opportunities during the day to do so.

6. For examples of evidence of owner sensitivity, see Alfred Moore to William Augustus Blount, September 22, 1835, box 193.21, folder 6, J. G. Blount Papers, North Carolina State Library and Archives, Raleigh. This letter concerns a Louisiana slave owner's efforts to buy the children of two adult slaves whom he already owned. In Horatio J. Eden, biographical sketch, Tennessee State Library and Archives, Nashville, Eden, a former slave, speaks kindly of his former owners. And see Rebecca J. McLeod to J. S. Beers, September 1, 1862, box 2, folder 25, Rosenberg Library, Galveston, Texas. In this letter, McLeod expressed interest in seeing that her slaves who were hired out were fed and clothed properly; that one girl not be separated from her mother, who was going blind; and that none of them be sold to settle any debts that her husband, recently deceased, might have owed. (McLeod's interests could also have been purely economical.) And see R. A. Adams to Mrs. Jno. W. Gilliam, January 29, 1855, box 2, folder 1850–1855, Slave Trade Papers, Alderman Library Archives, University of Virginia, Char-

lottesville. This document indicates that Adams was also in the process of settling her husband's estate. She had hired out all of the slaves, most of them with their families intact. It is also clear in this letter, however, that an elderly woman had not been placed, and Adams had apparently made no attempts to keep her with any of the other families. Because of the woman's age, Adams simply assumed that it would be impossible to place her.

7. Robert Winn Snead to Octavia Snead, November 17, 1861, verifax copy, Robert Snead Papers, Virginia Historical Society, Richmond (cited hereafter as VHS).

8. For an example of one slave owner's habit of providing more food to such women, see "Negro Account Books: Items given Negroes, 1817–1835," Massie Family Papers, University of Texas-Austin, Barker Texas History Center (cited hereafter as UT-BTHC).

9. Linda Brent (pseud. Harriet Jacobs), *Incidents in the Life of a Slave Girl*, ed. L. Maria Child (1861; San Diego: Harcourt, Brace, Jovanovich, 1973), p. 87.

10. Lizzie Bain to "sister," January 26, 1857, William T. Bain Papers, Perkins Library Archives, Duke University, Durham, N.C. The William Deveraux family papers located at UT-BTHC provide much detail about the maintenance of family connections among slaves through their owners and their owners' family. The Deveraux family, over the generations, lived in Georgia, Alabama, Louisiana, and Texas, and over the years the slave families were divided among various members of the white family. But the correspondence among the whites show attempts by the slaves to maintain contact with their own multigenerational, interstate family.

11. Rawick, Georgia, part 4, 13:102, 108. And for other examples of men and women's efforts to supplement the family diet, see ibid., part 3, 13:81–82, 156; part 4, 13:120.

12. Ibid., part 3, 13:191; Perdue et al., *Weevils*, pp. 201–2. Many former slaves distinguished between "taking" from the master and "stealing" from other slaves. In this regard, see George P. Rawick, *From Sundown to Sunup: The Making of the Black Community* (Westport, Conn.: Greenwood Publishing Co., 1972), p. 69; Eugene D. Genovese, *Roll, Jordan, Roll: The World the Slaves Made* (New York: Vintage Books, 1976), pp. 602–3. And see May Satterfield's discussion of her mother's conversations with her after emancipation. Satterfield related, "She tell me dat po' nigger had to steal back dar in slav'y eben to git 'nuf t' eat. White fo'ks so mean didn't eben want niger t' eat. Do nothin' but work day and night. Done heard her say she been in de field 'long side de fence many day an' git creasy [cress] an' poke sallet an' bile it 'dout a speck o' greese an' give it to us chillum 'cause de rashon de white fo'ks lounce [allowance] out fo' de week done give out. . . . She say dey eben had to steal apples an' stuff lak dat as much as dey was on de place." Satterfield apparently believed the slaves were stealing. Having been reared after freedom came, she had a code of ethics that defined taking something not belonging to oneself as stealing unequivocally. Still, she sympathized with her mother and other slaves and in fact went on to explain that slave owners forced slaves to learn to steal. See Perdue et al., *Weevils*, pp. 244–45.

13. Rawick, Alabama, 6:131; Georgia, part 1, 12:108; part 3, 13:150, 239; part 4, 13:103; Jasper Battle remembered that slave children wore "dresses" until they were about five years old, at which time boys got shirts. And Ed McCree remembered that they "wore shirts that looked lak nightgowns. You jus' pulled one of dem slips over your haid and went on' cause you was done dressed for the whole week, day and night." See Rawick, Georgia, part 1, 12:65; part 3, 13:60. It should be noted here that slave mistresses often made these basic clothes for the children. Sewing for the entire "household" was often one of the "plantation mistresses'" many duties.

14. Rawick, Alabama, 6:294–95; Brent, *Incidents*, pp. 17–18; Perdue et al., *Weevils*, p. 217.

15. Perdue et al., *Weevils,* p. 32.

16. Brent, *Incidents,* p. 9.

17. See, for example, Rawick, Alabama, 6:216, 295; Georgia, part 3, 13:19, 129.

18. Deborah Gray White, *Ar'n't I a Woman? Female Slaves in the Plantation South* (New York: W. W. Norton, 1985).

19. Rawick, Georgia, part 1, 12:40; part 4, 13:183, 259; Alabama, 6:343, 426; Thomas Webber, *Deep Like the Rivers* (New York: W. W. Norton, 1978), p. 174; Stacey K. Close, "The Role and Status of the Elderly Male Slave in the Plantation South" (master's thesis, Ohio State University, 1990), p. 6; Leslie Owens, *This Species of Property: Slave Life and Culture in the Old South* (Oxford: Oxford University Press, 1976), p. 203.

20. Benjamin Bedford to Julian Bedford, July 31, 1854, Benjamin W. Bedford letterbook, box 1, folder 2, Tennessee State Library and Archives, Nashville. And see Bedford's contract and instructions to his overseer on a Mississippi plantation, dated September 7, 1858. On the farm where Henry Wright lived in Georgia, the old woman who cared for the children also cared for the ill and did the cooking. See Rawick, Georgia, part 4, 13:198–99.

21. Rawick, Alabama, 6:90; Georgia, part 4, 13:186–87.

22. Rawick, Georgia, part 3, 13:287; Alabama 6:192, 429. For other examples of why mothers might not want their children to be kept in the nursery, even if their owners had provided one, see Georgia, part 4, 13:206–7, where Dink Walton Young describes the nursery in such a way that it sounds like an animal pen.

23. Rawick, Alabama, 6:27–32, 87, 316; Georgia, part 3, 13:229. Rush was born in 1828 and was probably one of the oldest living ex-slaves in the country at the time of the WPA interviews (cited n. 3). And as noted in the text, she lived on Saint Simons Island. It is possible that these women were following an African tradition. Certainly this was one of the places where Africanisms survived the longest. Also, see Richard Oxford's interview in Rawick, Georgia, part 3, 13:150, in which he notes, and it is either an exaggeration or evidence of a faulty memory, "women in dem days could pick five hundred pounds of cotton a day wid a child in a sack on dere backs." Men rarely picked five hundred pounds of cotton a day, and men generally outpicked women. But the point here is that some women performed field work while carrying their children.

24. Rawick, Georgia, part 4, 13:19.

25. Ibid., part 3, 13:265, 237; Alabama, 6:90.

26. Rawick, Alabama, 6:72, 413–18. On the granting of kinship titles, see Herbert G. Gutman, *The Black Family in Slavery and Freedom, 1750–1925* (New York: Vintage Books, 1977), pp. 220–29; White, *Ar'n't I a Woman?* p. 133.

27. Letter dated October 3, 1787, Edward Telfair Papers, Perkins Library Archives, Duke University; Daybook of Nicholas Edmunds, Edmunds Family Papers, box 3, section 7, pp. 13, 23, VHS.

28. See *Commonwealth v. Ally, property of George Millan,* Fairfax County Court, February 18, 1835, box 1969; *Commonwealth v. Kesiah, property of Henry L. Carter,* Henricho County Court, 5 May 1834, box 1969; *Commonwealth v. Lucy, slave of Judith F??e,* Richmond Hustings Court, 16 September 1852, box 1970; and *Commonwealth v. Lucy, slave of Thomas Batton,* Lewis County Court of Oyer and Terminer, 4 November 1819, box 1968, Auditor of Public Accounts Records, Virginia State Library and Archives (cited hereafter as APAR-VSLA). For some de-

tailed analyses of these and other Virginia cases involving slaves, see Philip J. Schwarz, *Twice Condemned: Slaves and the Criminal Laws of Virginia, 1705–1865* (Baton Rouge: Louisiana Southern University Press, 1988).

29. William Masie Account Books, February 27, 1844, p. 24; June 27, 1856, p. 35; February 7, 1861, p. 51; photocopy, VSLA. Liz, Rhoda, and Lucy are listed in Massie's 1862 Negro Account Books for having received certain clothes. Lizzie is listed as a house servant. In his "1862 List of Children to be Clothed," Liz is listed as having three children, and Rhoda is listed with three. See 1862 Negro Account Books, Massie Family Papers, UT-BTHC.

30. See Todd Savitt, *Medicine and Slavery: The Diseases and Health Care of Blacks in Antebellum Virginia* (Urbana: University of Illinois Press, 1978); and Savitt, "Smothering and Overlaying of Virginia Slave Children: A Suggested Explanation," *Bulletin of the History of Medicine* 49 (Fall 1975): 400–404. And for a discussion of the so-called suffocation of slave infants, see Michael P. Johnson, "Smothered Slave Infants: Were Slave Mothers at Fault?" *Journal of Southern History* 47 (November 1981): 493–520. I have used the term *infanticide* throughout, though some of these children were beyond the stage of infancy.

31. See T. S. Jones to John Jones, June 21, 1852, T. S. Jones Family Correspondence, Special Collections, Vanderbilt University Library, Nashville, Tenn.

32. *Commonwealth v. Amey, property of John Gresham,* King and Queen County Court of Oyer and Terminer, May 13, 1799, box 1966; and *Commonwealth v. Jenny, property of Peter Stratton,* Powhatan County Court of Oyer and Terminer, September 7, 1815, box 1967, APAR-VSLA; testimony of T. B. Barnet, n.d., Granville County Slave Records, North Carolina State Archives.

33. Gerda Lerner, *Black Women in White America: A Documentary History* (New York: Vintage Books, 1978), p. 38. It is important to note, however, that social science scholarship on postpartum depression has gone far beyond hormonal imbalance explanations. Some of these explanations that might be relevant in the case of slave women include "unresolved conflicts" regarding motherhood and mothering, physical exhaustion, and the trauma of childbirth itself. Brief discussions of this are included in Mary-Joan Gerson, Judith L. Alpen, and Mary Sue Richardson, "Mothering: The View from Psychological Research," *Signs* 9 (Spring 1984): 434–53; Ann Oakley, "A Case of Maternity: Paradigms of Women as Maternity Cases," *Signs* 4 (Summer 1979): 607–31.

34. Indeed, while the women were often charged with murder, a real issue in these legal proceedings was their crimes against property. That is, they had destroyed their masters' property.

35. Vincent Harding, "Religion and Resistance among Antebellum Negroes, 1800–1860," in August Meier and Elliot Rudwick, eds., *The Origins of Black Americans,* vol. 5 of *The Making of Black America* (New York: Atheneum, 1969), p. 190.

36. Quotations on the evidence of abortion are in Darlene C. Hine, "Female Slave Resistance: The Economics of Sex," *Western Journal of Black Studies* 3 (Summer 1979): 124–26; White, *Ar'n't I a Woman?* pp. 84–89.

37. Dorothy Sterling, *Black Foremothers: Three Lives* (Old Westbury, N.Y.: The Feminist Press, 1979), p. 11. Deborah Gray White, in *Ar'n't I a Woman?* provides examples of women being forced to marry or have sex with men chosen by their owners; of their refusing to have children by "husbands" forced on them by their owners; and of one woman killing her child because her mistress regularly beat the child. See pp. 85–88, 102–3.

38. Nancy Venture Woods to John Haywood, February 1825, box 19, folder 112, Ernest Haywood Papers, Southern History Collection, University of North Carolina, Chapel Hill.

39. It is entirely possible that Woods's daughter, the mother of most of these children, was not there because she was at her "prime" in terms of her productive labor capacity. Nancy Woods, however, was evidently past her prime when she was assigned to care for these youngsters when they were unable to care for themselves. By this process, their owner still benefited from Woods's labor and was at the same time relieved of caring for her and the children. This example is very similar to the one involving the elderly man, Payne, on p. 303.

40. Rawick, Georgia, part 4, 13:302–3; Alabama, 6:358, 343.

41. Perdue et al., *Weevils,* pp. 264–65; Rawick, Georgia, part 4, 13:296–97.

42. Genovese, *Roll, Jordan, Roll,* pp. 510–11.

43. Rawick, Georgia, part 3, 13:2, 17, 80, 104, 140, 214, 218, 237; part 4, 13:16, 120.

44. Ibid., Georgia, part 3, 13:88, 147; part 4, 13:101.

45. Ibid., Georgia, part 3, 13:47, 58, 72, 201, 237; part 4, 13:195.

46. Ibid., Georgia, part 1, 12:114; part 3, 13:71, 116, 133, 149; part 4, 13:16, 195; Alabama, 5:176, 181, 321, 429; Heloise M. Foreman, Lulu M. Wilson, interview transcript, UT-BTHC, p. 2.

47. Rawick, Georgia, part 3, 13:133, 269; part 4, 13:315, Alabama, 6:130.

48. Rawick, Georgia, part 1, 12:64.

49. Even more profoundly, the religious practices, folktales, and folk songs passed on by men and women, and the gang labor system of work itself, daily encouraged the formation of a collective consciousness that enhanced survival not only while enslaved but also after emancipation. See, especially, Levine, *Black Culture and Black Consciousness.*

15.

"SWEET GOOD MOTHERS AND YOUNG WOMEN OUT IN THE WORLD"

The Roles of Irish American Women in Late Nineteenth- and Early Twentieth-Century Worcester, Massachusetts

TIMOTHY J. MEAGHER

In 1913 the *Catholic Messenger,* an Irish newspaper in Worcester, Massachusetts, paused in the midst of an impassioned discussion of the "woman's issue" to look back to "the wholesome old time days which produced the sweet, good mothers, . . . and young women . . . out in the world . . . earning their daily bread." The *Messenger's* musing testified to the strength of Irish culture's singularly sharp distinction between the roles of married and unmarried women. Few Western cultures combined nineteenth-century Ireland's rigid and narrow limitations of married women's sphere with the latitude Irish culture afforded single women in their freedom to migrate and find employment. The American environment was far different from Ireland, but here too in America, or more specifically in the *Catholic Messenger's* city of Worcester, the sharp differentiation between the roles of married and unmarried women stubbornly persisted among Irish Americans until at least the early twentieth century. That did not mean that the lives of Irish women did not change in the new environment. Their lives did change and radically so, but only within the structure of Ireland's peculiarly dichotomized conceptions of women's place. Not until the 1910s or later did hints begin to appear in Worcester that that dichotomy was beginning to lose its force.

Perhaps all cultures make distinctions between the roles of married and unmarried women, but few seem to make such sharp, almost paradoxical distinctions as Irish culture did in the late nineteenth and early twentieth centuries. In Ireland for example the narrow domestic sphere of married women became so idealized

Reprinted from *U.S. Catholic Historian* 5 (1986): 325–44, by permission of the publisher.

that by 1923 the new Irish Free State constitutionally prohibited wives from working outside the home. Single Irish women, conversely, were not only permitted to
work outside the home but encouraged, perhaps even forced to migrate thousands
of miles in search of employment. The proportion of single women among Irish
immigrants to the United States was thus far higher than that among any other
American immigrant group, running to 60 percent or more by the turn of the
century.[1]

This sharp distinction in late nineteenth- and early twentieth-century Ireland
between the roles of married and unmarried women was not a peculiar and isolated
quirk in the Irish social system. Indeed, it was one of the natural results of the transformation of that social system itself by momentous economic and religious
changes. The same trends that forced up celibacy rates and the average age of marriage also had a significant effect on the roles of women. Those trends included the
conversion of Irish farms from tillage to grazing, the virtual elimination of the
landless laboring class, the transition from partible to impartible inheritance, and
the tightening discipline and puritanism of Irish Catholicism. Before the Famine,
Irish wives had performed numerous and varied roles on the farm. In the new grazing economy that spread across the island in the post-Famine era, the need for their
labor was severely reduced. Their sphere thus became increasingly restricted to domestic duties, principally the bearing and raising of children. Irish Catholicism, infused with new zeal by a devotional revolution at mid century, lent ideological
support to these economic changes by increasingly idealizing the role of motherhood. Unmarried Irish women also felt the effects of the changes. There was little
need for their labor on the family farm as well. Most of them could not realistically
hope to marry locally. Without job or marriage prospects in their own or nearby
villages they were forced to roam far and wide in search of employment and marital partners.[2]

This peculiar pattern born in the culture and economy of rural, largely
Catholic Ireland proved remarkably hardy among Irish immigrants and their children in urban and religiously diverse American environments. In Worcester, for example, the vast majority of single Irish women worked while their married sisters
were confined to the home to care for large families. This pattern contrasted
sharply with the roles their female Yankee neighbors played. Not only did a smaller
proportion of Yankee women work, but native-stock wives gave birth to fewer children than the Irish. Yankee wives, on the other hand, participated far more fully in
societies and clubs outside the home than did married Irish women.

In Worcester as in Ireland the notions of married women's roles remained severely restricted. For the Irish in Worcester, there appeared to be no conception of
a wife's role apart from the role of mother. Irish Catholic newspapers repeatedly

sang the praises of "sweet good mothers," the "anchors" of the home, "so holy so strong and so effective" in their family influence. Such lyricizing was not simply sentimental cant. Worcester's Irish Catholic editors expected all wives to be mothers. In 1918 the *Catholic Messenger* sternly warned that "the unfortunate creature who has willfully deprived herself of the glory of motherhood may now hang her miserable head in abject shame. God has not blessed all married persons with these proofs of his love; but they who have voluntarily refused this evidence of divine favor now stand forth as objects of scorn before God and man." Five years earlier the paper had more soothingly urged wives to combine "all their talents in one aim: the guidance of children."[3]

Irish American newspapers in Worcester almost always assumed that the women of their own group and religion were thoroughly committed to this ideal of motherhood. Indeed, for the *Catholic Messenger* and its predecessor, the *Messenger,* the issues of family morality seemed to offer a welcome opportunity to trumpet the virtues of their own people in contrast to the perversion and degeneracy of their Yankee Protestant neighbors. While celebrating the "Irish Catholic women of the modern age" who held fast to the motherhood ideals of the Old Testament, the *Messenger* and the *Catholic Messenger* often savagely ridiculed Yankee Protestants who practiced family limitation or race suicide. In 1913, for example, the *Catholic Messenger* sardonically suggested that native-stock Protestants should recall their missionaries to the immigrants in order to "gather native congregations . . . and teach them the law of the Lord on marriage."[4]

Undoubtedly the editors of Worcester's Irish newspapers were motivated by ethnic and religious rivalry in their incessant moralizing on motherhood and birth control issues. So long ridiculed for their own moral failings—drunkenness, brawling, and political corruption—Worcester's Irish Catholics could not pass up the opportunity to reply in kind on family issues, where they felt they now held the higher moral ground. Nevertheless, as Protestants in the city themselves admitted, the claims of Worcester's Irish papers seemed to be based on fact. In 1900, for example, only 8.3 percent of Irish immigrant women and 7 percent of second-generation Irish women in Worcester forty-five years of age or older and married ten to twenty years had no children. By contrast, 23.7 percent of the Yankee women in Worcester married for the same length of time had no offspring. Further, 83.5 percent of the Irish immigrant mothers and 80 percent of the second-generation Irish wives had more than two children, while only 34 percent of Yankee married women had that many.[5]

Enshrining motherhood as the central, indeed almost exclusive role of the wife, Irish Americans in Worcester denounced any diversions that might keep her from her true place at the "center of the family." In 1885 the Irish owned and edited

Worcester Daily Times worried anxiously over the poverty that seemed to be drawing mothers into the work force and thus disrupting the "sacred ties" of the family.
Nevertheless, though a large majority of Irish men remained blue-collar workers
until well into the twentieth century—a significant proportion of them no better
than unskilled workers—few Irish wives worked outside the home. In both census
years 1880 and 1900, the proportion of married Irish women working outside their
households was no more than 5 percent.[6]

As Worcester's Celts well knew, however, married Irish women might not be
forced out of the home by economic necessity but lured out by social or recreational distractions. In 1913, the *Catholic Messenger* bemoaned the disastrous effects
of "modern conditions," which caused so many American wives to become "frivolous butterflies." The paper even condemned new "labor saving techniques" that
seemed to permit mothers and wives too much free time. Earlier in the late nineteenth century, Irish magazines and newspapers in Worcester sternly warned young
women to reflect on the seriousness of their domestic duties before contracting
poor matches out of the pursuit of idleness and pleasure.[7]

Statistical evidence suggests that few Irish wives found the lure of the club or
the seashore so enticing that they would cross this stern advice offered by community spokesmen. In two of Worcester's most important Irish female clubs, for example, the Catholic Young Women's Lyceum and the Catholic Women's Club,
married women made up a distinct minority until the 1910s. In the Catholic
Women's Club, married women made up only 22 percent of the members in 1911.
By contrast, seven years before, 77 percent of the members of the Yankee Worcester Women's Club were married. Irish wives unaccompanied by their husbands
were also rare in the *Messenger's* and *Catholic Messenger's* annual summer listings of
vacationers at the seashore. In 1898 and 1913 fewer than 12 percent of the women
listed were married. Most Irish wives, it appeared, followed the example of the old-
fashioned wife who wrote to the *Messenger* in 1905 proclaiming that she would
never go away for the summer if her husband could not go too.[8]

While these Irish wives in Worcester remained restricted to domestic duties
just as married women in Ireland did, the vast majority of their Celtic daughters
and sisters, again as in Ireland, "were out in the world earning their daily bread."
Nearly 80 percent of Worcester's first- and second-generation Irish single women
worked outside the home in 1880 and 1900. As might be expected, given the
strength of Irish tradition, these women received strong support from many members of their community. In 1890, a young Worcester Irishman remarked approvingly in his diary on the great encouragement his girlfriend's family had given her
in the pursuit of her trade as a milliner. Four years later, "Anna" wrote a long article
for the locally published *Catholic School and Home Magazine* in praise of the "no-

bility of the working girl." In 1899, the *Messenger* asserted, "We flaunt our belief in the face of the fiercest opponent that our business woman is not less a woman with all [that] the ideal term implies." In the same article the paper even argued for equal pay for equal work. Later in the twentieth century, the *Messenger's* successor, the *Catholic Messenger*, excoriated critics who theorized about links between rising numbers of working women and increasing rates of prostitution: "The young working women is good and true . . . and to throw the onus of the evil of modern times upon her is a rank injustice."[9]

Despite this evidence of strong support, Irish Americans in Worcester nonetheless experienced some confusion in backing the right of their unmarried women to work. They recognized that prevailing American opinion accepted working women only grudgingly. The proportion of Yankee single women working outside the home in 1900, for example, was smaller than the percentage of unmarried working Irish women. More important, however, the Irish in Worcester seemed confounded by their own ideological premises. If Ireland had bequeathed them the custom of single working women, it had failed to provide them with a rationale for defending it. The Worcester Irish consistently argued that a woman's true sphere was the home, and her true role was as wife and mother. Even magazines published by Irish women in Worcester in the 1880s and early 1890s urged young women to help their mothers with housework lest they be unprepared for their own ultimate vocations as wives and mothers. Irish American men and women in Worcester also frequently referred to the "fanciful natures," "tenderness," and fragility of women. Catholic clergymen, in particular, insisted on the fundamental differences of the sexes. No less magisterial an authority than Cardinal James Gibbons, in an article published twice in the *Messenger*, argued that "both sexes should not engage in the same pursuits but rather each sex should discharge those duties which are adapted to its physical constitution and sanctioned by the civil canons of society." Gibbons severely condemned any diversion that "alienates the feminine spirit from its foreordained and guarded haven, the home." If this were true how could the Worcester Irish justify the right of women to stray from their true place into "the business world shoulder to shoulder with those of sterner sex"?[10]

Irish American spokesmen in Worcester, while stalwartly supporting the right of women to work, thus seemed to grope in confusion for some justification of their support. Their religion, so useful in buttressing their position on married women's roles, offered no help, except for an occasional statement suggesting the educational value of work for women. Surprisingly, no Irish Americans in Worcester made any reference to religious orders of women as examples of the worthiness of working single women. Most often Irish defenses of single working women in

Worcester fell back on arguments of economic necessity and family duty. While acknowledging that women sometimes worked for themselves, they hastened to add that they often worked because of the "force of circumstances," "to be helpful to their people," or for "the dear helpless ones" in their families.[11]

Such arguments may have had some foundation in fact, but they were conveniently fuzzy. No doubt the poverty of some Irish American families forced their daughters out into the world of work. Perhaps in the middle decades of the nineteenth century virtually all of Worcester's Irish daughters labored for households teetering on the brink of economic disaster. That did not appear to be the case in 1880 or 1900, however. In those two census years a large proportion of second-generation Irish working women came from families enjoying modest prosperity. From two-fifths to one-half of second-generation white-collar daughters, for example, lived in households that had two or more adult male wage earners. More important, even many of the second-generation Irish women, who might have entered the working world solely to aid their families achieved considerable occupational progress, progress which in turn bred self-confidence and self-respect.[12]

The vast majority of single immigrant Irish women began and ended their working careers at the bottom of Worcester's economic hierarchy; their second-generation Irish counterparts were, however, far more fortunate. In both 1880 and 1900 less than 1.2 percent of the unmarried Irish immigrant women in Worcester were skilled blue-collar or white-collar workers. Nearly half were domestic servants. Second-generation Irish women were better situated and prepared to take advantage of the Worcester economy's growing opportunities for women. As daughters in established households they had no need for the protective shelter that domestic service afforded immigrant girls who came to America without their families. More important, their American experience and education made them prime candidates for the hundreds of bookkeeping, sales, clerical, and other white-collar posts opening up in Worcester's economy at the end of the nineteenth century. By 1900 nearly a quarter of the unmarried second-generation Irish women of Worcester were white-collar workers. Most of these were clerks or saleswomen, but by 1910 nearly half the teachers in Worcester's school system were second-generation Irish women. A tiny number, but nonetheless worth noting, had even become doctors.[13]

Irish Americans of both sexes in Worcester were well aware of the self-esteem such progress inspired among second-generation Irish women. As early as 1888 the *Messenger* noted wryly that the success of Irish American women workers had undermined the "slavery" of Celtic sisters to their brothers' wishes in Hibernian families. The paper ruefully admitted that there would be no more cries of "get up to let your brother sit down" in Worcester's Irish families. In 1894 "Anna" also praised the working girl "as one who dares to be independent." That same year Alice

O'Hara, a Worcester schoolteacher, looked forward to the twentieth century when women would be able to remain unmarried and pursue a career without rousing public comment.[14]

Not all of the Irish in Worcester approved of the growing assertiveness of Irish women. Some Irish males found the new freedom and self-reliance of single Celtic women disturbing. The *Catholic Messenger,* for example, criticized working girls in 1915 for loafing downtown after work and not hurrying home to help their mothers. More alarming was the suspicion that Irish Catholic girls found Irish boys too lowly in status or uncultured to consider as marriage partners, thus preferring to marry outside the Church or to avoid marriage altogether. These charges seem inflated. Second-generation Irish women married late, but so did second-generation Irish men. Moreover, not only did the vast majority of first- and second-generation Irish women eventually marry, but the vast majority married Irish men. Such fears, nonetheless, once again testified to the rising self-esteem of second-generation women.[15]

Such comments perhaps also testified to the freedom single Irish women in Worcester—again, it appears, largely second-generation women—enjoyed in their recreational life. While, as noted, few married women journeyed to the seashore or the mountains without their husbands, numerous single Irish women did so, and without male supervision. As early as 1886, the *Messenger's* social columns were filled with the names of single Irish women spending time at the Rhode Island seaside or New Hampshire lake resorts. In August of 1898, for example, 60 of 74 vacationers recorded by the *Messenger* were single women. In the same month in 1913, 30 of 34 were unmarried females. As important, a large proportion of these summertime vacationers were white-collar workers, presumably of the second generation. In 1898, for example, of the women who could be traced in the city directory, nearly 80 percent were white-collar workers.[16]

Further evidence of the expanding horizons of these successful unmarried Irish American women can be found in their growing participation in societies and clubs. Until the 1880s there appeared to be no permanent formal associations for Irish women in Worcester, outside of parish sodalities and devotional societies. In 1886, however, a women's temperance, literary, and social organization appeared in Worcester. By the 1910s nearly a third of the Irish American societies and clubs in Worcester were women's organizations. Most of these clubs drew their members from the ranks of single women, and many seemed to appeal largely to the most successful of these unmarried women. In 1906, for example, 42 percent of the members of the Catholic Young Women's Lyceum were teachers. Another 15 percent were bookkeepers, clerks, or saleswomen. A similarly large proportion of the Catholic Women's Club members, 49 percent, were white-collar workers in 1911.[17]

The broadening sphere of unmarried Irish women's activities in Worcester extended even to participation in efforts to free their ancestral homeland. Indeed, Irish American women, the vast majority of them unmarried, played a vital role in Worcester's Irish nationalist movement as early as 1880. In November of that year they organized a branch of the Ladies Land League in the city. Over the next two years they raised at least $5,000 to support Irish peasants engaged in the land war in Ireland. This sum far exceeded the amounts raised by the city's more numerous male-dominated Land League branches. More important, the Worcester's Ladies Land League defied the conservative male leadership of the local Land League agitation by dispatching their funds to Patrick Ford, the leader of the nationalist movement's radical faction. The motto of the Worcester Ladies League was further evidence of the seriousness of their purpose: "The land of every country belongs to the people of that country. No alien rule. Out on the invader. Thousands for independence, not one penny for rent."[18]

Though Worcester's Irish American women would never again play as important a role in the local Irish nationalist movement as they did in the early 1880s, they continued to participate in nationalist causes. The Ladies Auxiliary of the Ancient Order of Hibernians, for example, frequently debated the "Irish question" and in the 1890s and early 1900s passed resolutions in support of Ireland's freedom. In 1916, after the British government announced its decision to execute the leaders of the abortive Easter Rebellion, a public meeting appointed four women (all of them unmarried) and four men to draft resolutions of protest.[19]

Though the sphere of activity for unmarried Irish women in Worcester was clearly larger than for their married sisters, it is important to recognize the limits placed on the freedoms of Worcester's Irish single women as well. Despite their occupational successes, they were not expected, nor did most of them themselves seem to expect, to pursue a career in place of marriage. Their organizations were also almost always founded and rigorously controlled by men, usually priests. Members of the Catholic Women's Club, for example, obeyed the precepts of their founder, Rev. John J. McCoy, "to the letter," even to the design of their clubhouse. Also, these organizations seemed to lag far behind their Yankee counterparts in their attention to publicly controversial issues such as education, housing, or public health reforms. The Catholic Women's Club, for example, devoted most of its meetings to discussions of poetry or cooking demonstrations long after the Yankee-dominated Worcester Women's Club had become seriously involved in crusades for clean milk and women's suffrage.[20]

Irish stands on the latter issue, women's right to vote and hold office, also suggest the limits Irish Americans placed on the freedom of married and unmarried women alike. Throughout the late nineteenth and early twentieth centuries, Irish

Americans, even many Irish women, in Worcester were fiercely hostile to women's suffrage. In 1895 Irish wards in the city voted overwhelmingly against a state referendum that would have allowed women to vote in municipal elections. Though women were allowed to vote in this election, very few Irish women did. By contrast, voters in the city's native-stock wards split almost evenly over the suffrage issue, and three to four times more Yankee women turned out to vote in these wards than in Irish districts. It is true that suffrage was a complicated issue. Even Worcester's Yankee newspapers acknowledged that at that time local pro-suffrage reformers were closely allied with Prohibitionists and anti-Catholic nativists. There were also some Irish American women who spoke kindly of the suffragettes, though not of the "militant" types. Nevertheless, the *Messenger*'s ridicule in 1898 of "amazons" who flocked to the state legislature in pursuit of suffrage seemed to reflect well the opinions of Worcester's Irish community in the late nineteenth century.[21]

This hostility to women's suffrage seemed to soften somewhat in the twentieth century. Most of the Worcester Irish did not embrace women's suffrage, but their active antagonism did appear to become muted. Some Worcester Irish even became supporters of the suffrage cause. In 1915, when the women's suffrage question appeared on the state ballot once again, the Irish-owned *Worcester Evening Post* proclaimed its "strict neutrality" on the issue. Nevertheless, the *Post* asserted "not only that the right to the ballot on equality with men should be given to women but that sooner or later it will be given to them." The *Post* qualified its support by invoking arguments tied to traditional notions of women's roles, contending that new women voters would concentrate on questions concerning the home and the child, such as the cost of living or the purity of food. Furthermore, the paper's own straw poll revealed that anti-suffrage sentiment remained strong among Irish males in the Knights of Columbus and the police department. The paper, however, consistently, if carefully, urged on the suffragettes. Even more important, Irish Catholic women, even some prominent in Church clubs, began to play important roles in Worcester's suffrage organizations. Miss Catherine Hagerty served as treasurer of the Worcester Woman's Suffrage League, and Miss Ellen Callahan, Dr. Anna Murphy, and Miss Maud Cheese held important positions in the city's Equal Franchise Club.[22]

This shift in attitudes on women's suffrage in the 1910s may have been indicative of more-general changes among Worcester's Irish Catholics in their conceptions of women's roles. There is evidence, for example, that Irish married women began to move beyond the narrow limits of their homes in the second decade of the twentieth century. Married women dominated some of the new Irish women's associations, such as the Ladies Catholic Benevolent Association, which appeared in the 1910s. Irish wives also predominated in the St. Agnes Guild, founded in 1913, which provided a wide range of social services for poor mothers and their children. Even more interesting perhaps, while married Irish women seemed to find more freedom in the 1910s, Irish men appeared intent in that decide on restricting the already broad sphere of activities afforded single Irish women. The *Messenger* and the *Catholic Messenger,* at least, became much more prudish in the early twentieth century than they had been in the 1880s and 1890s. An important part of this new puritanism was a vigorous condemnation of public entertainments, such as dance halls or non-Catholic boardinghouses, which might lead young Catholic women into sin. Thus while the evidence is sketchy, and far too limited for firm conclusions, it appears that the exaggerated distinctions between married and unmarried women inherited from Ireland may have begun to blur by the early twentieth century.[23]

Nevertheless, hints of such a trend should not obscure the seemingly remarkable endurance of such distinctions among the Worcester Irish. Born in rural Catholic Ireland, the ideal of "sweet good mothers and young women out in the world earning their daily bread" had nonetheless proved very resilient among the Irish in the industrial and religiously plural environment of Worcester, Massachusetts. Indeed, that conception continued to clearly distinguish the Worcester Irish from their native-stock neighbors and even to provoke spirited conflict with the Yankees over a number of key issues.

Despite the obvious differences between the environments of Ireland and Worcester, however, Irish attitudes seemed to persist in the new world because of the same combination of influences which had shaped them in the old. More specifically, religious norms and economic considerations seemed to combine in Worcester as they had in Ireland to maintain a dichotomized conception of women's roles among the Irish. Catholic values, for example, seemed critical to the definition of the Irish wife's role as mother and her sphere as home. Poor immigrant Irish women may have viewed a large family as a potential economic resource, but such economic considerations do not explain why second-generation women and white-collar Irish wives should give birth to children at about the same rate as their poorer Irish-born sisters. Catholicism then seems to have exerted significant influence in maintaining the ideal of motherhood and the consequent norm of restricted, married domesticity among the new, upwardly mobile generation. Economic considerations were very important, however, in shaping conceptions of the roles of single women. Irish families might forgo the economic contributions of wives working outside the home, but they encouraged—even expected—single Irish women to work "to help their people" or "save the dear ones." This attitude, born in Ireland and nourished by working-class conditions in American industrial cities like Worcester, seemed to persist even after it became clear that many Irish families did not need their daughter's wages, or that some Irish women discovered a new self-confidence and sense of independence in their work.[24]

Irish Americans thus seemed to conceive of women's roles in strict terms of duty. The wife's role was to be a mother, the daughter's role was to work. Worcester's Irish consistently attacked women who deviated from either of those norms. They condemned "idle," "frivolous" daughters who avoided work with the same vehemence that they attacked "irresponsible" wives who "flitted" from club to club neglecting their motherly chores or, worse yet, motherhood itself. The women graduates of Worcester's only Catholic high school expressed that view with some self-satisfaction in 1886: "Well for us that we have been taught not to take our place in the ranks of the pleasure seekers but among the toilers, working while young and we yet have time."[25]

Such support for the freedom of single women to work, however, had some unanticipated consequences in the new urban industrial environment of Worcester. In the new environment, unlike in Ireland, Irish women (especially American-born women) did not merely find work, they found positions of status as teachers, bookkeepers, clerks, and saleswomen. Such positions bred self-confidence and a sense of independence. The new environment also facilitated women's organizations and offered a variety of recreational outlets. Once unmarried women were permitted the freedom to work outside the household, it proved difficult to rein them in and restrict them to the natural place for all women: the home.

There were restrictions, however, even upon the broadly conceived spheres of single women. Almost all Irish women's organizations felt the heavy impress of male influence, particularly clerical male influence. More important, Irishmen seemed to place strict limits on the political roles of women. Here Irish attitudes were complicated—even paradoxical. Single Irish women freely joined efforts to liberate the ancestral homeland throughout the late nineteenth and early twentieth centuries, but the majority of Irish men and women seemed to oppose granting women the right to vote and hold office in America. In part their opposition seemed to stem from the nativist and Prohibitionist taint to the suffrage movement. The anti-immigrant and anti-Catholic tinge to the women's suffrage movement was noticeable throughout the United States but was particularly visible in Worcester. Nevertheless, it is difficult to imagine that the Irish in Worcester opposed suffrage only because some of their most bitter opponents backed it. It may be that the Worcester Irish suspected the suffrage movement because it granted the right of political participation to all women, married and unmarried. Not only might the working daughter or single woman plunge into the world of politics but so might the wife and mother, straying from her restricted sphere of the home. Furthermore the Irish community itself could not regulate women's political participation if enfranchisement were granted to all women. Irish nationalist activity by single women, on the other hand, threatened neither the mother's role nor the community's oversight of women's political activity. Finally, support for women's suffrage may have required a fundamental alteration in Irish concepts of women's nature, a reorientation of attitudes to accept women's basic similarities to men. This step the Irish of Worcester seemed reluctant to take.

The history of Worcester's Irish women in the late nineteenth and early twentieth centuries reveals a complicated pattern of continuity and change. While the American environment combined with religious norms to maintain sharp Irish distinctions between married and unmarried women's roles, that same environment permitted—even encouraged—significant changes in the status and freedom of single women. By the second decade of the twentieth century there were hints that this old dichotomy might be breaking down, suggesting, ironically, new restrictions on unmarried women as the spheres of Irish American wives broadened. The *Catholic Messenger*'s longing for "sweet good mothers and young women out in the world earning their daily bread" in 1913 may have been fond nostalgia for traditions that were already passing. Such a judgment may be too hasty, however, for in 1913 the *Messenger*'s lament still seemed a fair reflection of the attitudes of its own people as well as their ancestors of "old time days."

NOTES

This essay was originally presented at the Cushwa Center Conference on American Catholicism, October 4, 1985.

1. Mary T. W. Robinson, "Women in the New Irish State," in Margaret MacCurtain and Donnacha Corrain, eds., *Women in Irish Society: The Historical Dimension* (Dublin, 1978), pp. 168–70; Robert F. Kennedy, *The Irish* (Berkeley, 1973), p. 75.

2. Lawrence McCaffrey, *The Irish Diaspora in America* (Bloomington, Ind., 1976), p. 70; Kennedy, *The Irish*, pp. 8–10, 52–61, 75, 159–62, 173–77, 195–96, 202–3; Lynn Lees, *Exiles of Erin: Irish Migrants in Victorian London* (Ithaca, N.Y., 1979), p. 128; K. H. Connell, *Irish Peasant Society: Four Historical Essays* (Oxford, 1961), pp. 15–16, 50, 83; Garoid O'Tuathaigh, "The Role of Irish Women under the New English Order," Joseph J. Lee, "Women and the Church since the Famine," and Robinson, "Women in the New Irish State," in MacCurtain and O'Corrain, eds., *Women in Irish Society*, pp. 26–45, 58–70, 75–84, 168–70.

3. *Catholic Messenger*, July 5, 1918, June 20, 1913.

4. *Messenger*, March 28, 1902; *Catholic Messenger*, May 16, 1913; *Messenger*, July 27, 1903.

5. Samples one in nine Irish immigrants and one in twelve second-generation Irish from

the Census Manuscript Schedules, 1900 U.S. Census; sample one in twenty native born, native parents, ibid.; *Worcester Daily Times,* April 7, 1885.

6. Samples of immigrant and second-generation Irish, 1900 U.S. Census.

7. *Sacred Heart Calendar,* April 1891, p. 2. "Anna," "Home Corner," *Catholic School and Home Magazine,* March 1894, pp. 15–17; November 1893, pp. 251–52; June 1895, pp. 95–96; *Alumna,* July 1886, p. 1; *Catholic Messenger,* February 28, 1913.

8. *Messenger,* August 13, 20, 26, 1898; *Catholic Messenger,* August 15, 22, 1913; *Messenger,* July 18, 1905; *Catholic Messenger,* January 27, 1911; *Worcester House Directory* (Worcester, 1900), p. 523. In addition, all of the original officers of the Ladies Auxiliary of the Ancient Order of Hibernians were unmarried, and by 1901 all the officers of Division 11 Ladies Auxiliary of the AOH were single: *Messenger,* April 21, 1894, June 30, 1901. All but one of the officers of the St. Loretta Court of the Massachusetts Catholic Order of Foresters in 1900 were single: *Twenty-Second Annual Report of the Massachusetts Catholic Order of Foresters* (Boston, 1901).

9. Immigrant and second-generation Irish samples, 1900 U.S. Census; Stephen Littleton, Diaries, vol. 4, entry for January 7, 1890, American Antiquarian Society, Worcester; "Anna," "Nobility of the Working Girl," *Catholic School and Home Magazine,* March 1896, p. 13; *Catholic Messenger,* July 4, 1913; *Messenger,* October 28, 1899.

10. Robert Smuts, *Women and Work in America* (New York, 1959), p. 48; Hasia Diner, *Erin's Daughters in America: Irish Immigrant Women in the Nineteenth Century* (Baltimore, 1983), p. 74; *Alumna,* July 1886, p. 1; "Anna," "Home Corner," *Catholic School and Home Magazine,* December 1896, pp. 210–12; *Sacred Heart Calendar,* April 1891, p. 1; August 1891, p. 2; Alice L. O'Hara, "Women in the Twentieth Century," *Catholic School and Home Magazine,* June 1894, p. 2; "E. T. McG.," "Epigrams," *Catholic School and Home Magazine,* July 1895, pp. 115–17; "Anna," "Home Corner," *Catholic School and Home Magazine,* December 1896, pp. 210–11; "J. O.," "Heroines of Fiction Past and Present," *Catholic School and Home Magazine,* June 1894, pp. 63–64; *Catholic Messenger,* July 4, 1913.

11. *Messenger,* October 28, 1899; *Catholic Messenger,* July 4, 1915.

12. In 1880 45.5 percent of the white-collar daughters who lived in two-parent households lived in families where the father was a skilled or white-collar worker and there was one other working sibling, or the father was a semi- or unskilled worker and two brothers were working. In 1900 54.9 percent lived in such families. In 1880 38.6 percent of women industrial workers lived in such families, and in 1900 42.6 percent of women industrial workers lived in such families. Immigrant and second-generation Irish samples, 1880 and 1900 U.S. Censuses.

13. Immigrant and second-generation Irish samples, 1880 and 1900 U.S. Censuses. Between 1880 and 1900 the number of female clerical jobs, bookkeepers, clerks, saleswomen, and stenographers in Worcester grew 928 percent. The number of women teachers in Worcester grew 421 percent in the same period: *Tenth Census of the United States Taken in the Year 1880,* vol. 1, *Population* (Washington, D.C., 1900), p. 909; *Twelfth Census of the United States Taken in the Year 1900,* vol. 2, part 2, *Population* (Washington, D.C., 1903), pp. 599–602. Irish American women in Worcester were more successful in becoming teachers than their Celtic sisters in almost any other American city: *Reports of the Immigration Commission, 61st Congress, 3rd Session, Document no. 747, Abstracts of Reports of the Commission,* vol. 2, pp. 58–59.

14. "Anna," "Nobility of the Working Girl," *Messenger,* February 11, 1888; O'Hara, "Women in the Twentieth Century," pp. 90–91.

15. *Catholic Messenger,* July 1, 1915; *Messenger,* January 6, 1900, September 9, 1899; *Catholic Messenger,* February 28, 1913, March 1, 1908.

16. *Messenger,* August 1886, August 4, 11, 1888; August 13, 20, 26, 1898; *Catholic Messenger,* August 15, 22, 1913. Seventeen of twenty-two single women from the 1898 lists traced in the *Worcester City Directory* (Worcester, 1898) were white-collar workers.

17. *Messenger,* October 28, 1893, April 7, 1894, March 31, 1894, May 30, 1896; *Catholic Messenger,* February 8, 1907; *Worcester City Director* (Worcester, 1920); *Messenger,* February 16, 1906; *Catholic Messenger,* January 27, 1911; *Worcester City Directory* (Worcester, 1906), and *Worcester City Directory* (Worcester, 1911).

18. *Worcester Evening Post,* May 31, 1906; Richard O'Flynn Manuscripts, Folio 1, November 17, 1880, February 18, 1882, Treasure Room, Holy Cross College Library; *Irish World,* March 25, 1882.

19. *Catholic Messenger,* October 4, 1914; *Messenger,* September 20, 1902, January 22, 1905; *County Convention of the Ladies Auxiliary of the A.O.H.,* September 28, 1906, American Antiquarian Society, Worcester; *Catholic Messenger,* June 15, 1916.

20. *Messenger,* October 28, 1893, March 31, 1894; *Catholic Messenger,* February 8, 15, 1907; "Catholic Women and Temperance," *Catholic School and Home Magazine,* October 1894, p. 169; *Catholic Messenger,* February 13, 1914.

21. The vote in the three Irish wards was 68 percent to 32 percent opposed, and in the Yankee wards 51.1 percent to 49.8 percent opposed: *Worcester Spy,* November 6, 1895. The number of women registered to vote in the two Yankee wards was 713; the number in the three Irish wards was 180: *Worcester Spy,* October 17, 1895. For links between suffrage and Prohibition and nativism, see James Kenneally, "Catholic and Women's Suffrage in Massachusetts," *Catholic Historical Review* 53, no. 1 (April 1967): 43–57; and *Worcester Evening Gazette,* October 18, 1876, October 24, 1876. For Irish women's opinions on suffrage, see O'Hara, "Women in the Twentieth Century," p. 90; *Messenger,* July 29, 1893; "Booklover," *Catholic School and Home Magazine,* June 1895, p. 66. For the *Messenger's* opinion on "amazons," see *Messenger,* April 30, 1898.

22. *Worcester Evening Post,* October 6, 18, 23, 1915; Charles C. Nutt, *History of Worcester* (New York, 1919), 1:953, 4:30; *Messenger,* March 31, 1915.

23. For married women in organizations, see *Catholic Messenger,* August 15, 1913, September 30, 1915; *Catholic Free Press,* August 5, 1955. For new prudery and restrictions on single women, see *Messenger,* November 7, 1903, January 12, 1906; *Catholic Messenger,* October 18, 1910, April 18, 1913, October 3, 1913, February 13, 1914, March 20, 1914, March 29, 1918, July 12, 1918.

24. Special "dummy" variables were created to measure the effect of the wife's generation and the husband's occupation on the fertility of married Irish women in 1900. These variables were included in regression equations with the variables of age and number of years married. With the latter two variables controlled, the beta and F tests revealed that wife's generation and husband's occupation had very little effect on the fertility rates of married Irish women:

Wife's Generation	Beta	F
Age	-.28	11.163
No. of years married	.78	85.79
Generation	.03	.69

Generation measures the second generation's deviation from the immigrant norm.

Husband's Occupation	Beta	F
Age	-.27	10.7
Number of years married	.78	89.4
White-collar	-.01	.07
Unskilled and semi-skilled blue-collar	-.05	1.68

White-collar and unskilled and semi-skilled measure the deviation from a skilled norm.

25. *Notre Dame Alumna,* July 1886, p. 2.

16.

Jewish Mothers and Immigrant Daughters
Positive and Negative Role Models

SYDNEY STAHL WEINBERG

Male reminiscences and novels have created familiar stereotypes of the domineering "Jewish mother" and the struggle of sons for independence. This study suggests that such descriptions do not as readily apply to relationships between immigrant mothers and daughters.[1] The view presented here has grown out of an intensive oral history project, supplemented by traditional research in memoirs and autobiographies. The oral histories explore the lives of forty-six women who left Eastern Europe for the United States by 1925 and were old enough when they emigrated to have some memory of their early home.[2] These women differed in their area of birth, social class, and circumstances of departure.[3] Yet they had much in common. Despite the dislocations involved in entering a highly industrialized society, most of them emphasized the importance of their mothers as role models of some kind. The majority also felt that their order of birth and age at time of immigration determined relationships within their families.[4] Almost all the women interviewed shared the belief that one or both of these factors exerted a significant effect upon their lives.

Dora W., for example, believed that she had come to America at just the right age. As the third child and second of three daughters who had emigrated with her parents when she was eight years old, Dora felt that her relationship with her parents was better than that of her sisters because of her particular situation. "We were once in my house, my sisters and I," she recalled, "having discussions of older times. We spoke about our parents, and it was fascinating. You would think that the three of us had different sets of parents. And maybe we did. You wouldn't recognize *my* parents from what my older sister said or what my younger sister said." Dora went on to explain why she and her sisters held such diverse impressions. Her older sister hated her father for taking her away from Russia at fifteen, leaving behind school, a boyfriend, and a familiar life. A sensitive and educated girl, she was too old for school in America and had to work in a garment shop, where she was miserable. As the oldest daughter, she also bore heavy responsibilities for helping her mother at home. When she wanted to go out with friends or keep some of her salary for herself, her father refused to permit such liberties. She never managed to "Americanize," or to do the next best thing—marry an American man—and she blamed her father for her unfulfilled life. Dora's younger sister resented her parents for a different reason. She was born in America and shared the unfortunate trait of some American-born children—shame at being part of a foreign-born family. As the youngest, she was a favorite of her father and mother, but she wanted them to be like the parents of her American friends and felt embarrassed by their poor home on Manhattan's Lower East Side.

Dora, however, believed that she had "the best of both worlds." She remembered enough of her life in Russia to appreciate the difficulties her parents faced in leaving and creating a new life in America. Dora understood that they had done this for the sake of their children, and she felt that she had benefited from their decision more than her sisters. She had attended school here, as her older brother and sister could not, but she still had to make the effort to learn a new language and way of life, which her American-born sister took for granted. Thus, as poor as her family was, Dora knew that life was going to be better in America than it would have been in Russia; she always felt that she was "upward bound."

The sisters' differences in age shaped attitudes toward their parents and led to very different life experiences. Dora's older sister remained within the immigrant culture, while the youngest blamed her mother and father's foreign ways for preventing her from being accepted as "a real American." Dora believed that she alone had successfully bridged the gap between cultures and felt comfortable with both her European origins and her life in America.

Birth order was also crucial in determining a daughter's responsibilities in the home. Generally, older daughters were expected to act as their mothers' chief assistants in caring for the home and younger children. Particularly when families were poor, the daily struggle to put food on the table placed heavy burdens on these girls. Many older daughters felt overworked by their duties, cooking and cleaning and watching over their siblings. Some even took charge completely while their mother was out earning a living. "I had no freedom," asserted Rose G., echoing the statements of others, "no childhood at all." These women believed that their brothers had easier lives. Although boys, too, might leave school at a young age to work, their childhood years were relatively free of family obligations. Few attended day-long Hebrew schools, as they would have in Eastern Europe,[5] nor were they expected to help with the household chores and younger children. "My brother really enjoyed his life," recalled Fannie C. "I had all the responsibilities."

These attitudes are reflected in the different perceptions of their mothers' kitchens recorded by the sons and daughters of this generation. For boys, it was a refuge where they were coddled guests. In the memories of sons, the mother's performance of her chores assumes an almost mystical quality, as in Sholem Asch's *The Mother,* where in an impoverished family, "Sarah Rifke turns to her magical cooking pots to provide for her family. She could milk her pots as though they were cows. They never denied her anything. She gave them cold water and the pots yielded yesterday's carrot soup anew. . . . When the pots heard mother sigh it was as though she had repeated a secret incantation over them with which she adjured them to supply the pitifully meager bit of nourishment which was all she demanded for her large brood."[6] Alfred Kazin described his mother's Sabbath preparations in a similar manner. "By sundown," he wrote, "the curtains had been drawn, the world put to rights. Even the kitchen walls had been scrubbed and now gleamed in the Sabbath candles. On the long white tables were the company dishes." Kazin's mother accomplished her tasks without effort, almost magically. "When my father came home from work," he recalled, "she had somehow mysteriously interrupted herself to make supper for us, and the dishes cleared and washed, was back at her machine."[7] This was a woman's world, viewed through a romantic haze created by a complete lack of experience with the efforts it took.

Girls knew that it was hard work rather than magic that put food on the table. Because of the different roles mothers played in the lives of their male and female children, girls' perceptions of their mothers' chores were more precise than the descriptions recorded by sons. For older daughters, the family kitchen was a school and workshop where labor seldom ceased. Fannie C. remembered that her mother "was busy the whole day long. She was an immaculate housekeeper—she used to sew too. She made all my clothes. She always had people in, and she did everything herself. For Friday, she got up early to bake the challah [Sabbath bread] and the little cakes. Then she would make the gefilte fish and roll out dough to make the noodles." Before she was old enough to go to school, Fannie learned to help with these tasks. Anzia Yezierska, a well-known writer in the 1920s, provides a less rosy but equally graphic description of her mother, who "dried out her days fighting at the push-carts for another potato, another onion into the bag, wearing out her heart and soul and brain with the one unceasing worry—how to get food for the children a penny cheaper."[8] In their mother's lives, daughters saw with fear or anticipation what they themselves might become.

If sons generally held a favored position in the family, youngest children, even if they were girls, also had an easier time than their older siblings. They often escaped most household chores, and there were no younger children for them to care for. As the babies, they were frequently spoiled by parents or older sisters. As Dora W. explained the relationship within her own family, her father had mellowed and was less restrictive when she was growing up than he had been with his older children. Her brother and sister had to fight for their privileges, while she was permitted more freedom without a struggle. Part of this change she credited to age, but part was also due to the respect her father had for his more Americanized child. Gussie M. similarly attributed her mother's closeness to her youngest child to a change in attitude after emigrating. In her village of birth, children had been expected from their earliest years to labor for the family, with few rewards or thanks—a system similar to that of working-class families throughout the Western world in the nineteenth century, where parents considered children as "their own flesh, blood and labor supply."[9] When they came to the United States, however, Gussie's mother saw how people treated children—"with respect, with ice cream cones, and she learned." Her youngest daughter reaped the benefit.

Middle-class families in Europe and America, particularly in urban areas, were already treating young children *as* children rather than as an economic investment.[10] This did not mean that daughters no longer had obligations to the family, but rather that their efforts were often appreciated rather than taken for granted. If a daughter's work in the home or a factory was appreciated by her parents, it could provide a source of fulfillment and was not considered a chore. "I felt a great deal of responsibility towards my parents," observed Fannie C., "and I felt that they loved and appreciated me." Pauline H., who at fourteen had to keep house for her father and brothers, recalled with pride the words of praise she earned. "They used to say, '*A junge kindt un an alte kopf*' [a young child with an old, or wise, head]." Anna S., who ruined her health working to bring her parents to America, remembers her mother thankfully saying, "This is my daughter's miracle." Only when they were taken for granted did such women later resent their sacrifices.[11] In general, the closer the relationship, the more willingly did daughters assist their mothers, although all girls were expected to work in the home.

This relationship also helped determine a daughter's attitude toward contributing her wages to the family. In most Western nations, this was expected of working daughters,[12] and statistics indicated that girls contributed to a greater extent than their brothers.[13] A common refrain was "people were depending on me." Many women used the example of their mothers' selflessness to explain why they had been willing to work to help the family. Furthermore, despite the American emphasis on individualism, responsibility to one's family became a more generally accepted value after the onset of the Great Depression.[14]

Often older daughters helped support their families while brothers attended school,[15] but age just as frequently as sex determined whether a child attended school or went to work. In a Census Bureau survey of Jewish immigrants who were forty-five years and older in 1950, the men averaged 8.1 years of schooling and the women 5.8. But the years of education either sex achieved was low compared to that of their younger siblings. Among younger foreign-born Jews, twice as many boys as in the older group, but three times as many girls, graduated from high school. Children who came to this country younger thus had a greater chance of receiving a high school education, and the difference in years of education between girls and boys is narrow. Among the American-born men and women, many of whom were the youngest children of immigrant parents, the difference is insignificant.[16] Thus, although sons were initially favored slightly if a family could afford to permit only one of its children to remain in school rather than work, once financial security was established, younger children of both sexes had greater access to education than either their older sisters *or* brothers.

For older girls in particular, if the family needed their income, there were few options besides the factory. "We were the lost generation," observed Fannie K., who came to America at the age of twenty. "If we were born here, who knows what we could have been?" "I saved the family," recalled Anna S., who had worked steadily since she was fourteen, "but it almost killed me." These young women who had come too late to get an education themselves could sometimes cope with disappointment by transferring their desire for learning to the youngest child or children. Several women I interviewed went to high school and one even finished law school because older siblings had worked and insisted that they complete their education. They were aware of the sacrifices of these older sisters, and of their limited horizons regardless of talent or intelligence. "She was the oldest and I'm the youngest," mused Marie F., who became an opera singer. "It made all the difference in the world."

Apart from the order of their birth, an important influence on women's lives was the role their mothers had played in the family. Although many daughters became Americanized and most worked steadily before marrying, they did not assume that a homebound mother was less important than a wage-earning father. In fact, the most common observation about a mother was that she was "a great manager," when managing meant everything from looking after her husband's and children's needs, to taking in boarders and doing piecework, to controlling the family's expenditures—the key to most women's importance throughout urban society at that time.[17] The smooth functioning of the household thus depended on a wife's ability to "manage." Her sense of competence as well as her daughter's appreciation came from the ability—as one woman succinctly put it—"to make two pennies out of one." Rose G. remembered her mother "saving up the pennies she and her brother had earned—and every one counted. She used to say, 'My little bags will outlive other people's big sacks of money.' And they did, because she was very good at it." Women remembered such qualities and prided themselves on following their mothers' example. Rose L. recalled that "any money my husband had, he gave it to me. Thank God, like my mother, I was always a good manager."

These women learned from their mothers to place the well-being of their families before the demands of pride or status. Sometimes fathers became demoralized at having to accept a low-paying, low-status job in this country and never succeeded in earning enough to care for their families adequately. The wives of such men usually managed to keep food on the table by taking a temporary job or earning money in the home when times were hard. Status did not matter as much to these women. As Riva P. observed, for her mother "the important thing was that the family be taken care of." Ethel B.'s mother worked in her husband's business and secretly put away a small amount of money each week. When the business failed during the Great Depression, she had saved $1,000 to start over. Rose G., who still works at eighty-six, remembered that her mother loved going out to work with her husband. "She was happy when she was needed and busy," Rose observed, "like I am too."

Some young unmarried daughters, although very few in this survey,[18] had an ambivalent relationship with their mothers. One source of this ambivalence was based upon a subtle kind of rivalry. Although parents generally had emigrated so their children might lead an easier life, some mothers could not help envying the opportunities, which contrasted so vividly with their own limited lives. As a woman saw her daughter exceeding her in education, in adjusting to America, in possibilities for a satisfying life, the only advantage the mother held was in the performance of her housewifely duties. Thus, while she usually took pride in her daughter's accomplishments, a mother might at the same time withhold the finer points of cooking or baking and would give her instead the less skilled tasks to perform in the home.[19]

Parents could also be ambivalent about their children's "American" ways. Some mothers and fathers made great efforts to learn the language—more Jewish adults than those of any other immigrant group attended night school.[20] A few refused to permit books written in any language but English into their homes. Even if they sought to retain old customs, most parents nevertheless seemed proud of their Americanized children. Several women, who were the youngest children in the family and therefore the most Americanized, commented upon this pride and observed that in their parent's eyes they could do no wrong. Yet sometimes the apparent requirements of "Americanization" created tensions within families. Conflict could erupt over a daughter's decision to work on the Sabbath, spend money on clothing, attend dances or union meetings in the evenings, go to movies, and in general seek more freedom. Tanya N. had to leave home for a few days to avoid her father's wrath after she "bobbed" her long hair. Fannie C. resented her father's refusal to permit her to attend a high school prom with schoolmates. In many families, a daughter's desire to express her individualism, a trait fostered by American society, clashed with a parent's insistence on the primary importance of family needs or the assertion of patriarchal authority.[21] Urbanization and industrialization had altered life irrevocably, and a mother's homebound existence offered few clues to behavior in this new world. Girls would insist that parents did not understand them, and mothers could no more provide role models for these teenage daughters on the Lower East Side of New York than they could in the working-class areas of Białystok or Odessa.[22] Some young women working in factories found an alternative focus to family life in union activities or in socializing with their peers. Those who did not work lacked this option and their lives were more restricted. Some even chose to work because of the greater freedom this would gain for them; one fourteen-year-old girl decided to take a job when her mother told her that only those who worked needed new clothes and shoes.

Despite such conflicts, mothers seemed less likely than fathers to impose their values upon daughters. The term "fanatical," frequently applied to a dictatorial father, was never used to describe a mother, no matter how religious she was. Furthermore, mothers often served the function of mediator—a bridge between the old ways and the new, or simply between a rigid father and a daughter (or son) desiring more freedom.[23] For example, when Dora W. got a good job requiring her to work on Saturday, her father refused to speak to her for a year, but her equally pious mother accepted Dora's wages and eventually secured a reconciliation. When the mother of Mildred L., a simple, devout woman, learned that her troubled daughter was attending a Christian Science church, she kept it from her husband and told the girl, "If it's doing you good, it has to be good, and I want you to have it." Fannie K.'s mother, more religious than her father, accepted her daughter's lesser piety and helped hide from her husband the dresses Fannie bought lest he object to the unnecessary expense. Although mothers usually maintained their old-country traditions, they generally accepted their children's signs of entry into the modern world more readily than fathers. These women perhaps could vicariously achieve through their daughters a freedom they were seldom permitted in Eastern Europe. Possibly they believed that their own traditions might prevent their children from assimilating and thus reaping the benefits of becoming Americans.[24] Perhaps they simply wanted to keep peace within the family. Regardless of the reason, mothers seemed to accept the Americanization of their daughters with relative equanimity.[25]

Although ambition to be anything but a wife and mother was not considered appropriate for young women of any ethnic background,[26] Jewish immigrant mothers, while accepting traditional roles for themselves, sometimes encouraged their daughters' ambitions, or at least passed on a mixed message. The mother of Marie F., for example, opposed her going on the stage, preferring that she be "safely married," but when her daughter proved adamant, they both moved to Chicago to help with Marie's career. When Sophie Abrams Flint, as a child, read until late at night, her mother would wake up and say, "The light is still on? What do you expect to be, a doctor or a lawyer? What's the use of all this reading and writing? Don't be foolish, a woman never needs to know anything!" But Sophie would hear her mutter under her breath, "A talented child has hands of gold."[27] Despite the desire that their daughters marry, such mothers encouraged in them a sense of independence, sometimes without themselves being aware of it.[28]

Many mothers seem to have encouraged their daughters' desire for education in part because of their own thwarted ambitions or limited lives, and in part because they followed a timeworn tradition of wanting them to be self-supporting if necessary. Mollie Linker remembered her mother wanting something better for all her children but especially for the girls,[29] and the mother of Hattie L., who made a career out of helping other immigrants get settled, was proud when her daughter became a nurse. In Abraham Cahan's *The Rise of David Levinsky,* Dora, an illiterate immigrant woman, lives her life through her daughter, whom she views with a combination of pride and envy. "My own life is lost," she thought, "but she shall be educated."[30] This was a common attitude. Riva P.'s mother, like Dora, used to berate her daughter when she did poorly in school and tell her how lucky she was to be able to get an education. "If I were raised in this country," she told her repeatedly, "do you imagine what I would have become?" Very few mothers, though, would go as far as Kate Simon's did. "Study, learn. Go to college," she urged her daughter. "Don't get married, at least not until you can support yourself and make a careful choice. Or don't get married at all, better still."[31]

Even if a relationship between mother and daughter faced strains when a daughter was in her teen years, the tie usually became closer once the younger women married.[32] Possible tensions arising from a girl wanting to date, buy clothing, or lead a relatively independent life were replaced by concerns similar to those of the mother: how to manage a home, deal with a husband, and raise children. Mothers and daughters now would share more interests. They could help each other with shopping, household activities, and baby-sitting,[33] a connection common to women of other ethnic groups as well after a daughter's marriage.[34] At this point, young women could accept their mothers as role models. Women who wanted their lives to follow a different path were still aware of the effect their mothers exerted in forming their attitudes. "My life," asserted Rose Chernin, "you can only understand if you know my mother."[35]

Apart from learning housekeeping skills, many women had learned from observing their mothers how to make important decisions in their own homes while maintaining, for the sake of their husbands' egos, that these decisions were made by the men. Rose G., for example, insisted that she, like her mother, had continually deferred to her husband. "Louis," she remembered telling him, "please don't come down from your pedestal." In most cases, however, the creation of this male dominant role was a convenient fiction. Like Rose, Fannie C. asserted that her father made the decisions, but went on to explain that her mother had ways of getting what she wanted. "Many of the decisions my father made," Fannie concluded, "were really hers to start with. But as children we were under the impression that it was my father's decision." It was important that men *appear* to be the heads of the family, making all important decisions. The reality was somewhat different, as it was among other immigrant groups where it was important to maintain the public posture of male leadership.[36] In such families, the men were "ceremonial leaders," assuming credit for the decisions the women convinced them they had made on their own.[37] One woman described how she had learned this strategy from her mother: "She lets him think he is boss but when anything really important comes up she usually handles it without letting him know she is doing it. When it is disposed of, he pats himself on the back and claims all the credit. And she lets him get away with it, never contradicts him. She tipped me off to that system when I got married and I guess that is why my husband and I get along so well."[38] These women were, as Frances F. put it, "the power behind the throne." Many women acted in this circumspect way to help maintain the egos of husbands who had difficulty adjusting to low status and poorly paid jobs. In their households, as in those of their daughters, solutions to most problems were based on the input of both parents rather than imposed by the father alone, regardless of outward appearances.[39]

The way women ran a home and raised their children was also affected by what they had learned from their mothers. More than half the women in this survey asserted that they had consciously followed their mothers' example in their own marriages. Like many others, Jennie H. and Mollie Linker kept kosher homes more because their mothers did than because of religious conviction. "It's the heritage; it's embedded in me," Mollie explained. "I want my grandchildren to remember

. . . just like my children remember what my mother did." Her mother, the back-bone of the family, also taught her how to raise children—"Not to curse or raise the voice"—and, Mollie insisted, she was "the best teacher."[40] Many other women also emphasized that they had learned how to bring up their children from their mothers. Sometimes the similarities between their attitudes or mannerisms and those of their mothers took them by surprise: Rose G. remembered as a child mak-ing fun of her mother praying for her children. "Now," she observed with amuse-ment, "I'm doing the same thing."

Many women internalized their mothers' caring attitudes toward people. They insisted that they had learned to derive great satisfaction from helping others. Anna R. asserted that in this characteristic, she resembled her mother—a "people's per-son"—the kind of woman who, as Irving Howe described his own mother, "blooms through sustaining others."[41] Anna and Janet A. learned from their moth-ers to keep an open house and an open heart to anyone in need, not because it was an obligation, but because "it was the way to be." Hattie L. remembered her mother, not yet able to speak much English, traveling to Ellis Island to meet other immigrants and help them get settled. "She had nothing," Hattie recalled, "but she had her work. She had gratification. She became a real social worker, and that's what she left with me—it must have rubbed off." Hattie herself became a psychi-atric nurse. Quite possibly, these daughters also learned that such activities, which made the home the focus of social life, also enhanced their mothers' status in the family.[42]

A few women attributed a stoical acceptance of life's tribulations to their moth-ers' example. The mother of Fannie C. found life here more difficult than she had anticipated but ultimately accepted its limitations. She learned to seek satisfaction in her children, as did the mothers of Fannie G. and Riva P., who endured philan-dering husbands. Several women learned to face adversity with the saving grace of humor, as their mothers had done. Whenever she mispronounced an English word, instead of reacting with embarrassment, Janet A.'s mother would laugh at herself and go on with the arduous task of learning a strange language. The mother of Tanya N. also used humor to provide color to a drab existence. For example, a friend once asked her where she got all the sunflower seeds she liked so much. "I'll tell you," she replied. "When I scrub the floor, I also plant seeds between the boards. And in the summertime, I have sunflowers." "She was always imaginative," Tanya recalled. "Even when things were bitter, she never gave up. She understood her hardships and faced them with humor."

Among the majority of women who held such positive views of mothers, or felt that they had sacrificed for their children's welfare, relationships tended to be strong, with mothers often living near or with daughters after marriage. For example, Sara B., speaking of the nine years her mother had spent under her roof, observed, "I always felt that my mother was a *tsirung* in the house—something very beautiful and decorative." One woman, Minna S., instead of marrying, lived at home and cared for her mother devotedly until her death. Another, Rose S., married not so much to gain a husband but in the futile hope of finding in her new mother-in-law a replacement for her dead mother—her "best friend." Sometimes the connection persisted despite the effects of distance. Louise C., who fled a life of poverty in Russia, remained close to her mother through their correspondence. On the very day Louise left for the hospital to give birth to her first child, a letter arrived from her mother to urge her "to have the courage to give birth." "In spite of the fact that you were an ocean apart," observed Louise, "the umbilical cord was never really cut. The tie was there."

In a few families, however, relationships between mothers and daughters were distant. This situation generally occurred when a daughter rejected her mother as part of the East European background she wanted to shed, particularly when the parent was unwilling or unable to take any steps toward Americanization, or at least toward understanding the needs of a daughter who wanted to be "all-American." Shame at having an obviously foreign parent, unfortunately, was not unusual,[43] although it was seldom encountered in this survey. Some children were mildly embarrassed when parents came to school to speak to their teachers in inadequate English. Riva P. always felt that teachers looked down on her parents because of their accent. And although she loved them, she remembered thinking often, "I wish they were American!" Children might feel that they were judged by their parents. For this reason, in one of Anzia Yezierska's short stories a young girl works to no effect to modernize her dowdy, old-country mother. "I dressed her in the most stylish Paris models," she tells her brothers, "but Delancey Street sticks out from every inch of her. Whenever she opens her mouth, I'm done for."[44] This more intense kind of rejection was shared by a few women, like Mildred L., who was ashamed of her poor, illiterate mother and sought single-mindedly to dissociate herself from her and to become a "real American." She spent her money on scented soaps and fashionable clothing and chose only American-born friends whom she refused to bring home to meet her parents. "My growing up didn't do me any good," she stated, still passionate with feelings of deprivation after more than fifty years, "because I had nobody to learn from." Mildred had what sounds like a nervous breakdown at sixteen, which she attributed to the strain of trying to escape from her hated immigrant environment. Such daughters, as Sonya Michel has observed, may have suffered from a kind of identity crisis, because although they rejected the behavior and personality traits of their mothers, they had also internalized them and were therefore fearful of seeing these traits emerge in themselves.[45]

Thus, in the few instances where a daughter rejected a mother, she would still consider her a role model, but a negative rather than a positive example. "Everything that my mother did," asserted Gussie M., "I decided to do the opposite." One woman, an oldest daughter who had to forgo an education and stay home to help with the younger children without any appreciation, branded her mother's methods and attitudes "primitive" and swore to raise her own children in a more enlightened way.[46] Another, who saw her mother broken by the constant battle for survival, was obsessed by the desire to lead a different and better life. "Always I struggled," she recalled with passion, "never to be like mama."[47]

Despite such exceptions, most women felt close to their mothers and seem to have derived particular satisfaction from caring for them late in life. Jewish girls, and indeed girls of many ethnic groups, were socialized to assume such obligations, and there is little question that many achieved gratification from fulfilling what they perceived to be a filial responsibility.[48] After being widowed, the mother of Rose S. lived in turn with each of her three daughters, all of whom urged her to remain, but she refused to stay with her son and his wife. Hannah F. and her three sisters also fought over what they considered the privilege of caring for their mother, but again the brothers were not involved. Sons were expected to contribute financially to the care of an elderly parent, but this was the extent of their obligation. Their responsibility for a sister was even more limited. One dying mother told her devoted daughter that after her death the girl would be alone—a prophecy that became true—because her brother "is a man and will go his own way."[49] Women, not men, were expected to be the caretakers. When the mother of Rose G. was terminally ill with cancer, Rose left a good job to nurse her continuously for a year, with her brothers paying the bills and visiting every month or two. She remembered, as a child, her mother closing the eyes of her dead grandmother, and she felt privileged to do the same for her own mother. "It was no sacrifice," Rose insisted, for she had given this care not out of obligation but because of the example her mother had set before her. "It was a natural thing to do," she explained, "because she was always so sweet and self-effacing." Occasionally, the mother-daughter relationship was cemented late in life by this apparent role reversal—a daughter caring for her mother. Frieda M. observed that her mother "was never important to me until I had to take care of her. And then," she explained simply, "she was."

Although most daughters felt close to their mothers, even those who had been alienated gained insight into the older women's lives in their own mature years. The few women who believed their mothers had not loved them or treated them properly—all from very poor families—explained that they understood that their lives had been too bitter or harried to enable them the luxury of love. "My mother happened to be a selfish woman," observed Rose G. in discussing her own impoverished youth. But she went on to explain that her mother "had no real childhood" of her own and had suffered great deprivation that affected her attitudes. Jennie Herbst recalled her own mother's "caustic and sarcastic retorts" that often made her young daughter cry. "Love was never talked about," she remembered, "nor was there ever a gesture or intimation that such a thing existed between mother and child." Yet after Jenny married, she thought about her mother's sorry life "with pity and commiseration."[50] Even for these women, age brought reconciliation.

Thus, most women eventually seemed able to accept differences in values or behavior between themselves and their mothers[51] without simultaneously rejecting the parent. Perhaps one reason for this tolerance is that the majority of mothers had also accepted the values or behavior of their children, although they may not have shared them. Relatively few relationships seemed to founder on the shoals of intergenerational strife.

Few immigrant mothers could offer their daughters advice on how to be Americans—how to speak properly, dress, or behave—for in this country, as in the cities of Russia or Poland, the culture of young people was diverging from that of their parents. What young immigrant women *could* learn from their mothers, though, were the basic values and attitudes that would affect their lives as mature women, once the initial desire to "fit in" with American society was satisfied. Girls of every ethnic group learned from their mothers what it took to run a home properly. They saw their mothers shopping, baking, cooking, cleaning, sewing, managing the family's money, and sometimes earning it themselves. They learned how to do the emotional housework of dealing with the psychological needs of husbands and children. These mothers set important examples for their daughters in understanding how to approach life and relate to their families and others. Although girls could learn individual values from fathers, from mothers they absorbed a whole system of values that would affect them profoundly as adults—in a positive way if the relationship was sound, and negatively in the few cases where it was not.

As members of a generation that emphasizes self-fulfillment, we might not easily understand the satisfactions of those who lived their lives for and through others. Like their mothers, the women of the immigrant generation, whatever their ethnic origin, were socialized to consider others before themselves. Older daughters in particular seemed to bear more responsibility than either brothers or younger children, and the order of a girl's birth and her age at the time of emigration greatly affected her later life. It seems clear, though, that these Jewish immigrant daughters were profoundly influenced by their mothers' example of service and self-sacrifice. Yet they demanded something in return. These young women's attitudes toward their own sacrifices depended on the response of parents and siblings, and if their efforts were rewarded by an appreciative family, they, like their mothers, learned to achieve gratification from such a life. How these values are affecting the more varied lives of the next generation is an intriguing topic for further study.

NOTES

1. Among recent writers to be concerned with such issues are Sonya Michel, "Mothers and Daughters in American Jewish Literature: The Rotted Cord," in *The Jewish Woman,* ed. Elizabeth Koltun (New York, 1976), pp. 272–82; Kim Chernin, *In My Mother's House* (New Haven, 1983); Eleanor Mallach Bromberg, "Mother-Daughter Relationships in Later Life" (Ph.D. diss., Columbia University School of Social Work, 1982).

2. Women I have interviewed are identified only by their first name and last initial to preserve confidentiality, and quotations from their testimony are not footnoted. The author's complete name is given for published or other open sources, which are cited in the notes.

3. The first fifteen women interviewed were selected based upon the availability of informants. The second group of thirty-one were chosen in an attempt to achieve more balance in the following areas: area of birth, social class, circumstances of emigration (for example, did they emigrate alone or with parents), age at time of emigration, number of children in the family, and birth order of the informant.

4. These interviews were loosely structured, so although I had many specific questions, the women were free to emphasize what they believed were important factors in determining their lives. Initially, I had been seeking other information, but these two major points—the importance of mothers as role models and the significance of the child's birth order and age at time of emigration—emerged from the narratives of so many women that I realized they formed an important pattern, and I altered some of my subsequent questions accordingly. However, because of the advanced age of some of my informants, the fact that a few resisted talking about their parents, and because material from other sources is interspersed with evidence from the interviews, I make no claims for scientific methodology and avoid using percentages of the women interviewed to support a particular attitude. I do attempt to indicate whether an attitude or pattern of behavior was one shared by many women or a small minority—whether it seemed dominant or deviant.

5. In 1916, there were only two yeshivoth (Jewish high schools) in the United States, and only 24 percent of Jewish elementary school children received a Jewish education. See Charles S. Liebman, "Religion, Class and Culture in American Jewish History," *Jewish Journal of Sociology* 1 (December 1967): 227–42, esp. p. 231.

6. Sholem Asch, *The Mother* (New York, 1937), p. 10.

7. Alfred Kazin, *A Walker in the City* (New York, 1931), pp. 52, 53, 66–67.

8. Anzia Yezierska, "The Fat of the Land," in *Hungry Hearts* (Boston, 1920), pp. 208–9.

9. Mary Ryan, *The Cradle of the Middle Class: The Family in Oneida County, New York, 1790–1865* (New York, 1981), p. 26.

10. Joan Scott and Louise A. Tilly, *Women, Work and Family* (New York, 1978), p. 107.

11. Some examples of this resentment can be seen in Elizabeth W. Ewen, "Immigrant Women in the Land of Dollars, 1890–1920" (Ph.D. diss., SUNY, Stony Brook, 1979), pp. 126–27; Laura Schwartz, "Immigrant Voices from Home, Work and Community: Women and Family in the Migration Process, 1890–1938" (Ph.D. diss., SUNY, Stony Brook, 1983), p. 615; and Elizabeth Hasanovitz, *One of Them* (New York, 1918), p. 42.

12. Scott and Tilly, *Women, Work and Family,* pp. 108, 111, 115.

13. A Department of Labor survey indicated that sons gave an average of 83 percent of their wages to parents, while daughters gave 95 percent. See Schwartz, "Immigrant Voices," pp. 610–12.

14. Winifred Wandersee, *Women's Work and Family Values, 1920–1940* (Cambridge, Mass., 1981), p. 116.

15. This was a fairly typical pattern. See Schwartz, "Immigrant Voices," pp. 613–15.

16. Among twenty-five- to forty-four-year-old foreign-born males, 44 percent of males graduated from high school, while 36 percent of women in this age group did so. The median years of schooling for this male group was 10.9, for the women, 9.7. This is a narrower gap than for the older group, where the males had a median of 8.1 years of schooling, and the women 5.8. Among native-born children, in contrast, the gap between male and female education is narrower still. Males in the younger age group averaged 12.7 years of schooling, and 72 percent had at least completed high school, while women averaged 12.4 years of school, and 69 percent of them had graduated from high school. See census survey in Miriam Cohen, "From Workshop to Office: Italian Women and Family Strategies in New York City, 1900–1950" (Ph.D. diss., University of Michigan, 1978), p. 251.

17. See Scott and Tilly, *Women, Work and Family,* pp. 142–44, 205, and esp. p. 106.

18. Almost all the women whose mothers came to this country had a good relationship with them in their later years, and this might have modified memories of earlier strife. The few women who seem not to have been close with their mothers were reluctant to speak about them at all except to say that they were difficult people.

19. On this point, see Ruth Landes and Mark Zborowski, "Hypotheses Concerning the Eastern European Family," in *The Psychodynamics of American Jewish Life,* ed. Norman Kiell (New York, 1967), pp. 33–66, esp. pp. 36–37.

20. In Pittsburgh, one study indicates that Jews also had the lowest rate among immigrant families of the European language being spoken in the home. See Corinne Azen Krause, *Grandmothers, Mothers and Daughters: An Oral History Study of Ethnicity, Mental Health and Continuity of Three Generations of Jewish, Italian and Slavic American Women* (New York, 1978), p. 29.

21. On this important issue, see Elizabeth W. Ewen, "City Lights: Immigrant Women and the Rise of Movies," *Signs,* supp. to vol. 5, no. 3 (Spring 1980): 545–65, esp. pp. 549–50; Ewen, "Immigrant Women in the Land of Dollars," pp. 196–97, Schwartz, "Immigrant Voices from Home, Work and Community," p. 696.

22. In "Mothers and Daughters," p. 275, Michel pointed out that immigrant mothers were unable to provide their daughters with role models in the United States, but she seems to have assumed that what was true in youth remained constant throughout these women's lives.

23. See, for example, Beverly G. Bienstock, "The Changing Image of the American Jewish Mother," in *Changing Images of the Family*, ed. Virginia Tufte and Barbara Myerhoff (New Haven, 1979), pp. 173–91, esp. pp. 173–74, 177.

24. Michael R. Weisser, *A Brotherhood of Memory: Jewish Landsmanshaftn in the New World* (New York, 1985), p. 274.

25. Rudolph Glanz, *The Jewish Woman in America: Two Female Immigrant Generations, 1820–1929*, vol. 1: *The Eastern European Jewish Woman* (New York, 1976), p. 58.

26. Alice Kessler-Harris, *Out to Work: A History of Wage-Earning Women in the United States* (New York, 1982), p. 126.

27. Unpublished Manuscript Autobiography No. 92, YIVO Archives, New York.

28. On this point, see Alice Kessler-Harris, "Organizing the Unorganizable: Three Jewish Women and Their Union," in *Class, Sex and the Woman Worker*, ed. Milton Cantor and Bruce Laurie (Westport, Conn., 1977), p. 147.

29. Sydelle Kramer and Jenny Mazur, eds., *Jewish Grandmothers* (Boston, 1976), p. 98.

30. Abraham Cahan, *The Rise of David Levinsky* (1917; reprint, New York, 1960), pp. 242–43, 254–55.

31. Kate Simon, *Bronx Primitive: Portraits in a Childhood* (New York, 1982), p. 48.

32. This is generally true in mother-daughter relationships. See Edith Neisser, *Mothers and Daughters: A Lifelong Relationship* (New York, 1967), p. 170.

33. Bromberg, "Mother-Daughter Relationships," pp. 32, 210.

34. For example, among Italian women, see Janet Theophano, "'It's Really Tomato Sauce But We Call It Gravy': A Study of Food and Woman's Work among Italian-American Families" (Ph.D. diss., University of Pennsylvania, 1982), p. 135.

35. Chernin, *In My Mother's House*, p. 29.

36. On this point for Italian immigrant families, see Cohen, "From Workshop to Office," p. 52; and Leonard Covello, *The Heart Is the Teacher*, reissued as *The Teacher in the Urban Community* (Totowa, N.J., 1970), p. 210.

37. For this ceremonial role, see Barbara Myerhoff, *Number Our Days* (New York, 1979), p. 247.

38. WPA interview, transcribed in the 1930s, with Marie Esposito, a Jewish woman married to an Italian man. Cited in Schwartz, "Immigrant Voices from Home, Work and Community," pp. 586–87.

39. For a model of such family decision making, see Marilyn Manser and Murray Brown, "Bargaining Analyses of Household Decisions," in *Women in the Labor Market*, ed. Cynthia B. Lloyd, E. S. Andrews, and C. L. Gilroy (New York, 1979), p. 5.

40. Kramer and Mazur, *Jewish Grandmothers*, pp. 98–99.

41. Irving Howe, *A Margin of Hope: An Intellectual Autobiography* (New York, 1982), p. 7.

42. See, for example, Michelle Z. Rosaldo, "Women, Culture and Society: A Theoretical Overview," in *Women, Culture and Society*, ed. Rosaldo and Louise Lamphere (Stanford, Calif., 1974), p. 46.

43. For some examples, see Charlotte Baum, Paula Hyman, and Sonya Michel, *The Jewish Woman in America* (New York, 1976), pp. 205–6.

44. Yezierska, "The Fat of the Land," pp. 208–9.

45. Michel, "Mothers and Daughters," p. 278.

46. Kramer and Mazur, *Jewish Grandmothers,* p. 14.

47. Chernin, *In My Mother's House,* pp. 15, 39.

48. Bromberg, "Mother-Daughter Relationships," p. 239.

49. Esther Bender, "Looking Back," *National Jewish Monthly,* November 1977, pp. 28–34, esp. p. 34.

50. Jenny Herbst to Beatrice Weinreich, 18 September 1984, reprinted with permission of the author, YIVO Archives.

51. Bromberg, "Mother-Daughter Relationships," p. 35.

17.

SOCIAL, HISTORICAL, POLITICAL, AND CULTURAL SETTINGS OF JAPANESE AMERICAN MOTHERHOOD, 1940–1990

The Tradition of Amae, Gambare, *and* Gaman *in the American Midwest*

SUSAN MATOBA ADLER

Introduction

Kodomo no tame ni, meaning "for the sake of the children" in Japanese, is a common saying passed down through generations of Japanese American families.[1] For Japanese immigrant mothers it was considered an unquestionable imperative that they sacrifice everything for their children.[2] They did so just as their mothers had done for them, following Japanese tradition, which honors motherhood.

Contemporary Japanese society reflects the same orientation, as evidenced by the *kyoiku mamas* who contribute to their children's education and well-being with conviction and intensity.[3] "While the child is studying," writes Anne Imamura, "mother is close by rather than off doing things that interest her. Indeed living up to the model of mother as all-sacrificing constitutes a primary motivation for success in contemporary Japanese society."[4] The academic success of Japanese children is attributed to the mother's efforts to provide an environment that is conducive to learning. Japanese mothers succeed if they have fulfilled their honored role as a supportive parent.

Japanese American mothers who settled in the Midwest after leaving internment camps in the 1940s found themselves rearing children with advice from Doctor Spock, on the one hand, and by the methods of their Japanese mothers and mothers-in-law, on the other. Beginning with the Nisei generation, parenting approaches began to utilize professional resources as well as family and community practical knowledge.[5] But culturally, the bond of Japanese mother-child interdependency clashed with the goals of self-sufficiency and independence reflective of Western child rearing. Across the generations, Japanese American women have

351

been formulating their own integrated perspectives about the role of motherhood from two primary sources: practices and beliefs passed down through their families, and Euro-American conceptions of parenting gathered from American child development and medical experts. As postwar knowledge of Japanese culture emerged in the West, third- and fourth-generation mothers may have been indirectly influenced by contemporary stereotypes and accounts of Japanese motherhood, like the concept of the *kyoiku mamas.* This article examines the source of these differing child-rearing traditions and how midwestern Japanese American mothers experienced, interpreted, and resolved these bicultural tensions.

Generational groups of Japanese Americans have been identified by their proximity from the *Issei,* or the first group of Japanese to immigrate to the United States during the Meiji Era, 1867–1912.[6] The *Nisei* (second generation) were born in the United States and reared primarily on the West Coast or Hawaii, while their children, the *Sansei* (third generation), were reared throughout the United States in Asian, multicultural, or primarily Caucasian environments removed from large ethnic communities. Grandchildren of the Nisei, the *Yonsei* (fourth generation), include many *hapa* (biracial or half-Japanese) children, offspring of an increasing number of interracial marriages. Finally, full-blooded *Gosei* (fifth generation) tend to be found more often in areas where there is a large Japanese American community.[7] My research cohort included elderly Nisei women who settled in the Midwest after internment, middle-aged Sansei women who were reared in the Midwest in primarily white middle-class neighborhoods, and young adult Yonsei women who were highly assimilated into suburban midwestern communities.

Since antiquity, the expected role of a Japanese woman has been that of motherhood, which is highly respected in Japan.[8] Japanese American child rearing has its roots in the Japanese concept of *amae,* a term that was coined by the psychologist Takeo Doi and refers to the close interdependency between a Japanese mother and her child.[9] The *amae* relationship is described as one that allows permissiveness, since it is founded upon security and unconditional love. Psychological interdependence leads to a mutual responsiveness between a mother and her child in which dominance and authority are not linearly imposed from parent to child. In comparing Japanese *amae* and Western concepts of child development, it is clear that the Japanese stress the permanence of human relationships in which indulgences can be freely given and received without power differentials, whereas Western child rearing stresses separation and individuation within hierarchial systems.[10]

In her study of Japanese American *amae,* Amy Iwasaki Mass coined the phrase "indulgent love" to describe the behavior of many Issei, some Nisei, and some Sansei mothers. She interpreted *amae* as "the overall quality of nurturing, anticipating children's needs, and helping children achieve a high level of functioning."[11] In my study of midwestern Japanese American women, *amae* was described negatively by some Nisei and Sansei mothers as spoiling or pampering, yet versions of this behavior were evident across the three generations. For some women, the differing interpretations of *amae* within a family created bicultural tension over child-rearing approaches.

How "American," one might ask, are Japanese American mothers? Or conversely, how "Japanese" are they in terms of their beliefs about child rearing? I would venture to say that there is a great deal of diversity of views both within the ethnic group and, certainly, across the generations. And in some cases, divergent perspectives are expressed within families, where varying interpretations of the Japanese worldview lead to confusion. As one Sansei put it: "My personality fits with the American culture, it conflicts with the Asian . . . the problem was that I lived in an Asian culture family. So I learned the Asian skills (to serve others, to deify the family) better than the American. But I never learned to know my place." The more collectively oriented "Japanese way," as one Nisei described it, was in conflict with the need to survive in an individualistically oriented Western society. This was particularly true after World War II when the Nisei resettled throughout the country and found it prudent to remain "low key" as an ethnic and racial minority.

At home the Nisei were free to maintain a Japanese lifestyle, but in public they attempted to assimilate as much as possible, thus adopting a bicultural existence. In homes where the nuclear and extended family lived together, contrasting perspectives on child rearing between Issei grandmothers and Nisei mothers would often emerge. In other cases, siblings disagreed about child-rearing methodology. Despite internal conflict about practices within families, the real question was the continuity of Japanese culture and group identity: how much Japanese culture would be passed on to the Sansei, Yonsei, and Gosei generations?

Sociopolitical Contexts of Child Rearing

After the attack on Pearl Harbor, all Japanese Americans residing on the West Coast in what was considered the militarized zone were evacuated to inland relocation camps. It was in the camps that the Japanese American family systems began to break down. Traditional parental roles were difficult to maintain, and family cohesion decreased as children spent more time with peers rather than with family.[12] During and after the war, young adult Nisei began to leave the camps and secure jobs or to enroll in universities, in the Midwest and elsewhere. It was the overt racism of the internment that taught the Nisei to maintain a "low key" image in public and to become assimilated into mainstream society as quickly as possible. As a result, many Nisei identified themselves as 100% (or even 200%) "all American," leaving their ethnic identity and the language of their parents and ancestors dormant for generations.[13]

Nisei women, like their mothers, lived for and through their children, seeing their successes and failures as their own.[14] But, as they began to question, and then reject, the *amae* mother-child relationship, midwestern Nisei mothers began to rear their Sansei children to become more independent and self-sufficient. Some Nisei even moved their families away from ethnic neighborhoods (i.e., metropolitan Chicago) into the white suburbs so that their children could more readily integrate into Western society rather than maintain their "Japaneseness." As a result, many midwestern Sansei identified themselves as more "white" than Asian or Japanese. As one Sansei participant in my study put it: "While [I was] growing up my family put a low priority on things Japanese. My mother and grandmother many times voiced relief that they were free of the many Japanese obligations. They were into assimilation and they didn't look back . . . there was little nostalgia for the old country in our family." While growing up, these Sansei women assumed that differences between themselves and their Caucasian friends (and later their spouses) were merely individual rather than cultural.

The Sansei in my study had been educated (88 percent completed baccalaureate degrees, 65 percent earned graduate degrees) at the time of the Civil Rights movement, but few participated in any substantial way. Of the seventeen Sansei participants, only one actually participated in political demonstrations. In fact, they had been discouraged from active participation by their Nisei parents, who indicated that they were visible minorities among a sea of white faces and would therefore be remembered. Being singled out in a potentially negative context might bring attention, or even shame, to the family. (This perspective is consistent with the Japanese value of collective harmony expressed in such sayings as "Don't stick out" or "Don't be the nail that needs to be hammered down.") Although Asian American studies was becoming established on the larger midwestern campuses, many Sansei and Yonsei participants regarded ethnic identity as a personal rather than a political issue. The Yonsei learned about the internment of Japanese Americans and the Civil Rights movement in their high school history classes, and they too faced covert discrimination and stereotyping. But like their Sansei parents, midwestern Yonsei felt that discrimination and racism had very little impact on their daily lives, although they all had personal examples of both to share. In fact, some were inclined to attribute discrimination to gender rather than to race, feeling a greater affinity with the women's movement than the Civil Rights movement.

All participants though, regardless of generational group, were cognizant of the common stereotypes attributed to Asian Americans, Japanese, and Asian women. These stereotypes include the *model minority* stereotype, which focuses on high achievement and academic and economic success; the *exotic oriental woman* stereotype, which is based upon subservience and sexual desirability; and the *yellow peril* or *alien "Jap"* stereotype, which paints Japanese Americans as foreigners or non-Americans.[15] The Nisei were perhaps most affected by the *yellow peril* myth, while the Sansei and Yonsei faced the Asian female stereotype as a result of the many GIs stationed in Japan, Korea, and Southeast Asia who returned to the United States with Asian wives. A few Sansei participants thought the exotic oriental woman stereotype ludicrous when applied to themselves, while others recalled dating Caucasian males who "had notions of oriental beauties and of being served."

In my sample, feelings of "Japaneseness" varied considerably within all three generations (Nisei, Sansei, and Yonsei), from those who felt completely removed from their Japanese roots ("I see myself as a middle-class American woman," or "I don't know much about Japanese traditions") to those who actively sought to learn about contemporary Japanese culture, language, and traditions ("I want to go to Japan to learn about my heritage," or "I took Japanese in college to be able to speak to my grandmother"). The development of self-identity in relation to racial awareness was rarely discussed by Japanese American mothers. Children were simply given two seemingly contradictory messages: "Be proud of your Japanese heritage" and "You're 100 percent American." As one Sansei participant was told by her father, "Tell them you are American with a Japanese face."

Conversations with Japanese American Women

In comparing the child-rearing beliefs of midwestern Japanese American mothers across three generations, I conducted both in-depth individual interviews and multigenerational small group interviews. From these interviews I attempted to discern the interpretation these women held of the Japanese concept *gambare*. *Gambare* can be defined as perseverance or "keeping going" and has been used interchangeably with the term *gaman*, meaning endurance or tenacity. Some participants referred to both terms with the often repeated phrase "Do your best," focusing on the process of continually working toward a role perfectionism without consideration for outcome or reward. Rather than working toward a specific attainable goal, one learns the process of continually bettering oneself. Effort is more important than outcome. This interpretation is evident in the following

vignette, a conversation among participants of different generations. The generational group of each speaker is in parenthesis.

> "'Do your best' is what we always heard," said Mona (Nisei),
> "Do your best even if you're a street sweeper or you work at Mac-
> Donald's!" There was a quiet consensus of recognition.
> "Were we conditioned that way?" asked Chiyo (Nisei).
> "I think we were," answered a few women.
> "I don't think we were pressured," said Leia (Yonsei), "but we
> were expected to 'Do our best.' For me, this intense effort wasn't ex-
> ternal. I was self-driven. I know I learned that from my mother."
> Chiyo and Mona remembered knowing Leia's mother as a youngster
> in their small community of Japanese American families.
> Laughingly Chiyo (Nisei) said, "I guess we were obligated not
> to be a bum!" Others agreed. They couldn't imagine themselves as
> Japanese American bums.
> "You can see it through the generations," Mia (Nisei) added.
> "Yeah," Leia (Yonsei) agreed, "My uncles worked hard too. And
> they wanted to live up to their father's standards . . . my brilliant
> grandfather."

The concept of "Doing your best," of ultimate effort and the sense of perfectionism, and the associated emphasis on continual hard work, lead to the expectation of success, or as Chiyo noted, they were "obligated not to be a bum." I must
note here that although this was an ongoing theme in the interviews, some participants expressed reservation and annoyance that such high expectations were made
of them. *Gambare* would be considered futile by American standards based on
goals and competition, because it would be, as one Sansei suggested, "like the horse
following the carrot." The concept of *gambare* has essentially remained the same,
to work hard and persevere, but this imperative has been interpreted by Nisei, Sansei, and Yonsei to include both the process and the product. In Japanese culture, to
gambatte (verb form of *gambare*) means to continually work hard, to keep up the
struggle, regardless of outcome. Many participants, however, interpreted *gambare*
as positive motivation not unlike the Protestant work ethic. One works hard not
just to build fortitude but to succeed, and conversely, success will come if one always works hard. Thus, a cause-and-effect relationship is inherent in the process.

Several themes emerged on the topics of family cohesion, responsibility, and
obligation which indicated changing perspectives across the generations. Traditional family expectations brought by the Issei evolved as families experienced
internment, resettlement, acculturation, and intermarriage. After the war, mid-

western Nisei who did not maintain ongoing relationships with ethnic communities found it easy to phase out obligatory expectations like *koden,* reciprocal monetary gift giving at funerals, or *omiyage,* taking presents whenever you visit someone. The close family ties and the obligation to care for elders that were once maintained through the lineage of first-born sons changed to a maternal kinship pattern of Nisei sisters keeping family members connected.[16] The following vignette illustrates the continuity of family responsibility assumed by some midwestern Japanese American women.

> Fusako (Yonsei) shared her feelings of being responsible for her parents and grandparents. Perhaps, she noted, this was because she was the oldest child (there were no brothers in her family). Her sister didn't feel as obligated to care for her family.
>
> "I'm the only one that lives near my parents," said Akiko (Sansei), as she told of her mother's weekly visits when Erika (Yonsei) was young. "She invested a lot of time in you kids," Akiko said, looking at her daughter. Erika smiled and admitted that, even today as an adult, she has a close relationship with her grandparents and sees them on a regular basis. That relationship is something she always counts on.

It was clear that for most participants in my study, a combination of nuclear and extended family exerted more influence on child-rearing beliefs than did the Japanese American community, which in many cases was dispersed or even nonexistent. Child-rearing practices emerged as a result of individual modeling of both Japanese and mainstream Euro-American perspectives. But confusion regarding cultural difference permeated the relationships these women had with their mothers and contributed to the formation of their own perspectives on child rearing. This last vignette illustrates the desire to comprehend what was "Japanese" and what was "American" and the need for cultural integration.

> In an attempt to solicit feedback from the women present, Imoto (Sansei) shared a difference she perceived between Japanese American and Euro-American parents: the expectation that children should not bother adults. She spoke of a situation involving her nephew and a Caucasian neighborhood man. "I questioned her (Imoto's mother) about that . . . well, not to her face (laughter) . . . what would be wrong with Jimmy going over there?" Caucasian children interact freely with adults even demanding attention, Imoto noted, recalling the behavior of her Caucasian boyfriend's niece.

> Bonnie (Sansei) agreed with Imoto's mother, sharing that she doesn't allow her children to bother neighbors or go into their yards unless they have been invited. She compared the control she has over her children to a "bungee cord" approach. Yano (Yonsei) also agreed, explaining that her approach to her children's freedom to socialize is that "you have to wait until you're invited." Since other neighborhood children "just come over," her daughters couldn't understand Yano's rule. "But yet there's something in me that says," admitted Yano, "you don't impose on other people." Others readily agreed. "Those are regular values," concluded Chiyo (Nisei), "or just being thoughtful."

Not intruding upon the privacy of others and encouraging general politeness among children were considered common "American" values without consideration for the ethnic roots of collective responsibility and personal reserve. For these Japanese American mothers, their "Japaneseness" was not recognized as separate from their "Americaness," yet they knew they were passing on a legacy of family cohesiveness and the primacy of children that had roots in their heritage.

Continuity and Transformation of Culture

When an immigrant's culture meets a distinctly different dominant culture, most likely assimilation will occur, but the seeds of valued cultural concepts will be planted on foreign soil and nurtured in new and unique ways. This transformative process is what I believe happened to Japanese Americans over a period of five generations. Recent immigrants from Japan may share some common beliefs with the Issei, Nisei, Sansei, Yonsei, and Gosei, but not a past *American* history. The newest term, *Nikkei,* refers to anyone having racial and ethnic roots in Japan, a shared heritage but not necessarily a shared history.

My study illuminates the continuity and transformation of the concepts of *gambare, gaman,* and *amae* and the enduring belief in the primacy of family, children, and elders. Japanese American mothers across the generations have attempted to help their children accommodate to the demands of society while maintaining the moral and intellectual imperatives of their family belief systems. Fundamental concepts may have remained relatively intact while the contexts for applying the concepts have changed. It is also possible that Issei immigrants misinterpreted these Japanese concepts and that new definitions became the foundation for ideas thought to be Japanese.

The Issei reverence of motherhood reflected in the saying *Kodomo no tame ni* (for the sake of the children) appears still to be relevant for many midwestern Japanese American mothers. They invest time and energy in the care and education of their children, although intense sacrifice may not be a norm. And they are also concerned about the comfort and well-being of family elders. But the tradition of parents living with the eldest son or of extended family members providing child care for working parents has changed from an obligatory role to a commitment to family cohesion and to the development of strong interpersonal relationships among individual family members. The shift from an *amae*-like interdependency to a kind of monitored independence of both children and elders in retirement reflects the transformation of Japanese concepts across the generations. Some Sansei and Yonsei mothers in my sample attempted to discourage rather than encourage strong mother-child attachments with their toddlers, and elderly Nisei began to tell their Sansei children that they preferred to live alone or in a nursing home rather than in the households of their children.

The Euro-American emphasis on the nuclear family rather than the extended family, and on the husband-wife relationship rather than the mother-child relationship, has begun to change Japanese American families. But there is still a compelling desire for Japanese American mothers to nurture and support their children of all ages, and to care for and worry about their elderly parents until they pass away. This is evident in the decision of Sansei and Yonsei mothers who are doctors or lawyers to work part-time to rear their young children rather than build a practice or career; or to take time off from work to attend to a sick grandparent along with their Nisei mothers; or to provide opportunities for their children to spend time and to communicate with their grandparents. The Japanese American mother's need to continually facilitate the development of her children and her sense of responsibility for the welfare of her (and her husband's) parents appear to be a lasting legacy of her Japanese heritage.[17]

NOTES

This paper is based on my doctoral dissertation, "Midwestern Japanese American Women: Perspectives on Childrearing and Education across Three Generations" (University of Wisconsin-Madison, 1995). Unless otherwise cited, all quotations from Japanese American women are from this source.

1. This common saying was quoted from the brochure announcing the traveling Smithsonian Exhibition entitled *Strength and Diversity: Japanese American Women, 1885–1990*.

2. This sense of sacrifice and commitment to children was described in Lauren Kessler, *Stubborn Twig: Three Generations in the Life of a Japanese American Family* (New York: Random House, 1993). This theme is clearly reflected in some literature written by Japanese American

women (Jeanne Wakatsuki Houston and Akemi Kikumura come to mind) and in my conversations with midwestern Japanese American women.

3. C. Simons, "They Get By with a Lot of Help from Their Kyoiku Mamas," *Smithsonian,* March 1987, pp. 44–53.

4. Anne E. Imamura, "Introduction: Families as a Mirror of Society," in Barbara Finkelstein, Imamura, and Joseph J. Tobin, eds., *Transcending Stereotypes: Discovering Japanese Culture and Education* (Yarmouth, Maine: Intercultural Press, 1991).

5. Harry Kitano, "Differential Child-Rearing Attitudes between First and Second Generation Japanese in the United States," *Journal of Social Psychology* 53 (1961): 13–19.

6. For more information on the Meiji Reformation and Japanese immigration, see Harry Kitano, *Japanese Americans: Evolution of a Subculture,* 2d ed. (Englewood Cliffs, N.J.: Prentice Hall, 1976).

7. Stanford Lyman, *Color, Culture, Civilization: Race and Minority Issues in American Society* (Urbana: University of Illinois Press, 1994), describes the generational groups unique to the Japanese American ethnic group. Based upon a distinct period of immigration and the successive groups of offspring, Japanese Americans have been referred to as *Issei* (immigrants and the first generation to settle in America), *Nisei* (second generation and first-born Americans), *Sansei* (third generation), *Yonsei* (fourth generation), and *Gosei* (fifth generation). *Hapa,* meaning half Japanese, can be found in any generational group as a result of intermarriage, either interracial or within the Asian race. The currently used inclusive term *Nikkei* refers to anyone of Japanese heritage and encompasses all the previous groups as well as postwar immigrants and their children. For further information on Japanese American intermarriage, see Kitano and Akemi Kikumura, "Interracial Marriage: A Picture of the Japanese American," *Journal of Social Issues* (1973): 29; and H. R. Barringer, R. W. Gardner, and M. J. Levin, *Asian and Pacific Islanders in the United States* (New York: Russell Sage Foundation, 1993), based on the 1980 census.

8. Imamura, "Introduction"; Simons, "They Get By with a Lot of Help from Their Kyoiku Mamas."

9. In 1961 the Japanese American social psychologist Harry Kitano noted that there were different attitudes between the immigrant Issei and their American-born Nisei children about child rearing. The Japanese immigrant mothers were continually responsive to their children's needs, in accordance with their family tradition, whereas the Japanese American mothers tended to rely on advice from Western child development and medical professionals. The Japanese psychologist Takeo Doi, writing in 1962, described the strong interdependency between mother and child called *amae,* which is reinforced by Japanese society. This psychologically close relationship allows the child to behave in a demanding way assuming a sense of security and trust. See L. Takeo Doi, "*Amae:* A Key Concept for Understanding Japanese Personality Structure" (1962), in *Japanese Culture and Behavior: Selected Readings,* ed. Takie Sugiyama Lebra and William P. Lebra (Honolulu: University Press of Hawaii, 1974). Amy Iwasaki Mass studied this *amae* relationship in Japanese American families in 1986, describing it as indulgence and nurturance. See her "Amae: Indulgence and Nurturance in Japanese American Families" (Ph.D. diss., University of California, Los Angeles, 1986). My own study continues to probe the child-rearing attitudes of midwestern Japanese American women across three generations.

In Japanese culture there are other forms of *amae* defining relationships between husband and wife, employer and employee.

10. Merry White mentions the basic difference in *The Japanese Educational Challenge: A Commitment to Children* (New York: Kodansha International, 1987) but does not elaborate on the differing cultural interpretations. The mother-child *amae* relationship is based on psychological closeness, permanence of relationships, and interdependence within the family, while Japanese society provides clear hierarchial patterns defining behavior outside the family. In contrast, Western motherhood assumes parental authority and child compliance both inside and outside the home. Japanese American mothers found these differences confusing and contradictory, since they adopted Western patterns of parental authority while trying to develop close psychological relationships with their children. Without understanding the Eastern cultural context, Nisei and Sansei participants viewed the permissiveness and indulgences of *amae* as "spoiling."

11. Mass, "Amae."

12. Two resources, among many, written about the internment of Japanese Americans during World War II are Bill Hosokawa, *Nisei: The Quiet Americans* (New York: William Morrow, 1969); and Michi Weglyn, *Years of Infamy: The Untold Story of America's Concentration Camps* (New York: Morrow Quill Paperbacks, 1976).

13. The desire of Japanese Americans to be model citizens and to behave as the *hakugin* (Caucasians/whites) did is discussed in Roger Daniels and Harry Kitano, *American Racism: Exploration of the Nature of Prejudice* (Englewood Cliffs, N.J.: Prentice-Hall, 1970); Kessler, *Stubborn Twig;* and Mei Nakano, *Japanese American Women: Three Generations, 1890–1990* (Berkeley: Mina Press, 1990).

14. Nakano, *Japanese American Women.*

15. The "model minority" stereotype of high achievement, hard work, and model citizenship has been characterized by some Asian American scholars as having negative ramifications for all Asians and Asian Americans. This stereotype ignores diversity within the Asian American group based upon ethnic background, educational opportunity, immigration history, ethnic group history, and individual differences, and it establishes false expectations for all Asian Americans. For further critique and discussion, see Stacey Lee, *Unraveling the "Model Minority" Stereotype: Listening to Asian American Youth* (New York: Teachers College Press, 1996); D. Ogawa, *From Japs to Japanese: The Evolution of Japanese-American Stereotypes* (Berkeley: McCutchan, 1971); Ken Osajima, "Asian Americans as the Model Minority: An Analysis of the Popular Press Image in the 1960's and 1980's," in G. Y. Okihiro, ed., *Reflections on Shattered Windows: Promises and Prospects for Asian American Studies* (Pullman: Washington State University Press, 1987); Stanley Sue and Harry Kitano, "Stereotypes as a Measure of Success," *Journal of Social Issues* 29 (1973): 83–98; and Bob Suzuki, "Education and Socialization of Asian Americans: A Revisionist Analysis of the 'Model Minority' Thesis," *Amerasia Journal* 4 (1977): 23–52.

16. Sylvia Yanagisako, *Transforming the Past: Tradition and Kinship among Japanese Americans* (Stanford: Stanford University Press, 1985), describes how Nisei sisters transformed Japanese kinship patterns, creating ties that kept Japanese American families connected.

17. My study of midwestern Japanese American women reflects the perspectives of one subset of women and should not be generalized to all Japanese American women. But some of the themes on family, education, and the role of mothers that emerged in my study were also reflected in Nakano's *Japanese American Women.*

18

RECONSTRUCTING MOTHERHOOD: THE LA LECHE LEAGUE IN POSTWAR AMERICA

LYNN Y. WEINER

> In the 1950s: Formula was providing scientifically perfect food for babies. Anesthesia was saving mothers from the horrors of childbirth. Bottles were making it easy for anyone to care for the baby. Schedules and discipline from the moment of birth were preventing babies from ruling their parents' lives. . . . In 1956, seven women joined together in a movement that was to change the face of motherhood in America. They have devoted their lives to bringing mother and baby together again.
>
> —KAYE LOWMAN,
> The LLLove Story

For almost four decades, the La Leche League—a voluntary association of women—has championed its cause of "good mothering through breastfeeding" in the United States and around the world. Although the league has been largely overlooked in scholarly discussions of women in the postwar era, it represents an important piece in the puzzle of twentieth-century social history. The league's publication, *The Womanly Art of Breastfeeding,* has sold some two million copies since 1958, and millions of women have attended league support groups, read league literature, or otherwise encountered league ideology. By the mid-1980s, the league claimed over four thousand support groups in forty-eight countries, and in the United States it had a reputation among many women as the primary source of

Reprinted from *Journal of American History* 80 (1994): 1357–81, by permission of the publisher.

expertise on motherhood—a position held earlier by the United States Children's Bureau.[1]

The La Leche League was organized during a turbulent period when the social roles of American women as mothers and as workers were contested in both ideology and practice. Nineteenth-century middle-class cultural definitions had promoted "the intense, essentially private nature of the mother-child bond and the primary responsibility of mothers for the well-being of their children." In the mid-twentieth century, those definitions were challenged by developments in fertility patterns, new scientific childbirth and infant-feeding techniques, feminism, and the rapid growth of the female labor force. Science had entered the nursery, which growing numbers of women would soon leave behind.[2]

The La Leche League arose to defend traditional domesticity against the assaults of modern industrial life and to dignify the physical, biological side of motherhood in ways that proved to have surprising appeal to many Americans. Whereas the nineteenth-century version of middle-class "true womanhood" emphasized moral purity and piety in a secular and industrializing age, the league, in the scientific twentieth century, emphasized naturalism. Mother and baby were not so much icons of purity as symbols of nature and simplicity. But they were not just symbols. The founders of the league had a social outlook that can be called maternalist; that is, they implied that an empowered motherhood defined by "female" qualities would improve society. Their faith in this maternalist prescription enabled La Leche League women to focus their efforts. From the mid-1950s to the present, the La Leche League has pursued a steadfast mission: to "bring mother and baby together again" through the "womanly art of breastfeeding."

That mission attracted a variety of supporters. To those suspicious of the intrusion of experts into family life, the league presented a social role for mothers that restored a sense of autonomy to the private domestic realm. Health benefits to mother and child from breast-feeding, childbirth as a natural process, trust in one's own instincts—these notions found favor among women who questioned "scientific motherhood," an ideology initially developed during the late nineteenth and early twentieth centuries that promoted the authority of experts in the realm of child rearing. By the 1950s, "scientific motherhood" dominated mainstream approaches to family life. In addition, the social movements of the 1960s and 1970s welcomed the "natural" methods of the league and its challenge to the patriarchy of the medical establishment.[3]

The league grew rapidly, especially in the 1960s and 1970s. From one meeting of twelve friends in the fall of 1956, the number of league groups multiplied to 43 in 1961, 430 in 1966, 1,260 in 1971, and to about 3,000 in 1976. By 1981, some 17,000 women had been trained as league leaders. While it is difficult to ascribe credit for the rise in breast-feeding in the United States from the mid-1950s through the mid-1980s, the incidence of breast-feeding by new mothers grew from about 20 to about 60 percent.[4]

If some women saw the league's vision of motherhood as empowering and progressive, there was a catch. To meet league standards of on-demand breast-feeding, mother and infant must remain together. This was not too difficult in the 1950s, when fewer than one in five married mothers of young children under the age of six worked outside the home, but by 1980, that number had risen to almost one in two. As maternal employment norms changed, a posture critical of working mothers made the La Leche League seem increasingly conservative. Like maternalist ideologies of past centuries, La Leche League motherhood gave public purpose to the private activities of domestic life; like advocates of those past ideologies, too, the league urged that women subsume their individualism for the greater good of the family and society. This essay will introduce the history of the league and explore the paradox embedded in the league's maternalist ideology—the way in which it simultaneously promoted women's autonomy and restricted women's roles.[5]

At a picnic in the Chicago suburb of Elmhurst during the summer of 1956, two mothers—Mary White and Marian Tompson—sat under a tree nursing their babies. As other women approached them and admired what seemed a difficult and unusual task in an era when bottle-feeding was the norm, these mothers determined to help others learn the "womanly art" of breast-feeding. With five friends they formed the La Leche League, to give "mother-to-mother" help to women who wanted to nurse their infants. The "founding mothers" at first struggled to find a suitable name, for in those days, according to founder Edwina Froehlich, "you didn't mention 'breast' in print unless you were talking about Jean Harlow." The solution of "La Leche League" was offered by Mary White's husband, the obstetrician Gregory White, who often gave his pregnant patients medals from a shrine in St. Augustine, Florida, dedicated to a Spanish madonna, Nuestra Señora de La Leche y Buen Parto, or, loosely translated, "Our Lady of Happy Delivery and Plentiful Milk."[6]

The seven founders of the league were Roman Catholic, white, middle-class women who had become acquainted in two ways: through activism in the Christian Family Movement (CFM), an ecumenical Christian organization, and through a common interest in natural childbirth and breast-feeding. Like many white Americans in that era, all but one of the founders grew up in cities, but by the mid-1950s all but one lived in the suburbs. Three of the seven founders had college degrees; the husbands of most worked in professional occupations. Several of the founders were patients of Gregory White, who in his obstetrical practice favored natural childbirth procedures.[7]

The Christian Family Movement, established nationally in 1949, was an important influence on the early league's organization and outlook. The CFM organized small discussion groups focused on family and such social justice issues as civil rights, based on an "action cell" format developed by Canon Joseph Cardijn, who held that "like ministers to like"—workers to workers, businessmen to businessmen, married couples to married couples. Typically, a CFM group consisted of five or six couples who followed a program of discussion about theology and social action centered on family life; their concern was not just with "the betterment of their own family situations but also with the life of families everywhere." Members were encouraged to share their thoughts while receiving the moral support of the group for their actions, including activities the member "could not or would not do alone." The Young Christian Workers, a social action group for single people, similarly influenced league founders before they married; Froehlich was the groups's first national president.[8]

Using a model similar to that of the Christian Family Movement, the first La Leche group meeting was held in Franklin Park, Illinois, on an October evening in 1956. That night, the seven founders and five of their pregnant friends discussed a *Reader's Digest* article advocating breast-feeding. Soon, with thirty and forty women crowding into living rooms, the meetings had grown so large that new groups formed to accommodate the demand. League founders quickly developed a series of five rotating sessions on pregnancy, birth, infant feeding, nutrition, and child rearing. Women gathered in members' houses and studied the material that eventually became the basis for *The Womanly Art of Breastfeeding,* first published in 1958. One meeting was held every three weeks, so that over the course of four months a participant attended all five; men were often invited to an additional "For Fathers Only" meeting as well. These small group sessions were facilitated at first by the founders and later by "league leaders," women who had successfully breastfed their babies at least a year and shared the league's maternalist philosophy. The groups provided information and emotional support for women wanting to breastfeed. Founder Mary Ann Cahill suggested, "We were considered . . . extremely radical . . . and this is why the [groups] were so important, because they gave you contact with other women who were also kind of thinking crazy."[9]

The creation of small all-female groups of peers seems to have been an important source of the league's strength. The groups may have helped to break down the isolation of mothering in nuclear families—a growing problem during an era of rapid suburbanization and geographic mobility. In moving to the new postwar suburbs, many women moved farther away from relatives who in earlier times might have provided information and support for the task of mothering. One grandmother wrote the league, for example, that her daughter had moved away to a new city and felt lonely "until she discovered the existence of La Leche League there." Like the earlier CFM groups, the breast-feeding groups enabled women to practice collectively what might have been difficult for them to achieve on their own. And like the later consciousness-raising groups of the women's liberation movement, the breast-feeding support groups made common the problems of individual women and nurtured their sense of belonging to a special subculture. One league member, Mary Jane Brizzolara, recalled attending a meeting in 1957 and finding "instant rapport" with every woman in the room. "In those days, any woman who wanted to have her baby naturally and breastfeed it thought she was the only person in the world who wanted those things," she said, "but to go to that first meeting and discover a whole room full of women who had the same feelings and the same values—it was great."[10]

The woman-to-woman approach of the groups was also evident in the league's hot-line telephone service and its publications. The league from the start received letters and telephone calls from women seeking advice about specific breast-feeding problems. The founders answered these queries "at home surrounded by . . . babies and children," and it was in response to the "never-ending stream of mail and the frantic phone calls" that the first version of *The Womanly Art of Breastfeeding* was put together, in loose-leaf folders sold as a "Course By Mail." The league newsletter first appeared in May of 1958 and was meant "to keep mothers in touch and give them somebody else to relate to or identify with . . . because at that time few mothers had anyone in their circle of friends who was breastfeeding," recalled founder Marian Tompson. The newsletter featured communications, poetry, photographs, and articles by league members. By 1960, four years after the founding of the organization, its headquarters averaged three hundred telephone calls and four hundred letters monthly. One member explained the reason she turned to the league for information. "My doctor has never had a baby. My doctor has never nursed a baby . . . Sally Jones . . . has nursed three babies. Darlene Smith has nursed four. . . . So this is why I called them instead of my doctor." According to the league, breast-feeding was not a medical issue but rather a "womanly art," and "it's up to women who have learned it to pass it on." Emphasizing the experience and wisdom of mothers rather than the expertise of doctors, the league by the mid-1950s anticipated later feminist calls for a women's health movement by questioning the medicalization of birth and infant care and challenging the influence of "experts" on changing definitions of motherhood.[11]

As membership in the league grew, it attracted a wider range of supporters who did not share the Catholic roots of the founders. Photographs and letters in league publications identified women who were African American, Asian, and Hispanic as well as white, Jewish as well as Christian. In its writings the league itself maintained a nonsectarian posture. But women of color appear to have been in the minority of the membership. A 1970 survey by the psychologist Alice Kahn Ladas indicated that the majority of active league members were white, middle-class, native-born women, with those identifying themselves as either Catholic or of "no religious identity" present in larger numbers than in the general population. As membership grew, governance of league affairs broadened. While the founding mothers controlled both office hiring practices and the executive board that made policy directions well into the 1980s, local regional chapters (known as sections) were organized by the early 1960s. The first national league convention in 1964 drew some 425 mothers and 100 babies to the Knickerbocker Hotel in Chicago, after which coordinators were appointed on the national and state levels. By 1964, too, the league had become international, with 6 groups in other countries as well as 115 in the United States. Fifteen years later there were La Leche League groups in 42 countries around the world.[12]

Although the league's founders had not initially planned for any kind of growth or set up a formal organizational structure beyond that of a local "club for nursing mothers," the league did grow, in part because of its complicated interactions with larger social trends. Though founded by women enmeshed in a distinctive Catholic subculture, the league clearly spoke to the enthusiasm felt by many Americans in the 1950s for nuclear family life. That the league emerged when it did was not surprising. The "baby boom" peaked in the mid-1950s in the United States as fertility rates, which had been steadily declining for nearly two centuries, sharply rose, as did the rate of marriage. Women coming of age during the 1950s gave birth to an average of 3.2 children, compared to an average of 2.4 children for women reaching adulthood during the 1930s. The founders of the league had many more children than was common even for the baby boom. The seven La Leche League founders claimed a total of fifty-three offspring (an average of more than seven per mother); their families ranged from three to eleven children. While all seven founders were Roman Catholic, they have suggested it was not religious impulse but rather the desire to deal with the reality of households full of infants that motivated the league's beginning. Motherhood was clearly of central concern to these women, who chose to shape a public meaning for their private lives.[13]

The increased birth rate of the 1950s was accompanied by a pronatalist ideology, defined by the historian Elaine Tyler May as the "belief in the positive value of having several children."[14] Many Americans in the postwar years believed that personal happiness for both men and women was to be found in an intensive family life focused on children, and that full-time motherhood was the ultimate fulfillment of femininity. The league gave formal expression to these pronatalist ideals, asserting that motherhood was "natural" and beneficial to women, children, and the social order.

The popularity of the league also reflected unease with approaches to motherhood and family life common among physicians and other experts in the 1950s. The kind of motherhood experts advocated was anything but "natural"—instead it was "scientific." Professional advice was to replace maternal instinct, and so child-rearing manuals, mothers' clubs, and physicians' counsel brought "modern" ideas about motherhood into the home. Earlier maternalist women's groups, such as the National Congress of Mothers, had argued that motherhood was so important to society that women must be trained to "be the best mothers possible for the good of the race." A School of Mothercraft, for example, was established in New York in 1911 to train mothers in the "intelligent and efficient" art of child care. By the 1930s, the authority of professionals on the subject of motherhood was institutionalized in the disciplines of social work, child guidance, preschool education, and, above all, medicine. Scientific motherhood came to favor the bottle over breast-feeding, medicated hospital birth over natural home birth, and rigidly scheduled days and nights over a more fluid approach to time. Motherhood, in short, was to be controlled by experts rather than directed by instinct. Rationality and order—then important in such other arenas of industrial American culture as business, home economics, and education—informed proper mothering as well. Standards of efficiency, time, and measurement were to control a baby's day as well as a factory's routine.[15]

Bottle-feeding was the preferred way to nourish a baby in 1956. The incidence of breast-feeding at one week of age had fallen to about 18 percent, a decline from about 38 percent in 1948 and from over 80 percent before 1920. Bottle-feeding first became popular in the United States in the late nineteenth century in part because of concerns about high infant mortality rates among the urban poor. Middle-class women soon adopted the new infant feeding method because of a desire to be fashionable and scientific. The historian Rima Apple suggests that the introduction of infant formula and the rise of pediatrics as a medical field led to the development of a mutually advantageous relationship between infant food companies and physicians. Taking another perspective, the historian Harvey Levenstein has argued that the male physicians who were replacing midwives by the turn of the century, "perhaps afflicted by . . . prudishness . . . tended to shy away from urging breastfeeding by mothers."[16]

In the mid-twentieth century, bottle-feeding was a complicated and time-consuming affair. Mothers followed elaborate methods for preparing formula using evaporated, powdered, or whole milk; carefully calculated total milk volume spread over a certain number of bottles per day; and conscientiously sterilized bottles, rubber nipples, and bottle caps. Babies were often weighed before and after feedings. Advice books insisted that mothers consult their doctors about techniques and schedules; doctors were to "prescribe" breast-feeding or bottle-feeding and to mandate all aspects of mothering. Dr. Benjamin Spock, for example, in the 1946 edition of *The Pocket Book of Baby and Child Care*, offered advice on schedules "only for those parents who are unable to consult a doctor regularly" and suggested that ideally "your doctor will prescribe the baby's schedule on the basis of his needs, and you should consult him about any changes." A 1953 publication circulated by the Beech Nut Company, *Happy Mealtimes for Babies*, stated: "Before we go any further, let's emphasize one important point: your doctor knows your baby—and he knows you. How your particular baby should be cared for, *whether he's sick or well*, is a matter that should be decided by your doctor—not by the neighbors, relatives or books." The federal Children's Bureau, in the 1940 edition of its popular booklet *Infant Care*, offered a detailed daily schedule for infants, which could "be varied according to the directions of the physician."[17]

Childbirth, like infant feeding, was defined as "scientific" in the 1950s. Advocates of scientific motherhood had by the 1920s and 1930s labeled childbirth a medical problem rather than a natural function, in part as a response to high infant and maternal mortality rates. As childbirth became medicalized, control of the birthing process fell away from women and their midwives and into the hands of physicians. By the mid-1950s, 95 percent of all births in the United States took place in hospitals—compared to about 50 percent in 1940 and fewer than 5 percent in 1900—and a high proportion of those births involved the use of painkilling drugs, forceps, and other medical interventions. This medicalization of childbirth, begun earlier in the century in an attempt to secure safety and comfort for women, now was seen by some as unpleasant, alienating, and manipulative. Further, medicated childbirth affected infant feeding because a mother who was drugged could not nurse her baby. And delivery in a hospital affected feeding because without flexible nursery policies, the baby could be brought to the mother only at certain times of the day, leading to tightly scheduled feedings.[18]

Scientific motherhood was not uncontested. There was a "motherhood reform" community made up of people—health care providers as well as mothers and fathers—interested in returning mothering from the artificial or scientific to the "natural" sphere. By the mid-1950s there were throughout North America and

Europe critics representing a variety of social perspectives who challenged invasive childbirth methods, artificial infant-feeding techniques, and rigid child-rearing practices. Some, for example the British natural childbirth educator Grantly Dick-Read, believed that motherhood embodied "essential femininity" and that childbirth was "woman's supreme triumph." Others presented arguments for woman-centered childbirth or more general critiques of modern industrial life. La Leche League founders communicated with many of these varied reformers, including the advocates of family-centered maternity care who in 1960 formed the International Childbirth Education Association. League founders read about natural childbirth, nutrition, and child-rearing techniques in *Child-Family Digest,* published in the United States, and in the *Natural Childbirth Trust Newsletter* from Great Britain. They corresponded with Dick-Read about his manual *Childbirth without Fear,* and in 1957 they sponsored him as their first guest speaker. In short, they began to communicate, founder Froehlich recalled, with a growing network of "people who had this healthy thinking about the body."[19]

Much attention focused on how to feed infants—on schedules or on demand, by the bottle or at the breast. Breast-feeding support groups were active in California during the 1940s. In 1942, medical workers in Detroit, including psychiatrists, pediatricians, obstetricians, and allied professionals, founded the Cornelian Corner to advocate breast-feeding and relaxed approaches to child-rearing practices such as toilet training. The Cornelians were named for the legendary Roman matron Cornelia, who said of her children, "these are my jewels," and for the corner of the family kitchen toward which she turned while nursing. According to one observer, the Cornelians "say that in many ways we have forgotten that a baby is a baby. Rather he has been thought of as a piece of physiological machinery to be handled by standardized methods."[20]

The pioneering public health physician Alice Hamilton was an early critic of the trend toward bottle-feeding. She wrote the Children's Bureau in 1949 that "for years . . . I watched this increasing opposition on the part of physicians and nurses toward breastfeeding." Young mothers, she suggested, "nowadays are under the impression that suckling a baby is an unusual activity, granted only to the specially gifted," and she urged Katherine Bain, director of the bureau's Division of Research in Child Development, to publicize findings supporting the importance of breastfeeding. Bain responded, "As I go around the country it appears to me that more physicians are becoming interested in breastfeeding and that some mothers themselves are pressing for it. I hope that I am right."[21]

La Leche League leaders built strong ties with others in the international motherhood reform community of the postwar years, but they were especially influenced by two Chicago-area physicians critical of scientific motherhood: Gregory White, the husband of league founder Mary White, and White's former teacher, Herbert Ratner, a Chicago-area health commissioner. During the early 1950s, these doctors encouraged their patients to attempt home birth, natural childbirth, and breast-feeding, and they urged their patients to talk with each other about natural mothering techniques. Founder Mary Ann Cahill recalled how White recognized the importance "of mother-to-mother help in breastfeeding" and "recognized that one woman needed another" for advice and support. Several of the league's founders were patients of White and Ratner, who, with a medical advisory board, provided La Leche League with "credibility and acceptability in the scientific community." This was especially important during the early years of the organization, when some considered mothers talking about infant feeding to be, according to founder Froehlich, "interfering with medicine."[22]

Doctors Ratner and White urged league founders to broaden their interests from breast-feeding to the more general issue of mothering. Like many in the motherhood reform community, these men held an essentialist view of women that presupposed a natural and biologically based social role. To Ratner, breast-feeding symbolized woman's place in the social order. At the first league convention in 1964, his keynote address focused on the "art of mothering." He believed Americans had abandoned a family ideology that nurtured women and children. "Motherhood," he stated, "is an opportunity for growth. Three children nurture motherhood more than one. Each mothering experience enriches." He also suggested that women who bottle-fed their babies could too easily separate from them and "become vulnerable to other persuasions," and that a decision to bottle-feed "may be a sign of emotional difficulties in the mother." White also saw breast-feeding as a key to good motherhood. The mother who bottle-feeds, he stated, does not have high levels of prolactin, the hormone that contributes to milk production, and therefore she does not have the same physical feelings toward her baby. "She's handicapped," he said. "She may turn out to be a pretty good mother. But she could have been a lot better mother if she had breastfed." By 1958, league founders had begun to shape a maternalist philosophy centered on "good mothering through breastfeeding" that reflected this essentialist model of womanhood.[23]

At the heart of the La Leche League's philosophy was the notion that the needs of the infant—as interpreted by the mother rather than the doctor—should determine the practice and pace of mothering. League founder Cahill said that "one of our mottos was 'give the baby back to the mother, that's who it belongs to.'" The basic need of the infant was for mother's milk and for mother herself. Therefore breast-feeding and bottle-feeding were not two equally acceptable options for mothers, as the Children's Bureau and Dr. Spock had advised. In the words of a league publication, breast-feeding was a moral imperative, being no less than "God's plan for mothers and babies."[24]

Breast-feeding, as defined by the league, offered important advantages for the baby, the mother, and the social order. The first and most important beneficiary of breast-feeding was the child. According to the league, breast milk was the best infant food, fitted to the human digestive system; its use would lead to infant health, a gain in natural immunities, and the avoidance of allergies. A baby would also learn love and trust so that he or she might "go out and make a better world." The league advocated prolonged breast-feeding because its founders believed that the emotional and physical health of an infant was strengthened by allowing the child, rather than a doctor's chart, to determine the duration of breast-feeding and the initiation of weaning. The idea that the child, her needs interpreted by the mother, should set the schedule for feedings and later for weaning distinguished the league from physicians who favored a breast-feeding regimen regulated by external norms of time. Many medical authorities approved nursing for a short period, from a few days to nine months, and they usually mandated feeding on a strict schedule of every three or four hours. For example, Frederic H. Bartlett wrote in the 1943 edition of his best-selling guide *Infants and Children*, "If you have plenty of milk you should nurse . . . perhaps not longer than 7 months," and he recommended a regular feeding schedule of the "usual" hours of 6 A.M., 10 A.M., 2 P.M., 6 P.M., 10 P.M., and 2 A.M. But the league urged instead that mothers nurse their babies on demand for at least a year, and preferably longer. Let him nurse until he wants to stop," the league advised. "Your baby may need the special kind of mothering he gets from breastfeeding for a longer time than someone else's baby." Techniques for, and defense of, breast-feeding older toddlers have long been a common and controversial theme in league literature.[25]

Second, the league promoted breast-feeding as beneficial to the mother. Breast-feeding would get women back into shape after pregnancy, help prevent breast cancer, and provide a natural form of birth control. Perhaps most important, breast-feeding would facilitate a woman's realization of her full potential as a person. In the first league statement of policy, circulated in 1964, the leaders suggested that "a mother who chooses to mother through breast-feeding, finds it an excellent way to grow in mothering as her baby grows in years. And since the woman who grows in mothering thereby grows as a human being, any other role she may fill in her lifetime will be enriched and deepened by the insights and humanity she will bring to it from her experience as a mother." The basic requirement for successful child rearing was a full-time, attentive mother who understood and accepted her "special vocation in life." As a corollary, league writers urged women to avoid such "mother substitutes" as pacifiers, high chairs, baby carriages, playpens, and, of course, bottles.[26]

Finally, not only babies and women but also society would benefit from breast-feeding, because good mothering would foster trust and security in children who would become, as league founder Betty Wagner said, "secure, well-adjusted adults, healthy adults, who will make this world a better place to live." In this sense the La Leche League echoed earlier ideals of motherhood that directed women's energies into domestic activities and claimed a higher civic purpose in the raising of children. League leaders believed that breast-feeding "is the ideal way to initiate good parent-child relationships and to strengthen the family and hence the whole fabric of our society." League leaders also believed that their movement would promote social cohesion in another way. By emphasizing the common bond of gender, league leaders, like earlier maternalists, minimized class and racial distinctions between women. According to founder Marian Tompson, women who differed in other ways could meet on the "common ground" of breast-feeding.[27]

The league took the act of breast-feeding and transformed it to symbolize an entire agenda for motherhood. For nearly four decades, league founders consistently argued that breast-fed babies required a different type of mothering than did bottle-fed babies. "If you were breastfeeding in the way we were suggesting . . . on demand," said founder Wagner, "then your baby expected a lot more and you were responding differently to this baby, and so we had to bring in the mothering." "Good mothering through breastfeeding" meant communicating with the baby, providing full-time love and care, and "accepting that his wants and needs are the same." The mother, closely attentive to her child, should turn to natural instinct rather than to charts, books, or schedules.[28]

La Leche League leaders sometimes struck others as radical. Indeed, some of them welcomed the description. "Everything we did was radical," Cahill said, from supporting breast-feeding to advocating the later introduction of solid foods to "listening to the baby." They certainly offered a program radical in its challenge to basic assumptions of mid-twentieth-century American culture, whether patriarchal or feminist. In a society much taken with efficiency, the clock, and precision, league attitudes to time and nature can be described as preindustrial. The league encouraged women to let their babies, instead of the clock and the calendar, set the time for eating and the time for weaning, to orient themselves to a variable natural time pattern rather than a fixed schedule based on external authority. A 1962 poem in the newsletter was typical in its approach to time and nature:

Observe her, her child at her breast.
Pause from the day's whirling activity
and consider her meaningful passiveness . . .
Look closer.
Discern her faith, somewhat unique in
a mechanized world.
Faith in the quiet order of nature,
in the complete and unstinting productivity
of her healthy young body.
Faith in herself, in her womanliness.[29]

This faith in "God's plan" focused on interpersonal relationships and "meaningful passiveness," rather than schedules and other externally mandated norms of behavior. The league urged women to "refuse to accept the attempted mechanization of human beings or to abandon their true, womanly role."

The league also questioned the pervasive glorification of individual achievement in American society. It is not surprising that the league showed more sympathy with mothers driven to work outside the home by financial need than with those who prized the possibility of achievement offered by a public career. In the league outlook, achievement in this sense meant less than did connection with people. Not only the league but many Americans assumed that women were by nature more attuned to people than were men. One author widely cited by league members, Arlene Rossen Cardozo, argued in her 1976 book, *Woman at Home,* that a "male model" of achievement and success had misled feminists, who "fled home in imitation of Man. And the man of the day was the Hollow Man, the Computerized Man" who placed a success ethic higher than human relationships. In this cherishing of personalism and emphasis on the claims of others, league advocates echoed earlier maternalist ideologies and appealed to many American women in the twentieth century. The essentialism of the league, moreover, prefigured aspects of a later strain of radical feminism that was committed to preserving and celebrating gender differences.[30]

This personalism was clearly evident in the office procedures of the league, where human relationships held sway over rational, meritocratic bureaucracy. On office procedures, the league's policy has from the beginning been "nepotism reigns supreme." Other qualifications being equal, the hiring order is "Founding Mother's child" first, down a scale of five categories to "friends or neighbors" of league mothers and employees. Moreover, office hours have been geared to the school day to accommodate family needs of office staff, and there "is never a problem in taking time off to tend to a sick child." Similarly, the first national league convention in 1964 did not follow the usual methods of American business culture. Apparently, the hotel had not been asked before for diaper containers, cribs, and a "rock and rest" room, but the manager said, "Listen, when the business men come, they want a bar in every room and ice on tap. Your requests are a little different, but nothing we can't handle." Essential notions of womanhood, then, configured not only league ideology but the mundane workings of its organization as well.[31]

Radical or conservative, the league's philosophy raised questions about American mores. The La Leche League's emphasis on intensive mothering led its leaders to criticize the consumerist "happy housewife" image of the 1950s that was first labeled in Betty Friedan's 1963 best-seller, *The Feminine Mystique*. The happy housewife was concerned with appearances, of herself and of her house, and was above all a consumer of material goods. She was *not* first and foremost a mother. League leaders criticized this prescriptive image, urging mothers to attend to their children first. The league ran counter to American norms by implying that it was more important to build intense affectional ties between family members than to acquire and maintain the material trappings of a middle-class family. "What's important in your life," founder Mary White told a league convention in 1966, "is the people and not the things. And . . . especially while you have babies and small ones around, the most important people are your children." Time spent on housework, league leaders argued, was better spent with the family. Founder Cahill believed that to deemphasize housework was liberating. She said, "It was not unusual in those days for a mother to put the little one in the crib to entertain herself or to cry while mother spiffed up the house. You weren't to have dirty dishes in the sink, or unmade beds." Another founder, Viola Lennon, agreed that in the 1950s "the rules were very severe. . . . I think we were greatly responsible for changing the emphasis, that you were home to take care of the baby (instead of the house)."[32]

If the league's maternalism codified a social role for women within a family defined less by consumerism than by personalism, it also prescribed a domestic role for men. The league argued that a father should, by supporting and encouraging the mother, enable her to nurture the baby more completely. Fathers should focus on family life rather than on professional success alone; spend more time with their children, "because the joys of parenthood are meant to be shared"; and participate fully in domestic tasks, because the "authoritative, masculine man knows his dignity and stature are not in jeopardy when he performs a kitchen chore." The league newsletter on occasion published a June "Father's Day" issue that addressed such topics as how to offer support to a breast-feeding wife, and *The Womanly Art of Breastfeeding* discussed fatherhood in each edition. Just as the league helped shape a dimension of pronatalist womanhood, in its attention to fathers it helped shape notions of manhood in postwar American society.[33]

Some women and men rejected the philosophy of the league because they disliked its moral fervor, complaining that the league used scare tactics and dogmatism to inflict feelings of guilt on women who failed to breast-feed or breast-fed only a short time. Others argued that children who were breast-fed too long might become infantilized and have difficulty separating from their mothers, who were overeager to conform to maternalist ideology. League policy makers, recognizing that reputation, warned leaders to avoid overzealousness. "League mothers need to be . . . non-critical with their non-breastfeeding friends, instead of militant and crusading about the subject," the newsletter editor cautioned in 1972. "Because we know we're onto a good thing, we sometimes put people off. . . . We need to relax and appreciate other people . . . even when we don't agree with some of their ideas." Lennon suggested that the league's reputation for fanaticism came "out of the fact that when you're walking up hill, as the road gets steeper, you might . . . have leaders [who are militant]. I don't think as an organization, top level, we were militant, but . . . some of our leaders once in a while would . . . take a very aggressive stand." At a 1968 convention, a panel titled "Can Breastfeeding Be Carried Too Far?" discussed the public relations problem caused by the "holier than thou" attitude of some group leaders who were "more League than League" in their insistence on prolonged breast-feeding and full-time motherhood. The working or bottle-feeding mother, league leaders suggested, was not "beyond the pale"; league mothers should not criticize or pass judgment, but neither should they "carry acceptance to the point of imitation." More important was the effort to bring information on mothering through breast-feeding to all women, even to those who disagreed with league ideology. "Our goal," according to the league leaders' handbook, "is to avoid diluting the philosophy while helping a mother grow toward it—without antagonizing the mother along the way."[34]

During the late 1960s and after, falling fertility rates, the rise of feminism, and an increase in maternal employment inspired a lively debate among league members about the meaning of motherhood in American society. While the basic message—that the ideal role for women was full-time motherhood focused on the natural needs of the baby—remained constant, the public reception of that message changed. The league initially challenged scientific motherhood and promised to empower women by helping them reclaim the arts of childbirth and infant feeding from the domain of experts. Now, the league was vocally challenging employed motherhood. To the league, both practices—health professionals intervening in the realm of motherhood and women working outside the home—represented a falling away from nature in a scientific age. In both cases, the prescription for social health was a return to "natural" behavior by women, where mother and child would form a "nursing couple" to better reflect traditionalist values. Thus an ideology of maternalism that in the mid-1950s sounded radical and empowering thirty years later impressed some as "extremely conservative." Tompson, one of the founders, wrote in 1970 that breast-feeding *was* conservative because it "ranks in status with traditional values of God, motherhood, and love of country."[35]

The social context surrounding the league shifted dramatically from the time of its founding in 1956 through the 1980s. Fertility rates fell from a high in 1957 of 123 per thousand women between the ages of 15 and 44, to 96.6 in 1965, and to 66.7 in 1975. At the same time, economic pressures and opportunities for women outside the home increased. Maternal employment began a steady climb. In 1950, fewer than 12 percent of mothers with children under the age of six worked outside the home; by 1960, this had climbed to 19 percent, and by 1970, to 30 percent. By 1980, nearly 50 percent of mothers with children under six were in the labor force. These figures increasingly included the mothers of very young children. In 1978, the United States Census Bureau for the first time counted mothers of infants under the age of one year who were at work. That year, a startling 30 percent of mothers of infants were working, at least part-time; 41 percent of all mothers with children under the age of two were employed.[36] This "normalization" of maternal employment, combined with the growth of the feminist movement in the late 1960s and 1970s, put the league into sharpening conflict with women's lives and attitudes. The premise that a woman contributed to the world mainly by what she did within the home became anachronistic as family norms shifted to include maternal employment and less time-intensive child rearing. In response, league leaders and members increasingly addressed the issues of feminism and working mothers.

And yet the league flourished during these challenging years of social change. During the decade of the 1970s, the number of active La Leche League groups more than tripled, growing from 1,260 in 1971 to 4,327 ten years later. There were certainly many women claiming no allegiance to any philosophy other than traditional domesticity, and the league gave them a voice. But, in addition, the commonality between league practice and that of feminists and the counterculture may have overridden the ideological differences between them. League practice dovetailed, for example, with the "return to nature" ethos of the counterculture. Founder Lennon recalled that "by the time the '60s rolled around, people were beginning to accept certain things that were in 1956 really way out." League founders believed that the "hippie movement" aided in the popularization of the league "because they embraced all this natural stuff" and because their rebellion against the establishment included the medical establishment. Of the counterculture, founder Mary Ann Cahill said, "We were there, ready and in place when the big push came

from those people flocking to the La Leche League . . . they had the idealism, but
we had it all in place . . . they were looking for literature and information which
they were able to find from us."[37]

The alliance of the counterculture with the league and, indeed, a general
broadening of the league's constituency through the 1970s were not without tension. Many of the new members attempted to bring to the league agenda such issues as advocacy of natural foods, environmental politics, civil rights, home
schooling, and family planning; others wanted the group to take a stand on abortion. But the league cautioned against "mixing causes," arguing in its 1973 "Statement of Policy" that, whatever the merit of other concerns, the message about
mothering through breast-feeding must not be diluted. "People who support good
mothering," the league stated, "may reject the League if it seems to be part of another movement." Whereas other historical maternalist movements had encompassed a broader range of reforms, the league's belief in the importance of
breast-feeding as a key to good mothering pushed it to cast as wide a net as possible
over the varied female population of the late twentieth-century United States; advocacy of any other controversial cause might take away resources from the promotion of breast-feeding or, worse, might turn some potential breast-feeding
mother away.[38] With the practice of breast-feeding by a wider variety of women
came some interesting nuances, such as the popularization of the electrical breast
pump or the sight of a working mother nursing her baby at work. In both cases,
the spread of breast-feeding, although initially motivated by an interest in tradition
and naturalism, ironically helped blur long-standing demarcations between home
and work, and between nature and science.

Another source of league growth was its increasing acceptance in the medical
community. At first physicians who favored scientific motherhood considered the
league marginal, believing that "breastfeeding fell into the medical domain, and
that one nursing mother was not qualified to advise another." Gradually, however,
the league gained respectability. Although the founders believed that "most of the
questions and problems a nursing mother may encounter are not medical," they
stressed that they did not "intend to invade the jurisdiction of the physician." From
the beginning they consulted with physicians. They formed a "medical advisory
board" for editorial approval of materials and advice on specific medical problems.
By 1960, a physician in North Carolina cited the league's work favorably, saying
that it advocated "a revival of the age-old conviction that nature is more reliable
than science, that mother-love is more effective than aseptic precautions." In 1968
the *Journal of Pediatrics* published "A Salute to La Leche League International,"
cautioning the league against dogmatism but wishing them "continuing success."
Physicians spoke to mothers at league conventions. Informal programs for physi-

cians that were started in the late 1950s evolved into a Physician's Breastfeeding Seminar in 1973, which the American Medical Association and other medical groups recognized for continuing education credit. Local league groups facilitated hospital prenatal programs and initiated Information Service Centers to distribute breast-feeding information to mothers and health care professionals; by 1978 there were seventy centers, twenty of them in the United States. The league succeeded in winning public and professional support for its belief that the feeding of well babies was not a medical problem. More problematic was the reception of its maternalistic philosophy.[39]

The founders of the La Leche League have described themselves as early feminists, for they believed women should reclaim control of their bodies through natural childbirth and breast-feeding. An editorial in the league newsletter in 1966 stated that "feminism was with us long before Betty Friedan." In the early 1960s, league founders discussed Friedan's pioneering book, *The Feminine Mystique;* they remember agreeing with some of her views while rejecting her "negative analysis of motherhood." If they did not accept the feminist critique of gender roles, they too thought that women should not be subservient to men in the domain of mothering. In the 1963 edition of *The Womanly Art of Breastfeeding,* the authors wrote, "Breastfeeding is part of a womanly heritage, and it would naturally follow, in fact it seems almost inevitable, that mothers should initiate the revival in breastfeeding." Cahill recalled that when she was pregnant with her fourth child in 1955 she was looking "for ways to have a more natural delivery and then to breastfeed . . . because I wanted to be in control. I wanted to have some say in this. I did not want somebody to just knock me out and say, 'leave it to us, we'll take care of everything and you'll have the baby.'"[40]

Elements of the maternalist ideology of the La Leche League had a natural appeal for some late twentieth-century feminists. Although many of the women who launched the women's liberation movement of the 1960s and 1970s attacked motherhood as a patriarchal construct reproducing traditional relationships within the family, others argued for a feminist version of maternalism. Both league maternalism and feminism questioned the control of childbirth and child rearing by the medical establishment, and both promoted a collective female consciousness reinforced by small group meetings. The league shared the feminist conviction stated by the philosopher Joyce Trebilcot in 1984 that "mothering must now be defined and controlled by women."[41]

Feminists liked the league's emphasis on reclaiming the arts of breast-feeding and natural childbirth, but with some qualification. For example, the Boston Women's Health Book Collective, in the first edition of the widely read health manual *Our Bodies, Our Selves,* recommended *The Womanly Art of Breastfeeding,* "if you can get past the sickening stuff about [how] a woman's role is to bear and raise kids." Five years later, the collective, perhaps recognizing more common ground, wrote that *The Womanly Art of Breastfeeding* "will give you facts and confidence . . . but its philosophy is different than ours. We do not believe that breastfeeding has to dominate your life." The collective suggested, however, that the "women's health movement" could bring together "different groups of women." A medical sociologist stated in 1975 that breast-feeding was a feminist issue, asking, "Where and by whom are the definitions of woman's body made? Who will control how she uses it?"[42] Feminists applauded the league's involvement in legal cases involving women's right to breast-feed in public and at the workplace; the league also provided information for lawsuits and criminal charges concerning breast-feeding and maternity leave extensions, jury duty, women prisoners, child neglect, and child custody.[43]

By the late 1960s, league publications directly addressed feminism. Founder Mary White told the second international league convention in 1966 that most league women had wanted to "*be* somebody and get married too." And once women "accept—not just accept, but embrace wholeheartedly, the idea that mothering is a rewarding job, a job filled with all sorts of satisfactions, then we'll be able to see and enjoy all the benefits it has to offer." League members found satisfaction in embracing this active definition of motherhood. Beginning in the early 1970s, letters and articles in league publications debated the problem of woman's proper place. How should mothering be defined? What was a feminist? Could you be a feminist and a full-time mother? Readers thought so, the founding mothers thought so, and if their definition of feminism was dismissed by some, it nonetheless reflected the thinking of a significant number of American women. According to a 1972 survey, league members saw their organization as "traditionalistic in its advocacy of the family role of wife and mother [but] . . . liberating because it teaches members actively to define and achieve satisfying goals within this role." Members placed "their confidence in themselves and their sisters rather than passively following the advice of licensed professionals." Breast-feeding provided a link to other mothers and was therefore a sign of "womanly power."[44]

Many women writing to the league newsletter appropriated the language of feminism to argue that maternalism was liberating. In 1971, a league member from Ohio wrote, "I've been reading and hearing a lot about Women's Liberation and I think I would like to be liberated too! I want to be free to have my babies with dignity and joy. . . . I want to be free to nurse my baby on the delivery table. . . . I want to be free to, of all things, feed my baby when he is hungry. . . . Yes, I want to be liberated! I want to be free! I want to be free to be a woman!" A Chicago woman wrote that "the thrust of the Woman's Movement is toward each person being able to do what suits her best (and the League way of mothering suits me)." A league leader from Minnesota wrote the next year that the league reassured women that "mothering is a valid vocation" and "indeed, a 'liberating career.'"[45]

If league supporters often appropriated the language of feminism, most rejected feminist philosophy, especially the idea that women could work for wages and mother at the same time; they reacted to growing public acceptance of women workers with a strong reaffirmation of housewifery and motherhood. A woman's self-esteem and sense of worth, league representatives suggested, could be found at home as well as at work. The newsletter in the 1970s and 1980s printed reams of articles and correspondence about mothers who had planned to work or were working while their children were young but later decided to stay at home. In a typical letter of this kind, published in 1972, a woman who had planned to work after the birth of her child decided she could not leave her baby; she proclaimed, "The only stimulation I felt I needed was the stimulation of my baby nursing at my breast." Another writer suggested that sometimes women could combine family and career, if work was flexible enough, but if a woman *had* to work "one simply has to make the best of a bad situation." There is a decidedly defensive cast to many of these articles, as there is in publications promoted by the league "for the woman who chooses to stay at home to raise her family, and for whom forming close human relationships is the first priority." By the mid-1970s, even as membership continued to rise, the league seemed aware that the full-time mother devoted to the care of others, once in the mainstream, was now threatened by social change.[46]

League leaders strongly criticized the materialism and consumerism that, they believed, pushed women into the labor force. Many articles and letters from readers offered concrete ways in which families could survive on lower incomes by budgeting, bartering, and lowering living standards.[47] But others recognized the economic need pulling many women into the workforce and proposed maternalist public policies, such as mothers' pensions, to support women at home. In 1979, for example, founder Marian Tompson told a league conference, "In our society where two income families are close to becoming an economic necessity, traditional mothering is being systematically stamped out. What we desperately need are policies that will allow women the choice of staying home to care for their babies without having to opt for poverty. Breastfeeding, once considered a medical problem, now becomes a political issue."[48]

The league's service to working mothers was not consistent. Some La Leche League groups excluded working mothers, but others welcomed them. A 1984 survey found several groups in California, Connecticut, Florida, New Mexico, and New York that accepted or were oriented toward working mothers. The league has for over a decade been involved in peer-counseling programs for poor inner-city women, most of whom have to work for wages. League leaders estimated that by the 1980s, when membership began to slide after some twenty-five years of growth, up to half of the women attending meetings were employed outside the home. But if the league has in practice in some times and places been supportive and non-judgmental about working mothers, ideologically it has consistently valued full-time mothering for families. To be accredited as a group leader through the early 1980s, a woman "had to be pretty much at home" rather than at work.[49]

League founder Mary White expressed the organization's general attitude toward working mothers when she stated at a league conference in 1981 that "any weakening in the link between the mother and her baby endangers the future health and security of the child." She added: "We in La Leche have just as great an obligation to help [working mothers] . . . breastfeed their babies as we have any mother who comes to us for help . . . but, knowing what we know about mothering . . . shouldn't we want to do more? I think we must show all mothers how important full-time mothering is to their babies, to themselves, and to their whole families. How the needs of their babies are not only for mother's milk, or mother's breast, but for all of her." Each successive edition of *The Womanly Art of Breastfeeding* offered more acknowledgment of working mothers. The most recent (1991) edition contains a chapter on breast-feeding tips for working mothers, followed by a chapter titled "Making a Choice" that urges mothers to consider staying at home while their children are young. The league's philosophy, then, while acknowledging the tremendous changes in women's lives, has remained steadfast in its vision of breast-feeding and full-time parenting of young children as the essence of "good mothering."[50]

League maternalism, based on the notion of difference rather than equality between men and women, represented an important voice in the chorus of postwar interpretations of gender in the United States. The league embraced a biosocial understanding of women by defining female success and achievement through motherhood rather than through economics or politics. Because of the league's maternalism, which both asserted women's authority over the practice of motherhood and emphasized the importance of full-time motherhood, the group's history presents an interesting paradox. On the one hand, by the mid-1950s the league anticipated a strand of the feminist movement that was concerned with women's control over health care issues centered on childbirth and child rearing. On the other hand, by the early 1970s the league also challenged the emerging feminist ideology by questioning the consequences for children of the movement of women away from the home and into the workplace. In both cases, the league decried aspects of modern life that seemed to distance women from essentially natural behavior. The La Leche League reconstructed mothering in a way that was both liberating and constricting and so ironically offered both prologue and counterpoint to the emerging movement for women's liberation.

NOTES

1. La Leche League International, *The Womanly Art of Breastfeeding* (New York, 1991), back cover. For the house history of the La Leche League (LLL), see Kaye Lowman, *The LLLove Story* (Franklin Park, 1978). Overviews of women's changing status in the postwar United States include Eugenia Kaledin, *Mothers and More: American Women in the 1950s* (Boston, 1984); and Elaine Tyler May, *Homeward Bound: American Families in the Cold War Era* (New York, 1988). On the Children's Bureau as an earlier source of information on mothering, see Molly Ladd-Taylor, *Raising a Baby the Government Way: Mothers' Letters to the Children's Bureau, 1915–1932* (New Brunswick, 1986), pp. 1–3. Copies of *Leaven*—the publication for LLL group leaders— and other LLL documents cited in this paper are housed in the archives of the La Leche League, at their headquarters in Franklin Park, Illinois. See *Leaven* 3 (Summer 1967): 17; 8 (July–Aug. 1972): 19; and 5 (May–June 1969).

2. Nancy Schrom Dye and Daniel Blake Smith, "Mother Love and Infant Death, 1750–1920," *Journal of American History* 73 (Sept. 1986): 329–53, esp. p. 353. On the historical construction of motherhood, see ibid.; and Nancy Pottishman Weiss, "The Mother-Child Dyad Revisited: Perceptions of Mothers and Children in Twentieth Century Child-Rearing Manuals," *Journal of Social Issues* 34, no. 2 (1978): 29–45. On nineteenth-century domestic ideology, see the influential article by Barbara Welter, "The Cult of True Womanhood," *American Quarterly* 18 (Summer 1966): 151–74. The domestic ideology, of course, had long been challenged by the work behavior of those black, immigrant, and poor women who did not have the luxury of emulating an idealized middle-class motherhood supported by a male wage earner. On race, see Eileen Boris, "The Power of Motherhood: Black and White Activist Women Redefine the 'Political,'" *Yale Journal of Law and Feminism* 2 (Fall 1989): 27–31.

3. On the varying definitions of maternalism, see the group of papers edited by Lynn Weiner, "International Trends: Maternalism as a Paradigm," *Journal of Women's History* 5 (Fall 1993): 95–131. On scientific motherhood, which early advocates often called "trained motherhood," see Andrea Meditch, "In the Nation's Interest: Child Care Prescriptions, 1890–1930" (Ph.D. diss., University of Texas, Austin, 1981), pp. 166–78; and Rima D. Apple, *Mothers and Medicine: A Social History of Infant Feeding, 1890–1950* (Madison, 1987), pp. 97–113.

4. La Leche League International, "Statement of Policy," publication no. 2, May 1982, p. 2; *La Leche League News* 18 (July–Aug. 1976): 51; 23 (Jan.–Feb. 1981): 2, 5–6. The *News* was first published in May 1958; in 1985 it was retitled *New Beginnings*. See also La Leche League International, *The Womanly Art of Breastfeeding* (New York, 1983), p. 340; ibid. (1991), pp. 405–6. The later 1980s saw a decline in breast-feeding to 52 percent. These figures chart the numbers of women breast-feeding at the birth of their babies; the numbers fall off drastically as babies age

or when factors of race and class are taken into account. In 1984, about the peak of breast-feeding incidence in recent times, some 24 percent of women breast-fed their infants six months after birth; by 1989, the figure had declined to 18 percent. Jeanne Gatoura, "Reverse Trend: Its Benefits Notwithstanding, Breastfeeding Is Declining," *Chicago Tribune,* June 14, 1992, sec. 6, p. 12; Warren E. Leary, "Why Fewer Blacks Choose to Breast-Feed Than Do Whites," *New York Times,* April 7, 1988, p. B7; Kathleen G. Auerbach, "The Decline of Breastfeeding," *Mothering* 51 (Spring 1989): 76–79.

5. On maternal labor force statistics from 1950 through 1985, see Sara E. Rix, ed., *The American Woman, 1988–89: A Status Report* (New York, 1988), p. 127, table 3.1. On earlier expressions of domesticity, see Linda K. Kerber, *Women of the Republic: Intellect and Ideology in Revolutionary America* (Chapel Hill, 1980); and Kathryn Kish Sklar, *Catharine Beecher: A Study in American Domesticity* (New Haven, 1973).

6. Lowman, *LLLove Story,* pp. 11, 18; league founders Mary Ann Cahill, Edwina Froehlich, Viola Lennon, Betty Wagner, and the medical information liaison Julie Stock, interview by Lynn Weiner, March 21, 1989 (hereafter cited as league founders interview), transcript, p. 9 (in Lynn Weiner's possession); league founder Marian Tompson interviewed by Weiner, Nov. 5, 1990, audiotape and transcript, ibid. The other "founding mothers" of the LLL were Mary White and Mary Ann Kerwin.

7. Two of the founders' husbands were attorneys; the others were an accountant, a physician, an engineer, an Internal Revenue Service officer, and a machinist. Biographical material is available in "La Leche League—The Story of Our Life," *La Leche League News* 1 (May–June 1958): 1; Betty Wagner, "Ten Years of La Leche League," ibid., 8 (Sept.–Oct. 1966): 5; Lowman, *LLLove Story,* pp. 76–90; La Leche League International, *The Womanly Art of Breastfeeding* (Franklin Park, 1963), pp. 147–50; league founders interview, p. 1.

8. Lowman, *LLLove Story,* pp. 13, 78; *New Catholic Encyclopedia,* s.v "Christian Family Movement"; Christian Family Movement activist Patty Crowley, interview by Erin Roach Hupp, March 18, 1989, transcript (in Weiner's possession). The founders also mentioned the format of the Great Books discussion groups as an organizational model; see league founders interview, p. 7.

9. Lowman, *LLLove Story,* pp. 15–17. The publishing history of *The Womanly Art of Breastfeeding* has some interesting parallels to the publishing history of *Our Bodies, Our Selves,* the feminist health manual of the 1970s, which similarly began as a "kitchen table" publication and was later produced commercially. See Boston Women's Health Book Collective, *Our Bodies, Our Selves: A Course by and for Women* (Boston, 1972), pp. 1–2, 137–38; league founders interview, p. 5.

10. On families and suburbanization, see May, *Homeward Bound,* pp. 24–25; "Mail Bag," *Leaven* 5 (Mar.–Apr. 1969): 7. On consciousness-raising groups, see Blanche Linden-Ward and Carol Hurd Green, *American Women in the 1960s: Changing the Future* (New York, 1993), pp. 436–39. For a description of the early LLL groups, see Lowman, *LLLove Story,* p. 37.

11. Lowman, *LLLove Story,* pp. 24–25, 31; Kathleen Astin-Knafl and Hannah Meara Marshall, "National Survey of La Leche League Members," *La Leche League News* 17 (July–Aug. 1975): 51; Wagner, "Ten Years of La Leche League," p. 1.

12. See the summary of the survey, based on a sample of some 1,100 LLL members, in Al-

ice Kahn Ladas, "An Educator Looks at LLL," *La Leche League News* 12 (July–Aug. 1970): 54–55. See also "La Leche League—The Story of Our Life," p. 1; and Nell Ryan, "Editor's Echo," *La Leche League News* 11 (Jan.–Feb. 1969): 15.

13. Lowman, *LLLove Story,* pp. 14, 37, 75–90; May, *Homeward Bound,* pp. 136–37; Tompson interview, p. 1.

14. Elaine Tyler May argues brilliantly that in the postwar era the politics of the Cold War and fears about technological advances, consumerism, and women's emancipation contributed to a "contained" family life that offered security in an insecure world. May, *Homeward Bound,* pp. 208, 137–40.

15. Apple, *Mothers and Medicine,* pp. 97–113; Mary L. Read, *The Mothercraft Manual* (Boston, 1926), pp. 1–2; Nancy F. Cott, *The Grounding of Modern Feminism* (New Haven, 1987), pp. 169–70. On the influence of such psychologists as G. Stanley Hall on the first popularization of scientific motherhood in the late nineteenth century, see Barbara Ehrenreich and Deirdre English, *For Her Own Good: One Hundred and Fifty Years of the Experts' Advice to Women* (New York, 1978), p. 199. Hall, they suggest, "at the National Congress of Mothers meetings, seemingly trailing faint emanations of laboratory chemicals, promised a glorious union of science and motherhood." On scientific management and expertise in American life, see Cecelia Tichi, *Shifting Gears: Technology, Literature, Culture in Modernist America* (Chapel Hill, 1987).

16. "Comments on Breastfeeding," *La Leche League News* 4 (Sept.–Oct. 1962): 2; La Leche League International, *Womanly Art* (1991), p. 405; Apple, *Mothers and Medicine,* p. 153, table 9.1, 169; Harvey Levenstein, "'Best for Babies' or 'Preventable Infanticide'? The Controversy over Artificial Feeding of Infants in America, 1880–1920," *Journal of American History* 70 (June 1983): 88.

17. Dr. Benjamin Spock was certainly the most popular child-rearing authority in this era; over 30 million copies of his advice book were sold between 1946 and 1985. Apple, *Mothers and Medicine,* p. 119; Benjamin Spock, *The Pocket Book of Baby and Child Care* (New York, 1946), pp. 24, 52–76. For the Beech Nut quotation, see Barbara Katz Rothman, *In Labor: Women and Power in the Birthplace* (New York, 1982), p. 105. U.S. Department of Labor, Children's Bureau, *Infant Care* (Washington, 1940), p. 6.

18. Apple, *Mothers and Medicine,* pp. 173–74; Kaledin, *Mothers and More,* pp. 178–81; Ladd-Taylor, *Raising a Baby the Government Way,* pp. 14–15; Richard W. Wertz and Dorothy C. Wertz, *Lying-In: A History of Childbirth in America* (New York, 1979), p. 173.

19. League founders interview, p. 3; Kaledin, *Mothers and More,* pp. 178–81; Lowman, *LLLove Story,* pp. 21–24; Janet Carlisle Bogdan, "Childbirth in America, 1650 to 1900," in *Women, Health, and Medicine in America: A Historical Handbook,* ed. Rima D. Apple (New Brunswick, 1992), pp. 119–20; Grantly Dick Read, *Childbirth without Fear: The Principles and Practice of Natural Childbirth* (New York, 1944).

20. Charlotte Aiken to Clara E. Councell, Jan. 31, 1949, box 400, file 4–8–1–1, Records of the U.S. Children's Bureau, RG 102, National Archives, Washington, D.C.; Alice Hamilton to Katherine Bain, March 14, 1949, ibid.; J. C. Riddle to Robert Slade, Sept. 21, 1950, ibid. An officer of the General Federation of Women's Clubs wrote to the Children's Bureau in 1957 urging that it promote breast-feeding along the lines of a crusade she had witnessed in England in the 1920s. See Jessie Haver Butler to Bain, Jan. 19, 1957, box 611, ibid. On the Cornelians, see

Oscar B. Markey, "The Human Breast in the First Year of Life," paper presented to the American Orthopsychiatric Association, Feb. 24, 1950, pp. 9–11, box 400, ibid.; and Lawrence Gould, "How to Give Your Baby the Best Start in Life," *Family Circle Magazine,* Jan. 1949, p. 50.

21. Hamilton to Bain, Mar. 7, 1949, and Bain to Hamilton, Mar. 14, 1949, box 400, file 4–8–1–1, Children's Bureau Records.

22. Lowman, *LLLove Story,* pp. 14, 56; league founders interview, pp. 5, 6, 14; Apple, *Mothers and Medicine,* pp. 177–78.

23. League founders interview, p. 22; *La Leche League News* 1 (May–June 1958): 2; 6 (July–Aug. 1964): 2; Lowman, *LLLove Story,* pp. 48–49, 21.

24. League founders interview, p. 3; "We Believe," *La Leche League News* 6 (July–Aug. 1964): 1. For the Children's Bureau position of the late 1950s on the bottle versus breast-feeding that "women are not all alike; each one should have the individual consideration that her physician is in the best position to give," see Bain to Butler, Feb. 19, 1957, box 611, file 4–8–1–1, Children's Bureau Records. For a widely read opinion that bottle-feeding and breast-feeding were both acceptable, see Spock, *Pocket Book of Baby and Childcare,* pp. 30–80.

25. La Leche League International, *Womanly Art* (1963), pp. 7–9, 129–34; Frederic H. Bartlett, *Infants and Children: Their Feeding and Growth* (New York, 1943), pp. 4–5. Spock suggested nursing babies until they were ready for weaning to a cup, somewhere between eight and twelve months. See Spock, *Pocket Book of Baby and Childcare,* p. 47. Lowman, *LLLove Story,* p. 40.

26. Lowman, *LLLove Story,* p. 40; La Leche League International, *Womanly Art* (1963), pp. 9–12; *La Leche League News* 6 (July–Aug. 1964): 1–2; *Leaven* 6 (Jan.–Feb. 1970): 2.

27. League founders interview, p. 24; Tompson interview, p. 2; Lowman, *LLLove Story,* p. 40. On women's common bond, see Nancy F. Cott, *The Bonds of Womanhood: "Woman's Sphere" in New England, 1780–1835* (New Haven, 1977); and Sklar, *Catharine Beecher.*

28. League founders interview, p. 5; Lowman, *LLLove Story,* p. 40; *La Leche League News* 6 (July–Aug. 1964): 1. The use of the male pronoun is striking in this women's organization. The handbook said, "We appreciate and laud the fact that babies come in two genders, male and female. . . . In this book, we refer to baby only as 'he,' not with sexist intent, but simply for clarity's sake. Mother is unquestionably 'she.'" La Leche League International, *Womanly Art* (1983), pp. xvi, 48–51.

29. "The Modern Nursing Mother," *La Leche League News* 4 (Sept.–Oct. 1962): 9; league founders interview, pp. 21–22; E. P. Thompson, "Time, Work-Discipline, and Industrial Capitalism," in *Classes, Power, and Conflict: Classical and Contemporary Debates,* ed. Anthony Giddens and David Held (Berkeley, 1982), pp. 299–309; Meditch, "In the Nation's Interest," pp. 200–201.

30. Nell Ryan, "Editor's Echo," *La Leche League News* 11 (Sept.–Oct. 1969): 79; 6 (July–Aug. 1964): 5; Arlene Rossen Cardozo, *Woman at Home* (New York, 1976), pp. 3, 144–56. For a comparable understanding of gender differences, see Carol Gilligan, *In a Different Voice: Psychological Theory and Women's Development* (Cambridge, Mass., 1982). For a cultural feminist point of view, see Adrienne Rich, *Of Woman Born: Motherhood as Experience and Institution* (New York, 1976).

31. Lowman, *LLLove Story,* pp. 72–74, 41–42, 69.

32. Betty Friedan, *The Feminine Mystique* (New York, 1963); league founders interview, p. 9; Mary White, "What's in It for Mother?" *La Leche League News* 8 (Sept.–Oct. 1966): 9.

33. La Leche League International, *Womanly Art* (1963), p. 116; Robert A. Bradley, "Husband's Role in Breastfeeding," *La Leche League News* 5 (May–June 1963): 1–2; "To Father—With Love," ibid., 9 (May–June 1967): 2; David Stewart, "Good Fathering and a Successful Career: Can a Man Do Both?" ibid., 23 (Nov.–Dec. 1981): 111; Lowman, *LLLove Story,* p. 62; May, *Homeward Bound,* pp. 145–49.

34. League founders interview, p. 11; *La Leche League News* 10 (Sept.–Oct. 1968): 72–79; 14 (July–Aug. 1972): 51; *Leaven* 12 (Sept.–Oct. 1976): 23; La Leche League, "Statement of Policy" (1982), p. 2; Linda Stevely, ed., "Presenting the Philosophy—Mother-Baby Togetherness," *Leader's Handbook* (Franklin Park, 1981), p. 7.

35. League founders interview, pp. 11–12; Marian Tompson, "Memos from Marian," *La Leche League News* 12 (Mar.–Apr. 1970): 31.

36. U.S. Department of Commerce, Bureau of the Census, *Statistical Abstract of the United States: 1980* (Washington, 1980), p. 62, table 88; Kaledin, *Mothers and More,* p. 179; Lynn Weiner, *From Working Girl to Working Mother: The Female Labor Force in the United States, 1920–1980* (Chapel Hill, 1985), pp. 93, 97; Suzanne M. Bianchi and Daphne Spain, *American Women in Transition* (New York, 1986), p. 225.

37. League founders interview, p. 10; Marian Tompson, "Twenty-Five Years and Still Nursing," *La Leche League News* 23 (Sept.–Oct. 1981): 99.

38. Tompson interview, p. 3; *Leaven* 3 (Summer 1967): 17; 8 (July–Aug. 1972): 19; 12 (Nov.–Dec. 1976): 29–30; 5 (May–June 1969); Lowman, *LLLove Story,* p. 62; La Leche League International, "Statement of Policy," publication no. 2 (1973), p. 3. On the abortion issue, members of the league's executive board were "deeply disturbed about the trend toward devaluation of human life," but they still would not "mix causes" by taking a stand. See "From the Executive Board," *Leaven* 5 (May–June 1969): n.p.

39. La Leche League, *The Womanly Art of Breastfeeding* (Franklin Park, 1958), cover. See also *La Leche League News* 8 (Jan.–Feb. 1966): 11; and 18 (July–Aug. 1976): 50. La Leche League International, *The Constitutional By-Laws of La Leche League International* (Franklin Park, 1974), p. 2; Frank Howard Richardson, "Breast Feeding: Going or Coming? And Why?" *North Carolina Medical Journal,* Mar. 21, 1960, p. 11; "A Salute to La Leche International," *Journal of Pediatrics* 73 (July 1968): 161–62.

40. White, "What's in It for Mother?" p. 7; league founders interview, pp. 2, 21–22; La Leche League International, *Womanly Art* (1963), p. 151.

41. Joyce Trebilcot, introduction to *Mothering: Essays in Feminist Theory,* ed. Trebilcot (Totowa, 1984), p. 4. See also Friedan, *Feminine Mystique;* and Gayle Graham Yates, *What Women Want: The Ideas of the Movement* (Cambridge, Mass., 1975), pp. 154–58.

42. Boston Women's Health Book Collective, *Our Bodies, Our Selves: A Course by and for Women* (Boston, 1971), p. 111; ibid. (New York, 1976), pp. 312, 368; Datha Clapper Brack, "Social Forces, Feminism, and Breastfeeding," *Nursing Outlook* 23 (Sept. 1975): 557. For feminist appreciations of the work of the league, see ibid.; Rothman, *In Labor,* pp. 103–9; and Penny Van Esterick, *Beyond the Breast-Bottle Controversy* (New Brunswick, 1989), pp. 68–79. For a highly critical feminist analysis, see Deborah Gorham and Florence Kellner Andrews, "The La Leche

League: A Feminist Perspective," in *Delivering Motherhood: Maternal Ideologies and Practices in the Nineteenth and Twentieth Centuries,* ed. Katherine Arnup, Andrée Lévesque, and Ruth Roach Pierson (New York, 1990), pp. 238–69. Founder Marian Tompson recalled that feminists picketed some league meetings in Minnesota during the early 1970s. Tompson interview, p. 1.

43. The LLL also supported Iowa firefighter Linda Eaton in her legal battle to breast-feed her son at the fire station. See *La Leche League News* 21 (Mar.–Apr. 1979): 39–40; and Mary Lofton and Gwen Gotsch, *Legal Rights of Breastfeeding Mothers: USA Scene,* La Leche League Reprint no. 59 (Franklin Park, 1983). More recently, in 1991, the league testified on behalf of New Yorker Denise Perrigo, who was charged with child abuse and neglect in part because she was still nursing a two year old. *Chicago Tribune,* Feb. 9, 1992, sec. 1, p. 17.

44. White, "What's in It for Mother?" p. 7; Astin-Knafl and Marshall, "National Survey," pp. 49–51.

45. "Thoughts on Women's Liberation," *La Leche League News* 13 (Jan.–Feb. 1971): 3; 17 (Nov.–Dec 1975): 84; 10 (Jan.–Feb. 1968): 5–6; 13 (May–June 1971): 42; 20 (Jan.–Feb. 1978): 3. See also "Western U. S. Leaven Insert," *Leaven* 12 (May–June 1976): 2.

46. *La Leche League News* 14 (Jan.–Feb. 1972): 5; 14 (May–June 1972): 37; 14 (Sept.–Oct. 1972): 65–67; 14 (July–Aug. 1972): 61–62. See also Cardozo, *Woman at Home.* For positive comments about working mothers and feminism, see *La Leche League News* 13 (July–Aug. 1971): 62; 13 (Nov.–Dec. 1971): 86; 14 (Sept.–Oct. 1972): 65–67.

47. League founders interview, p. 13; *La Leche League News* 21 (Jan.–Feb. 1979): 6; 22 (Jan.–Feb. 1980): 11–12; 25 (Jan.–Feb. 1983): 1–2. See also La Leche League International, *Womanly Art* (Franklin Park, 1981), pp. 63–64.

48. *La Leche League News* 21 (Sept.–Oct. 1979): 86. For reference to a Chicago doctor's arguments for mothers' pensions, paid maternity leave, and work-site day-care centers, see ibid., 14 (Sept.–Oct. 1972): 66.

49. *Leaven* 21 (Apr.–May 1985): 43; league founders interview, p. 20; Tompson interview, p. 1. For an anecdote about the rejection of a working mother by a league group, see Sylvia Ann Hewlett, *A Lesser Life: The Myth of Women's Liberation in America* (New York, 1986), pp. 40–41. On low-income women and breast-feeding, see Gatoura, "Reverse Trend."

50. *La Leche League News* 23 (Sept.-Oct. 1981): 90–91; La Leche League International, *Womanly Art* (1991), pp. 159–90.

19.

Diversity in Women's Liberation Ideology
How a Black and a White Group of the 1960s Viewed Motherhood

M. RIVKA POLATNICK

Since the start of the contemporary women's movement in this country, women from many different backgrounds have been active for the cause. That diversity has been recognized least with regard to the initial period of the movement; the latter half of the 1960s. In this article I discuss two leading sixties radical women's groups that differed in their racial-ethnic and class composition.[1] The Mount Vernon/New Rochelle group consisted of Black women who were mainly from the lower working class or on welfare.[2] New York Radical Women was predominately White and middle-class. Both groups were the most militant women's liberationists in their own environment, but they fought for the cause in their own distinctive ways.

In studying these two groups, I was interested in how the women's social locations—especially their class positions and racial-ethnic identities—shaped their political approaches. Thus, I examined the evolution of each group's thinking in relation to the social and economic conditions of their lives. I compared the two groups' women's liberation ideologies, strategies, and actions.

One of the most striking contrasts between the ideologies was the Black group's much more positive view of the mother role. They considered it a source of power for women, whereas the White group saw it mainly as a locus of oppression. The Black women defined the mother role more broadly; it encompassed caring for all the children of their community and fighting for a better future for the community. The women's different social locations fostered different personal and political attitudes about mothering.

Reprinted from *Signs: Journal of Women in Culture and Society* 21 (1996): 679–706. Copyright © 1996 by the University of Chicago Press; reprinted by permission of the publisher.

In this article, I explore this area of contrast. I trace the groups' thinking on motherhood as they pursued their separate paths of women's liberation activism. Both groups were responding to the historical context of the latter 1960s; however, they stood in different relationship to the social, political, and economic trends of that period. Comparing their viewpoints reveals a complex interplay of commonality and difference. The discussion of women's "common differences" has become a central focus for the women's movement and women's studies. On the scholarly level, such discussion deepens our understanding of how gender interacts with other forms of inequality. On the political level, discussion of common differences "allows for new forms of recognition as we look *at* each other, as we try to imagine viable ways of joining our strengths" (Joseph and Lewis 1981, 13).

A growing body of literature on African American women and mothering has characterized their attitudes and practices as distinct from those of European Americans.[3] This literature examines how cultural influences and dynamics of class and race have shaped the mothering patterns. I examine those patterns, too, but emphasize how the groups' differing perceptions of motherhood affected their women's liberation ideologies.

Because even the language we use about motherhood may mean different things in different communities, I want to clarify my use of certain terms. By *mothering* I mean nurturing children, whether or not they are "one's own." I use *mother* to refer to the primary female long-term caregiver, whether she is the biological mother (*bloodmother*), the mother by formal or informal adoption, or a foster mother. Other women who help nurture her child are *othermothers* (Troester 1984; Collins 1987). I use both *motherhood* and *the mother role* to encompass all the dimensions of female parenting: bearing children, raising one's own children, and helping to nurture other children. I compare the groups' views on all these aspects of motherhood.

The Two Groups and the Research Process

The two groups I studied, located in the New York City area, helped pioneer the women's liberation cause in the latter 1960s.[4] Both had great influence through their writings, which were widely distributed and frequently published.

The Black group consisted of two networks of poor women in the neighboring cities of Mount Vernon and New Rochelle, New York, and a middle-class (Black) social worker who played a key catalyst role. When much of the Black movement was turning toward nationalism and "Black unity," the Mount Vernon/New Rochelle (MV/NR) group insisted on raising women's issues as well as class issues. They fought against sexism in the Black movement and struggled to understand the interactions of different forms of oppression. The MV branch, in their best-known manifesto ([Mount Vernon group] 1968a), defended Black women's right to use the (new) birth control pill, despite Black movement concerns that the pill was a tool of genocide. The group ran a "freedom school" for children, fostering radical ideas about race, class, and sex. In 1973, they cowrote (using the pseudonym "The Damned") a powerful book, *Lessons from the Damned: Class Struggle in the Black Community,* which included their account "The Revolt of Poor Black Women."[5] By the mid-1970s, with the economy worsening and the political climate shifting to the right, the MV/NR group had dissolved.

The predominantly White group, New York Radical Women (NYRW), was started mainly by young middle-class women with backgrounds in the Civil Rights movement or New Left who saw the need to organize separately from men to address women's oppression. Formed in 1967, NYRW helped launch an independent women's liberation movement. They produced the movement's first political/theoretical journal, *Notes from the First Year* (NYRW 1968). Group members wrote groundbreaking papers, including "The Women's Rights Movement in the U.S.: A New View" (Firestone 1968b), "The Myth of the Vaginal Orgasm" (Koedt [1968] 1970), and "The Politics of Housework" (Mainardi [1968] 1970). The NYRW organized the 1968 protest at the Miss America pageant that first made women's liberation a household word. The group played a central role in developing the movement practice of consciousness-raising (Sarachild 1968b). Some members helped lead the fight for abortion rights.

Early on, two main factions arose in NYRW: the "politicos," more tied to the New Left and its anticapitalist politics, and the "feminists," soon called "radical feminists," who insisted on an independent analysis grounded in women's experiences. The radical feminists produced most of the group's best-known writings and defined its public position regarding motherhood. I refer briefly to ideas of some politico women, but that faction did not really produce a coherent ideology concerning the mother role. The views on motherhood most characteristic of the group were those of the radical feminists. When NYRW fell apart in 1969, its radical feminist leaders remained prominent as activists and writers; I note some subsequent directions of their thinking.

In my research, I relied on primary documents from the 1960s through the early 1970s: published and unpublished writings by the groups and by prominent members, and notes and transcripts from meetings. I also interviewed, in the mid-1980s, six former members of the MV/NR group and fourteen from NYRW, mostly women who were central in shaping the groups' approaches. In the interviews, I sparked people's memories by showing them detailed chronologies I had pieced together of their group's development and activities.[6] The original interviews have been supplemented with ongoing conversations. Because subsequent experiences can color memories, I have used the interview material cautiously, giving more weight to information in the 1960s documents.

As a researcher, I had a different relationship with each group. I was a member of NYRW in its last few months (fall 1968 to early 1969) and stayed involved in those circles until I moved west in 1970. My insider status made me more aware of that group's internal disagreements and the stances of particular individuals, and the women talked to me more about those things. With the MV/NR group, I (middle-class and White) was an outsider in more ways than one, and I heard less about the group's internal dynamics. The former members I interviewed were wonderfully helpful but tended to present a more collective front and view of their history.

One way in which my personal concerns may have influenced this research is that I conducted it at a time when I was reconsidering my own child-free state. Already more than thirty-five years old, I was "up against the biological clock" and thinking that maybe I did want to have children after all. As a young woman in the late 1960s, I had internalized an attitude from my radical feminist circles that becoming a mother meant getting mired in women's oppression. By the early 1980s I had experienced a trend in White feminism toward revaluing motherhood (e.g., Love and Shanklin 1978; Friedan 1981), but I still associated it with being confined, curtailed, and diminished. Studying the MV/NR group had a profound effect on my feelings; the high regard these dedicated fighters against sexism, racism, and class exploitation had for the mother role touched me deeply. I did go on to have a child. My own assessment is that this research affected my personal views far more than my personal views affected this research. The contrast in attitudes about motherhood is apparent in the written record from the sixties.

The Mount Vernon/New Rochelle Group

When the women's liberation movement generated its first mass-market anthologies in 1970, the MV/NR group's writings appeared in three influential collections: Robin Morgan's *Sisterhood Is Powerful,* Toni Cade's *The Black Woman,* and Leslie Tanner's *Voices from Women's Liberation.* Yet scholars have overlooked this pioneering group. Elsewhere I present a fuller account of its history and discuss the reasons for its "invisibility" (Polatnick 1994, 1995), but here I focus on the development of the group's ideology about motherhood.

The MV branch of the group goes back to 1960, when the social worker and radical Pat R. began knocking on doors in the poor Black neighborhood as a "volunteer visitor" for the local Planned Parenthood.[7] That organization was concerned about a sharp rise in births among poor Black teenagers. Girls were having babies as early as age twelve or thirteen; by their early twenties, some already had six or seven children. Planned Parenthood wanted someone who could bring birth control advice to this community. Pat R., from the Black middle class, was a married woman in her thirties with three small children. She took on this task because she saw birth control as an important tool for women to gain some control over their lives: "You could only get birth control if you were married and middle class, able to afford a doctor."[8]

As Pat talked with women and girls in their apartments, the conversations ranged far beyond birth control. Women brought up their hassles with landlords, schools, hospitals, the Department of Welfare, and the men in their lives. Individual conversations evolved into group sessions. Over the next few years, Pat facilitated a process of radical political education. She helped the women draw connections between their daily problems and the larger system of social and economic relations. By the mid-1960s, together the women had developed a sophisticated analysis of racial, class, and sex oppression.[9]

Many participants in this network were mothers. The group included domestic workers, factory workers, welfare recipients, and schoolchildren. Some of the women had husbands or boyfriends living with them, but more typically their households consisted of women and children, often in extended family groupings.[10] Although poverty made rearing children difficult, female-centered networks of relatives, neighbors, and friends provided the help necessary for survival.

The high rate of teen motherhood in this community resulted from multiple factors. "When the sisters are real young and it's been bad for them at home," wrote the MV group, "pregnancy is sometimes their leap into 'independence'" (The Damned [1973] 1990, 100). With educational and job opportunities extremely limited, teenage girls saw no future more appealing than motherhood. Having a baby was their main route to adult status. Boyfriends pressured them to have sex without precautions, and they lacked access to contraceptives or abortion.[11] Some young women were having babies, the group noted, "because they (mistakenly) think it'll keep their man" (100).

The high birthrate was also fueled by positive feelings about motherhood. The emotional satisfactions of having a baby loomed large in this impoverished environment. Furthermore, the MV women's lives centered on kin and neighborhood networks in which mothers were the key figures. Being a mother was a major source of positive identity for these women.

Nonmothers in the group were involved in raising children too. As poor Black women, they tended to live with or near their relatives, sharing resources in order to survive economically and emotionally. They served as othermothers to younger relatives and to neighborhood children. Caring for children was a central, valued component of their adult role.

The MV group's first political actions (1964) grew out of their mothering responsibilities. Women from the network started a welfare rights group and organized a rent strike against poor housing conditions. In both cases, the women were fighting for basic needs—income and housing—for themselves and the children.

During these political struggles, the Mount Vernonites began distinguishing two types of mothers: those who put their man above their children, and those who put their children above "*any* man." The first type, "our dick-happy sisters," were "always longing for a man, fighting and woofing on other women" (The Damned [1973] 1990, 92). This type, observed Pat R., "had 'to ball' on Friday night or die. So they were the ones always looking for babysitters." The group began to view such women as "counterrevolutionary." The women fighting the welfare department and landlord were the ones who "put their children first."[12]

The group's evolving analysis of dick-happy sisters tied together issues of gender, race, and class. Those sisters were desperate to catch a man; they imagined that with a man they could be upwardly mobile and live happily ever after. Despite the realities of racial and class hierarchies, they were buying into the American Dream, "which included this whole system and a step up the ladder [for] them" ([MV group] 1968b, 2). They "couldn't face that the dream was never to be."[13] A dick-happy sister became dependent on men. She would "do anything to keep her man, including having children just for his satisfaction, not hers" (The Damned [1973] 1990, 69). Such women became self-destructive and destructive of their children—"leaving their children for some man." For the MV group, "our children came before *any* man" (ibid., 92).

The group had to mesh their political activities with their child-care responsibilities. When the women got together, children were often present. In a transcript of a 1969 discussion session, it is no surprise to find the notation "(Children's needs interrupt us)."[14]

In the group's political thinking, they were placing increasing importance on woman's role as socializer and teacher of the young. Pat R. had been inspired by Malcolm X when he told Black women in 1964 "that we were the real educators. We were the setter of fires that would burn until our people set themselves free. It was up to us to educate the coming generation to their historical responsibility to the oppressed and have-nots of the world" (Robinson 1969, 62–63).

In 1966, the group launched a project that became a major focus through the early 1970s: a Saturday afternoon freedom school for neighborhood children. Pat had been tutoring children, using her politically oriented, consciousness-raising approach, and they were learning far better than in the alienating public schools (The Damned [1973] 1990, 93). A number of the mothers wanted to help with this process and bring in more children.[15] In the freedom school, children learned about racial, class, women's, *and* children's oppression and discussed how to confront those issues in their daily lives. The MV women wrote in 1967 that they were focusing on "the children . . . the future and the revolution" ([MV group] 1967, 1).

By 1968, the group was getting involved in the issue of birth control. At the beginning of the decade, there had been a dramatic new development in reproductive technology: the pill. By the mid-1960s the MV women had access to it through Planned Parenthood. At first they were wary of the pill, but they began to see its significance for their self-determination. As Pat R. stated in 1967, "[The] black woman began popping those pills into her mouth and telling her husband and lover what she thought. . . . She had made an interior decision to control her own destiny."[16]

However, some voices in the Black movement were condemning use of the pill. In 1968, the MV women received a statement by the Black Unity Party of Peekskill, New York, which began, "The Brothers are calling on the Sisters not to take the pill. . . . To take the pill means contributing to our own *GENOCIDE*." The Unity Party said White supremacists were pushing birth control on Black women as the latest means of "Race Control." Blacks should view procreation as highly positive, they asserted. "When we produce children, we are aiding the REVOLUTION in the form of NATION building" (Black Unity Party 1968, 7).

The sisters of Mount Vernon wrote an angry response. "Poor Black sisters decide for themselves whether to have a baby or not to have a baby," they declared. They attacked poor Black men bitterly for failing to help them raise the children. The group agreed that "whitey" had genocidal motives. But the pill gave them "freedom to fight genocide of Black women and children. . . . Having too many babies stops us from supporting our children, teaching them the truth . . . and fighting Black men who still want to use and exploit us." The women challenged the motives of the middle-class "Black unity" brothers: "You want to use poor Black women's children to gain power for yourself" ([MV group] 1968a, 8).[17]

In formulating this response, the women had to reconcile their various political commitments in a climate of pronatalist pressure from the nationalists. The group believed birth control was essential for women's liberation. However, they also valued children, gave high priority to their care and education, and considered political work with children a vital contribution to social change. They reconciled these commitments by arguing that birth control meant they could be better mothers and teachers to the children they and their neighbors already had.

In their statement, the women described a negative scenario of motherhood and drew a parallel to the experiences of middle-class White women: "Poor black women would be fools to sit up in the house with a whole lot of children and eventually go crazy, sick, heartbroken, no place to go, no sign of affection—nothing. Middle class white men have always done this to their women—only more sophisticated like" ([MV group] 1968a, 8). However, the MV women defined the problem more in terms of having too many children than in terms of having children per se.

During 1968, Pat R. and the MV women connected with a network of young women in neighboring New Rochelle who became the other branch of the group.[18] These young women, just finishing high school, had been galvanized by the assassination of Martin Luther King, Jr., (April 1968) and had helped form an organization, Black Radicals Onward (BRO), which grew to several hundred members. Before long they were fighting male domination in BRO. The New Rochelle (NR) women were younger and slightly better off economically than the MV core activists, which had some effects on their outlook.[19]

These young women shared the MV branch's child-oriented values. The BRO organization that they helped create gave considerable emphasis to working with children. Among the community services BRO provided were baby-sitting, tutoring children, organizing weekend recreation programs, and running a freedom school (BRO 1969, 7).

For most of these NR young women, however, the idea of having children of their own had stayed on the back burner. As fifth graders they had been affected indelibly by the Civil Rights movement; they experienced a successful campaign to desegregate New Rochelle's public schools. Once they became part of BRO in high school, they centered their lives on political activism. When they graduated, a few had the chance to go to local colleges; some financial aid and support services had been established for Black students. The NR women thus had more incentives for postponing childbearing than their somewhat older and poorer sisters in Mount Vernon. However, like their MV sisters, they valued woman's role as mother. Over time, most did become mothers.

The favorable attitudes of the MV/NR women toward motherhood infused their theoretical work.[20] In 1969, women from both networks and Pat R. produced "A Historical and Critical Essay for Black Women in the Cities."[21] They wrote: "The woman's body, which receives, hosts, and gives forth the future of the species, is inherently powerful" (Haden, Middleton, and Robinson 1970, 320). At the beginning of human history, they argued, women and their children had constituted the human family, with the men only marginal figures. Men, however, feared women and their "inner and reproductive powers" and banded together to over-throw them and establish male domination (Robinson and Group 1969, 203). Men then created cultures based on "suppression of the female" (204) and of "things having to with the animal body" (200).

The group sounded an early warning against White male efforts to develop alternative means of reproduction: "[He] turn[s] his attention to the danger the woman's body has always posed to his rule. He struggles to perfect artificial insemination and a machine host for the human fetus. . . . Those white males who rule the free world (capitalist world) understand that if they are to keep their rule over women and so called lesser men, they must stop being dependent on their bodies and must perfect machines which they can control absolutely" (Haden, Middleton, and Robinson 1970, 321). The group invoked "our fearsome but inevitable historical duty to overthrow oppressive male authority and its system" (Robinson and Group 1969, 210).

In their last major project, the women, together with some freedom school children and sympathetic men, produced a book based on their experiences: *Lessons from the Dammed* (The Damned [1973] 1990). In *Lessons,* the women reaffirmed their support for birth control. They acknowledged that the White power structure had its own reasons for offering them contraceptives; nonetheless, they were glad to be "freer of our men-folk always messing over us, freer of the fear of unwanted babies." Again, they supported birth control by using a maternal rationale: "We can love the children who are already here" (100).

One essay in *Lessons* by "four 16-year-old young women" discussed the new type of family they hoped would replace "the capitalist system's family" (69). To fight for the new system and family, revolutionary children needed "the help of mommas who are not Dick-Happy, who struggle against being second to their man, who struggle for their children first, the man later" (71). The new family would have men "who love women like they love themselves"; it would have "mothers who put children first" (72).

Overall, then, the group placed great value on the mother role. They did express some negative feelings about its burdens. In particular, having too many children was perceived as a problem. It was also a mistake to have them for the wrong reasons: because of pressure from a man or in hopes of entrapping a man. The women certainly wanted to raise children under better economic and social conditions. And there was another side to their defiant pride about raising children without men: a strong desire for more male involvement. However, the group's positive views about motherhood far outweighed these negative considerations; the mother role itself was not the problem.

New York Radical Women

The NYRW (1967–69) displayed quite different attitudes about motherhood. Marilyn Lowen, married and a few months pregnant when she first came to a meeting, felt "an antagonistic thing from some women, an antichild thing. The women would be helping me find an abortionist." Lowen cautions against characterizing the whole group as antichild; however, the atmosphere certainly was not conducive to celebrating a pregnancy.[22] Rosalyn Baxandall, who was the only mother in the group's inner core, comments that "most radical feminists were not anti-child; they simply ignored children" (Baxandall 1994, 12).

Though a large number of women from a range of backgrounds passed through NYRW's open weekly meetings in Manhattan, the majority of the group and of its committed core were young Whites with college degrees. Some participants came from working-class backgrounds, but middle-class women were predominant and set the group's tone. Of the core members, most were single, heterosexual, and child free.[23]

These young women had grown up in the 1950s, under the powerful post–World War II ideology that women should find their complete identity and satisfaction in the wife/mother role. They had watched their mothers wrestle with the frustrations of trying to follow that script, or with the guilt and stress of being a "working mother." "Our mothers told us they loved being a wife and mother, but we felt their anger," comments (Chude) Pam Allen, cofounder of NYRW. "We were carrying a strong awareness of contradiction in our mothers' lives. We were left with a deep-seated fear that our lives would be destroyed, we'd be ruined, if we had kids. At some psychic level, we felt it was death."[24]

These young women for the most part had been educated alongside their male peers. Despite ongoing societal messages directing them toward marriage and motherhood, they were also oriented toward self-development and occupational achievement. Entering the workforce, they had encountered overt sex discrimination. But in the latter 1960s these young Whites saw new possibilities on the horizon. The recent civil rights laws and the growing women's rights agitation fueled their expectations or at least their determination that they would find satisfying, decent-paying jobs.

For the core members of NYRW, however, their passionate focus was the women's liberation cause. Some also had commitments to the Civil Rights movement or the New Left, but with this new cause they felt they were right at the cutting edge, pioneering a revolutionary social transformation. Most were also enjoying a single lifestyle with a degree of sexual freedom unprecedented for women of their social background.

Motherhood meant sacrificing these exciting new possibilities. As former member Ellen Willis put it: "I saw having children as the great trap that completely took away your freedom, that forced you into domesticity."[25] Alix Kates Shulman, a member with two small children, felt the same way: "From the minute my children were born, I felt excluded from the human race.... Though I loved mothering, I thought my life was over. I had given up my career [as a writer]. I thought I'd just have to hang around till I died."[26]

The negative attitudes of these middle-class White women toward motherhood reflected other realities of their lives. Many came from upwardly mobile or geographically mobile families no longer very connected to an ethnic community with traditional family-oriented values. Most of the women lived at some distance from parents and other relatives and barely knew their neighbors. Unlike the MV/NR women, the White activists typically were not around children in their daily lives. To them, motherhood implied being in an isolated situation, with little outside support. "Sisters" from the group lived in different areas of New York City and did not constitute the kind of community that helped mothers handle the day-to-day demands of child rearing.

Within NYRW, being a mother was definitely a minority status, in terms of both numbers and norms. Shulman, mother of two, remembers feeling "like some kind of Martian" to many nonmothers in the group. They seemed oblivious to her having to miss evening meetings because of child-care problems. In White radical feminist circles, she often got the sense that having a family was "an embarrassment," was "reactionary."[27] Ellen Willis, not a mother then, acknowledges that there was an "under-the-surface condescension toward mothers.... On some level was the ... feeling that women who were breaking with traditional roles were the ones who would be your *real* allies."[28] These activists would not have envisioned their allies as women who "put children first."

The group's first public action (January 1968) challenged conventional sex roles. In the context of an all-women's anti–Vietnam War protest in Washington, D.C., they organized a theatrical "Burial of Traditional Womanhood." The NYRW thought the peace protesters were wasting their time by appealing as wives and mothers to the male government; that approach pointed up how powerless women were in those roles. Instead, the group believed, women should challenge sex roles and organize to gain real power for women (Firestone 1968a). Speaking for NYRW, Kathie (Amatniek) Sarachild introduced what would become the group's main theme about mothering: women should "insist to men that they share the housework and child-care, fully and equally, so that we can have independent lives as well" (Sarachild 1968a, 21).

The group's views on motherhood were discussed further in their journal *Notes from the First Year* (NYRW 1968).[29] An article by Carol Hanisch and Elizabeth Sutherland (Martinez) asserted that women must be freed of the sole or primary responsibility for rearing children. Not only should men do an equal share, but eventually "new forms should replace today's nuclear family." That might mean "a combination of social and private care, totally socialized care, the extended family or whatever." Children were the "responsibility of the community" (1968, 15).

Two of the articles in *Notes from the First Year* cautioned women against being overly devoted to children. Hanisch and Sutherland cited this comment from a critic: "'Are you also advocating an end to families—putting all kids in nurseries? Kids need mother love or they'll grow up neurotic.'" The women answered: "'Mother love' can usually be translated as a woman finding her identity through another person. That's a terrible burden on the child. . . . It's also a paralysis of the woman's human development" (1968, 14). In another article, Firestone warned against "the special conditioning which women undergo . . . to put the interests of the male or the child above their own" (1968b, 4–5). The implication was that women should put themselves first.

Hanisch and Sutherland suggested that women needed relief not only from rearing children but also from bearing them: "Society cannot lay the responsibility for continuing the race solely on women. If there is any responsibility here, it's the responsibility of society to offer women all possible choices by developing new technology for continuing the species in other ways—so that the task not be unilaterally imposed on women" (1968, 14). Unlike the MV/NR group, these women thought alternative means of reproduction could serve women's interests.

The major theoretical treatise that came out of NYRW circles, Firestone's *The Dialectic of Sex* (1970), also endorsed alternative reproduction. Indeed, Firestone argued that for the first time in history women had a real chance for liberation *because* of developments in birth control and the prospect of test-tube babies.

Firestone regarded childbearing and child rearing as burdensome. Her depiction of motherhood in early human history contrasted sharply with that of the MV/NR group. The Black women had theorized that "the male's only role . . . was insemination. Then he drifted off, leaving the female to take care of herself during pregnancy, birth, and the nursing of the young" (Robinson and Group 1969, 200). Firestone asserted that, from earliest times, women's childbearing had made them dependent on men and subordinate (1970, 8–9). Women were less privileged biologically—subject to the "tyranny" of their reproductive systems (206). (What a contrast to the Black group's view of women's bodies as "inherently powerful.") Firestone stated that even the modern woman is "totally incapacitated" when she "bears children and takes care of infants" (48). Women had to be relieved of their childbearing function, and men had to share equally in the rearing of children (206).

Firestone proposed an alternative to the nuclear family for child rearing. About ten adults of different ages would contract to form a living unit for seven to ten years, in order to rear jointly several children. These could be children born to them, adopted, or (eventually) "produced artificially." In this arrangement, child rearing would be "so diffused as to be practically eliminated" (231).

Although Firestone's ideas were on the extreme end of the spectrum in NYRW, her writing did embody attitudes that were common in NYRW circles: that childbearing dragged you down, that child-care responsibility was mainly a burden, that having children meant being dependent on a man. Certainly not everyone endorsed test-tube babies, but most saw value in having the idea on the table. It challenged the whole mystique of motherhood as women's biological destiny.

A more immediate reproductive issue for NYRW was abortion rights. Most of these young women now had access to contraceptives—something very new but already starting to be taken for granted. For these women, the priority regarding reproduction was to make abortion legal; they still worried about an accidental pregnancy. In *Notes from the Second Year* (produced by Firestone and Anne Koedt in 1970, after NYRW had disbanded), a testimonial by "Barbara Susan" exemplified the concerns underlying NYRW's support for abortion rights. She told about having to leave college at seventeen and forfeit a scholarship because she had become pregnant and could not get an abortion. "In effect, I had no freedom to pursue the goals which I had set up for myself. . . . I no longer had control of my life" (Susan 1970, 94).

With other options to pursue, many of the young White women wanted to avoid the constraints of motherhood. Politically they argued that there should be no "mother role" distinct from the "father role," that both sexes should parent equally. The 1969 manifesto of The Feminists, one of the main radical feminist successors to NYRW, gave an explicit rationale for rejecting the mother role: "All contributions to society which do not add to the individual's unique development must be shared equally, e.g. all 'wifely' and 'motherly' duties. . . . We seek the self-development of every individual woman" (1969, 117).

By generalizing that the majority in NYRW looked unfavorably on the mother role, I do not mean to belie the actual range of opinions in the group, especially as the weekly meetings grew to fifty or sixty women, with new faces each time. Women who were mothers, however, tended not to keep coming. Several mothers helped create a splinter group, the New Women. Interestingly, key members of that group were White women married to Black men; perhaps they were influenced by

African American attitudes about motherhood. In any event, they did not have much impact in wider women's liberation circles (Echols 1989, 98).

Within NYRW, a few women aligned with the politico faction put forth ideas on motherhood different from the prevailing radical feminist viewpoint. Peggy Dobbins wanted the group to investigate the evidence of ancient matriarchy, but only a small minority were interested (Echols 1989, 113). (Chude) Pam Allen, who left the group after conflict with radical feminists, criticized them in a fall 1968 article for "their total rejection of all traditional women's roles, and especially their view of children as merely the means by which men enslave women" (Allen 1968, 9). Allen, too, was married to a Black man and, furthermore, had ties with Pat R. of the MV/NR group (the only link I uncovered between the two groups). Yet even Allen illustrates that the radical feminists' wariness of getting trapped by motherhood resonated with most young Whites in NYRW. Earlier I quoted Allen about the fear she and her peers carried out of the 1950s that "our lives would be destroyed . . . if we had kids." In 1974, when Allen did start trying to get pregnant, she made her husband agree that if they split up, "the child would go with *him*."[30]

In sum, the NYRW activists tended to regard motherhood mainly as a site of oppression. Freeing up women to do things other than mothering was their paramount consideration. Most of the core members never did become mothers. Although reasons cited by the women included fertility and health problems, negative perceptions of the mother role certainly played a part.

Common Differences

Class and race-ethnicity made a big difference in how these two groups of sixties women's liberationists viewed the mother role. Yet there also were important commonalities. I compare first their views on bearing children and then on rearing children.

Women's Liberation and Childbearing. A key commonality was that both groups considered birth control crucial for women's self-determination. Both believed developments in reproductive technology were bringing about a fundamental change in women's relationship to their reproductive capacity. Each group went out on a limb to support birth control—the Black group in their spirited defense of the pill, the White group in their demand for total repeal of antiabortion laws. The cutting-edge issue concerning birth control thus differed for the two groups, but they agreed on the basic principle that women should be able to limit their childbearing.

Both groups saw on the horizon the possibility of alternative reproduction, which would have momentous implications for women's status. They differed dramatically, though, on what those implications were. The Black group could envision alternative reproduction only as a tool of White male control. Some of the White women, by contrast, portrayed it as desirable or even essential for women's liberation. They did recognize that it could be used against women's interests. "To envision [alternative reproduction] in the hands of the present powers," wrote Firestone, "is to envision a nightmare" (1970, 200). Firestone had a solution, though: women must "seiz[e] control of" reproduction (11). The poor Black women did not imagine being in control of reproductive technology.

The Black group also viewed more favorably the biological processes of pregnancy and childbirth. They valued the female's "connection with nature" and criticized Western (male) culture for its repression of "things having to do with the animal body" (Robinson and Group 1969, 206, 200). In contrast, Firestone, taking NYRW's sentiments to a bold extreme, called pregnancy "barbaric" (1970, 198).

Most basically, the groups differed on whether women's childbearing ability was a source of power or a disadvantage. The MV/NR group reminded Black women that "no Black man gets born unless we permit it." Remembering this was "the first simple step to understanding the power that we have" (Haden, Middleton, and Robinson 1970, 324). Firestone, by contrast, wanted women freed from the "tyranny" of childbearing (1970, 206).

Women's Liberation and Child Rearing. With regard to the rearing of children, the groups' thinking differed in significant ways, but again I start by highlighting commonalities. The groups shared some perceptions about the toll taken by too heavy mothering responsibilities. The Black group's positive view of motherhood should not lead us to romanticize their mothering experiences. Their fears of being overburdened related mainly to having too many children, whereas the White group's fears related to having any children at all. In any event, the groups agreed that too much responsibility for children drains women.

Both groups favored a community-based mode of child rearing. However, intermixed with this commonality were differences. The Black women already had a somewhat communal mode, though based on female networks without extensive male involvement. For the White women, the goal of communal child rearing was more abstract; on the practical level it translated mainly to promoting publicly funded child-care centers. The White group focused mostly on demanding equal parenting from the biological fathers. The Black group emphasized that issue less, in part because they got more help from other women. Despite these differences, the groups agreed that children are the responsibility of the community.

Overall, though, the Black group put more value on women's child rearing.

That contrast reflected differences in the appeal of motherhood itself and also differences in what other opportunities were available. In the two social contexts, motherhood was a different experience, with different meanings and implications. For the Black women, mothers were part of family and community networks that assisted with everyday child rearing. To the White women, motherhood meant being isolated and being the sole child rearer. Scholars of African American mothering patterns have noted their more communal approach, and some connect it to West African cultural traditions (Sudarkasa 1981; Collins 1987, 1991, 1994; James 1993). Collins explicitly contrasts this "Afrocentric" approach with the "Eurocentric" perspective that mothering should take place within "a private, nuclear family household" (1987, 3).

African Americans adapted African traditions to fit their situation in the United States (Collins 1987). A communal approach to child rearing was functional under slavery, when biological mothers were separated from their children daily for long hours of labor, or permanently if the slave owner sold or gave away mother or child (White 1985). In more recent times, communal responsibility for children has served as a survival strategy for handling the stresses of poverty and racism (Stack 1974; Collins 1991, 119–23; James 1993).

African American attitudes about children and child rearing undoubtedly still reflect the experiences of slavery. "Having children ripped away from you is such a profound experience, it's got to stay in the bones and marrow of people."[31] Perhaps that historical trauma helps explain the typically child-centered values of Black communities. Under slavery, virtually the only unexpropriated labor was the women's domestic labor in the slave quarters (Davis 1971). Similarly, for many contemporary Black women locked into exploitative, unsatisfying jobs, mothering is the most meaningful labor available to them.

Historical factors related to class and race-ethnicity also shaped European-American mothering patterns (Cott 1977; Degler 1984; Coontz 1988). The middle-class ideal of the privatized full-time mother arose with the transition to a wage-labor economy. The husband was to provide full economic support through cash-generating activities outside the home, while the wife focused on homemaking and child rearing. (White male industrial workers also tended to adopt these gender ideals and fought to be paid a "family wage" sufficient to support a wife and children.) For the emerging middle class of the industrial era, capitalism weakened the ties between the nuclear family and its extended family and community. The men had more chances for economic success if they were willing to be geographically mobile. Thus, the economic possibilities for some sectors of the White male population fostered the ideal of the mother whose life revolved around nurturing her nuclear family.

Analyzing further the Afrocentric versus Eurocentric patterns sheds light on significant differences in the thinking of the two sixties groups. For African American women, mothering was a bridge into social activism. Nurturing children in their extended families "stimulated a more generalized ethic of care where Black women feel accountable to all the Black community's children" (Collins 1987, 5). The MV/NR women felt this broad accountability, which helped fuel their activism. To many NYRW members, motherhood and involvement with children implied withdrawal from activism.[32]

The Black group's association of motherhood with power mirrored West African culture and also reflected this link between mothering and activism. Collins asserts that "much of Black women's status in African-American communities stems not only from actions as mothers in Black family networks but from contributions as community othermothers" (1991, 132).

To the White group, motherhood entailed domestic confinement, economic dependence, and therefore powerlessness. These perceptions arose not simply out of a Eurocentric perspective but out of the distinctive climate of the 1950s, with its ultradomestic ideology for middle-class women. Some of the mothers of NYRW members had worked outside the home, but the fathers generally had provided the family's primary income. Members of NYRW were challenging the assumptions that mothers should be home full-time and depend economically on a man, but their image of motherhood was still shaped by those assumptions. For the MV/NR women, economic dependence on a man was rarely an option. The Afrocentric perspective regarded "providing as part of mothering" (Collins 1987, 5). To poor Black mothers, providing might mean having to go on welfare, another form of dependency, but motherhood did not connote dependence on a man.

To many of the young White activists, having children meant getting locked into women's oppression. It is no coincidence that the enormously popular article "The Politics of Housework," by NYRW member Pat Mainardi ([1968] 1970), which gave strategies for getting men to share the housework, portrayed a wife without any children. In struggles with a husband one could let the dishes pile up and the dust accumulate, but one could not leave children uncared for. Becoming a mother would mean losing the battle for equality. The trend toward postponing childbearing among the sixties generation of middle-class White women has been explained mainly in terms of the lure of careers. Though that factor was important, so too, I would argue, was the fear that having children meant being subordinate.

The radical activists I studied had a genuine commitment in the 1960s to transforming society. Nonetheless, the appeal of motherhood to these two sets of women depended to some extent on what other opportunities they saw—for advanced education, for meaningful employment, for a satisfying career. By the late

1960s, these were becoming possible for the middle-class Whites of NYRW, but were at best only minimally possible for the NR young women, and even less possible for the MV women. Though women from both groups considered themselves revolutionaries, their views on motherhood were affected by their prospects within the existing system.

The 1960s Context. Both of the groups developed their ideologies in relation to the specific historical context of the 1960s. However, they were differently positioned with regard to the developments of that decade, and different factors in the sixties environment were salient for each group. Especially important for the Black group was the influence of the Black movement. The movement's emphasis on serving the community encouraged the women to work closely with children, the community's future. But some of the young NR activists, in dedicating themselves to "the struggle," put off having children of their own. The slight improvement in educational and job opportunities for Black women in the late 1960s (a result mainly of the Black movement) also disposed some of the younger women to postpone motherhood. That postponement, only temporary in most cases, was a limited version of the avoidance of motherhood by many of the young White activists.

The 1960s developments in birth control technology had a liberatory effect on heterosexual women in both groups. But the Black women in the latter sixties had to deal with the strident pronatalism of some Black nationalists. Although the MV/NR group rejected the call to produce babies for the revolution, perhaps they were influenced to prioritize educating children for the revolution. This work did continue a long tradition of community othermothering. However, when the group repeatedly argued that using the pill let them be better nurturers of the children already here, I sensed a defensive need, specific to this time period, to define themselves through maternal concerns.[33]

For the White women, one of the most salient features of the 1960s was the lingering 1950s ideal of the full-time housewife/mother and their own strong reaction against it. That reaction was supported by a sense of alternatives opening up for them in the wake of civil rights activism and new laws against discrimination. Carrying the fight for equality into new realms of occupational life would be an exciting challenge. The women's deep involvement in a movement starting to have a major impact on the larger society made a domestically oriented mother role seem stifling. These factors, in conjunction with the profound liberatory impact (for many women) of the pill, help explain the vehemence with which some in the White group rejected the mother role.

Images of the Past, Visions of Liberation. Although I expected the groups' experiences to influence their political views on motherhood, I was surprised that their experiences seemed to influence even their historical theories of women's oppression. The Black group asserted that early womankind raised and provided for children without men. Women's reproductive role was revered, and they were the leaders of society until men overthrew them. The White group's most prominent theoretician, Firestone, saw primeval women as severely limited by their childbearing and dependent on men for survival. Women from both groups consulted anthropological studies but gravitated toward the theories that made the most sense to them given their life experiences. Each group asserted a version of prehistory that reflected their own perception of motherhood as powerful or as oppressive.[34]

In their vision of future liberation, the White group emphasized more than the Black group the need to do away with sex roles entirely. Within the Black group, the younger and slightly economically better-off NR women expressed more opposition to sex roles than did the MV women. The latter mainly wished men would pull their weight in terms of family and community responsibility; *which* tasks the men took on mattered less. But even the NR women thought White feminists were going too far in trying to break down all sex role distinctions. Neither branch of the Black group wanted to surrender the specialness of mothering in favor of a completely sex-neutral concept of parenting.

"Putting Children First." The MV branch's theme of "putting children first" provides a powerful example of the need to understand liberation ideology in context. At face value, that theme would be an anathema to the NYRW, who were battling traditional notions that women should sacrifice themselves and put their own needs last. However, for the Black group the theme expressed a commitment to the uplift of the whole community and to the struggle for a future free from racism, sexism, and class oppression.

That the Black group advocated putting children first points to a difference in the two groups' values. The MV/NR women were more deeply and consistently community oriented. In discussing the activism of Black "community othermothers" under conditions of racism and poverty, Collins notes that they model a value system of "connectedness with others" and "common interest," in which "ethics of caring and personal accountability move communities forward" (1991, 131–32). The NYRW, despite a commitment to collective struggle and a certain advocacy of communal values, showed a more individualistic orientation, with an emphasis on woman's development of self. Women, they argued, needed more freedom to pursue independent lives, to develop themselves as human beings. The White group's attention to women's self-development reflected their more advantaged position in the society's class and racial hierarchies.

Partial Perspective: The Contributions and Limitations of Each Approach

Each of these 1960s groups viewed the relationship between motherhood and women's liberation from their own angle of vision. Each group offered valuable ideas and insights, yet each group's perspective had its limitations.

The MV/NR group's genuine high regard for motherhood was an important message to a society that celebrated mothers at the superficial level but devalued them at deeper levels. Their community-based child rearing challenged the mainstream notion that the mother should handle all the parenting. By connecting mothering with community activism, the group countered the dominant image of the mother immersed in domesticity. Their child-centered values bade defiance to the societal obsession with self-interest and materialism.

However, the MV/NR group's commitment to putting children first had its problematic side. The MV branch posed women's choices as either putting the man first or putting the children first—putting themselves (or other women) first was not articulated as a possibility. Were these dedicated mothers caught in the sexist trap of putting their own needs last? Barbara Christian provides support for that interpretation: "The idea that mothers should live lives of sacrifice has come to be seen as the norm" in African American communities. When "women are reduced to the function of mother," this "often results in their loss of sense of self" (1994, 103, 116).

To some extent, the MV women's stance on motherhood was an adaptation to an oppressive reality. With few other ways to channel their abilities and creativity, they focused their efforts on nurturing the next generation. The women's devotion to children made the best of a bad situation.

The NYRW, operating in a different milieu, made a crucial contribution to women's liberation when they boldly rejected the mother role. By challenging the sacredness of motherhood, they helped to free up consciousness and validate other options for women.

It is understandable why NYRW did not celebrate motherhood, given its implications for them and the allure of new possibilities. However, a major problem with their approach was that, in rejecting the mother role, they seemed to be seconding male-dominated society's low estimation of child-rearing work. Though they insisted that men share in child care, they conveyed more sense of its burdens than its satisfactions.

By encouraging woman's self-development, NYRW offered an essential corrective to female socialization for self-sacrifice. Nonetheless, were the White women also reflecting middle-class values of individualism and self-interest? Would their message of self-development resonate with women like the MV activists? Though NYRW gave lip service to community, they did not address enough how to reconcile pursuing self-development with sustaining families (of whatever kind) and communities.[35]

If these two groups had engaged in ongoing dialogue about their common differences, could they have helped generate a more multifaceted understanding of motherhood, with a broad appeal to women of different backgrounds? For example, had the MV/NR group's perspective been integrated into mainstream feminist ideology, feminism might have avoided being branded with a simplistic antimother image, which began to plague it and alienate some mothers.

In a recent article, Collins argues that "feminist theorizing about motherhood reflects a lack of attention to the connection between ideas and the context in which they emerge." Although she is discussing feminist scholars rather than movement thinkers, her comments aptly sum up the lessons of my comparative study. She states that "the specific contexts in which [feminist scholars] are located provide the thought-models of how they interpret the world." Their theories are "valid as partial perspectives" but are not "generalizable to all women." Collins calls for "examination of motherhood and mother-as-subject from multiple perspectives." She concludes that "shifting the center to accommodate this diversity promises to recontextualize motherhood and point us toward feminist theorizing that embraces difference as an essential part of commonality" (1994, 61–62).

A Note on Subsequent Developments

Attitudes toward motherhood in the two groups' circles have not been static since the 1960s.[36] By 1983, when I conducted my initial interviews, there had been a certain convergence of the thinking in these two social contexts. The NR women noted that more young Black women were determined to get schooling and jobs, "not lookin' where the first thing I'm gonna do is get married and have kids."[37] Some of the NYRW members, up against the biological clock for childbearing, were feeling regrets about renouncing motherhood earlier.

In general, White feminists in the 1980s and 1990s have moved toward a higher valuation of motherhood. More middle-class White women are struggling to combine it with employment. Lower-working-class Black women are having a hard time handling that double workload too. In the early 1980s, the era of "Reaganomics," the NR women were seeing some breakdown of the extended family and friendship networks that shared in the rearing of children. In the early 1990s, the sociologist Collins observed that in many inner-city neighborhoods "the very fabric of African-American community life is being eroded by illegal drugs." The "entire community structure of bloodmothers and othermothers is under assault" (Collins 1991, 122). Whatever limited convergence has occurred in terms of the White women valuing motherhood more and the Black women having a less communal experience of motherhood, the contrasts between the conditions of life for these two populations of women are still stark.

Views about motherhood, children, and family remain an important area for feminists from diverse backgrounds to explore together.[38] In the 1980s, right-wing attacks on feminism as antimotherhood and antifamily put the women's movement on the defensive. If the movement in all its diversity can articulate a more unified yet nuanced position on family issues, perhaps it can regain some of the ideological initiative and have greater impact on public policy concerning mothers and families.

Conclusion

The social locations of these two 1960s groups of women's liberation activists shaped their thinking about the mother role. For the Black women, held down so strongly by racial and class oppression as well as gender oppression, motherhood offered significant meaning, satisfaction, and respect. Children represented the hope for a better future, and educating them to help transform the society constituted vital political work.

The White women, in contrast, rejected the mother role almost with a vengeance. This attitude arose from their socioeconomic location at a specific moment in history. Being aware of the factors that fostered this attitude helps us understand the antimotherhood tone that emanated from some White feminist circles.

For feminist scholars, this case study underscores the importance of recognizing the diverse forms women's liberation efforts have taken and the diverse ideologies activists in different communities have generated. Writers on the second wave should give more attention to the early approaches of women of color and working-class women, who were making pioneering efforts to integrate issues of class, race, and gender.[39]

With regard to the women's movement agenda of bridging divisions, this study illustrates that the different social contexts in which we operate can affect many aspects of our political approaches: how we picture women's status in prehistory, how we envision liberation, which issues we consider cutting-edge, how we argue for the same goal, or whether our meetings include children. The point is not to conclude that one approach is right and another wrong; different approaches arise from different realities. The main point for the women's movement is the need to address and encompass multiple realities.

To build alliances across racial-ethnic and class lines, women at minimum must share similar goals. Middle-class White women who do not put a strong priority on racial and economic justice will not succeed in allying with racially oppressed and economically deprived women. However, sharing similar goals does not guarantee being able to cooperate or work together. Connecting across racial-ethnic and class lines requires real effort to understand how our different social locations have shaped our perspectives, so that differences in thinking become a bridge to deeper mutual understanding, rather than a wedge for further division. Women must connect across divisions in order to transform the systems of class, race, and gender and make real again the 1960s promise of women's liberation.

NOTES

This article is dedicated to my beloved daughter, Esta. I thank the women I interviewed, whose help made this study possible. The research was supported in part by the Mabelle McLeod Lewis Fund. I received useful feedback on this material from my dissertation group and committee and on this article from Elaine Bell Kaplan, Patricia Guthrie, Colleen Fong, Ann Van de Pol, Barbara Paige, Chude Pam Allen, Pat Robinson, and the manuscript readers and editors of *Signs*. I also thank Cousin Bob for computer assistance and Barbara LaRocca and Esta J. P. Grill for their support.

1. In comparing Black and White, I use the term *racial-ethnic* to convey the intertwined realities of racial hierarchy and ethnic (subculture) difference. Like DeVault (1995, 628), "I rely on a view of race-ethnicity that sees both as socially constructed, though materially consequential, categories of social differentiation. . . . While there are clearly good reasons to distinguish differences labeled 'ethnic' and 'racial' for some purposes," for other purposes a clear distinction cannot or need not be made.

2. Although in the 1990s *African American* has become the preferred term, in writing about the 1960s I use the preferred term of that period, *Black*. I capitalize Black and White because they are not simply physical descriptions but social categories of racial-ethnic identification. The Black group, really a network of women from two neighboring communities, did not

have an official name. Their writings were published under several names, including "Pat Robinson and Group." In consultation with the members I interviewed, I chose to use "Mount Vernon/New Rochelle group," which recognizes the group's two branches and acknowledges collective effort rather than a single individual. The group members felt strongly about the latter point (see n. 7).

3. See Collins 1991, chap. 6, "Black Women and Motherhood," for a comprehensive discussion of this literature with references. See also James 1993.

4. "Women's liberation" refers to the more radical sector of the 1960s women's movement. The moderates and the liberals tended to talk about "women's rights."

5. The second edition (1990) has the same pagination and is identical to the original except for a new foreword and introduction.

6. These in-depth interviews were done in person, mainly in 1983. I used both specific and open-ended questions geared to the particular interviewee(s). In my five sessions with MV/NR group members, the number of interviewees ranged from one to three (a result of both circumstances and their preferences). I interviewed the NYRW members individually.

7. The group members asked me to use their first names and last initials only. The introduction to *Lessons* (The Damned [1973] 1990, 9) explains their viewpoint: "Please let our individual names pass away and be forgotten with all the nameless like us—and those too who went before and yet in reality made it possible for us to speak today." In my text, I honor the request. In citing their writings, I use full names if the original source did.

8. Pat R., interviews by author, New Rochelle, N.Y., September 7 and 28, 1983, transcript. Unless otherwise indicated, subsequent information about the MV branch is pieced together from the Pat R. interviews; Joyce H. and Catherine H., interview by author, Mount Vernon, N.Y., October 8, 1983, transcript; The Damned (1973) 1990, 89–101; and the group's other published and unpublished writings.

9. About fifteen to twenty women were involved in the group; the committed core numbered five to ten.

10. With regard to the participation of lesbians, I did not access enough information to make statements about this.

11. In the 1960s in New York, abortion was illegal except to save the mother's life. Poor Black teenagers in Mount Vernon rarely had the money or the desire to get a "back-alley" abortion. The idea of giving up a baby to an adoption agency was foreign to this community (though informal adoption by a relative or friend was accepted). In any event, adoption agencies usually had little interest in Black babies.

12. Patricia Robinson, "Revolt of the Black Woman," interview by Dan Georgakas, New Rochelle, N.Y., April 1967 (author's file, Women's Studies Program, San Jose State University, photocopy), 2–3.

13. Joyce H., interview.

14. "Rita," interview by Pat Robinson, Mount Vernon, N.Y., 1969 (author's files, Women's Studies Program, San Jose State University, photocopy), 3.

15. Catherine H. and Joyce H., interview. The school grew to thirty-five children, ranging in age from two to fourteen (The Damned [1973] 1990, 124).

16. Robinson, "Revolt of the Black Woman," 7.

17. An essay by Pat R. that the group distributed with their statement developed further the idea of children as an important resource (Robinson 1968).

18. The NR network numbered six to ten at the core and up to twenty counting marginal members.

19. Carrietta G. and Linda Landrine (she wanted her full name used), interview by author, New Rochelle, N.Y., October 9, 1983, transcript; Carrietta G., Linda Landrine, and Maureen W., interview by author, New Rochelle, N.Y., October 23, 1983, transcript. Unless otherwise indicated, subsequent information about the NR branch is pieced together from these interviews; The Damned (1973) 1990, 101–11; and the groups other published and unpublished writings. With regard to the NR women's class position, many of their mothers worked as domestics or as cleaning women in local hospitals; a few mothers were typists or nurses' aides. In the early 1950s, their fathers had held factory jobs, but by the 1960s most were unemployed or only marginally employed and had drifted away from their families. At the end of the 1960s, some of the young women were able to go to college. By the 1980s their occupations included social worker, elementary school teacher, and secretary (The Damned [1973] 1990, 104–5; interviews 1983).

20. A common question about my research has been: Were the group's ideas and writings really coming from the middle-class Pat R.? The group's process of developing ideas and writings was interactive and synergistic. Their political sophistication did reflect Pat R.'s involvement (more so for the MV than for the NR branch). However the MV/NR women, distrustful of middle-class Blacks, would not have responded to Pat R. with such heartfelt enthusiasm had she been imposing alien views rather than helping them develop and articulate their own understanding of the world. The group's politics were rooted in the realities and perspectives of poor women.

21. This essay was published in two somewhat different versions: Robinson and Group 1969; and Haden, Middleton, and Robinson 1970.

22. Marilyn Lowen, interview by author, New York, October 13, 1983, transcript. Unless otherwise indicated, subsequent information about NYRW is pieced together from the group's published and unpublished writings and my interviews with fourteen former members.

23. These generalizations about the core members should not gainsay the diversity among them: they came from different strata of the middle class and some from the working class. A substantial minority were married. The group grew to twenty or thirty regulars, and by fall 1968 the weekly meetings were drawing fifty to a hundred women (Echols 1989, 74). The peripheral participants were more diverse than the core in age and class. With regard to sexual orientation, see Echols's discussion of lesbianism in these circles (210–20).

24. (Chude) Pam Allen, telephone interview by author, San Francisco, January 1995.

25. Ellen Willis, interview by author, New York, October 14, 1983, transcript.

26. Alix Kates Shulman, interview by author, New York, October 29, 1983, transcript.

27. Ibid. Shulman noted that sometimes she was valued as a token mother, "their peculiar example of the real thing." In 1969 she gravitated to the radical feminist offshoot group Redstockings, which "tried to take account of most women's lives." There, motherhood was at least "a condition to be acknowledged and accounted for."

28. Ellen Willis, interview.

29. Although the articles were by different individuals, they grew out of group discussions and put forth a fairly consistent viewpoint.

30. (Chude) Pam Allen, telephone interview. Allen asked me to add that, when they actually split up some years later, she felt quite differently.

31. (Chude) Pam Allen, telephone conversation with author, San Francisco, August 10, 1995.

32. Although middle-class European American norms dictated a domestic focus for mothers, one strain of feminism in the latter nineteenth and early twentieth centuries ("social feminism") had maintained that women should extend their mothering skills to the larger community and society (Cott 1977).

33. Pat R. of the MV/NR group comments: "The abuse of children by dick-happy mothers was an important concern; it was happening around us at that time" (letter to author, September 4, 1995).

34. Pat R. points out that the NYRW were influenced by de Beauvoir's *The Second Sex* (1953), which promotes French anthropologist Lévi-Strauss's "thesis of motherhood as oppressive and women always under male superiority." The MV/NR women were persuaded more by "the 'old theorists' [Bachofen, Briffault, Morgan], supported by Engels, etc., who established the historical primitive equalitarian, matriarchal thesis. . . . Our MV/NR anthropological studies went back to Briffault and studies in early African history which were becoming abundant. We always had early childhood memories of women's strengths in plantation society, still extant even then. So the Briffault studies made more sense to all of us. The NR women paid more attention to Engels. They were into college studies and papers by then" (Pat R, letter to author, September 4, 1995).

35. In *Notes from the First Year,* Hanisch and Sutherland stated, "Just what new forms should replace today's nuclear family . . . is not for us to determine. Men too have a responsibility for working that out. More important, we reject the idea that women must come up with a perfect formula for the human race before their demands for liberation are met" (1968, 15).

36. For an insightful discussion of Black and White feminists' evolving views on motherhood, see hooks 1984, 133–46.

37. Carrietta G., interview, October 23, 1983.

38. Glenn, Chang, and Forcey 1994 is an excellent recent book in this vein.

39. This theme is developed further in Polatnick 1994.

REFERENCES

Sources in the reference list with an asterisk can be found in the personal files of the author, Women's Studies Program, San Jose State University; those with a dagger are available from Redstocking's Women's Liberation Archives, Archives Distribution Project, P.O. Box 2625, Gainesville, FL 32602.

Allen, (Chude) Pam. 1968. "What Strategy for Movement Women?" *Guardian,* October 5, 9.
Baxandall, Rosalyn. 1994. "Rosalyn Baxandall's Feminist Memoir." Manuscript, New York City.

Beauvoir, Simone de. 1953. *The Second Sex.* New York: Knopf.

*Black Radicals Onward (New Rochelle, N.Y.). 1969. *Harambee.* April 19.

†Black Unity Party (Peekskill, N.Y.). 1968. "Birth Control Pills and Black Children." *Lilith* (Seattle), Fall, 7.

Cade, Toni, ed. 1970. *The Black Woman.* New York: Signet.

Christian, Barbara. 1994. "An Angle of Seeing: Motherhood in Buchi Emecheta's *Joys of Motherhood* and Alice Walker's *Meridian.*" In Glenn, Chang, and Forcer 1994, 95–120.

Collins, Patricia Hill. 1987. "The Merging of Motherhood in Black Culture and Black Mother/Daughter Relationships." *SAGE: A Scholarly Journal on Black Women* 4 (2): 3–10.

———. 1991. "Black Women and Motherhood." In her *Black Feminist Thought,* 115–37. New York: Routledge.

———. 1994. "Shifting the Center: Race, Class, and Feminist Theorizing about Motherhood." In Glenn, Chang, and Forcey 1994, 45–65.

Coontz, Stephanie. 1988. *The Origins of Private Life: A History of American Families, 1600–1900.* New York: Verso.

Cott, Nancy. 1977. *The Bonds of Womanhood.* New Haven, Conn.: Yale University Press.

The Damned. (1973) 1990. *Lessons from the Damned: Class Struggle in the Black Community.* Ojai, Calif.: Times Change.

Davis, Angela. 1971. "Reflections on the Black Woman's Role in the Community of Slaves." *Black Scholar* 3 (4): 3–15.

Degler, Carl. 1984. *At Odds: Women and Family from the Revolution to the Present.* New York: Oxford University Press.

DeVault, Marjorie L. 1995. "Ethnicity and Expertise: Racial-Ethnic Knowledge in Sociological Research." *Gender and Society* 9 (5): 612–31.

Echols, Alice. 1989. *Daring to Be Bad: Radical Feminism in America, 1967–1975.* Minneapolis: University of Minnesota Press.

†The Feminists. 1969. "The Feminists: A Political Organization to Annihilate Sex Roles." In Firestone and Koedt 1970, 114–18. Also in *Radical Feminism,* ed. Anne Koedt, Ellen Levine, and Anita Rapone, 368–78. New York: Quadrangle, 1973.

†Firestone, Shulamith. 1968a. "The Jeanette Rankin Brigade: Woman Power?" In NYRW 1968, 18–19.

———. 1968b. "The Women's Rights Movement in the U.S.: A New View." In NYRW 1968, 1–7.

———. 1970. *The Dialectic of Sex.* New York: Bantam.

†Firestone, Shulamith, and Anne Koedt, eds. 1970. *Notes from the Second Year: Women's Liberation.* New York: Firestone and Koedt.

Friedan, Betty. 1981. *The Second Stage.* New York: Summit.

Glenn, Evelyn Nakano, Grace Chang, and Linda Rennie Forcey, eds. 1994. *Mothering: Ideology, Experience, and Agency.* New York: Routledge.

Haden, Patricia, Donna Middleton, and Patricia Robinson. 1970. "A Historical and Critical Essay for Black Women." In Tanner 1970, 316–24.

†Hanisch, Carol, and Elizabeth Sutherland [Martinez]. 1968. "Women of the World Unite— We Have Nothing to Lose but Our Men!" In NYRW 1968, 12–16.

hooks, bell. 1984. *Feminist Theory: From Margin to Center.* Boston: South End.

James, Stanlie M. 1993. "Mothering: A Possible Black Feminist Link to Social Transformation?" In *Theorizing Black Feminisms,* ed. Stanlie M. James and Abena P. A. Busia, 44–54. New York: Routledge.

Joseph, Gloria I., and Jill Lewis. 1981. *Common Differences: Conflicts in Black and White Feminist Perspectives.* Boston: South End.

†Koedt, Anne. (1968) 1970. "The Myth of the Vaginal Orgasm." In Firestone and Koedt 1970, 37–41. Also in several books, including *Radical Feminism,* ed. Anne Koedt, Ellen Levine, and Anita Rapone, 198–207. New York: Quadrangle, 1973.

Love, Barbara, and Elizabeth Shanklin. 1978. "The Answer Is Matriarchy." In *Our Right to Love,* ed. Ginny Vida, 183–87. Englewood Cliffs, N.J.: Prentice Hall.

†Mainardi, Pat. (1968) 1970. "The Politics of Housework." In Firestone and Koedt 1970, 28–31. Also in *Liberation Now! Writings from the Women's Liberation Movement* [comp. Deborah Babcox and Madeline Belkin], 110–15. New York: Dell, 1971.

Morgan, Robin, ed. 1970. *Sisterhood Is Powerful.* New York: Vintage.

*[Mount Vernon group]. 1967. Letter to the *National Guardian.* November. Photocopy.

†———. 1968a. "The Sisters Reply." *Lilith* (Seattle), Fall, 8. Also published as "Statement on Birth Control," in Morgan 1970, 360–61.

*———. 1968b. Letter to Women's Liberation Group in Canada. November. Photocopy.

†New York Radical Women (NYRW), eds. 1968. *Notes from the First Year.* New York: [NYRW].

Polatnick, M. Rivak. 1994. "The Wave and the Movement: Doing Justice to the Feminist Activism of Women of Color." Manuscript, San Jose State University.

———. 1995. "Poor Black Sisters Decided for Themselves: Case Study of '60s Women's Liberation Activism." In *Black Women in America,* ed. Kim Vaz. Thousand Oaks, Calif.: Sage.

†Robinson, Patricia. 1968. ["Poor Black Women"]. *Lilith* (Seattle), Fall, 9–11. Also published as "On the Position of Poor Black Women in This Country," in Cade 1970, 194–97.

———. 1969. "Malcolm X, Our Revolutionary Son and Brother." In *Malcolm X: The Man and His Times,* ed. John Henrik Clarke, 56–63. New York: Macmillan.

Robinson, Pat, and Group. 1969. "A Historical and Critical Essay for Black Women in the Cities, June 1969." In Cade 1970, 198–210.

†Sarachild, Kathie [Amatniek]. 1968a. "Funeral Oration for the Burial of Traditional Womanhood." In NYRW 1968, 20–22.

†———. 1968b. "A Program for Feminist 'Consciousness Raising.'" In Firestone and Koedt 1970, 78–80.

Stack, Carol. 1974. *All Our Kin.* New York: Harper & Row.

Sudarkasa, Niara. 1981. "Interpreting the African Heritage in Afro-American Family Organization." In *Black Families,* ed. Harriette Pipes McAdoo, 37–53. Beverly Hills, Calif.: Sage.

†Susan, Barbara. 1970. "An Abortion Testimonial." In Firestone and Koedt 1970, 94.

Tanner, Leslie B., ed. 1970. *Voices from Women's Liberation.* New York: Signet.

Troester, Rosalie Riegle. 1984. "Turbulence and Tenderness: Mothers, Daughters, and 'Othermothers' in Paule Marshall's *Brown Girl, Brownstones.*" *SAGE: A Scholarly Journal on Black Women* 1 (2): 13–16.

White, Deborah Gray. 1985. *Ar'n't I a Woman? Female Slaves in the Plantation South.* New York: Norton.

Part Four

PUBLIC POLICY

The concluding section of this volume explores critical links between mothers, mothering, and public policy. At different times in our history women have used their status as mothers to inaugurate, sustain, and achieve political agendas. In the nineteenth century "Home Protection" was the cry of the Women's Christian Temperance Union. It fought to outlaw the manufacture and sale of alcohol, which it believed posed a threat to the well-being of children and mothers. Today, saving lives is the aim of the organization known as Mothers Against Drunk Driving. In both cases, a reference to mothering sustains a political position.

The articles in this section point to four themes in the overlapping histories of American motherhood and American public policy. One is the way women use the rhetoric of motherhood to gain political and social authority in the hopes of controlling their own lives and the lives of others. A second is the flowering of maternalist discourse in the Progressive Era, when many women, organizations, and reformers attempted to make policies on the basis of the "needs" of mothers. While these groups sometimes disagreed over preferred ends, they shared the conviction that promoting public policy by referring to its effects on mothers was an effective strategy. Third, many groups understood that changing society meant reaching out to mothers, whether as the parents of school-age children, immigrants, or the parents of farm children who suffered from poor health. Finally, the articles illustrate how the work of mothering is inextricably intertwined with the economy; we cannot ignore the ways in which the marketplace influences the work and meaning of mothering.

The section opens with Linda Gordon's article on the voluntary motherhood movement of the late nineteenth century. Arguing that women had a maternal instinct and that motherhood was an exalted profession, proponents of voluntary motherhood demanded a more restricted sexual morality. They opposed contraception, which they feared would permit men to engage in extramarital sex, and vehemently supported the right of women to abstain from sex.

While voluntary motherhood demanded authority for women in the home, the National Congress of Mothers and Parent-Teacher Associations looked to gain power in the public arena. As Molly Ladd-Taylor explains, between 1890 and 1930 this organization sought to teach mothers how to care for their own offspring while simultaneously encouraging them to promote the well-being of all children. She contrasts their efforts with those of the National Association of Colored Women, which engaged in similar efforts but embraced a different interpretation of home and motherhood and thus evolved a different political strategy.

George Sanchez analyzes some of the efforts to "Americanize" immigrant Mexican women in California in the years from 1915 to 1929. A state-sponsored home teacher program tried to make Mexican mothers agents of cultural change; it encouraged them to adopt "American" health habits, cleanliness standards, dietary routines, and, later, family planning practices. At the same time, Mexican mothers were encouraged to work in the low-paid domestic labor market. These programs illuminate the assumptions made about Mexican and Euro-American mothering during the Progressive Era.

Concurrent with attempts to "Americanize" Mexican American mothers in California were programs to "modernize" farm mothers in Illinois. Lynne Curry's analysis of these efforts reveals much about the material conditions in which mothers struggled to rear their children. She also describes how farm women's organizations and Home Bureaus—clubs for rural women—began offering demonstration programs and traveling exhibits to educate women about modern health practices. Not surprisingly, mothers from larger, wealthier farms had greater access to these programs than those from smaller, poorer farms or from tenant farms.

Eileen Boris describes the fight to regulate industrial homework in the 1930s and 1940s as involving conflicting interpretations of "sacred motherhood." Businesses defended home manufacturing by arguing that it allowed mothers to rear their children while earning an income; opponents charged that homeworkers were doubly exploited by the demands of child care and the extremely low wages and long hours that homework demanded. Although reformers succeeded in outlawing homework for mothers, they did so, Boris argues, without challenging the gender division of labor, the devaluation of motherhood, or the continuing privatization of child care.

The section closes with Joanne Goodwin's reevaluation of the history of welfare and motherhood in the twentieth century. She argues that concepts of maternal wage earning and welfare dependency have changed over time, but in all cases the role of the marketplace and fiscal policies informed public policy. Beginning with the creation of state-supported mothers' pensions in the early twentieth century, Goodwin notes that women were pushed into the labor market in addition to being given benefits. After passage of the 1935 Social Security Act, federal resources became available to mother-only families. The treatment of women receiving Aid

to Dependent Children differed, however, from that of women given survivor benefits. In the postwar era, Aid to Families With Dependent Children was recon-
ceptualized to incorporate work incentives. Today, welfare programs are once again
being redesigned, and once again policy makers are grappling with the rhetoric and
realities of motherhood.

20.

Voluntary Motherhood
The Beginnings of Feminist Birth Control Ideas in the United States

LINDA GORDON

Voluntary motherhood was the first general name for a feminist birth control in the United States in the late nineteenth century.[1] It represented an initial response to feminists' understanding that involuntary motherhood and child raising were important parts of woman's oppression. In this paper, I would like to trace the content and general development of "voluntary motherhood" ideas and to situate them in the development of the American birth control movement.

The feminists who advocated voluntary motherhood were of three general types: suffragists; people active in such moral reform movements as temperance and social purity, in church auxiliaries, and in women's professional and service organizations (such as Sorosis); and members of small, usually anarchist, Free Love groups. The Free Lovers played a classically vanguard role in the development of birth control ideas. Free Love groups were always small and sectarian, and they were usually male dominated, despite their extreme ideological feminism. They never coalesced into a movement. On the contrary, they were remnants of a dying tradition of utopian socialist and radical Protestant religious dissent. The Free Lovers, whose very self-definition was built around a commitment to iconoclasm and to isolation from the masses, were precisely the group that could offer intellectual leadership in formulating the shocking arguments that birth control in the nineteenth century required.[2]

The suffragists and moral reformers, concerned to win mass support, were increasingly committed to social respectability. As a result, they did not generally advance very far beyond prevalent standards of propriety in discussing sexual matters publicly. Indeed, as the century progressed the social gap between them and the

Reprinted by permission of the author from *Feminist Studies* 1 (1973): 5–22.

Free Lovers grew, for the second and third generations of suffragists were more concerned with respectability than the first. In the 1860s and 1870s the great feminist
theoreticians had been much closer to the Free Lovers, and at least one of these
early giants, Victoria Woodhull, was for several years a member of both the suffrage
and Free Love camps. But even respectability did not completely stifle the mental
processes of the feminists, and many of them said in private writings—in letters
and diaries—what they were unwilling to utter in public.

The similar views of Free Lovers and suffragists on the question of voluntary
motherhood did not bridge the considerable political distance between the groups
but did show that their analyses of the social meaning of reproduction for women
were converging. The sources of that convergence, the common grounds of their
feminism, were their similar experiences in the changing conditions of nineteenth-
century America. Both groups were composed of educated, middle-class Yankees
responding to severe threats to the stability, if not dominance, of their class position. Both groups were disturbed by the consequences of rapid industrialization—
the emergence of great capitalists in a clearly defined financial oligarchy, and the
increased immigration, which threatened the dignity and economic security of the
middle-class Yankee. Free Lovers and suffragists, as feminists, looked forward to a
decline in patriarchal power within the family but worried, too, about the possible
disintegration of the family and the loosening of sexual morality. They saw reproduction in the context of these larger social changes, and in a movement for
women's emancipation, and they saw that movement as an answer to some of these
large social problems. They hoped that giving political power to women would
help to reinforce the family and to make the government more just and the economy less monopolistic. In all these attitudes there was something traditional as well
as something progressive; the concept of voluntary motherhood reflected this
duality.

Since we all bring a twentieth-century understanding to our concept of birth control, it may be best to make it clear at once that neither Free Lovers nor suffragists
approved of contraceptive devices. Ezra Heywood, patriarch and martyr, thought
"artificial" methods "unnatural, injurious, or offensive." Tennessee Claflin wrote
that the "washes, teas, tonics and various sorts of known appliances known to the
initiated" were a "standing reproach upon, and a permanent indictment against,
American women. . . . No woman should ever hold sexual relations with any man
from the possible consequences of which she might desire to escape." *Woodhull &
Claflin's Weekly* editorialized: "The means they [women] resort to for . . . prevention is sufficient to disgust every natural man."[3]

On a rhetorical level, the main objection to contraception[4] was that it was "unnatural," and the arguments reflected a romantic yearning for the "natural," rather pastorally conceived, that was typical of many nineteenth-century reform movements. More basic, however, particularly in women's arguments against contraception, was an underlying fear of the promiscuity that it could permit. The fear of promiscuity was associated less with fear for one's virtue than with fear of other women—the perhaps mythical "fallen" women—who might threaten a husband's fidelity.

To our twentieth-century minds a principle of voluntary motherhood that rejects the practice of contraception seems so theoretical as to have little real impact. What gave the concept substance was that it was accompanied by another, potentially explosive, conceptual change: the reacceptance of female sexuality. As with birth control, the most open advocates of female sexuality were the Free Lovers, not the suffragists; nevertheless both groups based their ideas on the traditional grounds of the "natural." Free Lovers argued, for example, that celibacy was unnatural and dangerous—for men and women alike. "Pen cannot record, nor lips express, the enervating, debauching effect of celibate life upon young men and women."[5] Asserting the existence, legitimacy, and worthiness of the female sexual drive was one of the Free Lovers' most important contributions to sexual reform; it was a logical correlate of their argument from the "natural" and of their appeal for the integration of body and soul.

Women's rights advocates, too, began to demand recognition of female sexuality. Isabella Beecher Hooker wrote to her daughter: "Multitudes of women in all the ages who have scarce known what sexual desire is—being wholly absorbed in the passion of maternity, have sacrificed themselves to the beloved husbands as unto God—and yet these men, full of their human passion and defending it as righteous & God-sent lose all confidence in womanhood when a woman here and there betrays her similar nature & gives herself soul & body to the man she adores."[6] Alice Stockham, a Spiritualist Free Lover and feminist physician, lauded sexual desire in men and women as "the prophecy of attainment." She urged that couples avoid reaching sexual "satiety" with each other, in order to keep their sexual desire constantly alive, for she considered desire pleasant and healthful.[7] Elizabeth Cady Stanton, commenting in her diary in 1883 on the Whitman poem "There Is a Woman Waiting for Me," wrote: "He speaks as if the female must be forced to the creative act, apparently ignorant of the fact that a healthy woman has as much passion as a man, that she needs nothing stronger than the law of attraction to draw her to the male."[8] Still, she loved Whitman, and largely because of that openness about sex that made him the Free Lovers' favorite poet.

According to the system of ideas then dominant, women, lacking sexual drives, submitted to sexual intercourse (and notice how Beecher Hooker continued the image of a woman "giving herself," never taking) in order to please their husbands and to conceive children. The ambivalence underlying this view was expressed in the equally prevalent notion that women must be protected from exposure to sexuality lest they "fall" and become depraved, lustful monsters. This ambivalence perhaps came from a subconscious lack of certainty about the reality of the sexless woman, a construct laid only thinly on top of the conception of woman as highly sexed, even insatiably so, that prevailed up to the eighteenth century. Victorian ambivalence on this question is nowhere more tellingly set forth than in the writings of physicians, who viewed woman's sexual organs as the source of her being, physical and psychological, and blamed most mental derangements on disorders of the reproductive organs.[9] Indeed, they saw it as part of the nature of things, as Rousseau had written, that men were male only part of the time, but women were female always.[10] In a system that deprived women of the opportunity to make extrafamilial contributions to culture, it was inevitable that they should be more strongly identified with sex than men were. Indeed, females were frequently called "the sex" in the nineteenth century.

The concept of maternal instinct helped to smooth the contradictory attitudes about woman's sexuality. In many nineteenth-century writings we find the idea that the maternal instinct was the female analogue of the male sex instinct; it was as if the two instincts were seated in analogous parts of the brain, or soul. Thus to suggest, as feminists did, that women might have the capacity for sexual impulses of their own automatically tended to weaken the theory of the maternal instinct. In the fearful imaginations of self-appointed protectors of the family and of womanly innocence, the possibility that women might desire sexual contact not for the sake of pregnancy—that they might even desire it at a time when they positively did not want pregnancy—was a wedge in the door to denying that women had any special maternal instinct at all.

Most of the feminists did not want to open that door either. Indeed, it was common for nineteenth-century women's rights advocates to use the presumed "special motherly nature" and "sexual purity" of women as arguments for increasing their freedom and status. It is no wonder that many of them chose to speak their subversive thoughts about the sexual nature of women privately, or at least softly. Even among the more outspoken Free Lovers, there was a certain amount of hedging. Lois Waisbrooker and Dora Forster, writing for a Free Love journal in the 1890s, argued that while men and women both had an "amative" instinct, it was much stronger in men; and that women—only women—also had a reproductive or "generative" instinct. "I suppose it must be universally conceded that men make the better lovers," Forster wrote. She thought that it might be possible that "the jealousy and tyranny of men have operated to suppress amativeness in women, by constantly sweeping strongly sexual women from the paths of life into infamy and sterility and death," but she thought also that the suppression, if it existed, had been permanently inculcated in woman's character.[11]

Modern birth control ideas rest on a full acceptance, at least quantitatively, of female sexuality. Modern contraception is designed to permit sexual intercourse as often as desired without the risk of pregnancy. Despite the protestations of sex counselors that there are no norms for the frequency of intercourse, in the popular view there are such norms. Most people in the mid-twentieth century think that "normal" couples have intercourse several times a week. By twentieth-century standards, then, the Free Lovers' rejection of artificial contraception and "unnatural" sex seems to preclude the possibility of birth control at all. Nineteenth-century sexual reformers, however, had different sexual norms. They did not seek to make an infinite number of sterile sexual encounters possible. They wanted to make it possible for women to avoid pregnancy if they badly needed to do so for physical or psychological reasons, but they did not believe that it was essential for such women to engage freely in sexual intercourse.

In short, for birth control, they recommended periodic or permanent abstinence. The proponents of voluntary motherhood had in mind two distinct contexts for abstinence. One was the mutual decision of a couple. This could mean continued celibacy, or it could mean following a form of the rhythm method. Unfortunately, all nineteenth-century writers miscalculated women's fertility cycle. (It was not until the 1920s that the ovulation cycle was correctly plotted, and until the 1930s it was not widely understood among American doctors.)[12] Ezra Heywood, for example, recommended avoiding intercourse from six to eight days before menstruation until ten to twelve days after it. Careful use of the calendar could also provide control over the sex of a child, Heywood believed: conception in the first half of the menstrual cycle would produce girls, in the second half, boys.[13] These misconceptions functioned, conveniently, to make practicable Heywood's and others' ideas that celibacy and contraceptive devices should *both* be avoided.

Some of the Free Lovers also endorsed male continence, a system practiced and advocated by the Oneida community, in which the male avoids climax entirely.[14] (There were other aspects of the Oneida system that antagonized the Free Lovers, notably the authoritarian quality of John Humphrey Noyes's leadership.)[15] Dr. Stockham developed her own theory of continence called "Karezza," in which the female as well as the male was to avoid climax. Karezza and male continence were whole sexual systems, not just methods of birth control. Their advocates expected the self-control involved to build character and spiritual qualities, while honoring, refining, and dignifying the sexual functions; and Karezza was reputed to be a cure for sterility as well, since its continued use was thought to build up the resources of fertility in the body.[16]

Idealizing sexual self-control was characteristic of the Free Love point of view. It was derived mainly from the thought of the utopian communitarians of the early nineteenth century,[17] but Ezra Heywood elaborated the theory. Beginning with the assumption that people's "natural" instincts, left untrammeled, would automatically create a harmonious, peaceful society—an assumption certainly derived from liberal philosophical faith in the innate goodness of man—Heywood applied it to sexuality, arguing that the natural sexual instinct was innately moderated, self-regulating. He did not imagine, as did Freud, a powerful, simple libido that could be checked only by an equally powerful moral and rational will. Heywood's theory implicitly contradicted Freud's description of inner struggle and constant tension between the drives of the id and the goals of the superego; Heywood denied the social necessity of sublimation.

On one level Heywood's theory may seem inadequate as a psychology, since it cannot explain such phenomena as repression and the strengthening of self-control with maturity. It may, however, have a deeper accuracy. It argues that society and its attendant repressions have distorted the animal's natural self-regulating mechanism and have thereby created excessive and obsessive sexual drives. It offers a social explanation for the phenomena that Freud described in psychological terms and thus holds out the hope that they can be changed.

Essentially similar to Wilhelm Reich's theory of "sex-economy," the Heywood theory of self-regulation went beyond Reich's in providing a weapon against one of the ideological bastions of male supremacy. Self-regulation as a goal was directed against the prevalent attitude that male lust was an uncontrollable urge, an attitude that functioned as a justification for rape specifically and for male sexual irresponsibility generally. We have to get away from the tradition of "man's necessities and woman's obedience to them," Stockham wrote.[18] The idea that men's desires are irrepressible is merely the other face of the idea that women's desires are nonexistent. Together, the two created a circle that enclosed woman, making it her exclusive responsibility to say no, and making pregnancy her God-imposed burden if she didn't, while denying her both artificial contraception and the personal and social strength to rebel against male sexual demands.

Heywood developed his theory of natural sexual self-regulation in answer to the common anti–Free Love argument that the removal of social regulation of sexuality would lead to unhealthy promiscuity: "In the distorted popular view, Free Love tends to unrestrained licentiousness, to open the flood gates of passion and remove all barriers in its desolating course; but it means just the opposite; it means the *utilization of animalism,* and the triumph of Reason, Knowledge, and Continence."[19] He applied the theory of self-regulation to the problem of birth control only as an afterthought, perhaps when women's concerns with that problem reached him. Ideally, he trusted, the amount of sexual intercourse that men and women desired would be exactly commensurate with the number of children that were wanted. Since sexual repression had had the boomerang effect of intensifying our sexual drives far beyond "natural" levels, effective birth control now would require the development of the inner self-control to contain and repress sexual urges. But in time he expected that sexual moderation would come about naturally.

Heywood's analysis, published in the mid-1870s, was concerned primarily with excessive sex drives in men. Charlotte Perkins Gilman, one of the leading theoreticians of the suffrage movement, reinterpreted that analysis two decades later to emphasize its effects on women. The economic dependence of woman on man, in Gilman's analysis, made her sexual attractiveness necessary not only for winning a mate but as a means of getting a livelihood too. This is the case with no other animal. In the human female it had produced "excessive modification to sex," emphasizing weak qualities characterized by humans as "feminine." She made an analogy to the milk cow, bred to produce far more milk than she would need for her calves. But Gilman agreed completely with Heywood about the effects of exaggerated sex distinction on the male; it produced excessive sex energy and excessive indulgence to an extent debilitating to the whole species. Like Heywood she also believed that the path of progressive social evolution moved toward monogamy and toward reducing the promiscuous sex instinct.[20]

A second context for abstinence, in addition to mutual self-regulation by a couple, was the right of the wife unilaterally to refuse her husband. This idea is at the heart of voluntary motherhood. It was a key substantive demand in the mid-nineteenth century, when both law and practice made sexual submission to her husband a woman's duty.[21] A woman's right to refuse is clearly the fundamental condition of birth control—and of her independence and personal integrity.

In their crusade for this right of refusal the voices of Free Lovers and suffragists were in unison. Ezra Heywood demanded "Woman's Natural Right to ownership and control over her own body-self—a right inseparable from Woman's intelligent existence."[22] Paulina Wright Davis, at the National Woman Suffrage Association in 1871, attacked the law "which makes obligatory the rendering of marital rights and compulsory maternity." When, as a result of her statement, she was accused of being a Free Lover, she responded by accepting the description.[23] Isabella Beecher Hooker wrote her daughter in 1869 advising her to avoid pregnancy until "you are prepared in body and soul to receive and cherish the little one."[24] In

1873 she gave similar advice to women generally, in her book *Womanhood.*[25] Elizabeth Cady Stanton had characteristically used the same phrase as Heywood: woman owning her own body. Once asked by a magazine what she meant by it, she replied: "Womanhood is the primal fact, wifehood and motherhood its incidents . . . must the heyday of her existence be wholly devoted to the one animal function of bearing children? Shall there be no limit to this but woman's capacity to endure the fearful strain on her life?"[26]

The insistence on women's right to refuse often took the form of attacks on men for their lusts and their violence in attempting to satisfy them. In their complaints against the unequal marriage laws, chief or at least loudest among them was the charge that they legalized rape.[27] Victoria Woodhull raged, "I will tell the world, so long as I have a tongue and the strength to move it, of all the infernal misery hidden behind this horrible thing called marriage, though the Young Men's Christian Association sentence me to prison a year for every word. I have seen horrors beside which stone walls and iron bars are heaven."[28] Angela Heywood attacked men incessantly and bitterly; if one were to ignore the accuracy of her charges, she could well seem ill-tempered. "Man so lost to himself and woman as to invoke legal *violence* in these sacred nearings, *should have solemn meeting with, and look serious at his own penis until he is able to be lord and master of it, rather than it should longer rule, lord and master, of him and of the victims he deflowers.*"[29] Suffragists spoke more delicately but not less bitterly. Feminists organized social purity organizations and campaigns, their attacks on prostitution based on a critique of the double standard, for which their proposed remedy was that men conform to the standards required of women.[30]

A variant of this concern was a campaign against "sexual abuses"—a Victorian euphemism for deviant sexual practices, or simply excessive sexual demands, not necessarily violence or prostitution. The Free Lovers, particularly, turned to this cause, because it gave them an opportunity to attack marriage. The "sexual abuses" question was one of the most frequent subjects of correspondence in Free Love periodicals. For example, a letter from Mrs. Theresa Hughes of Pittsburgh described

> a girl of sixteen, full of life and health when she became a wife. . . . She was a slave in every sense of the word, mentally and sexually, never was she free from his brutal outrages, morning, noon and night, up almost to the very hour her baby was born, and before she was again strong enough to move about. . . . Often did her experience last an hour or two, and one night she will never forget, the outrage lasted exactly four hours."[31]

Or from Lucinda Chandler, well-known moral reformer:

This useless sense gratification has demoralized generation after generation, till monstrosities of disorder are common. Moral education, and healthful training will be requisite for some generations, even after we have equitable economics, and free access to Nature's gifts. The young man of whom I knew who threatened his bride of a week with a sharp knive in his hand, to compel her to perform the office of "sucker," would no doubt have had the same disposition though no soul on the planet had a want unsatisfied or lacked a natural right.[32]

From an anonymous woman in Los Angeles:

> I am nearly wrecked and ruined by . . . nightly intercourse, which is often repeated in the morning. This and nothing else was the cause of my miscarriage . . . he went to work like a man a-mowing, and instead of a pleasure as it might have been, it was most intense torture. . . .[33]

Clearly these remarks reflect a level of hostility toward sex. The observation that many feminists hated sex has been made by several historians,[34] but they have usually failed to perceive that feminists' hostility and fear of it came from the fact that they were women, not that they were feminists. Women in the nineteenth century were, of course, trained to repress their own sexual feelings, to view sex as a duty. But they also resented what they experienced, which was not an abstraction but a particular, historical kind of sexual encounter—intercourse dominated by and defined by the male in conformity with his desires and in disregard of what might bring pleasure to a woman. (That this might have resulted more from male ignorance than malevolence could not change women's experiences.) Furthermore, sexual intercourse brought physical danger. Pregnancy, childbirth, and abortions were risky, painful, and isolating experiences in the nineteenth century; venereal diseases were frequently communicated to women by their husbands. Elmina Slenker, a Free Lover and novelist, wrote, "I'm getting a host of stories (truths) about women so starved sexually as to use their dogs for relief, and finally I have come to the belief that a CLEAN dog is better than a drinking, tobacco-smelling, venereally diseased man!"[35]

"Sex-hating" women were not just misinformed or priggish or neurotic. They were often responding rationally to their material reality. Denied the possibility of recognizing and expressing their own sexual needs, denied even the knowledge of sexual possibilities other than those dictated by the rhythms of male orgasm, they had only two choices: passive and usually pleasureless submission, with a high risk of undesirable consequences, or rebellious refusal. In that context, abstinence to ensure voluntary motherhood was a most significant feminist demand.

What is remarkable is that some women recognized that it was not sex per se, but only their husbands' style of making love, that repelled them. One of the women noted above who complained about her treatment went on to say: "I am undeveloped sexually, never having desires in that direction; still, with a husband who had any love or kind of feelings for me and one less selfish it *might* have been different, but he cared nothing for the torture to *me* as long as *he* was gratified."[36]

Elmina Slenker herself, the toughest and crustiest of all these "sex haters," dared to explore and take seriously her own longings, thereby revealing herself to be a sex lover in disguise. As the editor of the *Water-Cure Journal,* and a regular contributor to *Free Love Journal,*[37] she expounded a theory of "Dianaism, or Nonprocreative Love," sometimes called "Diana-love and Alpha-abstinence." It meant free sexual contact of all sorts except intercourse.

> We want the sexes to love more than they do; we want them to love openly, frankly, earnestly; to enjoy the caress, the embrace, the glance, the voice, the presence & the very step of the beloved. We oppose no form or act of love between any man & woman. Fill the world as full of genuine sex love as you can . . . but forbear to rush in where generations yet unborn may suffer for your unthinking, uncaring, unheeding actions.[38]

Comparing this to the more usual physical means of avoiding conception—coitus interruptus and male continence—reveals how radical it was. In modern history, public endorsement of nongenital sex, and of forms of genital sex beyond standard "missionary position" intercourse, has been a recent, post-Freudian, even post–Masters and Johnson phenomenon. The definition of sex as heterosexual intercourse has been one of the oldest and most universal cultural norms. Slenker's alienation from existing sexual possibilities led her to explore alternatives with a bravery and a freedom from religious and psychological taboos extraordinary for a nineteenth-century Quaker reformer.

In the nineteenth century, neither Free Lovers nor suffragists ever relinquished their hostility to contraception. But among the Free Lovers, free speech was always an overriding concern, and for that reason Ezra Heywood agreed to publish some advertisements for a vaginal syringe, an instrument whose use for contraception he personally deplored, or so he continued to assure his readers. Those advertisements led to Heywood's prosecution for obscenity, and he defended himself with characteristic flair by making his position more radical than ever before. Contraception was moral, he argued, when it was used by women as the only means of defending their rights, including the right to voluntary motherhood. Although "artificial means of preventing conception are not generally patronized by Free Lovers," he wrote, reserving for his own followers the highest moral ground, still he recognized that not all women were lucky enough to have Free Lovers for their sex partners.[39]

> Since Comstockism makes male will, passion and power absolute to *impose* conception, I stand with women to resent it. The man who would legislate to choke a woman's vagina with semen, who would force a woman to retain his seed, bear children when her own reason and conscience oppose it, would waylay her, seize her by the throat and rape her person.[40]

Angela Heywood enthusiastically pushed this new political line:

> Is it "proper," "polite," for men, to go to Washington to say, by penal law, fines and imprisonment, whether woman may continue her natural right to wash, rinse, or wipe her own vaginal body opening—as well legislate when she may blow her nose, dry her eyes, or nurse her babe. . . . Whatever she may have been pleased to receive, from man's own, is his gift and her property. Women do not like rape, and have a right to resist its results.[41]

Her outspokenness—vulgarity in the ears of most of her contemporaries—came from a substantive, not merely a stylistic, sexual radicalism. Not even the heavy taboos and revulsion against abortion stopped her: "To cut a child up in woman, procure abortion, is a most fearful, tragic deed; but *even that* does not call for man's arbitrary jurisdiction over woman's womb."[42]

It is unclear whether Heywood, in this passage, was actually arguing for legalized abortion; if she was, she was alone among all nineteenth-century sexual reformers in saying it. Other feminists and Free Lovers condemned abortion and argued that the necessity of stopping its widespread practice was a key reason for instituting voluntary motherhood by other means. The difference on the abortion question between sexual radicals and sexual conservatives was in their analysis of its causes and remedies. While doctors and preachers were sermonizing on the sinfulness of women who obtained abortions,[43] the radicals pronounced abortion itself an undeserved punishment, and a woman who had one a helpless victim. Woodhull and Claflin wrote about Madame Restell's notorious abortion "factory" in New York City without moralism, arguing that only voluntary conception would put it out of business.[44] Elizabeth Cady Stanton also sympathized with women who had abortions, and used the abortion problem as an example of women's victimization by laws made without their consent.[45]

Despite stylistic differences, which stemmed from differences in goals, nineteenth-century American Free Lovers and women's rights advocates shared the same basic attitudes toward birth control: they opposed contraception and abortion but endorsed voluntary motherhood achieved through periodic abstinence; they believed that women should always have the right to decide when to bear a child; and they believed that women and men both had natural sex drives and that it was not wrong to indulge those drives without the intention of conceiving children. The two groups also shared the same appraisal of the social and political significance of birth control. Most of them were favorably inclined toward neo-Malthusian reasoning (at least until the 1890s, when the prevailing concern shifted to the problem of underpopulation rather than overpopulation).[46] They were also interested, increasingly, in controlling conception for eugenic purposes.[47] They were hostile to the hypocrisy of the sexual double standard and, beyond that, shared a general sense that men had become oversexed and that sex had been transformed into something disagreeably violent.

But above all their commitment to voluntary motherhood expressed their larger commitment to women's rights. Elizabeth Cady Stanton thought voluntary motherhood so central that on her lecture tours in 1871 she held separate afternoon meetings for *women only* (a completely unfamiliar practice at the time) and talked about "the gospel of fewer children & a healthy, happy maternity."[48] "What radical thoughts I then and there put into their heads & as they feel untrammelled, these thoughts are permanently lodged there! That is all I ask."[49] Only Ezra Heywood had gone so far as to defend a particular contraceptive device—the syringe. But the principle of woman's rights to choose the number of children she would bear and when was accepted in the most conservative sections of the women's rights movement. At the First Congress of the Association for the Advancement of Women in 1873, a whole session was devoted to the theme "Enlightened Motherhood," which had voluntary motherhood as part of its meaning.[50]

The general conviction of the feminist community that women had a right to choose when to conceive a child was so strong by the end of the nineteenth century that it seems odd that they were unable to overcome their scruples against artificial contraception. The basis for the reluctance lies in their awareness that a consequence of effective contraception would be the separation of sexuality from reproduction. A state of things that permitted sexual intercourse to take place normally, even frequently, without the risk of pregnancy inevitably seemed to nineteenth-century middle-class women an attack on the family, as they understood the family. In the mid-Victorian sexual system, men normally conducted their sexual philandering with prostitutes; accordingly, prostitution, far from being a threat to the family system, was a part of it and an important support of it. This was the common view of the time, paralleled by belief that prostitutes knew of effective birth control techniques. This seemed only fitting, for contraception in the 1870s was associated with sexual immorality. It did not seem, even to the most sexually liberal, that contraception could be legitimized to any extent, even for the purposes of family planning for married couples, without licensing extramarital sex. The fact that contraception was not morally acceptable to respectable women was, from a woman's point of view, a guarantee that those women would not be a threat to her marriage.

The fact that sexual intercourse often leads to conception was also a guarantee that men would marry in the first place. In the nineteenth century women needed marriage far more than men. Lacking economic independence, women needed husbands to support them, or at least to free them from a usually more humiliating economic dependence on fathers. Especially in the cities, where women were often isolated from communities, deprived of the economic and psychological support of networks of relatives, friends, and neighbors, the prospect of dissolving the cement of nuclear families was frightening. In many cases children, the prospect of children, provided that cement. Man's responsibilities for children were an important pressure for marital stability. Women, especially middle-class women, were also dependent on their children to provide them with meaningful work. The belief that motherhood was a woman's fulfillment had a material basis: parenthood was often the only creative and challenging activity in a woman's life, a key part of her self-esteem.

Legal, efficient birth control would have increased men's freedom to indulge in extramarital sex without greatly increasing women's freedom to do so. The pressures enforcing chastity and marital fidelity on middle-class women were not fear of illegitimate conception but a powerful combination of economic, social, and psychological factors, including economic dependence, fear of rejection by husband and social support networks, internalized taboos, and, hardly the least important, a socially conditioned lack of interest in sex that may have approached functional frigidity. The double standard of the Victorian sexual and family system, which had made men's sexual freedom irresponsible and oppressive to women, left most feminists convinced that increasing, rather than releasing, the taboos against extramarital sex was in their interest, and they threw their support behind social purity campaigns.

In short, we must forget the twentieth-century association of birth control with a trend toward sexual freedom. The voluntary motherhood propaganda of the 1870s was associated with a push toward a more restrictive, or at least a more rigidly enforced, sexual morality. Achieving voluntary motherhood by a method that would have encouraged sexual license was absolutely contrary to the felt interests of the very group that formed the main social basis for the cause—middle-class women. Separating these women from the early twentieth-century feminists, with their interests in sexual freedom, were nearly four decades of significant social and economic changes and a general weakening of the ideology of the Lady. The ideal of the Free Lovers—responsible, open sexual encounters between equal partners— was impossible in the 1870s because men and women were not equal. A man was a man whether faithful to his wife or not. But women's sexual activities divided them into two categories—wife or prostitute. These categories were not mere ideas but were enforced in reality by severe social and economic sanctions. The fact that so many, indeed most, Free Lovers in practice led faithful, monogamous, legally married lives is not insignificant in this regard. It suggests that they understood that Free Love was an ideal not to be realized at that time.

As voluntary motherhood was an ideology intended to encourage sexual purity, so it was also a pro-motherhood ideology. Far from debunking motherhood, the voluntary motherhood advocates consistently continued the traditional Victorian mystification and sentimentalization of the mother. It is true that at the end of the nineteenth century an increasing number of feminists and elite women— that is, still a relatively small group—were choosing not to marry or become mothers. That was primarily because of their increasing interest in professional work, and the difficulty of doing such work as a wife and mother, given the normal uncooperativeness of husbands and the lack of social provisions for child care. Voluntary motherhood advocates shared the general belief that mothers of young children ought not to work outside their homes but should make mothering their full-time occupation. Suffragists argued both for making professions open to women and for ennobling the task of mothering; they argued for increased rights and opportunities for women *because* they were mothers.

The Free Lovers were equally pro-motherhood; they wanted only to separate motherhood from legal marriage.[51] They devised pro-motherhood arguments to bolster their case against marriage. Mismated couples, held together by marriage laws, made bad parents and produced inferior offspring, Free Lovers said.[52] In 1870 *Woodhull & Claflin's Weekly* editorialized, "Our marital system is the greatest obstacle to the regeneration of the race."[53]

This concern with eugenics was characteristic of nearly all feminists of the late nineteenth century. At the time, eugenics was seen mainly as an implication of evolutionary theory and was picked up by many social reformers to buttress their arguments that improvement of the human condition was possible. Eugenics had not yet become a movement in itself. Feminists used eugenics arguments as if they instinctively felt that arguments based solely on women's rights had not enough power to conquer conservative and religious scruples about reproduction. So they combined eugenics and feminism to produce evocative, romantic visions of perfect motherhood. "Where boundless love prevails . . ." *Woodhull & Claflin's Weekly* wrote, "the mother who produces an inferior child will be dishonored and unhappy . . . and she who produces superior children will feel proportionately pleased. When woman attains this position, she will consider superior offspring a necessity and be apt to procreate only with superior men."[54] Free Lovers and suffragists alike used the cult of motherhood to argue for making motherhood voluntary. Involuntary motherhood, wrote Harriot Stanton Blatch, daughter of Elizabeth Cady Stanton and a prominent suffragist, is a prostitution of the maternal instinct.[55] Free Lover Rachel Campbell cried out that motherhood was being "ground to dust under the misrule of masculine ignorance and superstition."[56]

Not only was motherhood considered an exalted, sacred profession, and a profession exclusively woman's responsibility, but for a woman to avoid it was to choose a distinctly less noble path. In arguing for the enlargement of woman's sphere, feminists envisaged combining motherhood with other activities, not rejecting motherhood. Victoria Woodhull and Tennessee Claflin wrote:

> Tis true that the special and distinctive feature of woman is that of bearing children, and that upon the exercise of her function in this regard the perpetuity of race depends. It is also true that those who pass through life failing in this special feature of their mission cannot be said to have lived to the best purposes of woman's life. But while maternity should always be considered the most holy of all the functions woman is capable of, it should not be lost sight of in devotion to this, that there are as various spheres of usefulness outside of this for woman as there are for man outside of the marriage relation.[57]

Birth control was not intended to open the possibility of childlessness but merely to give women leverage to win more recognition and dignity. Dora Forster, a Free Lover, saw in the fears of underpopulation a weapon of blackmail for women:

I hope the scarcity of children will go on until maternity is honored at least as much as the trials and hardships of soldiers campaigning in wartime. It will then be worth while to supply the nation with a sufficiency of children . . . every civilized nation, having lost the power to enslave woman as mother, will be compelled to recognize her voluntary exercise of that function as by far the most important service of any class of citizens.[58]

"Oh, women of the world, arise in your strength and demand that all which stands in the path of true motherhood shall be removed from your path," wrote Lois Waisbrooker, a Free Love novelist and moral reformer.[59] Helen Gardener based a plea for women's education entirely on the argument that society needed educated mothers to produce able sons (not children, sons).

Harvard and Yale, not to mention Columbia, may continue to put a protective tariff on the brains of young men: but so long as they must get those brains from the proscribed sex, just so long will male brains remain an "infant industry" and continue to need this protection. Stupid mothers never did and stupid mothers never will, furnish this world with brilliant sons.[60]

Clinging to the cult of motherhood was part of a broader conservatism shared by Free Lovers and suffragists—acceptance of traditional sex roles. Even the Free Lovers rejected only one factor—legal marriage—of the many that defined woman's place in the family. They did not challenge conventional conceptions of woman's passivity and limited sphere of concern.[61] In their struggles for equality the women's rights advocates never suggested that men should share responsibility for child raising, housekeeping, nursing, cooking. When Victoria Woodhull in the 1870s and Charlotte Perkins Gilman in the early 1900s suggested socialized child care, they assumed that only women would do the work.[62] Most feminists wanted economic independence for women, but most, too, were reluctant to recommend achieving this by turning women loose and helpless into the economic world to compete with men.[63] This attitude was conditioned by an attitude hostile to the egoistic spirit of capitalism; but the attitude was not transformed into a political position and usually appeared as a description of women's weakness, rather than an attack on the system. Failing to distinguish, or even to indicate awareness of a possible distinction between, women's conditioned passivity and their equally conditioned distaste for competition and open aggression, these feminists also followed the standard Victorian rationalization of sex roles, the idea that women were morally superior. Thus the timidity and self-effacement that were the marks of women's powerlessness were made into innate virtues. Angela Heywood, for example, praised women's greater ability for self-control and, in an attribution no doubt intended to jar and titillate the reader, branded men inferior on account of their lack of sexual temperance.[64] Men's refusal to accept women as human beings she identified, similarly, as a mark of men's incapacity: "Man has not yet achieved himself to realize and meet a PERSON in woman."[65] In idealistic, abstract terms, no doubt such male behavior is an incapacity. Yet that conceit failed to remark on the power and privilege over women that the supposed "incapacity" gave men.

This omission is characteristic of the cult of motherhood. Indeed, what made it a cult was its one-sided failure to recognize the privileges men received from women's exclusive responsibility for parenthood. The "motherhood" of the feminists' writings was not merely the biological process of gestation and birth but a package of social, economic, and cultural functions. Although many of the nineteenth-century feminists had done substantial analysis of the historical and anthropological origins of woman's social role, they nevertheless agreed with the biological determinist point of view that women's parental capacities had become implanted at the level of instinct, the famous "maternal instinct." That concept rested on the assumption that the qualities that parenthood requires—capacities for tenderness, self-control and patience, tolerance for tedium and detail, emotional supportiveness, dependability and warmth—were not only instinctive but sex linked. The concept of the maternal instinct thus also involved a definition of the normal instinctual structure of the male that excluded these capacities, or included them only to an inferior degree; it also carried the implication that women who did not exercise these capacities, presumably through motherhood, remained unfulfilled, untrue to their destinies.

Belief in the maternal instinct reinforced the belief in the necessary spiritual connection for women between sex and reproduction and limited the development of birth control ideas. But the limits were set by the entire social context of women's lives, not by the intellectual timidity of their ideas. For women's "control over their own bodies" to lead to a rejection of motherhood as the *primary* vocation and measure of social worth required the existence of alternative vocations and sources of worthiness. The women's rights advocates of the 1870s and 1880s were fighting for those other opportunities, but a significant change had come only to a few privileged women, and most women faced essentially the same options that had existed fifty years earlier. Thus voluntary motherhood in this period remained almost exclusively a tool for women to strengthen their positions within conventional marriages and families, not to reject them.

NOTES

1. The word "feminist" must be underscored. Since the early nineteenth century, there had been developing a body of population control writings which recommended the use of birth control techniques to curb nationwide or worldwide populations; usually called neo-Malthusians, these writers were not concerned with the control of births as a means by which women could gain control over their own lives, except, very occasionally, as an auxiliary argument. And of course birth control practices date back to the most ancient societies on record.

2. There is no space here to compensate for the general lack of information about the Free Lovers. There is a fuller discussion of them in my *Woman's Body, Woman's Right: A Social History of Birth Control* (New York: Viking Penguin, 1976). Some of the major Free Love writings include R. D. Chapman, *Freelove: A Law of Nature* (New York: author, 1881); Tennessee Claflin, *The Ethics of Sexual Equality* (New York: Woodhull & Claflin, 1873); Tennessee Claflin, *Virtue, What It Is and What It Isn't; Seduction, What It Is and What It Is Not* (New York: Woodhull & Claflin, 1872); Ezra Heywood, *Cupid's Yokes; or, The Binding Force of Conjugal Life* (Princeton, Mass.: Cooperative Publishing Co., [1876?]); Ezra Heywood, *Uncivil Liberty: An Essay to Show the Injustice and Impolicy of Ruling Woman without Her Consent* (Princeton, Mass.: Cooperative Publishing Co., 1872); C. L. James, *The Future Relation of the Sexes* (St. Louis: author, 1872); Juliet Severance, *Marriage* (Chicago: M. Harman, 1901); Victoria Claflin Woodhull, *The Scare-Crows of Sexual Slavery* (New York: Woodhull & Claflin, 1874); Woodhull, *A Speech on the Principles of Social Freedom* (New York: Woodhull & Claflin, 1872); Woodhull, *Tried as by Fire; or, The True and the False Socially* (New York: Woodhull & Claflin, 1874).

3. Heywood, *Cupid's Yokes,* 20; Claflin, *The Ethics of Sexual Equality,* 9–10: *Woodhull & Claflin's Weekly,* 1, no. 6 (1870): 5.

4. "Contraception" will be used to refer to artificial devices used to prohibit conception during intercourse, while "birth control" will be used to mean anything, including abstinence, which limits pregnancy.

5. Heywood, *Cupid's Yokes,* 17–18.

6. Letter to her daughter Alice, 1874, in the Isabella Beecher Hooker Collection, Beecher Stowe Manuscripts, Stowe-Day Library, Hartford, Conn. This reference was brought to my attention by Ellen Dubois of SUNY-Buffalo.

7. Alice B. Stockham, M.D., *Karezza: Ethics of Marriage* (Chicago: Alice B. Stockham & Co., 1898), 84, 91–92.

8. Theodore Stanton and Harriot Stanton Blatch, eds., *Elizabeth Cady Stanton as Revealed in Her Letters, Diary and Reminiscences* (New York: Harper & Bros., 1922), 2:210 (Diary, Sept. 6, 1883).

9. Ben Barker-Benfield, "The Spermatic Economy: A Nineteen Century View of Sexuality," *Feminist Studies* 1, no. 1 (Summer 1972): 53.

10. J. J. Rousseau, *Emile* (New York: Columbia University Teachers College, 1967), 132. Rousseau was, after all, a chief author of the Victorian revision of the image of woman.

11. Dora Forster, *Sex Radicalism as Seen by an Emancipated Woman of the New Time* (Chicago: M. Harman, 1905), 40.

12. Norman E. Himes, *Medical History of Contraception* (New York: Gamut Press, 1963).

13. Heywood, *Cupid's Yokes,* 19–20, 16.

14. Ibid., 19–20; *Woodhull & Claflin's Weekly* 1, no. 18 (September 10, 1870): 5.

15. Heywood, *Cupid's Yokes,* 14–15.

16. Stockham, *Karezza,* 82–83, 53.

17. See, for example, *Free Enquirer,* ed. Robert Owen and Frances Wright, May 22, 1830, 235–36.

18. Stockham, *Karezza,* 86.

19. Heywood, *Cupid's Yokes,* 19.

20. Charlotte Perkins Gilman, *Women and Economics* (New York: Harper Torchbooks, 1966), 38–39, 43–44, 42, 47–48, 209.

21. In England, for example, it was not until 1891 that the courts first held against a man who forcibly kidnaped and imprisoned his wife when she left him.

22. Ezra Heywood, *Free Speech: Report of Ezra H. Heywood's Defense before the United States Court, in Boston, April 10, 11, and 12, 1883* (Princeton, Mass.: Cooperative Publishing Co., n.d.), 16.

23. Quoted in Nelson Manfred Blake, *The Road to Reno: A History of Divorce in the United States* (New York: Macmillan, 1962), 108, from the *New York Tribune,* May 12, 1871, and July 20, 1871.

24. Letter of August 29, 1869, in Hooker Collection, Beecher Stowe Manuscripts. This reference was brought to my attention by Ellen Dubois of SUNY-Buffalo.

25. Isabella Beecher Hooker, *Womanhood: Its Sanctities and Fidelities* (Boston: Lee and Shepard, 1873), 26.

26. Elizabeth Cady Stanton Manuscripts, no. 11, Library of Congress, undated. This reference was brought to my attention by Ellen Dubois of SUNY-Buffalo.

27. See, for example, *Lucifer, The Light-Bearer* [ed. Moses Harman (Valley Falls, Kans., 1894–1907)] 18, no. 6 (October 1889): 3.

28. Woodhull, *The Scare-Crows,* 21. Her mention of the YMCA is a reference to the fact that Anthony Comstock, author and chief enforcer for the U.S. Post Office of the antiobscenity laws, had begun his career in the YMCA.

29. *The Word* (Princeton, Mass.) 20, no. 9 (March 1893): 2–3, emphasis in original.

30. See, for example, the National Purity Congress of 1895, sponsored by the American Purity Alliance.

31. *Lucifer,* April 26, 1890, 1–2.

32. N.a., *Next Revolution; or, Women's Emancipation from Sex Slavery* (Valley Falls, Kans.: Lucifer Publishing Co., 1890), 49.

33. Ibid., 8–9.

34. Linda Gordon et al., "Sexism in American Historical Writing," *Women's Studies* 1, no. 1 (Fall 1972).

35. *Lucifer* 15, no. 2 (September 1886): 3.

36. *The Word,* 1892–93, 20.

37. [Elmina Slenker], *Lucifer,* May 23, 1907; *Cyclopedia of American Biography,* 8:488.

38. See, for example, *Lucifer* 18, no. 8 (December 1889): 3; 18, no. 6 (October 1889): 3.

39. Heywood, *Free Speech,* 17, 16.

40. Ibid., 3–6. "Comstockism" is also a reference to Anthony Comstock. Noting the irony that the syringe was called by Comstock's name, Heywood continued: "To name a really good

thing 'Comstock' has a sly, sinister, wily look, indicating vicious purpose: in deference to its N.Y. venders, who gave that name, the Publishers of *The Word* inserted an advertisement . . . which will hereafter appear as 'the Vaginal Syringe'; for its intelligent, humane and worthy mission should no longer be libelled by forced association with the pious scamp who thinks Congress gives him legal right of way to and control over every American Woman's Womb." At this trial, Heywood's second, he was acquitted. At his first trial, in 1877, he had been convicted and sentenced to two years, of which he served six months; at his third, in 1890, he was sentenced to and served two years at hard labor, an ordeal that probably caused his death a year later.

41. *The Word* 10, no. 9 (March 1893): 2–3.

42. Ibid.

43. See, for example, Horatio Robinson Storer, M.D., *Why Not? A Book for Every Woman* (Boston: Lee and Shepard, 1868). Note that this was the prize essay in a contest run by the AMA in 1865 for the best antiabortion tract.

44. Claflin, *Ethics;* Emanie Sachs, *The Terrible Siren, Victoria Woodhull, 1838–1927* (New York: Harper & Bros., 1928), 139.

45. Elizabeth Cady Stanton, Susan B. Anthony, and Matilda J. Gage, eds., vol. 1 of *History of Woman Suffrage,* 597–98.

46. Heywood, *Cupid's Yokes,* 20; see also *American Journal of Eugenics* (ed. M. Harman) 1, no. 2 (September 1907); *Lucifer,* February 15, 1906; June 7, 1906; March 28, 1907; and May 11, 1905.

47. I deal with early feminists' ideas concerning eugenics in my book *Woman's Body, Women's Rights.*

48. Elizabeth Cady Stanton to Martha Wright, June 19, 1871, Stanton Manuscripts. This reference was brought to my attention by Ellen Dubois of SUNY-Buffalo. See also Stanton, *Eighty Years and More: Reminiscences, 1815–1897* (New York: Schocken, 1971), 262, 297.

49. Stanton and Blatch, *Stanton as Revealed in Her Letters,* 132–33.

50. *Papers and Letters,* Association for the Advancement of Women, 1873. The AAW was a conservative group formed in opposition to the Stanton-Anthony tendency. Nevertheless, Chandler, a frequent contributor to Free Love journals, spoke here against undesired maternity and the identification of woman with her maternal function.

51. *Woodhull and Claflin's Weekly* 1, no. 20 (October 1, 1870): 10.

52. Woodhull, *Tried As by Fire,* 37: Lillian Harman, *The Regeneration of Society,* a speech before the Manhattan Liberal Club, March 31, 1898 (Chicago: Light Bearer Library, 1900).

53. *Woodhull & Claflin's Weekly* 1, no. 20 (October 1, 1870): 10.

54. Ibid.

55. Harriot Stanton Blatch, "Voluntary Motherhood," in *Transactions of the National Council of Women of the United States, Assembled in Washington, D.C., February 22 to 25, 1891,* ed. Rachel Foster Avery (Philadelphia: J. B. Lippincott, 1891), 280.

56. Rachel Campbell, *The Prodigal Daughter; or, The Price of Virtue* (Grass Valley, Calif., 1885), 3. An essay read to the New England Free Love League, 1881.

57. *Woodhull & Claflin's Weekly* 1, no. 14 (August 13, 1870): 4.

58. In addition to the biography by Sachs mentioned above, see also Johanna Johnston, *Mrs. Satan* (New York: G. P. Putnam's Sons, 1967); and M. M. Marberry, *Vicky: A Biography of Victoria C. Woodhull* (New York: Funk & Wagnalls, 1967).

59. From an advertisement for her novel *Perfect Motherhood: or, Mabel Raymond's Resolve* (New York: Murray Hill, 1890), in the *Next Revolution*.

60. Helen Hamilton Gardner, *Pulpit, Pew and Cradle* (New York: Truth Seeker Library, 1891), 22.

61. Even the most outspoken of the Free Lovers had conventional, role-differentiated images of sexual relations. Here is Angela Heywood, for example: "Men must not emasculate themselves for the sake of 'virtue,' they must, they will, recognize manliness and the life element of manliness as the fountain source of good manners. Women and girls demand strong, well-bred, generative, vitalizing sex ability. Potency, virility, is the grand basic principle of man, and it holds him clean, sweet and elegant, to the delicacy of his counterpart." From *The Word* 14, no. 2 (June 1885): 3.

62. Woodhull, *The Scare-Crows;* Charlotte Perkins Gilman, *Concerning Children* (Boston: Small, Maynard, 1900).

63. See, for example, Blatch, "Voluntary Motherhood," 283–84.

64. *The Word* 20, no. 8 (February 1895): 3.

65. Ibid.

21.

"When the Birds Have Flown the Nest, the Mother-Work May Still Go On"

Sentimental Maternalism and the National Congress of Mothers

MOLLY LADD-TAYLOR

By 1914, so many middle-class mothers had taken up social service work that the novelist Dorothy Canfield Fisher concluded that all the publicity given to child care had caused "most matrons to turn naturally to some phase of similar activity in the community." According to Fisher, middle-aged women were making "themselves more useful to the world than ever before by applying to various forms of social uplift the experience, the poise, the knowledge of life which they have acquired in the years of their mothering."[1] Moved by the seemingly universal "pang of motherhood"—and certain that they had a special role to play in the community by virtue of being mothers—middle- and upper-class women joined mothers' clubs and parent-teacher associations in the thousands. Working on the local level and in the National Mothers' Congress, they educated themselves about the science of child development, distributed child-rearing information to the poor, and got involved in political matters relating to child welfare. Their maternalism was a bridge between mothers and experts, grassroots activists and political reformers, and between traditional and modern concepts of child care.

Motherhood was a central organizing principle of Progressive Era politics. Although it was also a unifying theme for a wide array of voluntary associations in the nineteenth century, between 1890 and 1920 it became an overtly political concern, inextricably tied to state building and public policy.[2] Virtually every female activist used motherhood rhetoric, and virtually every male politician appealed to motherhood. My book *Mother-Work: Women, Child Welfare, and the State, 1890–1930* examines the ideology of motherhood held by three groups of activists: sentimental maternalists of the National Congress of Mothers, progressive maternalists at the Children's Bureau, and feminists. All three groups built on the organizing power of motherhood during the Progressive Era, using motherhood rhetoric both to improve conditions for children and to advance women's status. All three also backed away from motherhood rhetoric in the 1920s, when tensions over women's role in public life and the state's responsibility for social welfare provoked a backlash against feminism and reform, and a bitter split among women activists. Despite, or perhaps because of, maternalist welfare successes during the 1910s, motherhood rhetoric stopped being a viable organizing tool for reform-minded women activists after 1925. Progressive appeals to motherhood were for the most part politically ineffective, and the language of motherhood increasingly became the preserve of conservative politicians and organizers.[3]

This chapter focuses on the National Congress of Mothers, which gave a unified voice to the thousands of white women who participated in mothers' clubs and parent-teacher associations between 1890 and 1930. Although it has generally been ignored by historians, the National Congress of Mothers played a critical role in the popularization of parent education and child psychology and in the expansion of American public education, health, and welfare services—especially mothers' pensions—in the early twentieth century.[4] By 1915 the National Congress of Mothers and Parent-Teacher Associations (the name was changed in 1908) had a paid membership of 60,000, a monthly journal called the *Child-Welfare Magazine,* and ties with mothers' organizations throughout the world. Five years later membership had reached 190,000, and by 1930 the National Congress of Parents and Teachers boasted almost 1.5 million members.[5] Each mothers' club or PTA paid dues to the National Congress and received the *Child-Welfare Magazine,* but the activities of local chapters varied widely. Some clubs, especially in the early days, were primarily discussion groups on child study; others were vehicles for socializing and entertainment. Some PTAs focused on the schools, while others were involved in a wide range of community activities. As the national organization grew, it became increasingly oriented to the schools.

The diversity in membership, the autonomy of local groups, and the fact that few clubs appear to have left records make the activities of the PTA difficult to document, but a tentative portrait of the organization can be drawn from published materials and local reports included in the *Child-Welfare Magazine* during the 1900s and 1910s. Like nineteenth-century clubs and charities, the Mothers' Congress distributed alms and was steeped in the ideology of friendly visiting; unlike them, it also called on federal and state governments to protect child health and welfare. Local clubs raised money for school supplies, such as playground equip-ment, and programs, such as kindergartens and hot lunches for children, until school districts began to provide funds themselves. Club mothers helped establish juvenile courts and baby clinics; they lobbied for state mothers' pensions laws, fed-eral health care legislation, financial aid to the schools, and censorship of "im-moral" books and films. In the 1920s, state and local PTAs helped the federal Children's Bureau administer the Sheppard-Towner Act. Yet despite working closely with government leaders to develop child welfare policies, PTA leaders in-sisted that woman's place was in the home and refused to endorse controversial is-sues such as woman suffrage.[6]

Most members of the National Congress of Mothers agreed on the dual aim of maternalism: to teach mothers how to care properly for their own children and to awaken their maternal responsibility to improve social conditions affecting all children. "The young mothers have all they can do within the home," wrote PTA president Hannah Schoff, "but when the birds have flown from the nest, the mother-work may still go on, reaching out to better conditions for other children." Underscoring both the private and public responsibilities of motherhood, Schoff insisted that "parents can never do their full duty for their own children . . . until they make it their business to see that all children have proper treatment and proper protection."[7] The two sides of maternalism are reflected in the aims of the National Congress: "To carry the mother-love and mother-thought into all that concerns or touches childhood in home, school, church or state; to raise the standards of home life; to develop wiser, better-trained parenthood; to bring into closer relation the home and the school."[8]

Sentimental maternalists were not only interested in child welfare; they also wanted to advance women's status. Yet while feminists and progressive women re-formers embraced modernity and women's expanding social roles, the leaders of the National Congress of Mothers held fast to the late nineteenth-century ideol-ogy of scientific motherhood. To the extent that they wanted to professionalize motherhood by bringing science and education to child rearing, it was at least ini-tially because they wanted women to be more content to stay at home in their tra-ditional roles. "It is because most women have not had the knowledge and training which would enable them to evolve the beautiful possibilities of home life that they have in many instances found that sphere narrow and monotonous," explained the organization's founder Alice Birney.[9]

The contradictions inherent in maternalism—that is, in idealizing women's place in the home while asserting their influence in politics and government—are illuminated in the history of the National Congress of Mothers. Internal politics and changing times brought a significant shift in the organization's public image.

Initially a model of respectability, opposed to woman suffrage and to women's professional involvement in social welfare administration (President Hannah Schoff even opposed the creation of the Children's Bureau in 1912), the National Congress of Mothers worked closely with progressive maternalists in the late 1910s. In the early 1920s, the PTA was listed as part of the international socialist conspiracy on the infamous Spider Web Chart, an effective piece of right-wing propaganda alleging a communist plot to take over the United States.[10] The resulting dissension within the PTA led the organization to withdraw from political controversy and to focus instead on parent education. By the end of the decade, the right-wing backlash to advances in social welfare policy and to women's visibility in public life had brought about the depoliticization of motherhood—and of the national PTA.

The National Congress of Mothers

At the end of the nineteenth century, many women exhibited a great deal of interest in an organization of mothers. When Alice Birney called the first meeting of the National Congress of Mothers in 1897, she expected seventy-five women to attend. Instead, over two thousand women and a handful of men poured into the meeting hall. They listened to lectures by G. Stanley Hall and the moral crusader Anthony Comstock and heard papers on maternal responsibility for home life, heredity, and character building. At the end of the meeting, they passed a series of resolutions on moral reform, child welfare, and parent education, which reflected the wide scope of their concerns. A White House reception, the wide press coverage, and the enthusiasm of the women who attended the first gathering attest to the broad interest in both the private and public aspects of mother-work.[11]

From its inception, the Mothers' Congress seemed as interested in preserving what it thought to be the traditional home as in distributing scientific information on child rearing to its members. Congress leaders idealized motherhood, took for granted the biological differences between men and women, and did not question men's authority in the family. According to Birney, mothers had been "divinely appointed to be the caretaker of the child," and they needed a "system of mutual aid" to help them meet this awesome responsibility. Membership in the National Congress of Mothers was not limited to biological mothers, however; it was also open to men and unmarried women, who "through their works have shown themselves possessed of the maternal instinct." Indeed, at one point the advisory council of the Mothers' Congress was made up entirely of men. The "love of childhood is a common tie, which should unite us in holiest purpose," Birney explained.[12]

The ideology of the Mothers' Congress was shaped to a great extent by the child study movement and its founder, the psychologist G. Stanley Hall. Hall was an educational reformer who criticized traditional rote learning as unnatural and insisted that children's health would improve if educational programs were shaped according to their "natural" needs. "The guardians of the young should strive first of all to stay out of nature's way," he proclaimed. Applying Darwin's theory of evolution to psychological development in his well-known theory of recapitulation, Hall maintained that every individual passed through successive developmental stages that retraced the evolution of the human race. Children's physical and mental well-being thus depended on their being treated differently at each developmental stage. Hall believed that preschool children should be allowed to express their instinctive (animal) desire for freedom and play, while older children in the "savage" stage needed external controls and habit training. Not until a young white man entered university did the psychologist think reason and intellectual learning should take precedence over physical health.[13]

Hall's evolutionary theory informed his understanding of woman's social role. Convinced that men and women had separate social functions because of their biological differences, he argued that (Anglo-American) women were by their very nature more intuitive and emotional than men and thus better suited to be moral teachers. The "body and soul" of womanhood was "more generic . . . nearer the child and shares more of its divinity than does the far more highly specialized and narrowed organism of the man," he told the National Congress of Mothers in 1905. Women's education should therefore focus not on intellectual development but on training for motherhood. "I do not know . . . whether the Holy Mother . . . knew how to read, but the whole world has united in reverence of her because she illustrated the complete glory of motherhood."[14]

Hall's idealized view of maternity, his racial concept of child development, and his scientific authority made him popular with the conservative leaders of the Mothers' Congress, who made him a featured speaker at their first convention. Elite club mothers saw in Hall's child study movement a way to dignify Anglo-American motherhood; as one female follower explained approvingly, child study would not "revolutionize all our educational methods . . . [but] confirm some good old-fashioned ways of training." Moreover, the imprecise methodology of the "science" of child study gave women a prominent, if subordinate, place in the movement. Hall declared that child study "should be preeminently the woman's science," and he encouraged mothers to make their own contributions to knowledge by studying their children. He got women to turn their homes into laboratories for child study and to keep "life books" recording the size, weight, and character development of their children. Even after 1900, when the theory of recapitulation fell into disfavor among psychologists, sentimental maternalists held on to child study ideas.[15]

Perhaps to defend the new—and unprecedented—mothers' organization from the criticism of conservatives, Alice Birney declared that all women on the board of the Mothers' Congress were "emphatically women of the home." In reality, however, their lives often contrasted with the domestic image they were trying to convey. Although Birney insisted that she spent most of her time at home with her children, "where all mothers belong unless they are so situated as to be compelled to earn a livelihood," she herself did not stay at home. Born in 1858 in Georgia and educated for one year at Mount Holyoke, Alice McLellan hoped for a career in medicine. She married in 1879 but was soon widowed and left with a small daughter to support, so she earned money selling advertisements in New York City. In 1892, she married the prominent Washington attorney Theodore Weld Birney, by whom she had two daughters. Birney came from a strong free-soil background and apparently encouraged his wife to establish a mothers' organization. When he died shortly after the National Congress of Mothers was founded, Alice Birney devoted herself to the organization. Her mother helped care for her children.[16]

Hannah Kent Schoff, who took over the presidency after poor health forced Birney to resign in 1902, also built an impressive career during her administration, which lasted until 1920. Despite her stated allegiance to traditional feminine values, Schoff operated successfully in the predominantly male political world. The wife of a prominent Philadelphia businessman and mother of seven, she fashioned the Mothers' Congress into an organization influential in local and national affairs. As president of the Philadelphia Juvenile Court and Probation Association, she drafted and secured the passage of bills setting up juvenile courts and a probation system for youth offenders in several states. Schoff persuaded President Theodore Roosevelt to endorse the juvenile court system and was the first woman invited to speak before the Canadian Parliament on the subject. She served as a consultant to the U.S. Bureau of Education, worked with the State Department to organize an International Conference on Child Welfare in 1908, and in 1910 was appointed U.S. delegate to the International Congress for Home Education in Brussels.[17]

Indeed, none of the early leaders of the Congress could be called typical mothers. Phoebe Hearst, the wife of the California senator and mother of publisher William Randolph Hearst, was the financial backer of the organization. The officers included the wives of the vice-president, the postmaster general, and three Cabinet members, the sister of the secretary of agriculture, and two daughters of the secretary of the navy. Theodore Roosevelt sat on the Advisory Council, and Frances Cleveland, wife of President Grover Cleveland, took an intense interest in the organization. Others well known in reform circles also participated in the Mothers'

Congress. The African American writer and activist Frances Ellen Watkins Harper and the suffragist freethinker Helen Gardener spoke at the first meeting. Among the delegates to the first Congress were Mrs. Luther Gulick, wife of the playground reformer, and Mrs. Max West, who sixteen years later would write the Children's Bureau publications on child care.[18]

Given their backgrounds, it is not surprising that the leaders of the Mothers' Congress believed that women had influence and did not need to vote. Although some club mothers were suffragists, and Congress leaders requested and received letters of support from Susan B. Anthony and Elizabeth Cady Stanton, they tried to suppress discussion of woman suffrage "lest inharmony arise."[19] In general, the National Congress of Mothers, like conservative women's groups today, was primarily concerned with asserting women's proper place in the home. Schoff, for example, believed that woman's influence was and should be based on motherhood. She thought that the "new woman" was more interested in self-fulfillment than the well-being of her children and vigorously opposed what she considered the "warped" values of wives who preferred "self-ownership," financial independence, and careers outside the home to child rearing. Theodore Roosevelt, an ardent supporter of the National Congress of Mothers, commended club mothers for their superiority to the "new woman" who sought a life outside of childbearing. A good mother was "sacred," he told them, but the woman who "shirks her duty, as wife and mother, earns the right to our contempt."[20]

As Roosevelt's attack on the new woman suggests, the maternalism of the Mothers' Congress derived much of its appeal from the gender and race apprehensions of the Anglo-American elite. At a time when immigration, the uncertain status of African Americans, and white women's increasing visibility in the public sphere generated cultural anxieties about "race suicide" and the decline of the family, Anglo-American club mothers clung to the traditions and social structure that appeared to provide them with dignity, authority, and security. They believed their status enhanced by rhetoric about maternal responsibility for racial progress and took advantage of the fear of race suicide by using eugenic arguments to insist that women should be treated with respect. As the suffragist freethinker Helen Gardener told delegates at the 1897 convention, "The race which is born of mothers who are harassed, bullied, subordinated, or made the victims of blind passion or power . . . can not fail to continue to give the horrible spectacles we have always had of war, of crime, of vice, of trickery . . . and, alas! of insanity, idiocy, and disease added to a fearful and unnecessary mortality."[21]

Maternalist politics were necessarily racial politics. As followers of G. Stanley Hall, PTA members naturally accentuated the role of heredity in the natural development of the child and in the "progress" of the race. They celebrated healthy and virtuous (white) women as mothers of the nation's citizen-soldiers and censured those whose heredity, homes, and family lives did not fit the ideal. "To bring a child into the world without a prospect of being able to provide food and clothes for its body, or instruction and training for its mind, is not only a crime against the unfortunate offspring," a speaker told the Mothers' Congress in 1897, "but a crime against society itself." More than a decade later, Hannah Schoff proclaimed that "every wrong condition that confronts our nation" could be traced to the home. "Infant mortality, juvenile delinquency, increase in divorce, race suicide, municipal and political corruption . . . have their root in the kind of care and training received in the home and its relation to that received out of it."[22]

Club mothers, no doubt convinced that heredity had made them fit to be parents, avowed that privileged women had a special responsibility for the nurture and care of the world's less fortunate children. Believing in the natural goodness of all children, yet appalled by cultural differences in child rearing and the grim conditions of urban poverty, the leaders of the Mothers' Congress urged their followers to become moral teachers of the poor. They called on "enlightened" club mothers to educate poor women about scientific methods of housekeeping and child rearing and about the "laws" of heredity. "Some people say that the first need of the submerged world is better tenements," a speaker told delegates to the first Congress. "But it seems to me that we must first elevate the woman herself, and then she will be capable of using a better tenement. The woman, the mother, must be helped by other women." Another speaker evinced the double edge of maternalism's regard for all children's welfare when she called on elite women to "love the children that belong to other people" while justifying their intercession into the family lives of the poor. "Your children belong to me, to the neighbors, to everybody else, to every one with whom they come in touch," she declared. "You can not keep them to yourself; you can not keep them within the narrow home circle—they belong to the world, and they should be so taught. They are only lent to you to care for, to help, until they can stand on their own feet and live their own lives independently of you." It was the duty of elite women to help disadvantaged children become good citizens by teaching their mothers scientific methods of housekeeping and child rearing and an appreciation of Anglo-American ways.[23]

The Work of the PTA

In its early years, the National Congress of Mothers focused more on educating individual mothers about child study and proper home life than on providing social services or welfare-state building. Under Birney's leadership, the Congress supported local child welfare charities and promoted parent-teacher cooperation, but made child study a priority. Club members discussed Hall's theories about child development in mothers' classes and clubs and distributed his questionnaires on imagination, religious sentiment, and fear to their children. Disseminating Hall's work to a wide audience, they played a leading role in popularizing child study.[24]

Following Hall, PTA leaders claimed that scientific knowledge about child development proved the need for school and welfare reform. By 1910, most mothers' clubs combined child study and maternal education with a variety of charitable and social services. The activities of the Gardner, Massachusetts, Parent-Teacher League were typical. In 1911, the league reported to the *Child-Welfare Magazine* that it published weekly newspaper articles and book lists on child development, ran a library on child welfare, and raised funds for educational projects, a playground, and a hot lunch program at a local school. In addition, it set up a pure milk station, collected money for a local tuberculosis society and fresh air camp, distributed Thanksgiving dinners and Christmas baskets to the poor—and provided child care during meetings so that more women would be able to attend.[25]

The move from friendly visiting to service providing to politics is evident in the PTA's work on child health, the preservation of which President Hannah Schoff called the "first duty of parents and society." Five of the twenty-three papers presented at the founding meeting in 1897 concerned health, a fact reflecting women's responsibility for taking care of ill children as well as the ideology of child study and eugenics. Initially, the health work of the Mothers' Congress was mostly educational and was organized on a private and voluntary basis; for example, club members distributed literature on the prevention of tuberculosis and organized classes and clinics on nutrition and hygiene. For the most part, such activities separated maternal education from other social reform efforts and attributed child death and disease to women's ignorance rather than to poverty or the environment. "Infant mortality exists because of lack of knowledge on the part of mothers as to care of babies," Schoff wrote; "only as mothers are instructed in infant hygiene can babies' lives be saved."[26]

In the 1910s, club mothers across the country made the provision of child health services a priority. A number of PTAs ran infant health clinics, where physicians and nurses, many of them women, examined, weighed, and measured children and instructed their mothers on nutrition and hygiene. In Providence, Rhode Island, the PTA conducted baby clinics in every school district. Volunteers treated sick infants and offered information and "cheer and encouragement" in Yiddish, Italian, French, Portuguese, Polish, and English. In 1914, the Springfield (Missouri)

Mothers' Congress announced in the *Child-Welfare Magazine* that it held fourteen free clinics, established a baby ward in a local hospital, and employed a visiting nurse. The same year, 845 women and 425 babies attended a child welfare station run by club mothers in Poughkeepsie, New York; 120 children between the ages of eight and twelve enrolled in their Little Mothers' Leagues. Another 503 mothers enrolled in a PTA-run Los Angeles children's center the first two months it was open in 1916. Significantly, the clinic did not serve the city's most disadvantaged families; the majority of clients were "American" and the wives of office employees or skilled workers (although the largest percentage had only an eighth-grade education). Several groups reported that, despite initial troubles getting women to attend, their health clinics had become so popular they had to turn people away. The services established by the PTA (and other voluntary women's organizations in the same years) served as a model for the prenatal and well-baby clinics later funded by the federal government under the Sheppard-Towner Act.[27]

Although many mothers' clubs provided much-needed health care to local women, some PTA baby contests and clinics focused more on physical beauty and eugenics than on the elimination of disease. The Erie, Pennsylvania, Mothers' Congress reported enthusiastically that better baby contests "standardized" the physical and mental equipment of childhood and gave mothers the chance to learn from physicians "wherein their children may be falling away from the point of perfection."[28] By publicizing a "normal" standard of health and development, such clinics legitimized a racially biased concept of health and beauty. This no doubt increased the anxiety of women who did not fit the ideal while elevating the status of Anglo-American mothers, whose social worth was enhanced by the supposedly superior physical characteristics of their children.

For many PTA members, it was but a short step from the voluntary provision of health services to involvement in politics. Finding the demand for health care great, but their own funds inadequate to meet the need, hundreds of local mothers' clubs lobbied the government for publicly funded child health services and worked with the federal Children's Bureau on its baby-saving campaign. The National Congress of Mothers and Parent-Teacher Associations helped the bureau distribute its child-care bulletins, publicize the need for birth registration, and organize government-sponsored health conferences; it was the only private organization acknowledged in the introduction to the Children's Bureau pamphlet *Prenatal Care.* The PTA's association with the Children's Bureau continued into the 1920s, when parent-teacher associations in forty-two states helped the Children's Bureau administer the child health programs of the Sheppard-Towner Act. Many clubs also worked with the Bureau of Education on the "summer round up" of preschool children, giving examinations to preschool children so that they would enter the first grade free of remediable physical "defects."[29] They thus went beyond their initial emphasis on education and friendly visiting to establish permanent publicly funded health services.

PTA efforts to improve education, like its work for health care, revealed the fluid boundaries between public and private. Local parent-teacher associations funded and administered numerous school programs before local governments began to do so. In 1914, for example, the Parent-Teacher League in Gardner, Massachusetts, gave the local school money for a music teacher, a piano, a playground apparatus, a manual training program, student hot lunches, an emergency medicine cabinet, individual towels, liquid soap, and electric lights. The Springfield, Missouri, Mothers' Club furnished books, clothes, and balls to school children and organized a crusade against cigarette smoking by schoolboys. PTA members throughout the country funded improvements on school buildings and grounds, taught cooking and sewing to schoolgirls, supervised the janitors who cleaned school buildings, and sought with varying degrees of success to influence the curriculum and format of the report card. They provided scholarships and clothing to poor children and raised money for higher teacher salaries and for better country roads so that rural children would find it easier to attend school.[30]

Since Birney was inspired by a meeting with kindergarten supporters to organize the Mothers' Congress, it was only natural that the PTA should make kindergartens a high priority. Delegates at the founding meeting passed a resolution calling for kindergartens in the public schools; in the 1910s the National Congress of Mothers and Parent-Teacher Associations worked with the National Education Association, the National Kindergarten Association, and the U.S. Bureau of Education to secure public funding for kindergartens. In 1913, after the California chapter secured legislation requiring school districts to establish kindergartens upon the petition of the parents of twenty-five children, the number of kindergartens in the state doubled within two years. After the Erie, Pennsylvania, Board of Education decided to abolish public kindergartens because they were too expensive and merely relieved "lazy" mothers of the care of their children, the PTA collected four thousand signatures on a petition and prevented their demise. By 1915, approximately 12 percent of the nation's children were educated in public kindergartens.[31]

Like other maternalists, elite PTA activists believed that they had both a special responsibility and a unique ability to nurture disadvantaged children. Convinced of the therapeutic power of mother-love, they worked to incorporate maternal values and "a little love" into the law and called on the state to protect and discipline children when their families could or would not. Countless mothers' clubs thus campaigned aggressively for mothers' pensions laws. Committed to the idea that "the personal care of a loving and wise mother is the greatest need of every child," sentimental maternalists expected that state-funded allowances to "deserving" mothers would permit poor women to stay home and nurture their children, instead of neglecting them by doing outside work or putting them in institutions.[32]

PTA leaders also tried to bring a motherly influence to bear on the criminal justice system. Indeed, President Schoff made juvenile correction her personal priority, revealing the deep connection she and other conservative maternalists perceived between child rearing and the prevention of crime and disorder. Schoff drafted several states' bills for juvenile courts, detention homes for children awaiting trial, and probation systems, and she served on the committee that appointed Philadelphia's first probation officers. Juvenile delinquents, truants, and runaways were "not hopeless criminals," she declared, but "victims of conditions for which they are not responsible." Most juvenile crime could be prevented if every child had "sympathetic, individual and intelligent guidance." Schoff believed that the juvenile court could provide individualized and parentlike care for troubled children. Under the probation system, "wayward" children were permitted to live at home, but they were supervised by a social worker who taught the entire family "better" ways of housekeeping and child rearing.[33]

Schoff's fear of crime and disorder also determined her views on child labor. In contrast to progressive women reformers—and many rank-and-file club mothers—who wanted to restrict all wagework of children under fourteen, Schoff worried that "extreme and rigid" child labor laws would result in "compulsory idleness" and crime. She insisted that work developed "manliness and the sense of responsibility" in boys, directing their boundless energy "into safe channels." If they were prevented from working, she contended, many would turn to criminal lives. Although she supported welfare state protection for "dependent" mothers and children, Schoff adamantly opposed it for able-bodied men and boys.[34]

Elite club mothers thus asserted themselves as guardians of all the nation's children. They tried to protect their morals by banning the sale and consumption of liquor and by censoring books and films they considered immoral. In 1917, for example, the Denver PTA presented a petition with ten thousand signatures to the Film Exchange Board and won a permanent committee to judge the suitability of films.[35] During World War I, the National Congress of Mothers and Parent-Teacher Associations supported the country's policy makers and enthusiastically joined the war effort. Schoff, like many club mothers, saw the war as a vindication of her views on education and health; she attributed the war to Germany's authoritarian educational system and pointed to the large number of men doing poorly on military physicals as evidence of the need for better education about hygiene.

Although the leaders of the Mothers' Congress opposed government attempts to introduce military training in schools—children needed the "chance to be children"—they eagerly disseminated pro-American propaganda to immigrants and encouraged local chapters to form committees on food and energy conservation. In 1918, according to the *Child-Welfare Magazine*, all twenty-two PTAs in Memphis, Tennessee, sold Thrift stamps, worked with the Red Cross, planted victory gardens, and discussed patriotism in meetings. Most also made sure that the American flag hung over local schools.[36]

Congress members also tried to protect the morality of the "boys" in military service. Club mothers provided a "home influence" for young soldiers by inviting them home for Sunday dinner and by setting up clubs equipped with pianos, Victrolas, pool tables, books, and magazines close to military training stations. "The conditions of camp life are necessarily abnormal," explained the *Child-Welfare Magazine*; "there is a special need of personal influence and hospitality of good mothers, who can be camp protectors."[37] While the boys protected world democracy, sentimental maternalists—in a dauntless effort to maintain control of the moral order—protected the boys.

Maternalism and the Politics of Race

The social and political perspective of mothers' club members was determined not only by their gender but by their race and class as well. White women's understanding of woman's place, their concept of race "progress," and their readiness to use the state to promote a certain kind of home life reflected the experience and social position of the Anglo-American elite. Still, the official view of the Congress on race was liberal for its time. Leaders of the National Congress of Mothers believed that women all over the world were joined in motherhood and subjection to male lust and could unite "on the common ground of their children's welfare." "The National Congress of Mothers, irrespective of creed, color, or condition, stands for all parenthood, childhood, home-hood," declared founder Alice Birney. "Its platform is the universe; its organization, the human race."[38]

Such liberal rhetoric notwithstanding, many white club mothers were ambivalent about the participation of racial ethnic women in their movement. The National Congress of Mothers encouraged immigrant and African American women to form (their own) mothers' clubs but rarely treated them as equal partners in the mothers' movement. The maternalist ideology of Anglo-American club mothers thus had a double edge. On the one hand, the idea that motherhood made women particularly concerned about children's welfare promised to cut across distinctions of race and ethnicity; on the other, the view that women were responsible for the bearing and raising of citizens established a hierarchy among mothers that distinguished between those raising desirable citizens and those raising bad ones. White club women's culturally specific understanding of "home-hood" and "human race" took the family lives of white middle-class Protestants as the norm; they frequently had little meaning for women of other social groups. For example, the PTA assumption that married woman's place was in the home implicitly reproached many African American wives, who were five times as likely as married whites to work outside the home.[39]

From its founding through the 1910s, the National Congress of Mothers and Parent-Teacher Associations saw itself as an organization speaking for women of all races and cultures. The *Child-Welfare Magazine* contained reports from mothers' clubs in foreign countries, including Palestine, Persia, China, Mexico, and England. It discussed conditions for women and children in these places and urged Americans to help women there establish mothers' clubs and kindergartens. Perhaps reflecting the abolitionist heritage of a few of its leaders, the Mothers' Congress also invited some prominent African Americans to speak at its annual meetings. At the founding convention, the writer and activist Frances Ellen Watkins Harper took advantage of the inclusive rhetoric of maternalism and delivered an eloquent address urging white mothers to treat black women with dignity and to help fund their mothers' clubs. "Has not the negro also a claim upon a nation?" Harper implored. "If you want us to act as women, treat us as women." "That the children of any race are the hope of that race is doubly true of all backward races," declared Anna Murray of the Colored Women's League, using language understandable to Anglo-American club mothers. Speaking at the 1905 convention of the National Congress of Mothers, she urged white women to nurture and guard as "the jewel of our civilization" children of every race.[40]

PTA interest in mothers' clubs in foreign countries and African American communities was doubtless motivated by genuine concern for child welfare, but it also manifested a colonial spirit. The same year that white club mothers listened to Anna Murray's plea for fair treatment of black children, they enthusiastically applauded Columbia University professor Samuel Lindsay's speech urging them to become "truly missionary" and extend their "noble endeavors" to the "less favored" people of Puerto Rico. "They will receive us, as their people received the armed troops of the United States in 1898, with joy and hospitality," Lindsay declared; "and we can thus help fulfill for them their highest hopes that dawned the day the American flag was first raised as a symbol of their new sovereignty."[41]

During World War I, Anglo-American club mothers avidly joined the wartime Americanization campaign. In 1918, the National Congress of Mothers and Parent-Teacher Associations established its own Department of Americanization, which promoted English language classes for mothers and kindergartens for immigrant children. Americanization literature characterized ethnic women as "timid," "shy," and "diffident," innocent victims of social upheaval and male lust, childlike in their need of guidance and assistance. Convinced that foreign-born women were more abused by their husbands than they were, PTA members assumed that immigrant women's inability to speak English and their isolation in the home devalued them in the eyes of their more Americanized husbands and children. They believed that immigrant men forced their wives into domestic servitude, factory work, or street life; and they tried to save immigrant women by promoting American values. Once foreign-born women learned American ways, maternalists thought, they would no longer allow their husbands to treat them as slaves.[42]

The maternalistic attitude PTA officials had toward immigrants and women of color pervaded their literature and clearly influenced their charity and welfare work. However, the activities of the Mothers' Congress should not be seen simply as an attempt by elite matrons to impose their values on the poor, for it is likely that many club mothers learned something from the contact they had with working-class women. Like clients of other social service agencies, immigrant and working-class women who attended PTA classes were probably "active negotiators in a complex bargaining."[43] Maternalist ideas about universal motherhood may have made space for them to make their own demands. Although future research is needed to determine the influence of the participants in PTA-run mothers' classes on the National Congress of Mothers, it is possible that contact with working-class women contributed to the organization's growing interest in social welfare reform.

In any case, white club mothers' condescending attitude toward immigrant women coexisted with a romanticized view of "simple" hard-working mothers. Elite women who felt idle and useless often idealized poor women who had jobs, earned wages, and thus contributed to the upkeep of their families. "Happy the woman whose husband is so poor that her actual labor is honestly needed in the house," mused the popular novelist Dorothy Canfield Fisher. "She is still in those halcyon days of economic simplicity. But woe to the prosperous woman, who . . . wastes and perverts her valuable productive energy."[44] Articles in the *Child-Welfare Magazine* urged club mothers to treat poor women with dignity. Like child-rearing experts who told mothers they could learn from their children, Congress leaders reminded their members that they could learn from the poor. According to the *Child-Welfare Magazine*, the "silk-clad woman" was "generally clever enough to appreciate and to admire" the spirit and determination of poor mothers who faced years of self-denial and poverty for the sake of their children. "The feeling of inferiority, of uselessness . . . may humiliate the idle woman," one author wrote, "but it is bound to do her good. It will certainly deprive her conversation of sweeping criticism on lives and conditions unknown to her. It will also utterly do away with many of her prejudices against the foreigner and it will make the 'let them eat cake' attitude impossible."[45]

While the *Child-Welfare Magazine* frequently ran articles on club mothers' relations with immigrants, it contained little discussion of PTA work among African Americans. There is no evidence of an explicit policy on race in the records of the National Congress of Mothers and Parent-Teacher Associations, but it is likely that, like the General Federation of Women's Clubs and the National American Woman Suffrage Association, the Congress discriminated against African Americans. Although a handful of black women participated in the predominantly white mothers' clubs and PTAs, integrated groups were apparently rare, no doubt owing to racially segregated schools and housing patterns as well as to prejudice among white women. Separate "colored" mothers' clubs and parent-teacher associations appeared during the 1920s. The National Congress of Colored Parents and Teachers formed in 1926 (the same year the first Native American parent-teacher association was established in North Dakota). By 1930, it had 14,000 members.[46]

A 1926 survey of PTA officers about "extension work" among African Americans reveals white women's ambivalence about people of color in the national organization. Only two-thirds (168 of 248) of Colored Parent-Teacher Associations surveyed were even affiliated with the state or national Congress of Parents and Teachers. Most state PTAs did not allow black women to participate as equals; a leader of the Ohio Mothers' Congress observed with apparent astonishment that "some colored [women] seem to resent the fact that they are not invited to be a member of committees or take part on program of local meetings." White women were reluctant to have black leaders in groups that were predominantly white. Although a black woman successfully served as president of the nearly all-white Washington PTA, the California experience was undoubtedly more common: "While colored people are a small minority all is well, but if they become active, white women drop out." Although some groups avoided the race question because they had separate organizations, conventions and banquets seemed to pose a particular problem when black mothers' clubs were affiliated with white groups. In Tennessee, black women were allowed to attend PTA conventions as visitors but had to sit in the rear, apart from other delegates. The Ohio Congress provided separate banquet tables for black and white women.[47]

Despite the active role African American women played in mothers' clubs and PTAs, there is only scattered reference to their activities in the *Child-Welfare Magazine*. The few reports from African American clubs describe activities almost identical to those undertaken by white clubs, perhaps because those activities were given special emphasis in a magazine whose readership was mostly white. For example, in 1916, the *Child-Welfare Magazine* reported that the six members of the Poplarville, Mississippi, Colored Mothers' Club paid tuition and bought books for orphaned students, furnished wood and crayons for their school, and were beginning to raise funds for a domestic science teacher.[48]

Although some black women worked with the National Congress of Mothers and Parent-Teacher Associations, most were active in clubs and organizations within the African American community. The most influential organization in the period of this study was the National Association of Colored Women (NACW), founded one year before the National Congress of Mothers, in 1896. Within twenty years, the NACW represented fifty thousand women in over a thousand clubs across the country.[49] Despite the many differences between the NACW and the PTA, a brief comparison of the two organizations reveals both the different nature of black women's welfare activism and the ways in which the politics of Anglo-American club mothers were determined by their race. White and black club women were similar in a number of ways: they used the rhetoric of motherhood, found close friendships and meaningful work through club activism, and emphasized both the private and public aspects of mothers' work—child rearing and child welfare. Both groups of women ran classes for mothers on child rearing and domestic science and donated clothing, fuel, food, and medicine to the poor. Both established social welfare institutions, such as schools, orphanages, and old age homes, and ran these services until their funding and administration were taken over by local governments.[50]

Yet, the leadership of the National Congress of Mothers and the National Association of Colored Women—and therefore the political styles of the two organizations—could hardly be more different. First, while no well-known white woman had the Mothers' Congress or the General Federation of Women's Clubs as her primary organizational affiliation, the NACW provided a home base for such prominent activists as Mary Church Terrell, Ida B. Wells, and Mary McLeod Bethune. (In that way, as well as in its support of women's right to vote, the NACW was more a counterpart of the predominantly white social settlements or suffrage organizations.) Second, the National Congress of Mothers had only two presidents between 1897 and 1920, while the NACW had six presidents in the same period, perhaps suggesting different ideas about leadership, democracy, and power. A third difference was the greater likelihood of African American club women to be highly educated married women with careers. In contrast to sentimental maternalists, most of whom were married women but did not have a paying job, and progressive maternalists, who tended to be single women with careers, a profile of 108 NACW members between 1896 and 1920 found that three-quarters were married and nearly three-quarters worked outside the home. (Only one-quarter had children, however).[51]

Overcoming obstacles that white club mothers did not have to face, NACW leaders listed impressive accomplishments outside the home, especially in the area of education. Mary Church Terrell, the organization's first president, was a graduate of Oberlin College and the first black woman appointed to the board of education in the District of Columbia. Margaret Murray Washington, second wife of Booker T. Washington and dean of women at Tuskegee Institute, was the editor of the NACW journal, *National Notes,* and served as its president from 1914 to 1918. Mary Talbert, NACW president from 1916 to 1920, was another Oberlin graduate. She served as assistant principal of a church in Little Rock, Arkansas, and went on to become the national director of the Anti-Lynching Crusaders in the 1920s. Mary McLeod Bethune, arguably the most influential African American woman in the first half of the twentieth century, served as NACW president from 1924 to 1928 before going on to found the National Council of Negro Women in 1935. One of seventeen children of slaves freed by the Civil War, Bethune rose to national prominence as founder and head of the school that became the Bethune-Cookman College and as president of the Florida Federation of Colored Women. She reached the peak of her influence during the New Deal, when as director of the Division of Negro Affairs in the National Youth Administration, she ensured that at least some of the benefits of the expanding U.S. welfare system reached the African American community.[52]

Black and white members of mothers' clubs also differed in their understanding of home and motherhood.[53] Both groups accepted women's responsibility for child rearing and used maternal imagery to further their cause. For example, Ida B. Wells described motherhood as "one of the most glorious advantages of the development of . . . womanhood," and the Chicago club activist Fannie Barrier Williams urged women to "become the civic mothers of the race."[54] However, the realities of mothering in a racist society made it impossible for African Americans to idealize motherhood in the same way as elite whites. For them, the legacy of slavery—when motherhood meant producing slave labor and possibly losing one's children through sale—and infant and maternal mortality rates at least double those of whites defined the maternal experience. Mary Church Terrell, who herself lost three children within days of their births, eloquently explained the differences to the National Congress of Mothers:

Contrast, if you will, the feelings of hope and joy which thrill the heart of the white mothers with those which stir the soul of her colored sister. Put yourselves for one minute in her place, (you could not endure the strain longer) and imagine, if you can, how you would feel if situated similarly—As a mother of the weaker race clasps to her bosom the babe which she loves as fondly as you do yours, her heart cannot thrill with joyful anticipations of the future. For before her child she sees the thorny path of prejudice and proscription which his little feet must tread. . . . So rough does the way of her infant appear to many a poor black mother that instead of thrilling with the joy which you feel, as you clasp your little ones to your breast, she trembles with apprehension and despair.[55]

For Anglo-American women, the home was a locus of socialization to train young children to be good citizens. For African Americans, it was a training ground for struggle as well. It was the place for "building up strength and righteousness in its sons and daughters, and equipping them for the inevitable battles of life which grow out of the struggle for existence."[56] African American mothers were responsible not only for teaching children to be honest and industrious workers and citizens but also for helping them fight discrimination and live with dignity in a racist world.

Black and white women activists also differed in their attitude toward the poor. Like white club mothers, African American activists were concerned with "proper" home life and social uplift and assumed the task of imparting these values to the poor. Membership in African American clubs was limited to members of "worthy" families, and organizational activities often reflected a condescending attitude toward the poor. At the second NACW convention in 1897, for example, Mary Church Terrell urged club women to establish kindergartens so that the "waifs and strays of the alleys [could] come in contact with intelligence and virtue." Nevertheless, elite black women were much more likely than Anglo-Americans to perceive their fate as being tied to that of the poor. As Fannie Barrier Williams explained, "The club movement among colored women reaches into the sub-social condition of the entire race. Among white women, clubs mean the forward movement of the best women in the interest of the best womanhood. Among colored women, the club is the effort of the few competent on behalf of the many incompetent; that is to say that the club is only one of many means for the social uplift of a race."[57]

The NACW motto, "Lifting as We Climb," expressed black club women's desire to close the gap between different social classes even as it reinforced the social values of the elite. NACW leaders shared the view, widely held by whites, that many poor black families were unstable; unlike whites, they attributed family instability not to individual moral failure but to the historical sexual exploitation of black women under slavery. Thus, while Anglo-American club mothers tended to blame individual men or women for what they considered dysfunctional families, NACW leaders considered the "improper" home life of an African American "more his misfortune than his fault."[58]

While white club mothers tried to preserve the concept of woman's sphere (at least in theory), racism made the ideology of separate spheres a luxury few blacks could afford. Unlike the Mothers' Congress, which generally disavowed politics even while it developed close relationships with government leaders and influenced the direction of public welfare policy, the NACW openly asserted the need for political power. For them, there was a special urgency to the maternalist dictum that mothers' responsibilities should extend beyond the private home to improve social conditions affecting children. Like white club mothers, the NACW was concerned with moral and domestic matters, such as temperance, social purity, and child study. Beyond them, black women also agitated around obviously political subjects not directly related to child welfare, such as lynching, the convict lease system, police brutality, and Jim Crow laws. A comparison of the 1904 resolutions of the National Congress of Mothers and the NACW is instructive. The Mothers' Congress advocated moral training in the public schools, opportunities for deaf children equal to those of "normal" youth, stricter laws against divorce, child labor legislation, and a probation system. The same year, the NACW endorsed temperance, educational mothers' meetings, and the elimination of immoral literature; it also condemned lynching, called for a boycott of segregated street cars, and urged members to study and prepare for woman suffrage.[59]

The welfare institutions established by black club women, like those established by whites, reveal the fluid boundaries between public and private agencies. Kindergartens, a priority because education was crucial to African American advancement and because so many mothers worked outside the home, were established through the effort of the entire community. Churches supplied fuel and rent money; individuals and organizations donated milk, bread, and clothing. In Washington, D.C., the Colored Women's League ran seven free kindergartens and several day nurseries serving more than one hundred children until they were incorporated into the public school system. The Gate City Free Kindergarten Association of Atlanta ran five kindergartens and two day nurseries in poor neighborhoods. Even after the Kindergarten Association became eligible for public funding by joining the Atlanta Community Chest in 1923, it continued to be financed largely by private fund-raising drives.[60]

African American women activists, with little hope of influencing white policy makers, naturally focused more on community self-help and building private welfare institutions than on public welfare reform. Still, some organizations—most notably the Atlanta Neighborhood Union—combined self-help and political pressure. Organized in 1908 by Lugenia Burns Hope, wife of the president of Atlanta University, the union made health care a priority, offering classes in prenatal and infant care, hygiene, and the treatment of tuberculosis. It also ran a dental clinic and enlisted volunteer nurses and doctors to visit patients in their homes. Yet despite its success at institution building within the black community, the union was unable to make significant and lasting improvements in white-controlled services. A vigorous campaign to improve the public schools succeeded in establishing an additional school for black children and in raising the salaries of black teachers but ultimately had little impact on Atlanta's racist school system.[61]

The inability of African American women to influence policy makers is especially striking when compared to white women's success. Between 1890 and 1920, European American women gained unprecedented influence in government and won important legislative victories, such as mothers' pensions, protective labor laws, and the vote. African American women and children, however, faced tightening segregation laws and increasing racial violence. Most were not covered by mothers' pensions and protective legislation, and, even after the passage of the woman suffrage amendment, many were denied the right to vote. Blacks were also excluded from the alliance white maternalists forged with government agencies; not until the 1930s did Mary McLeod Bethune have the ear of federal officials. Yet most white club mothers did not see racial discrimination or violence as child welfare concerns. The racial exclusivity of the National Congress of Mothers and its members' narrow understanding of child welfare—along with legal segregation, Jim Crow laws, and the stinginess of white taxpayers and politicians—ensured that public child welfare services remained inferior or unavailable in black communities even as they were improving in white ones.

Politics and the PTA in the 1920s

While the NACW asserted the importance of women's political activism from its inception, the increasing political involvement of the National Congress of Mothers and Parent-Teacher Associations during the Progressive Era seemed to many a significant break from the past. In the 1890s, white club mothers concentrated on discussing child study and distributing alms to the needy; twenty years later, even rank-and-file members helped run social service organizations and lobbied their legislators themselves. However, in the anticommunist climate of the early 1920s, PTA leaders divided over the direction they felt the organization should take. Moderates like Katharine Chapin Higgins (president from 1920 to 1923) made restructuring the organization and increasing membership a priority, while National Secretary Florence Watkins and Legislative Department head Elizabeth Tilton focused on progressive welfare reform. Under Watkins's leadership, the National Congress of Mothers and Parent-Teacher Associations joined the National Council for the Prevention of War and the Women's Joint Congressional Committee, a lobbying coalition of the major women's reform organizations. As a result, the PTA was listed on the widely circulated Spider Web Chart as one of fifteen "Socialist-Pacifist" women's organizations that were "an Absolutely Fundamental and Integral Part of International Socialism."[62]

The Red Scare of the early 1920s brought the long-standing political differences within the PTA to the surface. Members were sharply divided over the questions of women's involvement in politics and the state's responsibility for social welfare. The president of the Washington, D.C., PTA accused Florence Watkins of being a communist. Archconservative Brigadier-General Amos Fries, head of the Chemical Warfare Service of the War Department, and a PTA member and father of four, attacked the National Council for the Prevention of War as communist, leading PTA President Higgins to order Watkins to withdraw from the peace organization. (She had been a member of its executive board.) In 1923, several delegates to the PTA convention attempted to remove the peace and child labor planks from the platform. They had the support of ex-president Hannah Schoff, who urged delegates to stand by their government against advocates of disarmament and the child labor amendment, but the liberal platform prevailed.[63]

Most PTA members seem to have welcomed the Progressive Era politicization of motherhood, but the organization's growing involvement in civic and legislative work did not go unquestioned. A 1919 letter to the *Child-Welfare Magazine* objected that the PTA's political activities violated the principle of helping its "*own members* to be more capable in developing the bodies, minds and hearts of *their own* children." "The average homemaker is not and never should become a public woman," the author complained. "Discussion and analysis of the essentials of true home life and child character, seem to have given place to restoration through Juvenile Courts and general legal and social service work."[64]

Such political conservatism affected the style and program of the National Congress of Mothers and Parent-Teacher Associations, as the uncontroversial task of membership building gained prominence over child welfare. The slogan "A PTA in every school" was adopted in 1922. In 1923, national membership reached 532,000, up from 200,000 just three years earlier. Although the National Congress continued to support progressive legislation, such as disarmament, the child labor amendment, and a world court, these were the efforts of an active minority led by Watkins, and not the major focus of the organization. For example, although the PTA endorsed the child labor amendment and the outlawry of war in its 1927 resolutions, these issues took a back seat to less controversial aims such as "worthy home membership, sound health, mastery of tools, technics and spirit of learning, useful citizenship, and wise use of leisure."[65]

The decision to drop "mothers" from the name of the National Congress of Mothers and Parent-Teacher Associations in 1924 acknowledged the growing influence of experts and teachers in the organization—and indicated the end of sentimental maternalism. While the early leaders all claimed to be "women of the home," the PTA's fifth president, Ina Caddell Marrs, listed among her credentials a ten-year teaching career, as well as nine years of activism in the state and National Congress of Parents and Teachers and marriage to the superintendent of the Texas State Department of Education. Furthermore, as the PTA began to focus on parent education and the schools, its officers benefited from new career opportunities in those fields. In 1930 the organization received a grant from the Laura Spelman Rockefeller Memorial Foundation for a specialist in parent education and for publication of the *Parent Education Yearbook*. PTA leaders taught parent education in colleges, summer schools, elementary schools, and libraries.[66]

The changing focus of the National Congress of Parents and Teachers was reflected in the *Child-Welfare Magazine*. The journal stopped publishing reports on the activities of local mothers' clubs, the section entitled "State News," and articles on foreign-born mothers. Instead, it discussed health and safety in the schools, ways to protect children from "immoral" influences, and how to raise a "normal" child. The magazine published study questions, reading lists, advice from child psychologists and educators, and excerpts of popular child-rearing books, such as Douglas Thom's *Child Management*, Dorothy Canfield Fisher's *Mothers and Children*, and *Wholesome Childhood*, by Ernest Groves. Child psychology and parent education replaced benevolence and social reform as its focus. In contrast to the Gilded Age and Progressive Era, when the ideal mother was portrayed as a "social" mother involved in women's clubs or charities, the exemplary mother of the 1920s was focused on her own children. Middle-class mothers were no longer supposed to be active in maternal education or welfare work; they were supposed to spend their time studying the latest theories on child care so that they would be able to care for their own children. Indeed, the 1930 assertion of PTA President Minnie Bradford that child welfare and parent education were one and the same negated the previous emphasis on social change and reinforced the view that mothers, not poverty or the environment, were responsible for their children's problems.[67]

Despite the increasingly professional orientation of its national leaders, the PTA remained a grassroots organization never fully accepted by psychologists or professionals in parent education. For example, the Child Study Association of America, the most influential parent education group in the 1920s, worked closely with social and research scientists but remained aloof from the amateurish PTA. CSAA leader Sidonie Gruenberg considered the PTA useful for disseminating materials on parent education, but incompatible with serious group work. Two surveys of school superintendents also document their frustration with what they considered the lack of professionalism in the PTA. Administrators criticized PTA meetings for being too devoted to child welfare and entertainment. They objected that members overemphasized the defects in the school program, frequently supported teachers who were out of harmony with the school administration, and did not behave "professionally" or with appropriate deference to experts. Perhaps aggravated by politically active women whose interests sometimes conflicted with their own, male school administrators accused PTA members of making trouble and of being primarily interested in their own personal gain. They suggested that relations between the school staff and the PTA could be improved if mothers stayed out of politics and cooperated more closely with the schools. Like the authors of child-rearing manuals in the same decade, professional educators considered mothers an impediment to their children's development.[68]

In the end, sentimental maternalism was partly a victim of its own success. Although club mothers played a key role in the initial development of parent education and social welfare programs, the professionalization of those fields limited the role that women at the grass roots could play in their administration. As academic conferences replaced mothers' study circles, health clinics and kindergartens—services often initiated by white and black organized mothers—were incorporated into public and private agencies and run by professionals. Rank-and-file PTA members were no longer considered unpaid professionals administering charities and welfare programs but volunteers who assisted the professionals in their work.

Some of the social services initiated by clubs' mothers were run by the progressive reformers in the Children's Bureau network. Unlike sentimental maternalists, who disavowed the political nature of their work, and African American activists, who were unable to get the ear of white policy makers, progressive maternalists openly extended social motherhood into government, expanding state responsibility for child welfare while simultaneously creating professional opportunities for educated women. The maternalist ideology and activism of the Children's Bureau women was markedly different from that of the National Congress of Mothers.[69]

NOTES

1. Dorothy Canfield Fisher, *Mothers and Children* (New York: Henry Holt, 1914), 258–59.

2. Progressive Era maternalism had roots in the temperance, antislavery, and moral reform associations of the antebellum period. See Carroll Smith-Rosenberg, *Religion and the Rise of the City: The New York City Mission Movement, 1812–1870* (Ithaca, N.Y.: Cornell University Press, 1971); Mary P. Ryan, *Cradle of the Middle Class: Family and Community in Oneida County, New York, 1780–1865* (New York: Cambridge University Press, 1981); Barbara Epstein, *The Politics of Domesticity: Women, Evangelicalism, and Temperance in Nineteenth-Century America* (Middletown: Wesleyan University Press, 1981); Lori D. Ginzberg, *Women and the Work of Benevolence: Morality, Politics, and Class in the Nineteenth-Century United States* (New Haven: Yale University Press, 1990); Peggy Pascoe, *Relations of Rescue: The Search for Female Moral Authority in the American West, 1874–1939* (New York: Oxford University Press, 1990).

3. This is not to say that motherhood rhetoric ceased, only that it no longer had the ability to inspire a mass movement for welfare. Some progressive reformers in government continued to employ maternalist rhetoric. See Eileen Boris, "Regulating Industrial Homework: The Triumph of 'Sacred Motherhood'" in this volume.

4. Historians have generally ignored the PTA, even though it is one of the largest and most influential women's organizations in the twentieth century. No organizational history has appeared since Harry Overstreet and Bonaro Overstreet's *Where Children Come First: A Study of the P.T.A. Idea* (Chicago: National Congress of Parents and Teachers, 1949). Theda Skocpol's *Protecting Soldiers and Mothers: The Politics of Social Provision in the United States, 1870s–1920s* (Cambridge, Mass.: Harvard University Press, 1992), examines the contribution the National Congress of Mothers made to maternalist welfare reform; and Steven Schlossman discusses its role in the prewar child study movement in "Before Home Start: Notes toward a History of Parent Education in America, 1897–1929," *Harvard Education Review* 46 (Aug. 1976): 436–67. The Congress is also discussed briefly in Sheila M. Rothman, *Woman's Proper Place: A History of Changing Ideals and Practices, 1870–1930* (New York: Basic Books, 1978); and Deirdre English and Barbara Ehrenreich in *For Her Own Good: 150 Years of Advice to Women* (Garden City: Anchor, 1978).

5. The name of the National Congress of Mothers was changed to the National Congress of Mothers and Parent-Teacher Associations in 1908 and to the National Congress of Parents and Teachers in 1924. In order to avoid confusion and repetition of the cumbersome name, I have referred to the organization as the Mothers' Congress or by its current colloquial name, the

PTA, throughout the text. National Congress of Parents and Teachers, *Golden Jubilee History, 1897–1947* (Chicago: National Congress of Parents and Teachers, 1947), 72; Overstreet and Overstreet, *Where Children Come First,* 195–97, 203.

6. Overstreet and Overstreet, *Where Children Come First,* and the PTA's *Golden Jubilee History* provide the best summaries of the organization's activities. See also Julian Butterworth, *The Parent-Teacher Association and Its Work* (New York: Macmillan, 1929).

7. "Message from the President," *National Congress of Mothers' Magazine* 1 (Nov. 1906): 2; Hannah Kent Schoff, *The Wayward Child: A Study of the Causes of Crime* (Indianapolis: Bobbs-Merrill, 1915), 12.

8. The aims of the Congress were printed in every issue of the organization's magazine. Additional aims included kindergartens, laws caring for neglected and dependent children, the juvenile court, probationary care in individual homes rather than institutions, parent education, "high ideals" of marriage, the nation's responsibility to childhood, and surrounding childhood with "loving, wise care . . . that will develop good citizens, instead of law-breakers and criminals." See, for example, *Child-Welfare Magazine* 8 (Apr. 1914).

9. Mrs. Theodore W. Birney, "Need for Organization," in *Parents and Their Problems,* ed. Mary Harmon Weeks (New York: Ferd P. Kaiser Publishing Co., 1914), 8:32.

10. On the Spider Web Chart, see J. Stanley Lemons, *The Woman Citizen: Social Feminism in the 1920s* (Urbana: University of Illinois Press, 1973), 209–27; Nancy F. Cott, *The Grounding of Modern Feminism* (New Haven, Conn.: Yale University Press, 1987), 242, 249–50.

11. National Congress of Mothers, *The Work and Words of the National Congress of Mothers: First Annual Session* (New York: D. Appleton, 1897), reprinted in *National Congress of Mothers: The First Conventions,* ed. David J. Rothman and Sheila M. Rothman (New York: Garland Publishing, 1987).

12. Mrs. Theodore W. Birney, "The Congress Origins," in Weeks, ed., *Parents and Their Problems,* 8:25–27; PTA, *Golden Jubilee History,* 36–37; Mrs. Theodore W. Birney, "Official Call to Congress," in National Congress of Mothers, *Work and Words,* ix, 10.

13. Quoted in Schlossman, "Before Home Start," 442, and Susan Tiffin, *In Whose Best Interest? Child Welfare Reform in the Progressive Era* (Westport: Greenwood Press, 1982), 21. See Charles Strickland and Charles Burgess, eds., *Health, Growth and Heredity: G. Stanley Hall on Natural Education* (New York: Teachers College Press, Columbia University, 1965). For Hall's biography, see Dorothy Ross, *G. Stanley Hall, The Psychologist as Prophet* (Chicago: University of Chicago Press, 1972).

14. G. Stanley Hall, "New Ideals of Motherhood," in National Congress of Mothers, *The Child in Home, School, and State: Proceedings of the Annual Meeting* (Washington, D.C.: National Congress of Mothers, 1905), 27. For an interesting analysis of Hall's ideas about masculinity, see Gail Bederman, "Racial Pedagogy or the Big Stick? G. Stanley Hall, Theodore Roosevelt, and the Manly Quest to Civilize the Primitive" (Paper presented to the Organization of American Historians, Chicago, 1992).

15. Milicent W. Shinn, *The Biography of a Baby* (Boston: Houghton Mifflin, 1900), 5–6; Hall quoted in Ross, *G. Stanley Hall,* 260.

16. Birney, "The Congress Origins," 29; PTA, *Golden Jubilee History,* 24–28; Edward T. James, Janet Wilson James, and Paul S. Boyer, eds., *Notable American Women* (Cambridge, Mass.: Belknap Press, 1971), 1:147–48.

17. PTA, *Golden Jubilee History,* 48–67; James, James, and Boyer, eds., *Notable American Women,* 3:237–39.

18. PTA, *Golden Jubilee History,* 21; Frances Ellen Watkins Harper, "The Afro-American Mother," and "Appendix," in National Congress of Mothers, *Work and Words,* 67–70, 255.

19. "Miss Anthony's Advice to Mothers," *Woman's Journal,* Sept. 8, 1900, 285; "Mrs. Stanton to the Mothers' Congress," *Woman's Journal,* May 26, 1900, 162. Stanton wrote of the Mothers' Congress, "I deem this organization altogether the most important yet formed in any period or nation."

20. Hannah Kent Schoff, "The Childless Wife," *National Congress of Mothers' Magazine* 2 (Apr. 1908): 189; Theodore Roosevelt, "Address to Congress on the Welfare of Children," ibid., 174.

21. Helen Gardener, "The Moral Responsibility of Women in Heredity," in National Congress of Mothers, *Work and Words,* 135–36.

22. Alice Lee Moque, "Reproduction and Natural Law," in ibid., 125; "State News," *Child-Welfare Magazine* 6 (Nov. 1911): 108. For a useful discussion of the intersection of race and gender in American welfare reform, see Gwendolyn Mink, "The Lady and the Tramp: Gender, Race, and the Origins of the American Welfare State," in *Women, the State, and Welfare,* ed. Linda Gordon (Madison: University of Wisconsin Press, 1990), 92–122.

23. Lucy Bainbridge, "Mothers of the Submerged World," in National Congress of Mothers, *Work and Words,* 49, 51; Frances Newton, "The Mother's Greatest Needs," in ibid., 153.

24. See Schlossman, "Before Home Start," 443–44.

25. Overstreet and Overstreet, *Where Children Come First,* 150; "State News," *Child-Welfare Magazine* 5 (May 1911): 175.

26. Mrs. Frederic Schoff, "Guardians of Childhood in Home and Nation," *National Congress of Mothers' Magazine* 3 (Apr. 1909): 231–32; "President's Desk," *Child-Welfare Magazine* 6 (Mar. 1912): 215.

27. Sybil Avery Perkins, "Child Hygiene in the Rhode Island Congress of Mothers," *Child-Welfare Magazine* 5 (May 1911): 164–65; "State News," *Child-Welfare Magazine* 8 (Dec. 1913): 148; "State News," *Child-Welfare Magazine* 9 (Nov 1914): 103–5; *Child-Welfare Magazine* 11 (June 1917): 301. A PTA-sponsored Mothers' Education Center in Los Angeles reported a total of 14,097 cases. "Annual Report of Baby Week Extension Committee, Los Angeles Mothers' Education Center," enclosed in Louise C. Heilbron to Julia Lathrop, June 1, 1920, File 4–15–4–3, Children's Bureau Records, Central Files, 1914–50, Record Group 102, National Archives, Washington, D.C.

28. "State News," *Child-Welfare Magazine* 10 (Sept. 1915): 35.

29. U.S. Children's Bureau, *Prenatal Care,* Publication No.4 (Washington, D.C.: Government Printing Office, 1913), 5; U.S. Children's Bureau, *The Promotion of the Welfare and Hygiene of Maternity and Infancy for the Fiscal Year Ending June 30, 1929,* Publication No. 203 (Washington, D.C.: Government Printing Office, 1931), 24; PTA, *Golden Jubilee History,* 97.

30. "State News," *Child-Welfare Magazine* 5 (May 1911): 175; Mrs. Frederic Schoff, "The National Congress of Mothers," *Club Woman* 10 (Mar. 1903): 241.

31. PTA, *Golden Jubilee History,* 28–30; Overstreet and Overstreet, *Where Children Come First,* 49; "Legislative Work for Kindergartens," *Child-Welfare Magazine* 10 (Aug. 1916): 444; Bessie Locke, "Kindergarten Extension," *Child-Welfare Magazine* 12 (May 1918): 173; "Parent-

Teacher Associations of Erie Save Kindergarten System," *Child-Welfare Magazine* 7 (Dec. 1912): 116. On the kindergarten movement, see Michael Steven Shapiro, *Child's Garden: The Kindergarten Movement from Froebel to Dewey* (University Park: Pennsylvania State University Press, 1983); Elizabeth Dale Ross, *The Kindergarten Crusade: The Establishment of Preschool Education in the United States* (Athens: Ohio University Press, 1976); Karen Wolk Feinstein, "Kindergartens, Feminism, and the Professionalization of Motherhood," *International Journal of Women's Studies* 3 (Jan.–Feb. 1980): 28–38; Ann Taylor Allen, "'Let Us Live with Our Children': Kindergarten Movements in Germany and the United States, 1840–1914," *History of Education Quarterly* 78 (Spring 1988): 23–48.

32. Schoff, *The Wayward Child*, 80–81.

33. Ben B. Lindsey, "Present Outlook for the Juvenile Court," *National Congress of Mothers' Magazine* 4 (Dec. 1909): 103; Schoff, *The Wayward Child*, 9, 12–13, 80. The history of the juvenile court has been well documented. See, for example, Anthony M. Platt, *The Child Savers: The Invention of Delinquency* (Chicago: University of Chicago Press, 1969); and Steven L. Schlossman, *Love and the American Delinquent: The Theory and Practice of "Progressive" Juvenile Justice, 1825–1920* (Chicago: University of Chicago Press, 1977).

34. Schoff, *The Wayward Child*, 64–72.

35. "State News," *Child-Welfare Magazine* 11 (May 1917): 268.

36. "President's Desk," *Child-Welfare Magazine* 12 (May 1918): 162; "President's Desk," *Child-Welfare Magazine* 11 (June 1917): 277; Mrs. Frederic Schoff, "Some Vital Questions of the Hour for Mothers," *Child-Welfare Magazine* 11 (June 1917): 285–87; "State News," *Child-Welfare Magazine* 12 (May 1918): 184.

37. "State News," *Child-Welfare Magazine* 11 (Aug. 1917): 345; "President's Desk," *Child-Welfare Magazine* 12 (Mar. 1918): 114–15.

38. Quoted in PTA, *Golden Jubilee History*, 35.

39. Jacqueline Jones, *Labor of Love, Labor of Sorrow: Black Women, Work, and the Family from Slavery to the Present* (New York: Basic Books, 1985), 65–66.

40. Frances Ellen Watkins Harper, "The Afro-American Woman," in National Congress of Mothers, *Work and Words*, 67–71; Mrs. Anna Murray, "The Negro Children of America," in National Congress of Mothers, *The Child in Home, School, and State*, 174.

41. Dr. Samuel McCune Lindsay, "Children of Porto Rico," in National Congress of Mothers, *The Children in Home, School, and State*, 135.

42. "President's Desk," *Child-Welfare Magazine* 12 (May 1918): 163; U.S. Bureau of Education, *The Kindergarten as an Americanizer* (Washington, D.C.: Government Printing Office, 1919), 1–2; Mrs. Jeremiah Rhodes, "Department of Americanization," *Child-Welfare Magazine* 14 (Oct. 1919): 44.

43. Linda Gordon, "Family Violence, Feminism, and Social Control," *Feminist Studies* 12 (Fall 1986): 471.

44. Fisher, *Mothers and Children*, 280–81. The book was commended in the *Child-Welfare Magazine* 21 (Oct. 1926): 91.

45. Mary Mumford, "The Public School and the Immigrant," *Child-Welfare Magazine* 4 (Apr. 1910): 232.

46. PTA, *Golden Jubilee History* 58, 101; Overstreet and Overstreet, *Where Children Come First*, 268–69.

47. "Report of National Chairman on Extension of Work Among Colored People," Box 11, Folder 224, Elizabeth Tilton Papers, Arthur and Elizabeth Schlesinger Library on the History of Women in America, Radcliffe College, Cambridge, Mass.

48. "President's Desk," *Child-Welfare Magazine* 10 (Mar. 1916): 230–31. See Mrs. Booker Washington, "Negro Women's Club Work," *Club Woman* 10 (May 1903): 297.

49. Paula Giddings, *When and Where I Enter: The Impact of Black Women on Race and Sex in America* (New York: Bantam, 1984), 94–95. On the National Association of Colored Women, see Wilson Moses, *The Golden Age of Black Nationalism, 1850–1925* (Hamden, Conn.: Archon, 1978), chap. 5; Charles Harris Wesley, *The History of the National Association of Colored Women's Clubs: A Legacy of Service* (Washington, D.C.: NACWC, 1984); Elizabeth L. Davis, *Lifting as They Climb: The National Association of Colored Women* (Washington, D.C.: NACW, 1933); Tullia K. Brown Hamilton, "The National Association of Colored Women, 1896 to 1920" (Ph.D. diss., Emory University, 1978).

50. For an analysis of the differences between black and white women's welfare activism that is not limited to these two organizations, see Linda Gordon, "Black and White Women's Welfare Activism," *Journal of American History* 78 (Sept. 1991): 559–90. Recent works on black women's reform activism include Dorothy Salem, *To Better Our World: Black Women in Organized Reform, 1890–1920* (Brooklyn, N.Y.: Carlson Publishing, 1990); Cynthia Neverdon-Morton, *Afro-American Women of the South and the Advancement of the Race, 1895–1925* (Knoxville: University of Tennessee Press, 1989); Jacqueline Rouse, *Lugenia Burns Hope: Black Southern Reformer* (Athens, Ga.: University of Georgia Press, 1989); Anne Firor Scott, "Most Invisible of All: Black Women's Voluntary Associations," *Journal of Southern History* 56 (Feb. 1990): 3–22; Darlene Clark Hine, "'We Specialize in the Wholly Impossible': The Philanthropic Work of Black Women," in *Lady Bountiful Revisited: Women, Philanthropy, and Power*, ed. Kathleen D. McCarthy (New Brunswick, N.J.: Rutgers University Press, 1990); Gerda Lerner, *The Majority Finds Its Past* (New York: Oxford University Press, 1979), chap. 6. See also the documents in Edyth L. Ross, ed., *Black Heritage in Social Welfare 1860–1930* (Metuchen, N.J.: Scarecrow Press, 1978).

51. Hamilton, "The National Association of Colored Women," 39–51. In her comparison of black and white women activists, Linda Gordon found that 85 percent of the black women married, although many "led lives quite independent of their husbands." Gordon, "Black and White Visions of Welfare," 568.

52. Davis, *Lifting as They Climb*, 132–80. Biographical information on Terrell and Bethune can be found in Barbara Sicherman and Carol Hurd Green, eds., *Notable American Women: The Modern Period* (Cambridge, Mass.: Belknap Press, 1980), 76–80, 678–80. See Dorothy Sterling, *Black Foremothers: Three Lives* (New York: Feminist Press, 1979), for information on Terrell and Ida B. Wells.

53. See Eileen Boris, "The Power of Motherhood: Black and White Activist Mother-Work in the Community: Women Redefine the 'Political,'" *Yale Journal of Law and Feminism* 2 (Fall 1989): 25–49.

54. Quoted in Salem, *To Better Our World*, 268 n. 31.

55. Mary Church Terrell, "Greetings from the National Association of Colored Women," *National Association Notes* 2 (Mar. 1899): 1. Eileen Boris notes that in the manuscript version, the

word "weaker" is crossed out and "oppressed" scratched in above. Boris, "The Power of Motherhood," 36.

56. Quoted in Giddings, *When and Where I Enter*, 100.

57. Terrell quoted in Salem, *To Better Our World*, 31; Williams excerpted in Gerda Lerner, *Black Women in White America* (New York: Vintage, 1972), 575–76. See also Beverly W. Jones, "Mary Church Terrell and the National Association of Colored Women, 1896–1901," *Journal of Negro History* 67 (Spring 1982): 20–33; and Farah Jasmine Griffin, "'A Layin' on of Hands': Organizational Efforts among Black American Women, 1790–1930," *Sage* (Student Supp., 1988): 23–29.

58. "Home Influences among Colored People," *National Association Notes* 1 (May 15, 1897).

59. *The Club Woman* 10 (Aug. 1904): 27; *National Association Notes* 8 (Oct. 1904).

60. Louie D. Shivery, "The History of the Gate City Free Kindergarten Association," excerpted in *Black Heritage in Social Welfare*, ed. Ross, 258–63; Lerner, *Majority Finds Its Past*, 88; Neverdon-Morton, *Afro-American Women*, 142–43.

61. See Rouse, *Lugenia Burns Hope;* Jacqueline Rouse, "Atlanta's African-American Women's Attack on Segregation, 1900–1920," in *Gender, Class, Race and Reform in the Progressive Era,* ed. Noralee Frankel and Nancy S. Dye (Lexington: University Press of Kentucky, 1991), 10–23; Louie D. Shivery, "The Neighborhood Union," in *Black Heritage in Social Welfare,* ed. Ross, 264–81; Ralph E. Luker, "Missions, Institutional Churches, and Settlement Houses: The Black Experience, 1885–1910," *Journal of Negro History* 69 (Summer/Fall 1984): 101–13.

62. Cott, *Grounding of Modern Feminism*, 249.

63. Florence Watkins to Elizabeth Tilton, Dec. 12, 1922, Mar. 21, 1923, and May 4, 1923, Folder 246, Elizabeth Tilton Papers, Schlesinger Library.

64. "The Vital Object of the Congress of Mothers," *Child-Welfare Magazine* 13 (June–July 1919): 281. See also James Killius, "What's the Matter with the PTA Movement?" *Child-Welfare Magazine* 17 (Feb. 1923): 224–26, and the responses in March and May 1923.

65. PTA, *Golden Jubilee History,* 82–84; "1927 Resolutions," *Child-Welfare Magazine* 21 (Aug. 1927): 558.

66. PTA, *Golden Jubilee History,* 102, 109; Orville Brim, *Education for Childrearing* (New York: Russell Sage Foundation, 1959), 330.

67. PTA, *Golden Jubilee History,* 119. According to Roberta Wollons, the Child Study Association of America, the major parent education organization in the 1920s, also retreated from social reform in the 1920s. Wollons, "Educating Mothers: Sidonie Matsner Gruenberg and the Child Study Association" (Ph.D. diss., University of Chicago, 1983), 311. See Steven L. Schlossman, "Philanthropy and the Gospel of Child Development," *History of Education Quarterly* 21 (Fall 1981): 275–99; and Schlossman, "The Formative Era in American Parent Education: Overview and Interpretation," in *Parent Education and Public Policy,* ed. Ron Haskins and Diane Adams (Norwood, N.J.: Ablex, 1983), 7–39.

68. Wollons, "Educating Mothers," 245–46; Julian Butterworth, *The Parent-Teacher Association and Its Work* (New York: Macmillan, 1929), 40. The results of a questionnaire distributed by the PTA to school superintendents in Iowa were reported in "State News," *Child-Welfare Magazine* 14 (Apr. 1920): 251.

69. See Molly Ladd-Taylor, "'The Welfare of Mothers and Babies Is a Dignified Subject of Political Discussion': Progressive Maternalism and the Children's Bureau," in *Mother-Work: Women, Child Welfare, and the State, 1890–1930* (Urbana: University of Illinois Press, 1994), 74–103.

22.

"GO AFTER THE WOMEN"
Americanization and the Mexican Immigrant Woman, 1915–1929

GEORGE J. SANCHEZ

The Americanization of the [Mexican] women is as important a part as that of the men. They are harder to reach but are more easily educated. They can realize in a moment that they are getting the best end of the bargain by the change in relationships between men and women which takes place under the new American order. . . . "Go after the women" should become a slogan among Americanization workers, for after all the greatest good is to be obtained by starting the home off right. The children of these foreigners are the advantages to America, not the naturalized foreigners. These are never 100% Americans, but the second generation may be. "Go after the women" and you may save the second generation for America.

—ALFRED WHITE, AN AMERICANIZATION TEACHER
OF MEXICAN GIRLS, 1923

One reaction to Mexican immigration to the United States in the early twentieth century was the establishment of programs aimed at Mexican women explicitly for the purpose of changing their cultural values. Americanization programs directed toward Mexican immigrants during one of the periods of massive movement across the border are an important contrast to the debates in Congress and among the American public on the utility of unrestricted Mexican immigration. These programs attempted to transform the values of the Mexican immigrant after arrival and encouraged them to conform to the American industrial order in

Reprinted from the Stanford University Center for Chicano Studies Research Working Series, vol. 6, 1984, with the permission of the author.

a prescribed manner. Older Mexican women were seen as primary targets because of their important role in homemaking and child rearing, but when they proved difficult to Americanize these programs refocused their efforts upon the adolescent American-born Chicana.

The Mexican immigrant woman, therefore, was confronted with the reality of integrating two conflicting cultures. She would be attributed with both the positive and negative sides of "La Malinche"—both mother of the Mexican people and traitor to the Mexican race—by members of her own community. Anglo-Americans also classified her as the individual with the most potential either to advance her family into the modern, industrial order of the United States or to inhibit them from becoming productive American citizens. Solutions to the "Mexican problem" were placed squarely in her lap.

Paradoxically, the Chicano family has traditionally been viewed as the one institution in Mexican American life that has consistently resisted the forces of assimilation in the United States. According to the argument advanced by Chicano scholars, the stability and insularity of the Chicano family has acted as a fortress against alien cultural values. Chicanas, in particular, have been seen as the "glue" that keeps the Chicano family together, and they have been designated as the individuals responsible for the maintenance of Mexican tradition. The tenacious insistence of social reformers that Mexican women could cast off vestiges of traditional culture calls this assumption into question.

This study will examine the nature of the "problem" of Mexican immigrant women as defined by Americanization programs in California during the period 1915–29. It will also examine the "solutions" offered by these programs, and the relative success or failure of reformers to carry out their mission of Americanizing Mexican immigrant women in the 1920s. The study is based on the writings of Americanization instructors who worked with Mexican immigrant women during the period and on the literature produced by the California Commission of Immigration and Housing, the primary governmental body involved with the state's immigrant population. I have analyzed this literature in order to assess the assumptions these reformers made about the role of women, the family, and work in Mexican culture and American society in the years before the Great Depression. Prior to that, however, Americanization programs must be placed in the context of Mexican immigration to the United States and the variety of responses to it.

The Nature of Mexican Immigration

The movement of Mexicans across the border into the United States increased substantially in the early twentieth century, although immigration from Mexico had been growing since the late 1880s. At its peak from 1910 to 1930, Mexican immigration increased by at least 300 percent.[1] The industrial expansion of the economy in the Southwest created an escalating demand for low-wage labor, and Mexicans took advantage of the economic opportunities available. The development of a transportation system in northern Mexico in the early part of the century facilitated the movement by connecting the populous central plateau of Mexico with the American Southwest. This railroad connection provided the means by which many migrants could escape the political, economic, and social disruption of the Mexican Revolution of 1910. World War I drew workers into war industries and the military, and the subsequent labor vacuum created an additional incentive for American employers to encourage immigration from Mexico. In fact, employers were able to pressure the federal government to establish a temporary admissions program for Mexican workers which served as a catalyst for increased immigration from 1917 to 1920. Although this enlarged flow was temporarily slowed during the recession of 1921, it grew to unprecedented levels during the rest of the decade as restrictions upon European and Asian immigration forced more employers to turn to workers from south of the border.[2]

The volume of this migration was nothing less than staggering. Approximately 100,000 persons of Mexican descent or birth lived in the United States in 1900; by 1930, this figure had climbed to 1.5 million. More than one million Mexicans— about 10 percent of Mexico's population—had entered the United States from 1910 to 1930. In 1930, 94 percent of the foreign-born Mexicans living in the United States had immigrated since 1900, and 64 percent had entered since 1915.[3]

Movement into the urban centers of the Southwest and Midwest from the countryside characterized this population shift. The Mexican population in Los Angeles more than tripled during the 1920s, making the Los Angeles barrio the largest Mexican community in the world outside of Mexico City. The Mexican populations of San Antonio and El Paso (and Texas in general) experienced between 50 and 100 percent growth in this decade. Even more dramatic was the establishment of completely new centers of Mexican population in the Midwest. The combined Mexican population of Ohio, Illinois, Indiana, and Michigan experienced a 669.2 percent growth in the 1920s, almost all of it concentrated in urban areas, particularly Chicago and Detroit. By 1930, one of every two Mexicans in the United States lived in an urban setting.[4]

The rapid increase in the numbers of Mexican urban dwellers completely transformed the Mexican communities that had existed before the turn of the century. Pressures on available housing in the barrios led to overcrowded, unsanitary living conditions and eventually forced many residents to move away from traditional centers of Mexican settlement. Barrios expanded rapidly during the World

War I years, and newcomers from Mexico no longer entered a well-defined, tight-knit community.[5] The fact that most Mexican migrants to the cities came from the ranks of Mexico's rural poor added burdens on community resources. In addition, the economic position of these migrants in the cities was tenuous at best. At the conclusion of World War I many Mexicans lost their new-found industrial jobs to returning servicemen, and the 1921 depression encouraged rural workers to seek refuge in urban areas already burdened with unemployment.[6]

The nature of Mexican immigration also recast the dynamics between men and women in the barrios. Throughout the first three decades of the twentieth century, men outnumbered women among Mexicans traveling northward at an average ratio of five to four. The greater the distance from the Mexican border and the more rural the community, the lesser the presence of Chicanas and the fewer the number of Chicano families. Chicago by 1930, for example, had 170 Mexican males for every 100 Mexican females, while El Paso had a Mexican male-to-female ratio of 86/100 in the same year. Urban communities as a whole by 1930 had a Mexican male-to-female ratio of 116/100, compared to a 148/100 ratio in rural communities. Los Angeles in this period maintained a fairly even sex ratio, attracting many Mexican immigrant families and balancing single-male immigration from Mexico with male out-migration into California's rural areas.[7]

Cities in the American Southwest also served as focal points for the reconstituting of Mexican familial constellations and the construction of new families north of the border. Los Angeles was often the end point for a reunification of extended families through a chain migration that saw a male head of household venture out alone for work in the United States and, once settled, send for his wife and children, and frequently other kin such as brothers, sisters, cousins, and parents. These extended family networks were crucial both in dealing with the disorienting aspects of migration—finding jobs, living in temporary homes, and possible sickness or death—and in reinforcing native customs, values, and institutions from Mexico.[8] Although few single women emigrated to Los Angeles alone, single Mexican males—known as "solos"—often established themselves in the city, married American-born Chicanas, and began families of their own. One study of 769 Mexican households in Los Angeles during the 1920s revealed a high birthrate in Mexican families compared to Anglo-American families, and an average number of children per family of 4.3.[9] Clearly, the lives of most Mexican immigrant women and men centered on their families in the early twentieth century.

"The Mexican Problem"

The response of Anglo-Americans to this influx of Mexican migrants ranged widely. Restrictionists, consisting primarily of organized labor and nativists, sought to limit the migration; employers fought to keep Mexican immigration unrestricted; and a third group, whom I shall call "Americanists," viewed the restrictionist debate as a secondary concern to the Americanization of the migrants to ensure their cultural allegiance to the United States after arrival.[10]

The most vocal respondents were the restrictionists, who wanted to see Mexican immigration contained, stopped, even reversed. Organized labor, under the auspices of the American Federation of Labor, viewed Mexican immigrants as cheap labor who would compete with "American" workers. Samuel Gompers urged Congress to include Mexico in the quota restrictions, arguing that Mexicans would not be content with farm labor and would soon attempt to enter the trades in the cities. Only months before his death in 1924, Gompers expressed concern that in Los Angeles "it appeared to me that every other person met on the streets was a Mexican.[11]

In addition to economic interests, racial attitudes influenced restrictionist sentiments. Nativists, including Anglo-American politicians, academics, reporters, and others who believed in Anglo-Saxon racial superiority, waged the longest and most virulent campaign against unrestricted Mexican immigration. After successfully pushing Congress to severely limit immigration from Asia and southern and eastern Europe in 1920, nativists were dismayed to discover that immigration law still allowed for the widespread introduction of "foreigners" whom they considered just as, if not more, unassimilable and undesirable. These nativists called for restriction on racial grounds based on the "Indian" or "Negro" makeup of the Mexican, the social threat to "American standards of living," and a view of the Mexican as an unstable citizen in a democracy.[12] Kenneth L. Roberts, writing in the *Saturday Evening Post,* expressed the nativist sentiments clearly when he stated that in Los Angeles one can "see the endless streets crowded with the shacks of illiterate, diseased, pauperized Mexicans, taking no interest whatever in the community, living constantly on the ragged edge of starvation, bringing countless numbers of American citizens into the world with the reckless prodigality of rabbits."[13]

In contrast to the restrictionists, southwestern employers, particularly railroad, agricultural, and mining companies, defended unrestricted Mexican immigration on economic grounds. They were no less racist in their attitudes but stressed the economic advantage of Mexican labor, arguing that "white" laborers would not and should not perform this work. According to these employers, Mexican labor provided the most desirable option for filling their labor shortages and was vital for the

survival of their industries. To counteract the racial and political arguments that restrictionists were making, employers stressed that the undesirable traits outlined by
nativists actually benefited American society; the Mexican worker, they argued,
provided the perfect, docile employee, had no interest in intermixing with Americans, and in fact returned to Mexico once their labor was no longer needed. W. H.
Knox, of the Arizona Cotton Growers' Association, belittled nativist fears by asking, "Have you ever heard, in the history of the United States, or in the history of
the human race, of the white race being overrun by a class of people of the men-
tality of the Mexicans? I never have. We took this country from Mexico. Mexico
did not take it from us. To assume that there is any danger of any likelihood of the
Mexican coming in here and colonizing this country and taking it away from us,
to my mind, is absurd."[14]

While the battle between restrictionists and employers raged in legislatures
and newspaper editorial pages, a third group took a different approach in dealing
with the "Mexican problem." Initially, the base of support for the "Americanist"
position came from progressive social reformers, many of whom were middle-class
Anglo-American women dedicated to the social settlement movement and the Social Gospel tradition. These individuals felt that society had an obligation to assimilate the Mexican immigrant and hoped to improve societal treatment of
immigrants in general. However, as World War I heightened anxieties concerning
immigrants, nativist sentiment began to affect Americanization efforts through the
"100 Percent American" movement, which wanted to ensure the loyalty of the immigrant to the United States. Additionally, big business took an interest in the
Americanization movement, since it wanted a method to combat radicalism
among foreign-born workers. Employers supported efforts to produce loyal, obe-
dient employees, with at least one ultraconservative business group in Los Angeles
encouraging a "superpatriotism," which included upholding the "open shop."[15]
With this uneasy alliance of support, Americanization activities spread throughout
the country in the late 1910s and 1920s, and programs situated in the Southwest had
as a primary target the Mexican immigrant.

In California, such "Americanists" first wielded power with the election of a
Progressive governor, Hiram Johnson, in 1910. Johnson secured passage of legislation in 1913 establishing a permanent Commission of Immigration and Housing,
which investigated the working and living conditions of all immigrants in the state
and spearheaded efforts to teach English to foreigners and to involve them in
Americanization programs.[16] Though governmental bodies and private organizations in other states also sought to Americanize Mexicans, California's program was
the most complete attempt to bring together government, business, and private
citizens to deal with the "problem of the immigrant" in a scientific and rational

fashion. The commission successfully recruited university academics, religious social workers, government bureaucrats, and middle-class volunteers.

Unlike the restrictionists and the employers, these reformers considered the Mexican immigrant to be similar to European immigrants in California at the time. In their eyes Mexicans might have presented a greater challenge than did Italians or Jews, but they found nothing endemic to the Mexican character that would prevent their eventual assimilation into the "American way of life." What distinguished such Americanization efforts from the social settlement response to European immigrants before World War I, however, was the lack of a focus on "immigrant gifts" to American society.[17] In the 1920s, little value was given to Mexican culture in Americanization programs; rather, Americanists saw immigrant traditions and customs as impediments to a rapid, thorough integration into American life.

Americanizing the Mexican Woman

As the commission expanded its Americanization programs, commissioners began to center their attention on the Mexican immigrant woman and her potential role in the cultural transformation of her family. In 1915, the state legislature had passed the Home Teacher Act, which allowed school districts to employ teachers "to work in the homes of the pupils, instructing children and adults in matters relating to school attendance, . . . in sanitation, in the English language, in household duties, . . . and in the fundamental principles of the American system of government and the rights and duties of citizenship."[18] In the war years, the home teacher became the centerpiece of Americanization efforts aimed at the Mexican family.

Why did the Mexican immigrant woman become the target of Americanization programs? First, Mexican women were seen as being primarily responsible for the transmission of values in the home. According to the strategy advocated by the Americanists, if the Mexican female adopted American values, the rest of her family would certainly follow suit. Pearl Ellis, who worked with Mexican girls in southern California throughout the 1920s, stressed the important "influence of the home" in creating an employee who is "more dependable and less revolutionary in his tendencies. . . . The homekeeper creates the atmosphere, whether it be one of harmony and cooperation or of dissatisfaction and revolt."[19]

Motherhood, in fact, became the juncture at which the Mexican immigrant woman's potential role in Americanization was most highly valued. By focusing on the strategic position of the mother in the Mexican family, Americanization programs hoped to have an impact on the second generation of Mexicans in the

United States, even if the immigrant generation itself turned out less malleable than expected. Since the father's role in parenting was assumed to be minimal, co-operation of the Mexican mother was crucial. Americanization ideology was undeniably infused with the traditional American belief in an exalted role of the mother in shaping the future political citizenry of the republic.[20] In the most grandiose visions of Americanists, the role of the mother loomed incredibly large: "As the mother furnishes the stream of life to the babe at her breast, so will she shower dewdrops of knowledge on the plastic mind of her young child. Her ideals and aspirations will be breathed into its spirit, molding its character for all time. The child, in turn, will pass these rarer characteristics on to its descendants, thus developing the intellectual, physical, and spiritual qualities of the individual, which in mass, are contributions to civilization."[21]

Besides creating a home environment that fit in an industrial order, the Americanization of Mexican women was valued for the direct benefits American society might gain from labor-force participation of female immigrants. Mexican women were seen as prime targets for meeting the labor need for domestic servants, seamstresses, laundresses, and service workers in the Southwest. Black and European immigrant women had not migrated to the American Southwest in large enough numbers to fill the growing demand in these areas. Ironically, in 1908 a Bureau of Labor inspector had regretfully noted that Mexican "immigrant women have so little conception of domestic arrangements in the United States that the task of training them would be too heavy for American housewives."[22] A decade later, Americanization programs were busy training Mexican women to fulfill these tasks.

Importantly, the conflict between the private responsibilities of American women to their homes and families and the public roles women began to play as workers and citizens in the 1920s were not addressed in Americanization programs.[23] Americanists were too interested in the contribution Mexican women could make in the transformation of their families from a rural, preindustrial people to an urban, modern American unit to worry about "women's proper place." Herbert Gutman, in his important book *Work, Culture, and Society in Industrializing America,* has examined the "recurrent tension" produced when immigrant men and women new to the American industrial order came in contact with the rigorous discipline of the factory system.[24] Because the Southwest lagged behind the rest of the nation in industrialization, local reformers were anxious to introduce Mexican women and men as rapidly as possible into a growing industrial society and to inculcate Mexican families with a "Protestant work ethic." To achieve these ends, the public and private responsibilities of women were blurred, and in fact Americanists discovered a peculiar way in which to economize their energy by taking care of both issues at once. By encouraging Mexican immigrant women to wash, sew, cook, budget, and mother happily and efficiently, Americans would be assured that Mexican women would be ready to enter the labor market while simultaneously presiding over a home that nurtured American values of economy.

Americanists viewed the ability to speak English as the most fundamental skill necessary for the assimilation of the immigrant, both female and male. English instruction was intended to provide the immigrant with much more than facility in the common language of the United States; it also sought to imbue the foreigner with the values of American society. The commission recommended in 1917 "that employers of immigrants be shown the relation between a unified working force, speaking a common language, and industrial prosperity."[25] In 1918, Mrs. Amanda Matthews Chase, a home teacher in southern California working for the commission, developed a primer for teaching English to foreign-speakers by covering "the most essential elements in the home teaching curriculum" and by associating these "with the pupils' own lives and affairs."[26] For example, home teachers were instructed to teach the following song to immigrant women (to the tune "Tramp, Tramp, Tramp, the Boys are Marching"). The song was intended to instruct them about women's work while they learned twenty-seven new English words:

> We are working every day,.
> So our boys and girls can play.
> > We are working for our homes and country, too;
> We like to wash, to sew, to cook,
> We like to write, or read a book,
> > We are working, working, working every day.
> Work, work, work,
> We're always working,
> > Working for our boys and girls,
> Working for our boys and girls,
> For our homes and country, too—
> > We are working, working, working every day.[27]

Despite the concerns of reformers, Mexican women continued to lag behind men in learning the English language. A study of 1,081 Mexican families in Los Angeles conducted in 1921 found that while 55 percent of the men were unable to speak English, an overwhelming 74 percent of the women could not speak the language. Similar gaps existed in English reading and writing.[28] Americanists blamed the patriarchal, outmoded nature of the Mexican family for this discrepancy. "The married Mexican laborer does not allow his wife, as a rule, to attend evening classes," reported Emory Bogardus, a sociologist at the University of Southern California.[29]

Getting the Mexican woman out of her home became a priority for Americanization programs because Americanists saw this as the only avenue available for her intellectual progress and, of course, the only method by which Americanists could succeed in altering her values. Americanists consistently criticized the alleged limitations placed upon the Mexican wife by her husband as traditional and unprogressive. Home teachers visited each Mexican home in their districts individually in order to gain the trust of family members and gradually encourage the husband to allow his wife to attend English-language classes. The scheduling of alternative classes in the afternoons for wives and mothers facilitated this process.[30] According to one Americanization instructor, if left in the home, the Mexican woman's "intellectual ability is stimulated only by her husband and if he be of the average peon type, the stimulation is not very great." The Mexican home, according to the same teacher, "being a sacred institution, is guarded by all the stolid tradition of centuries."[31] If the Mexican home remained such a fortress, Americanists would not be able to accomplish their mission among the Mexican immigrant population.

Americanization programs did not, however, intend to undermine the traditional Mexican family structure; rather, these programs depended on the cohesiveness of the Mexican family to achieve their goal of assimilation. Home teachers, even when they did get Mexican women out of the house to attend class, encouraged the acquisition of traditionally feminine skills which could then be utilized within the confines of the household. The conscious strategy of these reformers was to use the Mexican woman as a conduit for creating a home environment well suited to the demands of an industrial economy. In the ditty "The Day's Work," for example, home teachers utilized the following sequence of English phrases to emphasize a woman's contribution to this new order:

> In the morning the women get breakfast.
> Their husbands go to work.
> Their children go to school.
> Then the women get their houses in good order.
> They give the baby its bath.
> They wash, or iron, or cook.
> They get the dinner.
> After dinner they wash the dishes.
> Then they sew, or rest, or visit their friends, or go to school.
> The children must help to cook the supper and wash the dishes.[32]

Changing Family Habits

Two particular areas in which the Mexican female was regarded as crucial in transforming outdated practices in the home were diet and health. Americanization programs encouraged Mexican women to give up their penchant for fried foods, their too frequent consumption of rice and beans, and their custom of serving all members of the family—from infants to grandparents—the same meal. According to Americanists, the modern Mexican woman should replace tortillas with bread, serve lettuce instead of beans, and broil instead of fry. Malnourishment in Mexican families was not blamed on lack of food or resources but on "not having the right varieties of foods containing constituents favorable to growth and development."[33]

Food and diet management became tools in a system of social control intended to construct a well-behaved citizenry. A healthy diet was seen not only as essential for proper health but as fundamental for creating productive members of society. In the eyes of reformers, the typical noon lunch of the Mexican child, thought to consist of "a folded tortilla with no filling," became the first step in a life of crime. With "no milk or fruit to whet the appetite," the child would become lazy and subsequently "take food from the lunch boxes of more fortunate children" in order to appease his or her hunger. "Thus," reformers alleged, "the initial step in a life of thieving is taken."[34] Teaching immigrant women proper food values would keep the head of the family out of jail, the rest of the family off the charity lists, and save taxpayers a great amount of money.

Along with diet, health and cleanliness became watchwords for Americanization programs aimed at Mexican women. One of the primary functions of home teachers was to impress upon the minds of Mexican mothers and mothers-to-be "that a clean body and clean mind are the attributes of a good citizen."[35] Reformers working with Mexican women were warned, however, that their task would be a difficult one. "Sanitary, hygienic, and dietic measures are not easily learned by the Mexican. His philosophy of life flows along the lines of least resistance and it requires far less exertion to remain dirty than to clean up."[36] The lack of cleanliness among Mexicans was blamed for their poor state of health, and this connection was the main reason why the stereotype of the "dirty Mexican" brought concern to the Anglo urban dweller. According to an eminent sociologist working with Americanization programs, Anglo-Americans "object to the presence of Mexican children in the schools that their children attend, for fear that the latter will catch a contagious disease. A relatively permanent form of racial antipathy is the result."[37]

The ability of Americanization teachers to inculcate "American" standards of diet, health, and cleanliness among Mexican women was not considered the only essential component in creating a healthy home environment, however. All of the gains made by these programs would be lost if the Mexican female bore too many of these nascent citizens. Americanists worried that without limiting family size, the Mexican mother would be unable to adequately train each individual member of her household.

Control of immigrant population growth was a long-standing concern both of those who defined themselves as progressives and of nativists. Fears of "race suicide" had existed in the Anglo-American mind since the late nineteenth century, when Americans had first encountered immigrant groups who exhibited a greater propensity to repopulate themselves than native-born Americans. When this fear was applied to the Mexican immigrant, both nativists and Americanists shared a common concern: the nativist wanted to control Mexican population growth for fear of a "greaser invasion," while Americanists viewed unrestricted population growth as a vestige of Old World ways that would have to be abandoned in a modern industrial world.

Mexican women, according to Americanization strategy, should bear the brunt of the responsibility for family planning. Americanists gave a variety of reasons for the presumed inability of Mexican women to control reproduction: (1) lack of training in sex matters and a primitive sexuality; (2) early marriage of girls because of tradition and the "inherent sentimentality" of the Mexican female; and (3) religiously based opposition to birth control.[38] Despite these barriers, Americanization teachers reported that Mexican mothers were beginning to exhibit discomfort with large families, occasionally inquiring about birth control measures, and warning other women to delay marriage on the grounds of "much work, too much children."[39]

The Mexican Woman as Worker

Americanists viewed such evidence of changing attitudes as a hopeful sign, because limited reproduction opened up new opportunities for Mexican women inside and outside the home. Inside the home, Mexican women could devote more time to the "proper" raising of fewer children and the creation of an "American" home environment. Outside the home, it enabled new possibilities for female employment by freeing Mexican women from the heavy burden of constant child rearing. Traditionally, Mexican women had not engaged in wage labor outside the home because of their duties to reproduce and maintain the family unit. If a

Mexican immigrant woman worked, it was usually before marriage in her late adolescent or early adult years.[40]

The new demands of the industrial American Southwest, however, created a need for low-paid, low-status labor at tasks that had traditionally been performed by women inside the home. The labeling of domestic service, clothing manufacture, laundry, and food service as "women's work" presented a problem to employers in these industries in the Southwest. Employers were forced to search for an alternative female labor supply because of restrictions placed upon Asian and European immigration, the paucity of black migration to the Southwest, and the growing demands of Anglo middle-class families for these services. Despite all the traditional objections to Mexican women working outside the home, Americanization programs actively sought to prepare Mexican immigrant women for entrance into these sex-segregated occupations.[41]

The fact that these employment opportunities were in occupations that utilized traditionally female forms of labor made it easier for Americanists to advocate instruction in these tasks without upsetting the traditional social order within the Mexican family. For example, skill at needlework was viewed in Americanization programs as an inherited trait among Mexican women, passed down through generations. Americanization teachers were directed to "strive to foster it in them [so] that we may not lose this valuable contribution to our civilization with the passing of time." This form of encouragement, according to reformers, should be started as early as possible—by the third year in school at least—since Mexican girls were apt to drop out of school at an early age and would "miss out" on this opportunity to gain "greater respect for the school and for our civilization."[42]

Whatever success Americanization programs had in promoting greater standards of cleanliness and efficiency in home management were seen as having a double benefit for American society. For example, Americanists stressed the ability to set a table and to serve food properly. Table etiquette not only encouraged Mexican women to aspire to arrange their family's meals by American standards but also discouraged "sloppy appearance and uncleanliness of person [that] would not be tolerated in a waitress and would be the cause of no position or losing one already obtained."[43] Americanists also reasoned that the burden on a private citizen employing a Mexican woman as a domestic servant would be lightened if that woman had already been adequately trained through their programs. As one social worker stated in the late 1920s: "Americans want household help for two or three days a week, and they can, if they will, take Mexican women and teach them. It requires patience to be sure, but there are large numbers of Mexicans who can fill the household gap if the proper conditions are made."[44]

Additionally, encouraging Mexican women to engage in hard work was viewed as an important facet in "curing" the habits of the stereotypical "lazy Mexican." According to one Americanization teacher, "Quien sabe?" (who knows) was the philosophy of all of Mexico, and the inability of Mexicans to connect the things that are valued as worthwhile to the effort necessary to obtain them made Mexican laborers inefficient.[45] Another felt that "the laziness of Mexicans" was due to "climate conditions and inherited tendencies" which only hard work could root out.[46] Consequently, putting Mexican women to work would have the effect of promoting discipline in them, which in turn would encourage them to pass on a similar level of self-control to their children.

The Failure of Americanization

Did these programs, in fact, change Mexican family practices and produce "citizens of the republic" who adopted American values and customs? Certainly Americanization programs did produce Mexican converts to the American way of life. Many immigrant women flocked to programs that promised greater social freedom for them, and healthier, more contented lives for family members. By and large, however, Americanization programs failed to change the fundamental cultural practices of Mexican immigrant families for two principal reasons: (1) Mexican immigrants in the 1920s never fully committed themselves to integration into American life. Even when changes in cultural practices did occur, Americanization programs had little role in directing this evolution. (2) The various forces behind Americanization programs never assembled an optimistic ideological approach that might have attracted Mexican immigrant women. Instead, they presented a limited, inconsistent scheme that could not handle the demographic realities of the Mexican immigrant community.

Indeed, most Mexican immigrant families remained unaffected by Americanization efforts throughout the 1920s. A government study in 1930 found that the Mexican immigrant population in California, who had the lowest rate of naturalization of any immigrant group in the state in 1920, actually experienced a decline in the ratio of naturalized Mexicans among the total alien Mexican population from 1920 to 1930.[47] Mexican women remained very unlikely to pursue American citizenship or to encourage family members to do so. In fact, in a study conducted in 1923, 55 percent of the Mexican immigrants surveyed considered it their duty to remain politically loyal to Mexico, while almost all of the rest refused to answer the question.[48]

Within the home, little cultural change among the Mexican population was evident. A Mexican sociologist, Manuel Gamio, found that although material possessions often did change, Mexicans immigrants retained their ethics, culture, and loyalty to Mexico to a very large extent.[49] In fact, as the Mexican barrios grew extensively during the 1920s, the need for Mexicans to interact with Anglos lessened. Mexicans were more likely than ever to retain their own cultural values, because they experienced minimal contact with Anglo institutions.[50]

The one area in which change is apparent is that of female employment. Textile factories, laundries, hotels, wholesale and retail stores, and bakeries all seem to have been successful in recruiting Mexican women as employees during the 1920s in Los Angeles.[51] Few of these women, however, entered these industries as a result of Americanization efforts; rather, most had little choice in the matter. A study of Mexican women working in Los Angeles industries conducted in 1928 concluded that 62 percent of the women interviewed entered their occupations because of poverty or economic necessity. Moreover, nine-tenths of these women were unmarried, most were under the age of twenty-three, and two-thirds had been born in the United States.[52] It appears that unmarried older daughters would be the first women to seek employment, rather than older, married Mexican women, because this pattern was more familiar in Mexico and more acceptable in the family and community.[53]

Americanization programs did seem to encourage acculturation among the second generation, although not always in exactly the manner intended. The change in cultural values among children born or raised in the United States often led to conflict with Mexican immigrant parents. The sociologist Emory Bogardus noted that during the late 1920s and early 1930s Mexican girls often ran away from home in order to seek pleasure or to avoid parental discipline and control.[54] One Mexican immigrant mother explained: "The freedom and independence in this country bring the children into conflict with their parents. They learn nicer ways, learn about the outside world, learn how to speak English, and then they become ashamed of their parents who brought them up here that they might have better advantages." Another Mexican mother placed the blame squarely on American values: "It is because they can run around so much and be so free, that our Mexican girls do not know how to act. So many girls run away and get married. This terrible freedom in this United States. The Mexican girls seeing American girls with freedom, they want it too, so they go where they like. They do not mind their parents; this terrible freedom. But what can the Mexican mothers do? It is the custom, and we cannot change it, but it is bad."[55]

Rather than providing Mexican immigrant women with an attainable picture of assimilation, Americanization programs could only offer them idealized versions of American values. In reality, what was achieved turned out to be little more than

second-class citizenship. The most progressive assumptions behind Americanization programs were never fully shared by the government or business interests involved, and thus they could never be fully implemented. One Americanization
teacher who spent the decade working with Mexican immigrants noted with disappointment in 1923 that the newly elected governor of California had eliminated
financial provisions for the Americanization program in the public schools from
his budget.[56] At least one historian has concluded that the "love affair between the
progressive and the businessman" in California inevitably led, in the 1920s, to a
blunting of "the cutting edge of progressive social reform."[57] By 1927, the ambivalence of the reformers became apparent when the Commission of Immigration and
Housing itself sided with restrictionists, called for an end to unlimited immigration from Mexico, and blamed immigrants for "causing an immense social problem in our charities, schools and health departments."[58] Caught in the middle of a
growing debate surrounding Mexican immigration, social reformers were never
able to argue forcefully for their own particular program for dealing with the "Mexican problem."

The halfhearted effort of administrators of Americanization programs limited
available personnel and resources and ensured that the programs would never be
able to cope with the volume of Mexican migration. The barrios expanded so
quickly in the 1920s that any single Americanization teacher found it impossible to
keep abreast of the number of new Mexican families in her district who needed a
resumption of her program from scratch. Newer areas of Mexican settlement were
usually beyond the reach of established Americanization programs entirely. Furthermore, Mexicans experienced a high degree of geographic mobility in this period that easily wiped out whatever progress had been made by programs in a given
community. According to the historian Richard Romo, fewer than one-third of
Mexicans present in Los Angeles in 1917–18 were present in the city one decade
later.[59] The Americanization teacher Amanda Chase acknowledged the extent of
this problem when dealing with Mexican women: "I have had in my class record
book this year the names of about half as many Mexican women as there are Mexican families in the district. But a third of them moved to other districts."[60] Mexican women could not hope to develop allegiances to the United States when the
economic condition of their families forced them to migrate repeatedly in search
of an economic livelihood.

In the end, Americanization programs never had the time to develop sufficiently to offer a solution to the problems of Mexican immigrants in the United
States. With the stock market crash of 1929 and the subsequent Great Depression
of the 1930s, all attempts to Americanize Mexican immigrant women came to an
abrupt end. Rather than searching for ways to assimilate Mexican immigrants,

American society looked for methods to be rid of them altogether. About 500,000 Mexicans left the United States during the 1930s under strong pressure from the government, and up to one-tenth of these individuals had resided in Los Angeles.[61] Americanists joined in these efforts to repatriate Mexican residents; their commitment to improving the conditions of the Mexican female had no place in an economically depressed America.

However short-lived, Americanization programs offer us a unique opportunity to examine the assumptions made about both Mexican and American culture and to scrutinize the values of the Progressive Era in its waning moments. For a time, a certain group of American citizens felt that the Mexican immigrant woman could be fit into American society, but only in a particular fashion. Her role in the creation of a new industrial order would be to transform her own home into an efficient, productive family unit, while producing law-abiding, loyal American citizens eager to do their duty for capitalist expansion in the American Southwest. Furthermore, once she had learned proper American home care, she would help solve "the servant problem" in Anglo-American homes by providing a cheap but efficient form of domestic labor. Americanists felt that they were offering Mexican women an opportunity that they could ill afford to turn down. Apparently most Mexican women in the United States did just that.

NOTES

1. Jose Hernandez Alvarez, "A Demographic Profile of the Mexican Immigration to the United States, 1910–1950," *Journal of Inter-American Studies* 25 (1983): 472.

2. Mark Reisler, *By the Sweat of Their Brow: Mexican Immigrant Labor in the United States, 1900–1940* (Westport, Conn.: Greenwood Press, 1976), pp. 14–17, 41–42, 55–58.

3. Richard Romo, "Responses to Mexican Immigration, 1910–1930," *Aztlan* 6, no. 2 (1975): 173; Romo, "The Urbanization of Southwestern Chicanos in the Early Twentieth Century," *New Scholar* 6 (1977): 194.

4. Romo, "Urbanization," pp. 194–95; Reisler, *Sweat*, p. 267.

5. For Los Angeles, see Richard Romo, *East Los Angeles: History of a Barrio* (Austin: University of Texas Press, 1983), pp. 77–79; for El Paso, see Mario T. Garcia, *Desert Immigrants: The Mexicans of El Paso, 1880–1920* (New Haven: Yale University Press, 1981), pp. 141–43.

6. Romo, "Responses," p. 182; Reisler, *Sweat*, p. 50.

7. Alvarez, "Demographic Profile," pp. 481–82; Romo, "Urbanization," pp. 195–96.

8. Mario T. Garcia, "La Familia: The Mexican Immigrant Family, 1900–1930," in *Work, Family, Sex Roles, Language: The National Association of Chicano Studies, Selected Papers 1979*, ed. Mario Barrera, Alberto Camarillo, and Francisco Hernandez (Berkeley: Tonatiuh-Quinto Sol International, 1980), pp. 120–24.

9. Romo, *East Los Angeles*, pp. 52, 83; Alvarez, "Demographic Profile," p. 482.

10. My categories largely correspond with those of John Higham in his discussion of the restrictionist debate surrounding European immigration, with one notable exception—unlike the Mexican community, European immigrant groups themselves often produced political leaders and organizations who joined employers in fighting against restriction; John Higham, *Strangers in the Land: Patterns of American Nativism, 1860–1925,* 2d ed. (New York: Atheneum, 1963), pp. 301–7.

11. Reisler, *Sweat,* p. 169; Romo, "Responses," p. 187.

12. Reisler, *Sweat,* pp. 151–69.

13. Kenneth L. Roberts, "The Docile Mexican," *Saturday Evening Post,* March 10, 1928, p. 43.

14. U.S. Congress, House, Committee on Immigration and Naturalization, *Hearings on Temporary Admission of Illiterate Mexican Laborers,* 69th Congress, 1st sess., 1926, p. 191; and ibid., *Hearings on Seasonal Agricultural Laborers from Mexico,* p. 46.

15. Higham, *Strangers,* pp. 234–63; Edwin Layton, "The Better America Federation: A Case Study of Superpatriotism," *Pacific Historical Review* 30 (1961): 137–47.

16. Spencer Olin, *California's Prodigal Sons: Hiram Johnson and Progressives, 1911–1917* (Berkeley: University of California Press, 1968), pp. 76–80.

17. See Higham, *Strangers,* pp. 116–23; and Allen F. Davis, *Spearheads for Reform: The Social Settlements and the Progressive Movement, 1890–1914* (New York: Oxford University Press, 1967), pp. 84–102, for a fuller discussion of the treatment of immigrants by social settlements.

18. California, Commission of Immigration and Housing (CIH), "The Home Teacher, Immigrant Education Leaflet No. 5" (San Francisco, 1916), p. 8.

19. Pearl Idelia Ellis, *Americanization through Homemaking* (Los Angeles: Wetzel Publishing, 1929), p. 31.

20. See Linda Kerber, *Women of the Republic: Intellect and Ideology in Revolutionary America* (Chapel Hill: University of North Carolina Press, 1980), for the origins of this ideology.

21. Ellis, *Americanization through Homemaking,* p. 65.

22. See Mario T. Garcia, "The Chicana in American History: The Mexican Women of El Paso, 1880–1920—A Case Study," *Pacific Historical Review* 49 (May 1980): 326.

23. Interestingly, the clash between domestic duties and work outside the home became a much addressed, yet unresolved, issue in the 1920s among middle-class, college-educated Anglo-American women—the very group recruited to become Americanization teachers. See Carl Degler, *At Odds: Women and the Family in American from the Revolution to the Present* (Oxford: Oxford University Press, 1980), pp. 411–13; and Lois Scharf, *To Work and to Wed: Female Employment, Feminism, and the Great Depression* (Westport, Conn.: Greenwood Press, 1980), pp. 21–43.

24. Herbert G. Gutman, *Work, Culture, and Society in Industrializing America* (New York: Vintage Books, 1977), p. 13.

25. California, Commission of Immigration and Housing, "A Discussion of Methods of Teaching English to Adult Foreigners, with a Report on Los Angeles County" (Sacramento, 1917), p. 21.

26. California, Commission of Immigration and Housing, "Primer for Foreign-Speaking Women, Part II," compiled under Mrs. Amanda Matthews Chase (Sacramento, 1918), p. 3.

27. Ibid., p. 5.

28. Jay S. Stowell, *The Near Side of the Mexican Question* (New York: George H. Doran, 1921), p. 102.

29. Emory S. Bogardus, *The Mexican in the United States* (Los Angeles: University of Southern California Press, 1934), p. 81.

30. CIH, "Discussion of Methods," pp. 12–14.

31. Alfred White, "The Apperceptive Mass of Foreigners as Applied to Americanization, the Mexican Group" (master's thesis, University of California, 1923), p. 30.

32. CIH, "Primer," p. 9.

33. Ellis, *Americanization through Homemaking*, pp. 19, 21, 29.

34. Ibid., p. 26.

35. Ibid., p. 47.

36. Ibid., p. 64.

37. Bogardus, *The Mexican*, p. 33.

38. Bogardus, *The Mexican*, p. 25; Ellis, *Americanization through Homemaking*, pp. 61–62.

39. Bogardus, *The Mexican*, p. 26.

40. Garcia, "La Familia," pp. 124–27.

41. For an excellent discussion of occupational sex segregation in this period, see Ruth Milkman, "Women's Work and the Economic Crisis: Some Lessons from the Great Depression," *Review of Radical Political Economics* 8 (Spring 1976): 75–78.

42. Ellis, *Americanization through Homemaking*, pp. 15, 13.

43. Ibid., p. 35.

44. Bogardus, *The Mexican*, p. 43.

45. White, "Apperceptive Mass," p. 20.

46. Ellis, *Americanization through Homemaking*, p. 43.

47. California, "Mexicans in California: Report of Governor C.C. Young's Mexican Fact-Finding Committee" (Sacramento, 1930), pp. 61–74.

48. Evangeline Hymer, "A Study of the Social Attitudes of Adult Mexican Immigrants in Los Angeles and Vicinity" (master's thesis, University of Southern California, 1923), p. 51.

49. Manuel Gamio, *Mexican Immigration to the United States: A Study of Human Migration and Adjustment* (1930; New York: Dover, 1971), pp. 172–73.

50. Romo, *East Los Angeles*, p. 162.

51. Ibid., p. 118.

52. Paul S. Taylor, "Mexican Women in Los Angeles Industry in 1928," *Aztlan* 11, no. 1 (1980): 103.

53. Garcia, "La Familia," p. 127. This pattern is similar to that found among Italian immigrant families. See Virginia Yans-McLaughlin, *Family and Community: Italian Immigrants in Buffalo, 1880–1930* (Ithaca: Cornell University Press, 1977), pp. 180–217.

54. Bogardus, *The Mexican*, pp. 56–57.

55. Ibid., pp. 29, 28.

56. White, "Apperceptive Mass," p. 3.

57. Jackson K. Putnam, "The Persistence of Progressivism in the 1920's: The Case of California," *Pacific Historical Review* 35 (1966): 398.

58. California, Commission of Immigration and Housing, "Annual Report" (Sacramento, 1927), p. 8.

59. Romo, *East Los Angeles,* pp. 124–28.

60. CIH, "The Home Teacher," p. 3.

61. Abraham Hoffman, "Mexican Repatriation Statistics: Some Suggested Alternatives to Carey McWilliams," *Western Historical Quarterly* 3 (October 1972): 391–404; Hoffman, *Unwanted Mexican Americans in the Great Depression: Repatriation Pressures, 1929–1939* (Tucson: University of Arizona Press, 1974).

23.

MODERNIZING THE RURAL MOTHER
Gender, Class, and Health Reform in Illinois, 1910–1930

LYNNE CURRY

"What? Town Children Healthier Than Ours?" the monthly magazine *The Farmers' Wife* expressed dismay at this revelation to its readership of some 750,000 rural women nationwide. Yes, Carroll Streeter's column went on to say, the evidence appeared to be unmistakable. Physical examinations of pre-school-aged children in Illinois had revealed that rural children averaged 2.13 "significant defects," whereas those from the city averaged but 1.64. "For several years it has been increasingly apparent," commented one Illinois Department of Public Health official, "that the large cities are coming to be more healthful than the small communities and farming districts."[1]

In the period from 1910 to 1930, Illinois reformers counted country children among the primary casualties of the poor health conditions their investigations began to uncover in small towns and rural communities throughout the state. Many urban-based health reformers also agreed, however, that it was rural *mothers* who should be held responsible for this regrettable state of affairs. "Better living is a condition largely controlled by women," declared the Illinois nurse Katherine Olmsted, speaking on maternal welfare work in rural areas at a 1919 meeting of the American Association for the Study and Prevention of Infant Mortality. Women's intrinsic control over the quality of country life, Olmsted continued, placed the obligation for better "social conditions, better amusements and better health protection" squarely on the shoulders of rural wives and mothers.[2]

During the nineteenth century, advocates on behalf of the nation's physical well-being had shaped a distinctly gendered discourse of preventive health promotion.[3] Many reformers had shared an underlying assumption that protecting health, especially that of infants and young children, represented a natural and universal function of motherhood. Thus, mothers filled a highly specialized and demanding role within the particular vision of health reform reformers promulgated.

Increasing sophistication in understanding the etiology of infectious disease had led reformers to promote the "modernization" of mothers' traditional functions in safeguarding their family's health through intensive programs of "scientific" education in child care, nutrition, and domestic hygiene.[4] By the turn of the century, many of these urban-based, elite activists argued that such specialized functions of motherhood entitled women to take a leading public role in advancing the health and welfare of American society at large.[5]

But by tradition rural mothers had also played a prominent role in health care. Because they were geographically isolated, country dwellers had a long history of relying on self-help for dealing with accidents and disease, and rural mothers commonly acted as their family's primary medical practitioner. Farming manuals such as the *Practical Farmer,* for example, recommended a well-stocked medicine chest and a book of instructions as necessities for every rural wife and mother.[6] In 1919, the *Literary Digest* reported one survey's finding that farm women spent an average of thirty days per year nursing the illnesses of family members. An observer of rural life in Illinois went so far as to declare that "on the farm the mother of the house is the health department."[7] Crusaders for rural health fully realized the strategic necessity of keeping farm mothers at the center of their campaign. The domestic economist Juliet Lita Bane, conducting research for a master's thesis at the University of Chicago, concluded that while rural people must be urged to utilize whatever public health facilities were available to them, "a great deal of responsibility will rest upon the housewife and there are certain facts that she should know and certain principles that she should observe in safeguarding herself and her family against ill health and contagious diseases. She should have time to acquaint herself with the information necessary to do her part well."[8]

Bane's use of the word "housewife" is noteworthy, for it reveals an important underlying tenet of rural health reform in this period. Farm women had not experienced the "separation of spheres" between work and home that had come to characterize the urban middle class since the nineteenth century. Most rural wives and mothers, still engaged in their traditional economic activities, lacked sufficient quantities of both time and energy to devote to a rigorous study of "scientific motherhood," much less to engage extensively in public activities off the farm. Reformers like Bane realized that the farm mother's special responsibilities for improving rural health would exact stringent new demands on her time and resources. Women's traditional productive burdens on the farm must therefore be alleviated in order to allow them to participate fully in new rural health improvement initiatives. "It is poor business from every standpoint," declared Florence E. Ward of the United States Department of Agriculture, "if work out of doors means overstrained

nerves and muscles resulting from an attempt to take on these duties without releasing any household tasks, or if it means neglect of housework or sacrificing attention to children, with a consequent lowering rather than raising of the standard
of living."[9]

Ideally, then, the farm mother would come to resemble more closely her urban
middle-class sister in the definition and conduct of her womanly duties. A mother's
responsibilities on the family farm must be updated and "modernized" in order to
render her a more effective health care provider within the farm home, as well as a
vigorous advocate for public health in the rural community at large. Of course, the
general state of health among country dwellers was not actually deteriorating in the
early twentieth century; rather, public health conditions in small towns and rural
communities had simply failed to keep pace with the advances already achieved in
many American industrial cities.[10] Nevertheless, the compelling link between better health and social progress forged by health crusaders in this era conferred upon
rural mothers in Illinois a prominent new role in the general advancement of their
state. The time had come for rural motherhood to be recognized as an important
public, as well as private, vocation.

Illinois reformers' "discovery" of the poor health conditions that plagued many
of the state's small towns and farming communities followed upon several decades
of vigorous public health activity in Chicago.[11] A number of factors had conspired
to impede the development of an equally extensive public health movement in the
rural region downstate from that city. First, widespread alarm caused by the sheer
numbers suffering from epidemic diseases during Chicago's precipitous growth
had prompted the formation of a municipal board of health as early as the 1830s.
By contrast, poor public health conditions had been much less visible in the
sparsely populated countryside; although epidemics of contagious diseases such as
cholera, typhoid fever, and smallpox also visited rural dwellers with regularity, they
rarely made headlines outside of local areas.[12] As a consequence, downstate Illinois
did not develop a solid public health infrastructure to deal adequately with the numerous health problems that were chronic to the region. A statewide board of
health was not organized until 1877, and it remained underfinanced, unsupported,
and politically unpopular well into the twentieth century.[13]

Second, Chicago's health reformers had tended to focus on public health problems as an *imported* phenomenon, the unfortunate result of a large influx into the
city of foreign immigrants whose supposedly backward superstitions and careless
Old World customs had resulted in disproportionately high rates of disease and
death.[14] Urban-based health advocates only belatedly acknowledged that unsanitary conditions and ignorance of proper hygiene practices also prevailed

throughout many of the state's rural communities, where the residents were over-whelmingly native-born.[15] When public health officials did finally turn their at-tentions downstate, they were shocked to learn that rates of typhoid fever, tuberculosis, and maternal and child mortality in a number of rural counties were as high as those to be found in the poorest, most overcrowded tenement districts of Chicago. "Just across the boundary line from Chicago," Harriet Fulmer of the Illinois State Association for the Prevention of Tuberculosis declared, "is a territory covering six hundred square miles, populated by a quarter of a million people, who need as much instruction as the most benighted region of the United States, as far as matters of health are concerned."[16] A 1915 survey conducted by the University of Illinois found that just 2 percent of farm homes in the southern third of the state had acquired indoor toilets, while fully 59 percent of farm families there still regu-larly drank water from uncovered wells.[17] State public health investigators visiting White County, in the southeastern corner of the state, deemed only 4 of the 119 outdoor privies they inspected to be "fairly decent."[18] It is not surprising, then, that the incidence of typhoid fever had remained significantly high in the state's south-ernmost region.[19]

In addition, unlike Chicago, the downstate region lacked an organized net-work of middle-class and elite women activists whose civic endeavors called atten-tion to the special role of mothers in health reform. But country life was undergoing dramatic changes in the early twentieth century, a transformation clearly reflected in Illinois as the proportion of rural to urban residents steadily dwindled. In 1900, the urban and rural populations in Illinois were roughly equiv-alent. By 1920, however, a two-to-one majority lived in towns and cities; by 1930, nearly three out of four Illinois residents were urban dwellers.[20] At the same time, economic stratification among rural dwellers themselves became decidedly more pronounced as the high cost of newly available farm machinery drove many smaller and less productive farmers off the land.[21] By the 1910s such major changes in the state's agricultural economy had begun to produce a solid core of relatively pros-perous and progressively minded farm women whose own mobilization to improve the public's health mirrored the activities of their middle-class sisters in the city. While the Illinois State Department of Public Health provided the main institu-tional leadership for rural health reform in this era, farm women and their newly emerging organizations served as a vital link between the state's decidedly meager public health system and its rural downstate communities.

Like its urban equivalent, rural public health reform contained a distinctly gendered dimension. In the pages of social reform and progressive farm journals, in papers delivered at public health conferences, and in numerous published surveys of rural communities, farm mothers and their babies were portrayed as the primary victims of the unsanitary, unventilated, and disease-ridden conditions plaguing the countryside; rural uplifters commonly offered dismal maternal and infant mortality statistics as graphic evidence of an overall decline in the quality of agrarian life. "The problem of the farm woman," declared the *Literary Digest,* "finally has assumed proportions sufficiently alarming to call forth . . . a note of warning to the country." Surveys conducted by the USDA and the federal Children's Bureau led some reformers to conclude that high rates of rural infant mortality had become so distressing they were actually driving young women away from the family farm. Few girls contemplating their futures as wives and mothers, they concluded, would choose to remain on the farm where "child life is at a premium. . . . The farmers' wife too often sees the cradle emptied for the grave."[22]

If farm mothers represented objects in the rural health campaign, however, they could also be counted among its most active agents. Like their city sisters, women in downstate communities used the gendered language of maternalism to promote the cause of health reform. But the distinctive vernacular these women employed also reflected their evolving identity as members of an emerging rural middle class. The fact that so many country dwellers suffered from poor health was often expressed in the form of a *grievance* by newly affluent farm women, a protest that the health conditions they endured in the country appeared grossly substandard when compared to those of their social and economic counterparts in the city. By the early twentieth century, a sanitary home, healthy family, and clean community had come to symbolize social respectability for urban wives and mothers, and prosperous farm women claimed these benefits as an entitlement of their new class status.[23]

Relatively high rates of maternal and infant death, for example, connoted a certain backwardness and even ignorance among the rural population, and farm women's discussions of public health issues reflected their chagrin over this disagreeable fact of rural life. Farm babies *should* be healthier than their country cousins, asserted *The Farmer's Wife,* because of the advantages posed by "heaven's sunshine and the fresh, pure air." Unfortunately, it was becoming increasingly evident that this was not the case, and in fact city children appeared to be the healthier group. "Since we are obliged to admit this," *The Farmer's Wife* continued, "we should know why these apparently favorable circumstances are not working, in all cases, to the advantage of our country children."[24] Middle-class farm mothers' own concerns regarding rural health conditions indicated their sensitivities about the implied inferiority of country life compared to that of the city which the mounting evidence seemed to suggest. Accordingly, the public health activities these women supported reflected their overriding concerns with cleaning up rural communities, purchasing commodities to make farm homes more hygienic, and acquiring specialized domestic skills such as nutrition planning to better protect their families' health.[25]

The Agricultural Press

The farm press became one of the most important vehicles for carrying on the rural health campaign among middle-class farm women in Illinois. By the early twentieth century, the overwhelming majority of Midwestern farm women could read,[26] and because of their geographic isolation from urban political and economic centers, the woman on the farm depended upon the information she garnered from agricultural journals and popular magazines. A 1915 survey of 38,000 homes (nearly 12 percent of all farm households in the state) found that 68 percent subscribed to a weekly newspaper, 68 percent took a farm journal, and 54 percent received a popular ladies' magazine.[27] Progressive farm journals such as *The Farmer's Wife* frequently extolled the virtues of the "wide-awake" farm woman, whose vigorous efforts to render herself knowledgeable about all aspects of farm home management served to distinguish her from her poorer, less enlightened rural sisters.

The "wide-awake" mother required access to the most up-to-date medical information, and many Illinois farm publications urged women to submit their own questions on preventive health care. Articles offering advice on the hygiene of pregnancy and infancy became an extremely popular feature among the rural female readership, and by the 1910s most farm periodicals carried these items regularly. In 1915 the editor of *The Farm Home,* a Springfield periodical, announced that a child hygiene column would now appear as a regular feature; he also invited mothers to send in photographs of their babies, from which would be selected the most robust examples of infant vitality for publication in subsequent issues.[28] The new child care column included information on the normal growth of a baby, precautions for bottle-feeding ("cooking" water, for example, to ensure sterilization), weaning, recording the child's birth, the dangers of elixirs and "soothing syrups" (which often contained narcotics or alcohol), and the proper accessories for furnishing a nursery. The health care advice offered in farm journals, whether by a physician, feature columnist, or women's editor, reflected contemporary sensibilities about the inherent value of fresh air and sunshine as well as the growing understanding of the role played by bacteria, carried by water, milk, or flies, in causing disease.

The peril posed by disease-carrying flies, in fact, played as a constant theme in advice columns read by farm mothers. "Is the fly dangerous?" the *Illinois Farmer and Farmers' Call* asked rhetorically. "He is man's worst pest and more dangerous than wild beasts or rattlesnakes." The fly stood accused of carrying diseases such as typhoid fever, tuberculosis, and infant summer complaint "on his wings and his hairy feet"; indeed, the fly frequently appeared as Evil Incarnate in accompanying illustrations. "He may call on you next," warned one columnist in "The Fly Catechism": "Where is the fly born? In manure and filth. Where does the fly live? In every kind of filth. Is anything too filthy for the fly to eat? No . . . How shall we kill the fly? Kill the fly in any way, but kill the fly."[29]

Although they were an inevitable presence on the farm, in the wake of rural public health reform efforts flies became a potent symbol of a farm mother's ignorance and even negligence. "One mother did not believe a little fly could hurt her young," *The Farmers' Wife* intoned melodramatically. "One by one she laid away her babies until now they are three silent empty places in her heart."[30] As the medical historian Naomi Rogers has observed, the association between dirt, flies, and disease, although not always scientifically valid, nevertheless so compellingly combined morality with science that by the early twentieth century it had become a crucial cultural signpost for distinguishing "rich from poor, native-born from immigrant, the ignorant and careless from the informed and responsible."[31] Rogers's insight helps us to understand the vehemence with which flies came under attack in publications written for an audience of middle-class farm women in this period. Farm women's magazines could be unequivocal in their condemnation of slovenly farm mothers. A mother's failure to educate herself about proper child hygiene measures, the *Illinois Farmer and Farmer's Call* admonished, constituted criminal negligence, since "in this day and age there is no excuse for such ignorance."[32] Sensitive to such exacting critiques of rural motherhood, middle-class farm mothers now dutifully screened windows, poured lime into privy vaults, and slaughtered untold numbers of flies with the paddles, sticky paper, kerosene oil, and insecticide powders advertised regularly in the pages of farm journals.

Guaranteeing a sanitary and healthful environment for their families meant that farm mothers also needed to acquire indoor plumbing and toilet facilities, sufficient supplies of clean water and milk, and newly available commercial cleaning products such as Lysol disinfectant. A major survey undertaken by the USDA in 1913 revealed that a major complaint among farm women was the lack of indoor plumbing in their homes. While they decried the inconvenience, the survey's respondents also demonstrated their growing awareness that many commonplace facts of country life such as outdoor privies, shallow wells, and uncovered cisterns actually posed a serious hazard to their family's health. Further, these relatively affluent women felt that they fully *deserved* the benefits of modern technologies already widely available in the homes of their middle-class urban counterparts.[33]

"There's no farm wife who doesn't work hard enough to deserve the last notch in modern conveniences," one Illinois woman declared in a letter to *The Farmer's Wife*. Asserting that the acquisition of indoor plumbing represented nothing less than a matter of basic self-respect, this woman defiantly signed herself "I Won't Be a Hick."[34]

But while middle-class women in rural Illinois were gaining the wherewithal to obtain these commodities, the patriarchal economic arrangement of American farming meant that cash resources remained almost exclusively under the control of their husbands. This discrepancy between her own rising expectations and the farm resources she actually controlled did not go unnoticed by the "wide-awake" farm mother herself. Many rural women expressed resentment about the disproportionate share of attention being given (by the government as well as by their husbands) to the modernization of agricultural production while the crucial work of human reproduction remained in the Dark Ages. They complained that their husbands were willing to purchase modern equipment for the field but balked at investing money in indoor plumbing or electricity for the home. "For a number of years," one Illinois woman protested, "the average farmer has had his county soil expert and crop advisor, cow testing association and so forth, with all the latest inventions in farming apparatus . . . while the farmer's wife, in the majority of cases is plodding on in the same old way her mother did before her."[35] Farm mothers' own call for elevated hygiene standards in the home represented an assertion of both their traditional place as family medical practitioner and their right to perform that important role using the latest, most advanced means available. But, in conveying their desire for modern technologies, these women were also challenging—if somewhat obliquely—the unequal status they continued to endure on the family farm.[36]

Citing exhaustion as a major cause of their own poor health, women writing to farm journals frequently decried the plight of the overworked—and undervalued—farm wife. The *Journal of Home Economics* reported on one study's finding that farm women in Illinois and Indiana worked an average of thirteen hours per day year-round, including Sundays. The women's enumerated duties included the preparation of meals, care of the house, sewing, laundry, marketing, caring for children, poultry and dairy work, orchard and yard work, and procuring farm and household supplies. "Care of the sick," an item not originally included in the survey's list of chores, apparently constituted a substantial part of the farm woman's workload, for this item was written in by the respondents themselves.[37] Acutely aware of the enormity of their own workload, rural women in Illinois were not averse to voicing their complaints. Mrs. Fannie Tilton of Hoopeston proclaimed before a local country women's club that while the annual Chautauqua was of immense value in "bringing a bit of pleasure into the sordid lives of us farm women, . . . we want a little recreation oftener than once a year."[38] A woman writing in *Wallace's Farmer* applauded the idea of vacation camps for farm women, which had recently been established in Iowa and Illinois ("No Husbands, No Children, No Dishwashing or Chickens for One Glorious Week").[39] A Champaign County magazine claimed that one farm wife had calculated the total cash value of her work to be $61,630.55, a sum exceeding the entire real estate value of her farm. "If a reasonable commercial value were placed on the work of the women and children on the farm," the *Banker-Farmer* declared, "it would equal in dollars and cents the total real estate value of our nation."[40] The *Literary Digest* facetiously suggested that farm women stage a strike to protest their hours and working conditions.[41]

Farm Women's Organizations

Midwestern women have a long history of participation in agrarian reform, but by the turn of the century the nature of their activities began to reflect both a rising concern with rural health matters and the growing influence of the new field of home economics.[42] In 1898, women in the Illinois Farmers' Institute founded a separate Department of Household Science within the organization.[43] Nora Mabel Dunlap, the department's first director, urged farm women throughout the state to take an active leadership role in improving rural health as a means of advancing agrarian life. (The Dunlaps resided on a 320-acre farm in Champaign County and managed another 1,820 acres elsewhere. The wife of an Illinois state senator, Mrs. Dunlap's own particular commitment to the cause of rural health reform reportedly stemmed from the loss of all four of her children in infancy and early childhood.)[44] Topics pertaining to domestic hygiene and community sanitation consistently filled the department's agenda. Women gathered at the annual meeting in 1923, for example, heard a lecture on rural sanitation by Dr. Thomas H. Leonard of the State Department of Public Health, complete with slides illustrating the proper and improper construction of water wells.[45]

Programs for rural homemakers enjoyed a boost in 1914 when Congress passed the Smith-Lever Act, which provided federal funds for agricultural education services. Intended to further the extension work already being carried out by agricultural colleges, the USDA also perceived the need for "more definite instruction in domestic and sanitary science and household art than is given to mixed [male and female] audiences of the Farmers' Institutes."[46] Home extension services were

founded on the USDA's belief that increasing access to modern conveniences facilitated the farm woman's entrance into civic life by both diminishing her daunting workload on the family farm and enhancing communication among activist
rural women. The importance of farm women's role in advancing country life, it
seems, now required a higher degree of gender-specialized training than the older,
more traditionally structured Farmers' Institutes could offer.

In Illinois, Smith-Lever funds appropriated through the University of Illinois
helped to sustain the county-based rural women's clubs known as "Home Bureaus," which were designed to serve as female, household-oriented counterparts
to the male, field-oriented Farm Bureaus. Club women supplemented the federal
funds with their annual membership fees. The university provided extension
agents known as home advisors, who traveled to local meetings to present lectures
and demonstrations on various topics pertaining to farm household management.
Extension agents also trained Home Bureau members to organize and carry out
some of the demonstration work themselves.[47] Within five years, seventeen county
Home Bureaus with a combined membership of nearly ten thousand women had
become active throughout the state.[48] In 1918, the USDA investigator Anne Evans
reported that such organizations did indeed appear to be reducing "the sense of
drudgery" among rural women, and she illustrated her point with a description of
the thriving Household Science Club of Wyanet, Illinois; members delivered papers, listened to outside speakers on various domestic science topics, and planned
and executed their own community improvement projects.[49]

Farm mothers' special responsibility for the physical well-being of their families meant that health topics occupied a position of central importance in home extension programs, and subjects such as the care of the sick at home, emergency first
aid, and household sanitation became steady fare at Home Bureau meetings. In
1915 the University of Illinois extension service hired a public health nurse, Fannie
Brooks, to supervise all health education activities within the state. Brooks developed an ambitious—and for busy farm mothers, an exceedingly demanding—
"positive health program" with which she intended "to stimulate self-study to
attain health individually, to improve household sanitation including the disposal
of sewerage and the improvement of the water supply, to arouse interest in community health, and to obtain community sanitary conditions tending to promote
health." Traveling exhibits known as "movable schools" brought preventive health
demonstrations and exhibits to small towns and rural areas throughout the
state. From 1915 to 1916, for example, a movable school featuring the subject
"nursing and health" traveled to twenty-six counties in Illinois. Home demonstration agents gave 168 lectures on preventive health care in conjunction with
this traveling exhibit, which made its appearance at high schools, Sunday

schools, women's club meetings, and the Illinois Chautauqua. Over 32,000 people reportedly came to see movable school exhibits that year.[50]

A special aim of Brooks's positive health program was to provide information on prenatal and infant care to the women of downstate Illinois.[51] In cooperation with the Illinois State Department of Public Health, Brooks conducted lectures, supervised traveling well-baby clinics, and set up child welfare displays at local Home Bureau meetings. In discussing preventive health care, Brooks made a special point to urge her female audiences to avoid relying on patent medicines, a long-held rural custom which particularly concerned health reformers in this era.[52] Brooks even devised a chart on which individuals could keep track of their health habits, including the number of hours they slept, the glasses of water they drank, and the amount of exercise they received each day. "If you follow this daily health program," she instructed them, "you will realize that patent medicines are unnecessary."[53]

Activities emphasizing the health of infants and children found an especially receptive audience among rural mothers in Illinois. In the period from 1917 to 1918, for example, 4,431 women throughout the state attended home extension lectures on child health and infant feeding. The Home Bureau agent Clara Brian related the story of one mother who, having followed the extension service's advice on infant feeding, referred to her child as "our Home Bureau baby, because she is so healthy and well."[54] The women of the Champaign County Home Bureau even took partial credit for a perfect score received at a baby contest held at the 1924 State Fair. Baby Graycroft's success was largely due, they asserted, to the fact that his mother "secured help from the extension service on prenatal feeding, and afterwards followed out the Home Bureau program in nutrition and child feeding supplemented by conferences with the home advisor."[55]

Rural health reform represented one crucial piece of a larger message promoted by the USDA's home extension service: the improvement of country dwellers' health was integrally tied to their acquisition of household technologies designed to make farm homes more efficient and hygienic places.[56] Home extension programs specifically targeted an emerging group of progressively minded, better educated, and relatively prosperous farm women in Illinois. A series of talks on the topic of children's health, for example, covered a range of subjects including nutrition, proper clothing, personal hygiene, home sanitation, lighting, heating, and even household budgeting.[57] Similarly, Home Bureau agent Clara Brian organized "equipment tours" in which she drove around McLean County demonstrating vacuum cleaners, chemical toilets, gas mangles for ironing, and power washing machines in farm homes.[58] The club women in Brian's audience may well have been impressed by such newfangled technologies, but only the relatively affluent could actually acquire them. Census data reveal that as late as 1920 only 11 percent of Illinois farm families had plumbing installed in their homes, while less than 10 percent of farm homes in Illinois were wired for electricity at this time.[59]

Although home extension programs clearly promoted the USDA's own consumerist agenda, it is important to keep in mind that a large measure of the initiative for such programs came from the club members themselves. Home Bureau members planned and organized their own meetings, selected program topics, and invited guest speakers; extension agents' salaries were always at least partially supported by local membership fees. Middle-class clubwomen in rural areas and small towns often initiated their own projects designed to improve community health standards through the Home Bureaus. In 1919, for example, members of the Williamson County Home Bureau enlisted the aid of public health officers in exterminating the breeding places of flies. The women then extended their campaign by delivering addresses on "the necessity of having a clean town" to audiences at moving picture shows; they even spoke to local meetings of the miners' union. When in 1926 three cases of typhoid fever were reported in Champaign County, women of the local Home Bureau supervised a survey of the water quality of all wells used by local school children. The same year, Champaign County Home Bureau members announced their plans for a "positive health campaign," urging local physicians, dentists, and nurses to assist them in "making wives capable of cooperating with doctors" by training them in home nursing procedures.[60]

For its part, the home extension service actively encouraged this kind of female initiative. The home economics pioneer Isabel Bevier claimed that, upon her arrival at the University of Illinois, she found local women to be "handicapped" in their efforts at leadership in male-dominated farm organizations. "Most of the plans were made and executed by the men," Bevier recalled. "In those days, women were very timid, afraid of the sound of their own voice in a public audience."[61] Years later, Bevier looked back with pride at the near-miraculous transformation in farm women's organizations she had witnessed:

> In the women's session of the Farmers' Institute twenty years ago, the majority of the women were over fifty years old, a rather phlegmatic group somewhat wearied with the struggle. . . . Now the average age I would guess is under forty—women who are in the midst of the battle. They are well-groomed, their stockings are silk, their skirts and hair are short, and their heels are too high for comfort. Their minds are eager, alert, hungry for information on child care and training, on house furnishing, on dyeing, on kitchen equipment, and on numberless other points.[62]

In advancing the front lines of health reform, these "modern" mothers in the small towns and rural areas of downstate Illinois asserted their rightful place as custodians of family and community health. But in so doing, they also served as active agents in a larger social reform program whose ultimate aim represented nothing less than the modernization of rural life throughout the state.[63]

Conclusion

Carroll Streeter's expression of alarm over the poor state of health being "discovered" among country children is emblematic of the discourse surrounding the rural health campaign in Illinois in the period from 1910 to 1930. Chicago-based health reformers had long portrayed public health problems as products of dirty, congested cities and overcrowded slum tenements inhabited by foreign immigrants. That equally dismal public health conditions could be found among so many native-born country dwellers in downstate Illinois only served to dramatize for many the urgent need to "rescue" agrarian life by carrying the gospel of good hygiene to small towns and rural villages throughout the state. The rhetoric of the Illinois rural public health campaign in this period depicted mothers and children as the primary victims of the appallingly unsanitary health conditions to be found lurking on the family farm.

At the same time, however, the farm mother herself shouldered much of the responsibility for bringing about the desired change. Public health reformers assigned a new emphasis and value to the farm mother's traditional role as her family's chief medical practitioner. This role became upgraded to one of critical importance in ensuring the progress of rural life in the new century. Like her urban middle-class sister, the "modern" farm mother could no longer expect to be excused for any lapses in vigilance over the health of her family, the hygiene of her home, or the sanitation of her community.

But rural mothers also vigorously promoted the Illinois campaign, and because it was consistent with their customary health care duties on the family farm, many downstate women *took upon themselves* the responsibility for improving rural health. By the early twentieth century good health had been clearly established as a badge of social respectability, and upwardly mobile farm women were decidedly discomfited at the revelations of disease, ignorance, and apparent maternal negligence in their midst. Middle-class farm women's own formulations of rural health problems construed poor public health conditions as symptoms of their *oppression* in agrarian life. On the one hand, these women saw themselves as unfairly lagging behind their city sisters in the acquisition of labor-saving devices that would enable them to triumph over the drudgery in their lives and the ill health in their homes. On the other hand, many expressed resentment at their subordinate status on the family farm, where men's work was granted more worth than their own—largely unrecognized—labors.

Significantly, crusaders for rural health in Illinois did not demand that all country dwellers acquire equal access to adequate health care services. The "modern" approach to health reform required farm families to make a considerable financial investment in new technologies for improving sanitary conditions both inside and outside the farmhouse, an investment clearly beyond the means of many rural dwellers in this era. The daunting workload still carried by most farm mothers meant that time-consuming activities promoting health in the rural community remained prohibitive for all but the relatively well-to-do. The geographical distribution of the newly forming Home Bureaus in this period is revealing, for they appeared disproportionately in the state's northern and central counties, where farmers tended to be more prosperous and their material circumstances distinctively advantageous in comparison with the state's southern counties. In 1919, for example, fifteen Home Bureaus operated in the northern two-thirds of Illinois while only two had been organized in the southern third.[64] A 1928 study of home extension services in Vermilion County, in the central portion of the state, found that participants were more likely to be from larger, wealthier, family-owned farms. Conversely, the study found that tenant farmers and women from the county's smaller farms participated much less frequently in home extension activities.[65]

Thus, the "modernization" theme that permeated rural health reform activities during the period from 1900 to 1930 meant that the campaign served best those farmers who found themselves prospering amid the rapid social and economic changes that had come to characterize downstate Illinois. At the same time that rural mothers were taking up the banner of public health reform from their city sisters, agricultural life itself was becoming increasingly stratified by class. In the movement toward healthier communities and more hygienic homes in Illinois, the "wide-awake" farm mother was not about to be left behind.

NOTES

1. Carroll P. Streeter, "What? Town Children Healthier Than Ours?" *The Farmers' Wife* 30 (October 1927): 519–20.

2. Katherine M. Olmsted, "Problems of Maternal Welfare Work in Rural Communities," *Transactions of the Ninth Annual Meeting of the American Association for the Study and Prevention of Infant Mortality* (Baltimore: Franklin Printing, 1919), pp. 207–14. Poor public health

conditions among country dwellers challenged many urban-based, middle-class reformers' largely romanticized beliefs about the inherent virtues of agrarian life. In 1908, anxieties about a perceived decline in the quality of rural life had prompted the formation of the Country Life Movement, the "rural arm" of Progressive Era reform. See, for example, William L. Bowers, *The Country Life Movement in America, 1900–1920* (Port Washington, N.Y.: Kennikat Press, 1974); David B. Danbom, *The Resisted Revolution: Urban America and the Industrialization of Agriculture, 1900–1930* (Ames: Iowa State University Press, 1979); Katherine Jellison, *Entitled to Power: Farm Women and Technology, 1913–1963* (Chapel Hill: University of North Carolina Press, 1993); Don S. Kirschner, *City and Country: Rural Responses to Urbanization in the 1920s* (Westport, Conn.: Greenwood, 1970); Roy V. Scott, *The Reluctant Farmer: The Rise of Agricultural Extension to 1914* (Urbana: University of Illinois Press, 1970).

3. Suellen Hoy, *Chasing Dirt: The American Pursuit of Cleanliness* (New York: Oxford University Press, 1995), pp. 15–25; Regina Markell Morantz, "Making Women Modern: Middle Class Women and Health Reform in the Nineteenth Century," in *Women and Health in America*, ed. Judith Walzer Leavitt (Madison: University of Wisconsin Press, 1984), pp. 346–58; Nancy Tomes, "The Private Side of Public Health: Sanitary Science, Domestic Hygiene, and the Germ Theory, 1870–1900," *Bulletin of the History of Medicine* 64 (Winter 1990): 509–39.

4. There is a substantial historiography concerning changing conceptualizations of health and disease in the United States during the nineteenth century. See, for example, John C. Burnham, "Change in the Popularization of Health in the United States," *Bulletin of the History of Medicine* 58 (1984): 183–97; John Duffy, *The Sanitarians: A History of American Public Health* (Urbana: University of Illinois Press, 1990); Samuel H. Preston and Michael R. Haines, *Fatal Years: Child Mortality in Late Nineteenth Century America* (Princeton: Princeton University Press, 1991); George Rosen, *Preventive Medicine in the United States, 1900–1975* (New York: Science History Publications, 1975); Paul Starr, *The Social Transformation of American Medicine* (New York: Basic Books, 1982). The historian Molly Ladd-Taylor points out that, by the century's end, a number of scientific advances in the etiology of disease had rendered mere "mother-love" insufficient for proper middle-class parenting (*Mother-Work: Women, Child Welfare, and the State, 1890–1930* [Urbana: University of Illinois Press, 1994], 4). See also Rima D. Apple, *Mothers and Medicine: A Social History of Infant Feeding, 1890–1950* (Madison: University of Wisconsin Press, 1987), pp. 97–113.

5. Women's public activism on behalf of maternal and child health at the turn of the century was integrally tied to the building of the American welfare state. A rich historiography exploring these links is growing in volume as well as depth. See, for example, *Women, the State, and Welfare*, ed. Linda Gordon (Madison: University of Wisconsin Press, 1990); Gordon, *Pitied But Not Entitled: Single Mothers and the History of Welfare, 1890–1935* (New York: Free Press, 1994); Alisa Klaus, *Every Child a Lion: The Origins of Maternal and Infant Health Policy in the United States and France, 1890–1920* (Ithaca: Cornell University Press, 1993); *Mothers of a New World: Maternalist Politics and the Origins of Welfare States*, ed. Seth Koven and Sonya Michel (New York: Routledge, 1993); Ladd-Taylor, *Mother-Work;* Meckel, *Save the Babies;* Sonya Michel and Robyn Rosen, "The Paradox of Maternalism: Elizabeth Lowell Putnam and the American Welfare State," *Gender and History* 4 (Autumn 1992): 364–86; Robyn Muncy, *Creating a Female Dominion in American Reform, 1890–1935* (New York: Oxford University Press, 1991); Sandra Schackel, *Social Housekeepers: Women Shaping Public Policy in New Mexico,*

1920–1940 (Albuquerque: University of New Mexico Press, 1992); Kathryn Kish Sklar, *Doing the Nation's Work* (New Haven: Yale University Press, 1995); Theda Skocpol, *Protecting Soldiers and Mothers: The Politics of Social Provision in the United States, 1870s–1920s* (Cambridge: Cambridge University Press, 1992).

6. Ella J. Harvey, "Short Cuts in Family Doctoring," *The Practical Farmer Short Cuts for Busy Farmers, Their Wives and Families* (Philadelphia: Practical Farmer Company, 1899). Descriptions of folk medicine practiced by rural mothers may also be found in a number of interviews in the Rural Illinois Oral History Project, University of Illinois, Springfield.

7. "Some Solid Reasons for a Strike of Farm-Wives," *Literary Digest* 63 (December 20, 1919): 74–78; Clair S. Adams, *A Rural Survey in Illinois* (New York: Board of Home Missions of the Presbyterian Church in the U.S.A., n.d.), p. 20.

8. Juliet Lita Bane, "Betterment of Living Conditions Among Rural Women" (master's thesis, University of Chicago, 1919).

9. Florence E. Ward, *The Farm Woman's Problems* (Washington, D.C.: Government Printing Office, 1920), p. 22. Ward was in charge of extension work with women at the USDA. For a discussion of Ward and the USDA home extension service, see Jellison, *Entitled to Power*, pp. 34–37.

10. Danbom, *Resisted Revolution*, p. 9.

11. Interestingly, health reformers' initial lack of attention to rural dwellers is paralleled by current historiography, which has tended to overlook the distinctive ways in which public health efforts evolved in rural areas. Recently, Richard A. Meckel has challenged historians of public health to investigate areas outside of large cities. "Judging Progressive Era Infant Welfare in Light of *Fatal Years*—and Vice-Versa," *Bulletin of the History of Medicine* 68 (1994): 105–12.

12. Although systematic mortality statistics were not kept in Illinois before 1880, there is ample anecdotal evidence from country dwellers themselves attesting to the prevalence of sickness in the region throughout the nineteenth century. See, for example, Eliza W. Farnham, *Life in Prairie Land* (Urbana: University of Illinois Press, 1988); Isaac D. Rawlings, *The Rise and Fall of Disease in Illinois* (Springfield: Illinois State Department of Public Health, 1927). Charles Dickens had found southern Illinois singularly unappealing when he toured the United States in 1842, and he subsequently portrayed the harrowing health conditions he had encountered in his novel *Martin Chuzzlewit*. Transcripts of the Rural Illinois Oral History Project, housed at the University of Illinois at Springfield, contain reminiscences concerning outbreaks of a number of communicable diseases even well into the early twentieth century.

13. Thomas Neville Bonner, *Medicine in Chicago, 1850–1950* (Urbana: University of Illinois Press, 1991), pp. 175–98. Of the 1,100 individual public health districts established in the state, only 248 had health officers, and only 9 of these were full-time positions. Public health officials in Illinois were politically appointed, and as late as 1919 only 169 district health officers had received any medical training. Seba Eldridge, *Social Legislation in Illinois* (Rockford, Ill.: W. M. Shimmin, 1921), pp. 57–58; Rawlings, *Rise and Fall*, pp. 127–35.

14. The historian Richard A. Meckel describes the American infant welfare campaign's preoccupation with ethnic cultural differences as the cause of high rates of infant mortality. *Save the Babies: American Public Health Reform and the Prevention of Infant Mortality, 1850–1929* (Baltimore: Johns Hopkins University Press, 1990), p. 131. See also Hoy, *Chasing Dirt*, pp. 87–121; Alan M. Kraut, *Silent Travelers: Germs, Genes and the "Immigrant Menace"* (Baltimore: Johns

Hopkins University Press, 1994). Naomi Rogers argues that health reformers' fixation on disease transmission as a foreign phenomenon in this period actually blinded them to understanding the etiology of polio. *Dirt and Disease: Polio before FDR* (New Brunswick: Rutgers University Press, 1992).

15. Midwestern farmers, including those in Illinois, were overwhelmingly white and native-born in this period. Although the black population nearly quadrupled in Illinois, the number of African American farmers actually declined, from 1,486 in 1900 to 893 in 1920. United States Bureau of the Census, *Fourteenth Census of the United States,* vol. 6 (Washington, D.C., 1920), pp. 376–85. For a discussion of the racial and ethnic composition of Midwestern farmers, see Jellison, *Entitled to Power,* pp. 5–10. On African Americans in rural Illinois, see Jane Adams, *The Transformation of Rural Life: Southern Illinois, 1890–1900* (Chapel Hill: University of North Carolina Press, 1994), pp. 216–17; Shirley J. Carlson, "Black Migration to Pulaski County, Illinois, 1860–1900," *Illinois Historical Journal* 80 (Spring 1987): 37–46; Donald F. Tingley, *The Structuring of a State: The History of Illinois, 1899 to 1928* (Urbana: University of Illinois Press, 1980), p. 284.

16. Harriet Fulmer, "Rural Nursing Service in Cook County," in *Rural Health,* Proceedings of the Second National Country Life Conference (Chicago: American Country Life Association, 1919), pp. 59–65.

17. "Address, January 1917, Resume of the Report of the Farm Home Survey by Charles L. Stewart," Isabel Bevier Papers, University of Illinois at Urbana-Champaign Archives. See also Edward Bartow, *Chemical and Biological Survey of the Waters of Illinois,* University of Illinois Bulletin, Water Survey Series, no. 7 (Urbana: University of Illinois, 1909), p. 79.

18. I. A. Foster and Harriet Fulmer, "A Health Survey of White County, Illinois," *Illinois Health News* 2 (February 1916): 19–36.

19. In 1926, when mortality from typhoid in the northern and central counties of Illinois had dropped to 1.3 and 3.3 per 100,000, respectively, the rate in the southern one-third of the state remained at 11.8. "Northern Babies Fare Best," *Illinois Health News* 13 (August 1927): 253–59.

20. Population of Illinois, 1890–1930

Year	Population	% Urban	% Rural
1890	3,826,352	44.9	55.1
1900	4,831,550	54.3	45.7
1910	5,638,591	61.7	38.3
1920	6,485,280	67.9	32.1
1930	7,630,654	73.9	26.1

Adapted from John Clayton, *The Illinois Fact Book and Historical Almanac, 1637–1968* (Carbondale: Southern Illinois University Press, 1970), p. 38. The vast majority of these rural-to-urban migrants ended up in Chicago, whose population grew by almost 50 percent in this period. By 1930, Chicago's residents outnumbered the total rural population of the state by 1.5 million. Kirschner, *City and Country,* p. 13.

21. Tingley, *Structuring of a State,* pp. 40–43; H. E. Hoagland, "The Movement of Rural Population in Illinois," *Journal of Political Economy* 20 (November 1912): 913–27.

22. "Why Young Women Are Leaving Our Farms," *Literary Digest* 67 (October 1920): 56–57.

23. Morantz, "Making Women Modern," pp. 346–58; Rogers, *Dirt and Disease,* p. 7; Tomes, "The Private Side of Public Health," pp. 509–39.

24. Ella S. Webb, "Good Health: Why Country Babies Are Not Well Developed," *The Farmers' Wife* 17 (December 1914): 213.

25. The rural health crusade in Illinois paralleled public health activities among both African Americans and whites in the rural South. As in Illinois, public health work was severely undersupported in the South, and therefore middle-class women volunteers played a crucial role in carrying out these campaigns at the local level. See, for example, John Ettling, *The Germ of Laziness: Rockefeller Philanthropy and Public Health in the New South* (Cambridge, Mass.: Harvard University Press, 1981); Susan Lynn Smith, "'Sick and Tired of Being Sick and Tired': Black Women and the National Negro Health Movement, 1915–1950" (Ph.D. diss., University of Wisconsin, 1991).

26. Census data for 1910, for example, show that only 2.0 percent of rural adult females in Illinois were illiterate, as compared to 3.7 percent of the general adult population of the state. Cited in Jellison, *Entitled to Power,* p. 11.

27. Ward, *The Farm Woman's Problems;* "Address, January 1917," Isabel Bevier Papers. A discussion of the traditional importance of the rural press within the lives of American country dwellers may be found in Robert G. Hays, ed., *Early Stories from the Land: Short-Story Fiction from American Rural Magazines* (Urbana: University of Illinois Press, 1995).

28. Charles F. Mills, "Proud of Your Baby?" *The Farm Home,* March 1915, p. 18.

29. "The Fly Catechism," *Illinois Farmer and Farmers' Call,* July 15, 1912, p. 13.

30. Theora Carter, "Keep Flies Off Your Baby," *The Farmers' Wife* 17 (May 1914): 19.

31. Rogers, *Dirt and Disease,* p. 7. See also Morantz, "Making Women Modern."

32. "Responsibility of Mothers," *Illinois Farmer and Farmer's Call,* January 15, 1912, p. 22.

33. Many survey respondents deplored the lack of *information*—as well as technology— available to them for ensuring basic sanitation levels in the home. Jane B. Knowles, "'It's Our Turn Now': Rural Women Speak Out, 1900–1920," *Women and Farming: Changing Roles, Changing Structures,* ed. Wava G. Haney and Knowles (Boulder, Colo.: Westview Press, 1988), pp. 303–17. See also Deborah Fink, *Agrarian Women: Wives and Mothers in Rural Nebraska, 1880–1940* (Chapel Hill: University of North Carolina Press, 1992); Jellison, *Entitled to Power,* pp. 10–15, 34.

34. "Letters from Our Farm Women," *The Farmer's Wife* 32 (August 1929): 12. This shift in middle-class farm women's perceptions about their appropriate class and gender role is well illustrated by Joan Jensen's observation that the houses of wealthier farm families in this period began to have smaller kitchens, separate dining rooms, and larger parlors; in other words, the middle-class farm home was increasingly arranged around an ideal of female domesticity rather than of farm women's productivity. Introduction to her *Promise to the Land: Essays on Rural Women* (Albuquerque: University of New Mexico Press, 1991).

35. "What We Ourselves Want," *The Farmer's Wife* 17 (September 1914): 100.

36. Jellison has pointed out that the implied feminist critique of the patriarchal structure of the family farm represented by such complaints went largely unnoticed by the USDA; agricultural policies never challenged patriarchal economics in American farming. *Entitled to Power,*

pp. 17–18. I note, however, that Florence Ward, head of women's extension work at the USDA, did advocate the development of farm women's own money-yielding activities so that they could make home improvements themselves, avoiding conflicts with their husbands about how cash resources would be invested. Ward, *The Farm Woman's Problems*, p. 16.

37. Ilena Bailey, "A Study of the Management of the Farm Home," *Journal of Home Economics* 7 (August–September 1915): 348–53. As late as 1929, when the standard industrial work week had been reduced to forty-two hours, farm women still worked an average of sixty-three hours per week. Donald B. Marti, *Women of the Grange: Mutuality and Sisterhood in Rural America, 1866–1920* (New York: Greenwood Press, 1991), p. 73.

38. Fannie G. Tilton, "The Value of the Country Club to the Country Woman," *Illinois Farmer and Farmers' Call,* August 1, 1911, p. 13.

39. A Farm Woman, "At a Farm Women's Vacation Camp," *Wallace's Farmer,* June 17, 1927, p. 7.

40. Mrs. Phoebe V. Warner, "What's the Farm Woman Worth?" *The Banker-Farmer* 6 (September 1919): 12.

41. "Some Solid Reasons for a Strike of Farm-Wives," pp. 74–78. The subject of the potential damage posed by overwork and exhaustion to farm women's health was not always treated so lightheartedly. Farm women's grievances also reached the federal Children's Bureau through its correspondence program. Rural women's letters requesting advice in preparing for childbirth and the hygiene of pregnancy and infancy reflected conditions so distressing that they inspired the Children's Bureau to launch a series of studies of maternal health in rural communities. The historian Alisa Klaus believes that the anecdotal evidence gathered from these studies led bureau officials to conclude that rural women's geographic isolation and heavy physical workload were, to a considerable extent, the underlying causes of high rates of maternal and infant mortality. *Every Child a Lion,* pp. 238–39.

42. Sophonisba Breckinridge, *Women in the Twentieth Century: A Study of Their Political, Social and Economic Activities* (reprint, New York: Arno Press, 1972); Knowles, "'It's Our Turn Now,'" pp. 311–12.

43. Farmers' Institutes were a popular means for agrarian men and women to meet for educational lectures, discussions, and entertainment. Sponsored by state-level departments of agriculture and by agricultural colleges, nationwide participation in the institutes topped 500,000 by 1900. Clarence Beaman Smith and Meredith Chester Wilson, *The Agricultural Extension System of the United States* (New York: John Wiley, 1930), pp. 28–31; Knowles, "'It's Our Turn Now,'" pp. 303–19. Illinois was one of four states to form a women's auxiliary within the Farmers' Institute; nine states organized separate institutes for men and women. Scott, *The Reluctant Farmer,* pp. 120–21.

44. Nora Mabel Dunlap, "Address," Farmers' Institute, Department of Household Science, Annual Program, 1913, Champaign County Home Bureau and Home Extension Records, Champaign County Historical Society Archives; "Who Are the Master Farm Homemakers?" *The Farmer's Wife* 32 (March 1929): 40–41; "Mrs. Dunlap Started It All," *Champaign-Urbana Courier,* April 21, 1968, pp. A12–13.

45. Thomas H. Leonard, "Rural Sanitation," *Illinois Farmers' Institute, Department of Household Science, Yearbook 1923* (Springfield: Illinois State Journal, 1923), pp. 190–95.

46. Quoted in Knowles, "'It's Our Turn Now,'" p. 310. Extension activities created a huge

bureaucracy in the USDA; in the period from 1890 to 1920, the department's size increased over thirtyfold. Fink, *Agrarian Women*, p. 27.

47. In the summer of 1915, the women of Kankakee County organized the first Home Bureau under the auspices of the Smith-Lever Act, raising $1,500 to employ an extension agent. "Let Us Counsel Together," *The Farmer's Wife* 18 (September 1915): 78; Jellison, *Entitled to Power*, p. 21. The organization of home extension services in Illinois was somewhat unique in that the Home Bureaus were established and maintained completely independently of the Farm Bureaus. Smith and Wilson, *The Agricultural Extension System*, pp. 59–69, 192–93; *The County Home Bureau in Illinois* (Urbana: University of Illinois Agricultural College and Experiment Station, 1922); M. C. Wilson, W. H. Smith, and Kathryn Van Aken Burns, *Measuring the Progress of Extension Work*, Cooperative Extension Service Circular no. 104 (Urbana: University of Illinois, 1929).

48. "Home and Household," *The Prairie Farmer*, October 4, 1919, 30; Juliet Lita Bane, "Home Economics Extension Service in Illinois," typescript, n.d., Lita Bane Papers, 1919–54, Box 1, University of Illinois at Urbana-Champaign Archives.

49. Anne M. Evans, *Women's Rural Organizations and Their Activities*, USDA Bulletin no. 719 (Washington, D.C.: Government Printing Office, 1918).

50. "Household Science Extension Report, 1915–1916" and "1916–1917"; "Home Economics Extension Report, 1916–1917," Isabel Bevier Papers, Box 1.

51. "Outlook and Adjustment Conferences Material, 1928–1929," Isabel Bevier Papers, Box 2.

52. The historian James Harvey Young asserts that patent medicines among rural dwellers represented a market of over $74 million annually in the early twentieth century. *The Medical Messiahs: Quackery in Twentieth-Century America* (Princeton: Princeton University Press, 1967). Public health investigators surveying White County, Illinois, were alarmed to find that the use of patent medicines containing alcohol seemed to be especially common among young women in that "dry" county. Foster and Fulmer, "Health Survey," pp. 30–31.

53. *The Home Bureau Bulletin* 6 (August 1926), Champaign County Home Bureau and Home Extension Records, Champaign County Historical Society Archives; "Home Economics Extension Report, 1917–1918," Bevier Papers, Box 1.

54. "Home Economics Extension Report, 1917–1918," Bevier Papers, Box 2; *The Extension News* 1 (November 1918); *The Extension News* 12 (November 1930).

55. *The Home Bureau Bulletin* 6 (November 1924), Champaign County Home Bureau and Home Extension Records.

56. The historian Harvey Green has pointed out the increasing popularity in this period—in the kitchens of both town and country women—of white tile floors and walls, white enamel appliances and tables, and stainless steel accoutrements, all designed to emulate the environment of the modern sanitary hospital. *The Uncertainty of Everyday Life, 1915–1945* (New York: Harper Collins, 1992), pp. 184–85. See also Hoy, *Chasing Dirt*, pp. 157–63.

57. Juliet Lita Bane, "Notes for Talks Regarding Home Economics," n.d., Lita Bane Papers, Box 1; "Outlook and Adjustment Conferences Material, 1928–1929," Isabel Bevier Papers, Box 2.

58. Brian reportedly logged a total of 3,354 automobile miles in 1919 alone. See Margaret

Esposito, *Places of Pride: The Work and Photography of Clara R. Brian* (Bloomington, Ill.: McLean County Historical Society, 1989), pp. 12–17.

59. Cited in Jellison, *Entitled to Power,* p. 55. The disparity between the USDA's and farmers' definitions of the "needs" of farm women led to periodic tensions, especially in the early years of the home extension service. The profession of home extension agent was dominated by young, single, college-educated women who conceivably had little in common with farm wives and mothers. See, for example, Mamie Bunch, "A Course for Home Demonstration Agents: The Illinois Plan," *Journal of Home Economics* 11 (October 1919): 431; Rhondal McKinney, "Clara Brian: Home Bureau Photographs, 1919–1926," exhibition catalog (Bloomington, Ill.: McLean County Historical Society, n.d.), p. 4.; Cynthia Sturgis, "'How're You Gonna Keep 'Em Down on the Farm?': Rural Women and the Urban Model in Utah," *Agricultural History* 60 (Spring 1986): 182–215.

60. *The Extension News* 1 (April 1919), Agricultural Extension News and Extension Notes, Box 1, University of Illinois at Urbana-Champaign Archives; *The Home Bureau Bulletin* 6 (August and November 1926), Champaign County Home Bureau Records.

61. Juliet Lita Bane, *The Story of Isabel Bevier* (Peoria, Ill.: Charles A. Bennett, 1955), pp. 58–59. During the early years of Isabel Bevier's tenure at the University of Illinois, women in the Illinois Farmers' Institute were so distrustful of her emphasis on abstract theoretical science and experimental methods that they nearly forced her resignation from the university. They did succeed in closing down the university's fully electrified and equipped demonstration home (complete with the latest in furnishings brought down from Chicago), which they viewed as irrelevant to the work they actually did on the farm. Bevier, in turn, expressed a certain amount of contempt toward the women of the Illinois Farmers' Institute, whose own efforts on behalf of farm women's advancement she once described as being "haphazard" and "well-intentioned but uneducational." Laura Shapiro, *Perfection Salad: Women and Cooking at the Turn of the Century* (New York: Farrar, Straus, and Giroux, 1986), pp. 184–85; Knowles, "'It's Our Turn Now,'" p. 311.

62. Bane, *The Story of Isabel Bevier,* p. 86. As historians of women's household labor have pointed out, the proliferation of various "labor-saving" devices for the home have not necessarily reduced the amount of work performed by women; they have only changed the nature of that work. Ruth Schwartz Cowan, *More Work for Mother: The Ironies of Household Technology from the Open Hearth to the Microwave* (New York: Basic, 1983); Dolores Hayden, *The Grand Domestic Revolution: A History of Feminist Designs for American Homes, Neighborhoods, and Cities* (Cambridge, Mass.: MIT Press, 1981); Susan Strasser, *Never Done: A History of American Housework* (New York: Pantheon, 1982).

63. Although not as prominent in Illinois, rural health reform activities that specifically targeted high rates of maternal and child death were also carried out in this period by the women of the federal Children's Bureau. Alisa Klaus argues that these programs more directly addressed the feminist implications of health reform in this period, since Children's Bureau researchers interpreted high rural maternal mortality rates and the lack of medical resources available to rural women as evidence of *all* women's oppression. *Every Child a Lion,* p. 230.

64. The fifteen northern Home Bureau counties were Adams, Champaign, Hancock, Kane, Kankakee, LaSalle, Livingston, Logan, McHenry, McLean, Macon, Madison, Mercer,

Tazewell, and Vermilion. The southern Home Bureau counties were Saline and Williamson. "Home and Household," *The Prairie Farmer,* October 4, 1919, p. 30. Agricultural census data for 1920 reveal that the average dollar value per acre for farms in the twenty counties at the state's northern end ranged from $135.62 to $269.49, while for the twenty counties at the state's southern end this measure ranged from $23.74 to $111.19. United States Bureau of the Census, *Fourteenth Census of the United States,* 6:365–85; Tingley, *Structuring of a State,* 41.

65. Wilson, Smith, and Burns, *Measuring the Progress of Extension Work.*

24.

REGULATING INDUSTRIAL HOMEWORK
The Triumph of "Sacred Motherhood"

EILEEN BORIS

In 1934 Katherine Budd, a thirty-four-year-old deserted mother of two, sued the National Recovery Administration (NRA) for prohibiting her from making artificial flowers at home. Asking "What harm can it do anyone if I work in my room and make a few dollars a week to keep a home together for my children?" Budd challenged the right of the New Deal agency to ban industrial homework, piecework done in the home for an outside manufacturer. Defended by the employer-backed Homework Protective League and supported by much of the anti–New Deal press, Budd presented herself as the embodiment of wronged womanhood: "I earned that money working in a clean, sunny room in my own home, working about 5 hours a day and having plenty of time for my housework. If the blue eagle code provisions continue, I must go to work in some loft—if I can get a job—and my children, perhaps, to an orphanage."[1]

Budd and her defenders viewed the homework ban as an infringement on a woman's right both to work and to care for children, but social planners and social feminists thought the NRA codes a powerful tool to sweep away the evil of the sweatshop and its "child," industrial homework. In the eyes of most New Dealers, industrial homework curtailed factory employment, undercut wage and health standards, and lowered family purchasing power, thus impeding the recovery effort. Equally important from their viewpoint, such labor commercialized the home, undermining, as the Labor Department's Women's Bureau put it, "the normal demands of home and children upon the housewife and mother." Restricting industrial homework through the NRA codes of fair competition would bolster factory employment and would ultimately aid the New Deal to put "the forgotten man" back to work. It would make possible for millions the long-sought "family

Reprinted from *Journal of American History* 71 (1985): 745–63, by permission of the publisher.

wage," an income high enough for a man to support his nonwaged wife and children. By making homework less profitable for manufacturers, regulation would prove a powerful first step toward its abolition.[2]

Industrial homework persisted during the Great Depression, little changed from the system that had evolved alongside the nineteenth-century shift of most industry from the household to the factory. A form of production whereby the domestic locale becomes the scene of wage labor, homework represented a logical choice for firms in the secondary sector of the economy. Workers were generally paid by the piece, with material supplied by and returned to the employer. Beset by seasonality, highly competitive markets, undercapitalization, and frequent changes in product, manufacturers in the garment and related industries, such as those producing artificial flowers and embroidery, found flexibility through the homework system. They saved on plant overhead, shifting costs onto the employee, who not only had to supply her own sewing machine but also risked losing wages for "below standard" work. Employers could drop homeworkers, reduce their loads, and lower piece rates as the market demanded, or they could substitute homeworkers for factory employees during periods of labor militancy.[3]

Though employers could not directly control the work rhythms of homeworkers, they could demand that work be returned daily, speeding up a woman's own internalized clock—ticking, as one put it, "morning at the needle, noon at the needle, night still at the needle." Fifty to sixty hours of homework per week, squeezed among familial duties, were not uncommon throughout the period. Pay was often one-third or less of that for comparable factory jobs—when the work could be compared, since homeworkers more often engaged in time-consuming hand processes. "Sweating" dominated homework, not only because piece rates were low but also because the length of the working day stretched to meet employer deadlines as well as to maintain an individual's customary level of earnings. In rural areas, where women could find no other form of wage labor, and in urban areas, where a large immigrant family workforce existed, manufacturers took advantage of the sexual segregation of labor—in the market and between the market and the home—to hire women as homeworkers and to pay them at minimal rates. Though the decentralized and quasi-legal nature of the work made it almost impossible to count the numbers involved, the NRA homework committee estimated approximately 154,000 homeworkers in the early 1930s, fewer than in periods of economic expansion but still far too many at work under such exploitative conditions.[4]

The 1934 NRA ban on homework in some 108 industries represented the federal government's first real effort to regulate such labor and, as such, served to reinforce the major goals of the New Deal. The National Industrial Recovery Act of 1933 was the Franklin D. Roosevelt administration's initial attempt to reorganize an

ailing business system. Through tripartite governing boards, composed of representatives of business, labor, and government, industries would draw up codes of
fair competition to regulate themselves. Only section 7(a) of the act—which mandated inclusion of labor standards for minimum wages and maximum hours and
which encouraged collective bargaining—dictated the content of the codes. Prohibiting industrial homework became a way to maintain labor standards; homework bans, written into the codes for the majority of industries where the large
amount of homework seriously undermined hour and wage decrees, set industry-
specific timetables for its abolition. Despite organized labor's lobbying for provisions in the codes that would increase the number of jobs by making homework
immediately unprofitable, wage differentials between "inside" and "outside" work
persisted during transition periods of up to a year demanded by employers before
implementation of the codes could take effect. Nonetheless, both government and
labor felt that they could proceed on the basis of the various provisions in the codes
to begin eliminating homework. What the NRA attempted, in brief, was to provide a structure for a number of competing interests—organized labor, small and
big business, consumers, government administrators, and reformers—to collectively stabilize production. The homework bans would be a key component in the
process.[5]

Scholars have considered the NRA in two contexts. The first, seen in the work
of the historian Ellis Wayne Hawley, analyzes the agency in terms of a persistent
tension within the American political economy between Jeffersonian decentraliza-
tion, individualism, liberty, and antitrust, on the one hand, and Hamiltonian cen-
tralization, order, collective organization, and monopoly, on the other. The
second, represented by the political sociologist Theda Skocpol, points to the NRA
as evidence for the autonomous functioning of the state—that is, for the way in
which the state serves as an arena for struggle among competing groups, even
within the capitalist class, rather than as a handmaiden to a monolithic capitalism.
That neo-Marxist framework nicely meshes with Hawley's more empirical account
of the NRA, but neither approach addresses itself to the impact of NRA policies
on women's lives or, more generally, to the sex-gender division of labor, the process
by which work is separated into male and female categories. The Skocpol approach, however, can be adapted for an understanding of the process by which
public policy itself has shaped the larger social relations of gender, with the state as
a battleground for the social construction of the female life cycle as well as for the
division of labor.[6]

While women historians have begun to consider the impact of the New Deal
on women's status, they have mostly focused on the role of women policy makers,
the debates surrounding married women's work, and the decline of feminism and

women's position during the depression decade.[7] Analysis of the NRA's attempt to regulate homework not only connects those themes in the new historiography but also suggests the complex, not necessarily intended effects of public policy—here formulated by women—on the structures of gender dominance and subordination. By considering the impact of the New Deal on the position of women as a group, we can more fully understand the gender inequalities built into the welfare state. The question of ending homework raises the problematic issue of protective legislation for women in all its ambiguities: how a regulation that greatly curtailed the exploitation of women and children could also reinforce—and perhaps extend—the sex-gender division of social life.

Whether to regulate or to abolish homework during the 1930s generated a sharp debate over women's place within the political economy. Motherhood as symbol and reality stood at the center of the debate. Soon after the NRA codes went into effect, during the winter of 1934, NRA administrators and the Labor Department realized that the prohibitions against homework discriminated against certain workers—people with disabilities, those caring for them, and those too old to adjust to factory labor. Fearing a political backlash and desiring to ease the burden of the prohibition, they drew up an executive order, signed by President Roosevelt in May 1934, exempting such workers from the homework provisions of the NRA codes. On presenting a doctor's certificate to their state department of labor, such workers could obtain a homework permit. Over the next year about 2,600 such permits were issued, over half of them for New York State (the center of the homework system), for all the major types of homework. Although that number seemed to represent only a small percentage of all homeworkers, administrators believed that they were on the way to ending the practice.[8]

Who would fall under the executive order was hardly a foregone conclusion, however. NRA administrators, basically a male group, were open to including widows with preschoolers and even mothers with small children and unemployed husbands. As one argued, however "pitiful and small the earnings," homework was "an important part of the home economy, and one cannot ignore it, for to do so would be a grave injustice and would tend to add to the great want that already exists." Others emphasized the political consequences "of flatly denying homework certificates to nursing mothers, because of the manner in which this information could be used by anti-administration papers."[9] But the women of the Labor Department, veterans of the National Consumers' League crusade against child labor and of the Women's Trade Union League (WTUL) fight for protective legislation, saw excluding mothers from the ban as de facto nullifying the prohibitions. Not only were the majority of homeworkers mothers, thus making regulation impossible if mothers were included, but also mothers and their offspring—considered potential child laborers—were precisely the group that the women reformers would save from the exploitation of homework and would restore to a "normal" family life—that is, one with a male breadwinner, a housewife, and children. Or, as Clara Beyer, then of the Labor Department's Children's Bureau, put it, "in some instances where it might be possible for a woman to support (more or less) a family by homework, this would be too great a temptation for a husband who loved leisure more than honor to continue idle."[10]

Beyer and the other women of the Labor Department belonged to what one historian has called "the New Deal network of women." Composed of social workers, Progressive reformers, and Democratic party stalwarts, the network played a key role in shaping New Deal social-welfare policy. Led by Eleanor Roosevelt, Secretary of Labor Frances Perkins, and Democratic National Committee Women's Division chief Mary Dewson (former president of the New York Consumers' League), the network women were a distinguished group. Many were college-educated, most married or widowed. Those with children, such as Beyer, had taken time out from paid labor while their children were young. For over two decades those women fought for improved living and working conditions for all, but especially for women and children, whom they saw as the most vulnerable. As members of the WTUL, they sought to defend "sacred motherhood," the abuse of which the WTUL symbolized in a portrait of a woman nursing her infant amid the filth and disarray of a sweatshop. As leaders in the National Consumers' League, they lobbied for child-labor laws, for the Sheppard-Towner Act, concerned with maternal and child health, and for other protective legislation. They saw suffrage as a means to gain those other ends rather than as a goal in itself. Contrasting themselves to the self-proclaimed feminists of the National Woman's Party, the New Deal women rejected the label "feminist" and called themselves social reformers. Historians, however, have renamed them "social feminists," because their fight for women's rights focused on improving the living and working conditions of the majority of laboring women rather than on an abstract legal equality.[11]

Those women believed, with Eleanor Roosevelt, that "women *are* different from men." From Florence Kelley, the pioneer investigator of factory conditions for women workers and longtime secretary of the National Consumers' League, they learned that "sex is a biological fact. The political rights of citizens are not properly dependent upon sex, but social and domestic relations and industrial activities are." For Beyer, difference never meant that "women are inferior or superior to men"; rather, the fact that women bear children meant that women needed special protections, enforced by the state, because "their instability [in the labor force], their lack of skill, and their extreme youth" inhibited trade-union organiza-tion among them. Beyer argued: "Women will continue to bear children and cer-tain physiological corollaries to this fact will continue to exist. Exposure to strain and overfatigue in the childbearing period, and wage-earning women are almost all in this period of life, is reflected in higher morbidity of working women than of working men, and in the excessive sickness and death-rate of children of working mothers." Here biological difference justified legislation for "industrial equality with men" rather than exclusion of women from industry.[12]

Within that framework, Beyer and other social feminists further distinguished the young and single from married women. When they spoke about "industrial," or protective, legislation for women, they were thinking of unmarried women in their late teens and early twenties, the majority of women in industry.[13] For those women, the social feminists saw legislation as a prelude to unionization or, at least, a means to better working conditions and thus improved health and living stan-dards. But when it came to the mother in industry, they preferred she return to the home, a home free from industrial work, to prevent neglect of her children. Just as the New Deal women based their critique of the industrial workplace on the im-pact it could have on childbearing, so they criticized homework and other forms of paid labor for their potential to disrupt actual motherhood. Thus, they did not dis-sent from the near-universal belief that child care was a mother's responsibility. In response to the often repeated argument that "mothers with young children should be allowed to do homework," Beyer asked, "Is it socially desirable for a mother with a four months old baby and three other children under 6 to work 33 hours a week for $1.75; or for a mother with 4 children under 5 to work an average of 4 hours a day and receive 63 cents for her weeks work?" More than any other paid labor, in-dustrial homework interfered with women's social obligation to their children.[14]

Despite their disapproval of mothers' working, when it came to analyzing the actual situation of women workers, New Deal women displayed a sensitivity to the power relations within families that led to an understanding of the double expro-priation of women's labor power. Women's Bureau field investigators were quick to point out how homeworkers generally had to care for house and children as well as to finish bundles of garments. The investigators were condemning women for ne-glecting their home duties, though they usually reported houses as clean and well kept. But they also recognized "the double day." The Women's Bureau understood the economic hardships of women, how discriminatory firings of married and older women from office, shop, and factory forced them into "parasitic" homework as their only option. "Obviously," one report stated, "women who earn such low wages cannot be self-supporting." Yet a major goal of the Women's Bureau was to improve the economic conditions of women. Its opposition to industrial homework, then, reflected a complex set of beliefs: (1) that mothers ought not to work and that homework most undermined motherhood because its low piece rates meant long hours, "jeopardizing their health and family life"; and (2) that working women belonged in the factory in order to benefit from minimum wages and better working conditions, thus to have a real chance at economic independence.[15]

In charge of labor standards, Labor Department women had the final say over President Roosevelt's May 1934 executive order. They excluded mothers from the homework exemptions. In turn, that exclusion set the stage for a series of vitriolic attacks in the press and for a number of court suits brought by business groups on behalf of homeworking mothers. The anti–New Deal press fueled the controversy with sensationalist headlines: the *Carbondale (Illinois) Free Press* proclaimed, "Mother Denied Right to Work by President"; and the *New York Daily News* announced, "Two Mothers Draw Fire of NRA in 'Sweatshop War.'" Cartoons ridiculed the NRA, such as the one in the *Chicago Tribune* of August 1, 1934, that pictured New Dealers as "ogres, academic braintrusters, swinging a huge club at a small, helpless woman behind whose skirts children crouch in terror."[16] Hiding behind the figure of the mother, however, was the Homework Protective League, an organ of the National Hand Embroidery and Novelty Manufacturers Association. A small group of employers who depended on homeworkers, the association objected to being included in the code for the Pleating, Stitching and Bonnaz and Hand Embroidery Industry, a code dominated by larger manufacturers who relied on machine production. The Homework Protective League adopted three major tactics: it argued before the NRA that its members fell under another code, that of art needlework, which contained a homework provision; it lobbied for the inclusion of mothers in the executive order; and, after those tactics failed, it attempted to overturn the NRA decision through a series of court cases on behalf of mothers denied the right to work at home. In its opposition to any homework prohibition, the Homework Protective League represented only a fragment of the business-class, labor-intensive employers with the most to lose through prohibition, but its court cases generated much adverse publicity and deeply worried NRA officials.[17]

The case of Katherine Budd brought notoriety to the executive order, as the *Chicago Tribune* cartoon suggests. This Italian-American mother was a skilled artificial-flower maker who earned eighteen dollars per week, a substantial wage for the period. Though Budd hardly typified the poor, desperate women in whose name the Homework Protective League spoke, as NRA officials were quick to point out, her situation nonetheless was a common one. She lived in her parents' mortgaged Brooklyn home with three unemployed brothers and two sisters employed as stenographers. Her father was a bartender out of work from ill health, and her mother, whose eyesight suffered from years of homework, was "too nervous" to care for the children. Like her mother, she had long worked for the Jacob de Jong firm, a supporter of the Homework Protective League. Moreover, Budd held a personal grievance against the NRA, whose minimum-wage rules she judged had cost her a job as a telephone operator. Those circumstances made Budd a willing litigant. Throughout the summer and autumn of 1934, through one legal maneuver after another, the Homework Protective League kept the Budd case before the public. In July the New York attorney general held that the rule prohibiting homework by mothers was unconstitutional; in October a lower court overturned the ban on the basis of state laws permitting homework under specified circumstances. Eventually, a higher court nullified those rulings, sustaining the state Schanckno Act, which gave precedent to federal over state legislation. In the meantime, however, the league had effectively disrupted administration of the homework codes in New York.[18]

The Homework Protective League understood the depression era segmentation of the labor market in a manner not apparent in Roosevelt administration discussions; its arguments reflected the actual division of labor by sex, ethnicity, and life cycle at the time. According to one league petition, because homeworkers were performing women's work, they were "*not* depriving men workers of jobs, because the men who are skilled in this kind of needlecraft are negligible in number." Moreover, the homeworkers did not "keep the rank and file of women in industry from jobs," because "the majority are of foreign birth and training, coming from countries where it was considered an art and incumbent upon every young girl to be taught to do fine crochet and embroidery work." In contrast, "our American girls," the petition asserted, "become teachers, stenographers, bookkeepers, lawyers, reporters, instead."[19] That, too, was for the most part true, although the categorization of "American" jobs confused working-class with middle-class occupations. Native-born women in fact dominated professional and white-collar work, though young, second-generation ethnic women had begun to enter the clerical field. Most embroiderers were of Italian or Mexican descent, and a high proportion of urban homeworkers were immigrants or the daughters of immigrants. In rural areas, such as upstate New York and New England, native-born women worked at home as part of the customary organization of production in certain industries (that is, gloves in Fulton County, New York; wood shoe heels in New Hampshire). The Homework Protective League recognized that homeworkers were a particular segment of the labor market and that homework was a phase of the female lifework cycle. The businessmen of the league put occupations dominated by single women in one labor market and claimed homework for the poor widow and the mother with an unemployed husband: women without male breadwinners, either through unemployment, divorce, death, illness, or desertion.[20]

What was at stake, in the Homework Protective League's mind, was the best interests of the children. Although "some foes of homework have argued that the children should be sent to institutions and thus leave their mothers free to work in shops and factories," the league contended, "any student of family welfare will admit that the child is best off under its mother's care." By "institutions," the league meant child-care centers; such a designation drew on popular prejudices against separating children from their mothers and on the reality that churches, welfare agencies, and charities ran most child-care facilities. Ironically, "the foes of homework" also agreed that mothers ought to care for their children; they merely recognized that the pressures of homework increased the difficulty of carrying out that task.[21]

The Homework Protective League petitioned in the name of sacred motherhood; it even adopted the rhetoric of feminism. One favorable lower-court decision, according to the Tammany Hall politician and league lawyer Julius Hochfelder, settled for all times "the question that women are also people." Yet the league's other arguments—that the provisions in the homework codes violated the "constitutional" right to work as well as the general rights of employers, that the work process of the home crafts were incompatible with a factory environment, that cheap foreign imports would ruin them if forced to produce in a factory—exposed the league as merely the voice of certain marginal capitalists.[22] That the press and the administration took league arguments so seriously suggests the powerful appeal that could be made in the name of sacred motherhood.

Individual businessmen offered similar arguments for the continuance of homework. Ephraim Bros. Headwear Company, a manufacturer of cheap women's knitted headwear for chain stores and mail-order houses, offered the kind of response that the NRA received from textile firms queried about their business practices. While this New York City business paid a union scale for its machine-made goods as dictated by the Millinery Code, some 25 percent of its production was completed by women crocheting at home. Ephraim Bros. argued that a homework ban would force them to lose a quarter of their total sales. In words that characterized the combination of racist and sexist assumptions used to justify homework, Frank Ephraim wrote: "The best hands for this type of work are the Italian and Spanish women who are adept as a result of a training since childhood. These women are mainly housewives and could not leave their homes to work in a factory." Moreover, he contended, "owing to the slow process in the production of a single hat," the work could only be done at home. A code provision that made sense for manufacturers who catered to department stores and speciality shops through a higher-priced good—the types who dominated the Millinery Code Authority—actually discriminated against firms such as Ephraim Bros. with a chain-store market, and thus with lower unit price, firms that relied on homework for increased flexibility. The latter firms feared bankruptcy if they obeyed the code prohibitions.[23]

The sexual division of labor that assigned certain tasks to women also justified homework as women's work. According to the Troy, New York, neckwear firm Cluett, Peabody and Company, only women could perform handwork because "the very nature of the work required that skill found in the housewife and the young woman brought up at home and taught the art of hand needlework." A local physician reaffirmed the ideological connection of women's work with motherhood when he proclaimed that "those who most needed the work and those who were best able to do the work" were the same: "those with little children who should not be left alone if their mothers went into the factory to work." As Cluett's director of employment explained, "When we looked into it we were not surprised to find that this skill in hand sewing was acquired to a very great extent by the fact that the operator was forced to stay at home." Women agreed that they possessed such a skill; many reported to Women's Bureau investigators, as well as to aid societies and employer representatives, that they lacked other skills. According to the Women's Bureau, "they fear that as inexperienced help they will be unable to make the Code minimum and thus be discharged [from nonhandwork factory labor] by the employers."[24] Together, homework and domestic labor formed a self-contained circle, sharpening certain skills to the neglect of others, thus lending weight to the belief that women were perfect handworkers, ideal for homework.

No less than the Homework Protective League and other business apologists, organized labor presented a portrait of mothers suffering—though not from lack of homework. The WTUL, along with the International Ladies' Garment Workers' Union, the Amalgamated Clothing Workers of America, the United Hatters, Cap, and Millinery Workers Union, and the glove and neckwear unions, fought for outright prohibition. Like the Women's Bureau, the unions pointed out the social and economic cost of homework, including the opportunity it gave employers to chisel and the impossibility of unionizing its isolated workers. But sacred motherhood also stood at the heart of their discourse. Homework degraded motherhood, forcing a woman "to exploit her own children and to neglect her home and her children" to earn a mere three to six dollars per week, according to Elsie Gluck of the Labor Conference on Homework. But placed in a factory, with a workday that began at 8:30 A.M. and ended at 5:00 P.M., Gluck contended, the same woman earned between twenty and twenty-four dollars per week and had "time to attend to her household and . . . income enough to get occasional supplementary help."[25] Yet here was no real suggestion about how women were to redivide their domestic labors. Given the customary assignment of housework and child care to women and the already full allocation of women's wages to other items in family budgets, few women would take up Gluck's suggestion and hire "occasional" help. Because organized labor and the Women's Bureau focused on conditions in the paid labor force, because they considered the work of married women and mothers as temporary responses to economic hard times, neither seriously analyzed the question of child care as part of the problem of women's employment. Central to their policy remained the ideal of the family wage and the concept of full-time motherhood, or, as Women's Bureau head Mary Anderson, a former leader in the WTUL, argued, "The only thing to do about homework is to abolish it and to arrange for higher wages for the breadwinner in a family so that his wife and children do not have to supplement the family income by doing homework, or, if there is no regular breadwinner, to provide pensions or relief."[26]

The portrait of the homeworker as drawn by government, labor, and business was not far from the truth. The overwhelming majority of homeworkers in the 1930s, as earlier, were ethnic married women in their child-bearing years, with another cluster of women in the over-fifty age category. According to one survey in 1934, over 75 percent of all homeworkers had one or more dependents, close to 90 percent viewed themselves as housekeepers, and over a third of their husbands were unemployed at the time. These homeworking families tended to have more children and younger, preschool children. The women preferred homework because they thought they could continue caring for children, the elderly, or the disabled. Mrs. Thomas D. Herb of Bechtelsville, Pennsylvania, typified the average homeworker when she pleaded: "I have tow kids and my husband has oly 2 days work and we can hardly live from it. You can think whats 2 day pay it. my kids are to little to let home alone. Perhap yous let me take work home from the factory so that I can earn a few dollars for my kid clothes and eats." Also typical was fifty-five-year-old, disabled Stella Rock of Chicago, who wrote: "I have no one to help me. I want to make my own way. I just can't get anything to do." Others discovered it impossible to make ends meet merely by taking in boarders, while those older women who had never worked in factories found they were not fast enough to earn the rates set by NRA codes and, consequently, were fired. For these women, too, homework seemed the only way to cope with the depression.[27]

Women worked for the family, not for pleasure, though a few women reported pride in fine stitchery or joy in putting bows on shoes. Such pride in work, however, grew within a familial context; as one Chicana from Texas boasted: "The work isn't easy. Very, very fine and close. It's not every family that can do the very fine work." The taking in of gloves to stitch or tags to string or flowers to assemble must be seen as a strategy to sustain the working-class family or to increase its standard of living, with the available work passed among kinswomen even if only one woman's name appeared on company records as the employee. Although the practice had been common among families whose men held casual, unskilled, or seasonal jobs or whose cultural values discouraged married women from working outside the home, the need for the homeworker's meager wages—rarely above five dollars per week—intensified with the economic collapse. As a group of Philadelphia knitters told the Women's Bureau, "If regular wage earners were employed they would gladly give up homework as it brought so little income for the time spent and the home duties neglected. They would rather have their husband and grown children employed than eke out a sparse existence on homework."[28]

Child care was the major reason why women accepted homework, though many homeworkers also objected to the way that such labor disrupted their domestic work. Over and over again, Women's Bureau field investigators heard from women how reluctant they were to leave their children with other people, even family members. These women had always "supervised" their children; they feared bad "influences"; they believed child care their responsibility. Mrs. P., a woman who "said that she would never take so much work that she would be unable to care for the children," exemplified those numerous cases "of having children and needing additional income, but being unable to leave the children, or at least unwilling to do so." Women who entered the factory after the NRA denied their applications for exemption from the code prohibitions expressed anxiety about their homes and children. Among a group of Troy, New York, neckwear sewers, the Women's Bureau cited Mrs. Z., who worried "about children having responsibility of locking the house before they go to school"; Mrs. M., "about care of child during vacation"; and Mrs. D., about an ill toddler kept by a neighbor. A local observer, opposed to mothers' working away from their children, stated that "one mother had a miserable time learning her work in the factory because her little girl, whom she left for a kind neighbor to care for, cried all day for her mother while she was away at work." He argued that "many of these homeworkers are not of the type who could complacently put their children [in day care] where they would be exposed to the various hazards that are necessarily present in any heterogeneous group of children however carefully supervised. Is it right that they should be compelled to do so?" he asked the NRA.[29]

The arrangements made by factory workers in Troy reveal how the burden of child care fell on individual mothers. Though the city had two sliding-scale day-care centers, one of which took infants, only two out of twenty interviewees placed children in them. The majority relied on the public schools without making any arrangements for the hours before and after school or during lunch. A few could draw on grandmothers or husbands; others paid a neighbor to watch younger siblings. Such arrangements, including a reluctance to use institutional centers, resembled those reported to the sociologist Gwendolyn Hughes in the mid-1920s. Most women who entered the factory during the NRA period could make some kind of child-care arrangements. But the responsibility for doing so was the women's. That such child-care work added to their hours of labor went unrecognized by the same NRA officials who called evenings spent getting lunches ready for children to take to school or to day care "free" (as opposed to taken up with homework). The privatization of child care, an outcome of a general attitude that mothering was not work, reinforced the set of beliefs that judged waged labor for mothers socially undesirable even if necessary for some families. Yet the opposition of the mothers themselves to institutional child care provided a barrier that New Deal reformers, given both their political pragmatism and their own social beliefs, never attempted to breach.[30]

Because homework was a family strategy to overcome hard times, husbands, children, and relatives joined mothers in performing the work, especially in unskilled jobs such as sewing men's garters. More hands meant a larger output, thus higher wages. The pressures of homework—speedup during the rush season, sudden drops in the piece rates, new and more complicated patterns for the same rate—could suspend gender-based work assignments within families. If only on a part-time basis, unemployed or underemployed men found themselves doing "women's work," such as threading lace. Recognizing the value of a highly skilled or proficient sewer's labor power, some husbands joined children in relieving mothers of laundry, cleaning, and other household tasks during the rush season. Mrs. L., a lace threader, reported to Women's Bureau investigators in 1934: "Last week was a hard one. I started work at 9:30 A.M. and worked until 11:30 P.M. every day, with 2 hours taken out at noon and at night for cooking meals, washing dishes, etc., or 10 hours a day for 6 days." During part of that time, Mrs. L.'s husband and her fifteen-year-old son helped her thread lace; together they made almost thirteen dollars, the minimum weekly wage under the NRA lace code. Yet Mrs. L. actually worked fourteen hours per day for the six days, if we count hours taken out for household tasks. Whatever redivision of labor occurred within homeworking families, whatever "help" husbands and children provided, for the most part homework meant a stretch out of the working day, and for that reason many women complained that homework disrupted their housekeeping, exhausted them, and made them nervous. The structural role of industrial homework, then, was to mediate between the family's need for cash income and its reliance on the domestic nonwage labor of women. It thus helped to sustain the very sex-gender division of labor that made it seem natural.[31]

Just as homework reflected the sex-gender division of labor between the home and the society, so it fed into the segmentation of the labor market. In the ladies' handbag industry, for example, work done in the factories consisted only of cutting, and only men were cutters—a gender-based assignment prevalent throughout the garment trade. The cutters earned a minimum wage, but the piece rate paid to homeworkers, even with their long hours, made it impossible for women and children to earn the minimum. While the NRA codes would bring sewing into the factory, nothing in the codes would transform preexisting sexual divisions within occupations. Indeed, the codes maintained wage differentials between women and men, a discrimination condemned by the Labor Department women but ultimately accepted because the code minimums still had the effect of raising women's overall wages, even if they remained lower than men's.[32]

Homework was curtailed but not abolished during the two years before the May 1935 Supreme Court decision nullifying the NRA. Pennsylvania reported a drop in homework, and investigators from the National Child Labor Committee found less of it inside New York tenements. Neckwear manufacturers, for example, set up stitch shops in factories, though they returned to homework in the post-NRA period. "Of 75 firms surveyed for effects of home work prohibition," reported Secretary of Labor Perkins, "only one discontinued the line of goods on which home workers had been employed." Once working "inside," former homeworkers overwhelmingly reported a preference for factory work. According to the Women's and the Children's Bureaus, neither manufacturers nor homeworkers suffered "undue hardship" from the homework prohibition.[33]

The NRA experience, however, reinforced the conviction among Labor Department officials that homework could not be regulated and had to be prohibited. New York State's model regulatory system, with its certification and detailed record-keeping processes for both employers and homeworkers, had proved cumbersome despite the best intentions of its administrators. Not only was it difficult to calculate minimum-wage compliance by comparing homework with "inside" operations, but the understaffed inspection force also found it near impossible to check for the presence of illegal homeworkers and child laborers. NRA code authorities also ran into numerous roadblocks. The attempt to set piece rates was flawed, given the frequent changes in the labor process in these fashion-conscious industries and the different jobs done by homeworkers and factory workers. That only a few exceptional homeworkers could earn the hourly rates set by the industrial codes "led to a great deal of false reporting," with workers admitting to field investigators that employers premarked their record-keeping cards with the number of hours necessary to add up to the minimum wage. Employers were responsible for much of the hindrance by subverting the codes, whether through use of subcontractors, through "buy back" schemes (whereby they presumably sold the material to the homeworker and then bought the product back), or through sheer coercion of factory employees forced to take work home. When states with vigilant labor commissions, such as New York and Pennsylvania, attempted to enforce antihomework regulations, manufacturers sent work across state lines to New Jersey and as far away as Texas and Puerto Rico. Moreover, lack of uniformity in the codes themselves encouraged much "bootlegging" and jockeying among manufacturers for inclusion under those codes that still permitted homework. Only where unions were strong, as in the men's and women's garment industries, did the code authorities meet with success.[34]

The passage of the Fair Labor Standards Act (FLSA) of 1938 finally gave Beyer, then deputy director of labor standards, a mechanism to prohibit industrial homework. Section 8 of the act provided "that wage orders issued shall contain such terms and conditions as the Administrator finds necessary to carry out the purposes of such orders, to prevent circumvention or evasion thereof, and to safeguard the minimum wage rates established therein." Homework undermined the minimum-wage provisions of the FLSA, Beyer argued, because it was impossible to determine the number of hours worked, even in cases where pay records were accurate. Because women were working at home, their household duties interrupted their homework, making it difficult to measure the end of one activity and the beginning of another. Uncertainty over the number of persons actually doing the work, no matter what employers recorded, further brought into question the number of hours worked as reflected by overall wages. Moreover, many homeworkers never appeared on payrolls, especially those on relief who feared losing their benefits, while others proved too transient for investigators to check on. The NRA experience thus reinforced Beyer's belief that only legal prohibition could end homework. It also suggested, she stated during FLSA hearings, that both manufacturers and homeworkers would "adjust" to its end. In the early 1940s, amid growing fears of a wartime labor shortage and an actual increase in homework in nonessential and luxury industries, the secretary of labor used the FLSA finally to ban homework in women's apparel and related industries.[35]

Banning industrial homework in the early 1940s was a significant step in raising the standard of living and ending the superexploitation of women workers. But the context in which early New Deal prohibition took place strengthened the culturally dominant association of women with motherhood and of mothers with the home. This history suggests the power of gender ideologies—that is, our mythologies about womanhood and manhood—in shaping public policy, revealing that the welfare state is not sex-neutral. Both business proponents and New Deal opponents of homework relied on the same concept of motherhood to argue for diametrically opposite government policies. For business, female responsibility for child care made homework "logical." The same notion of "sacred motherhood," the image skillfully employed by the WTUL nearly three decades earlier, meant for New Dealers, women reformers, and organized labor that mothers ought not to work for wages. They thought that if the number of factory jobs increased, if employment picked up for men, then homeworkers—that is, mothers with small children—could stay at home and avoid debilitating factory labor. Administrators realized that individuals would suffer but felt "perhaps, in the long run, with increased factory employment those families which are now distressed by a prohibition of homework will benefit after an adjustment to changing conditions, by more steady employment at higher wages for at least one or more members of the family."[36] By fighting for a family wage and for mothers' pensions, policies that encouraged mothers to stay at home, New Dealers justified that actual division of economic life into men's and women's spheres, thus leaving women with responsibility for the home and simultaneously rationalizing their inferior pay in the labor market.

Yet the consequence of homework regulation went beyond a simple sex-gender division of labor. Because the industries most involved employed women in heavy concentrations, homework prohibition would have little impact on occupational segregation by sex. Men would not fill the new "inside" jobs presumably created with the end of homework, but women without children and those willing and able to make child-care arrangements could. Banning homework restricted the work options open to mothers as a group with the unintended impact of reinforcing occupational clustering among women and, consequently, of feeding into a division of labor determined by kinship position. New Deal regulation of industrial homework, thus, left an ambiguous legacy for mothers who needed to work. Protecting such women from an abusive labor system, FLSA bans interfered with the home's customary role as a place for women's paid labor. Since such policies developed in a context that reluctantly accepted mothers' participation in the labor force and that never tied the problem of mothers' employment to child care, they increased the difficulty women have had in finding paid labor that complements their family work.[37]

Despite the best efforts of the New Dealers, industrial homework still exists. It subsided during the quarter-century boom following World War II; however, in the unstable economy of the 1970s and 1980s, homework again became a production strategy in old industries, such as garments, as well as in new ones, such as microcomputers. While recent immigrants from Asia and Latin America found themselves in home sweatshops not unlike those which once dominated New York's Lower East Side, a new generation of "Katherine Budds," supported by Ronald Reagan's deregulatory-minded administration, sought to overturn the FLSA ban on homework. That they could defend homework as "ideally suited for mothers with small children" reminds us that the ideal of sacred motherhood, so central to the NRA years, continues to frame our public discourse.[38]

The "right" of mothers to work for wages at home, a "right" bestowed only by our cultural construction of motherhood, continues to conflict with the rights of all workers to minimum wages, maximum hours, and other fair-labor standards, rights guaranteed by law and by union contract. As long as our present gender-based social arrangements remain—including the devaluation of motherhood as well as a wage and occupational structure that leaves women with lower earnings than men—this conflict will persist. Letting women take in homework, as some propose today, hardly solves the problem of living-wage work for mothers but does serve to erode necessary labor legislation for both men and women. Instead of dismantling the welfare state, we must reorganize it to promote gender equality.

NOTES

1. *Washington Star,* May 14, 1934, p. 1.

2. *The Commercialization of the Home through Industrial Home Work* (Washington, D.C., 1935), p. 33; Martha May, "The Historical Problem of the Family Wage: The Ford Motor Company and the Five Dollar Day," *Feminist Studies* 8 (Summer 1982): 399–424.

3. *Commercialization of the Home through Industrial Home Work,* pp. 1–2; Oscar W. Rosenzweig, "N.R.A. and Industrial Homework," Mar. 19, 1936, pp. 1–11, "Reports" folder, box 8387, Records of the Homework Committee, Records of the National Recovery Administration, RG 9, National Archives; "Industrial Home Work," typescript [ca. 1939]; "Homework: Progress in Control, Laws, Orders, Resolutions, Reports on Shipment" folder, box 1602, Records of the Women's Bureau, RG 86, National Archives; "Industrial Homework during Business Depression," [State of New York, Department of Labor] *Industrial Bulletin,* 11 (Feb. 1932): 132–34.

4. Mary Loretta Sullivan and Bertha Blair, *Women in Texas Industries: Hours, Wages, Working Conditions, and Home Work* (Washington, D.C., 1936), p. 74; *Commercialization of the Home through Industrial Home Work,* pp. 3–4, 17–26; New York Department of Labor, Division of Women in Industry, "Problems of Homework," Feb. 26, 1934, pp. 1–3, "Reports" folder, box 8387, Records of the Homework Committee; Miss Jean Flexner and Miss Shinner, "A Study of Industrial Home Work in the Summer and Fall of 1934: A Preliminary Report to the National Recovery Administration," [1934], pp. 10–22, ibid.; Rosenzweig, "N.R.A. and Industrial Homework," p. 24.

5. *Commercialization of the Home through Industrial Home Work,* pp. 41–48. The code for infants' and children's wear, for example, had an "effective date" of Apr. 9, 1934, for the end of homework, but it prohibited only machine sewing at home. Ibid., 43.

6. Ellis Wayne Hawley, *The New Deal and the Problem of Monopoly: A Study in Economic Ambivalence* (Princeton, 1966), pp. 3–146, 472–94; Theda Skocpol, "Political Response to Capitalist Crisis: Neo-Marxist Theories of the State and the Case of the New Deal," *Politics and Society* 10, no. 2 (1980): 155–201. The concept of a sex-gender division of labor draws on recent feminist and Marxist feminist theory. By "gender" I mean the socially constructed categories of

"masculine" and "feminine." By adding "gender" to the term "sexual division of labor," I am emphasizing the social and cultural construction of the division of labor into women's work and men's work. Gayle Rubin, "The Traffic in Women: Notes on the 'Political Economy' of Sex," in *Toward an Anthropology of Women,* ed. Rayna R. Reiter (New York, 1975), pp. 157–210; Heidi Hartmann, "The Unhappy Marriage of Marxism and Feminism: Towards a More Progressive Union," in *Women and Revolution: A Discussion of the Unhappy Marriage of Marxism and Feminism,* ed. Lydia Sargent (Boston, 1981), pp. 1–42; Iris Young, "Beyond the Unhappy Marriage: A Critique of the Dual Systems Theory," in ibid., pp. 43–70; Ann Ferguson and Nancy Folbre, "The Unhappy Marriage of Patriarchy and Capitalism," in ibid., pp. 313–38; Mary McIntosh, "The State and the Oppression of Women," in *Feminism and Materialism: Women and Modes of Production,* ed. Annette Kuhn and Ann Marie Wolpe (London, 1978), pp. 254–89.

7. Susan Ware, *Beyond Suffrage: Women in the New Deal* (Cambridge, Mass., 1981); Ware, *Holding Their Own: American Women in the 1930s* (Boston, 1982); Lois Scharf, *To Work and to Wed: Female Employment, Feminism, and the Great Depression* (Westport, Conn., 1980); Susan D. Becker, *The Origins of the Equal Rights Amendment: American Feminism between the Wars* (Westport, Conn., 1981); Winifred D. Wandersee, *Women's Work and Family Values, 1920–1940* (Cambridge, Mass., 1981). For a perspective complementary to my own, see Wandersee, "A New Deal for Women: Government Programs, 1933–1940," typescript, 1983 (in my possession).

8. "Minutes," Mar. 19, 1934, "Committee, N.R.A. Homework" folder, box 8385, Records of the Homework Committee; "Number of Certificates Issued, Refused, Revoked, and Cancelled to and including May 27, 1935, According to States Reporting," "Appendix" folder, box 8383, ibid.

9. O. W. Pearson to Earl Dean Howard, Mar. 30, 1934, "Correspondence" folder, box 8383, Records of the Homework Committee; O. W. Rosenzweig to Clara Beyer, Aug. 29, 1934, "Committee, N.R.A. Homework" folder, ibid.

10. "Report on Homework by o. W. Rosenzweig, Chairman, N.R.A. Homework Committee," [1934], p. 15, "Committee, N.R.A. Homework" folder, Records of the Homework Committee; "Minutes," Mar. 13, 1934–Aug. 31, 1934, ibid.

11. Becker, *Origins of the Equal Rights Amendment,* pp. 197–234; J. Stanley Lemons, *The Woman Citizen: Social Feminism in the 1920s* (Urbana, 1973), pp. 181–208; Jane Humphries, "Women: Scapegoats and Safety Valves in the Great Depression," *Review of Radical Political Economics* 8 (Spring 1976): 98–121; Ware, *Beyond Suffrage,* esp. pp. 1–42, 87–115. Ware emphasizes that "women in the network enjoyed their own careers, especially if they did not have children at home, but they still held fairly traditional attitudes when it came to other women" (ibid., p. 184).

12. Ware, *Beyond Suffrage,* p. 14; Florence Kelley, "Shall Women Be Equal before the Law? No!" *Nation,* Apr. 12, 1922, p. 421; Clara Mortenson Beyer, "What Is Equality?" *Nation,* Jan. 31, 1923, p. 116.

13. W. Elliot Brownlee and Mary M. Brownlee, *Women in the American Economy: A Documentary History, 1675 to 1929* (New Haven, 1976), pp. 1–40; Alice Kessler-Harris, *Out to Work: A History of Wage-Earning Women in the United States* (New York, 1982), pp. 180–214.

14. Florence Kelley, "Married Women in Industry," *Proceedings of the Academy of Political Science* 1, no. 1 (1910): 90–96. Finding mothers' working regrettable but necessary, Kelley approved of European state-supported child-care centers. See also "Suggestions for Possible Use at

Hearing on Conflicts in the Homework Provisions (Particularly relating to Pleating and Stitching Code)," n.d., attached to Lucy Manning to Rosenzweig, Nov. 19, 1934, "Labor, U.S. Department of" folder, box 8386, Records of the Homework Committee.

15. "Industrial Home Work: Summary of the System and Its Problems," n.d., p. 11, "Industrial Homework General" folder, box 8384, Records of the Homework Committee; "Industrial Home Work," typescript, [ca. 1939], pp. 1, 3.

16. "Report on Homework by O. W. Rosenzweig," p. 35; *Chicago Tribune*, Aug. 1, 1934, p. 1; *Carbondale Free Press*, July 31, 1934; *New York Daily News*, Oct. 3, 1984, p. 36.

17. Anna M. Rosenberg to Rosenzweig, Aug. 8, 1934, "Homework Protective League" folder, box 8384, Records of the Homework Committee; "Activities of Hochfelder-Zahn Group, Submitted by Herman W. Berger, Legal Counsel for the Code Authority for the Pleating, Stitching, and Bonnaz and Hand Embroidery Industry" to Rosenzweig, Aug. 7, 1934, pp. 1–6, ibid.; Ivar Axelson, "Report on the Subversive Activities of the National Hand Embroidery and Novelty Manufacturers Association, Inc. and Its Secretary, Mr. J. Zahn. From Code Authority for the Pleating, Stitching, and Bonnaz and Hand Embroidery Industry," n.d., pp. 1–6, ibid.; "Attached Wire–Homework," attached to M. D. Vincent to James Cope, Aug. 15, 1935, ibid.; Anna W. Hochfelder to Donald R. Richberg, Oct. 1, 1934, ibid.; Julius Hochfelder to Franklin D. Roosevelt, May 19, 1934, "Hochfelder" folder, ibid.; Julius Hochfelder to Code Authority for the Pleating, Stitching, and Bonnaz and Hand Embroidery Industry, Oct. 29, 1934, ibid.

18. "State of New York, County and City of New York, ss: Katherine S. Budd (Aug 22, 1934), signed David H. Gottlieb, W. H. Schleichter, Notary Public, Bronx Co. Clerk #89, H. L. Buck," affidavit, "Budd Case" folder, box 8382, Records of the Homework Committee; John J. Taylor, "Re: Mrs. Kitty Budd, 411 Caton Ave., Brooklyn, New York," Aug. 16, 1934, ibid.; W. H. Schleichter, "Re: Mrs. Kitty Budd employee of Jacob de Jong, Inc., 19 West 36th St., New York City," Aug. 15, 1934, ibid.; *Carbondale Free Press*, July 31, 1934; *Chicago Tribune*, May 15, 1934, p. 1; *New York Evening Sun*, July 18, 1934, pp. 1, 24; *Washington Herald*, July 20, 1934, p. 7; *New York Times*, July 24, 1934, p. 37; Oct. 3, 1934, p. 14; Oct. 4, 1934, p. 42.

19. Anna Hochfelder, "Preliminary Memorandum of the Homeworkers' Council of the Homework Protective League of the United States," Mar. 3, 1934, pp. 2–3, "Homework Protective League" folder, box 8384, Records of the Homework Committee.

20. "Leather and Woolen Knit Gloves" folder, box 8385, ibid.; "New Hampshire" folder, box 8383, ibid. While no exact figures can be obtained, given the elusive and marginally legal quality of homework, this impression comes from the published and unpublished studies of the Women's Bureau. In Connecticut in 1930–31, for example, three-fifths of the 140 families interviewed had no regular wage earners other than homeworkers. Of 79 embroiderers interviewed in Philadelphia in 1934, 28 were on relief after being denied homework certificates. Caroline Manning and Harriet A. Byrne, *The Employment of Women in the Sewing Trades of Connecticut: Hours and Earnings, Employment Fluctuations, Home Work* (Washington, D.C., 1935), p. 32; Women's Bureau, "Visits to Homeworkers in Philadelphia, 1934–35," typescript, May 29, 1935, "Industrial Homework—Working Papers—Statements—Bill Draft" folder, box 1603, Records of the Women's Bureau.

21. A. Hochfelder, "Preliminary Memorandum of the Homeworkers' Council," p. 2; "Suggestions for Possible Use at Hearing on Conflicts in the Homework Provisions," n.d., attached to Manning to Rosenzweig.

22. *New York Daily News,* Oct. 3, 1934, p. 36; Rosenberg to Rosenzweig, Aug. 8, 1934, "Homework Protective League" folder, box 8384, Records of the Homework Committee; A. Hochfelder, "Preliminary Memorandum of the Homeworkers' Council," pp. 1–8. For New Deal reaction, see citations in n. 17.

23. Frank Ephraim to Rosenzweig, Feb. 23, 1934, "Request for Information and Materials" folder, box 8382, Records of the Homework Committee; Hawley, *New Deal and the Problem of Monopoly,* pp. 3–149.

24. R. O. Kennedy to R. Smith Payne, Oct. 22, 1934, "Men's Neckwear Industry" folder, box 8385, Records of the Homework Committee; Crawford R. Green to Kennedy, Oct. 16, 1934, ibid.; Rosenzweig to Green, Nov. 28, 1934, ibid. Significantly, as Clara Beyer pointed out to Rosenzweig, "Cluett-Peabody were the originators of homework in the necktie industry." Formerly a union shop in New York City, in 1927 the company moved upstate to get away from the union. Beyer to Rosenzweig, Nov. 5, 1934, ibid.

25. *Women's Wear Daily,* Mar. 19, 1934, p. 28; *New York Times,* Oct. 12, 1934, p. 31; Nov. 24, 1934, p. 14; *New York Evening Post,* Jan. 22, 1935, p. 7.

26. Wandersee, *Women's Work and Family Values,* pp. 27–54; *Women at Work: The Autobiography of Mary Anderson as Told to Mary N. Winslow* (Westport, Conn., 1951), p. 244; Virginia Kerr, "One Step Forward—Two Steps Back: Child Care's Long American History," in *Child Care—Who Cares? Foreign and Domestic Infant and Early Childhood Development Policies,* ed. Pamela Roby (New York, 1975), p. 90.

27. Mrs. Thomas D. Herb to N.R.A. Homework Committee, June 1934, "Correspondence" folder, box 8383, Records of the Homework Committee; Stella Rock to N.R.A. Homework Committee, June 18, 1934, ibid.; Susan Atwood to N.R.A. Homework Committee, Mar. 12, 1934, ibid.; Nellie Swartz, "Some Social and Economic Aspects of Homework," in State of New York, Department of Labor, *Special Bulletin* (New York, 1929); Flexner and Shinner, "Study of Industrial Home Work in the Summer and Fall of 1934," pp. 7–26; Sullivan and Blair, *Women in Texas Industries;* Manning and Byrne, *Employment of Women in the Sewing Trades of Connecticut;* Harriet A. Byrne and Bertha Blair, *Industrial Home Work in Rhode Island, with Special Reference to the Lace Industry* (Washington, D.C., 1935); Raymond A. Walsh to Payson Irwin, Feb. 8, 1934, "Men's Neckwear Industry" folder, box 8385, Records of the Homework Committee. Of the homeworking women, few were black, for historically black women have been consigned to domestic service and low-paid agricultural and manufacturing jobs. Spanish-speaking women, in contrast, often took on homework, especially in Texas and Puerto Rico; not only were other gender, race, and class-specific jobs lacking for them in those regions, but the "machismo" of their culture perhaps prescribed the home as the married women's workplace. Elizabeth Pleck, "A Mother's Wages: Income Earning among Married Italian and Black Women, 1896–1911," in *A Heritage of Her Own: Toward a New Social History of American Women,* ed. Nancy Cott and Elizabeth Pleck (New York, 1979), pp. 367–93; Rosalinda M. Gonzáles, "Chicanas and Mexican Immigrant Families, 1920–1940: Women's Subordination and Family Exploitation," in *Decades of Discontent: The Women's Movement, 1920–1940,* ed. Lois Scharf and Joan M. Jensen (Westport, Conn., 1983), pp. 59–84.

28. Sullivan and Blair, *Women in Texas Industries,* p. 72; Manning and Byrne, *Employment of Women in the Sewing Trades of Connecticut,* pp. 25–40; Byrne and Blair, *Industrial Home Work in Rhode Island,* p. 8; Women's Bureau, "Visits to Homeworkers in Philadelphia," p. 2.

29. Mary Skinner and Ruth Scandrett, "Report on the Investigation of Industrial Home Work in the Men's Neckwear Industry, Troy, New York," 1934, pp. 14–15, "Men's Neckwear Industry" folder, box 8385, Records of the Homework Committee; Green to Rosenzweig, Dec. 19, 1934, ibid.

30. Rosenzweig to Green, Nov. 28, 1934, "Request for Information and Materials" folder, box 8382, Records of the Homework Committee; Gwendolyn Hughes Berry, "Mothers in Industry," *American Academy of Political and Social Science* 143 (May 1929): 319–21; Ware, *Beyond Suffrage,* pp. 87–115; Scharf, *To Work and to Wed,* pp. 110–38; Judith Sealander, *As Minority Becomes Majority: Federal Reaction to the Phenomenon of Women in the Work Force, 1920–1963* (Westport, Conn., 1983), pp. 27–94.

31. Byrne and Blair, *Industrial Home Work in Rhode Island,* p. 8; Manning and Byrne, *Employment of Women in the Sewing Trades of Connecticut,* p. 29; Flexner and Shinner, "Study of Industrial Home Work in the Summer and Fall of 1934," p. 42; Women's Bureau, "Visits to Homeworkers in Philadelphia," p. 2; Rubin, "Traffic in Women"; Young, "Beyond the Unhappy Marriage"; Ferguson and Folbre, "Unhappy Marriage of Patriarchy and Capitalism"; McIntosh, "State and the Oppression of Women"; Hartmann, "Unhappy Marriage of Marxism and Feminism."

32. "A Sweatworker" to N.R.A. Labor Department, Mar. 4, 1934, "Ladies Handbags" folder, box 8385, Records of the Homework Committee; Kessler-Harris, *Out to Work,* pp. 262–65.

33. Bureau of Women and Children, "Industrial Home Work in Pennsylvania under the NRA," Mar. 1935, "Pennsylvania" folder, box 8389, Records of the Homework Committee; Cornelia Lyne to Rosenzweig, Aug. 7, 1935, "Correspondence" folder, box 8383, ibid.; Frances Perkins to Hugh Johnson, July 2, 1934, "Labor, U.S. Department of" folder, box 8386, ibid.; Perkins to State Labor Commissioners and Labor Organizations, Mar. 20, 1945, folder 148, box 10, Clara Beyer Papers, Schlesinger Library, Cambridge, Mass.; U.S. Department of Labor, Children's Bureau, *Industrial Home Work under the National Recovery Administration* (Washington, D.C., 1934).

34. Flexner and Shinner, "Study of Industrial Home Work in the Summer and Fall of 1934," pp. 44–45; U.S. Department of Labor, Division of Labor Standards, "Proceedings, Conference of State Industrial Homework Law Administrators," June 16, 1937, "Homework—Progress in Control, Laws, Orders, Resolutions, Reports of Shipment" folder, box 1602, Records of the Women's Bureau; Beyer to Rosenzweig, Sept. 24, 1934, "Labor, U.S. Department of" folder, box 8386, Records of the Homework Committee.

35. Clara Beyer, "Prohibition of Home Work in the Gloves and Mittens Industry," Mar. 2, 1942, typescript, pp. 1–18, "Industrial Homework Working Papers" folder, box 1604, Records of the Women's Bureau; Ruth Scandrett, "Mrs. Beyer's Statement for Hearing on Women's Apparel Industry," July 26, 1941, pp. 1–21, ibid.; "Prohibition of Industrial Home Work in the Button and Buckle Industry," n.d., typescript, pp. 1–22, ibid.; State of New York, Department of Labor, Division of Women, Child Labor and Minimum Wage, "Trends in Homework Industries in New York State," Aug. 1944, typescript, pp. 5–8, folder 153, box 10, Beyer Papers; "Report on Industrial Home Work—International Association of Government Labor Officials," 1944, typescript, p. 7, ibid.

36. Rosenzweig to Mrs. Emery A. Brownell, Oct. 30, 1934, "Men's Neckwear Industry" folder, box 8385, Records of the Homework Committee.

37. Maxine L. Margolis, *Mothers and Such: Views of American Women and Why They Changed* (Berkeley, 1984), pp. 186–234; Scharf, *To Work and to Wed*, pp. 159–65; Ruth Milkman, "Organizing the Sexual Division of Labor: Historical Perspectives on 'Women's Work' and the American Labor Movement," *Socialist Review* 10 (Jan.–Feb. 1980): 95–150.

38. Laura C. Johnson and Robert E. Johnson, *The Seam Allowance: Industrial Home Sewing in Canada* (Toronto, 1982), pp. 54–57; Hardy Green and Elizabeth Weiner, "Bringing It All Back Home," *In These Times*, Mar. 11–17, 1981, pp. 8–9; Philip Mattera, "Home Computer Sweatshops," *Nation*, Apr. 2, 1983, p. 392; *Daily Labor Report*, Feb. 18, 1981, sec. A, pp. 11–13; ibid., July 14, 1981, sec. F, p. 21; *New York Times*, Mar. 10, 1981, p. 1; *Wall Street Journal*, June 30, 1980, p. 15.

25.

"Employable Mothers" and "Suitable Work"

A Reevaluation of Welfare and Wage Earning for Women in the Twentieth-Century United States

JOANNE L. GOODWIN

U.S. welfare policy has yet to adequately address a mother's two work roles—caregiving and wage earning. These two responsibilities have produced conflicting policy responses, sometimes within the same historical period. Citizens and legislators have raised concerns about mothers who worked too much outside their homes; or conversely, mothers who did not work enough to support their families. These contradictions are reflected in the language and practice of welfare policy. During the twentieth century, programs such as mothers' pensions gained public support by promising to subsidize some mothers to raise their children. That language changed after World War II to reflect an expectation that women must enter the workforce to earn, as in the workfare initiatives of the late twentieth century. In contrast to the shift in language over time, the practice of encouraging wage earning has demonstrated remarkable continuity.

Similarly, the scholarship on gender and welfare has focused on one, not both, of women's responsibilities.[1] Little scholarly attention has been paid to the relationship between wage earning and welfare for the years preceding World War II. Instead, the standing interpretation for both mothers' pensions and Aid to Dependent Children explains these programs as policies that supported women to stay at home. Whether viewed as a maternalist policy designed to protect motherhood, as presented in Theda Skocpol's recent work, or as a restrictive policy that regulated women's behavior, as described by Linda Gordon, the leading scholarship discusses these programs as a relationship between government and families.[2]

In contrast, a secondary theme in welfare literature, the labor regulation thesis, focuses on wage earning to the exclusion of gender or family issues. According

Reprinted from the *Journal of Social History* 29 (1995): 253–74, by permission of the publisher.

to Frances Fox Piven and Richard Cloward, welfare policy encourages earning regardless of sex, family status, or race and cares little about the protection of family life or the maintenance of traditional gender relations. In fact, both scholars dismiss gender as a central element in welfare's operation. Piven and Cloward's focus on the intersections between markets and welfare policy could have filled this gap in the literature, but their insistence on gender's irrelevance and the primacy of the market over all other factors has kept the interpretations divided between class conflict and gender conflict.[3]

This article argues that policies for impoverished, mother-only families can best be explained by considering the public sector's relationship to both markets and families. This survey of the evolution of such policies illustrates that the expectation to earn has long been a component of public aid for women, even during the early twentieth century, when the greatest support for a maternal endowment existed. The connection between wage earning and welfare, I argue, redirects us to understand the role of politics in the development of the programs and in the debates over public spending, and its impact on potential beneficiaries of public aid. By following the transitions in the policies from state-level work rules to federal policy, and eventually to the Supreme Court's legitimation of work requirements, this article offers new perspectives on the relationships among gender, race, and welfare during the twentieth century.

The article is organized around three eras of significant transition in public provision. It begins with the origins of public aid to impoverished mothers through the mothers' pension programs of the early twentieth century. The policy that rapidly passed state legislatures, largely owing to its appeal to support women to rear their children at home, operated as little more than a wage subsidy. Faced with contests over public spending, the program applied exclusionary criteria, among them a woman's ability to earn. The second period examines the Social Security Act and the development of two provisions for mother-only families: Aid to Dependent Children (1935) and Survivors' Benefits (1939). The Social Security Act retained the language of maternal support, but federal policy administrators never enforced this goal. Rather, state and federal governing bodies jockeyed for a workable position between federal regulation and states' rights. The compromise that resulted allowed states to implement work rules. These rules expanded the definition of parental support beyond the male breadwinner to include maternal provision as both wage earner and care provider. The "able worker" and "employable mother" criteria worked hand in glove with moral and racial criteria to limit access to benefits. The third section of the article discusses the development of federal work rules in the context of postwar transitions in the economy and civil rights. By the 1960s, welfare policy accommodated state work rules and progressively strengthened earning requirements within federal law—not as a mediator of labor but as a mediator of political pressure and public spending.

Mothers' Pensions, 1911–1935

Throughout the nineteenth century, two groups made up the largest number of poor relief recipients. Mother-only families were consistently the single largest group using both public and private agencies. The exceptions to this pattern existed during periods of massive unemployment, when the second group, unemployed men, turned to poor relief for aid for their families. The long-term need of female-headed families and the intermittent use of relief by male-headed families has been recognized by scholars as the economic consequences of historic social relations. Men, it was assumed, would leave relief as work opportunities returned. Women, however, were more likely to need aid for longer periods owing to child-rearing obligations and the low wages received for women's work.[4]

The first major transition in provision for impoverished women came with the mothers' pensions laws. Advocates recognized that charity was insufficient, demeaning, sporadic, and inadequate to meet the needs of families in an industrial nation. Social scientists noted the correlation between wage earning, poverty, and mother-only families. Juvenile court judges and settlement workers wanted to change child welfare policy that took children from their families and placed them in institutions. A gender-conscious mobilization of traditionalist women's groups and progressive settlement house workers called for maternal subsidies to support women to raise their children at home.[5]

The arguments for pensions varied. A traditionalist appeal could be found among members of the National Congress of Mothers. One member, Mrs. G. H. Robertson, urged her coworkers to support the mothers' pension laws to strengthen the bonds of family life. "These friendless mothers are our especial responsibility." Having grown up "to believe in marriage and home-building," Robertson asked her supporters to not "let them find it a tragedy." She called for a national commission and appropriations to aid mother-only families, by which she meant deserted wives, never-married women, and widows with young children.[6] Others on the progressive edge of this movement called for social insurance for mother-only families. They wanted the government to provide insurance to poor mothers that was similar to private insurance benefits. Citing legal precedent for a wife's claim of support when the husband had property, Sophonisba Breckinridge asked if the same premise of a woman's entitlement would not apply to the woman whose husband died and left no property. "Whether it be termed a pension for the mother, . . . or pay for her services as agent of the court, or a grant in aid of family life—it should be available, sufficient in amount, regular in payment, dignifying in its assurance of the community's concern for the well-being of her group."[7] A diverse group of supporters with a wide range of motivations built support for the new policy and succeeded in passing legislation in a majority of states.

Illinois was the first to pass a state-wide enabling law in 1911, but other states followed quickly. Two years later, eighteen additional states passed mothers' pension legislation. By 1921, forty states and the territories of Alaska and Hawaii had some form of provision for the support of dependent children in their own homes.[8]

Grace Abbott, director of the U.S. Children's Bureau during the 1920s, explained the rapid spread of mothers' pension legislation in terms of the debate over the value and appropriate location of women's work. Abbott believed the public accepted the new programs because they recognized that "the contribution of the unskilled or semi-skilled mothers in their own homes exceeded their earnings outside of the home." She added that "it was in the public interest to conserve their [women's] child-caring functions." Abbott's assessment emphasized the well-documented evidence on women's poor working conditions, and raised the issue that different causes of poverty could demand different solutions. But she presented an overly optimistic view of the state's interest in providing funds for these programs.[9]

Abbott's statement outlined three problems in creating social policy for mother-only families. The first issue referred to the disparity women faced in the workforce. Occupational segregation and job crowding limited women's work options. Years of research by Abbott's colleagues in the Department of Labor and the nation's settlement houses had documented that the majority of wage-earning women worked in sectors characterized by long hours and low wages. These features made self-sufficiency, let alone support of a family, difficult if not impossible. Abbott's sister, Edith Abbott, had written the pioneering book on the economic status of women workers in the United States—a book that highlighted the structural barriers faced by women wage earners. In addition, Grace Abbott understood very well the opposition women faced from trade unionists in improving these labor conditions for working women. The majority of women could not work their way out of poverty as men theoretically were able to do, and useful social policy would need to recognize these facts.[10]

Second, Abbott recognized that the prevalent cultural view of women's primary duty as a mother had played a significant role in the rapid spread of mothers' pension laws. The National Congress of Mothers and the General Federation of

Women's Clubs—two organizations with the largest membership of any women's groups in the early twentieth century—promoted the maternal role over any other. Abbott acknowledged the views of these traditionalist women's groups with her reference to the "public's interest to conserve [women's] child-caring functions." She also knew that social theorists blamed working women for family fragmentation and juvenile delinquency. Any social policy for mother-only families would have to incorporate these ideas into its plan.

The part that Abbott portrayed too rosily—the third problem in creating new policy for mother-only families—was the public's willingness to pay for a subsidy for female-headed families. As director of the Children's Bureau, she was intimately aware of meager family stipends, requirements for women to earn, and the differential treatment of mothers based on their race, marital status, and in some cases family size. At the level of implementation, the public discourse that endorsed aid to impoverished mothers met a serious challenge from an equally strong demand for families in poverty, whether male-headed or female-headed, to earn their way to self-sufficiency. A conundrum evolved at the level of implementation. Aid for mother-only families would be endorsed, but a municipality could not possibly support all mothers in need of aid. Consequently, in county after county, administrators of the program developed a variety of screening mechanisms, including one that considered the mother's "ability to earn."[11]

A specific example from Chicago demonstrates the use of work requirements. When first passed in 1911, the mothers' pension law authorized that public funds could be provided to parents for the support of their underage children. That provision included single- as well as two-parent families, it listed no limits on the size of grants, nor did it describe other eligibility requirements. The Chicago program became the focus of national attention and debate because of its size and the involvement of its notable reform community. By the next meeting of the state legislature, political pressure had forced a revision of the law and created one of the most restrictive measures at the time (1913). New eligibility rules restricted grants to widows and wives of disabled men; children under the legal work age, which was fourteen years at the time; and citizens.[12]

Wage earning became intertwined with public aid in two ways—through the law and through denied eligibility. The law stated that a mother "may be absent [from home] for work a definite number of days each week to be specified in the court's order," and women received an examination to determine the degree to which they could earn wages.[13] The history of Mary Legaikas, referred to in the case records of the juvenile court as Mrs. C, illustrates a common situation for pensioned mothers.

In June, 1913, Mrs. C, a Polish woman, applied for a pension for her
two children aged 8 and 5 years because she found it impossible to
earn enough to support them. Her husband had died of heart disease
in 1909, leaving some insurance, but the money had been used for
paying funeral bills, debts, and living expenses. The family had been
compelled to ask help from the county agent and the united charities a number of times during the four years following the death of
the father. A stepson had gone to work at the age of 14, but Mrs. C
found him so unmanageable that in 1911 she sent him to his uncle in
Tennessee. Mrs. C had been earning only $10 a month by sweeping
in a school.[14]

The juvenile court's caseworkers estimated this family's budget at thirty-four dollars a month and granted the two children a pension of ten dollars each. The pension, along with Legaikas's earnings of ten dollars a month, left the family only four
dollars short of their needs. When Legaikas developed health problems from cleaning the school, caseworkers helped her find a job cleaning in a bank, where she
earned two dollars more a month. Mary Legaikas's story was recorded as a "success"
among pensioned families, but her wage earning was not exceptional. Approximately one-half of the women who received pensions in Chicago during the first
fifteen years of its operation engaged in wage earning.

The second way in which wage earning became a component of the mothers'
pension program was the practice of denying women aid on the basis of their "potential to earn." Although all able-bodied women were urged to find some type of
employment, African American women were believed to be more able to find
work. A combination of job segmentation, which retained certain classes of jobs
for blacks, and the perception that "black women had always worked" led to this
racialist perception. For example, take the case of an anonymous African American
woman who had received a pension for her five children until the 1913 revision
made her ineligible. At that point, she turned over the home responsibilities to her
fifteen-year-old daughter and went out to work. Two years later, when the law became more inclusive, the woman reapplied for a pension but was denied on the basis that she was "a good wage earner." The court gave precedence to her role as an
earner over that of a caretaker for her dependent children and refused even a subsidy for the children, such as that received by the Legaikas family.[15]

The expectation that women who received mothers' pensions would also work
for wages was not unique to Chicago. A Children's Bureau study published in 1923
found that local administration frequently encouraged wage earning by mothers to
meet the gap between family needs and pension stipends. The report noted:

> In each place studied there were some mothers who did not have as
> much free time to devote to their children as was considered desir-
> able. Some mothers were working because there was no other way to
> get an adequate income for the family, although the physical strain
> of work in addition to the care of the house and the children was
> probably more than they could long endure. . . . In many instances,
> however, it was believed that some money-earning occupation on
> the part of the mother was a wholesome influence in the family life.[16]

Slightly over half—52 percent of the 942 women included in the study—earned
to support the family. Twice as many worked outside the home for wages as those
who did piecework at home. Furthermore, nearly half (48 percent) of those who
worked outside the home worked three or more full-time days per week.[17]

The mothers' pension program in practice diverged quite significantly from
the initial proposals of its proponents, and its public benefits were distributed dif-
ferentially on several grounds. Fiscal and political pressures combined with moral
and racialist ideologies to shape the policy in its implementation. Rather than a
right or entitlement, mothers' pensions became a needs-based program. From this
perspective, it is apparent that using economic criteria like one's ability to earn allowed local administrators broad discretion in providing or withholding benefits.
This perspective on the linkage between public aid and work requirements places
the failure of women's employment policies in stark relief. The competition between self-sufficiency and care-taking contributed to the weakness of the program
at this early stage. To what degree did these ambiguities accompany the program
in the transition from locally administered, state-level programs to a federally supported policy in the Social Security Act?

Aid to Dependent Children, 1935–1962

Historians have looked upon the great safety net of social provision set in place by
the Social Security Act as the foundation of the modern welfare state, albeit a limited one. The exclusion of domestic service and agricultural work from social insurance benefits resulted in a two-tier system that protected some workers and not
others. Furthermore, many New Deal programs inscribed with family wage ideals
limited women's access to social security by emphasizing their primary responsibility within the home, as Linda Gordon has argued. Yet, as this section will illustrate, the practice of welfare continued to blur women's dual roles. Most important,

the meaning of parental support—as a male contribution to the family—changed. In the decades following passage of Aid to Dependent Children, state and local governments increasingly passed rules that linked welfare with wage earning.

The Depression all but dismantled the state mothers' pension programs. The policy had existed in 1,600 counties in 45 states by 1931, but during the next two years, counties began to drop the program. Declining revenues limited the number of families able to receive the aid, and social services went through a period of considerable fluctuation during the first years of the economic crisis. The Children's Bureau reported that 90 counties had stopped their programs between 1931 and 1933. Some counties retained the program but added rules that excluded families on the basis of race or family size. Many cities simply kept eligible but unfunded people on a waiting list. In Chicago, 1,434 families received mothers' pensions in 1935, but the waiting list for the program contained an additional 7,942 families. The public relief department carried 3,870 additional families who could have qualified for mothers' pensions, if additional funds had been available.[18]

During the first few years of the Depression, social service agencies made repeated attempts to convince the federal government of the severity of the economic crisis and the necessity for federal intervention for unemployed families. By 1935, federal funds helped states establish relief and employment programs. That same year, after much debate and compromise, Congress passed a set of provisions designed to provide a safety net for American workers and their families called the Social Security Act. The act had two components: one for social insurance and one for public assistance. Promoters of social insurance met with some success particularly in the provisions for unemployment insurance and old age insurance, but the program had many shortcomings. The social insurance provisions covered limited areas of work and by contemporary estimates excluded about one-half of the working population. In addition, the categories of coverage excluded a majority of women and minority workers. These omissions led to a compromise position to maintain the relief programs; thus the public assistance section of the Social Security Act included categorical aid to the disabled, the aged, and dependent children.

Title IV included provisions for Aid to Dependent Children (ADC) and specifically authorized funds for the support of families "who have been deprived of parental support or care by reason of the death, continued absence from the home, or physical or mental incapacity of a parent."[19] As such, supporters maintained their ideal "to enable the mother to stay at home and devote herself to housekeeping and the care of her children."[20] In addition, ADC expanded the benefits of mothers' pensions in two important ways. First, a state's acceptance of the program and its federal funds obligated it to implement the program in every county in the state, share costs with counties, and coordinate the program from one central agency. Mothers' pensions never had this breadth of coverage. Second, ADC expanded eligibility to include deserted, separated, and unmarried mothers. Only a few states had previously passed such inclusive eligibility.

On the other hand, ADC passed Congress with a series of compromises that reduced the scope of the act and left considerable control to local administration. Southern congressmen had effectively eliminated a provision in the original legislation that would have standardized benefits to all recipients by requiring states to provide "a reasonable subsistence compatible with decency and health." That stipulation in the policy would have authorized an equitable provision of public aid regardless of race, a goal they perceived to be incompatible with southern social relations. Congressional compromises also allowed localities the flexibility to limit eligibility for ADC relative to their resources. Some states continued to use the "ability to earn" criterion as a mechanism for limiting benefits and, in some cases, aiding local labor markets.[21]

The creation of categorical aid to dependent children complicated policy for female-headed families. Congress divided public provision into two categories during its debates over the Social Security Act. Social insurance covered those determined to be "employable," while an extended welfare system covered those people determined to be "unemployables." This policy decision continued to muddy the definition of women's work and fostered a situation in which mother-only families remained outside provisions in employment programs or social insurance yet had access to only the minimal resources through ADC. The 1939 amendment to the Social Security Act resolved this situation for one group of mothers. Survivors Insurance for Widows of Workingmen secured benefits for the wives and children of male workers in covered industries. This provision of insurance became the "counterpart of the protection of the wage-earner and his aged wife or widow."[22]

The Social Security Act's contributory system, therefore, institutionalized a division between female-headed families. Wives of industrial workers received a social security insurance payment sufficient to maintain the family. There would be no economic means test, no periodic inspections of the home, no rules governing the behavior of the widow or her children. Justification for the grant came entirely from the male earner's contributions, and it was seen as an extension of the social insurance package for those men working in the specific covered industries. The second group of mother-only families received benefits from the categorical relief program of ADC. If one's husband had worked in agriculture, service, or trades that remained outside the umbrella of social insurance, one received no survivor's benefits. If a woman's husband divorced, deserted, or separated from her, or if she never married, she must first apply for benefits and then be subject to regulation and scrutiny.[23]

To what degree did the earlier practices, which expected mothers on aid to supplement family income with wages, continue during these years? To answer that question we need to turn first to the relief programs that characterized New Deal measures well beyond the passage of the Social Security Act in 1935. Several states took years to put these plans in place. As categorical relief was transferred from the federal emergency programs to state and local governments, some areas failed to raise funds for the aged, the blind, and dependent children. In general, work projects under the Federal Emergency Relief Administration (FERA) or the Works Progress Administration (WPA) characterized mother-only families as "unemployable" and designated work relief projects predominantly for male heads of families. Exceptions existed, however.[24]

The line between government work relief, welfare, and low-wage work could be particularly narrow. In Minneapolis, employers' associations frequently pressured the public welfare department to limit eligibility and reduce stipends. In 1936, hundreds of women who received direct relief had their grants cut. An investigation into the welfare board's action revealed that the department had "made an organized effort to force single girls who are on relief to accept jobs as domestics in homes at starvation wages." The opposition charged the state with forcing women to accept work at substandard rates.[25] In Virginia, Washington, D.C., South Dakota, and New Jersey, local relief agencies closed welfare cases when local agricultural employment or domestic service was available. FERA supported workers' choices to refuse private sector employment when wages were too low, conditions poor, or the prospect of being paid doubtful. At the same time, the agency maintained that available seasonal employment "such as harvesting of tobacco and cotton" should be taken by the able-bodied in lieu of relief.[26] Urban workers also blended direct relief with wage earning. A study of city workers in 1934 found that over one-half of those who used both relief and earnings worked nearly full-time. Service occupations, particularly servants, hotel and restaurant workers, cleaners, and laundresses exhibited higher incidences of this pattern. The combination of private wages and public relief raised the concern that federal funds served as wage subsidies. These incidents anticipated similar charges by civil rights lawyers thirty years later.[27]

The Woodrum Act of 1939 changed the eligibility for the WPA and explicitly excluded anyone who could meet ADC eligibility. This effectively eliminated work programs as an avenue of support for female-headed families at a time when ADC administration was overwhelmed by demand. Women who received ADC probably continued to supplement it when and wherever possible, despite legislative language that discouraged earning.

The intermingling of race and gender ideas with labor segmentation was also evident. A study of the administration of ADC in southern states explained the underrepresentation of African American women on welfare as a result of local culture and attitudes. A field supervisor explained the discrepancy between need and coverage as "a unanimous feeling on the part of the [welfare] staff and board that there are more work opportunities for Negro women. . . . The attitude that 'they have always gotten along' and that 'all they'll do is have more children' is definite." Referring again to the local southern welfare board, the study reported that local administrators "see no reason why the employable Negro mother should not continue her usually sketchy seasonal labor or indefinite domestic service rather than receive a public assistance grant."[28] Over the next twenty years, other states would expand their expectations of mothers to earn.

Between 1935 and the early 1960s, state governments contested, challenged, and changed the meaning of "parental support" in ADC. The original provision intended to aid children whose fathers had died, deserted them, or suffered from a long-term disability. Consequently, the language of the act defined eligible children as those who had "been deprived of parental support or care." To the authors of the Social Security Act, this phrase meant that fathers would provide the income and mothers would provide the care. However, parental support came to mean a mother would assume both roles, as the pattern of mixing relief and wage earning crystallized into policy in some locations during the 1940s and 1950s. Louisiana adopted the first "employable mother" rule in 1943, only eight years after passage of the Social Security Act. The state maintained that all capable women with children over the age of seven years who received public aid could be denied assistance when field work was available. Georgia implemented a similar rule in 1952 but lowered the children's age to three years.[29] The federal Bureau of Public Assistance did not support compulsory earning by mothers, but the agency proved unable to control the practice or maintain desired standards of care. Having been given the leeway to set limits on aid, states used criteria such as family size or structure, residency, and "employable mother" rules to reduce public costs and address local political demands. Local control over eligibility also gave governing bodies the flexibility to address taxpayers' complaints and to retain "customary" practices of race relations. The Bureau of Public Assistance responded with additional regulations but was unable or politically unwilling to challenge the many and varied state departures from federal rules. It has been estimated that "two-thirds of eligible dependent children" remained uncovered by ADC in 1940.[30]

The dual roles imposed upon poor women can also be seen in the competing directions of federal welfare legislation during the 1950s. Federal initiatives attempted to strike an uneasy balance between "strengthening family life" through reinforcement of women's traditional caretaking roles, while encouraging parents "to attain the maximum of self-support." To move toward the first goal, Congress passed a caretaker grant that made a specific provision for "the mother or other relative" in its 1950 Social Security Act Amendments. The grant brought ADC in line with other categorical aid provisions, such as Old Age Assistance or Aid to the Blind, and some promoters hoped that this additional stipend would decrease the need for women to earn.[31]

But efforts "to attain the maximum of self-support" may be found in two restrictive measures passed with the same amendments. The Notification of Law Enforcement Officers had a direct effect because it required welfare officials to notify the police when a deserted child received aid. The Knowland amendment legitimated a reduction of public aid during labor force shortages. Although it was directed at unemployment insurance, not ADC specifically, the measure paralleled those mentioned above in Minneapolis during the Depression, or in the various counties that closed welfare cases when field work became available. It foreshadowed the ability of states to circumvent federal initiatives.[32]

When federal legislation first adopted employment policies in 1962, it was following the practice of a majority of states. Thirty-three states had work requirements in their ADC regulations, and many included a provision that could deny aid if employment was refused.

Federal Employment Policy in Aid to Families with Dependent Children, 1962–1972

Most commentators refer to the Family Support Act of 1988 as the turning point in work requirements for women on Aid to Families with Dependent Children (AFDC). That statute placed responsibility for the financial support of children upon both parents. It implemented firm measures to collect child support from fathers, and it provided funds for employment and training. The Family Support Act has been characterized as a profound change in welfare policy that created a new dilemma about the role of mothers. Yet, as this section demonstrates, the federal government made a commitment to mandate earning from women on AFDC much earlier, and the courts legitimated requirements to earn. These precedents by the legislative and judicial branches validated the authority of localities to control public costs.[33]

Why did federal policy change during the 1960s? The literature offers three explanations. Social scientists most frequently cite postwar demographic patterns and argue that ever increasing numbers of female-headed families relied on public support, which resulted in a welfare crisis. This occurred at the same time that greater numbers of women entered the workforce at all economic levels. A shift in public values in regard to working mothers corresponded with the rise of mother-only families on AFDC and led to the decline of protective, maternalist sentiments. Yet, even though demographics reshaped postwar welfare, the poor had always been asked to contribute to their support. The shift in social values toward wage earning for mothers applied more to middle-class women than to poor women. The second explanation places the motor of change in labor regulation. Evident throughout U.S. history, labor controls became a justified practice in the postwar years as local administrators expanded or contracted welfare eligibility in accordance with local labor demand and public budgets. Labor segregation accounted for the disproportionate exclusion of certain groups and fostered racial discrimination. As this article discusses, lawyers challenged labor regulation in the states during the 1960s and 1970s. Yet as a comprehensive explanation of change, labor regulation does not explain the absence or outright failure of work policies in some areas. The third explanation argues that welfare attempted to regulate women's sexual behavior, particularly through the use of "suitable homes" and "fit mother" criteria, regulations that cut women off grants if their personal behavior deviated from official rules. Welfare policies clearly tried to regulate women's sexual behavior; however, the bulk of evidence demonstrates that the policies sought to reduce the size of public aid rather than control household labor or childbearing.[34]

None of these explanations alone explains the shift in federal policy at the time, and they only marginally address the political context of the change. Furthermore, the sketchy historical accounts of "employable mother" rules mistakenly suggest that these state laws were overturned. In fact, the opposite occurred.[35] This section will demonstrate that by the 1960s support for female-headed families had become politically and economically unfeasible. The needs of states to control their expenses featured prominently in both political arguments and court cases. Federal welfare policy placed wage-earning expectations upon both parents and as such accommodated itself to and expanded upon state "employable mother" rules. While exemptions from work rules still existed when family conditions or child-care demands necessitated, these care-based ethics could also be suspended by local decisions. The increase in work requirements for all women receiving AFDC in the decades following World War II had its roots in the political as well as economic struggles of welfare policy.

During the 1960s, the central assumption guiding federal welfare policies was continued economic growth. John Kenneth Galbraith, in his influential 1958 book, *The Affluent Society*, predicted that the expanding postwar economy provided the opportunity for increased governmental spending in the public sector—spending that could reduce the degree of poverty in America. Michael Harrington described specific sectors of poverty in the United States in *The Other America,* published in 1962, and also called for massive increases in federal funding. Influential members of the Kennedy and Johnson administrations lobbied for targeted interventions, and yet the plans employed relied on fiscal measures. The Council of Economic Advisors designed conservative measures like tax decreases to spur economic growth, and job training—not job creation—to address unemployment.[36]

Social science research, available to policy makers at the time, contradicted the thesis that economic growth alone could reduce the incidence of poverty. Structural barriers to employment emerged during the postwar era that made it more difficult to work one's way out of poverty. The mechanization of agriculture, beginning in the 1940s and continuing for two decades, reduced the need for manual labor in the cotton fields of the South and displaced thousands of African American and white field workers. Thousands of people migrated to the cities of the Northeast, upper Midwest, and Pacific Coast to fill the wartime demand for labor but lost those jobs in the postwar demobilization. The aged and children, groups outside the labor force, made up significant sectors of the poor. Policy makers had firm evidence by 1963 that "technological change, shortages of decent paying jobs, and racial discrimination" rested at the core of rising poverty rates, as James Patterson has noted. Yet, policy makers adopted fiscally conservative antipoverty strategies and created programs that relied on individual initiative.[37]

William Julius Wilson described the increased rates of poverty for urban racial minorities relative to the effects of migration, economic restructuring, and social isolation. The migration of southern blacks to northern cities during the 1940s and 1950s expanded the population of those cities with disproportionate numbers of unskilled workers, many of whom were young. At first, higher paying industrial jobs existed, and later civil rights legislation opened those jobs to blacks, but in about a generation the national economy shifted from one based on manufacturing and industry to one that focused on "higher-order service provision." The inner-city poor typically attained less education, which placed them at a disadvantage for these new jobs. Manufacturing jobs left the industrial Northeast and Midwest and relocated in other regions of the country or outside the United States entirely. The expansion of lower-order service jobs between 1975 and 1985, which could have supplied new jobs to low-skill workers, occurred outside the inner city. Wilson's structural analysis moved the discussion of rising poverty rates away from behavior to focus on larger economic transitions and their relation to poverty rates. His thesis raised questions about the inherent inadequacies of welfare reforms that relied on wage earning for self-support during periods of declining job availability.[38]

Wilson's study concentrated on male unemployment in inner cities. The increased rates of poverty for female-headed families, which had risen significantly in the postwar decades, would decline, Wilson argued, as the economic prospects of African American men improved and expanded the "marriageable pool." This part of his thesis has been challenged on two specific points. It perpetuated an analysis of women as economically reliant on men, and it consequently obscured the two challenges historically faced by women: their responsibility for child care and their weak position in the wage economy.

Women were certainly affected by the declining financial fortunes of men, but additional economic trends after the war had an impact. The expanding service sector created a demand for workers in this low-skill, low-wage sector, and women continued to move into the labor market in greater numbers. But the characteristics of these jobs—wage ceilings, absence of benefits (particularly health care and child care), and little correlation between productivity and wage increases—made it difficult, if not impossible, for women supporting families to get ahead.

Federal welfare reform proposals began to openly discuss work incentives for women receiving AFDC in 1962. Over the next thirty years, continuing to date with the Clinton administration's welfare reform proposals, the central premise of these reforms has been to increase women's wage-earning contribution. The 1962 Social Security Amendments allowed states to add unemployed fathers to AFDC benefits, and in so doing provided the first language for work requirements in federal AFDC rules. The Kennedy administration wanted to emphasize services that would enhance both parents' efforts to become self-supporting. It provided funds for the reimbursement of child care expenses to encourage women to work, but the amount allocated remained relatively small. Disincentives remained in the program, in the form of a 100 percent wage deduction from welfare benefits.

By the mid-1960s, the growing number of families receiving AFDC, the rise in the number of never-married mothers receiving assistance, and the increased costs to localities created what academic and popular commentators referred to as a "welfare crisis." States and cities cut welfare budgets to reduce caseloads, but despite these attempts budgets continued to expand. The War on Poverty programs included employment programs, but they solicited primarily unemployed men and teenagers. Neither the employment programs nor the work requirements for mothers proved effective in moving people into self-supporting jobs. By 1967, public support for social programs waned in the context of an expensive war in Vietnam, continued social protest, and unrest in the nation's cities. Politicians found that their constituents were a receptive audience for calls to reduce welfare costs. Their arguments focused on personal behaviors—illegitimacy and a lack of the work ethic—as the source of the enlarged social programs. Wilbur Mills, representative from the state of Arkansas and chair of the House Ways and Means Committee, played a major role in the campaign to restrict benefits to AFDC and require wage earning.

The 1967 Social Security Act Amendments attempted to correct the ineffectiveness of the earlier provisions. Those amendments, referred to as the Work Incentive Program (WIN), created a plan for comprehensive services, job training, and employment. Congress authorized funds for job training and child care. WIN's incentive allowed a woman to keep part of her earnings in addition to her AFDC benefit, thus eliminating the 100 percent tax on earnings. Women could keep the first thirty dollars and one-third of any additional amount earned. The measure included stiff penalties, however, and benefits could be canceled for anyone who refused to participate or refused to accept employment. WIN also allowed exemptions for mothers with children sixteen years or younger in deference to caretaking responsibilities, yet by the end of 1971, Congress passed the Talmadge amendments, which expanded the work component. They required all recipients to register for jobs and lowered the age exclusion to six years of age. States received a mandate to submit 15 percent of their AFDC families for jobs or training.[39]

The discussion surrounding work requirements in 1967 and 1971 illustrated clearly that, lip service to motherhood aside, the priority in the law was to reduce AFDC rolls and the corresponding public costs of those programs. The House Ways and Means committee report on the Social Security Act in 1967 expressed its concern "over the rapidly increasing costs to the taxpayers" and the expanding numbers receiving public aid. The report linked the program's expansion to greater numbers of female-headed families and an increase in "out of wedlock" children receiving aid. The report also made it clear that the committee members were aware of an "increasingly critical public attention" to AFDC. Yet, WIN had limited success placing AFDC recipients in jobs. Too few people received referrals to work programs, less than 2 percent obtained jobs, and the majority of those jobs were at low wages. Furthermore, WIN prioritized recipients for training and placement. Fathers received preferential treatment and were thought to be the most able to reenter the market. Single mothers and married women followed. While it was politically and fiscally imperative to increase work requirements, the federal government left the details to the states.[40]

Federal policy did not seek to macromanage labor supply, but at the same time it did not enforce rules that would prohibit states from passing work rules. The following discussion of two seminal court cases reveals that in some locations, state and local public welfare administrators managed the size of their programs using "employable mother" criteria to exclude otherwise eligible families. As mentioned earlier, thirty-three states had work requirements in their welfare codes before 1962. A close examination of these two cases—one in Georgia that provided the first constitutional test on employment as an eligibility requirement, and one in New York that eventually led to the Supreme Court decision—illustrates the emerging legal position on the relationship between women's wage earning and receipt of AFDC. In both cases, the courts reaffirmed a state's right to make wage earning a condition of aid.[41]

During the late 1960s and early 1970s, civil rights and antipoverty lawyers presented cases before state courts and the U.S. Supreme Court in an effort to eliminate racial discrimination in welfare policy and to expand the rights of the poor. The Supreme Court decided in favor of expanded legal protection for welfare recipients and overturned several state laws between 1968 and 1973. These cases ended the "substitute father" laws that had required financial support from nonrelated men, and residency requirements. They also entitled recipients to due process through hearings regarding their case. But state and Supreme Court decisions that involved issues of employment and the control of public costs fared less favorably. The majority of the Supreme Court believed that welfare represented an experiment in "cooperative federalism" and as such required a delicate balance between state and federal powers. Success in these relations depended upon "considerable latitude" granted to the states. Nowhere is that more apparent than in the "employable mother" rules. The first constitutional test of the "employable mother" rule occurred in Georgia in 1968 as part of a larger civil rights legal campaign.[42]

Georgia legislators had historically resisted public provision for female-headed families. The state had the dubious distinction of being one of two states that had not enacted any form of mothers' pensions as late as 1931. By 1938, the state temporarily lost federal matching funds for ADC because it had established a racial quota system. Over the next two decades, African Americans consistently received less access to ADC than whites relative to their population and need. In 1951, the Georgia state legislature passed the first law in the country that denied aid to "more than one illegitimate child of a mother." The following year, the law was repealed on constitutional grounds, but the state legislature implemented a plan that would achieve similar goals. The plan comprised several measures that would establish paternity for all children, enforce "substitute father" liability, enact suitable home rules, and require wage earning. The "employable mother" rule is the only limitation among these that has not been discussed in the literature.[43]

Georgia's "employable mother" rule required all able-bodied mothers to work when "suitable work" was available, and when they were not needed in the home.

This policy had many characteristics of earlier practices in various regions of the country; yet, the Georgia case was distinctive for its subtext of gender and racial expectations regarding employability. Georgia defined "suitable work" as employment in line with a woman's "training and experience." It allowed for individual aptitude, but it also classified types of work appropriate to women workers, for example, domestic service. The rule further defined work as that which kept "with the prevailing wage scale and working conditions in the community." The county boards of welfare could use their discretion about "the habits and customs prevalent in the community" to determine if a woman was able to engage in part-time or full-time work. The language of the rule and the flexibility it granted to local boards to make decisions based on existing community "habits and customs" created an opportunity for discriminatory practices in the context of Georgia's previous history of aid to dependent families and the period's racial politics.[44]

In the fall of 1966 and spring of 1967, several African American welfare recipients working with C. B. King, an Albany, Georgia, attorney known for his litigation of civil rights cases, and Jack Greenberg, Charles Jones, and Stephen Ralston of the NAACP Legal Defense Fund, challenged Georgia's regulation. The lawyers for the plaintiffs argued that county welfare boards cut black families off AFDC when agricultural work or domestic service was available. The boards assumed the work to be full-time employment and eliminated any supplemental aid from public funds to those families. The rule violated their constitutional rights, compelled women to leave their young children, maintained "a stable underpaid agricultural labor force," and fostered racial discrimination.[45]

The plaintiffs' case focused on three parts of the "employable mother" rule. First, the rule made work mandatory for any mother who received aid. It stated that she "must accept available 'suitable' employment" if it provided necessary "safeguards" for her children. Second, the rule allowed county welfare boards located in areas with seasonal employment to "designate such periods as periods of full-time employment," and to deny aid to AFDC applicants and close current cases during those months. The fact of actual employment was secondary to the premise that work was available. Third, the rule distinguished between full-time and part-time employment and denied supplementary aid to full-time workers regardless of their need. The defendants in the case, officials of the county and state welfare departments, argued that Title IV of the Social Security Act called for parental responsibility for the support and care of the child. Mothers, they argued, had the same standard of responsibility as fathers. This position collapsed any division of labor between parents and placed the burden of both on the single mother.

The Fifth Circuit Court of Appeals found Georgia's Public Welfare "employable mother" rule valid and within constitutional protections. Women must accept employment when it was available. The case did result in a change of policy on the second and third points, however. Before the case went to court, the state department of welfare revised two parts of the rule. Actual employment replaced presumed seasonal employment, and the distinction between full-time and part-time workers was modified. Shortly before the finding of the Court of Appeals, the plaintiffs added charges against the federal and regional representatives of the U.S. Department of Health, Education, and Welfare who had approved the plan, and filed the case in U.S. District Court. The District Court agreed with the Court of Appeals and supported the work requirement in Georgia's plan. The judges found "there is no federally protected right of [a] mother to refuse employment while receiving assistance and remaining at home with her children." But the District Court did agree that Georgia had violated the Fourteenth Amendment's equal protection clause by denying aid to full-time workers and thus "discriminating on [the] basis of source of income."[46]

The plaintiffs' lawyers succeeded in eliminating discriminatory practices in the receipt of AFDC. The decision allowed women to combine public aid with full-time wages, a benefit previously denied. This had particular importance considering the low wages of the work. But the plaintiffs had hoped to challenge broader premises of welfare law—the "right not to work outside the home" and the segregation of employment patterns.

The issue of work requirements in AFDC reached the Supreme Court in 1973. The case involved public assistance recipients who had challenged New York State's requirement that people must accept jobs as a condition of eligibility. This case followed the implementation of WIN, and the plaintiffs sought to have the federal provisions supersede the state work rules. WIN offered greater support services and broader exemptions from employment. The District Court agreed, but the state appealed the decision.

The U.S. Supreme Court upheld New York State's work program, but the majority and minority reports offer an illustrative comparison of the issues surrounding employable mothers. At the center of the majority decision was the state's right to control work policies as a way to manage costs. Justice Powell, writing for the majority, rejected the claim that WIN superseded state plans. If Congress wanted that to be the case, it could have stated so directly, he argued. Furthermore, a system that gave the federal government sole jurisdiction over work programs presented several problems. The federal government would have "the exclusive manner of applying the carrot and stick" in employment policies. To give the federal government such powers, Powell continued, "could impair the capacity of the state government to deal effectively with the critical problem of mounting welfare costs and the increasing financial dependency of many of its citizens." The opinion affirmed the state's authority to set guidelines requiring self-support, limit expenses to those "most in need," and adopt mechanisms "to cope with the fiscal hardships enveloping many state and local governments." The decision set forward the Supreme Court's belief in the necessity of flexibility in allowing states to manage the fiscal politics of their welfare programs.[47]

Justice Thurgood Marshall wrote the dissent with Justice William Brennan joining. The dissent articulated two major objections: the justices had misinterpreted Congress's intent in establishing a federal work program, and they granted more extensive powers to states than the Court's earlier decisions had authorized. On the first point, Marshall argued that Congress had specifically designed a program of training, education, and employment in the 1967 WIN program. It represented a "carefully coordinated system" built upon a foundation of support services, designed to shape skills that could lead to real jobs and self-support. Congress recognized that the success of such a plan demanded supervision and evaluation, and made such provisions, Marshall continued. It did not envision a system of state make-work programs, such as New York State's, nor that employment would become a condition of welfare. On the second point, Marshall chastised the justices for their interpretation of states' rights. States had been granted flexibility in the Social Security Act in two areas: the allocation of resources and the establishment of standards of need. The majority opinion erred when it allowed states to propose "additional conditions of eligibility" such as work requirements, Marshall argued.[48]

Marshall's dissent also cautioned his peers and the public about the problems inherent in work programs. He acknowledged that the original intention of ADC had failed in practice, and mothers had often left home to earn additional income. But he questioned the purpose, efficacy, and potential abuses of work programs. What kind of job could be required—work for which one was trained and from which one could derive self-support, or any job designated by the welfare authority? The latter had proved to be the case in state experiences, and as ex-director of the NAACP Legal Defense Fund, Marshall was well aware of the way local boards had operated. Yet, in the context of growing impatience with increased public expenditures, rising unemployment, and inflation, the American public expressed overt hostility toward welfare, and the courts reinforced the authority of states to mandate earning by mothers.[49]

Two points may be drawn from this overview of twentieth-century policies for impoverished mother-only families. First, no analysis of public aid to mother-only families will ever fully evaluate the development of policy if it focuses only on the relation between states and families. It must add markets to that analysis. Women had to balance wage earning with welfare receipt even though policy did not provide many resources to do so. The findings presented here challenge the standard interpretations that public aid removed women from the workforce. In fact, the studies from the early twentieth century show a rate of employment among women receiving mothers' pensions at nearly 50 percent, much higher than scholars have previously thought. The evidence also indicates that the practices of the 1910s and 1920s continued through the following decades, although more case studies are needed for the 1930s and 1940s. The New Deal social policies that privileged male workers and identified mothers as "unemployables" because of their home responsibilities contributed to a false dichotomization of poor women's experience. So too did the attitudes of organized labor and social insurance proponents that failed to incorporate mother-only family issues into plans for universal social security. The flexibility granted to local welfare boards allowed officials to deny full or partial grants to women on the basis of their "ability to earn." Local administrators determined eligibility, not through standardized budgets or uniform rules, but in consideration of fiscal management and, in some areas, labor needs. Furthermore, an examination of wage earning and welfare explains links between race and welfare in specific local economies. Some women, like southern African Americans, had historically been marked as "more employable," and the "employable mother" rules required wage earning in racially segregated areas of the labor force. The continued use of work rules allowed state policies to operate in tandem with these racially constructed labor practices.

During the 1960s, the issue of wage earning became more visible at the national level. Civil rights lawyers challenged laws at the same time that city and state officials charged welfare recipients with fraud and castigated them for lacking initiative. Within this context, a federal policy emerged that insisted upon wage-earning requirements for mothers. Its history raises implicit concerns about the success of employment solutions in welfare reform. While welfare has changed in many ways over the century, the barriers women face supporting themselves—locating child care and working in low-wage sectors—have remained fairly constant. The provision of supplemental services may have the greatest long-range impact on self-sufficiency in families, but the additional costs of these programs continue to raise political opposition.

The second point to be drawn from this overview is the significant presence of fiscal politics in shaping programs at the local and federal levels. Politicians, policy administrators, and constituents repeatedly attempted to limit the size and cost of their programs, with varying success. By 1981, fiscal politics and budget reduction became so central to federal welfare reform that the Omnibus Budget Reconciliation Act (OBRA) eliminated the "work incentives" built into the policy since the early 1960s. OBRA eliminated deductions for work-related expenses including day care and gave no incentive for earned wages. The requirements to earn stayed in place, however. At the state level, experimental programs in work training and education have seen periodic cutbacks if not complete reduction of their budgets. Ironically, at a time in American politics when "family values" dominated political discourse, welfare policy expressed those values by eclipsing women's caregiving role in the family. If welfare policy continues to emphasize wage earning, politicians and planners will need to convince the public of the long-term benefits that additional expenditures in child care, training, and education will bring. They will need to address, finally, the specific challenges presented by the poverty of mother-only families.

NOTES

This research received financial assistance from the Nevada Humanities Committee and the University of Nevada–Las Vegas Graduate College. I would like to thank Terry McDonald, James Patterson, Colin Loader and the anonymous readers of the *Journal of Social History* for their helpful comments on earlier versions of this article. David Anderson provided helpful research at an early stage of this project.

1. The research on gender and the welfare state has developed into a complex and theoretically varied body of literature. For the most fully developed argument on maternalist social policy, see Theda Skocpol, *Protecting Soldiers and Mothers: The Political Origins of Social Policy in the United States* (Cambridge, Mass., 1992); and Seth Koven and Sonya Michel, eds., *Mothers of a New World: Maternalist Politics and the Origins of Welfare States* (New York, 1993). The most helpful overview of Aid to Dependent Children may be found in Linda Gordon, *Pitied but Not Entitled: Single Mothers and the History of Welfare* (New York, 1994). Recent work on gender and welfare states in Europe offers an interesting comparison to the United States on this point. For example, see Alisa Klaus, *Every Child a Lion: The Origins of Maternal and Infant Health Policy in the United States and France, 1890–1920* (Ithaca, 1993); Susan Pedersen, *Family, Dependence, and the Origins of the Welfare State: Britain and France, 1914–1945* (New York, 1993); and Miriam Cohen and Michael Hanagan, "The Politics of Gender and the Making of the Welfare State, 1900–1940: A Comparative Perspective," *Journal of Social History* 24 (Spring 1991): 469–84.

2. Linda Gordon and Theda Skocpol discuss their different understandings of gender and welfare in *Contention* 2 (Spring 1993): 157, 185.

3. Frances Fox Piven and Richard Cloward, *Regulating the Poor: The Functions of Public Welfare* (New York, 1971); Piven and Cloward, "Welfare Doesn't Shore Up Traditional Family Roles: A Reply to Linda Gordon," *Social Research* 55 (Winter 1988): 631–47; Michael Katz, *The Undeserving Poor: From the War on Poverty to the War on Welfare* (New York, 1989). For analyses of work and welfare since the 1960s, see Mimi Abramovitz, *Regulating the Lives of Women: So-*

cial Welfare Policy from Colonial Times to the Present (Boston, 1988), 338–42. Roberta Spalter-Roth and Heidi Hartmann have written several pieces on the inadequacies of contemporary work policies as antipoverty plans. For example, see Roberta Spalter-Roth, Heidi Hartmann, and Linda Andrews, *Combining Work and Welfare: An Alternative Anti-Poverty Strategy,* A Report to the Ford Foundation from the Institute for Women's Policy Research (Washington, D.C., 1992).

4. Excellent overviews of the history of welfare may be found in James Patterson, *America's Struggle against Poverty, 1900–1935* (Cambridge, Mass., 1986); and Michael Katz, *In the Shadow of the Poorhouse: A Social History of Welfare in America* (New York, 1986). For particular studies on women in poverty, see Linda Gordon, *Heroes of Their Own Lives: The Politics and History of Family Violence, Boston 1880–1960* (New York, 1988); and Beverly Stadum, *Poor Women and Their Families: Hard Working Charity Cases, 1900–1930* (Albany, 1992).

5. For the origins of mothers' pensions, see Mark H. Leff, "Consensus for Reform: The Mothers' Pension Movement in the Progressive Era," *Social Service Review* 47 (1973): 397–417; Skocpol, *Protecting Soldiers and Mothers.*

6. Quotation is from Mrs. G. H. Robertson, "The State's Duty to Fatherless Children," *Child Welfare Magazine,* January 1912, 156–60. A good source on the contemporary debate surrounding mothers' pensions may be found in *Proceedings,* National Conference of Charities and Corrections (Fort Wayne, 1912).

7. Sophonisba P. Breckinridge, "Neglected Widowhood in the Juvenile Court," *American Journal of Sociology* 16 (July 1910): 67.

8. U.S. Department of Labor, Children's Bureau, *Mothers' Aid, 1931,* Publication No. 220 (Washington, D.C., 1933), 2.

9. Grace Abbott, *The Child and the State, Select Documents,* vol. 2 (Chicago, 1938), 229, cited in Winifred Bell, *Aid to Dependent Children* (New York, 1965), 6.

10. Edith Abbott, *Women in Industry: A Study in American Economic History* (New York, 1910).

11. The problem of insufficient funding and work requirements was discussed in several Children's Bureau reports. For example, see U.S. Children's Bureau, *Minimum Standards for Child Welfare Adopted by the Washington and Regional Conference on Child Welfare,* 1919, Publication No. 62 (Washington, D.C., 1920), 10; ibid., *Proceedings of the Conference on Mothers' Pensions, Providence, Rhode Island, June 28, 1922,* Publication No. 109 (Washington, D.C., 1922), 11, 24; ibid., *Standards of Public Aid to Children in Their Own Homes,* by Florence Nesbitt, Publication No. 118 (Washington, D.C., 1923), 17–20. For a discussion of settlements' racially based views on working mothers, see Ruth Crocker, *Social Work and Social Order: The Settlement Movement in Two Industrial Cities, 1889–1930* (Urbana, 1992).

12. *Laws of Illinois,* Forty-Seventh General Assembly, 1911, 126; *Laws of Illinois,* Forty-Eighth General Assembly, 1913, 129.

13. *Laws of Illinois,* Senate Bill No. 300, 48th General Assembly, 1913, 129.

14. U.S. Department of Labor, Children's Bureau, *The Administration of the Aid-to-Mothers' Law in Illinois,* by Edith Abbott and Sophonisba Breckinridge, Publication No. 82 (Washington, D.C., 1921), 35–36.

15. Ibid., 109–10. The majority of denied pensions were refused on the assessment of adequate means of support. Forty-nine percent were deemed economically sufficient, 37 percent

were legally ineligible, and 12 percent were either uncooperative or unfit. Economic sufficiency also provided the single largest reason for removing women from the program once they had been accepted. Cook County, Ill., Board of County Commissioners, *Charity Service Reports,* County Agent Report (1911–1917) and Juvenile Court, Mothers' Pension Department (1918–1927).

16. The study took data from large, medium, and small cities and one rural county. Children's Bureau, *Standards of Public Aid to Children in Their Own Homes,* 17.

17. Ibid., 20.

18. Grace Abbott, "Recent Trends in Mothers' Aid," *Social Service Review* 8 (June 1934): 208; Grace Abbott, *From Relief to Social Security: The Development of the New Public Welfare Services and Their Administration* (Chicago, 1941), 183.

19. Grace Abbott, *The Child and the State,* vol. 2 (Chicago, 1938), 309–12.

20. U.S. Committee on Economic Security, *Social Security in America: The Factual Background of the Social Security Act as Summarized from Staff Reports to the Committee on Economic Security* (Washington, D.C., 1937), 223.

21. For an overview of ADC, see Bell, *Aid to Dependent Children;* and Gordon, *Pitied but Not Entitled.* Grace Abbott describes the circumstances surrounding the construction of the provision in *From Relief to Social Security,* 279.

22. "Final Report of the Advisory Council on Social Security," 30, Grace and Edith Abbott Papers, Special Collections, Joseph Regenstein Library, University of Chicago, Chicago.

23. Linda Gordon, "Social Insurance and Public Assistance: The Influence of Gender in Welfare Thought in the United States, 1890–1935," *American Historical Review* 97 (February 1992): 19–54.

24. Some women did receive work relief, but their participation was restricted by quotas; restrictions on the types of jobs, such as sewing; and a wage scale that remained lower than men's wages. Elizabeth Faue, *Community of Suffering and Struggle: Women, Men, and the Labor Movement in Minneapolis, 1915–1945* (Chapel Hill, 1991), 132–33; Nancy E. Rose, "Gender, Race, and the Welfare State: Government Work Programs from the 1930s to the Present," *Feminist Studies* 19 (Summer 1993): 319–42.

Also, see Claudia Goldin, "The Changing Economic Role of Women," *Journal of Interdisciplinary History* 13 (Spring 1983): 707–33; Ruth Milkman, "Women's Work and the Economic Crises, Some Lessons from the Great Depression," in *A Heritage of Her Own,* ed. Nancy Cott and Elizabeth Pleck (New York, 1979), 507–37; and Grace Abbott, citing a Children's Bureau study of the 1921–22 depression and its effect on families, in *From Relief to Social Security,* 125.

25. Faue, *Community of Suffering and Struggle,* 119–20, 154–55.

26. Federal Emergency Relief Administration, *Monthly Report, July 1 to July 30, 1935* (Washington, D.C., 1935), 49.

27. Ibid., 9–11.

28. Mary S. Larabee, "Unmarried Parenthood under the Social Security Act," *Proceedings of the National Conference of Social Work* (Washington, D.C., 1939), 447–49.

29. Bell, *Aid to Dependent Children,* chap. 6. For the Georgia case, *Anderson v. Burson,* 300 F. Supp. 401 (1968).

30. Scholars disagree on the explanations for the bureau's ineffectiveness. Piven and Cloward argued that the principle of local responsibility, which retained significant control at

the local level, was deliberate and functional to local labor demands. Piven and Cloward, *Regulating the Poor*, 128–30. Patterson found the federal bureau unable to act alone in the absence of "potent lobbies" or organizations of the poor. Patterson, *America's Struggle against Poverty*, 68, 87. Yvonne Zylan's political analysis of ADC in the postwar years suggests that the "backlash" on ADC programs, particularly in the states, might have been tempered had organized women mounted some political opposition. Zylan has found that, in contrast to organized women's support for mothers' pensions in the early twentieth century, there is no evidence for support of the ADC program at mid-century. Yvonne Zylan, "Constructing the Patriarchal Welfare State: Aid to Dependent Children and the Politics of Gender, 1945–1960," unpublished paper.

31. *New York Times*, 18 August 1950, p. 14, col. 2. Abramovitz believes states pressured the federal government to add the caretaker grant to help relieve some of the costs; Abramovitz, *Regulating the Lives of Women*, 316, 322; Patterson, *America's Struggle against Poverty*, 88.

32. The Knowland amendment effectively allowed states to cut workers' benefits during a labor shortage, even a strike. President Truman and organized labor spoke out against the measure as one that would seriously challenge a worker's right to reject employment at substandard wages. *New York Times*, 12 August 1950, p. 1, col. 4; 29 August 1950, p. 20, col. 6.

33. Aid to Dependent Children was renamed Aid to Families with Dependent Children in the 1962 revisions. Family Support Act, *Statutes at Large*, 100th Cong., 2d Sess., 102 Stat. 2343 (1988).

34. Social scientists have explained the shift toward increased federal work expectations as part of a transition that replaced social workers' influence over policy with that of economists. Irwin Garfinkle and Sara McLanahan, *Single Mothers and Their Children: A New American Dilemma* (Washington, D.C., 1986); Katz, *The Undeserving Poor*. For labor regulation theory, see Piven and Cloward, *Regulating the Poor*. For sex regulation theory, see Abramovitz, *Regulating the Lives of Women*.

35. The "employable mother" rule has been included among the state welfare laws overturned by the courts. Instead, as this article discusses, the courts reaffirmed a state's right to require work. Piven and Cloward, *Regulating the Poor*, 308; and Patterson, *America's Struggle against Poverty*, 179.

36. John Kenneth Galbraith, *The Affluent Society* (Boston, 1958); Michael Harrington, *The Other America* (New York, 1962); Katz, *The Undeserving Poor*, 91–94.

37. For example, see Nicholas Lemann, *The Promised Land: The Great Black Migration and How it Changed America* (New York, 1991), 345. The impact specifically on African American women is discussed in Jacqueline Jones, *Labor of Love, Labor of Sorrow: Black Women, Work, and the Family from Slavery to the Present* (New York, 1985), 235–68, 301–10. Also, see Patterson, *America's Struggle against Poverty*, 136.

38. William Julius Wilson, *The Truly Disadvantaged: The Inner City, the Underclass, and Public Policy* (Chicago, 1987), chap. 2, especially 33–41; and chap. 4, especially 160–61.

39. Ibid., 39; Patterson, *America's Struggle against Poverty*.

40. *Report of the House Committee on Ways and Means*, Social Security Amendments of 1967, H.R. Rep. No. 544, 90th Cong., 1st Sess., 95–96. On the limits of WIN, see Patterson, *America's Struggle against Poverty*, 176; Abramovitz, *Regulating the Lives of Women*, 332.

41. *Anderson v. Burson*, 300 F. Supp. 401 (1968); *New York State Department of Social Services v. Dublino*, 93 S.Ct. 2507 (1973). For a legal review that applies a patriarchal analysis, see

Sylvia A. Law, "Women, Work, Welfare, and the Preservation of Patriarchy," *University of Pennsylvania Law Review* 131 (May 1983): 1249–339.

42. Jack Greenberg, *Crusaders in the Courts: How a Dedicated Band of Lawyers Fought for the Civil Rights Revolution* (New York, 1994). The court cases are, respectively, *King v. Smith,* 88 Sup. Ct. 2128 (1968); *Shapiro v. Thompson,* 89 Sup. Ct. 1322 (1969); and *Goldberg v. Kelly,* 397 Sup. Ct. 254 (1970).

43. Children's Bureau, *Mothers' Aid, 1931.* South Carolina was the other state. Act No. 445, Georgia Laws 1951, pp. 692–93, cited in Bell, *Aid to Dependent Children,* 71, 35; Georgia, Department of Public Welfare, *Public Assistance Manual,* Pt. III, Sec. V, p. 15 (1952).

44. Regulations, *Georgia Manual of Public Welfare Administration,* Part III, Sec. V-C(3)(b)(2), cited in Brief for Plaintiffs (October 12, 1966), p. 11, *Anderson v. Burson* RG 21, U.S. District Court, No. District of Georgia, Atlanta Division, Box 880.

45. According to Stephen Ralston, King contacted the NAACP Legal Defense Fund. Personal correspondence, Stephen Ralston, Senior Staff Attorney, NAACP Legal Defense and Educational Fund, Inc., December 24, 1993. Complaint, June 5, 1967, *Anderson v. Burson* RG 21, U.S. District Court, No. District of Georgia, Atlanta Division, Box 880.

46. *New York Times,* 8 October 1967, p. 38, col. 3; *Anderson v. Burson,* 300 F. Supp. 401 (1968).

47. *New York State Department of Social Services v. Dublino,* 93 S.Ct. 2507 (1973), 2512–13.

48. Ibid., 2522.

49. Ibid., 2520.

BIBLIOGRAPHY
Selected Further Readings

I. Social Construction of Motherhood

Berch, Bettina. "Scientific Management in the Home: The Empress's New Clothes." *Journal of American Culture* 3 (Fall 1980): 440–45.

Bloch, Ruth H. "American Feminine Ideals in Transition: The Rise of the Moral Mother, 1785–1815." *Feminist Studies* 4 (1978): 100–126.

Bose, Christine E., Philip L. Berano, and Mary Malloy. "Household Technology and the Social Construction of Housework." *Technology and Culture* 25 (January 1984): 53–82.

Boydston, Jeanne. "To Earn Her Daily Bread: Housework and Antebellum Working-Class Subsistence." *Radical History Review* 35 (April 1986): 7–25.

Burnham, John C. "Why Did the Infants and Toddlers Die? Shifts in Americans' Ideas of Responsibility for Accidents—From Blaming Mom to Engineering." *Journal of Social History* 29 (1996): 817–37.

Cowan, Ruth Schwartz. *More Work for Mother: The Ironies of Household Technology from the Open Hearth to the Microwave.* New York: Basic Books, 1983.

Davis, Richard A. "Working Women and the Popular Print Media: A Changing View of Motherhood." *Free Inquiry in Creative Sociology* 18 (May 1990): 43–47.

Dennis, Paul M. "Between Watson and Spock: Eleanor Roosevelt's Advice on Child-Rearing from 1928 to 1962." *Journal of American Culture* 18 (1995): 41–50.

Formanek-Brunell, Miriam. "In the Dolls' House: The Material Maternalism of Martha Chase, 1889–1914." Pp. 61–89 in *Made to Play House: Dolls and the Commercialization of American Girlhood, 1830–1930.* New Haven: Yale University Press, 1993.

Gomersall, Meg. "Education for Domesticity? A Nineteenth-Century Perspective on Girls' Schooling and Education." *Gender and Education* 6 (1994): 235–47.

Grant, Julia. "Caught between Common Sense and Science: The Cornell Child Study Clubs, 1925–1945." *History of Education Quarterly* 34 (1994): 433–52.

Green, Harvey. *The Light of the Home: An Intimate View of the Lives of Women in Victorian America.* New York: Pantheon Books, 1983.

Hill, Shirley A. "Motherhood and the Obfuscation of Medical Knowledge: The Case of Sickle Cell Disease." *Gender and Society* 8 (March 1994): 29–47.

Kaplan, E. Ann. *Motherhood and Representation: The Mother in Popular Culture and Melodrama.* New York: Routledge, 1992.

Kuhn, Anne L. "Gentle Ruler." Pp. 149–72 in *The Mother's Role in Childhood Education: New England Concepts, 1830–1860.* New Haven: Yale University Press, 1947.

Letherby, Gayle. "Mother or Not, Mother or What? Problems of Definition and Identity." *Women's Studies International Forum* 17 (1994): 525–32.

MacPike, Loralee. "The New Woman, Childbearing, and the Reconstruction of Gender, 1880–1900." *NWSA Journal* 1 (1989): 368–97.

May, Elaine Tyler. *Homeward Bound: American Families in the Cold War Era.* New York: Basic Books, 1988.

Sandelowski, Margarete. "Separate, but Less Unequal: Fetal Ultrasonography and the Transformation of Expectant Mother/Fatherhood." *Gender and Society* 8 (1994): 230–45.

Sklar, Kathryn Kish. "Victorian Women and Domestic Life: Mary Todd Lincoln, Elizabeth Cady Stanton, and Harriet Beecher Stowe." Pp. 20–37 in Collum Davis, et al., eds., *The Public and Private Lincoln: Contemporary Perspectives.* Carbondale: Southern Illinois University Press, 1979.

Slatkin, Wendy. "Maternity and Sexuality in the 1890s." *Woman's Art Journal* 1 (1980): 13–19.

Solinger, Rickie. "'A Complete Disaster': Abortion and the Politics of Hospital Abortion Committees, 1950–1970." *Feminist Studies* 19 (1993): 241–68.

Ulrich, Laurel Thatcher, *Good Wives: Image and Reality in the Lives of Women in Northern New England, 1650–1750.* New York: Oxford, 1980.

Van Horn, Susan Householder. *Women, Work and Fertility, 1900–1986.* New York: New York University Press, 1988.

Weiss, Nancy Pottisham. "Mother: The Invention of a Necessity: Dr. Benjamin Spock's *Baby and Child Care.*" *American Quarterly* 29 (1977): 519–47.

———. "The Mother-Child Dyad Revisited: Perceptions of Mothers and Children in Twentieth-Century Child Rearing Manuals." *Journal of Social Issues* 34 (1978): 29–45.

II. Control of Reproduction

Albiston, Catherine. "The Social Meaning of the Norplant Condition: Constitutional Consideration of Race, Class, and Gender." *Berkeley Women's Law Journal* 9 (1994): 9–57.

Brodie, Janet Farrell. *Contraception and Abortion in Nineteenth-Century America.* Ithaca: Cornell University Press, 1994.

Daniels, Cynthia R. *At Women's Expense: State Power and the Politics of Fetal Rights.* Cambridge, Mass.: Harvard University Press, 1993.

Desmond, Ann M. "Adolescent Pregnancy in the United States: Not a Minority Issue." *Health Care for Women International* 15 (August 1994): 325–31.

Endres, Kathleen L. "'Strictly Confidential': Birth-Control Advertising in a 19th-Century City." *Journalism Quarterly* 63 (Winter 1986): 748–51.

Gordon, Linda. *Woman's Body, Woman's Right: A Social History of Birth Control in America.* Rev. ed. New York: Penguin Books, 1990.

Jarrell, Robin H. "Native American Women and Forced Sterilization, 1973–1976." *Caduceus: A Museum Journal for the Health Sciences* 8 (December 1992): 45–58.

Kunzel, Regina. *Fallen Women, Problem Girls: Unmarried Mothers and the Professionalization of Social Work, 1890–1945.* New Haven: Yale University Press, 1993.

———. "Pulp Fictions and Problem Girls: Reading and Rewriting Single Pregnancy in the Postwar United States." *American Historical Review* 100 (1995): 1465–87.

Lippman, Abby. "Mother Matters: A Fresh Look at Prenatal Testing." *Issues in Reproductive and Genetic Engineering* 5 (1992): 141–54.

Losure, Mary. "'Motherhood Protection' and the Minnesota Birth Control League." *Minnesota History* 54 (1995): 359–70.

Marsh, Margaret, and Wanda Ronner. *The Empty Cradle: Infertility in America from Colonial Times to the Present.* Baltimore: Johns Hopkins University Press, 1996.

Newcomer, Susan. "Out of Wedlock Childbearing in an Ante-Bellum Southern County." *Journal of Family History* 15 (1990): 357–68.

Rapp, Rayna. "Women's Responses to Prenatal Diagnosis: A Sociocultural Perspective on Diversity." Pp. 219–33 in Karen H. Rothenberg and Elizabeth J. Thomson, eds., *Women and Prenatal Testing: Facing the Challenges of Genetic Testing.* Columbus: Ohio State University Press, 1994.

Reed, James. *From Private Vice to Public Virtue: The Birth Control Movement and American Society since 1830.* New York: Basic Books, 1978.

Rodrique, Jessie M. "The Black Community and the Birth-Control Movement." Pp. 333–44 in Ellen Carol DuBois and Vicki L. Ruiz, eds., *Unequal Sister: A Multicultural Reader in U.S. Women's History.* New York: Routledge, 1990.

Sandelowski, Margarete J. "Failures of Volition: Female Agency and Infertility in Historical Perspective." *Signs* 15 (1990): 475–99.

Solinger, Rickie. "The Girl Nobody Loved: Psychological Explanations for White Single Pregnancy in the Pre–Roe V. Wade Era, 1945–1965." *Frontiers* 11 (1990): 45–54.

———. *Wake Up Little Susie: Single Pregnancy and Race before Roe v. Wade.* New York: Routledge, 1992.

Vinovskis, Maris A. "An 'Epidemic' of Adolescent Pregnancy? Some Historical Considerations." *Journal of Family History* 6 (1981): 205–30.

III. Childbirth and Infant Care

Apple, Rima D. *Mothers and Medicine: A Social History of Infant Feeding, 1890- 1950.* Madison: University of Wisconsin Press, 1987.

Baird, Nancy Disher, and Carol Crowe-Carraco. "A 'True Woman's Sphere': Motherhood in Late Antebellum Kentucky." *Filson Club History Quarterly* 66 (July 1992): 369–94.

Blum, Linda M. "Mothers, Babies, and Breastfeeding in Late Capitalist America: The Shifting Contexts of Feminist Theory." *Feminist Studies* 19 (Summer 1993): 291–311.

Bogdan, Janet Carlisle. "Childbirth in America, 1650–1990." Pp. 101–20 in Rima D. Apple, ed., *Women, Health, and Medicine in America.* New York: Garland Publishing, 1990; New Brunswick: Rutgers University Press, 1992.

Campbell, John. "Work, Pregnancy, and Infant Mortality among Southern Slaves." *Journal of Interdisciplinary History* 14 (1984): 793–812.

Carson, Carolyn Leonard. "Maternity Care in the Progressive Era: The Elizabeth Steel Magee Hospital." *Pittsburgh History* 77 (Summer 1994): 77–87; (Fall 1994): 116–129.

Craig, Lee A. *To Sow One Acre More.* Baltimore: Johns Hopkins University Press, 1993.

Dye, Nancy Schrom, and Daniel Blake Smith. "Mother Love and Infant Death, 1750–1920." *Journal of American History* 73 (1986): 329–53.

Elder, Glen H., Jr. "Scarcity and Prosperity in Postwar Childbearing: Explorations from a Life Course Perspective." *Journal of Family History* 6 (Winter 1981): 410–33.

Eyer, Diane E. *Mother-Infant Bonding: A Scientific Fiction.* New Haven: Yale University Press, 1992.

Golden, Janet. *A Social History of Wet Nursing in America: From Breast to Bottle.* New York: Cambridge University Press, 1996.

Hoffert, Sylvia D. *Private Matters: American Attitudes toward Childbearing and Infant Nurture in the Urban North, 1800–1860.* Urbana: University of Illinois Press, 1989.

Jacobsen, Cheryl Rose. "Lifting the Curse of Eve: Women Writers and Advice Literature on Childbirth." *Women's Studies in Communication* 18 (1995): 135–51.

Johnson, Michael P. "Smothered Slave Infants: Were Slave Mothers at Fault?" *Journal of Southern History* 47 (1981): 493–520.

Jones, Kathleen W. "Sentiment and Science: The Late Nineteenth-Century Pediatrician as Mother's Advisor." *Journal of Social History* 17 (1983): 79–86.

Leavitt, Judith Walzer. *Brought to Bed: Child-Bearing in America, 1750–1950.* New York: Oxford University Press, 1986.

McMillen, Sally. *Motherhood in the Old South: Pregnancy, Childbirth, and Infant Rearing.* Baton Rouge: Louisiana State University Press, 1990.

Niethammer, Carolyn. "The Dawn of Life: Childbirth in Native America." Pp. 1–22 in *Daughters of the Earth: The Lives and Legends of American Indian Women*. New York and London: Macmillan, 1977.

Rockwell, Susan L. "The Delivery of Power: Reading American Indian Childbirth Narratives." *American Indian Culture and Research Journal* 19 (1995): 71–85.

Scharf, Lois. "'I Would Go Wherever Fortune Would Direct': Hannah Huntington and the Frontier of the Western Reserve." *Ohio History* 97 (1988): 5–28.

Scholten, Catherine M. "'On the Importance of the Obstetrick Art': Changing Customs of Childbirth in America, 1760–1825." *William and Mary Quarterly* 34 (1977): 426–45.

Treckel, Paula A. "Breastfeeding and Maternal Sexuality in Colonial America." *Journal of Interdisciplinary History* 20 (1989): 25–51.

Waite, Gloria. "Childbirth, Lay Institution Building, and Health Policy: Traditional Childbearing Group, Inc., of Boston in a Historical Perspective." In Barbara Bair and Susan E. Cayleff, eds., *Wings of Gauze: Women of Color and the Experience of Health and Illness*. Detroit: Wayne State University Press, 1993.

IV. Social and Cultural Settings

Abbott, Devon. "'Commendable Progress': Acculturation at the Cherokee Female Seminary." *American Indian Quarterly* 3 (Summer 1987): 187–201.

Blackburn, George, and Sherman L. Richards. "The Mother-Headed Family among Free Negroes in Charleston, South Carolina, 1850–1860." *Phylon* 42 (March 1981): 11–25.

Bloom, Florence Teicher. "Struggling and Surviving: The Life Style of European Immigrant Breadwinning Mothers in American Industrial Cities, 1900–1930." *Women's Studies International Forum* 8 (1985): 609–20.

Brady, Marilyn Dell. "Organizing Afro-American Girls' Clubs in Kansas in the 1920s." *Frontiers* 9 (1987): 69–73.

Braund, Kathryn E. Holland. "Guardians of Tradition and Handmaidens to Change: Women's Roles in Creek Economic and Social Life during the Eighteenth Century." *American Indian Quarterly* 14 (Summer 1990): 239–58.

Devens, Carol. "'If We Get the Girls, We Get the Race': Missionary Education of Native American Girls." *Journal of World History* 3 (Fall 1992): 219–37.

Dill, Bonnie Thornton. "Our Mothers' Grief: Racial Ethnic Women and the Maintenance of Families." *Journal of Family History* 13 (1988): 415–31.

Diner, Hasia R. *Erin's Daughters in America: Irish Immigrant Women in the Nineteenth Century*. Baltimore: Johns Hopkins Press, 1983.

Ewen, Elizabeth. *Immigrant Women in the Land of Dollars: Life and Culture on the Lower East Side, 1890–1925.* New York: Monthly Review Press, 1985.

Fink, Deborah. *Agrarian Women: Wives and Mothers in Rural Nebraska, 1880–1940.* Chapel Hill: University of North Carolina Press, 1992.

Gilmore, Melvin. "Notes on Gynecology and Obstetrics of the Arikara Tribe of Indians." *Papers of the Michigan Academy of Science, Arts, and Letters* 14 (1930): 71–81.

Gordon, Linda, and Sara McLanahan. "Single Parenthood in 1900." University of Wisconsin Institute for Research on Poverty, Discussion Paper no. 919–90, June 1990.

Harley, Sharon. "For the Good of Family and Race: Gender, Work, and Domestic Roles in the Black Community, 1880–1930." *Signs* 15 (1990): 336–49.

Jones, Jacqueline. "'My Mother Was Much of a Woman': Black Women, Work, and the Family under Slavery." *Feminist Studies* 8 (Summer 1982): 245–69.

Labbe, Dolores Egger. "Mothers and Children in Antebellum Louisiana." Louisiana History 34 (1993): 161–73.

Lamphere, Louise. *From Working Daughters to Working Mothers: Immigrant Women in a New England Industrial Community.* Ithaca: Cornell University Press, 1987.

Lebsock, Suzanne. "Free Black Women and the Question of Matriarchy: Petersburg, Virginia, 1784–1820." *Feminist Studies* 8 (1982): 271–92.

———. "'We Have Not Lived for Ourselves Alone': Women and Domesticity in Antebellum Petersburg." *Virginia Cavalcade* 33 (1983): 53–63.

Litt, Jacquelyn. "Mothering, Medicalization, and Jewish Identity, 1928–1940." *Gender & Society* 10 (1996): 185–98.

Lomawaima, K. Tsianina. "'You're a Woman, You're Going to Be a Wife'." Pp. 81–99 in *They Called It Prairie Light: The Story of Chilocco Indian School.* Lincoln: University of Nebraska Press, 1994.

Mathes, Valerie Sherer. "Nineteenth Century Women and Reform: The Women's National Indian Association." *American Indian Quarterly* 14 (1990): 1–18.

May, Martha. "The 'Good Managers': Married Working Class Women and Family Budget Studies, 1895–1915." *Labor History* 25 (1984): 351–72.

McMillen, Sally. "Mothers' Sacred Duty: Breast-Feeding Patterns among Middle- and Upper-Class Women in the Antebellum South." *Journal of Southern History* 51 (1985): 333–56.

Messina, Elizabeth G. "Narratives of Nine Italian American Women: Childhood, Work and Marriage." *Italian Americana* 10 (1992): 186–202.

Miranda, Gloria E. "Hispano-Mexican Childrearing Practices in Pre-American Santa Barbara." *Southern California Quarterly* 65 (1983): 307–20.

Newcomer, Susan. "Out of Wedlock Childbearing in an Ante-Bellum Southern County." *Journal of Family History* 15 (1990): 357–68.

Niethammer, Carolyn. *Daughters of the Earth: The Lives and Legends of American Indian Women.* New York: Macmillan, 1977.

Parrino, Maria. "Education in the Autobiographies of Four Italian Women Immigrants." *Italian Americana* 10 (1992): 126–46.

Pease, Jane H., and William H. Pease. *Ladies, Women, and Wenches: Choice and Constraint in Antebellum Charleston and Boston.* Chapel Hill: University of North Carolina Press, 1990.

Powers, Marla N. "The Americanization of Indian Girls." *Society* 24 (Jan.–Feb. 1987): 83–85.

Roberts, Patricia Margaret. "Unmarried Motherhood: Childhood Experiences Described by 22 Adults Whose Mother Was Unmarried When They Were Born." *Health Care for Women International* 15 (1994): 77–86.

Ryan, Mary P. *The Empire of the Mother: American Writing about Domesticity, 1830–1860.* New York: Haworth Press, 1982.

Scott, Anne Firor. "Sisters, Wives and Mothers: Self-Portraits of Three Eighteenth-Century Women." Pp. 38–55 in Nancy A. Hewitt, ed., *Women, Families, and Communities: Readings in American History,* vol. 1. Glenview, Ill.: Scott, Foresman, 1990.

Theriot, Nancy M. *The Biosocial Construction of Femininity: Mothers and Daughters in Nineteenth-Century America.* New York: Greenwood, 1988.

Treese, Lorett. "'Why, It's Mother': The Italian Mothers' Clubs of New York." *Italian Americana* 9 (1990): 25–41.

Weinberg, Sydney Stahl. *The World of Our Mothers: The Lives of Jewish Immigrant Women.* Chapel Hill: University of North Carolina Press, 1988.

Weiss, Julie H. "Mothers as Others: The Construction of Race, Ethnicity, and Gender in Self-Help Literature of the 1940s." *Women's Studies in Communications* 18 (1995): 153–63.

West, Elliot. "Beyond Baby Doe: Child Rearing on the Mining Frontier." Pp. 179–92 in Susan Armitage and Elizabeth Jameson, eds., *The Women's West.* Norman: University of Oklahoma Press, 1987.

White, Deborah Gray. *Ar'n't I a Woman? Female Slaves in the Plantation South.* New York: W. W. Norton, 1985.

V. Mothers and Public Policy

Abel, Emily K. "Appealing for Children's Health: Conflicts between Mothers and Officials in the 1930s." *Social Service Review* 70 (1996): 282–304.

———. "Benevolence and Social Control: Advice from the Children's Bureau in the Early Twentieth Century." *Social Service Review* 68 (1994): 1–19.

Berry, Mary Frances. *The Politics of Parenthood: Child Care, Women's Rights and the Myth of the Good Mother.* New York: Viking, 1993.

Boris, Eileen. *Home to Work: Motherhood and the Politics of Industrial Homework in the United States.* New York: Cambridge University Press, 1994.

Bridgforth, Lucie Robertson. "The 'New' Woman in an Old Role: Maternal-Child Health Care in Memphis." *West Tennessee Historical Society Papers* 40 (1986): 45–54.

Chamallas, Martha, and Linda Kerber. "Women, Mothers, and the Law of Fright: A History." *Michigan Law Review* 88 (February 1990): 814–64.

Enstam, Elizabeth York. "They Called It 'Motherhood': Dallas Women and Public Life, 1895–1918." Pp. 71–95 in Virginia Bernhard, ed., *Hidden Histories of Women in the New South.* Columbia: University of Missouri Press, 1994.

Goodwin, Joanne L. "An American Experiment in Paid Motherhood: The Implementation of Mothers' Pensions in Early Twentieth-Century Chicago." *Gender & History* 4 (1992): 323–42.

Gordon, Linda. *Pitied But Not Entitled: Single Mothers and the History of Welfare.* New York: Free Press, 1994.

———. "Single Mothers and Child Neglect, 1880–1920." *American Quarterly* 37 (1985): 173–92.

———, ed. *Women, the State, and Welfare.* Madison: University of Wisconsin Press, 1990.

Howard, Christopher. "Sowing the Seeds of 'Welfare': The Transformation of Mothers' Pensions, 1900–1940." *Journal of Policy History* 4 (1992): 188–227.

Jacobs, Renee. "Iroquois Great Law of Peace and the United States Constitution: How the Founding Fathers Ignored the Clan Mothers." *American Indian Law Review* 16 (1991): 497–531.

Klaus, Alisa. *Every Child a Lion: The Origins of Maternal and Infant Health Policy in the United States and France, 1890–1920.* Ithaca: Cornell University Press, 1993.

Koven, Seth, and Sonya Michel, eds. *Mothers of a New World: Maternalist Politics and the Origins of Welfare States.* New York: Routledge, 1993.

Ladd-Taylor, Molly. *Mother-Work: Women, Child Welfare, and the State, 1890–1930.* Urbana: University of Illinois Press, 1994.

———. *Raising a Baby the Government Way: Mothers' Letters to the Children's Bureau, 1915–1932.* New Brunswick: Rutgers University Press, 1986.

Mathes, Valerie Sherer. "Nineteenth Century Women and Reform: The Women's National Indian Association." *American Indian Quarterly* 14 (1990): 1–18.

Meckel, Richard A. "Educating a Ministry of Mothers: Evangelical Maternal Associations, 1815–1860." *Journal of the Early Republic* 24 (1982): 403–23.

———. *Save the Babies: American Public Health Reform and the Prevention of Infant Mortality, 1850–1929.* Baltimore: Johns Hopkins, 1990.

Mettler, Suzanne B. "Federalism, Gender, and the Fair Labor Standards Act of 1938." *Polity* 26 (1994): 635–54.

Michel, Sonya, and Robyn Rosen. "The Paradox of Maternalism: Elizabeth Lowell Putnam and the American Welfare State." *Gender & History* 4 (1992): 364–86.

Muncy, Robyn. *Creating a Female Dominion in American Reform, 1890–1935.* New York: Oxford, 1991.

Riley, Susan E. "Caring for Rosie's Children: Federal Child Care Policies in the World War II Era." *Polity* 26 (1994): 654–75.

Rose, Margaret. "'From the Fields to the Picket Line: Huelga Women and the Boycott,' 1965–1975." *Labor History* 31 (1990): 271–93.

Schackel, Sandra. "Better Mothers, Better Babies: The Effects of Maternity and Infancy Work." Pp. 29–59 in *Social Housekeepers: Women Shaping Public Policy in New Mexico, 1920–1940.* Albuquerque: University of New Mexico, 1992.

Shelton, Brenda K. "Organized Mother Love: The Buffalo Women's Educational and Industrial Union, 1885–1915." *New York History* 67 (1986): 155–76.

Stehno, Sandra M. "Public Responsibility for Dependent Black Children: The Advocacy of Edith Abbott and Sophonisba Breckinridge." *Social Service Review* 62 (1988): 485–93.

Stiles, Julie A. "Nineteenth-Century Child Custody Reform: Maternal Authority and the Development of the 'Best Interests of the Child' Standard." *Probate Law Journal* 6 (1984): 5–32.

Swerdlow, Amy. *Women Strike for Peace: Traditional Motherhood and Radical Politics in the 1960s.* Chicago: University of Chicago Press, 1993.

Tuominen, Mary. "Gender, Class, and Motherhood: The Legacy of Federal Child Care Policy." *Affilia* 7 (1992): 8–25.

Vogel, Lise. *Mothers on the Job: Maternity Policy in the U.S. Workplace.* New Brunswick: Rutgers University Press, 1993.

Weiner, Lynn Y. *From Working Girl to Working Mother: The Female Labor Force in the United States, 1820–1980.* Chapel Hill: University of North Carolina Press, 1985.

CONTRIBUTORS

Susan Matoba Adler is assistant professor of education at the University of Michigan-Flint, where she teaches early childhood education. Her research is in the areas of ethnic minority families and the cultural context of learning.

Rima D. Apple is professor in the School of Human Ecology, with a joint appointment in the Women's Studies Program, at the University of Wisconsin, Madison, where she teaches the history of motherhood. Her most recent book is *Vitamania: Vitamins in American Culture.* She is currently writing a book tentatively titled "The Perfect Mother."

Marilyn S. Blackwell teaches history at the Community College of Vermont and the University of Vermont. She is writing a book, tentatively titled "Entitled to Relief: Poor Women, Charity, and Medicine, 1900–1920."

Eileen Boris is professor of history at Howard University. Her most recent book is *Home to Work: Motherhood and the Politics of Industrial Homework in the United States.* She is currently writing on work, welfare, and the understanding of sex and gender since World War II.

Lynne Curry is assistant professor of history at Eastern Illinois University. She is completing a book tentatively titled "Modern Mothers in the Heartland: Gender, Health, and Progress in Illinois, 1900–1930."

Ruth Feldstein teaches history and literature at Harvard University. Her forthcoming book is tentatively titled "Making 'Moms' and 'Matriarchs': Dangerous Women, Race, and American Liberalism, 1930–1965."

Janet Golden is associate professor of history at Rutgers University, Camden. Her most recent book is *A Social History of Wet Nursing: From Breast to Bottle.* She is currently writing a cultural history of fetal alcohol syndrome.

Joanne L. Goodwin is an assistant professor of history at the University of Nevada, Las Vegas. Her forthcoming book is titled *Gender and the Politics of Welfare Reform.* She is currently writing about work and welfare in the 1960s and 1970s.

Linda Gordon is professor of history at the University of Wisconsin-Madison. Her most recent book is *Pitied But Not Entitled: Single Mothers and the History of Welfare.* She is currently writing about an encounter between Mexicans and Anglos in early twentieth-century Arizona.

Molly Ladd-Taylor is associate professor of history at York University in Toronto.

Her most recent book is *Mother-Work: Women, Child Welfare, and the State, 1890–1930.* She is currently working on a study of eugenic sterilization in Minnesota.

Judith Walzer Leavitt is professor of the history of medicine, history of science, and women's studies at the University of Wisconsin-Madison and associate dean for faculty in the Medical School. Her most recent book is *Typhoid Mary: Captive to the Public's Health.*

Jan Lewis is a professor of history at Rutgers University, Newark. She is completing a book, tentatively titled "Women, Slaves and the Creation of a Liberal Republic."

Kenneth A. Lockridge is professor emeritus at the University of Michigan and professor of history at the University of Montana. His most recent book is *On the Sources of Patriarchal Rage: The Commonplace Books of William Byrd and Thomas Jefferson and the Gendering of Power in the Eighteenth Century.*

Margaret Marsh is professor of history at Temple University. Her most recent book is *The Empty Cradle: Infertility in America from Colonial Times to the Present,* coauthored with Wanda Ronner.

Joan J. Mathews is associate director of the Burn and Shock Trauma Institute at the Loyola University Medical Center. Her recent publications focus on cost-saving strategies in clinical settings.

Timothy J. Meagher is archivist and museum director at the Catholic University of America. He recently coedited, with Ronald Bayor, a collection of essays entitled *The New York Irish.*

M. Rivka Polatnick is associate professor at San Jose State University, where she teaches women's studies. Her current interests include ways for women to reduce their double workloads and ways to carry forward the momentum of the 1995 World Conference on Women.

Loretta J. Ross is founder and executive director of the Center for Human Rights Education in Atlanta. She is writing a book entitled "Black Abortion."

Marylynn Salmon is research associate in the History Department at Smith College. Her most recent book is *The Limits of Independence: American Women 1760–1800.*

George J. Sanchez is director of the American Culture Program and associate professor of history and American culture at the University of Michigan, Ann Arbor. He is the author of *Becoming Mexican American: Ethnicity, Culture and Identity in Chicano Los Angeles, 1900–1945.*

Stephanie J. Shaw is an associate professor in the departments of history and black studies at Ohio State University. Her most recent book is *What a Woman*

Ought to Be and to Do: Black Professional Women Workers during the Jim Crow Era.

Wendy Simonds is assistant professor of sociology at Georgia State University. Her most recent book is *Abortion at Work: Ideology and Practice in a Feminist Clinic.*

Laurel Thatcher Ulrich is Phillips Professor of Early American History and professor of women's studies at Harvard University. Her most recent book is *A Midwife's Tale: The Life of Martha Ballard, Based on Her Diary, 1785–1812.* She is currently writing a book on textiles in the social history of early America.

Sydney Stahl Weinberg is professor of history and director of the Master of Arts in Liberal Studies Program at Ramapo College of New Jersey. Her main interest is the history of immigrant women.

Lynn Y. Weiner is associate professor of history and associate dean of arts and sciences at Roosevelt University. She is the author of *From Working Girl to Working Mother: The Female Labor Force in the United States, 1820–1980.* She is currently studying working mothers and the changing culture of family life in the twentieth-century United States.

Kathleen Zadak is head nurse of a trauma patient care unit at the Loyola University Medical Center. She remains interested in issues of women's health.

Index

A. H. Robins Company, 261

Abbott, Edith, 542

Abbott, Grace, 542–43

Abbott, John, 54, 61, 63

Abell, Mrs. L. H. G., 222

abortions: and African American women, 174, 260–64, 268–75, 308–9, 313; fight for right to, 391, 401, 402; illegal, 268–75, 412n. 11; medical claims regarding, 221; in nineteenth century, 431, 433–34, 442n. 43; under slavery, 308–9, 313; in *True Story,* 116, 123–24; and Virginia gentry, 212n. 31

Adams, R. A., 314n. 6

The Adams Women (Nagel), 215n. 48

ADC. *See* Aid to Dependent Children

Adler, Susan Matoba, 296, 351–61

adoption: and African Americans, 412n. 11; by infertile couples, 218–19, 224–26, 233; loss associated with, 117, 119

The Affluent Society (Galbraith), 551

Africa, 266, 404, 405

African Americans: discipline issues of, 147; discrimination against, 543, 546, 547–49, 551, 552, 555–56, 559; as emotional, 143–44, 148; fertility rates of, 228; genocide fears of, 260, 267, 269, 272–75, 391, 395; as grieving mothers, 4, 131–70; infertility among, 232; media directed at, 145, 149, 152, 168n. 112, 265, 268, 271; middle-class, 137–38, 163n. 55; and mothers' movement, 456, 459–64, 467; northward migration of, 552; in paid labor force, 136–38, 161n. 34, 457, 463, 536n. 27, 544, 548, 549, 559; and reproductive issues, 174, 259–77; as slaves, xiv–xv, 86n. 3; as wet nurses of white children, 86n. 3; white fears con-cerning, 450; white rape of, 145, 309, 463; and women's liberation movement, 389–98, 402–11

agricultural work, 545, 548, 549, 552, 556

Aid to Dependent Children (ADC), 420–21, 539, 540, 545–50, 555, 563n. 33. *See also* Aid to Families With Dependent Children (AFDC)

Aid to Families With Dependent Children (AFDC), 421, 550–57, 563n. 33. *See also* Aid to Dependent Children (ADC)

Aid to the Blind, 550

Aidyll (author), 120

alcohol: in childbirth, 183, 186, 189; move-ment against, 419

Ali, Muhammad, 155

Allen, (Chude) Pam, 398, 402, 414n. 30

Allin, Abby, 118

amae, 352–54, 358, 359, 361n. 10

Amalgamated Clothing Workers of Amer-ica, 526

amenorrhea. *See* menstruation

American Academy of Pediatrics, 285

American Association for the Study and Prevention of Infant Mortality, 495

American Child Hygiene Association, 97

American College of Nurse Midwives, 285

American College of Obstetricians and Gynecologists (ACOG), 283, 285, 289

American Federation of Labor, 479

"Americanists," 479, 480–81. *See also* assimi-lation

Americanization. *See* assimilation

American Ladies' Magazine, 56–57, 64

American Medical Association, 97, 248, 379, 442n. 43

WOMEN AND HEALTH SERIES
Cultural and Social Perspectives

Rima D. Apple and Janet Golden, Editors

The series examines the social and cultural construction of health practices and policies, focusing on women as subjects and objects of medical theory, health services, and policy formulation.

Making Midwives Legal.
Childbirth, Medicine, and the Law
second edition
Raymond G. DeVries

The Selling of Contraception.
The Dalkon Shield Case, Sexuality, and Women's Autonomy
Nicole J. Grant

And Sin No More.
Social Policy and Unwed Mothers in Cleveland, 1855–1990
Marian J. Morton

Women and Prenatal Testing.
Facing the Challenges of Genetic Technology
Edited by Karen H. Rothenberg and Elizabeth J. Thomson

Women's Health.
Complexities and Differences
Edited by Sheryl Burt Ruzek, Virginia L. Olesen, and Adele E. Clarke

Listen to Me Good.
The Life Story of an Alabama Midwife
Margaret Charles Smith and Linda Janet Holmes